The Alan Dale
BIBLE

The Alan Dale
BIBLE

Winding Quest & New World

Combined and Revised

Kevin
Mayhew

First published in 2002 by
KEVIN MAYHEW LTD
Buxhall, Stowmarket, Suffolk IP14 3BW
Email: info@kevinmayhewltd.com

9 8 7 6 5 4 3 2 1 0

ISBN 1 84003 887 X
Catalogue No 1500493

Cover design by Angela Selfe
Edited by Peter Dainty
Typesetting by Richard Weaver

Printed and bound in Great Britain, by The Bath Press, Bath.

Foreword

When Alan Dale's *Winding Quest* and *New World* first appeared in the 1960s they were rightly welcomed and acclaimed as a refreshing and illuminating presentation of 'the heart' of the Old and New Testaments. It is no wonder that in the decades that followed they went on to be used widely by teachers and preachers in many schools and churches, as well as by those who simply wanted to know what the Bible was all about.

The Bible is not an easy book to read or to understand. That is why Alan Dale's version of it is so essential in the modern world, when many people have either never read it, or, having read some of it, misunderstand it. Alan Dale's aim was to make the Bible as alive and relevant and full of meaning for others, especially for young people, as it was for him. And he successfully achieved that aim both by drawing on the best modern scholarship available, and also by applying all his own gifts as a storyteller and poet, biblical scholar and man of faith. To read his accounts is to enter into the biblical world and discover, or rediscover, the essence of its message – that God is, and always has been, at work among us, challenging us with his Word and showing us his Way.

The Alan Dale Bible brings *Winding Quest* and *New World* together under one cover, with biblical references in the text and a new index at the end to make it easy to use and follow. Some of the language has been updated to comply with changing times; but 99.9 per cent of it is in Alan Dale's original words – as simple, direct, thrilling, thought provoking, striking, challenging, moving and inspiring as ever.

I feel privileged to have had a part in the publication of *The Alan Dale Bible*, especially if it means that many new readers will benefit from his writings. I am particularly grateful to Alan's widow, Mrs Phyllis Dale, who has taken a keen interest in this republication, and who, with her family, has offered wise and helpful advice concerning the changes that have been made.

PETER DAINTY – EDITOR

Contents

Note: 'GOD' translates 'Yahweh'; 'God' other divine names. 'South' translates 'Judah'; 'North' 'Israel' (see pp. 687-689).

THE OLD TESTAMENT

'WINDING QUEST'

Preface

Here is protest: the protest of a small highland people against the 'beasts' of brutal military empires; the protest of individuals against a baffling and apparently meaningless universe.

Here is the protest of a small people – far enough away for us to look at what was happening with clear eyes and to see in their experience a parable of the total human situation; yet brought close to us by the magic of enduring speech, the speech of people who had their backs to the wall and their lives at stake, who had once been slaves and who, after several hundred years of political independence, saw their city lie in ruins, a mass of debris – and survived.

Here is the protest of individuals –

> What do we gain by endless toil,
>   sweating under the hot sun?
> Families come and families go,
>   only the earth goes on for ever . . .
> What has been will be,
>   what's done must be done again,
>   there's nothing new under the sun!
> *Ecclesiastes 1:3-4, 9*

and –

> Our enemies have thrown us back
>   plundering to their heart's desire –
> we are butchered like sheep,
> scattered all over the world . . .
>   a byword and a laughing-stock
>   to everybody.
> *Psalm 44:10-11, 13*

and –

> Why should we be doomed
>   to grope our way blindfold
>   shut in by God's unceasing No?
> *Job 3:23*

and yet (one can say of God in spite of everything) –

I shall lack nothing –
   he lets me lie down on green grass,
   leads me by quiet streams,
   renews my strength.
He guides me along right tracks
   because he is what he is;
   when I go through the pitch-black gorge,
   nothing frightens me . . .
God's home is my home
   for ever!

Whatever else may be said of the Old Testament, nobody who has really read it would ever call it dull. It is crowded with colour – little, tidy, dogmatic minds may think too much colour. People speak their minds – paint even their kings in earthy colours. Here is rebel – and 'establishment'. The Old Testament is a bewildering book largely because so many voices are speaking. They are asking 'Why?' – speaking for themselves, and speaking for obscure men and women all over the world and in every century. The very variety ensures that everybody somewhere will hear their own voice.

The Old Testament is a lively book; it is also an important one. It is a pioneering book, asking, for the first time in human history (before the Greeks to whom we owe so much) and in language that can still speak directly to our imagination, ultimate questions about the meaningfulness – or meaninglessness – of human experience, questions which serious men and women have been asking ever since and which they – especially young people – are asking today.

There are no short answers to such questions – it sometimes seems that all we can do is to get the questions straight. Everybody, anyhow, has to ask their own questions and seek their own answers in their own way – learning from others but doing their own thinking, 'listening to all but giving their soul to none'. Here is a living introduction to this perennial enquiry.

The Old Testament is an important book for a further and more impressive reason: this is no academic debate. These writers speak from a threatened country or from exile in a foreign land; they speak frankly and directly – even brutally – with a contempt for conventional cant. There are questioners and doubters among them, but their profoundest minds believe they have found both the secret of living as human beings in a dehumanising situation and the clue to the making of a genuinely human world. They are searching for a new world and they speak to those in every generation who care. Here is a community of men and women –

'growing not as any collective urge
would have them
(in its own placable image) but into
their own more wayward value – strong,
untidy, original, self-possessed.'*

It is the *reading* of the Old Testament that matters – not just *reading about* it. I offer this version of the heart of it to all who care. I once thought it was a book of little significance today – until I started to read it again for myself. I had to learn how to come to terms with it the hard way, and I owe an immense debt to the Old Testament scholars who helped me; I made this version in the light of their discoveries and insights. This is how I read it and I offer it as first steps to the reading of the splendid modern translations of the full text.

But there is one thing to remember. I have spoken about the Old Testament as if it were a book in the ordinary sense of that word. It is not, of course. It is more like a library of books, written at different times by different authors. The collection and editing of these books were carried out by many editors over a period of many centuries; the final discussion about what books should be included did not take place until the year 90 of our era. The books themselves are very varied in style and contents. Here is prose – history, biographies, diaries, tracts for the times, short stories, legal documents; here, too, is poetry – ballads, love lyrics, dramatic poetry, hymns, prophetic poems.

The Old Testament, in a word, is like a shelf of books, and there is no more need to start at the traditional beginning than to read a shelf of library books by beginning with the one on the left. So we shall begin to read, not at the traditional beginning which you will find in the editions of the full text, but at an important and dramatic moment in the story of the Hebrew people (*Brief Hour of Glory*).† We then look

* Alan Brownjohn, from *For My Son* (Penguin Modern Poets)
† See also John Bowden, *What About the Old Testament?*

back over their past history as they remembered it (*Memories of the Past*). In *The Death of Two Cities* we see how they became the victims of powerful military empires. We then turn to see how they mastered their tragic suffering (*Making Sense of the Story*) and what they learned from it (*Enduring Convictions*). These, then, will be our first steps into the Old Testament.

Prelude

How can they live in GOD's Way?

Farmer
    ploughing the field, proud of his goad,
    driving his oxen, lost to the world,
    talking, talking of cattle,
    following the furrow by day,
    fattening the heifers by night?

Blacksmith
    sitting by his anvil in a world of pig-iron,
    scorched by the forge, fighting the furnace heat,
    deafened by hammers' din, rapt in his pattern,
    firm to finish his work, fashioning it into the night?

Potter
    working at his wheel, turning it with his feet,
    lost in his task of making up his tally,
    slapping and puddling the clay,
    engrossed in his glazing,
    staying awake cleaning out his kiln?

Such workers trust their hands;
    their craftsmanship is their wisdom.
Without them cities would be empty –
    nobody living there,
    nobody coming and going.
You won't hear them in the City Council
    or see them sitting in the Assembly;
you won't find them among the judges –
    they can't make head or tail of the Law;
they don't talk like scholars –
    they can't quote the critics.

Yet
they hold the world in their hands;
    their worship is in their work.
Ecclesiasticus 38:25-39

Brief Hour of Glory

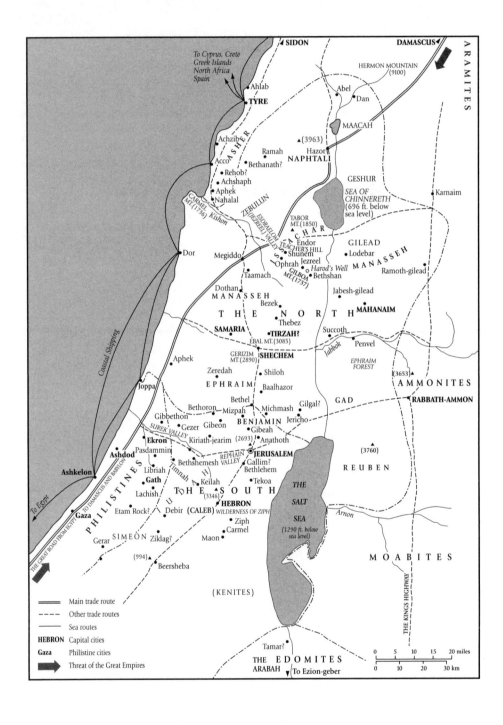

Introduction

About the year 1000 BCE,* 250 years after the escape from Egypt under the leadership of Moses, David became king of the South in Hebron City in the southern highlands. This was a turning point in the story of the Israelite people. Before this, they had been a tribal league whose story we will come back to later. Now they were to become a nation, the most powerful small nation in the Middle East. King David captured an old Canaanite fortress, Jerusalem, and made it his new capital. Here he established his court and government and ruled as a great king. And at his court, for the first time, records were made of the story of this remarkable rise to power and nationhood.

Up to this time, little had been written down. There had not been peace enough for writing; holding the highlands, fighting with the fortified cities or the camel-riding nomads from the eastern deserts, had drained the energy of the scattered tribes. The stories of these exciting days were handed on, from generation to generation, as tribal traditions, recited at the religious festivals at the central tribal shrine. Now there was peace and time to put the stories down in writing.

Most important of all, they were able to write down accounts of what was happening in their own time. They began to make official records – lists of army officers and their exploits, court documents, temple records. It was at Solomon's court that the first history books in the world were written, 500 years before historical writing began in Greece. So, in the 80 years following David's coronation in Hebron, the Israelites moved out into the light. They had strong memories of the decisive 200 years or so that followed their escape from Egypt, memories which governed their lives in this historic moment and which were to govern their lives over the succeeding centuries. But they were now standing on their own feet, building an empire which was to stretch from the far north to the Egyptian frontiers.

The world lay before them. The dreams and hopes and convictions of Moses could now be made a living reality. They could be GOD's people as God intended them to be. They had a capital city and an empire; their country was to be the centre of the new world. The glory of these days was to sustain them even in the darkest hours of disaster; it haunts the Jewish people still.

* Before the Common Era.

It will be best for us to get to grips with the story that lies behind the Old Testament at this historic moment in the fortunes of the Israelite people. Their tribal past, remembered in their traditions, lies behind them; the future is as yet all unknown. We can see what kind of people they were. We can see them, through the eyes of a contemporary, as real people, facing the same kind of human situation all people have to face, and not, as they have been so often presented to us, as 'pious puppets in a fairy tale'. This – or something very much like it – actually happened. This is the real world; if religion is to mean anything at all, it has to make sense in this kind of world and help people to live in it and deal with it.

The sources that these first historians used were varied.

When the story begins, the Philistines – the 'Sea Peoples' as the Egyptians called them – were already masters of the plain that lies between the highlands and the sea, and they were about to launch their attack on the highlands. For information about these days, the writers had only the popular stories which circulated among the Israelite tribes; only a few of these – like *The Philistine Attack* (the story of the Ark) with which we begin – had already been written down.

However, for the stories of the two great commanders, who became their first kings, they had written documents as well as popular tales. The kind of men Saul and David were and what they had tried to do was public knowledge. They were not far-off, misty figures; many of the men from whose lips the stories come had marched with them on their campaigns. Their stories give us, as it were, 'snapshots' of their commanders, vivid glimpses of incident and character. Here is no step-by-step account of all that happened, set in chronological order; many of the details of the various campaigns are now lost for ever – for example, the campaigns of David's Philistine War, when he subdued the five proud cities. But here is enough to see what kind of world it was, what sort of men they were and what they were trying to do. The stories are among the great stories of the world.

In addition, for the end of this part of the story, the writers had a vivid contemporary account, *The Court History*, written, it may be, by one of David's high officers. It is the account of the last days of David when he was no longer the able and vigorous king he had been (he is now painted as a disillusioned old man) and there was a harem quarrel about who should succeed him. A modern scholar writes:

This document . . . has the factual accuracy of contemporary chronicle. But, unlike the mere annalist, the writer reveals the relationship of character with event, and of one event with another, by the sheer skill of his narration. In the whole of the Old Testament, only the work of the Yahwist is comparable with the superbly simple prose of *The Court History*. As history, it is unequalled in ancient Hebrew literature. At this period, and for centuries afterwards, the neighbouring civilisations produced nothing comparable. The writer has seen history made in David's reign; and when, probably in the reign of Solomon, he wrote his narrative, he himself made literary history.*

* G. W. Anderson, *A Critical Introduction to the Old Testament*, p. 80. The 'Yahwist' is the name used for the author (or authors) of the 'first national history' (referred to as 'J') which we use for the Story of Moses (pp. 91-114) *What Kind of World Do We Live in?* and *What Kind of People Should We Be?* (pp. 292-328).

The Philistine Attack

The Opening Battle *1 Samuel 4:1-7, 9-14, 16-18*

War at last broke out between the Philistines in their fortified cities on the plain and the Israelites on the highlands.

The Philistines began it – they called out their army and took up their position at Aphek on the road to the north. The Israelites took the field against them at a place called the Stone of Help.

Battle lines were drawn up, and in the general fighting that followed the Israelites were defeated – many of their soldiers lay dead on the battlefield.

Back at the Israelite camp, there was heated debate among the sheiks.

'Why has GOD routed us like this,' they asked, 'and let the Philistines defeat us? Let us take the Ark out from the temple at Shiloh. If we've got it with us, GOD will rescue us from our enemies however strong they are!'

They sent to Shiloh and fetched the Ark. Hophni and Phinehas, sons of the aged priest Eli, were its guardians. There was a tremendous shout as the Ark was carried into the camp. The Philistine soldiers heard it across the valley.

'What are they shouting about over there?' they were asking one another.

Scouts soon brought the news – the Ark had been brought from Shiloh. The Philistines were in a panic.

'A god has come down to the camp!' they shouted. 'We're lost!'

'Screw up your courage!' said their officers. 'Be the soldiers you are! You're not going to be the slaves of these bandits, are you? We've defeated them before. You're soldiers – get on with the fighting!'

They fought hard, and the Israelite soldiers broke and fled in disorder, nobody bothering about what happened to his comrade. The Ark was captured and its guardians, the sons of the old priest Eli, were killed.

A soldier escaped from the battlefield and ran all the way to Shiloh in the highlands, his clothes torn and earth on his head to mark his grief.

The old priest Eli was sitting on a seat near the town gate, looking down the road, wondering anxiously what had happened to the Ark. The soldier ran into the town and told the bad news. There was uproar in the streets and Eli heard the wailing.

'What's all this wailing about?' he asked the men standing near.

The soldier himself ran across and told him.

'I'm the soldier from the camp,' he said. 'I escaped this morning from the battlefield.'

'How did the fighting go, my son?' asked the old man.

'Our soldiers fled in panic,' he said. 'There have been heavy casualties – your two sons are dead and the Ark's been captured!'

At the word 'Ark', the old man fell back from his seat by the gate. He broke his neck and died – he was a very old and heavy man.

The Capture of the Ark

1 Samuel 5:1-12; 6:1-5, 7-10, 12-14, 16; 7:1

The Philistines carried the captured Ark to Ashdod, took it to the temple of their god Dagon and set it beside his image there.

Early next day, worshippers found the image of Dagon lying face down on the ground in front of the Ark. They put the image back in its place. Next morning the same thing happened. This time its head and its broken hands were lying on the floor beside the platform – nothing was left of Dagon but his trunk.

Worse followed: plague broke out in the city – people were suffering from boils.

'The Ark's not staying here,' they said. 'It's destroying both us and our god!'

A council of the Philistine chiefs was called.

'What are we going to do with it?' people of Ashdod asked them.

'Let it go to Gath,' they said.

That's where they took it; and then there was trouble there. The city was in a panic; young and old were struck with boils.

They sent the Ark on to Ekron, and there was uproar in that city.

'Have they brought the Ark round here to kill us?' they protested.

Another council of chieftains was called.

The people of Ekron were in no doubt what should be done.

'Send the Ark back to where it belongs,' they said. 'We want no more deaths here.'

Panic had spread throughout the city. Many people were dead or plague-stricken, and there was uproar in the streets.

The Ark had now been seven months in Philistine territory. The priests and diviners were called together to advise the chieftains what to do with it and how to send it home.

'If you're going to send it home,' they said, 'don't send it home empty. You must send an offering to the God of the Israelites with it to acknowledge your guilt. Then you will be healed and you will find out why the God of the Israelites is against you.'

'What sort of offering?' they asked.

'Five golden plague-boils,' they said, 'and five mice, one of each for each of the cities; the plague attacked you all and your chieftains. Give honour to the Israelite God; perhaps he will relax his grip on you and your gods and your land. Then get a new farm cart ready and two milking cows that have not yet been trained to pull carts. Hitch the cows to the cart, but keep their calves at home, away from them. Put the Ark on the cart and put your offering in a box beside it. Let car and cows go, and watch what happens. If the Ark goes back to Israelite territory – to Bethshemesh over there – you will know that the Israelite God is the cause of all your trouble. If it doesn't do that, then we can be sure that he had nothing to do with the plague – it was just an accident.'

The Philistine chieftains followed this advice. They took two milking cows, hitched them to a cart, and shut their calves up.

The cows made straight for Bethshemesh, keeping to the road and lowing as they went. They just went straight on. The Philistine chieftains followed them to the borders of Bethshemesh – and watched what happened.

It was wheat harvest in the valley and the townspeople were out reaping. They suddenly saw the Ark and ran excitedly to meet it. It came into farmer Joshua's field and stopped by the Great Stone there. So they broke up the wood of the cart, made a fire and sacrificed the cows as an offering to GOD.

The Philistine chieftains went back to Ekron.

Some time later, the citizens of Kiriath-jearim came and took the Ark to their own town and put it in Abinadab's house on the hill. They made his son, Eleazar, its guardian.

The Beloved Captain

Saul was a Northerner; the stories that now lie before us, we must remember, are Southern stories, and Southerners disliked Saul just because he was a Northerner. In their account of these times they 'write him down', and forget that it was the North that first realised the great danger they were all in and did something about it.

Saul is indeed 'the Beloved Captain' – he never had to face (as David did) any rebellion against his authority. We shall see later how loyal David was to him in spite of the trouble that arose between them. He was a deeply religious man and never turned his back on his country's enemies. But the task was too great for him – you can't fight trained soldiers with tribal levies.

'Where have you been?'

1 Samuel 9:1-8, 10-14, 18-27; 10:1-7, 9-11, 13-16

Kish, a rich farmer of the Benjamin clan, lived in the central highlands. Saul was his son, a handsome young man, head and shoulders taller than most of his fellows; there was not a handsomer young man in the country.

One day the farmer found that some of his donkeys had strayed away.

'Take one of the farm lads,' he said to Saul, 'and go and find them.'

The two of them searched everywhere in the highlands, but no donkeys were to be found. They came at last to a small Benjamin town.

'We'd better go home,' Saul said to the boy. 'It won't be the donkeys my father will be worried about – it'll be us.'

'Wait!' said the boy. 'There's a man of God in the town here. Everybody talks about him – what he says always comes true. Let's go into the town; perhaps he can tell us where the donkeys are.'

'Well,' said Saul, 'suppose we do – what are we going to pay him with? We've no present to give him; our bags are empty.'

'I've got a silver coin,' said the boy. 'We can give him that to tell us what to do.'

'All right,' said Saul. 'Let's try.'

They went toward the town.

The town was built on a hill, and girls were coming down the road to draw water from the well.

'Is the seer at home?' they asked the girls.

'Yes,' they said, 'he's ahead of you, over there. He's just go here; we're going to have a sacrifice today on the hill. You'll easily find him when you get into the town – you may catch him before he goes to the hill for the meal there. Be quick – you may meet him now.'

Just as they got to the town gate, the seer (Samuel by name) was coming out of it on his way up to the hill.

Saul met him in the gateway.

'Can you tell me where the seer lives?' he asked.

'I am the seer,' said Samuel. 'Go ahead of me to the hill – you must share the meal with me there. Tomorrow I'll send you on your way, and tell you what you want to know. Forget about the donkeys – they've been found. Who are GOD's people waiting for? Isn't it you – and your family?'

'My tribe doesn't count,' said Saul, 'it's the least important in the land. My family doesn't count, either – we're nobody that matters. Why do you talk to me like this?'

Samuel just took Saul and the boy to the high hill, the holy place of the town, and into the guest-chamber. There were about 30 people there at the sacred meal. He set the two of them at the head of the table.

He turned to the cook.

'I told you to put a joint aside,' he said. 'Serve it now.'

The cook set the shoulder and fat tail in front of Saul.

'That was kept for you,' Samuel said to Saul. 'Eat it with the guests. It was kept for this important moment.'

So Saul shared the meal with Samuel.

They all went down the hill back to the town. Saul was given a bed on the flat roof of the house, and went to sleep.

At dawn, Samuel called up to him.

'Get up,' he said. 'I want to send you on your way.'

Saul got up, and he and Samuel went out into the street, and walked along until they came to the outskirts of the town.

'Tell the boy to go on ahead,' said Samuel.

The boy went on.

'Stand here,' Samuel said to Saul. 'I must tell you what GOD has said.'

He took some oil, poured it on Saul's head and kissed him (as if he were crowning a king).

'GOD anoints you as the leader of his people,' he said. 'You are to be their king and rescue them from their enemies who are attacking them on all sides. A sign will prove this to you. At Rachel's Tomb you'll meet two men who'll tell you that the donkeys have been found and that your father's worrying about you now. Then when you come to the Tabor Oak, three men, on their way to Bethel, will meet you. They will be carrying their gifts for the sacrifice there – one carrying three kids, another three bread loaves, the third a skin of wine. They will greet you and offer you two loaves – take them. After that you will come to God's Hill – there's a Philistine outpost there. A company of prophets will be marching down from the high hill there, playing on musical instruments, speaking excitedly words from GOD. GOD's spirit will seize you, and you will join them and speak as they do – you will become an inspired man. When all this has happened, you must do as you think best – GOD will be with you!'

Saul said goodbye to Samuel.

All happened as Samuel had said. When Saul's friends saw him acting like a prophet they were amazed.

'What's happened to Saul?' they asked. 'Has he joined the prophets?'

His uncle met them.

'Where've you been?' he asked.

'Looking for the donkeys,' said Saul. 'When we couldn't find them, we went to Samuel.'

'Oh!' said his uncle. 'And what did he talk to you about?'

'The donkeys,' said Saul. 'He told us they'd been found.'

Crowned King   *1 Samuel 11:1-11, 15*

A month later, Ammonite tribesmen, under their chieftain Nahash, attacked Jabesh town.

'We'll submit,' said the townsmen, 'if you make a binding treaty with us.'

'I'll make a treaty with you all right – on one condition,' said the chieftain. 'I'll gouge all your right eyes out and make you a disgrace to all your fellow countrymen!'

'Give us a week's armistice, then,' said the townsmen. 'Let us send messengers to our countrymen. If nobody comes to our rescue, we'll surrender to you!'

The messengers came to Saul's town, Gibeah. They had just told their news – there was a great noise of wailing people – when Saul came home from the fields driving his oxen before him.

'What's the matter?' he asked.

They told him.

GOD's spirit seized him when he heard the news. In a blaze of anger he cut his oxen into pieces, and sent couriers with the pieces to his fellow countrymen everywhere, with a proclamation:

'Follow me! Anyone who doesn't will have his cattle cut up like this!'

The fear of GOD fell upon everyone, and they rallied as one man.

The roll-call was held at Bezek, and Saul gave the Jabesh messengers their orders. 'Go home,' he said. 'Tell your fellow-townsmen that they will be rescued by noon tomorrow.'

There was great rejoicing in Jabesh town, and the townsmen sent word to the Ammonite chieftain.

'We will surrender tomorrow,' they said. 'You can do what you want with us.'

Saul marched all night with three companies. They stormed the Ammonite camp in the darkness before dawn. The fighting went on till noon – the Ammonite survivors fled in all directions, every man for himself.

The Israelite people gathered at Gilgal, and there Saul was crowned king in GOD's presence; there was a religious service with a sacrifice to GOD – and great celebrations.

Backs to the Wall   *1 Samuel 13:1-3, 5-7, 15-18*

Saul (now 50 years old) set about dealing with the Philistines. He organised an army and sent the rest of the tribal levies home. Two thirds of the men, under his own command, were encamped at Michmash and in the highlands of Bethel; one third, under his son Jonathan's command, were encamped at Gibeah in the Benjamin hills where they destroyed the Philistine outpost.

News reached the Philistine cities – 'The highlanders have revolted.' They called out their troops, marched into the highlands and occupied Michmash. This threw the Israelites into a panic – they knew they were now in grave danger. They left their villages, and hid themselves anywhere they could – in caves, holes, rocks, tombs or wells – or fled over Jordan River to the eastern mountains.

Saul held a roll call of his troops; they numbered about 600 men. He and Jonathan now set up camp at Gibeah. The Philistines held Michmash and sent out three raiding parties to capture strategic points in the highlands – towards Ophrah (Gideon's home town), Beth-horon and the hill looking down the Valley of the Hyenas toward the desert.

The Michmash Pass   *1 Samuel 13:23; 14:1-31, 36-46*

The main body of the Philistines at Michmash pushed out an outpost to the heights above the Michmash Pass.

One day Jonathan spoke to his young armour-bearer.

'Let's go and have a look at the Philistine outpost over there on the other side of the pass,' he said.

Saul had taken his stand, with his six hundred soldiers, outside Gibeah where he had his headquarters under the pomegranate tree by the threshing-floor. Jonathan had said nothing about his plans to his father; even the soldiers didn't know he had gone off.

Now on the other side of the Michmash Pass there were two steep cliffs, one on each side, north and south. (Their local names were 'Slippery Rock' and 'Thorny Rock'.)

'Let's go over to these heathen Philistines,' said Jonathan. 'GOD will be on our side, perhaps – he doesn't depend on numbers.'

'Go ahead,' said his armour-bearer. 'I'm your man!'

'Now listen,' said Jonathan. 'We'll let them see us. If they shout at us, "You stay where you are till we get at you!" we'll just stay put. But if they shout, "Come on up and try your luck!" then up we go. That's a sure sign GOD's put them at our mercy.'

They both stepped out and let themselves be seen.

'Look,' shouted the Philistine sentries, 'the highlanders are coming out of their hide-outs!'

The sentries hailed the two men.

'Come on up!' they shouted. 'We'll show you a thing or two!'

'After me!' ordered Jonathan. 'GOD's put them at our mercy!'

He scrambled up on his hands and knees, the soldier after him. They caught the sentries by surprise (they had no idea there was a path up the cliff). Jonathan knocked them down and his armour-bearer killed them off – twenty men on a narrow ledge.

Panic spread throughout the Philistine camp – and beyond. There happened to be an earthquake just at that moment too; the Philistine army and the raiding columns were terrified and the panic became a rout.

The Israelite look-outs in Gibeah were watching the Philistine camp and saw the soldiers suddenly scattering in all directions.

'Who's missing?' asked Saul. 'Find out!'

Jonathan and his armour-bearer were missing at the roll-call.

'Bring the Ark here,' said Saul to Ahijah its guardian.

While Saul was talking like this to the priest, the uproar in the Philistine camp grew louder.

'Wait,' said Saul.

He and his men raced over to the fight. Everybody seemed to be fighting everybody else; it was complete chaos. Even the Israelites who had gone over to the Philistines and were serving with their army deserted and joined Saul and Jonathan. Men who had been hiding in the highlands came out and joined in the pursuit. So GOD rescued the Israelites that day.

But Saul made a big mistake. He had put all his soldiers under oath – 'Cursed be the man who eats anything until evening, until I have had my revenge on my enemies'.

The soldiers were exhausted; nobody had eaten anything all day, not even the honeycombs in the open fields which the bees had abandoned. The oath had frightened them.

Jonathan knew nothing about all this. Walking along, he pushed his staff into a honeycomb and put some of the honey into his mouth with his hand. It did him good. Then a soldier told him about the oath.

'My father's made it very hard for the soldiers,' was all Jonathan said. 'See how much better I am with a little taste of honey. If the soldiers could have eaten when they wanted to today – there's plenty of loot – what a victory it would have been! We would have wiped them out!'

That day the Israelites fought the Philistines from Michmash to Aijalon, although they were weak with hunger.

'And now for a night attack!' ordered Saul. 'Loot until dawn and finish them all off!'

'As you command,' his men said.

'Let us ask GOD first,' said Ahijah the priest.

So that is what Saul did.

'Shall I go after the Philistines?' he asked. 'Will you make us the victors?' GOD gave no answer.

'Somebody's broken the oath,' said Saul. He ordered all the officers to meet and find out who the culprit was.

'By the GOD who rescues us,' he said, 'the culprit shall die – even though he is Jonathan, my son!'

The soldiers stood in silence.

'We'll soon find out,' said Saul. 'All of you shall be on one side – I and Jonathan on the other.'

'As you command,' said the soldiers.

Saul prayed to GOD.

'O GOD, 'he said, 'why haven't you given me an answer today? Guide the lots, and if the guilt is mine or Jonathan's, give *Urim*; if it is the soldiers', give *Thummim*.'

Jonathan and Saul were chosen.

'Now cast lots between me and Jonathan,' said Saul.

Jonathan was chosen.

'What have you done?' said Saul. 'Tell me!'

'I used my staff and tasted a bit of honey,' he said. 'I am ready to die.'

'And die you shall!' said Saul.

The soldiers protested.

'Jonathan die?' they shouted. 'Jonathan who rescued us today? Never! By GOD, not a hair on his head shall fall on the ground. He's been GOD's fellow-worker today!'

So the soldiers ransomed Jonathan and saved his life. Saul called off the pursuit of the Philistines; by now they had retreated to their cities.

Night in the Valley

1 Samuel 28:4-25

The last great battle was about to begin. The Philistines had massed their forces in the Jezreel valley with Shunem as headquarters. Saul and his men pitched camp on Gilboa Hill. Saul surveyed the Philistine troops massed in the valley below. What he saw filled him with fear and foreboding. He prayed to GOD, but GOD was silent. Whatever he tried – dreams, the stones,* prophets – he got no answer.

'I must get help from someone,' he said to his officers. 'Find me a woman who can conjure up the dead – I'll try her.'

'There's a woman in the valley below,' they told him, 'at Endor.'

He disguised himself as a private soldier and went, with two of his men, out into the night.

'You're a woman who can conjure up the dead,' he told the woman. 'Use your art to tell me my fortune – let me talk to the man whose name I'll give you.'

'You know Saul's orders,' said the woman. 'He's banished witches and wizards. You're trying to trap me, aren't you? You know I'll be put to death if I'm found out.'

Saul put her at her ease.

---

* The flat stones called 'Urim' and 'Thummim'. See under 'Notes on Some Important Words and Names' (p. 685).

'As GOD lives,' he said, 'you're quite safe; our visit tonight won't get you into trouble.'

'Who do you want to talk to?' she asked.

'Samuel,' he said.

When she heard the name of 'Samuel', she screamed and turned on Saul. 'Why have you played this trick on me?' she said. 'You are Saul himself!'

'Don't be frightened,' he said. 'Tell me what you are seeing.'

'A ghost,' she said, 'coming up out of the ground.'

'What's it look like?' asked Saul.

'An old man,' she said, 'an old man wrapped in a cloak.'

Saul knew it was Samuel, and he bowed to the ground before him.

'Why have you disturbed me,' asked Samuel, 'bringing me back like this?'

'I'm at my wits' end,' said Saul. 'The Philistines are attacking me in force, and GOD has left me and won't listen to my prayers any more. So I've called you back – tell me what I'm to do.'

'If GOD won't have anything to do with you,' said Samuel, 'why ask me? This is GOD's will: tomorrow you and your sons will die in battle – the Israelites will be defeated.'

Saul fell full length on the floor; Samuel's words terrified him. He hadn't any strength left – for a whole day and a whole night he'd eaten nothing. The woman knelt down beside him and saw his look of terror.

'I've done what you told me to,' she said. 'I've done it at the risk of my life. Now listen to me, please. Let me get you something to eat. You need a bit of food if you're going to get back to the camp.'

'No,' he said, 'I couldn't touch anything.'

The three of them – his two men and the woman – went on arguing with him. At last he gave way. He got up and sat on the bed in the room. The woman killed a calf she had and made unleavened cakes from some flour. She made a meal for the three men. They ate it and went back to the camp in the darkness.

Death on the Hill   *1 Samuel 31:1-13*

The Philistines launched their attack. The Israelites broke before them and left their dead and dying on the slopes of Gilboa Hill. The Philistines made for the king's standard and round it raged the fiercest fighting. Saul's sons were killed and, at last, the Philistine archers found their mark – Saul was badly wounded in the stomach.

'Draw your sword,' he said to his armour-bearer. 'Finish me off. I don't want these heathen beasts to come and make sport of me.'

His armour-bearer was too frightened to obey; so Saul got hold of his own sword and threw himself on it. At the sight of his dead king, the armour bearer threw himself on his own sword and died by his side. So Saul and his sons and his armour-bearer died together on the same day.

When the Israelites on the other side of the valley saw the rout of their own men, they abandoned their towns in panic.

Next day, the Philistine soldiers came back to the battlefield for booty. They found Saul's body and the bodies of his three sons where they had fallen on Gilboa Hill. They cut off Saul's head and stripped his body of his armour.

They sent heralds back to their own cities with the good news of victory. They announced it to the people in the streets and to the gods in their temples; they put Saul's armour in the temple of Astarte and hung his body on the wall of Bethshan.

News of all this reached the citizens of Jabesh-Gilead in the highlands east of Jordan River. A company of their bravest soldiers marched through the night across the river, to Bethshan, and took Saul's body – and those of his sons – down from the city wall. They carried them back home and buried their ashes under the tamarisk tree in their town. Everybody went into mourning for a week.

Salute to the Dead   *2 Samuel 1:1-27*

David (whose story we still have to tell) was stationed at this time in Ziklag, a small town far away in the south. He had been out raiding and had only been home a day or two.

A young man, with his clothes torn and earth on his head, came running into the town. He threw himself on the ground in front of David in homage.

'Where have you come from?' asked David.

'I've escaped from the Israelite camp on Gilboa,' he said.

'What happened?' asked David. 'Tell me.'

'It was just a rout,' said the man. 'There are many killed and wounded on the battlefield. Saul and Jonathan are dead.'

'How do you know?' asked David.

'I just happened to be on Gilboa Hill. Saul was leaning on his spear. The Philistine chariots and cavalry were charging down on him. He turned round, saw me and called me over to him. "Here, sir!" I said. "Stand beside me," he said, "and put me out of my misery – I'm in terrible pain and I can't die." I did what he ordered me; he couldn't have lived much longer, I'm sure. I took the crown from his head and the armlet from his arm. Here they are. They are yours, my lord.'

'Where do you come from?' David asked.

'I'm the son of an Amalekite immigrant,' he said.

'What?' said David. 'Weren't you too overawed to kill GOD's anointed king?'

'Here!' David called to one of his young soldiers. 'Strike him down!' The soldier struck him dead.

'You signed your own death warrant,' said David. 'Your own words – "I killed the king" – are evidence against you.'

David and his men tore their clothes in their grief, lamenting and fasting for all who had died in the battle and for the whole tribal league. So they spent the day until darkness fell.

This is the 'Lament' which David composed about Saul and Jonathan:

O Captain,
   dead in the highlands!
Heroes fallen
   in the thick of the fight!

Keep the news from Gath,
    no word of it in Ashkelon's streets –
    lest Philistine girls start singing,
    heathen girls make merry.

O Gilboa Hill! No dew be on you!
No rain fall on you, you fields of death!
The hero's shield, the king's sword
   were stained there
   with dead men's blood,
   strong men's flesh.

Jonathan's bow faced the foe,
   Saul's sword wreaked havoc –
Saul and Jonathan,

loved and lovely,
together in life and death,
swifter than eagles,
stronger than lions!

Girls in the villages,
cry your eyes out for Saul;
he clothed you in scarlet and splendour,
he braided your dresses with gold!

Alas for the heroes
fallen in the fierce fighting!

O Jonathan, my heart breaks for you,
my brother, my closest friend!
You loved me more dearly
than any woman could!

Alas for the dead heroes!
Alas for their broken swords!

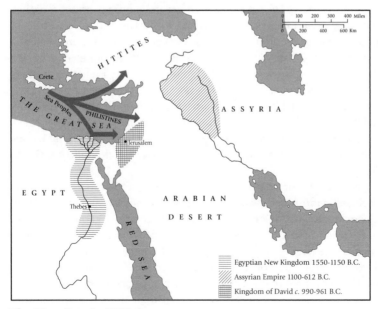

The Near East in 1000 BCE

The Great King

The story of King David begins before Saul's death and we must now go back in time in order to tell it. King David is one of the outstanding kings in history, although his empire was a small affair beside the great empires of Egypt and Assyria. It was only because, as we have said, these powerful empires were having trouble at home and had no time for foreign adventures that David could dominate the small countries of the Middle East as he did.

His character and achievements made him the most famous Israelite king; later centuries were to remember him as the ideal king – a sort of King Arthur – beside whom all other kings were judged. When, after the Exile, small groups of Jews returned to build their city but had no king of their own (they were part of the vast Persian Empire), they began to dream that one day God would again give them a king like David.

Saul had failed to drive the Philistines back to the plain and defeat them; David believed God had called him to carry out this task. He saw plainly that it could not be done with unreliable tribesmen whose interest very rarely went beyond their tribal boundaries and who were not capable of sustained warfare. He set himself to create a proper state, a nation, with a central government and a standing army. He enlisted and trained his famous 'Foreign Legion' from soldiers who had served under him in his days as a freebooter in the hills or as an officer under one of the Philistine chieftains. He was a great soldier and many Philistine soldiers were glad to serve under him. The Captain of his 'Foreign Legion' was a Philistine, and one of his most loyal officers, Captain Uriah, was a Hittite.

But David, like Saul, was a deeply religious man and cared greatly that the Israelite people should really be GOD's People. The tribal league had failed. David set himself to create a nation which could be GOD's People.

The new nation, including as it did Philistines and Canaanites as well as Hebrews, made a great change in Israelite religion. It brought them into close touch with neighbouring peoples; the new capital city itself ('David's Town', 'Zion') had been a Canaanite fortress with its temple and priests. The Israelites believed GOD had chosen it as his 'place' and David as his king. So for them the nation was founded on a new Covenant – a covenant made by God with David (representing the people). Many Israelites, especially in the North, had their doubts about all this, as we shall see.

David was a great man and a great king; a thousand years later one of his descendants – Jesus – was to deal with the problems he faced in a very different way and to call into being a new 'People of God' which would transcend national politics and be a world community.

Captain of the King's Bodyguard

Called to the Court   *1 Samuel 16:14-23; 18:1-9*

Saul suffered from sudden and unreasoning fits of terror.

'Some evil demon's tormenting you,' his courtiers told him. 'Let us find a clever harpist – you've only to give us the command; he can soothe you with his music when these fits of terror seize you.'

'Good,' said the king. 'Find me a clever musician and bring him to court.'

'I know of a man who can play the harp,' said one of the pages. 'He's the son of Jesse, a farmer in Bethlehem.'

Saul asked Jesse to send his son David to court. Jesse sent him – along with a present of five loaves of bread, a skin of wine and a kid. Saul took a great fancy to him and made him his armour-bearer.

'I like David very much,' he sent word to his father. 'Let him become one of my officers.'

Whenever he had his fits of terror, David played his harp. The king was soothed, the fits passed and he felt himself again. He took David into his service, and wouldn't let him go home.

Jonathan, Saul's son, and David became bosom friends and swore an oath of friendship with one another; in proof of his friendship, Jonathan gave his royal cloak to David, along with his weapons – his sword and his bow – and his belt.

David proved a first-class soldier. Saul promoted him to the rank of Commander-in-Chief. Everybody liked him – even the king's officers. He was a popular hero. When he came back from a campaign, village girls came out to meet him, dancing to music and singing songs. One of the popular songs of the day ran –

'Saul has killed his thousands –
David his tens of thousands.'

Saul didn't like that! 'Tens of thousands to David,' he growled, 'but only thousands to me!'

That's how his jealousy of David started; from now on he kept an eye on him.

The King's Daughter   *1 Samuel 18:20, 22-29; 19:11-17*

Michal, Saul's daughter, fell in love with David. When Saul heard about it, he seemed very pleased; but he had his own reasons. He told his courtiers to find out what David himself thought.

'Get him talking,' he said. 'You can start him off with something like this: "You're a lucky fellow – you're on the right side of the king, and we are all your friends. Is it such a wild dream to think of being the king's son-in-law?"'

This was the way the conversation went when David was present.

'Nonsense,' he said. 'I'm nobody; you talk as if anybody could become the king's son-in-law!'

His words were reported to the king.

'Tell him I want no marriage present,' said Saul, 'but that there's one thing I would like: a little revenge on my enemies – the death of a hundred Philistine soldiers.'

The officers quickly told David. He thought it was an easy way of becoming the king's son-in-law. So he called out to his men, raided the Philistines, and killed two hundred of them. He brought back to Saul evidence that he had killed them, and claimed his right to be his son-in-law.

So Saul gave David his daughter Michal in marriage. He knew in his heart that David was a good man and that Michal was really in love with him. But all this deepened his jealousy of David; and he began to plan his murder. One night he sent agents to keep watch outside David's house, with orders to murder him as he left home next morning.

Michal got wind of her father's plans and told David.

'Get out tonight,' she said. 'If you don't, you're as good as dead.'

She let him down through a window and he got away and made good his escape. Michal then took the household gods and put them in his bed, with a goat's-hair pillow at its head and a cloak covering gods and pillow.

When David didn't come out of the house in the morning, Saul ordered his agents to break in and arrest him. Michal faced them and told them he was ill.

Saul wasn't being stopped by that. He ordered his agents to bring him, bed and all; he would see him killed himself. The agents soon discovered the trick – there were household gods in the bed with the pillow at its head!

'Why have you played this trick on me?' Saul asked his daughter. 'You helped him to escape and get away – and you know he's my enemy!'

'He made me do it,' she said. 'He said he'd kill me if I didn't.'

Escape to Nob *1 Samuel 21:1-9*

David reached Nob where the priest was a man called Ahimelech. Ahimelech saw him coming and ran out to meet him.

'Why are you alone?' he asked. 'And where are your men?'

'I'm on a mission from the king,' said David, 'and on the king's orders, it must be kept secret. I am meeting my troops at a rendezvous. What have you got to eat? Give me four loaves of bread – or anything else you can lay your hands on.'

'There's only sacred bread here,' said the priest. 'There's no ordinary bread. Have your soldiers kept free from women?'

'Indeed they have,' said David. 'We maintain the sexual taboo whenever we go out on raids. Their equipment is dedicated to GOD.'

So the priest let him have the sacred bread. (This is special bread kept only for the worship of GOD; it is always replaced with fresh bread on the day it is taken away.)

'Haven't you got a spare sword or spear here?' asked David. 'The king's mission was so urgent that I left unarmed.'

'Goliath's Philistine sword is kept here,' said the priest. 'It's wrapped in a cloth over there behind the image. You can take it if you want to. We haven't anything else.'

'Fine! Let me have it,' said David. 'There isn't another sword like it!'

All this time, one of Saul's soldiers happened to be staying in the temple – Doeg, an Edomite, Saul's strongest cattleman. He was under a vow to GOD which he had to carry out in the shrine itself.

Outlaw

The Massacre at Gibeah *1 Samuel 22:6-18*

News about David and his men and where they were reached Saul at Gibeah. He was holding court at the time, sitting, spear in hand, under the tamarisk tree on the high hill. His officers were standing at attention round him.

'I've got something to say to you, men of Benjamin,' he said to them. 'Will this Bethlehem farmer David give you fields and vineyards – will he make you commanders of regiments and companies – that none of you breathed a word to me that my son Jonathan had actually set one of my officers up as my rival?'

'I've seen David,' called out Doeg the Edomite. 'I saw him at Nob. He came while I was staying in the temple there. The priest Ahimelech prayed to God for him, fed him and gave him Goliath's sword.'

Saul sent for Ahimelech and his assistant priests and commanded them to attend court.

'Now listen, Ahimelech,' said Saul.

'I am at your majesty's service,' said Ahimelech.

'What's this conspiracy against me about?' asked Saul. 'Why have you sided with David? I hear you've fed and armed him – and prayed to GOD for him. Why? He's now set himself up as my rival; he's out looking for me!'

'What else could I do?' asked Ahimelech. 'David's your son-in-law, the captain of your bodyguard, one of the most important men here in your court. If I couldn't trust *him*, whom could I trust? Is praying to GOD for him an irreligious thing to do? I deny your charge against me. You have no reason to suspect me of conspiracy. I don't know what you're talking about.'

'I've already passed the death sentence on you,' said Saul, 'and on your fellow priests.'

The King turned to Doeg.

'You kill them,' he ordered.

Doeg stepped forward and killed them. Eighty-five men died that day.

The Relief of Keilah Town   *1 Samuel 23:1, 5, 7-13*

David heard that the Philistines were raiding Keilah Town; they had surrounded it and were looting the threshing floors. He immediately went to the town's rescue. He and his men routed the raiders and carried off their cattle.

Saul heard about all this.

'GOD's put him just where I want him,' he said. 'He's gone inside a walled town – he's walked into a trap!'

He called his army out; he would go down and catch him in the town.

Now Abiathar, the son of Ahimelech – the priest Saul had murdered – had escaped from Nob and joined David; and he had brought the ephod with him to Keilah. When Saul's plans were reported to David, he called Abiathar to him.

'Bring the ephod here,' he ordered.

Then he prayed to GOD.

'O GOD,' he prayed, 'will Saul attack me here, as the reports say? Tell me, I am your servant.'

'He will,' said GOD.

'Will the citizens of this town hand me and my men over to him?'

'They will,' said GOD.

David acted straightaway. He marched his 600 men out of the town and they lived as guerrillas in the hills. Saul heard of David's escape and called off his expedition.

Hachilah Hill   *1 Samuel 26:1-22, 25*

The people of Ziph took the news that David was hiding near them to Saul in Gibeah. He called out his crack troops and marched to the wilderness of Ziph to hunt him out. He pitched camp on Hachilah Hill on the road facing 'The Desert'.

David was out in the rough moorlands when he heard that Saul was tracking him down. He sent scouts to find out where he was.

Then he moved quickly. He marched by night to the outskirts of Saul's camp. Saul and his commander-in-chief, Abner, were asleep – Saul lying in the trench, the soldiers in the tents around him as guard.

David called two men, the Hittite Ahimelech and Abishai.

'Which of you will go down with me to the camp – to Saul?' he asked.

'I will,' said Abishai.

So, through the darkness, the two men stole down to the camp. There was Saul lying asleep in the trench – his spear stuck in the ground at his head, Abner and the soldiers lying around him.

'GOD has put your enemy at your mercy,' whispered Abishai. 'I'll pin him to the earth with his own spear. One stroke's enough.'

'No murder,' said David. 'Saul is GOD's anointed king – murder of GOD's anointed king is a dreadful thing. In GOD's name, no murder! We'll leave him in GOD's hands, to die an ordinary death or meet a soldier's violent end. But GOD forbid that I should lay my hand on his anointed king. Get the spear at his head, and the water-jug there – and let's get out!'

So they took the spear and the water-jug from near Saul's head and slipped away. Nobody saw or heard them, and nobody woke up. They were all sound asleep.

David crossed the valley and stood at a safe distance on a hilltop on the other side. He was so far off that he had to shout as loud as he could to be heard.

'Why don't you answer, Abner?' he shouted.

'Who are you,' Abner shouted back, 'calling up the king like this?'

'You're a fine soldier!' shouted David. 'You're the finest soldier of them all! What sort of guard is this to keep over his majesty the king? Didn't you know there's an assassin prowling round? What a soldier you are! By GOD, you ought to be executed for sleeping – you're supposed to be on guard, you know! Do you want proof? See where the king's spear and his water-jug are now – not at his head!'

Saul, awake by now, recognised David's voice.

'Is that you, my son David?' he called.

'It is, your majesty,' David shouted back. 'And let me finish what I have to say. Why do you hunt me like this? What have I done wrong? If GOD's made you do this, let us ask his forgiveness; but if it's just slander, GOD's curse be on the slanderers – they have driven me out of the company of GOD's people and tried to make me a foreigner. Don't let my blood be spilt in this foreign countryside. You're hunting me like a hawk hunting a partridge in the highlands!'

'I'm in the wrong,' said Saul. 'Come back to me, my son David. I'll do you no more hurt; you treated me as the real king today. I've been a fool and done a dreadful thing.'

'The king's spear is here,' called David. 'Let one of the soldiers come over and fetch it.'

'GOD bless you, my son David,' said Saul. 'You've a great future in front of you!'

David went on his way and Saul went home.

A Highland Farmer   1 Samuel 25:1-25, 27-28, 32-44

There was a rich farmer in Maon, Nabal by name, who owned a farm at Carmel Town. He was a farmer in a big way; he had three thousand sheep and a thousand goats. His wife, Abigail, was an able and attractive woman. The man himself was just the opposite, a rude and coarse fellow.

It was the sheep-shearing season and Nabal was at his farm. David was out on the moors. Someone told him about Nabal and his sheep-shearing. He sent ten young soldiers to the farm.

'Go to Carmel Town,' he told them, 'and see Nabal. Give him my regards. Wish him many happy returns – and good luck to himself and his family and farm. Then give him this message: "I've heard that sheep-shearing has begun. Your shepherds have been in my neighbour-hood. We didn't molest them and they lost nothing all the time they were on the moors. Ask them – they will tell you. So treat these young soldiers well; after all, it's a festival. Give them something – whatever you like – and don't forget me, your friend."'

The men met Nabal, gave him David's message and waited for an answer.

'Who's David?' was all they got. 'There are hundreds of slaves running away from their masters nowadays. Good God, must I take what I've got ready for my own shearers – my bread and wine and meat – and give it to any Tom, Dick or Harry? How do I know where you've come from?'

The men went back to David and told him what had happened. He mustered his men.

'Buckle your swords on,' he commanded.

He left two hundred men with the baggage and marched with four hundred to the farm.

Meanwhile, when David's messengers had left the farm, one of the servants had gone to Nabal's wife, Abigail.

'Look,' he said, 'David sent some of his men to our master with his greetings, and all he could do was to shout at them. When we were out on the hills, the men were very good to us – they didn't molest us at all and we lost nothing all the time we were with them. They were like a wall round us day and night while we were looking after the sheep near them. You'd better do something about it – our master will really be in trouble if you don't. He's a brute of a fellow; nobody can talk to him.'

Abigail didn't wait a moment. She collected two hundred loaves, two skins of wine, five sheep ready for cooking, five pecks of roasted corn, a hundred bunches of raisins and two hundred fig cakes. She packed them on donkeys and told her servants to go on ahead – she would follow them. She didn't say a word to her husband.

She was riding on her donkey under the cover of the hill; David and his soldiers were moving down the opposite hillside towards her. They suddenly met.

'I've been wasting my time looking after this fellow's property out on the moors,' David had been thinking. 'He's lost nothing – and this is how he repays me! God help me, if I leave any of his men alive by dawn!'

Abigail got quickly off her donkey, and threw herself at David's feet.

'I am the one to blame,' she said. 'Let me tell you my side of the story. Take no notice of this brute of a fellow, Nabal; he's a fool by name and a fool by nature. I didn't know anything about the soldiers my lord sent – I didn't even see them. I've brought a present for my lord; let your soldiers have it.'

'Thank GOD for sending you to me today,' exclaimed David. 'Blessings on you! You're a sensible woman. And you've saved me from an act of bloodshed, from taking GOD's law into my own hand! I can see that

GOD himself has been behind all you've done. But by GOD! if you hadn't been so quick off the mark, there wouldn't have been a man left alive on Nabal's farm by dawn!'

He accepted her present.

'Go home in peace,' he told her. 'See, I've listened to your story – I've done what you asked me.'

When Abigail got home to the farm, she found Nabal still feasting – very merry and as drunk as a lord. So she waited until next morning when he's slept off his drunkenness. Then she told him what had happened – who the soldiers really were and what she'd done about it. At her words, Nabal had a stroke and fell unconscious on the floor. He had another stroke ten days later, and this stroke killed him.

'Blessed be GOD!' said David when he heard of Nabal's death. 'He avenged the insult Nabal gave me – and he stopped me taking the law into my own hands. Nabal got what he deserved!'

David had been very attracted by Abigail, and he now started to court her. Then he sent some of his men to her on her farm with a proposal of marriage. When they told her who had sent them, she got up and bowed herself to the ground. Her thoughts were: 'I would be glad to be just a slave-girl in his home, let alone his wife!' She quickly got herself ready. She mounted a donkey, and five of her maids went on foot. They followed David's soldiers back to camp, and she and David were married.

(David now had two wives – he was already married to a Jezreel girl, Ahinoam. Saul had divorced him from his daughter Michal and had married her to Paltai, a Gallim man.)

Philistine Commander

Flight to Gath   *1 Samuel 27:1-4, 7-9, 11, 10, 12, 5-6*

'One of these days Saul will get me,' thought David. 'The best thing I can do is to cross over into Philistine territory. It's the only way to get out of his clutches. He'll give up when he knows he can't catch me in his own territory.'

David marched his six hundred men across the frontier to the Philistine town of Gath. He went over to its chieftain Achish, and he and his men settled in the town. When news of David's flight reached Saul, he gave up his attempt to capture him.

David spent sixteen months in Philistine territory. He and his men set off, raiding the various tribes in the Negeb as far as the Egyptian border. His raids followed a similar pattern: all the tribes-people – men and women – were killed; all livestock – sheep, cattle, donkeys, camels – were driven away and all clothing seized. He brought them all back to Achish.

(He regularly killed all men and women, rather than bring them back as prisoners to Achish, to stop any information about his movements reaching Saul. He made this his settled policy while in Philistine territory.)

To Achish's regular question, 'Where've you been raiding today?' David always gave a vague answer.

'Oh, in the Negeb,' he would say, and add 'of Judah' or 'of the Jerah-meelites' or 'of the Kenites' in an offhand way.

Achish came to trust David.

'His own people will have finished with him,' he would think. 'I can count on him as a permanent officer of my army – he'll never dare to go home.'

When some time had passed, David spoke to Achish.

'If you are satisfied with my service,' he said, 'let me be stationed in one of the country towns – you don't need me in the city here.'

Achish appointed him to the small town of Ziklag, in the south on the road to Beersheba.

Commander of the Bodyguard   *1 Samuel 28:1-2; 29:1-4, 6-11*

At last the Philistines called out their forces for a full-scale war against the Israelites.

'I expect you to fight with my army,' Achish told David.

'Certainly!' said David. 'You'll see what kind of soldier I am!'

'Fine!' said Achish. 'I promote you commander of my bodyguard.'

The Philistines assembled their forces at Aphek across their northern border. The Israelite camp lay at Harod in the Jezreel Valley. The Philistines held a march-past – the chieftains with their regiments and companies, David and his men bringing up the rear under Achish of Gath.

The Philistine High Command protested.

'What are these highlanders doing here?' they asked.

'You know,' said Achish. 'It's David who deserted from Saul. He's been with me for a year or more now. He's given excellent service – I've no complaints at all.'

The Philistine officers were in an ugly mood.

'Send him packing!' they said. 'Let him get back to the town where you stationed him. He's not taking part in this battle – he'll turn traitor as soon as the fighting begins. What better way could he find of putting himself right with his king than by turning on our own troops?'

Achish called David over to him.

'As GOD lives,' he said, 'you are an honourable man, and, as far as I am concerned, you should be marching with me in this campaign. I've no complaint to make about you from the day you entered my service, but the High Command doesn't approve of you. Go back – and go without any fuss – I don't want any trouble with the other chieftains.'

'But what have I done?' asked David. 'Have I ever done anything as an officer of yours which disqualifies me from fighting your enemies by your side?'

'You are a magnificent officer,' said Achish. 'But the fact is this. The High Command have made it plain that you are not to have any part in this campaign. Your orders are to go at first light tomorrow – you and your soldiers – back to Ziklag. Don't take this badly; you know what I think of you. But at dawn tomorrow, you must be gone.'

So, at first light, David and his men marched off, back through Philistine territory, as far south as Ziklag – three days' march. The Philistine army moved north, through the Megiddo Pass, and then eastwards to Jezreel Valley.*

Back to Ziklag   1 Samuel 30:1-4, 6-24, 26

By the time David got back, Amalekite tribes had raided the Negeb and sacked Ziklag and burned it to the ground. They had marched away all the women they found there – young and old. What David found was a burned town – wives, sons and daughters all gone. The soldiers broke down in an agony of grief. David himself was now in real danger. His soldiers were so bitter and grief-stricken that they talked of stoning him there and then.

He turned to Abiathar the priest.

'Bring the ephod here,' he commanded.

He put a question to GOD: 'Shall I go after that mob? If I do, shall I capture them?'

'Go after them,' said GOD. 'You will certainly capture them and rescue the prisoners.'

---

* For the story of the battle between the Philistines and the Israelites, see p. 35.

David set out with all his six hundred soldiers. He reached Besor Ravine. Here he left two hundred men who were too exhausted to go further. He and the other four hundred men went on.

In the open country his men found an Egyptian lying half-dead on the ground, and brought him to David. They gave him something to eat – bread, a fig cake and two bunches of raisins – and some water to drink. That brought him round; he had been starving for three whole days.

'Who owns you?' asked David, 'and where do you come from?'

'I'm an Egyptian,' he said, 'and my master's an Amalekite. I was taken ill three days ago, and he left me to die. We'd been on a raid into the Negeb. We burned down Ziklag town.'

'Will you guide me down to these raiders?' asked David.

'I'll guide you,' he answered, 'but swear to me that you won't kill me or hand me over to my master.'

He led David down – and there they were, spread over the whole countryside, eating and drinking and dancing. They had captured a vast amount of loot in Philistine territory. David attacked them and routed them; the fighting went on from dawn to dark and into the next day. The only men to escape were four hundred young men who fled on camels.

David recovered all the loot that had been taken at Ziklag. The prisoners were all safe. His men took possession of all the livestock they found in the Amalekite camp – sheep and cattle – and drove them away to shouts of 'David's Booty!'

He returned to Besor Ravine. The two hundred men left there came out to meet him and his men. David saluted them. Some of the meaner-minded soldiers who had taken part in the fighting objected to the two hundred sharing in the loot.

'They didn't fight – they don't get anything,' they said. 'Let them take their wives and children and go!'

'Not on your life,' said David. 'GOD has given us all this booty and saved our lives and given us the victory – who's going to think like you? No! The men who guard the baggage and the men who fight share alike!'

When David got back to Ziklag he sent part of the loot to the elders of his own tribe – Judah – and to his friends there, with this message: 'Here's a present for you from the loot of GOD's enemies!'

King of the South

Crowned at Hebron   *2 Samuel 2:1-10*

David had only been two days back at Ziklag when news of Saul's death on Gilboa Mountain reached him.*

'Shall I leave Ziklag,' he asked GOD, 'and go up to one of the towns in the Judean highlands?'

'Yes,' said GOD.

'Where shall I go?' David asked.

'To Hebron,' said GOD.

So David marched with his men to Hebron and settled in the surrounding villages. They took their wives and families with them; David took both his wives, Ahinoam of Jezreel and Abigail, Nabal's widow from Carmel.

The men of Judah came and crowned David as their king.

The story of how the men of Jabesh-Gilead had buried Saul's body was told to David. He was deeply moved and sent a message to the town: 'Blessings on you for your loyalty to Saul and for seeing to it that he was properly buried. May GOD show steadfast love and faithfulness to you! I shall not forget; I will see that you get a proper reward for what you have done. May you always show such a brave and valiant spirit. King Saul is dead; the men of Judah have crowned me as their king!'

Meanwhile, Saul's commander-in-chief, Abner, had escorted Saul's son, Ishbaal, across Jordan River and crowned him king of the Northern tribes in Mahanaim in the highlands. Only the Southern tribe of Judah acknowledged David as king.

The Battle of Gibeon   *2 Samuel 2:12-32; 3:1*

Abner, the Northern commander, set out from Mahanaim, with the Northern army, crossed River Jordan and marched to Gibeon on the eastern edge of Saul's own tribal territory of Benjamin, northwest of the fortified Canaanite city of Jerusalem. Joab, David's commander, marched north from Hebron, with David's army. The two armies met at Gibeon Pool.

'Let the lads try their luck,' Abner said to Joab. 'Let's have a trial of strength.'

'Yes, let them fight it out,' said Joab.

* See p. 37.

So they counted off soldiers from each side by number – twelve Benjamites and twelve of David's men. It was bloody fighting. Each soldier seized his opponent with one hand by the hair of his head, and with his other hand plunged his sword into his side. Both fell dead together.

Fierce fighting now broke out between the armies, and David's soldiers routed the Northerners.

Joab's brother, Asahel, a divisional commander, was a famous runner who could run (as the saying went) 'as fast as a wild gazelle'. He marked down the Northern commander, Abner, and ran after him, never letting him out of his sight.

Abner rounded on him.

'Are you Asahel?' he called out.

'I am!' he shouted back.

'Then clear off and tackle a common soldier,' he said. 'Take his armour for loot!'

Asahel still kept on his track.

'I've told you to clear off,' called Abner. 'Stop following me, or I'll kill you. How could I look your brother in the face then?'

But Asahel wouldn't be put off. So Abner struck him in the stomach with a backward blow. The spear came out at his back, and Asahel fell dead in his tracks.

Asahel's two brothers, Joab the commander-in-chief and Abishai, were hot on Abner's trail. At sunset they reached Ammah Hill on the desert road. The Northern soldiers formed a solid phalanx behind Abner on the brow of the hill.

'Is there no end to the fighting?' Abner called out. 'It can only bring bitterness for us all. How much longer have we got to wait for you to call off the pursuit and stop kinsman fighting kinsman?'

'By GOD!' said Joab, 'if you hadn't spoken we would have gone on fighting all night!'

Joab gave the command for the bugle to be blown. The Southern army halted; the pursuit of the Northern soldiers was over and there was no more fighting.

Abner moved that night along the Jordan Valley, forded the river and marched all morning to reach the eastern capital, Mahanaim, by noon.

At a roll-call of the Southern army, Joab listed the casualties of the fighting: on the Southern side, nineteen dead (besides Asahel); on the Northern side, three hundred and sixty dead. He and his men marched southwards all through the night and reached Hebron at daybreak.

They carried Asahel's body with them and buried him in his ancestral tomb in Bethlehem town.

The war between North and South – between Saul's family and David – went on and on. David had the better of the fighting; the Northern resistance began to give way before his growing military strength.

Rebellion in the North

Abner became the most powerful man in the North – his influence grew and grew. He took a fancy to one of Saul's secondary wives called Rizpah.

'What game are you up to,' King Ishbaal asked him, 'sleeping with one of my father's wives?'

This touched Abner on the raw.

'Am I scum from the South?' he exploded, 'I – who've stood by Saul's family and saved you from David's attacks? And you go and spread scandal about a woman at this time of day!'

The king was reduced to silence; he was thoroughly scared.

Abner now sent a secret message to David at Hebron, the Southern capital.

'If you'll come to an agreement with me,' he said, 'all my influence in the North is at your disposal. I will arrange for the North to crown you king.'

'Excellent,' David's answer came back. 'I will certainly come to an agreement with you. I have only one condition. When you come to negotiate the terms of the treaty, you must bring Michal, Saul's daughter, with you.'

At the same time, David sent an official request to King Ishbaal: 'I demand the surrender of Michal my wife – I was betrothed to her.'

King Ishbaal commanded Michal to go with Abner's mission to the South. Her husband followed her for miles along the road, in great distress, until Abner ordered him home.

Now Abner had already had secret talks with leading men in the North about the future of the kingship. There was a growing movement to make David king instead of Ishbaal. Abner urged immediate action. He put the same point to the leaders of Saul's own tribe, Benjamin. He had done all this before he set out on his mission to David to tell him about the friendly feeling towards him in the North – especially among the leaders of Saul's own tribe.

So, when he and the twenty men accompanying him reached Hebron, David gave them a banquet.

'I will now go back and rally the North to your side,' Abner told David, 'and get them to make a treaty with you. You can be king over as wide a kingdom as you wish.'

David sent him back under safe conduct.

Just then the Southern commander-in-chief, Joab, came in from a raiding expedition. Abner by now had set off back for the North. Joab soon learned what David had done – let Abner, the Northern commander-in-chief, visit him and go away under safe conduct.

He went straight into the king's presence.

'What have you been up to?' he blurted out. 'You've had a visit from Abner, have you? And you've given him a safe conduct home? Don't you know he only came here spying and making a fool of you? And you let him get away!'

He stormed out of the king's presence, and sent some of his soldiers after Abner at Sirah's Pool and brought him back to Hebron. Joab beckoned him over to the side of the town gate, as if he was going to talk to him, man to man. He stabbed him in the stomach and killed him – that would pay him back for murdering his brother Asahel.

The murder was quickly reported to David.

'I and my kingdom have had no part in this. GOD knows that!' he exclaimed. 'May Joab and all his descendants suffer for it – may they be sick, lepers, beggars or murdered!'

He ordered the whole court to go into mourning. Abner was buried in Hebron. King David walked behind the bier and there was loud wailing at the graveside; everyone wept openly. King David himself made this lament for Abner:

'That Abner should die
    a peasant's death –
    hands not handcuffed,
    feet not fettered!
You died
    at the hands of villains!'

The wailing went on.

The court tried to persuade David to take some food.

'No!' said David. 'May GOD punish me if I eat any food until after sunset!'

The people were impressed; David had done the right thing and it was clear to everybody that he had nothing to do with Abner's murder.

'A great commander has died today,' King David told his court. 'I am a crowned king, but it breaks my heart. I'll not have cruelty like the cruelty of these men. May they suffer for their crime!'

Assassination   *2 Samuel 3:6-8, 11-39*

There was panic in the North when news of Abner's murder reached there. King Ishbaal himself was a very frightened man.

One day two of his guerrilla leaders, Rechab and Baanah, entered the palace. It was early in the afternoon, the hottest time of the day. The king was taking his siesta; the woman in charge of the palace gate had been sifting wheat and had drowsed off. Two men slipped quietly past, broke into the royal bedroom and murdered the king in his sleep. They cut his head off and made off with it. All afternoon and through the darkness of the night they hurried south by way of Jordan Valley and reached Hebron. They sought an audience with King David.

'Here is King Ishbaal's head,' they said. 'He was your enemy – he would have killed you if he could. GOD has seen justice done on Saul's family!'

'By GOD who has never failed to rescue me when my life's been in danger,' David exclaimed, 'I know how to treat men like you! I killed the fellow who brought me news of Saul's death; he thought he'd make something out of such "good news". He did – he died. How do you think I'll treat thugs like you who murder a good man asleep in his own home? You're not fit to live!'

He called out his bodyguard and they killed them both, there and then. They cut off their hands and feet, and hung their bodies up by Hebron Pool.

The North Goes Over to David   *2 Samuel 5:1, 3*

All the Northern tribes now sent their leaders south to Hebron to King David.

'Look, they said to King David, 'we come, not as your enemies, but as your kinsmen – to crown you as our king.'

And they crowned him king of the North.

The Philistine War
2 Samuel 5:17-19, 25; 21:15-22; 23:8-12, 18-39, 13-17

This startled the Philistines. They called out their army in force, marched into the hills and occupied the whole Rephaim Valley to the south-west of Jerusalem. Their plan was to drive a wedge between South and North and capture David. But when David's scouts brought news of enemy movements, he made Adullam Fort, fifteen miles south-west of Jerusalem, his headquarters.

'Shall I attack the Philistines?' he asked GOD. 'Will you deliver them into my hands?'

'I certainly will,' said GOD.

David went into the attack and routed the Philistines all the way from Gibeon north of Jerusalem as far as Gezer in the Philistine Plain.

There are many stories told of David and his officers and their exploits in the Philistine War.

Once, when David and his men were fighting, he fell from sheer tiredness. Benob, a Philistine hero, wearing a belt of honour and with a bronze spear weighing thirteen pounds, took him prisoner and was going to kill him. Captain Abishai came to his rescue and struck the Philistine dead. David's officers were alarmed at the risks he was running. They vowed to take no chances.

'Keep out of the fighting,' they told him. 'We don't want you killed – you're the only hope of our people.'

In another battle in Gob, Sibbecai the Hashathite killed a Philistine called Saph. In another battle in the same countryside, Elhanan, an officer from David's own town of Bethlehem, slew Goliath of Gath whose spear was as big as a bough of a tree. Once, when the fighting had reached the Philistine city of Gath, Jonathan, David's nephew, killed a giant of a man (who had six fingers on each hand and six toes on each foot) when he stood up and taunted the Israelite soldiers. All these were members of the Scimitar Brigade.

Here is the roll-call of David's officers.

There were three commanders over the army. These are some of their expoits.

The first commander was Ishbaal the Hachmonite – he was famous for winning a fight against great odds, armed only with a spear.

The second commander was Eleazar. He was once with David in a tight corner in Pasdammim. The Philistine troops were pushing the Israelites back. But the battle was saved by Eleazar who stood his ground and fought on till his arm was almost too tired to lift and his hand felt as if it was glued to his sword. But he rallied his men to victory – all that was left was the looting!

The third commander was Shammah the Hararite. The fighting at a place called 'Jawbone' was swaying round a plot of ground, a lentil garden. The Israelite soldiers began to give way, but Shammah stood boldly in the middle of the lentil plot and refused to give ground – it turned the tide of the battle.

Under the Three Commanders were Thirty Captains.

The most famous and the leader of the Thirty was Abishai, brother of Joab, David's commander-in-chief. He once killed three hundred men with his spear. That made his reputation. Although he became leader of the Thirty he never reached the rank of the Three Commanders.

Among the other captains was Benaiah, a born soldier about whom many stories were told: how he once killed two Moabite heroes; how he fought with a lion in a pit on a snowy day and killed it; how he slew a giant of an Egyptian. He had only a club, but he attacked the armed Egyptian, wrenched the spear out of his hand, and killed him with his own spear. Benaiah was a very famous soldier. David made him Captain of his Bodyguard.

The Thirty Captains came from very different places. Several came from David's own town of Bethlehem or the countryside round about it. Others came from north of Galilee Lake, the mountains east of Jordan River, from the Plain between the mountains and the sea, from south of the Salt Sea, from the old Southern capital Hebron. Two came from Saul's own town of Gibeah. Two were foreigners, one an Ammonite and one a Hittite – of whom we shall hear more.

There's a famous story about three of the Thirty Captains. It happened when David was besieged by Philistine troops in the Adullam Fort in the Rephaim Valley – about three or four miles from his home town of Bethlehem, where the Philistines had an outpost.

One day, David was very thirsty. 'What wouldn't I give for a drink of Bethlehem water from the well by the city gate!' he exclaimed.

Three of his captains overheard him. Without telling anybody, they broke through the Philistine lines, went to Bethlehem, drew some water from the well by the city gate, and brought it back to David.

He wouldn't drink it. 'GOD forbid that I should do such a thing!' he said. 'This is the blood of men who took their lives in their hands – can I drink water as costly as that?' He poured it out as an offering to GOD, and refused to quench his thirst with it.

King of the South and North

New Capital

2 Samuel 5:6-11

North and South each had their own capital city – Mahanaim in the North and Hebron in the South. David, now he was king of the South and North, decided to establish a new capital city for the new nation. Near the borders of North and South lay the fortress of Jerusalem, controlling the road between them. It was still in Jebusite hands – it had never been captured. This, he made up his mind, should be his new capital city.

David besieged Jerusalem with his troops.

'You can't capture us!' the Jebusite soldiers laughed at them from the city walls. 'Blind and lame men could guard our gates!'

They knew David couldn't storm the walls. But he broke into the fortress nevertheless.

David may have captured it in this way (the actual text is obscure):

Jerusalem city had no natural water supply; the citizens had to sink a deep shaft down to the spring outside the western wall. They thought this was quite safe, for the water rose and filled the bottom of the shaft. But for a short time each day the water level dropped. David may have done what nobody had ever done before – sent some of his commando troops up the shaft while the water was low. They had just time to climb up it. They took the fortress by surprise; before the guards realised what was happening, David's soldiers had opened the city gates and his troops stormed in.

He made the citadel his palace – he called it 'Davidstown' – and built the city proper inwards from the Great Tower.

David now became a powerful king; GOD was with him.

He made treaties with neighbouring kings. For example, he hired, by treaty, Tyrian workmen – carpenters and stonemasons – to build his palace.

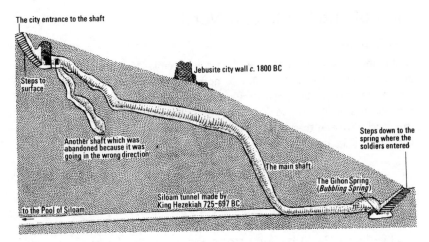

The city entrance to the shaft

Steps to surface

Jebusite city wall *c.* 1800 BC

Another shaft which was abandoned because it was going in the wrong direction

The main shaft

Steps down to the spring where the soldiers entered

The Gihon Spring (*Bubbling Spring*)

to the Pool of Siloam

Siloam tunnel made by King Hezekiah 725-697 BC

The water tunnel cut through the rock in the Jebusite city of Jerusalem (before 1000 BCE). This is the water tunnel David's soldiers climbed to get inside the city. (The plan is foreshortened, which makes the shaft look steeper than it really is.)

One Religious Centre for South and North   *2 Samuel 6:1-12, 16, 20-23*

The Ark of GOD had stayed until now in the house of Abinadab on the hill – the men of Kiriath-jearim had taken it there when the Philistines sent it back.

King David now mustered his army and set out to bring it to Jerusalem. They took it from Abinadab's house and put it on a new cart. Two sons of Abinadab – Uzzah and his brother – guided the cart. Uzzah walked beside it; his brother walked in front. The king and the people formed a procession, dancing wildly and singing to the music of guitars, harps, tambourines, bells and cymbals.

They reached a certain threshing-floor. Suddenly the oxen stumbled and Uzzah put out his hand to steady the Ark. He collapsed and died beside it – GOD was angry with him for touching it. King David was vexed at what GOD had done and he was afraid of him.

'How can I do anything with the Ark now?' he asked.

He changed his mind about taking it to Davidstown and left it in the house of Obed-Edom the Philistine. Here it stayed for three months – lucky months for Obed-Edom and his family. When the king learned that nothing unlucky had happened, he decided that it would be safe to bring it to Davidstown. He set out and brought it to his city in a joyous procession.

As the Ark was being carried into the town, Michal was watching the procession from a palace window. She saw the king leaping and dancing with religious fervour; and she despised him for acting as she thought no king should.

'The king has been a fine king today,' she sneered, 'walking naked for slave-girls to laugh at – like a village peasant!'

'I will dance for GOD if I think I ought to,' David retorted. 'He chose me, anyhow, instead of your father, and he made me king of his people. I will dance and make merry before him, if I want to. I'll make myself "like a village peasant", as you put it, and you can sneer at me as much as you like! But slave-girls won't laugh at me – they know what I'm doing and honour me for it.'

He treated her no more as his wife.

The Court History

David and Meribaal

2 Samuel 9:1-3; 4:4; 9:4-11

'Jonathan was a sworn friend of mine,' said King David one day. 'I wonder if any of his father's family are still alive, that I may show kindness to them for Jonathan's sake.'

Now it happened that one of Saul's courtiers, a man called Ziba, was still living in one of the villages. He was summoned to court.

'So you're Ziba, are you?' the king asked him.

'I am,' he said.

'Tell me something,' said the king. 'Are any of Saul's descendants still alive?'

'There's a grandson,' he said, 'a lame son of Jonathan's. He was only five years old when news of his father's and his grandfather's deaths on Gilboa Mountain was brought from the battlefield. His nurse picked him up and ran away into hiding. But she stumbled as she ran and dropped him. He was hurt and has been lame ever since. He's called Meribaal.'

'Where is he now?' asked the king.

'Oh, he's living with Machir's family in Lodebar.'

King David summoned Meribaal to court.

He came, and bowed to the ground in homage.

'Meribaal!' said the king.

'Here I am, Your Majesty,' he said.

'There's nothing to be frightened of,' said David. 'Your father was my friend and I must fulfil my promise to him. I am going to give you back all your grandfather's estates. I want you to live here as a member of my court.'

'Who am I, for you to treat me like this?' said Meribaal. 'I'm just a useless nobody.'

The king spoke to Ziba.

'I have given back to your master's son all the estates of his grandfather,' he said. 'These are your orders: you and your family are to take charge of the estates and bring the produce to Meribaal. He will live here at my court.'

'I will carry out your orders to the letter, Your Majesty,' said Ziba.

So Meribaal lived with King David as though he were one of his own sons.

The Ammonite War

East of the River   *2 Samuel 10:1-19; 11:1*

Not long afterwards, the king of Ammon, east of Jordan River, died. His son, Hanun, succeeded him.

'The dead king was a good friend of mine,' thought David. 'I will offer my friendship to his son to show my respect for his father.'

He sent ambassadors to the Ammonite capital, Rabbah, to offer his sympathy to the new king.

The Ammonite sheiks had different views.

'You don't think David sends ambassadors here just out of respect for your father, do you?' they said to the king. 'It isn't sympathy they're bringing – it's a clever move to see the city at first hand. They are just spies, trying to find out how it can be captured.'

King Hanun insulted the ambassadors. He shaved off half their beards and ripped off their clothes below their waist and sent them packing.

The men went back embarrassed and ashamed. News of the insult went ahead of them. When David heard of it, he sent officers to meet them with orders for them to stay at Jericho – where they had crossed the river – till their beards were grown again; and then to come up to the capital.

The Ammonites knew that they were now in serious trouble. David wasn't the sort of man to let an act like this pass unchallenged. So they made a treaty with the Aramaeans in the north under which they were to take into their pay some thousands of infantry.

David called out his army and sent his commander-in-chief, General Joab, to deal with the matter.

The Ammonites drew up the main body of their troops in front of the city gates; the foreign infantry were kept as a mobile force out in the open countryside.

Joab noted their strategy: he was to be attacked both in the front and in the rear. So he made his plans. He led his crack troops against the Aramaean force in the open country; he put his brother, Abishai, in charge of the main army and posted him against the main body of the Ammonite troops in front of the city. Battle orders to Abishai were: 'You come to my help if the battle goes against me; I will come to your help if you find the Ammonite army too strong to deal with. Be of good heart. Let us play the man today, for our people and the cities of our GOD! The issue is in GOD's hands!'

Joab and his crack troops attacked the Aramaeans out in the open countryside and routed them. When the main body of the Ammonite army saw what was happening they gave way under Abishai's attack and withdrew into the city. Joab did not feel strong enough to besiege a fortified city; he abandoned the attack and marched back to Jerusalem.

Events now took a serious turn.

The Aramaeans resented being beaten by the Israelites. They rallied their main forces and came into the war – Hadadezer, their king, wasn't going to let troops of his be routed like this. He sent his commander-in-chief, Shobach, with a large army into Ammonite territory and they took up their position at Helam.

News reached David. He called out his army and reserves, crossed Jordan River and advanced to Helam. He struck swiftly and destroyed the Areamaean army. The Aramaean casualties were heavy; Shobach, the commander-in-chief, himself died of wounds.

The Aramaean sheiks admitted defeat, sued for peace and surrendered to David. They left the Ammonites to deal with their own problems.

The following year, after harvest (when fighting was usually begun again), David sent his commander-in-chief to ravage the Ammonite countryside and to lay siege to their capital city, Rabbah. David himself stayed in Jerusalem.

A Foul Crime   *2 Samuel 11:2-27; 12:1-7, 9, 13-24*

Late one afternoon David got up from his siesta and strolled to and fro on the flat roof of the palace. He looked down over the neighbouring courtyards and caught sight of a woman – a very beautiful woman – bathing. He sent one of his officers to find out who she was: she was Bathsheba, he was told, the wife of one of his Thirty Captains – Uriah the Hittite – who was on active service at the siege of Rabbah, the Ammonite capital.

He sent an officer to bring her over to the palace. They slept together that night and she went home. She became pregnant and saw to it that the king knew what had happened.

He acted quickly. He sent a dispatch to the commander-in-chief at the front, ordering Captain Uriah home on leave. The captain was sent home to report to the palace. The king discussed the war with him, and then told him to go home and enjoy his leave.

Captain Uriah left the palace with the present the king gave him. But he wouldn't go home to his wife; he slept with the guard posted at the palace gate. This was reported to the king.

'My dear fellow,' the king said to him, 'you've had a long journey. Why didn't you go home?'

'The troops are under canvas,' Captain Uriah answered. 'The Ark is at the front. General Joab and Your Majesty's soldiers are sleeping on the bare ground. You don't think I could just go home and have a good meal and go to bed with my wife – as if was no war on? By GOD, I am a soldier, not a civilian!'

'Well, then,' said the king, 'you can stay in the palace tonight. Tomorrow, I'll let you get back to the fighting.'

Next morning, the king invited Captain Uriah to share the royal table with him, and plied him with wine till he was drunk. He was too drunk to return to the front. He went and slept that night with the officers of the guard. But he still wouldn't go home.

Next morning the king sent a dispatch to his commander-in-chief, General Joab. Here are the brutal words:

'Order Captain Uriah into the front line where the fighting is fiercest. Then suddenly fall back and leave him to his fate.'

He gave the dispatch to Captain Uriah himself to deliver to the commander-in-chief.

General Joab surveyed the siege and stationed Captain Uriah opposite the enemy's crack troops. It was at this point that the enemy then struck in force. Quite a number of officers were killed in the fighting. Captain Uriah was among them.

The commander-in-chief then sent a dispatch back to the king with a full report of the battle.

'When you've given this report to the king,' he told the officer taking the dispatch, 'he may be bitterly angry. If he says to you, "Why did you press the fighting so close to the city? Don't you know the danger of fighting right under the walls? Why did you go so near?" – just say these words: "Your officer, General Uriah, died in the fighting too."'

The officer left for Jerusalem and gave King David the full report of the battle – just as his commander-in-chief had ordered. The report angered him and he turned on the officer – just as the commander-in-chief expected.

'The enemy were out in strength,' replied the officer. 'They attacked us out in the open and we drove them back to the city gate. The archers on the wall shot a storm of arrows down on your troops. A number of Your Majesty's officers were killed – about eighteen of them. Captain Uriah was among the dead.'

'Take this message back to General Joab,' King David told his officer. 'Tell him this to encourage him: "Don't let this incident depress you. You have to be prepared for all sorts of casualties in war. Mount a stronger attack on the city and take it by storm."'

The news of Captain Uriah's death was given to his wife, and she went into mourning for him. As soon as the funeral rites were over King David sent for her and took her into his harem. In due time she gave birth to a son.

The way King David had treated Captain Uriah and his wife was wrong in GOD's eyes. He sent the Prophet Nathan to tell him so. This is how Nathan told him:

'Two farmers – one very rich and one very poor – lived in the same country town,' he told King David as if he were reporting a case for him to deal with. 'The rich farmer hardly knew how many flocks and herds he had, he had so many. The poor farmer had practically nothing except one little ewe-lamb. He had bought it and reared it; it grew up like a member of the family, sharing his food and drinking from his cup and sleeping in his arms. It was like a child to him.

'One day a traveller arrived at the rich farmer's house. And what did he do but take the poor farmer's little ewe-lamb to feed his guest – he was too mean to kill a sheep or an ox of his own.'

David was furious.

'By God!' he told Nathan. 'The fellow ought to die! Hadn't he a touch of pity in him? I'll see he pays back four times more than he took from the poor farmer!'

'You're the man I'm talking about,' said Nathan. 'These are GOD's words: "Why have you slighted me by doing this hateful thing – murdering Captain Uriah and stealing his wife?"'

'I have sinned,' said the king, 'and I have sinned against GOD himself.'

'GOD has forgiven you; you shall not die,' said Nathan. 'But the baby will die; you treated GOD with contempt.'

Nathan went home.

When the baby was taken very ill, King David prayed to GOD. He refused to eat anything and spent the nights lying in sackcloth on the ground. Some of the older courtiers came and tried to make him get up from the ground. But he stayed where he was and wouldn't have any meals with them.

A week later the baby died, and there wasn't a courtier who dared breathe a word about it to him.

'He wouldn't listen to us when the baby was alive and we tried to talk to him,' they said. 'Now the baby's dead, he'll do something desperate if we tell him.'

King David saw his courtiers whispering together and he guessed what had happened.

'Is he dead?' he asked.

'Yes, he is,' they said.

He got up from the ground, washed and anointed himself, changed his clothes and went into GOD's house to pray. He then went back to the palace, called for a good meal (which was quickly brought to the royal table) and ate it up.

His courtiers thought he was acting strangely.

'When the baby was alive,' they said to him, 'you ate nothing and wept; now he is dead, you get up and have a good meal!'

'As long as the baby was alive,' said the king, 'there was hope GOD would have pity on me and let him live. Now he is dead, what's the point of fasting? Can I bring him back again? I shall go to him, but he will never come back to me.'

Some time later, Bathsheba bore another son to David. His name was Solomon.

The End of the War

2 Samuel 12:26-31

General Joab, acting on King David's orders, made a full-scale attack on Rabbah, the Ammonite capital. He captured the Water City, and sent an urgent dispatch back to Jerusalem.

'I have made an attack on Rabbah,' he informed the king, 'and I have taken the King's Pool by storm. Bring the rest of the army and come yourself and capture the main city. I don't want to be known as the conqueror of Rabbah – as I shall be if I storm it alone.'

So the king mustered the rest of the army, marched to Rabbah and took it by storm. The crown of Milcom, the Ammonite god, was captured – it was made of silver and gold, and set with a very costly jewel. David tried it on.

A great deal of loot was captured in the city; the citizens were organised into labour gangs with saws and iron picks and axes, and set to forced labour in the brick-kilns.

The other Ammonite cities were captured and treated in the same way. Then David and his army marched back to Jerusalem.

Southern Rebellion

A Sordid Beginning

2 Samuel 13:1-17, 19-22

It began with a harem intrigue. Amnon and Absalom were half-brothers, both sons of King David but with different mothers. Amnon fell madly in love with Tamar, Absalom's beautiful sister. He was so tormented with his love for her that he made himself ill. But she was quite out of his reach; she was a virgin, and was confined to her mother's quarters in the royal harem.

Now Amnon had a friend, Jonadab, a nephew of the king and a very crafty man.

'My dear prince,' he said one day, 'you look haggard and ill. What's the matter? Won't you tell me your secret?'

'I'm just desperately in love with Tamar,' said Amnon.

'I'll easily put that right,' said Jonadab. 'You go to bed and pretend to be ill. When your father comes to see what's the matter with you, tell him you can't eat anything. And then go on to tell him that if Tamar came and cooked some choice food in your own room, that would give you an appetite. Ask him to let her come and look after you.'

Amnon thought it a clever idea; he took to his bed and pretended to be ill.

His father came to see him.

'If Tamar came,' Amnon told him, 'and made a couple of cakes while I watch, that would give me an appetite. Let her come.'

So King David summoned Tamar to the Palace.

'Go to your brother Amnon's house,' he told her, 'and get him a meal.'

Tamar found Amnon in bed. She got him a meal of cakes. She kneaded the dough, made the cakes and baked them. Amnon watched.

The she took the pan and served the cakes. But Amnon wouldn't touch them.

'Clear the room,' he ordered.

When everybody had gone, he told Tamar to bring the cakes into the inner bedroom.

'I'd rather have them from you,' he said.

Tamar did as she was told; and as she handed him the cakes, he caught hold of her.

'Come to bed with me, my sister,' he pleaded.

'No! no! no! my brother!' she protested. 'You mustn't dishonour me like this. It isn't right. You mustn't rape me. Where should I hide my shame? And you'll be held as one of the most vicious scoundrels in the country. Speak to the king – he'll let us marry.'

Amnon just wouldn't listen. With his greater strength, he overpowered her and raped her.

His love suddenly turned to bitter hatred; he hated her now more than he had ever loved her. He ordered her out of the house.

'No!' she said. 'Sending me off like this is worse than the wrong you've already done me.'

He ignored her and called his servant.

'Put this woman out,' he ordered, 'and lock the door behind her.'

The servant pushed her out into the street, and bolted the door.

Tamar was beside herself. She threw dust on her head, tore her royal dress, and, with her hand on her head, went screaming home.

Her brother Absalom met her.

'Has your brother Amnon been with you?' he asked. 'Well, keep your mouth shut – he is your brother – and forget it.'

So Tamar stayed in Absalom's house; she was broken-hearted.

When King David heard about it all, he was very angry indeed, but he did nothing. Amnon was his eldest son and he didn't want to hurt him.

But with Absalom it was a different matter. He never spoke to Amnon again, one way or another. He just hated him with a deadly hatred for raping his sister.

Absalom's Revenge   *2 Samuel 13:23-37*

Two years went by. Absalom was holding a sheep shearing at a place called Baal-Hazor, some fifteen miles north-east of Jerusalem; and he invited all the royal princes.

He sought an audience with his father.

'I've a sheep-shearing festival soon,' he said. 'It would be fine if Your Majesty and the court would attend.'

'No, my son,' said the king. 'We should be too great a burden.'

Absalom pressed his father to come. He firmly refused but gave him his blessing.

'Well,' said Absalom, 'if you won't come, at least let my brother Amnon join us.'

'Why Amnon?' asked the king. 'Why should he go with you?'

Absalom wouldn't be put off. So the king let Amnon go along with the other princes.

Absalom prepared a royal banquet. But he gave secret orders to his servants.

'Make a careful note of this: when Amnon has got a little drunk, I shall call out, "Down with Amnon!" Then you must kill him. There's nothing to be frightened about – I am giving the orders. Be bold like men!'

So Absalom's orders were carried out. All the other princes rose from the table, mounted their mules and escaped.

News went ahead of them and rumour had it that all the princes had been murdered – there were no survivors. The king tore his clothes and lay flat on the ground; all his courtiers tore their clothes in grief.

But Jonadab, the king's nephew, spoke up.

'Your Majesty,' he said, 'you mustn't believe a mere rumour like this. Only one prince is dead – and it's Prince Amnon. Absalom has had one grim purpose ever since Amnon raped his sister Tamar. Your Majesty mustn't get the idea that all the princes are murdered. Only Prince Amnon is dead.'

Meanwhile the sentry saw a crowd of men coming down the hill on the Horonaim road. He reported to the king.

'Look, Your Majesty,' Jonadab said. 'The princes are here. It's exactly as I said.'

He had hardly finished speaking when the princes entered the palace. They were weeping; the king and the whole court broke into bitter weeping too.

Absalom himself escaped to Talmai, king of Geshur, east of Jordan River.

Back in Favour   *2 Samuel 13:38-39; 14:1-13, 15-24, 28-33*

Three years went by. The king had got over the shock of Amnon's murder and now was pining for the exiled Absalom. General Joab noticed his mood. He knew it was no good talking plainly to him; so this is what he did. He sent to Tekoa, some ten miles south of Jerusalem, for a wise woman who lived there.

'I want you to dress up as a mourner,' he told her. 'Put on funeral clothes, and look as if you have been mourning the death of your husband for a long time. Don't freshen yourself up in any way. Then I want you to seek an audience with the king, and I'll tell you what I want you to say.'

So he rehearsed with her the speech he wanted her to make.

The woman asked for an audience with the king. She fell down on her face in homage.

'Help me, Your Majesty!' she cried out. 'Oh help me!'

'What do you want me to do?' asked the king.

'I am a widow,' she said. 'My husband died a long time ago. I'm in real trouble. My two sons had a violent quarrel while they were out working in the field; one of them struck his brother and killed him. The whole clan is now up in arms. They want me to hand the murderer over to them – death is what he deserves, they say, and they mean it. But if they kill him, my husband will have no heir. They would take my last hope from me. My husband will have neither name nor descendant left in the world.'

'Go home,' said the king. 'I will give the necessary orders, and you will be all right.'

'I don't want any guilt to fall on Your Majesty or your throne,' said the woman. 'The guilt all lies on me and my family.'

'If anybody interferes with you,' said the king, 'report him to me. I'll see to it that he causes you no further trouble.'

'Will you swear this by GOD's name?' asked the woman. 'I'm frightened of the blood-avenger and what he might do – he might kill my son.'

'In GOD's name,' said the king, 'not a hair of his head shall be cut off!'

'Might I talk plainly to Your Majesty?'

'You may,' said the king.

'I'm really talking about Absalom,' said the woman. 'Why is he still banished – an evil for the whole country and a very wrong thing in itself, as Your Majesty has admitted in what you have just said to me? That's why I came with my story to you. You represent God. You know how to tell right from wrong. I wanted you, Your Majesty, to pass judgement on my case so that you could pass judgement on your own. Your word is final.'

'Tell me everything,' said the king. 'I want you to give me a plain answer to a plain question.'

'Ask me any question you like, Your Majesty,' said the woman.

'Has General Joab put you up to this?' he asked.

'You have asked a plain question; I'll give you a plain answer,' said the woman. 'Yes, he has. He told me what to say. He wanted Your Majesty to look at the whole matter of Absalom's banishment in a new light. Your Majesty has GOD's wisdom – you know everything.'

The king summoned General Joab into his presence.

'I grant you your wish,' he told him. 'Recall Prince Absalom.'

General Joab bowed to the ground in homage.

'I thank Your Majesty,' he said. 'You have granted my request; I know now how highly you think of me.'

He set off straightaway for Geshur and escorted Prince Absalom back to Jerusalem.

But the king had further orders: Absalom was to be confined to his own house; he was not to set foot in the palace.

So Absalom stayed in his own house in Jerusalem; for two whole years he and his father never met.

At last, Prince Absalom sent for General Joab – he wanted him to speak to the king. Joab refused to meet him. He refused a second time, when Absalom sent for him.

'You know that field of General Joab's,' said Prince Absalom to his courtiers. 'It's the field next to mine – the field where he's growing barley. Burn it down.'

They set the field on fire.

This soon brought General Joab round to Prince Absalom's house.

'What are you up to?' he asked. 'Your men have burned my field down!'

'Well, what do you expect?' said the prince. 'I sent for you twice. I want you to see my father and tell him that I might as well have stayed in Geshur as stay confined to this house. I want justice. If I deserve death tell him to put me to death.'

General Joab sought an audience with King David and told him what Prince Absalom had said. The king summoned the prince into his presence. Prince Absalom bowed to the ground in homage, and King David kissed him. He was back in favour.

Open Rebellion   *2 Samuel 15:1-12*

Prince Absalom was now a free man. The first thing he did was to set himself up with a royal chariot and horses, and fifty runners to go before him. Every morning he would go down and stand by the road leading to the city gate (where the king held his Court of Justice). He would stop everybody who was going along to the Court.

'Where do you come from?' he would ask.

'From such and such a district,' the man would answer.

'What's the trouble?'

The man would tell him.

'You've got a very good case,' he would say. 'But you won't get any justice from the king.'

Or sometimes –

'If only I were appointed the supreme judge! If only everybody with a dispute or lawsuit would come to me! I'd see he got justice!'

When any man came to him to pay his respects, Prince Absalom would offer his hand and embrace and kiss him. This is how he treated everybody who came to the Court of Justice; and in this way he won the loyalty of many citizens.

This went on for four years.

Then the prince sought an audience with his father.

'May I have permission to go to Hebron to discharge a vow I made to GOD?' he asked. 'I made the vow when I was living in Geshur; I promised GOD that, if he would bring me back to Jerusalem, I would worship him in Hebron.'

'Certainly,' said his father.

So he set off for Hebron.

At the same time, he sent secret agents everywhere with these orders: 'At the sound of the bugle, shout, "Long live King Absalom in Hebron!"'

Two hundred invited guests went along with him, but they went quite innocently – they hadn't any idea what was afoot. The prince also summoned Ahithophel, the king's Counsellor, to come from his town of Giloh.

The rebellion spread far and wide.

Flight from Jerusalem   *2 Samuel 15:13-24, 27-37*

News of the revolt was brought to King David – it was clear that the Southern clans had gone over to Prince Absalom. He ordered the court to escape.

'We must get out as quickly as we can,' he said. 'If we stay we shall be captured. A sudden attack by Absalom and we are finished. He'll put the city to the sword.'

'As Your Majesty commands,' said his courtiers. 'We are your officers.'

So the king and his court left the city. The secondary wives were left to take care of the palace.

At the last house on the edge of the city a halt was made while the king watched the march past of his Foreign Legion – Cretans and Philistines and the Gath Battalion of six hundred men under the commander Ittai.

He called Captain Ittai over to him.

'There's no need for you to come,' he said. 'Go back and take service under the new king. You are a foreigner and an exile from your country. It isn't long since you came here. Why should I make you a vagabond like myself – I haven't any idea where I'm going. Go back with your men. May GOD be kind and faithful to you!'

'Not on your life, Your Majesty,' said Captain Ittai. 'I'm not going back! I am an officer under command – where you go, I go, come life, come death!'

'Very good,' said the king. 'March on!'

Captain Ittai marched on with his soldiers and camp-followers. The crowds watching were in tears as the procession moved by. The king crossed the Kidron Valley and took the desert road.

Zadok and Abiathar, the priests, were carrying the Ark of GOD. They had set it down until everybody had marched past.

The king went over and spoke to Zadok.

'Look,' he said, 'I want you to go straight back to the city, you and Abiathar and your two sons Ahimaaz and Jonathan. Keep your eyes open and keep me informed. I will stay by the Fords and wait there for any news you can get to me.'

So Zadok and Abiathar took the Ark of GOD back to Jerusalem and stayed there.

King David slowly climbed the slopes of the Olive Hill. He was in tears. He'd drawn his cloak over his head and was walking barefoot. The men with him walked up the hill with covered heads and in tears, too.

Someone told the king that Ahithophel was among the rebels on Absalom's side.

'May Ahithophel give bad advice, O GOD!' he said.

He had just come to the top of the hill where there was a shrine when he suddenly met his old friend Hushai the Archite, with his coat torn and earth on his head.

'If you come along with me,' the king said to him, 'you'll only be a burden. But you can be a real help if you'll go back to the city. Get on the right side of Absalom. Tell him that once you were his father's courtier, and that now you will be his. You may get a chance of confusing Ahithophel's advice to my advantage. Then you can get all the palace news to me. Tell Zadok and Abiathar anything you find out. Their sons will bring it to me.'

Hushai reached the city just as Absalom was entering it.

Stories of the Flight   *2 Samuel 16:1-14*

Over the top of the hill, the king met Ziba, Meribaal's servant. He was driving two donkeys laden with bread, raisin cakes, summer fruits and wine.

'What are all these for?' he asked.

'The donkeys are for Your Majesty's family to ride on,' said Ziba. 'The bread and fruit are for the soldiers. And someone will need the wine if he faints on the desert march.'

'Where's Meribaal?' asked the king.

'Back in Jerusalem,' said Ziba. 'He thinks the country will give him back his grandfather's kingdom.'

'I see!' he said. 'All Meribaal's estate is now yours.'

'I give you the homage which is your due, Your Majesty' said Ziba. 'May you always think kindly of me.'

As the king reached Bahurim Village, a man called Shimei came running out cursing and throwing stones at him, although his Guards were marching on each side of him.

'Down with you! Down with you, you murderer, you scoundrel!' he shouted. 'You usurped Saul's throne and now GOD is avenging the murder of Saul's family! He's made your son Absalom king! You are a murderer, that's why you've come to this miserable end!'

(Shimei was a Benjamite like Saul.)

'Why should Your Majesty let a wretch like this curse you?' asked Captain Abishai. 'Let me go over and knock his head off!'

'You're a violent lot, you and Joab!' said the king. 'You can't quarrel with a fellow like this and his curses – perhaps GOD himself inspired him.'

He turned to his court.

'My own son,' he said, 'the son of my own body, would kill me if he could; who can blame this Benjamite for doing what my own son does? Let him go and let him get on with his cursing – GOD has inspired him to curse me. I pray that GOD won't forget me; he may turn his curse into blessing!'

King David and his soldiers marched on along the road and ignored him. Shimei ran along with them, on the hillside above, cursing and throwing stones. They came at last, dead-tired, to the Fords. It was good to drink the cold water.

Absalom Occupies Jerusalem   2 Samuel 16:15-23; 17:1-23

Prince Absalom and the Southern rebels were now masters of Jerusalem. Ahithophel was his Chief Adviser.

David's friend, Hushai, sought an audience with the prince.

'Long live the king!' he said.

'This is a queer sort of loyalty,' said the prince. 'Why aren't you with your old friend?'

'My place is here,' he replied, 'with the king that GOD and his people have chosen. Here I stay. Besides, whose officer shall I be? His son's – I will serve you as I served your father.'

The prince summoned his chief adviser, Ahithophel.

'Give us your advice,' he said. 'What do you suggest we should do now?'

'Make it clear that you have completely broken with your father,' he said. 'Nothing would make this clearer than your taking his secondary wives as your own wives. He left ten of them to look after the palace. That will stiffen the resistance of your followers.'

So they set up the bridal tent on the roof of the palace. All his followers could now see that he intended to be the real king.

'There is another urgent matter,' said Ahithophel. 'Give me the army tonight and I will attack King David while he's tired and exhausted – that will put him in a panic. His troops will scatter and I can get him by himself and kill him. I will unite the whole country behind you. The fact is that there is one man – and one man only – who stands in your way. Deal with him and the whole country will be at peace.'

This seemed like excellent advice to the prince and his court.

'I would like to know what Hushai would advise,' he said.

Hushai was summoned to the court and told about Ahithophel's plans.

'What do you think?' asked the prince. 'Don't be frightened to disagree – I want your own unbiased judgement.'

'I don't really think that is good advice,' said Hushai. 'I'll give you my reasons. You are dealing with veteran soldiers – the Guard will fight to the death like a wild bear robbed of her cubs. Your father is a seasoned soldier – you won't find him where you think you will. He won't be with his troops tonight; he'll be in hiding in some ravine or other. You'll certainly have some casualties in the first attack. It would be easy to make that look like defeat. You've got men with lion's courage, but they know David's reputation as a hero and they know how the Guards fight.

'What I would suggest is this: attack David with overwhelming force; call upon the whole country and march yourself as their commander-in-chief. Then, whenever you attack him, you can utterly outnumber his forces and wipe them out, Guards and all. If he retires into a fortified city, you will be strong enough to storm it and destroy it.'

The prince and the whole court now voted for Hushai's plan as better than Ahithophel's.

Hushai told Zadok and Abiathar what had happened at court – Ahithophel's plans and his own proposals.

'Get the information to King David immediately,' he told them. 'Warn him not to stay at the Fords tonight but to get over to the other side of Jordan River. He is in great danger.'

Now Jonathan and Ahimaaz were hiding at Rogel Well. A girl used to go from time to time and tell them what was happening. On this occasion a boy saw them, and Prince Absalom was told about them. They left Rogel Well in a hurry and got as far as Bahurim Village, and took refuge with one of the villagers. They climbed down into the pit in the courtyard, and his wife covered it with a sheet and scattered grain on top of it – there was nothing to make anyone suspect anything. Rebel officers from Jerusalem tracked them down to the village.

'They went on through the ravine,' she said.

The officers searched everywhere in vain, and at last went back to Jerusalem to report.

When all was clear, the two men climbed out of the pit and found King David at the Fords.

'Up, and over the river!' they told the king, 'Don't waste any time.' They gave him a detailed account of Ahithophel's plans.

King David and his troops struck camp and crossed Jordan River. By dawn all of them were on the eastern bank.

Ahithophel knew that Prince Absalom had made a fatal mistake in not taking his advice. He saddled his donkey, and went back to his home town. He put all his affairs in order, and then hanged himself. He was buried in his father's grave.

David in Mahanaim *2 Samuel 17:24-29*

King David marched into the eastern mountains and reached Mahanaim.

Prince Absalom and his troops crossed Jordan River, marched on into the Gilead Highlands and set up camp there. (He had made General Amasa his commander-in-chief instead of David's commander-in-chief, General Joab.)

North-west of Jordan River, the men of Ammon and Gilead rallied to David in Mahanaim. Couches, rugs, basins and earthen vessels were brought along; wheat, barley, meal, parched corn, beans, lentils, honey, curdled milk, sheep and calves were given freely.

'They must be starving after the march through the wild mountains,' people said.

Among those who gave freely were, for example, Shobi the Ammonite (he lived in Rabbah, the capital city), Machir from Lodebar, and the Gileadite Barzillai from Rogelim.

King David now reviewed his troops and reorganised the command. He formed three army corps, under three commanders – General Joab, General Abishai (his brother) and Captain Ittai, the commander of the Foreign Legion. He proposed to lead the troops himself as commander-in-chief. His generals strongly objected.

'No!' they said. 'If we are routed, they won't bother about us. You are worth ten thousand soldiers; it would be the end of us if you were killed. You must stay in Mahanaim. You can survey the course of the battle and send reinforcements when they are needed.'

'I accept your judgement,' he said.

So he took the salute, standing by the side of the city gate; the regiments and battalions marched by.

He gave special orders to his three commanders about Absalom.

'Don't be hard on the young man,' he said,' for my sake.'

This was made clear in army orders.

The battle took place in the forest south of Mahanaim. The rebels were routed by David's veteran soldiers. There were terrible casualties. The fighting spread over the whole countryside; more died in the forest than died on the battlefield.

In the confusion of the fighting, Prince Absalom stumbled accidentally into a body of David's soldiers. The mule he was riding bolted into the forest under the branches of a great oak tree and his hair got caught in the branches. He was left hanging between heaven and earth.

A soldier reported the incident to General Joab.

'I saw Prince Absalom hanging from an oak tree,' he said.

'You stand there and just tell me you saw him!' exclaimed the general. 'Why didn't you kill him there and then? I would have rewarded and promoted you.'

'I wouldn't lay my hands on the king's son for a thousand pounds,' said the soldier. 'You know what the king's orders are. If I'd played the traitor and disobeyed them at the risk of my life, I'd be quickly found out – and you wouldn't have lifted a finger to help me at the court martial!'

'I'm not standing here arguing with you all day,' snapped the general. So he took three spears and drove them into the prince's heart while he was still alive and hanging from the oak tree.

He then sounded the 'Cease Fire', calling off the pursuit and withdrawing his troops. Soldiers threw Prince Absalom's body into a hole in the forest and built a pile of stones over it. The surviving rebels made off home.

David Hears the News

Ahimaaz, son of Zadok the priest, spoke to General Joab.

'Let me be the first with the good news,' he asked. 'Let me tell King David how GOD has routed the rebels!'

'Not today,' said the general. 'Not today. Another day perhaps. You're not the right kind of messenger to announce the prince's death.'

He called one of the foreign soldiers of the Guards.

'Go and tell the king what you've seen,' he commanded.

The guardsman saluted and ran off.

'Let me run after him,' said Ahimaaz. 'I don't care what happens!'

'Why risk it?' said the general. 'It won't pay!'

'I don't care,' said Ahimaaz. 'I'm going!'

'All right,' said the general, 'you run!'

Ahimaaz ran off, and, taking the road through the Jordan Plain, overtook the guardsman.

King David was sitting in the open space between the outer and inner gates of Mahanaim City. A sentry, stationed at the top of the outer gate, was watching the road.

'There's a man running alone!' he called out.

'He's bringing news of the battle, then,' said the king.

As the man came nearer, running fast, the sentry saw another man running behind him.

'There's another man running after him,' he shouted down to the guard below.

'He's bringing news, too,' said the king.

'The first man looks to me like Ahimaaz,' the sentry shouted down. 'Only Ahimaaz runs like this!'

'A good man,' said the king, 'and good news.'

Ahimaaz reached the gate.

'All's well!' he shouted as he saluted. 'Praise God! the rebels are routed, Your Majesty!'

'Is the young prince safe?' asked the king.

'There was such a hullabaloo when General Joab sent me off,' he said, 'I don't know what it was all about.

'Step aside,' said the king, 'and stand here.'

He stood at ease and waited.

The guardsman came running in.

'Good news for Your Majesty!' he reported. 'GOD has rescued you from the rebels.'

'Is the young prince safe?' asked the king.

'May all your enemies and all rebels die as he died!' said the guardsman.

King David broke down and burst into tears. He stumbled up to the guardroom over the gate; and all the way he kept saying, 'O my son, Absalom – my son – my son Absalom! I would rather have died myself! O Absalom, my son, my son!'

Angry Soldiers   *2 Samuel 19:1-8*

General Joab was told how the king had taken the news – broken with grief for his dead son. There was no victory parade. News of the king's grief dampened the spirits of all his soldiers. They walked about the city in silence; you would have thought they had lost the battle and were ashamed of their cowardice. All the time King David could think of nobody but his dead son; he had pulled his cloak over his face and kept on saying, again and again, 'O my son Absalom! Absalom, my son, my son!'

General Joab went to the palace and rebuked the king to his face.

'You have shamed your own soldiers,' he said curtly, 'soldiers who have saved your life and the lives of all your family. This is a nice state of affairs – you love those who hate you, and hate those who love you! It's quite obvious that neither officers nor men mean a thing to you. What a happy man you'd be if we were all dead and Absalom was alive! Stand up and be a man! Go out and congratulate your soldiers. By GOD, there'll not be a soldier in the city tonight if you don't! That will teach you – you've never had to face anything like that since you were a young soldier yourself!'

The king got up and took his seat at the gate.

News spread throughout the city, and the soldiers crowded round.

The March Back to Jerusalem   *2 Samuel 19:8-40*

There was chaos throughout the whole country. The rebels were back in their own homes and people everywhere were talking.

'What's happened to the king?' they were asking. 'He was our hero in the early days. He put the Philistines in their place. But his own son Absalom drove him out of the country and we crowned him king! Now *he's* dead! Why is David idling in Mahanaim? Why does nobody do anything about bringing him home?'

News of this country-wide gossip was reported to King David. He sent a message to Zadok and Abiathar in Jerusalem:

'Call a meeting of the leaders of the Southern tribe of Judah and put this to them: "Why should you – members of my own clan, my blood-relations – be so slow to get me, your king, back home?" Tell General Amasa: "We are close kinsmen. I'll see to it that you are commander-in-chief instead of General Joab."' So David again won the affections of the leaders of his own clan. There was a unanimous decision to invite him and his court back to his capital city.

He set off on the march home and reached Jordan River. The Southern clansmen came as far as Gilgal to escort him across.

Shimei – the Benjamite from Bahurim Village, who had cursed David when he was escaping – eagerly joined the Southern clansmen at the head of a thousand Benjamites. Ziba, who had helped the king in his escape, was there too, with fifteen sons and twenty slaves. Indeed he had made sure of getting to the river before the king arrived and had crossed the ford to the eastern side to escort him across and see to his needs.

King David was about to cross the river when Shimei threw himself on the ground before him.

'I pray Your Majesty not to hold me guilty,' he said. 'I remember with shame how I treated Your Majesty when you were escaping from Jerusalem. I hope you won't hold it against me now; I know what a terrible thing I did. Today, you see, I am the first of the Northern clansmen to come and greet Your Majesty.'

'He cursed GOD's anointed king,' General Abishai broke in. 'Is he going to get away with it?'

'You and your brother!' said King David, 'What bitter men you are! You're talking like my enemy! On such a day as this, it is unthinkable that any man should be put to death. I am king again – and I know it!'

He turned to Shimei.

'You shall not die!' he said. 'This is my solemn promise!'

Meribaal, Saul's lame grandson, was there too. He had gone into mourning from the day the king escaped from the city until the day of his return in safety.

'Why didn't you go with me into exile, Meribaal?' asked the king.

'Your Majesty,' he said, 'my servant Ziba betrayed me. I told him to saddle the donkey – I am lame and if I were to overtake Your Majesty I had to ride. What he did was to slander me. Your Majesty is the representative of God. Punish me as you please. I've no right to complain –

my whole family were at your mercy when you called me to share Your Majesty's royal table.'

'You talk a lot,' said the king briefly. 'You and Ziba can share your estates between you.'

'He can take it all!' exclaimed Meribaal. 'I'm only too glad to have Your Majesty safe home again!'

Then there was Barzillai the Gileadite. He had come up to Mahanaim from his village of Rogelim and travelled with the king all the way to Jordan River. He was an old man, 80 years of age, and a very rich farmer. He had seen to the king's needs all the time he was in Mahanaim.

'You must come along with me,' said the king to him. 'In Jerusalem I can look after you in your old age.'

'I am now 80 years of age,' said Barzillai. 'I haven't many more years to live. I'm an old man – I can't tell the taste of one thing from the taste of another, and I'm too deaf to hear the singers. There's no point in my going with Your Majesty and living in your palace. I should only be a burden. I haven't done much – I don't deserve such handsome treatment. Let me go back to my home town and die there by my father and mother's grave. My son here can go with Your Majesty – give him what you would have given me.'

'Your son shall come with me, indeed,' said the king. 'I will treat him as you wish. And if there's anything I can do for you, tell me and I will do it.'

The troops began to ford the river, and the king followed. He kissed Bazillai goodbye, and the old man went home.

The king reached Gilgal, escorted by Southern clansmen and some Northerners.

Northern Rebellion   *2 Samuel 19:41-43; 20:1-2, 4-22*

The Northern clansmen had already begun to make trouble. They sought an audience with King David while he was still in Gilgal.

'Why have the Southern clansmen stolen a march on us?' they asked. 'Why should they step in and escort Your Majesty and his court over Jordan River?'

'It's obvious,' retorted the Southerners. 'He's our fellow-clansman. What on earth is there in that to make you angry? We haven't sponged on him. We haven't kidnapped him!'

'We have ten shares in the king to your two,' they retorted, 'and we've an older history – we were in this land first! Why slight us like this? Weren't we the first to talk of escorting the king back to his capital?'

But the Southerners shouted the Northerners down.

Now there was a scoundrel of a man among the Northerners – Sheba from King Saul's clan, the Benjamites. He sounded the war-cry:

We don't belong to David!
We've nothing to do
with the Bethlehemite farmer!
Back to the North!

Some of the Northerners, led by Sheba, rose in rebellion. The Southerners rallied to King David and escorted him from Gilgal to Jerusalem, his capital city.

'Muster the Southern clansmen,' the king commanded General Amasa, 'and report to me in three days' time.'

At the end of three days, there was no sign of General Amasa.

The king ordered General Joab to deal with the Northern rebellion.

'Take the Guards,' he commanded, 'and hunt Sheba down. He'll do us more harm than Prince Absalom. If he wins over the fortified cities, we're in grave difficulties.'

General Abishai and General Joab called out the Guards and marched north.

At the great stone in Gibeon, they came face to face with General Amasa. General Joab was wearing his uniform. His sword was in its sheath and was fastened by a girdle over it. It fell out as he went forward and dropped on the ground. He picked it up with his left hand, as he greeted General Amasa.

'How are you?' he asked, and took the general's beard in his right hand to kiss him. General Amasa hadn't noticed the sword in his left hand. General Joab jabbed his sword in General Amasa's stomach, and he died without a second blow.

The two generals – Joab and Abishai – went on after Sheba.

One of the guardsmen stood over General Amasa's body shouting, 'Let everyone who's a friend of General Joab's and is for King David, follow the General!'

The body lay in the middle of the road in a pool of blood with a crowd round it. A soldier dragged it off the road into a field and covered it with a cloak. The soldiers marched on after General Joab.

Sheba had moved rapidly north to Abel Town, some twenty-five miles north of Galilee Lake. His fellow clansmen rallied round him and occupied the town. General Joab caught him there, and besieged him. He set his soldiers to build a mound against the rampart and to batter the city walls down.

Then a wise woman stood on the outer city wall and called down to the soldiers below.

'Listen to me! Listen to me!' she shouted. 'Tell General Joab to come here. I want to talk to him.'

General Joab approached the wall.

'Are you General Joab?' she asked.

'I am,' he answered.

'Listen to me,' she said.

'I'm listening,' he said.

'There's an old proverb,' she said. 'It says: "In Abel disputes are settled." You are destroying a city where GOD's people can settle their disputes. Why destroy GOD's heritage?'

'I don't want to do that,' answered General Joab. 'I'm no destroyer or vandal. That's not the issue. There's a man inside the city who has raised his hand against King David – Sheba's his name. Hand him over and I'll withdraw.'

'Then,' said the woman, 'his head shall be thrown over the city wall to you!'

So she talked the city over to her way of thinking. They executed Sheba and threw his head over the city wall to General Joab.

The general sounded the retreat and withdrew from the city. The soldiers went home and General Joab reported to the king in Jerusalem.

Palace Plot

1 Kings 1:1, 5-53

King David was now a very old man and needed nursing. Prince Adonijah – born after Absalom and a good-looking man – began to talk publicly about being his father's successor on the throne. Like Absalom, he was a favourite son; David let him do what he liked.

So Adonijah now set himself up as king – with a chariot and horsemen and fifty soldiers to lead his cavalcade, just like Absalom in his bid to be king. He came to an understanding with General Joab, the commander-in-chief, and Abiathar the priest, men who had been loyal to King David.

He failed to win the support of the priest Zadok, the prophet Nathan and the Guards and Captain Benaiah.

His coronation was arranged. A sacrificial feast was held by the Serpent's Stone near Fuller's Well in the Kidron Valley south-west of the city. He invited all his brother princes and the royal officials, but not Nathan or Captain Benaiah or the Guards – or his brother Solomon. The coronation ceremony began.

News of all this soon spread. The prophet Nathan went immediately to Bathsheba, David's favourite wife, the mother of Solomon.

'Have you heard what's happening?' he said. 'Prince Adonijah is being crowned king – without His Majesty knowing anything about it. Your life and Prince Solomon's are in danger. Let me give you some advice. Seek an audience with the king and say this to him: "Didn't Your Majesty promise me that your son, Prince Solomon, should succeed to the throne? Why, then, is Prince Adonijah being crowned king?" I'll wait till you've started talking to him and then come hurriedly into the room and support what you are saying.'

Bathsheba went into the king's bedroom where the nurse was looking after him. She bowed in homage.

'What do you want?' he asked.

She said what Nathan had told her to say.

'You don't know what's happening,' she went on. 'You swore that my son Solomon should succeed you. But the coronation of Prince Adonijah is taking place at this moment. All the princes are there – and Abiathar the priest and General Joab. But Prince Solomon hasn't been invited. The whole country is waiting to know whom Your Majesty will announce as your successor. As things are going, I and Prince Solomon will just be treated as rebels on your death!'

It was at this point that the prophet Nathan came into the room.

'Nathan the prophet asks for an audience with Your Majesty,' the king was told.

Nathan bowed before him in homage.

'Has Your Majesty made a royal proclamation that Prince Adonijah shall succeed to the throne?' he asked. 'He is holding his coronation ceremony at this very moment. The princes and General Joab and Abiathar the priest are attending the coronation banquet. The whole company have raised the cry "Long live King Adonijah!" I haven't been invited – nor has Zadok nor Captain Benaiah nor Prince Solomon. Has Your Majesty commanded this coronation ceremony without a word to us, your officers?'

'Call Bathsheba over to me,' said the king.

She came and stood in front of him.

'In GOD's name who has always come to my rescue,' he said, 'what I promised to do I will do – and I will do it now.'

Bathsheba bowed in homage.

'Long live Your Majesty!' she said.

'Call Zadok and Nathan and Captain Benaiah into my presence,' he commanded.

The three men stood before him.

'Order my officers on parade,' he said. 'Escort Prince Solomon, mounted on my royal mule, to Bubbling Spring in the Kidron Valley. Let Zadok and Nathan crown him. Let the bugles blow and let everybody shout "Long live King Solomon!" Escort him to the throne-room and let him take possession of my throne. He shall be my successor and king of the whole country, North and South. This is my will.'

'As Your Majesty commands,' said Captain Benaiah. 'May GOD confirm Your Majesty's decision. As GOD has blessed Your Majesty, may he bless King Solomon. May his reign be greater even than Your Majesty's!'

Zadok, Nathan, Captain Benaiah and the Guards escorted Prince Solomon, riding on the king's mule, to Bubbling Spring. Then Zadok the priest anointed Prince Solomon king. The bugle was blown, and the soldiers and the crowds shouted, "Long live King Solomon!" With flutes playing, the Guards escorted the new king back into the city. The noise was tremendous.

Prince Adonijah and his guests further down the valley heard the shouting – the feast was almost over.

'What does the shouting mean?' asked General Joab.

While he was asking the question, Jonathan, Abiathar's son, burst in.

'Come in!' Prince Adonijah called out. 'A good man like you must be bringing good news.'

'I'm not,' he said. 'The shouting you heard was the shouting at Prince Solomon's coronation. King David has made a royal proclamation. Zadok and Nathan and Captain Benaiah and the Guards have carried it out. The noise you heard was the royal procession going back into the city. What is more – Solomon has taken his seat on the royal throne. All King David's officers are now congratulating him on his decision, and he is acknowledging them. He has confirmed his proclamation.'

The guests were terrified and were soon gone. Prince Adonijah was so frightened that he ran to the royal shrine and clung to the altar there.

'King Solomon must first promise not to murder me!' he kept saying.

All this was reported to King Solomon.

'If he keeps straight,' he said, 'he's safe enough. One slip, and he'll be a dead man.'

King Solomon ordered Prince Adonijah into his presence.

He was brought from the altar and he bowed in homage before the new king.

'Go home,' said King Solomon.

Not long after that, the old king died.

Memories of the Past

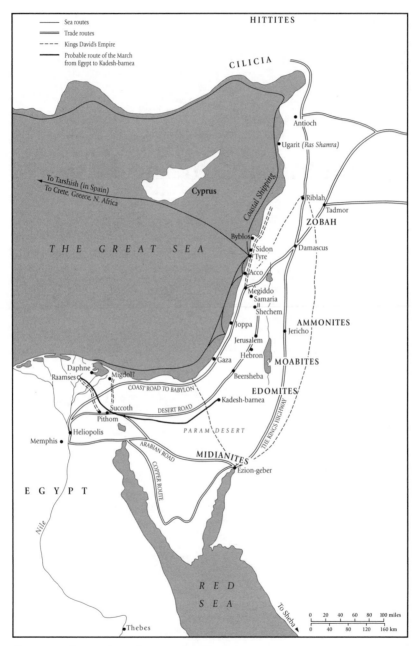

The route of Moses' march across the desert

Introduction

The Israelites had come into the highlands with firm convictions about their destiny: they were 'GOD's People'.

Many of them held these convictions strongly; they knew what they believed. Many others had only a vague idea of what it was all about. Some held no deep convictions at all. This variety of attitude and conviction is what we find in all societies, even in the closely-knit societies of the ancient world. But there was a peculiar strength about the common convictions of the Israelite people in these early days of their history which marked them off from their neighbours. This strength stemmed from the insight and greatness of Moses and the profound meaning which he helped them to find in their dramatic escape from Egypt.

The story of their brief hour of glory which we have just read has only given us glimpses of these profound common convictions; we must turn now to look at them in greater depth.

We find them embodied in their 'tribal traditions' which were recited regularly at their religious festivals by the guardians of the sanctuaries at Shiloh and Hebron (afterwards at Bethel and Jerusalem). These traditions were gathered together and written down in King Solomon's time.

Tribal traditions, handed on by word of mouth from generation to generation, are not like written contemporary records; but we know now that they can give us a reliable picture, in broad outline, of the decisive events through which the people who cherished them have lived. They also have a value which written records can never have. The form in which we have them has been given to them through their being recited again and again in worship; they express, therefore, the common convictions of a whole society – the recital year by year at their religious festivals was a public statement of their faith. For at these festivals they were not merely celebrating important events that had happened in the past; they were declaring their enduring meaning – a meaning which still gave purpose to their own lives.

The Israelite people believed that, under GOD, they owed their convictions to one man, Moses – one of the greatest men who has ever lived, to judge by his influence over the later history of the world. These central convictions were two: that they owed everything to GOD and what he had done for them; and that they were his 'People' and live in his Way.

It was only when their city was in ruins and their national life destroyed that they really discovered on what strong foundations these convictions were built. As we read these old traditions about their escape from Egypt, their march across the desert, what happened at 'GOD's Mountain', and their settlement in their new homeland, we must keep our eyes open for the 'growing points' of this old story, and remember that we are watching the beginnings of a faith that three thousand years later will grow into the faith of a Dietrich Bonhoeffer or of a Martin Luther King.

In the very early days, before they became a people or a nation, the ancestors of the Israelites belonged to many different tribes with many different names. They had no one common name – except the contemptuous name given them by their powerful neighbours: 'Hebrews' – 'freebooters'. This is the name we will use in this part.

Escape from Egypt: Moses

Moses was the founder of Israelite religion. He dominates the traditions his people handed down of their escape from Egypt and their march to their homeland. His great achievement was to weld the very mixed company of tribesmen he led out of Egypt into a people with common religious convictions. The traditions do not hide from us the fact that he had to face disaffection and even rebellion. But he is one of the outstanding leaders in world history. His courage and vision stand out in these stories his people told of him. His courage he shared with many of his soldiers; his vision was something new which we look for in vain in the worship of the surrounding peoples of his time.

His vision can be put quite simply. From the point of view of the his-torian, the story of the Hebrew labourers was just the story of an escape across the frontiers. It must have been so common a story that no mention of it is to be found in Egyptian records. It would have passed unnoted and unrecorded − but for Moses. To him this was not just an escape − it was a deliverance. Here was a god who came to a people who were at the lowest level of human society − slaves in the Egyptian labour gangs − and acted for them though they never expected help and had not even asked for it. This is the key to the importance of these old stories: it is the first step towards the adult and mature faith of the Israelite prophets and of Jesus. So GOD for Moses was Deliverer and Saviour of his people: and this faith of his was embodied in the 'Covenant' established at 'GOD's Mountain'.

There is much in these stories which, as we might expect, is crude and far from what Jesus was to believe. Their idea of GOD, for example, as the friend of the Hebrews but the enemy of the Egyptians was too naïve − and yet something that we should not be surprised to find among rebel slaves. But their central convictions that they owed every-thing to GOD was not mistaken. Moses saw that if GOD rescued them like this, he must be master of history and nature. He did not see this with all the fullness with which the prophets, some five hundred years later, were to see it. But he saw it and saw it clearly. He transformed an apparently insignificant border incident into a turning point in the religious history of the world.

Egyptian Labour Corps

Exodus 1:8-12, 22

A new Pharaoh had risen to power in Egypt – a Pharaoh who cared nothing for the fact that the Hebrew Joseph, more than a hundred years before, had been viceroy of Egypt.

'We'd better beware,' he said one day to his ministers. 'There are too many of these Hebrews about – they are far too strong for us to feel safe. If we're ever at war, they'll go over to the enemy and make good their escape.'

So orders were given to break their spirit. They were conscripted into labour gangs (as if they were prisoners of war) and forced to work on the building of new store-cities in the Nile Delta near the Bitter Sea. But this hard slavery made no difference; their numbers kept on growing, and they even emigrated into other parts of the country. The Egyptians loathed them.

Pharaoh gave brutal orders.

'Throw their baby boys into the river,' he ordered. 'You needn't bother about the baby girls – they can live.'

Incident on a Building Site

Exodus 2:11-22

Moses had been brought up at the royal court, away from his fellow-countrymen.

He went out one day to see what was happening to the men in the labour gangs. He soon found out how savagely the Egyptians were treating them – he actually saw an Egyptian officer strike down one of his fellow-countrymen. He looked round to see if anyone else was in sight – they were alone. He killed the officer and buried his body in the sand.

Some time later, he went out again to see what was happening and found two Hebrew labourers fighting. One was obviously a bully.

'What are you beating him up for?' he asked.

'Hello, who made you boss round here?' the man sneered. 'Are you going to murder me as you murdered the officer?'

That scared Moses.

'Everybody knows about it,' he thought.

He got out of Egypt as quickly as he could and went as far as the tribal territory of the Midianites. He came to an oasis and sat down by the well. Seven shepherd girls, daughters of the priest there, brought their sheep to the well to water them. They were filling the trough with water when some shepherds came along and began to drive them off. Moses went to their rescue and helped them to water their sheep.

'You've got back early today,' said their father when they got home.

'An Egyptian rescued us from the shepherds,' they said. 'He even drew the water and helped us to water the sheep.'

'Well – where is he?' he asked. 'You haven't left him at the well, have you? Go and fetch him at once – we can at least give him hospitality.'

That's how Moses came to stay in the Midianite encampment. He stayed there a long time; he married one of the priest's daughters, and his son was born there.

The Mountain Experience

Exodus 3:1-14, 16; 4:1-4, 6-7, 10-12, 19-20

This is the story of how GOD called Moses to his great work. We must remember that it is a tribal tradition, not a contemporary record; and that it was a story the Israelites were to think about and live by through the centuries.

The story is how the name of the Hebrews' God was revealed to Moses as 'Yahweh'. The Midianites (among whom he was now living) and some Hebrew tribes had always used this name for God; others had not known it – it was a new name to them. We do not know what the name 'Yahweh' originally meant (perhaps it was 'Storm God'); but it was given a new meaning for the Hebrews through their experience of being rescued from Egypt. Later, as in the story below, they were to explain it as 'I AM WHO I AM' (or 'I WILL BE WHAT I WILL BE') because in Hebrew the words 'I am Yahweh' and 'I am who I am'* sound somewhat alike.

What is important for us is not what the name originally meant but what it meant to the people who used it. And to Moses it meant a new idea of God as the 'Living God' who made himself known in ordinary human experience. Moses saw God in action in the rescue of the small, insignificant and hopeless group of slaves from Egypt. He was not just a tribal god (as he was for their tribal ancestors) and he was not like the gods of the surrounding nations, a nature god. He was Lord of history

* The words 'I am' in Hebrew are much stronger than our 'I am'; they mean 'I am present and active'.

and of nature. We have put this in our own language; the tribes whose stories we are reading put it in their cruder, more limited way. It was a new idea of God; this is what lies behind this story of how GOD revealed his name to Moses.

Moses spent his time looking after his father-in-law's sheep. One day he found himself in the western part of the desert.

He looked – a bush was on fire, but the fire went on burning brightly.

'I must have a look at this remarkable sight,' thought Moses. 'I wonder why the bush doesn't burn out.'

GOD saw that Moses went out of his way to have a look at it.

'Stay where you are,' he said. 'Take your sandals off. You are standing on holy ground. I am your ancestors' God.'

Moses hid his face; he was frightened at meeting God like this.

'I have seen the brutal treatment of my people in Egypt,' GOD went on. 'I have heard their cry for help under their savage foremen. I know what they are going through and I have come down to rescue them. I'm going to send you back to bring them out of Egypt.'

'But – I'm not the man to rescue them,' said Moses.

'I'll stand by you,' said God. 'And this will prove to you that I myself have given you your orders: when you've escaped from Egypt, you shall worship me here on this mountain.'

'But if I go back to Egypt,' said Moses, 'and tell the Hebrew labourers that their ancestral God has sent me to them, they'll only say, "Well, you tell us what his name is, then." What shall I say?'

'I AM* – that is my name,' said God. 'Tell them that I AM has sent you to them. Go and get the heads of the great families together. Tell them that the God of their fathers has appeared to you, and that he told you to tell them this: "I have been watching. I have seen what you are going through in Egypt. I promise to rescue you from this savage suffering."'

'They won't believe a word I say,' said Moses. 'They won't even listen to me. They will say, "GOD never appeared to you!"'

'What's that in your hand?' asked GOD.

'A staff,' said Moses.

'Throw it on the ground,' said GOD.

Moses threw it on the ground – it became a snake. He jumped away from it.

* In the earliest form of the story, this would probably read 'I am Yahweh' ('I am GOD'). Later editors put 'I AM' (what, for them, was the meaning of the name) in its place.

'Stretch your hand out,' said GOD, 'and take it by the tail.'

He stretched his hand out and caught hold of it – it was a staff in his hand again.

'Put your hand inside your shirt,' said GOD.

He put his hand inside his shirt. He pulled it out – it was snow-white with leprosy.

'Put your hand inside your shirt again,' he said.

He put his hand in. When he pulled it out, it was his healthy hand once again.

But Moses hadn't finished.

'O GOD,' he said, 'I'm a poor speaker. I always was, and I still am – even though you have spoken to me. I never know what to say.'

'Who made man's mouth?' asked GOD. 'If a man is dumb or deaf, seeing or blind, who makes him so? Is it not I who am GOD? Go – I'm your mouth, I'll give you the words you must speak. Back to Egypt! The men who wanted to kill you are all dead.'

So Moses took his wife and son, put them on a donkey and went back to Egypt.

Audience with Pharaoh   *Exodus 4:29-31; 5:1-23; 6:1*

When Moses got there he called all the heads of the great families of his people together. He told them what GOD had said to him, and proved that GOD had really spoken to him by the signs of the 'staff' and the 'hand'. They took him at his word. When they heard what GOD had said – that he had come to his people and seen all they were going through – they bowed their heads in worship.

Some days later, Moses and some of the Hebrew leaders went to Pharaoh.

'These are the words of GOD, the God of the Hebrew labourers: "Let my people go – they must hold a religious festival in the desert",' Moses told him.

'Who's he?' sneered Pharaoh. 'Why should I take any notice of him and let them go? I know nothing about him. I'll not let them go.'

'But our GOD has made himself known to us,' said Moses. 'Let us go forty or fifty miles into the desert and offer our sacrifices to him – terrible things might happen to us if we don't.

'You are just stopping the people working!' Pharaoh said. 'Mind your own business!'

'They're a lazy lot,' he thought to himself, 'and you'd give them a holiday, would you?'

So, that same day, he gave new orders to the Egyptian officers in charge of the labour force.

'No more straw for the brick-making,' he said. 'I won't have that any more – let them get their own straw. But I want the same number of bricks as before – no slackening off! They're a lazy lot – that's why they want to go off to the desert. Make them work harder. Take no notice of their lies.'

The officers went out.

'New orders of the day from Pharaoh,' they announced. '"No more straw. Get it yourselves when you can find it. But no change in the number of bricks to be made!"'

So the labourers had to go all over Egypt trying to find stubble for straw.

The officers kept shouting at them – 'Today's work's got to be finished today, just as before!'

They beat up the Hebrew foremen.

'Why haven't you got the right number of bricks today? You used to get them made all right!'

The foremen appealed to Pharaoh.

'Why are you treating us like this?' they pleaded. 'You give us no straw but tell us to make bricks. We are beaten up. It's all your officers' fault.'

'Lazy, lazy, lazy!' said Pharaoh. 'That's why you want to go off to the desert. Get back to work! No straw – but bricks as usual!'

The foremen saw that they had an impossible task – the number of bricks demanded was beyond all reason.

As they came out from the palace, they met Moses waiting for them.

'GOD will put you in your place,' they said. 'We're now the scum of the earth to Pharaoh and his officers. You've just given them the chance they wanted – they'll soon have us all dead men.'

Moses prayed to GOD.

'Why have you treated these men so brutally?' he said. 'And why did you ever send me? We've had nothing but disaster ever since I came here with your message. You haven't rescued us at all!'

'You'll see how I'll deal with Pharaoh,' said GOD. 'It won't be a matter of "letting the people go" – he'll make them go!'

Egyptian Disasters

Exodus 7:14-18, 20-21, 23-25; 8:1-4, 8-15, 20-32;
9:13-14, 20-21, 23-30, 33-34; 10:1, 5-11, 13-26, 28

We do not know what actually happened in Egypt; all we can say is that some natural disasters struck Egypt and Moses saw in them GOD coming to the rescue of the Hebrew labourers.

'Pharaoh's a stubborn man,' GOD said to Moses. 'He just won't let the people go. Tomorrow morning, meet him on the river bank as he is going to bathe. Tell him this: The God of the labourers sends me to you with this message: "Let my people go to hold a pilgrimage festival in the desert. You have not done what I told you. You shall learn that I am GOD. I will strike the Nile water. The fish will die; the water will stink – nobody will be able to find any to drink."'

GOD struck the river. The fish died; the water stank – nobody could drink it.

Pharaoh went into his palace – he wasn't at all troubled. The Egyptians had to dig in the ground for water; they couldn't stomach the river water.

A week passed.

'Go to Pharaoh,' said GOD to Moses. 'Tell him: These are GOD's words: "Let my people go to worship me. If you still say No, I will infest the whole countryside with frogs. You'll have frogs everywhere – in your palace and royal bedroom and on the royal bed, and in the houses of your ministers and citizens and in ovens and kneading bowls. They'll come swarming out of the Nile."'

And so it happened.

'Ask GOD to take the frogs away,' said Pharaoh to Moses, 'away from me and my people. I'll let the labourers go on their pilgrimage.'

'When?' asked Moses. 'What are your orders?'

'Tomorrow,' said Pharaoh.

'As you command,' said Moses. 'You shall learn that there is no one like our GOD. The frogs will leave you and your houses.'

Moses left the palace. He did what he had promised and prayed to GOD about the frogs. And GOD did what Moses asked him. The frogs died out – in house, courtyard and field. They were piled up in heaps and there was a terrible stench. When Pharaoh saw that it was all over, he was as stubborn as ever.

'Get up early tomorrow morning,' said GOD to Moses. 'Wait for Pharaoh as he's going down to the river to bathe. Tell him: These are GOD's words: "Let my people go to worship me. If you won't, I'll send swarms of insects everywhere – in the houses, on the ground, to your ministers and your common people alike. There shall be no insects where the labourers live; that will prove to you that I am GOD even here in Egypt. This shall all happen tomorrow."'

That's just what GOD did. The insects came – into the palace and into the houses of Pharaoh's ministers. Everywhere the insects ruined the land.

Pharaoh summoned Moses to the palace.

'You can go and worship,' he said, 'but you must stay in Egypt.'

'No,' said Moses. 'At our religious festivals we sacrifice animals. Egyptians would stone us if we did that sort of thing here. We must go right out into the desert; it is there we must do what GOD commands.'

'Well, I'll let you go to the desert for your festival,' said Pharaoh, 'but you mustn't go far. Now pray to GOD for me.'

'Look,' said Moses, 'I am leaving your presence; I will ask GOD to get rid of the insects tomorrow. But we don't want any double-dealing from you. We don't want to find you saying No to us again.'

Moses went out from the palace and prayed to GOD. And GOD did what Moses asked and got rid of all the insects – there was not an insect left.

But Pharaoh was just his old stubborn self. He wouldn't let the people go.

'Get up early tomorrow morning,' said GOD to Moses. 'Stand in the presence of Pharaoh. Tell him: These are GOD's words: "Let my people go to worship me. You are still being proud and stubborn – refusing to let them go. So tomorrow I will send a violent hail-storm, a storm more terrible than any of you Egyptians have ever known in all your history. You had better get your livestock – and everything else you've got out in the fields – under shelter. Nothing out of doors will survive this storm."'

Some Egyptian ministers had begun to take GOD seriously; they quickly got animals and slaves indoors. Those who dismissed the whole thing as nonsense, of course, left their slaves and animals out in the open.

Then the thunder and lightning began. The hailstones were bigger than anybody had ever seen; they struck everything down – man and animal, plant and tree. Only where the Israelite labourers lived was there no storm.

Pharaoh sent for Moses.

'I'm a guilty man,' he said. 'Your GOD is in the right; we are all in the wrong. Pray to him – the storm has lasted long enough. I will let you go. You can get out right away.'

'When I've left the city,' said Moses, 'I will pray to GOD. The thunder and hail will stop. The earth is GOD's – remember that! But I know you and your ministers – you don't yet take GOD seriously.'

Moses went out of the palace and out of the city, and prayed to GOD. The thunder and hail stopped and there were clear skies.

But Pharaoh and his ministers hadn't changed at all. They were as stubborn as ever – when the storm was over.

'Go into the presence of Pharaoh,' said GOD to Moses. So Moses went to the palace.

'These are the words of GOD, the God of the labourers,' he said. "How long are you going to be stubborn? Let my people go to worship me. If you still say No, I will bring swarms of locusts into Egypt – you won't be able to see the ground you walk on. They'll eat up everything – everything the hail left, every tree left standing. They will swarm into your palaces, and into the houses of your ministers and common people alike. Neither your fathers nor your grandfathers ever saw a plague of locusts like it."'

Moses turned on his heel and left the palace.

Pharaoh's ministers now spoke up.

'How long is this man going to be a menace to us all?' they asked. 'Don't you know that Egypt is ruined already? Let the labourers go to worship their GOD.'

They brought Moses back to the palace.

'You can go to worship your GOD,' said Pharaoh. 'But who's going?'

'All of us,' said Moses, 'young and old, sons and daughters, flocks and herds. We must hold a proper festival.'

'Not on your life!' said Pharaoh. 'Children indeed! What scheming idea have you got into your heads? Let me be plain: only the labourers themselves can go to worship their GOD. That's what you wanted, isn't it?'

Moses was roughly dismissed from the royal presence.

An east wind blew all that day and night. And next morning the locusts were everywhere. Dense swarms settled over the whole land. Nobody had ever seen anything like it. The countryside was dark with locusts, everywhere everything was eaten up – plant, fruit, tree and grass, every bit of green.

Pharaoh sent hurriedly for Moses.

'I stand guilty – in GOD's sight and in yours,' he said. 'Forgive me, I beseech you, this once. Ask GOD to take this deadly plague away.'

Moses went out of the presence of Pharaoh and prayed to GOD.

GOD changed the wind into a very strong west wind which blew the locusts into the Sea of Reeds. There wasn't a locust left in Egypt.

But Pharaoh was as stubborn as ever.

'I will send a great darkness over the whole land of Egypt,' said GOD to Moses.

The whole sky went black. Nobody could see anybody else; people had to stay indoors. But it was daylight where the labourers lived.

Pharaoh sent for Moses.

'Go and worship,' he said, 'and you can take your children with you. But you must leave your livestock behind.'

'We need them,' said Moses, 'we need them for the festival sacrifices. We must take them all; we shan't know what we need until we get there. We won't leave an animal behind.'

'Get out,' said Pharaoh, 'and see that you never come into my presence again. I'll have you executed if you do.'

'As you say,' said Moses. 'I won't.'

The Last Night   *Exodus 11:1-6; 12:21-23, 27, 29-39*

This is a story of an epidemic which was so widespread that it reached the Pharaoh's palace itself. The death of the Crown Prince was for Egyptians a terrible disaster, for he was thought by them to be a divine being.

'There's yet one more plague for Pharaoh and the Egyptians,' GOD said to Moses. 'He will let you go after this one. And when he does, he'll make you go – and make you go in a hurry. Give the people these orders: Every man and every woman must borrow gold and silver jewellery from their Egyptian neighbours.'

The Egyptian people began to feel some sympathy for the Hebrew labourers. Indeed the man Moses was accepted as an outstanding leader by both Egyptian ministers and ordinary people.

Moses gave the people further orders from GOD.

'These are GOD's words,' he told them. '"At midnight I will deal with the Egyptians. The plague will be so widespread it will reach even the palace. It will infect the cattle too. There shall be wailing all over Egypt – wailing such as was never heard before and will never be heard again."'

Moses called the heads of the Hebrew families together and gave them their orders.

'You must carry out these orders family by family,' he said. 'Kill a lamb. Take a bunch of the hyssop plant, dip it in the blood and smear it on the outer door of your house – on the lintel and the two door-posts. And stay indoors all night. GOD will be passing through the whole of Egypt bringing death to the Egyptians. When he sees the smear of blood on your door, he will pass by and forbid the Destroyer to bring death to any in your house.'

The people bowed their heads in worship.

At midnight it happened. The Crown Price of Egypt died – and many others. Cattle suffered too.

Pharaoh, ministers and common people got up out of bed, and there was wailing all over Egypt. Death was everywhere.

In the darkness of the night, Pharaoh summoned Moses to the palace.

'Get up and get out,' he said, 'out from among my people. Go and worship GOD, as you said you wanted to. Take all your cattle, if you want to, and get out. And bless me too.'

The people of Egypt were in a panic to get rid of the labourers.

'If they stay here,' they said, 'we'll all be dead!'

It all happened so suddenly, that the Hebrews couldn't finish baking their bread – they had to pick up the unleavened dough, wrap up the kneading bowls in their cloaks and carry them on their shoulders. They had already carried out Moses' orders and borrowed silver and gold and clothing from their Egyptian neighbours. There had been no trouble about that – their neighbours had been very friendly.

They set out from Rameses and got as far as Succoth. They were a mixed crowd – labourers who were not Hebrews escaped with them. And there were large herds of cattle.

The Sea of Reeds

Exodus 13:20-22; 14:5-6, 10, 13-14, 19-25, 27, 30-31; 15:21

The Hebrew name for this sea is 'Yam suph'; the second word is from an Egyptian word meaning 'reed' or 'papyrus'; and the first word can mean 'sea' or 'marsh'. The sea is not the Red Sea, but a reed marsh or lake not far from the Mediterranean coast. We owe the use of the name 'Red Sea' for this sea to the Greek translation of the Old Testament.

They left Succoth and set up camp at the border fortress of Etham on the edge of the desert.

They travelled day and night. GOD guided them – a column of cloud by day, a column of fire by night. The cloud and the fire were always ahead of the moving people.

Pharaoh now changed his mind.

'What on earth have we done?' he said. 'We've lost our labour gangs.'

He ordered his chariot force out in pursuit.

The Hebrews were in a panic. They turned on Moses, talking like the slaves they were.

'Weren't there graves enough in Egypt,' they said, 'that you'd got to bring us out here to die in the desert? Is this what all your talking about "rescue" means? Didn't we tell you in Egypt to let us alone? Living as slaves in Egypt is better than dying in the desert.'

'Don't panic,' said Moses. 'Stand firm. GOD will rescue you – and rescue you today. You see that Egyptian army over there – you will never see it again. GOD's on your side – you've only got to stand your ground.'

The column of cloud moved from ahead of them and stopped behind them – between the camps of the Egyptian army and the escaping people. The cloud remained dark. Thus the camps were out of touch with each other throughout the night. GOD drove the sea back by a strong east wind, the sirocco, all night, and Moses and the people crossed over in safety.

The Egyptians followed them far into the water.

Just before dawn next morning, GOD looked down from the column of cloud towards the Egyptian army and threw it into panic.

'GOD's on their side!' the Egyptian soldiers shouted to one another.

When daylight came, the sea fell back to its steady flow. The Egyptian troops were caught and GOD swept them away.

That's how GOD rescued the Hebrew labourers from the attack of the Egyptian army. They saw the dead bodies of Egyptian soldiers lying on the seashore. They held GOD in awe and put their trust in him and Moses, his messenger.

And they made this song:

Sing to GOD –
    he marches in triumph;
horse and rider
    he has sunk in the sea.
He shall reign
    for ever.

Stories of the Desert March

Exodus 15:22-25; 16:2; 17:1-2, 4-6, 8-13

The marchers went on into the desert which lay to the east of Egypt – marching for three days across a waterless stretch of salty ground.

They came at last to the water hole called 'Bitter Springs'. The water was undrinkable.

The people soon began to grumble again; they still showed how slavery had sapped their courage. And, of course, they blamed Moses for everything.

'What are we going to drink?' they asked.

Moses prayed to GOD.

GOD showed him a tree and he threw it into the water; that sweetened it.

They came to another waterless stretch of the desert where there was a great rock. Again the marchers blamed Moses.

'Get us water to drink,' they said.

'Why do you go for me?' asked Moses. 'Why do you argue with GOD!'

Moses prayed to GOD.

'These people will lynch me,' said Moses. 'How am I to handle them?'

'Go ahead of the people,' said GOD. 'Take some of the heads of the great families with you – and the staff you used when you struck the waters of the River Nile. See – I will stand in front of you on the rock there. Strike the rock. Water will gush out – the people can drink that.'

That's what Moses did.

One day they were attacked by wandering Amalekite tribesmen.

'Pick some of the men,' said Moses to Joshua, 'and go out and fight these tribesmen. Tomorrow I will stand at the top of the hill.'

Joshua attacked the Amalekite tribesmen; and Moses, with two of his leaders, climbed the hill.

The fight went first this way and then that. The Hebrews beat the tribesmen back whenever Moses lifted his hand; whenever he dropped it, the tribesmen drove them back.

At last Moses got very tired. So the two leaders with him got a large stone for him to sit on, and they stood on each side of him and held his hands up.

They stood like that, holding his hands steady, till darkness fell.

The fight ended with the defeat of the tribesmen.

At the Mountain: the Covenant   *Exodus 18:1-8, 11-27*

Here we come to the story of the event which embodies Moses' second great conviction: that GOD, who rescued the tribes from Egypt, had called them to be his people. At a great religious assembly on 'GOD's Mountain' he made this clear.

We do not know where the mountain was. It has two names – Horeb and Sinai – in the Hebrew stories. It was a mountain associated with the Midianites and their worship, the people among whom Moses had his great experience. The Midianites were roving people; the mountain may have been in their old territory east of Aqabah Gulf or nearer Kadesh Oasis. It is not likely to have been the present Mount Sinai.

The idea of a Covenant between God and humankind was a new idea and it expressed Moses' new conviction about God and what he is like. He is a God who comes into personal relationship with those who worship him, offering them his friendship and asking for their trust – and their trust in him must be expressed by living in his Way. This is the fact that lies behind these popular stories. We cannot now know what actually happened in this decisive religious event, but the new insight into God's nature and God's Way is the foundation of all later understanding for both Jews and Christians. Everything rested on their conviction that GOD had rescued them from slavery.

The Covenant was, on GOD's part, the offer of his love and care – 'I am your God; I rescued you from Egypt'. On humanity's part, it meant trusting him and living in his Way. 'Living in GOD's Way' was embodied in the 'Ten Words' ('Ten Commandments').

News about Moses and what GOD had done for him and his people reached his father-in-law, the Midianite priest. He had been taking care of his wife and his two sons. He now came to meet Moses in the desert and brought them with him. He found him camped at the Holy Mountain, 'GOD's Mountain'.

'Your father-in-law is on the way here – and your family is with him,' Moses was told.

Moses went out to meet him and received him with proper courtesy. They asked after each other's health, and went into the tent together. He told his father-in-law how GOD had rescued them from Egypt and about the rough time they'd had on the desert march.

'Blessed be God,' said his father-in-law. 'Now I know what our GOD is really like – he is the God who rescues his people and defeats the proud Egyptians. Now I know he is the greatest of the gods.'

And there, at the Holy Mountain, his father-in-law led their worship of GOD. They offered a sacrifice and shared in a sacred meal together.

Next day, Moses held a law-court in the presence of the people; he was busy from dawn to darkness. His father-in-law sat watching.

'What do you think you are doing?' he asked Moses. 'Why do you tackle this by yourself – the court sessions just go on and on.'

'It's the people,' said Moses. 'They keep on coming to me for justice. When there's a dispute, they bring it to me and I have to pronounce judgement and show them what God's law is.'

'This is no way to do it,' said his father-in-law. 'You'll just get worn out. It's too big a job – you can't do it alone.'

'Listen to me,' he went on. 'I'll tell you what to do. This is how God's work should be done. Share the work out with able and trustworthy men – the sort of men who can't be bribed – and give them various ranks. You will represent the people before God – and make God's Way clear to them, how day-to-day life must be lived. They will carry on the ordinary day-to-day court work. All really important matters will be referred to you. That will make it easier for you, and they can share the work with you. If you deal with the work in this way, God will give you the strength you need, law won't break down and the people will go home knowing justice has been done.'

Moses reorganised the work of the law-courts as his father-in-law suggested.

He said goodbye to him, and his father-in-law set off home.

The Hebrews set up camp facing the Holy Mountain, and Moses climbed up to the top of it. GOD called to him.

'Tell the people: I am Lord of the whole earth,' said GOD. 'They shall be my own people – if they listen to me and walk in my Way.'

Moses told the people what GOD had said.

'We will do all he tells us,' they said.

Moses went back up the mountain with their answer.

'Go down again to the people,' GOD said. 'They must wash their clothes and be ready to come into my presence in two days' time. Set boundaries round the mountain. These are my orders: "Do not climb the mountain – or even walk on the edge of it. Anybody found on the mountain will be executed. He must be executed by stoning or shooting – he himself must not be touched. Animals must be dealt with in the same way."'

Moses came down the mountain, back to the camp. He got the people ready to go into GOD's presence.

'You must be ready in two days' time,' he said. 'While you are getting ready, there must be no sexual intercourse.'

On the second morning, a storm broke over the mountain. The lightning flashed and the thunder boomed; smoke rolled over it, like smoke belching out of a kiln. And there was an earthquake. GOD was coming down in fire.

GOD called Moses to the mountain top.

'Go down to the people,' he said. 'If they cross the boundaries of the mountain to see what is happening, many of them will die.'

'They can't climb the mountain,' said Moses. 'We have had your strict orders.'

'But go down again to them,' said GOD. 'None of them must try to come into my presence and risk violent death.'

So down Moses went and made it quite clear to the people.

These are the Ten Words GOD gave the people:

'I am your GOD. I rescued you from Egypt where you lived as slaves.

'You must worship no other gods;
You must not make any images to worship;
You must not use my name in wrong ways;
You must do no work on the Sabbath;
You must never despise your father and mother;

You must not kill;
You must not commit adultery:
You must not steal;
You must not bear false witness against anybody;
You must not covet anybody else's family property.'

The Making of the Covenant   *Exodus 24:3-8*

Moses came down from the mountain and gave the people the 'Ten Words'.

'What God commands, we will do,' they said. They were all agreed.

Moses wrote down GOD's 'Ten Words'.

He rose at dawn next day. At the foot of the mountain he built an altar and set up twelve pillars. Then the Covenant between God and the people was confirmed. There was a great sacrifice, carried out by the young men. Moses took half the blood in bowls, and half the blood he splashed on the altar. He read the 'Ten Words' so that all the people could hear them.

'All GOD commands, we will do,' said the people. 'We will obey him.'

Moses splashed the blood in the bowls on the people.

'This is the blood of the Covenant,' he said, 'the Covenant GOD has made with you and set out in the "Ten Words".'

The March to the River   *Numbers 10:29-33*

Hobab, a leader of the Blacksmith Tribes, was camping nearby.

'We are striking camp,' Moses told him. 'We are setting out for the homeland GOD has promised us. March with us. You won't lose by it – you can share with us in the good things GOD will give us.'

'No,' said Hobab. 'I'm not going with you. I'm going home to my fellow tribesmen.'

'Please don't leave us,' said Moses. 'You know we have to cross the desert – you can be our guide. If you'll act as guide, we'll treat you as GOD has treated us.'

So they left the Holy Mountain and went out into the desert on the first lap of their journey. The Ark of GOD was carried ahead of the march to make clear which oasis should be their camping place.

There was a hard core of trouble-makers in the camp – strangers who had joined them. They had got thoroughly tired of desert food; and everybody – Hebrews and all – just dreamed of gorging themselves with meat.

'Oh for a piece of meat to eat,' they grumbled. 'We can still taste the fish we had in Egypt – the cucumbers, the melons, the leeks, the onions, the garlic! But it doesn't make a bit of difference. We are as hungry as hunters – and all we've got to look at is this wretched manna!'*

Moses heard all this – the men were standing at their tent-doors – and he didn't like it. GOD was angry too.

Moses prayed to GOD.

'Why have you led me into all this trouble?' he asked. 'What have I done that you let me carry the heavy burden of looking after all these people alone? I'm not their mother! I'm not responsible for them. You treat me like a nursemaid – "Carry them in your arms" is what it all comes to! Where do you think I can get meat to give them? "Get us meat, get us meat!" is what they are forever saying!'

'I'll deal with the matter,' said GOD. 'Tell the people: These are GOD's orders – "Get ready to come into my presence tomorrow; and you shall have meat to eat. I know what you've been saying – 'We had a grand time in Egypt, but there's nobody to give us one here.' But now you'll eat meat till you are sick of it!"'

'But where are you going to get the meat from?' asked Moses. 'Kill all the livestock? All the fish in the sea wouldn't be enough!'

'Do you think I've lost my power?' asked GOD. 'You will find out whether I can do what I say or not!'

So Moses went out to tell the people.

A great wind blew up and drove quails in from the sea. A mass of them dropped on the ground all round the camp.

All that day and night and all next day the people were out gathering quails. Even the man who gathered least gathered as much as a donkey could carry on ten journeys!

But as soon as they ate the quail meat, plague broke out and many people died.

The place where it happened had a sinister name – it was called 'Boundary Graves'.

---

* 'There is still manna today in the inland region of the Sinaitic peninsula, and it is even called *mann* by the nomadic inhabitants of this region. It is a sort of drop-like formation on the leaves of the tamarisk tree or shrub . . . formed of the secretions produced by the sting of the tree louse.' (North, *Exodus* p. 132).

One day, on the march, Moses sent some of his men on ahead.

'Go up into the Negeb over there,' he told them, 'and explore the highlands. Find out what the country is like – whether the soil is rich or poor, what kind of people live there (their strength and numbers), what their settlements are like (camps, like ours, or walled towns), if it is wooded country. Be bold. And bring back some samples of the plants they grow.'

The men went north into the Negeb, as far as the old fortified town of Hebron on the summit of the highlands, where the descendants of the legendary giants – 'necklace' people – lived. They found a rich valley. It was the beginning of the grape harvest; so they cut a branch with a single cluster of grapes, and two of the men carried it on a pole. They picked pomegranates and figs as well.

Then they went back to the Hebrew encampment.

'We carried out your orders,' they reported. 'It is a rich and fertile land – this is the sort of fruit which grows there. But the people are a different matter. They are big men – descendants of the giants of old; their towns are large and strongly fortified.'

Caleb – one of the scouts – reassured the people.

'Let us march there at once and capture the territory,' he said. 'We could take it in our stride.'

'That's not true,' said the others. 'We can't capture it – they're far too strong for us.'

The people were in a panic.

'Let's choose another captain of our own,' they said, 'and be off back to Egypt!'

'How long will these people go on despising me?' asked GOD. 'None of them shall ever see their new homeland. Caleb's a different sort of man – he's got the right spirit and his whole heart's in the march to the new land I'm giving you. I'll give him the countryside he's just explored – he and his descendants shall live there. But now, here are your orders: "Tomorrow you all go back – back to the desert and the Sea of Reeds."'

When Moses told the people GOD's orders, they were very dismayed.

They got up at dawn next day and marched to the highlands.

'We have done wrong,' they said to Moses. 'Here we are – we'll capture the highlands GOD has promised us.'

'Why are you now defying GOD's clear command?' said Moses. 'You can't win. Stop this march; you'll only be beaten back by the highlanders – GOD is not on your side. The highlanders stand across your path; you will just die fighting. You are defying GOD; he is not on your side.'

But they stubbornly went on, though neither the Ark of GOD nor Moses left the camp.

They were badly defeated. The highlanders rushed down from the hills and swept them as far south as Hormah, east of Beersheba.

Numbers 16:1-2, 12-15, 25-34

Two men, Dathan and Abiram, rebelled against Moses and spread rumours in the camp.

Moses sent for them.

'We are staying where we are,' they sent back word. 'You add one thing to another. You brought us from a rich and fertile country, and all we get is death in the desert. And then you play the tyrant over us. You promised to guide us to another rich and fertile land and make us owners of fields and vineyards – and see where you've got us. You're just hoodwinking the people. We stay here.'

Moses was very angry.

He protested to GOD.

'Don't take any notice of their complaints,' he said. 'I'm innocent – I've never robbed anybody or done anybody any harm.'

He went into the camp, with other leaders, to deal with Dathan and Abiram face to face.

'Have nothing to do with these men,' he told the people. 'If you do, you will suffer their fate as well.'

The crowd moved away. Dathan and Abiram, with their families, stood outside their tent-doors.

Moses spoke to the crowd.

'This will prove that I've done what I have done because GOD told me to,' he said. 'I've done nothing of my own accord. If these men die an ordinary death, the common fate of us all, GOD has not sent me to be your leader. But if GOD makes a great hole swallow them up, then you will know what kind of men they are.'

He had scarcely finished speaking when there was an earthquake.

Dathan and Abiram and all their families fell to their death in a great hole in the ground and vanished from sight.

The crowd scattered in panic. They feared the same fate.

Moses sent a messenger to the court of the king of Edom, east of Jordan River.

'We are your kinsmen,' ran the message. 'You will have heard of the hard times we have had. Our ancestors settled in Egypt. The Egyptians treated us brutally; but GOD heard our cry for help and rescued us. We are now encamped at Kadesh, on the edge of your territory. May we have your permission to pass through? We will keep clear of fields and vineyards; we will leave the wells alone (rain-water will be enough for us). We will march by the King's Highway, and keep to it until we are out of your territory.'

'You'll keep out of our territory altogether,' was the Edomite answer. 'If you try to enter it, we will call out our army.'

The Hebrews tried again.

'We will stick to the King's Highway,' said their second message. 'All we want is your permission to march through your territory. Nothing more.'

'No,' was the answer – and the calling out of the army.

That settled it. The Hebrews set off from Kadesh but they had to find another way round.

The Death of Moses *Deuteronomy 34:1-6, 10; Numbers 12:6-8*

They reached the edge of the Jordan Valley – the high hills which look down on Jericho, the City of Palms. They had made themselves masters of the territory between the rivers, the Arnon and the Jabbok.

From the top of a high mountain GOD showed Moses the land on the other side of the valley.

'This is the land I promised your ancestors,' he said. 'I have let you see it from a distance. You yourself will not cross the river.'

Moses died there. He was buried in a valley in Moabite territory. His grave is unknown.

Moses was a great man. No prophet has ever been as great as he was – he talked to GOD face to face.

'To a prophet
    I, GOD, show myself
    in vision or speech or dream,'
        says GOD.

'But with my servant Moses
    I am different –
my people's destiny
    is in his hands.
I speak with him face to face,
    never in riddles.
He sees me
    as I really am.'

In the Highlands

In the central highlands (where little fighting is recorded) Hebrew tribes who had not been in Egypt were already in occupation; here the invading Hebrews, after overwhelming a few fortified towns, joined up with their kinsmen in the Shechem area and established themselves in the hills round Shechem City. Fighting took place in the south, and fortified cities like Lachish were destroyed about this time; the attack here seems to have been made, not by Joshua but by other Hebrew tribes from the south. There was fighting in the north, too; the fortified city of Hazor was destroyed about this time.

Many of the stories in Joshua seem to be late popular accounts which were told when people had forgotten what really happened; the earliest accounts which told of hard and scattered fighting or of peaceful penetration seem to have been discarded. An early account survives in the first chapter of Judges, and we give it first.

We give, secondly, the account of the great assembly of the Hebrew tribes in the central highlands when they renewed the Covenant together.

The old tribal stories in Judges show how slow and difficult settlement in their new homeland was; we give some of them here.

The Settlement *Judges 1:1-3, 10-17, 19, 21-27, 29-31, 33-35*

The Hebrews asked GOD what he wanted them to do now.

'Which of us must attack the highlands first?' they asked.

'The people of Judah,' said GOD. 'See, I am giving them the country to rule over.'

The people of Judah discussed the situation with their kinsfolk, the people of Simeon.

'Help us to invade the territory given to us,' they said. 'If you will share in the attack, we will help you in your fighting.'

Hebron, in the Negeb, was attacked and captured. Then they moved on to Debir whose old name was Kiriath-sepher ('Book City' – perhaps 'The City of the Writers' Guild').

Caleb was fighting alongside the men of Judah.

'Whoever attacks and captures Kiriath-sepher,' he said, 'can marry my daughter, Achsah.'

His nephew, Othniel, captured it and married her.

When they met her father, Othniel urged Achsah to ask him for some fields as part of her dowry.

She got down from the donkey she was riding.

'What do you want?' asked her father.

'You have given me some dry Negeb countryside,' she said. 'Give me some springs as well.'

So Caleb gave her the Upper Springs and the Lower Springs.

Hobab, the Smith, who had been Moses' guide, fought alongside the men of Judah. He came up from the City of Palms with them and was fighting for them to the south of Hebron. Then he went off to live with the Amalekites.

The men of Judah and Simeon went off and captured Hormah.

GOD helped the men of Judah in their fighting in the highlands. But the fortified towns of the plain were too strong for them – the soldiers of these towns fought with iron chariots.

Nor could the men of Benjamin capture Jerusalem where the Jebusites lived.

The men of Joseph marched against Bethel, twelve miles north of Jerusalem. GOD helped them too.

When they reached Bethel, they sent scouts out to reconnoitre the town. They saw a man walking out of the town into the countryside.

'Show us how to get into the town,' said the scouts, 'and we'll look after you.'

He told them what they wanted to know, and they sacked the city. The informer and his family were given their freedom, and went off to live in Hittite territory.

The men of Manasseh went north, to the valleys between the Jordan and the sea.

The fortified cities of Bethshan (in the Jordan Valley), of Taanach (seventeen miles west of Bethshan), Dor (on the coast) and Megiddo (in the Esdraelon Valley) – all these held out against them.

Nor did the men of Ephraim drive out the citizens of the fortified city of Gezer – they all settled down together.

The same thing happened with the men of Zebulun when they attacked the towns of Kitron (near Acco) and Nahalal (which was about three miles west of Nazareth).

The men of Asher could not capture the fortified towns of Acco and Sidon – nor Ahlab, Achzib, Helbah, Aphik and Rehob. Like their kinsmen in the south, they settled down together with citizens of these towns. They were not strong enough to drive them out.

The men of Naphtali fared the same way when they attacked the fortified towns of Beth Shemesh ('House of the Sun') and Beth-anath ('House of Anath').

The Amorites drove the men of Dan into the highlands – they were masters of the plains and they held on to their towns.

(So the Hebrews settled in the sparsely-populated highlands; the fortified cities of the plains remained unconquered.)

The Meeting at Shechem

Joshua, who had served under Moses as one of his commanders, became the great hero of the settlement in Palestine. He was the leader of the tribes who penetrated the central highlands by way of the Jordan Valley. He later came to be thought of as the hero of all the Hebrew tribes throughout the whole of the occupied territory in the south and north as well as in the central highlands. His greatness lies in the fact that he was the man who saw to it that the vision of Moses was not lost.

The meeting at Shechem is a renewal of the Covenant, a call to the tribes to take up, under their new conditions, the work of Moses and to be 'GOD's People' in their new homeland.

Joshua 24:1-15, 18-19, 21-25

When the worst of the fighting was over, Joshua called a great meeting of the Hebrew tribesmen – the heads of the great families and tribal leaders – in Shechem.

He recited the history of the tribes – what GOD had done for them – from the days when their ancestors had lived beyond the Euphrates River. He reminded them of the hard times in Egypt, GOD's rescue of them, the march across the desert and the fighting with hostile tribes. Now they were in the homeland GOD had given them – land on which they themselves had never laboured and towns they themselves had not built.

'You must now choose,' said Joshua, 'whom you are going to worship – your ancestral God or the gods of the land here. I know what I'm going to do – I and my family will choose GOD and be loyal to him.'

'We, too,' said the people, 'will be loyal to GOD – he is our God.'

'You can't serve GOD and the gods of the peoples around you as well,' said Joshua. 'If you worship GOD, you must worship him alone.'

'It's GOD we want to be loyal to,' said the people.

'You are your own witnesses,' said Joshua, 'that you have chosen GOD to give your loyal service to him.'

'We are witnesses,' they said.

'If there are any foreign gods worshipped among you,' said Joshua, 'get rid of them now. You must give your whole hearts to GOD.'

'We will serve GOD,' said the people. 'What he commands we will do.'

So that day Joshua and the people renewed the Covenant with GOD.

Tribal Stories

The Ballad of Kishon River   *Judges 5:3-31*

Let the whole world listen –

I will sing – I will sing to GOD,
I will praise the God of his people.

When GOD came out of the southern highlands,
    marching through the Edomite mountains
    through earthquake and drenching rain and cloudburst,
    the mountains quaked before him,
    before GOD, the God of his people.

Caravans were gone from the high roads,
    travellers were taking the byways,
    villages were deserted, deserted –

    until you arose, O Deborah,
    arose a mother among GOD's people.

There was not a blacksmith to be found,
    not a soldier left in the city –

not a shield or a lance
among the forty thousand of GOD's people.

My heart goes out to the captains,
    the volunteers in the villages.
Bless GOD! Tell the good news!
You, riding on tawny asses,
    you who sit on rich carpets
    and you who travel on foot!

Above the chattering at the well
    GOD's triumphs will be told
    the triumphs of his villagers!

To the city gates marched GOD's people:
'Awake, awake, Deborah!
Awake, awake, strike up the song!
Up, Barak, seize your prisoners,
    Son of Abinoam!'

Those that were left marched down like nobles,
    GOD's people marched down like heroes.

The men of Ephraim surged into the valley,
    'We are with you,' came the Benjamin battle cry!

From Manasseh came down the commanders.
From Zebulun came down the marshals!

The chieftains of Issachar followed Deborah.
The men of Naphtali rallied to Barak,
    into the valley they stormed at his heels!

The men of Zebulun recklessly courted death.
The men of Naphtali were in the thick of the fighting.

There was a lot of arguing in Reuben –
    lounging among the sheepfolds,
    listening to the shepherds piping!

The men of Gad stayed beyond Jordan River,
  the men of Dan idled by Galilee Lake,
  the men of Asher lounged by their Great Sea landings!

The kings came and fought!
The Canaanite chieftains fought;
  but at Taanach, by Megiddo streams
  they seized no loot of silver:
  from the sky the stars were fighting,
  the wheeling stars against Sisera.

The Kishon River swept them away,
  the raging torrent, the Kishon River.

March on, my soul, march on!

Loud hammered the hoofs
  of the galloping, galloping horses.

'Curses on the town of Meroz,' said GOD's messenger,
  'bitter curses on all who live there.
They did not come to GOD's help,
  to GOD's help like heroes.'

But happiest of women be Jael,
  of Bedouin women the happiest!
Water he asked,
  but she gave him milk in a royal bowl.

Then she picked up a hammer,
  with her right hand a workman's hammer;
  she struck Sisera a blow,
  she crushed his head –
  she shattered and smashed his temple.
At her feet he sank, he fell,
  lifeless he lay –
  at her feet he sank, he fell
  dead where he fell.

Through the window she peered,
    gazed, Sisera's mother, through the lattice window.
'Why is his chariot so slow,
    why linger his chariot's hoof beats?'
Her knowing ladies-in-waiting tell her –
    indeed she keeps telling herself –
'They're finding and sorting the booty, of course!
A girl or two for each soldier!
Loot of dyed cloth for Sisera,
    dyed cloth embroidered;
two pieces of dyed cloth embroidered
    for my shoulders!

So perish all your enemies, O GOD!
But let your friends conquer
    like the rising sun!

Gideon *Judges 6:11-19, 21-24, 34; 7:1, 9-15, 17, 20-21; 8:4-9, 11-21, 24-27*

At Ophrah, in the Jezreel Plain, there was an oak tree. It belonged to a man called Joash whose son was called Gideon. The Midianites – camel-riding nomads from the desert – were raiding the Hebrew villages.

Gideon was threshing wheat, but not openly on the village threshing-floor. He was beating a few sheaves of wheat down on the floor of the winepress, to keep it out of sight of the raiders. GOD's messenger came and sat down under the tree.

'GOD is with you, brave hero,' he said.

'Then tell me,' said Gideon, 'if GOD is on our side, why has there been all this raiding? What about all those wonderful deeds we've been told of from the past – the deliverance from Egypt, and all that? But now GOD has deserted us and given the Midianites a free hand!'

GOD turned to him.

'You're a leader,' said GOD. 'Go and rescue your fellow countrymen from the raiders. Am I not sending you?'

'Tell me, sir,' said Gideon, 'how can I rescue my fellow countrymen? We're the poorest clan in Manasseh; and I carry no influence at all in my clan.'

'I will be on your side,' said GOD. 'You shall wipe out the raiders to the last man.'

'Don't go away, I beg you,' said Gideon. 'Wait here till I come back with my present for you.'

'I'll stay till you come back,' he said.

Gideon went inside. He prepared a kid and made unleavened cakes with some flour. He put the meat in a basket and the broth in a pot. He brought them back to the oak tree and offered his present to his visitor.

GOD's messenger lifted his staff and touched the meat and the cakes. A flash of fire from the rock burned them all up. Gideon then knew for certain that he was GOD's messenger.

'O GOD!' he said. 'I have seen you face to face – I'm a doomed man!'

'You are quite safe,' said GOD. 'Don't panic, you won't die.'

Gideon built an altar on the spot. He was filled with GOD's spirit and mustered his clan to follow him. They got up early and set up camp near Harod Well. The raiders' camp lay to the north of them, by Teacher's Hill in the valley of Jezreel.

That very night, GOD spoke to him.

'Get up and go down to the camp. It's yours,' he said. 'If you are too scared to go alone, take your servant Purah with you. Listen to the raiders talking. That will give you courage enough to attack the camp.'

They both crept down to the camp and got close to the tents of the outposts. A man was talking.

'I've just had a strange dream,' he was saying. 'I saw a loaf of barley bread come tumbling into the camp. It smashed a tent flat.'

'I know what that means,' said his comrade. 'It's Gideon's army. It means we're beaten.'

When Gideon heard that, he said a prayer to GOD and went back to his own men.

'Up!' he said. 'GOD's giving the raiders into our hands!'

He divided his three hundred men into three companies and gave them jars with torches inside.

'Watch me,' he said. 'When we reach the tents, make sure you do just what I do. And when I blow the trumpet, shout "For GOD and for Gideon!"'

They reached the camp about midnight, just after the guard had been changed. They surrounded it, smashed the jars with a loud noise, waved the torches in their left hands and held their swords in their right hands.

'For GOD and for Gideon!' they shouted.

The camp awoke and stampeded down the valley and over the Jordan. Gideon had only three hundred men, but they followed the raiders across the Jordan and into the eastern highlands. They reached the town of Succoth, dead-tired.

'Give us some food,' Gideon said to the townspeople. 'We're tired out with chasing the Midianite chieftains.'

'Have you caught them,' they sneered, 'that we should feed you and your soldiers?'

'All right,' he said, 'when I've caught them, I'll thrash you with thorns and thistles!'

The same thing happened at Penuel.

'When I've come back in triumph,' he told the townspeople there, 'I'll tear down the tower of your town!'

He followed the caravan road and caught the raiders off their guard. The chieftains escaped. He went after them and caught them; and the raiding army melted away. He turned for home.

He passed by Succoth and captured a Succoth boy out in the fields. He asked for the names of the town's officers and wrote down a list of them – seventy-seven of them, all told. He entered the town.

'Here are the Midianite chieftains,' he said. 'What about your sneering now?'

He arrested the town officials, got hold of some thorns and thistles and taught them a lesson. He didn't forget the townspeople of Penuel, either. He tore down their tower and executed their officials.

Then he turned to the two Midianite chieftains.

'What about the men you murdered at Tabor in the Jezreel Valley?' he asked.

'They were like you, every one of them,' they said. 'They had a royal look about them.'

'They were my brothers,' he said, 'sons of my own mother. By GOD! – if you had let them live, I wouldn't be executing you now!'

'Kill them!' he said to his eldest son.

The boy was frightened; he was only a boy and he wouldn't draw his sword.

'Kill us yourself,' said the chieftains. 'It needs a man's strength.'

Gideon killed them both, and he took the crescents from the necks of the camels.

'I've one thing to ask,' he said to his soldiers. 'Let each of you give me the earrings of the men he's captured.'

'That we will,' they said.

They spread out a cloak on the ground and threw the earrings into it. There was a great weight of gold. Gideon made an idol of it and set it up in his own town of Ophrah.

Abimelech

Abimelech was one of Gideon's sons – born to him by a Shechem slave-girl, a Canaanitess.

He went to Shechem to meet his relatives and the members of his mother's clan.

'Start this rumour going round the city,' he said. '"Is it better to have a lot of Gideon's sons ruling over you or to have just one man your ruler?" and don't forget that Abimelech's a member of our clan.'

This is how his relatives talked; the citizens thought it wasn't a bad idea. 'After all,' they said, 'he's one of us.'

The town treasury was kept in the temple of the local god, 'The Lord of the Covenant'. The officials of the town took money from the temple and gave it to Abimelech who hired some devil-may-care ruffians with it. He went to Ophrah, his father's home town not far away, and murdered all but one of his half-brothers on the same stone slab.* Only Gideon's youngest son, Jotham, managed to hide himself and escape.

The citizens of Shechem gathered at the Great Tower of the city and crowned Abimelech king by the oak tree of the Sacred Pillar.

Shechem city lay in a valley between two mountains; Gerizim Mountain lay to the south. When Jotham – the one son of Gideon to escape – heard the news he climbed the mountain and shouted down to the citizens below.

'Citizens of Shechem!' he called. 'Listen to me – and GOD may listen to you. Here's a story:

Once upon a time the trees set out to elect their king.
They said to the olive tree – 'Be our king!'
'Do you think I've no rich oil left,' said he, 'the oil that adorns both
    gods and humans, that I should go swaying over trees?'
So the trees asked the fig tree.
'Do come and be our king,' they said.
'Do you think I've no sweet rich figs left,' he said, 'that I should go
    swaying over trees?'
So the trees asked the vine.
'Do come and be our king,' they said.
'Do you think I've no wine left,' said he, 'the wine that cheers both
    gods and humans, that I should go swaying over trees?'
At last, the trees had to go to the thorn-bush.

* To give his act the look of a legal execution (or possibly sacrifice).

124

'Do be our king,' they said.

'Well,' said the thorn-bush, 'if you're serious about it, come and shelter in my shade. But, if you're not, let the thorn-bush burst into flames and start a forest fire!'

'You see the point? If you're serious about Abimelech, well and good – have a happy time together. But if you're playing a game, Abimelech will burst into flames; and you'll all be burned – citizens, fortified tower and Abimelech himself.'

Jotham then made off. He settled at a place called 'The Well' – out of reach of Abimelech.

Three years later there was trouble in Shechem; the citizens fell out with Abimelech. They didn't hesitate to do him whatever mischief they could. Important roads crossed at Shechem. So they set men in ambush on the hilltops, robbed the passers-by and kept the money for themselves – that touched Abimelech's pocket. He soon learned about their treachery.

He rounded up his men, divided them into three companies and lay in ambush in the fields. He waited until he saw the people coming out of the city. He and his company made a dash for the city gate and captured the entrance square. The other two companies attacked the people in the fields.

It was a hard fight all day. But Abimelech captured the city, killed its citizens, razed the walls and buildings to the ground and sowed the place with salt* – all but the strong Great Tower in the Temple of the 'Lord of the Covenant' outside the city.

Crowds had packed in here to escape the havoc within the walls. When they heard what Abimelech had done, they crowded into the underground crypt of the tower. Abimelech and his men climbed the hill, cut down the brushwood, carried it back on their shoulders and put it on the crypt. Then they set it all on fire. About a thousand people died.

Abimelech went on to Thebez, besieged it and captured it.

The Great Tower there was inside the city. It was crowded with citizens. They barred the doors and climbed on to the roof.

Abimelech attacked it. He went towards the tower door to set it on fire; a woman on the roof pushed over a heavy millstone and it caught him on the head and broke his skull.

'Draw your sword and kill me,' he said to his armour-bearer. 'I don't want people to say that a woman killed me.'

His armour-bearers carried out his orders.

When his soldiers saw that he was dead, they went home.

* An idiom meaning 'made it utterly desolate'.

Danite Stories *Judges 14:1-3, 5-20; 15:1-17; 16:4-31*

The Danite tribes were settled in the neighbourhood of the Philistine 'Five Cities' and had become their vassals. Later they were to march north and capture, with great brutality, a town north of Galilee Lake. The stories about Samson are really 'tall stories' of the tribe's imagined prowess in dealing with the Philistines – when they were far enough away to tell them! They are popular stories – Samson was a legendary hero. Later historians were a little doubtful even then about some of these stories (to get over the difficulty they tried to think of Samson as a sort of 'Man of GOD' – we have not given their later account of this).

If we are tempted to dismiss these stories out of hand, let us remind ourselves of the brutalities of our own century – even in our 'Christian' west. A good world has to grow out of the world as it is; we shall see that the Israelite prophets saw this quite clearly. Their greatest men were later to condemn this violence and inhumanity in unambiguous words (see pp. 224, 266).

a) Popular Stories of the Plain

Samson lived in a Southern village near Zorah, fifteen miles west of Jerusalem, on the borders of the plain where the Philistines, the Sea Peoples, lived. He went one day down to the Philistine town of Timnah, four miles across the valley, and a Philistine girl caught his eye. When he got home he told his father.

'I saw a Philistine girl in Timnah,' he said. 'I want to marry her – make the arrangements.'

'Can't you find a girl in your own clan or people, that you have to go off and marry a girl from these heathen foreigners?'

'You get her for me,' said Samson. 'I like her.'

Samson went back to Timnah. Just as he came to the town's vineyards, a young lion sprang at him with a roar. GOD's spirit filled him with tremendous strength. He had nothing in his hands, but he tore the lion to pieces as though it had been a kid. He said nothing about what he had done to anybody, but went on down into the town and met the girl again. He really liked her. On a later visit to the town, he went out of his way to see what had happened to the lion's carcase; there was a swarm of bees inside – and honey! He scraped the honey out with his hands and ate it as he walked along. When he got home, he gave some to his parents, but he didn't tell them where he got it from.

He went down to Timnah for his wedding feast. The people there chose thirty friends to attend him.

'Let me ask you a riddle,' he said. 'The feast lasts seven days. If you can solve it before it ends, I'll give you thirty fine linen sheets and thirty gold dresses. If you can't, you'll give the same to me.'

'Out with your riddle,' they said. 'Let's hear it.'

'Here it is,' he said:

'From the eater came something to eat,
from the strong came something sweet.'

For three days they tried to solve it, but it beat them.

'Coax your husband to give you the answer,' they said to his wife. 'If you don't we'll set the whole house on fire. Did you invite us here just to ruin us?'

His wife tried tears.

'You don't love me,' she sobbed. 'You just hate me. You haven't told me the answer!'

'I haven't told it even to my parents,' said Samson. 'Why should I tell it to you?'

She went on badgering him for the rest of the feast. At last he could stand it no longer, and he told her.

On the last night, just when the marriage ceremony was about to be completed, the guests gave him the answer –

'What's sweeter than honey?
What's stronger than a lion?'

'If you hadn't ploughed with my heifer, you wouldn't have solved my riddle,' said Samson.

Off he went to the Philistines in Ashkelon – twenty-four miles there and twenty-four miles back. He killed thirty men, looted the gold dresses he wanted and gave them to the wedding guests. Blazing with anger he strode off home. Her father gave his wife to his best man!

It was wheat harvest.

'I think I'll visit my wife,' said Samson, and he went down to Timnah with a kid to give her. He had no idea what had happened after he strode out of the wedding feast. He thought the marriage ceremony had been completed.

Her father stopped him.

'I thought you'd finished with her,' he said. 'I gave her to your best man. Take her younger sister – she's a more attractive girl!'

'I'll be quits with these Philistines this time,' Samson told himself. 'I'll give it to them hot!'

He caught three hundred jackals. He tied each pair of jackals tail to tail, fastened a torch between their tails and lit the torches. He turned the lot loose into the standing corn of the Philistine farmers. What a fire!

'Who's the villain who's done this?' asked the farmers.

'Samson,' was the general opinion. 'You know what happened at his wedding.'

So they went off into the town, and burned his father-in-law's house down with the girl and her family inside.

'If this is the sort of thing you'll do,' said Samson, 'I'll not leave you alone until I've got my own back!'

He rushed at them, hitting left and right with his great strength and killed many of them. Then he went off and lived in a cave at Etam Rock.

The Philistines raided a town of the Judah clan.

'Why are you treating us like enemies?' asked the Judeans.

'We want Samson,' they said. 'We are going to give him a bit of his own medicine.'

So a large company of the citizens went down to Etam Rock.

'This is Philistine country – you know that,' they said to Samson (who was not of their tribe), 'why harm us?'

'I only treated them as they treated me,' he answered.

'Well, we're not having it,' they said. 'We're going to take you prisoner and hand you over to the Philistines.'

'Promise me you won't kill me yourselves,' said Samson.

'We promise,' they said. 'We just want to get hold of you and hand you over. We don't want to kill you.'

They bound him with two new ropes, and took him up from the cave in the Rock.

Outside the town, the Philistines rushed at him shouting.

GOD's spirit seized Samson and he broke free – in a flash he'd snapped the ropes like burning flax and his handcuffs like melting wax. He saw a fresh jawbone – a donkey's. He picked it up and felled a thousand Philistines with it. Hence the saying –

'With a red donkey's jawbone I have reddened them red,
with a red donkey's jawbone I have felled a thousand men.'

He threw the jawbone away.

Samson fell in love with a girl in the Sorek Valley – Delilah.

The five Philistine chieftains came to her.

'Coax him,' they said, 'and find out the secret of his great strength – how we can master him and bind him and make him helpless. We'll pay you well – £50 each.'

'Do tell me why you're so strong,' she said to Samson, 'and how you can be bound helpless.'

'Seven fresh undried bowstrings will do it,' he said. 'That'll make me as weak as an ordinary man.'

The Philistine chieftains got seven fresh undried bowstrings for her, and she tied him up with them. Men were lying in ambush in the inner room.

'Samson! Samson!' she shouted. 'The Philistines are here!'

He snapped the bowstrings as a strand of tow snaps at the touch of fire – he was as strong as ever.

'You're just playing with me,' said Delilah. 'You're lying to me. Go on – tell me how you can be tied up!'

'Try new ropes – really new ones,' he said. 'That'll make me as weak as an ordinary man.'

She tried new ropes.

'Samson! Samson!' she shouted. 'The Philistines are here!'

Again, men were waiting in ambush in the inner room.

He snapped the ropes like thread.

'You're just playing with me,' said Delilah. 'You go on telling me lies. Now, how can you be tied up?'

Samson had long hair.

'Weave the seven locks of my hair into the loom there,' he said, 'and beat them in with the loom pin. That will do it.'

While he was sleeping, that's what Delilah did.

'Samson! Samson!' she shouted. 'The Philistines are here!'

He started up and pulled up the loom with his hair.

'You don't trust me at all,' said Delilah. 'How can you say you love me? You're just laughing at me – and you've done it three times now! I still don't know why you're so strong – you won't tell me.'

She went on badgering him and getting at him till he was sick of the whole thing and told her his secret.

'I've never had my hair cut off,' he said. 'I'm under a vow. I should be just like an ordinary man if my hair were cut off – my strength would vanish.'

Delilah knew that he was now telling the truth. She went for the Philistine chieftains.

'Come back once more,' she said. 'He's told me the truth this time.'

They came back; and this time they brought the money with them.

Samson went to sleep with his head on her lap. She beckoned one of the men and had his hair cut off.

'Samson! Samson!' she shouted. 'The Philistines are here!'

He woke up.

'I'll escape,' he thought, 'as I've escaped so many times before. I'll shake myself free.'

He did not know that GOD had left him; the Philistines got hold of him, put his eyes out, took him down to Gaza and bound him with bronze fetters. He spent his time grinding corn in the prison mill. His hair, however, began to grow again.

The Philistine chieftains gathered in the temple for a great sacrifice to their god Dagon, and to celebrate the capture of Samson with public games.

'Dagon has captured our enemy, Samson, for us!' they shouted.

When the crowd saw their god Dagon they sang his praises:

'Dagon has captured him –
Samson our enemy,
destroyer of our land,
murderer of our people.'

They were in high spirits.

'Bring him in to entertain us!' they went on shouting.

Samson was brought from prison, and entertained them with exhibitions of his strength.

Then they put him to stand between the pillars. A boy was holding his hand.

'Let me feel the temple pillars,' he said to the boy. 'I want to lean against them.'

The temple was crowded with men and women. The chieftains were there, and about three thousand climbed on to the roof to watch the entertainment.

'O GOD,' prayed Samson, 'remember me. Give me my strength again – just once again, O GOD. I want to get my revenge on the Philistines for the loss of my two eyes.'

He grasped the two central supporting pillars with both his arms and threw his weight against them.

'Let me die with the Philistines,' he said.

He pulled with all his strength and the temple fell in on chieftains and crowd. The death toll was greater than all those he had already killed.

His relatives came and took his body away. They buried him in their ancestral tomb, between Zorah and Eshtaol.

b) The March to the North   Judges 17:1, 5, 7-13; 18:1-29

A prosperous farmer, Micah, lived in the central highlands. He had his own shrine; he had carved an idol and household gods, and made his son his priest.

A young man from the south was wandering through the country. He belonged to the Southern tribe of Judah, his home town was Bethlehem and he was a member of the priestly clan. He was looking for somewhere to live. He came one day into the highlands and stopped at Micah's farm.

'Where are you from?' asked Micah.

'Bethlehem,' he said. 'I'm a priest from Judah. I am wandering about the country to settle down where I can.'

'Just the man I'm looking for!' said Micah. 'Stay with me, and be a father and a priest to me.'

Micah treated him like one of his own sons. He became his priest and one of the family.

'I know GOD will be good to me now,' said Micah. 'I've got a real priest.'

At that time the Danites wanted to get away from Philistine country and find a home of their own. They sent five of their bravest men to explore the north country and find out what it was like.

They came into the highlands and lighted on Micah's farm – a good place to spend the night. They recognised the southern accent of the young priest.

'Who brought you here?' they asked. 'What are you doing here?'

'The farmer took me on as his priest,' he said.

'Pray to GOD for us, then,' they said. 'Find out whether our expedition will be a success.'

'Go in peace,' he said. 'Your expedition is in GOD's care.'

The five men left the farm and went on to the north of Galilee Lake and found a quiet and unsuspecting town, Laish, a remote place, far from anyone, and especially from their overlords, the Sidonians. It had everything they could ask for. They went back home.

'How did you get on?' everybody asked.

'Come with us,' they said. 'We've found the very place. Let's attack it!'

They all set out for the north, women and children and livestock going on ahead, six hundred soldiers bringing up the rear. They climbed the hills and camped at Kiriath-jearim. Then they pushed on into the central highlands and made for Micah's farm.

'Do you know, there's an idol on this farm,' said the five scouts to their comrades, 'and household gods. Don't waste this piece of good luck.'

They went towards the buildings and found the young priest's house and greeted him. The soldiers stood at the open gate while the five scouts seized the idol and its belongings.

'What are you up to?' the priest protested.

'Sh-sh,' they said. 'Keep your mouth shut. Come along with us and be father and priest to us. A whole tribe's better than one man's family, isn't it?'

The priest was delighted. He picked up the idol and its belongings and went off with them.

The soldiers turned round and marched off. They had gone some distance along the road before Micah could muster the men in the nearby houses and overtake them. He shouted to them to stop.

The soldiers turned round.

'What's the trouble?' they asked. 'And why this mob?'

'You take my gods – gods I made myself – and my priest,' shouted Micah, 'and you walk away and leave me with nothing – and then ask what the trouble is!'

'Keep your voice down,' said the soldiers. 'Some of us might lose our tempers – and then you and your men would lose your lives!'

The soldiers marched on north – with the god and the priest. Micah knew he was beaten and went home.

The Danites came at last to Laish in its lonely valley. They killed the people who lived there and burned the town to the ground – there was nobody to stop them. They then rebuilt it and made it their headquarters. They changed its name to Dan.

The Death of Two Cities

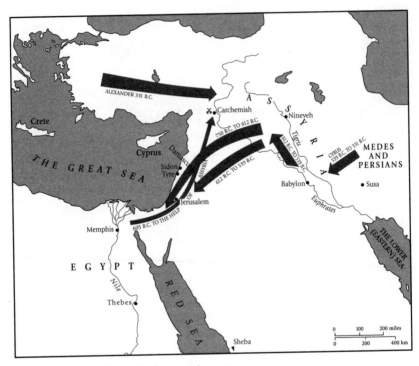

The Near East, 8th to 2nd centuries BCE

Introduction

We must now take the story up again, at the point where we laid it down at the end of *Brief Hour of Glory.*

We have seen what kind of people the Israelites were, and how they became a nation; and we have seen something, too, of the religious convictions that sustained them.

The vision of Moses and King David is not in doubt. But is this the way it is to be worked out? The next four hundred years provided the answer. We turn now to see what happened.

At first glance, the story that follows reads as if it might have come from the pages of any national history: military dictatorship; bitter hostility between North and South; civil war; invasion and the death of cities and villages; and all through, intrigue, assassination, exploitation, rebellion. Why is this story a special story? Perhaps that is the point – it isn't; it is, so far, a recognisable, human story provoking the question 'Why?' as appalling suffering always does. Here, in their own words, is their own account of these fateful years – contemporary narrative, official document, prophetic history, popular story.

But there *is* something special about the story. It reads like the story of the end; in fact, it is the story of a new beginning. Within fifty years of the final disaster in 586 BCE, a handful of men and women returned to rebuild the ruined city and begin life again as 'God's People'. How did this happen? What kept the vision of Moses and David alive?

The Death of Two Cities is, as a matter of fact, only part of the story. There is another part yet to be told: the rise of the great prophets, only glimpsed in the histories. These men, lacking political power, were critics of king and people; they saw, when statesmen were blind, the coming political disaster, but they interpreted it, not as the defeat of Moses' vision but as God's judgement on his own people for betraying it. To get the full picture of what happened, we must read both *The Death of Two Cities* and *Making Sense of the Story.*

New King, New Ways

A Brutal Beginning

1 Kings 2:13-46

Prince Adonijah came to Bathsheba, King Solomon's mother, and bowed in homage before her.

'Do you come as a friend?' she asked.

'Yes,' he said, 'as a friend. I want to talk to you.'

'Go on,' she said.

'I ought to have been king, you know,' he said. 'I am King David's eldest surviving son, and the whole country expected me to succeed him. All that's changed now. My younger brother is king – so GOD determined it. I've got one thing to ask you – don't say No.'

'Go on,' she said again.

'Ask King Solomon if he will let me marry Abishag. He won't refuse me if you ask him.'*

'All right,' she said. 'I'll do what you want.'

She sought an audience with the king.

He stood up to receive her, bowed and then ascended the throne. A throne was brought for Bathsheba and she sat at his right hand.

'I've something to ask you,' she said. 'I hope you won't say No.'

'All right, mother,' he said. 'I won't say No. Tell me what you want.'

'Let Abishag be given in marriage to Prince Adonijah,' she said.

'Why Abishag to Prince Adonijah?' said the king in anger. 'You might as well tell me to give him the whole country! You know he is my elder brother. This is a plot – Abiathar the priest and General Joab have got a finger in it! By GOD! Adonijah shall pay for this with his life! And he shall die today!'

He ordered Captain Benaiah of the Guards to execute Prince Adonijah immediately; the order was carried out.

The king then dealt with Abiathar the priest.

'Home to your village of Anathoth!' he commanded. 'I'd have you executed too – but for two things: you carried GOD's Ark in my father's time and you stood by him in his darkest days.'

He deprived him of his priestly office.

When General Joab heard what had happened to Prince Adonijah and Abiathar the priest, he fled to the Tent of GOD and clung to the altar.

* Abishag was one of King David's wives. Prince Adonijah was still thinking of keeping his claim to the throne alive.

136

'Go and kill him,' the king commanded Captain Benaiah, when he heard what he had done.

'In the name of the king, come out!' Captain Benaiah commanded the general.

'If I'm to die,' said General Joab, 'I'll die here.'

The captain hesitated to kill him in the very Tent of GOD itself, and went back to report to the king.

'Let him die as he asks!' said the king. 'Kill him and get him buried! He was a bloody man in his day; I don't want the guilt of his reckless crimes put on me or my father's house. He murdered General Abner and General Amasa in cold blood without a word to my father. He must pay for his own bloody deeds. I'm not having the peace of my father's dynasty put to risk.'

Captain Benaiah went back and killed General Joab where he was. The general's body was buried in his own desert home.

King Solomon made Captain Benaiah his commander-in-chief; and appointed Zadok the priest to take Abiathar's place.

He then turned to deal with the Benjamite Shimei.

'Live here in the city,' he ordered, 'and stay here. You are under house-arrest. One step outside across the Kidron Brook – and you are a dead man. Do you understand?'

'Fair enough,' said Shimei. 'You command, I obey.'

Three years went by.

Then, one day, two of Shimei's slaves escaped to the Philistine city of Gath. When Shimei heard of their escape, he saddled a donkey and went off to Gath to get them back.

It was reported to the king that Shimei had been to Gath and back. He called Shimei into his presence.

'You swore to me by GOD that you would stay in your house,' he said, 'and I made it clear that one step outside would mean your death. You gave your word – why haven't you kept it? You were my father's bitter enemy – you know that. Now you'll pay for the wrong you did him.'

He turned to General Benaiah.

'Execute him,' he commanded.

That is how King Solomon established his authority and made certain there would be no such internal rebellions as his father had had to deal with.

Border Rebellions

1 Kings 11:14-22, 23-25

King Solomon, however, had some trouble on his borders. Prince Hadad, of the royal house of Edom, was one who caused trouble. When General Joab had won the Edomite War in King David's days, he and his troops had stayed in the country for six months, carrying out mopping-up operations and exterminating every able-bodied man they could find. Prince Hadad and a number of royal officers had escaped to Egypt – he was only a small boy at the time. They marched south through Midian, crossed the Paran Desert west of the Gulf of Aqabah (where they enlisted some tribesmen) and reached Egypt. The Pharaoh welcomed Prince Hadad and gave him a house and land and a food allowance. They got on so well together that he married a princess, Queen Tahpenes' sister. His son Genubath grew up in the palace with the royal princes.

When Prince Hadad heard of King David's death and the murder of General Joab, he judged it the right moment to make a bid for Edomite freedom.

'Let me go home,' he said to the Pharaoh.

'Why go home?' asked the Pharaoh. 'You don't lack anything here, do you?'

'No,' he said, 'but I must go home.'

He went and made himself master of Edomite territory in the east towards the desert. He was a dangerous enemy all King Solomon's days.

Another trouble-maker was King Rezon in the north. He had escaped from his overlord, King Hadad of Zobah, and become a guerrilla leader, roaming the northern highlands. He went back to Damascus City, made it his headquarters and was crowned king. He, too, was a trouble to King Solomon throughout his reign.

Oriental Despot

King David had built his empire on the old tribal league; he respected the ancient loyalties of his people. But both the rebellions he had to face arose from old tribal suspicions. King Solomon learned from his father's experience. He made up his mind to break with the past and build a new kind of empire. He and his son were to find out that tribal loyalties ran more deeply and more strongly than they thought.

Government Reorganisation *1 Kings 4:1-7, 27-28*

The king set about reorganising the whole empire. These were the officers he appointed:

> In charge of the Calendar – Azariah, Zadok's son;
> Adjutant-general – Ahijah;
> Secretary of State – Jehoshaphat;
> Commander-in-chief – General Benaiah;
> Priests – Zadok and Abiathar;
> Chaplain and Adviser – Zabud, the prophet Nathan's son;
> Director of the Labour Corps – Adoniram.

These were posts of cabinet rank which King David had established. To these King Solomon added two new posts:

> Chief of Provincial and District Administration – Azariah;
> Prime Minister (or Vizier) and Mayor of the Palace – Ahishar.

The king further reorganised the districts into which the whole country was divided, cutting across the old tribal boundaries. There were to be twelve new districts (as there had been twelve tribal districts), each under a District Officer, each to be responsible for one month a year for the maintenance of the palace (seeing that the king had all he needed) and the entertainment of royal visitors and delegations. The districts were also responsible for the supply of barley and straw for the new courier-service, arranging for it to be delivered at the various courier-stations.

Foreign Alliances

Political alliances were often confirmed by a royal marriage. Two powers above all others were important to Solomon – Egypt to the south; and the Phoenicians who controlled all the coast to the north-west and whose sea trade was expanding (they were later to found colonies in Cyprus, Sicily and Sardinia and beyond).

a) Egypt *1 Kings 3:1; 9:16*

King Solomon had a marriage-alliance with the Pharaoh of Egypt and married an Egyptian princess. Since he was still building his new palace and the temple and the new city wall, he housed her in Davidstown, the old city where King David had lived. For dowry, the Pharaoh gave the princess Gezer Town; he attacked the city for this purpose, captured it, burned it to the ground and killed its inhabitants. King Solomon later built a special palace for her.

b) Tyre   1 Kings 5:1-17; 7:13-14; 5:11

On hearing of King Solomon's coronation, King Hiram of Tyre sent his congratulations to him by the hand of royal officers – he had always been a good friend of his father's. King Solomon returned his compliments and proposed a commercial treaty between the two countries. He wanted timber from the great cedar and pine forests of Lebanon and he offered to pay for it with an annual consignment of wheat and oil.

He also needed to hire skilled craftsmen – one of the most famous he later hired was Hiram (his father was a Tyrian who had married an Israelite widow), an outstanding worker in bronze.

So the two kings signed a treaty between their two countries.

National Defence

a) Key Cities   1 Kings 9:15-22

After King Solomon had finished the building of his capital city – his new palace, the temple, the citadel and the new city wall – he fortified six chariot cities as key cities for the defence of the heartland of his empire:

Hazor, north of Galilee Lake, facing north;

Megiddo, guarding the pass through the Carmel mountain range (both these cities lay on the great trade route which ran from Egypt, along the plain, past Megiddo and then on across the Esdraelon Plain, along the shore of Galilee Lake, through Hazor and on to Damascus City);

Gezer (which King Solomon rebuilt), Bethoron and Baalath which guarded the western approaches to Jerusalem from the plain between the central highlands and the sea;

Tamar, south of the Salt Sea, facing Edomite territory.

The royal army was stationed at these points. It could be quickly organised to meet invasion, internal rebellion or troublesome border vassals.

b) The Chariot Force

The chariot was a military weapon King David had never tried to develop. It had been used by the Philistines and the Canaanite cities. Now the old Israelite tribal territory and the Canaanite fortified cities were welded together into one country, King Solomon made his chariot force the main arm of his army.

1 Kings 10:26

King Solomon raised a strong striking force of 1400 chariots and 1200 cavalry; they were stationed in the six chariot cities and in the capital city, Jerusalem.

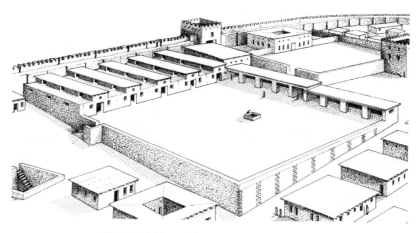

The Megiddo stables as they once looked.

Trade

King Solomon's genius was for trade and industry. His country lay across the roads from Egypt to Northern Syria and from Syria to the Red Sea; he saw how important these roads were. The city of Tyre was expanding its trade across the Great Sea; King Solomon sought to have good relations with it.

a) Red Sea Trade   *1 Kings 9:26-28; 10:11, 22*

King Solomon built a fleet of ships, hiring craftsmen from the Tyrian shipbuilding yards. He built ships at the port of Ezion-geber, on the east shore at the top of the Aqabah Gulf of the Red Sea (in Edomite territory) and they were manned by Tyrian and Israelite officers and men – the Tyrians bringing their wide experience of the seas. The fleet went on regular trading voyages – sailing as far as Ophir, on the north-east shores of Africa – and brought back large cargoes of gold, sandalwood and precious stones.

Both King Solomon and King Hiram had fleets trading along the coasts of the Red Sea. King Solomon also had a fleet of 'refinery' ships sailing from the copper refinery of Ezion-geber. Once every three years the fleet of 'refinery' ships would come back laden with gold, silver, ivory, apes, and peacocks.

b) The Arabian Trade

King Solomon was interested not only in the sea routes down the Red Sea but also in the overland caravan trade with the south. His interests went as far south as the south-eastern tip of the Arabian peninsula where the Sabeans lived – nomads who had settled down as a kingdom on the trade route which led from the shores of the Indian Ocean to Palestine. The story that was told of the Queen of Sheba's visit to Solomon's court reflects the popular interest in these far-flung adventures of his.

1 Kings 10:1-10, 13

The Queen of Sheba (the Sabeans), so the story goes, was so impressed by King Solomon's fame, that she came with a great retinue of her officers to Jerusalem City, with camel trains carrying spices and gold and precious stones. It was his wisdom that drew her. They talked together and she spoke freely to him, asking questions and listening to his answers – he seemed to know everything. All she saw, too, took her breath away – his new palace, the rich food at the royal table, the seating of his officers, the attendance and dress of his waiters and his cup-bearers, the sacrifices he offered in the temple. She was overwhelmed by it all.

'The reports I heard in my own country,' she told him, 'were reliable reports. But I didn't believe them – until I came here and saw with my own eyes. And now I know they weren't even half the truth – your wisdom and your wealth make a mockery of them. How happy your wives and your ministers! And how blessed is your GOD!'

She gave the king a splendid present – gold and spices and precious stones. The king never again received so splendid a gift.

He returned her kindness and gave her all she asked for. Then she and her retinue went back home.

c) The Copper Industry

Copper was plentiful in the territory to the south of the Salt Sea, and mines had been worked there from earliest times. King Solomon developed this and built in Ezion-geber the largest refinery that we know of in the Ancient Near East. He opened mines and built furnaces, and the copper was refined and worked into ingots in the great refinery. He must have had the help of Tyrian craftsmen. He built a 'refinery' fleet, as we have seen, ships like the Tyrian ships built for the transport of smelted metal. King Solomon needed the copper for use at home and to exchange for foreign goods.

d) The Trade in Horses and Chariots

King Solomon built up, as we have seen, a powerful chariot force. But he neither manufactured chariots nor bred horses; Egypt made the finest chariots and Cilicia bred the best horses. Hence he had to buy chariots from Egypt and horses from Cilicia. Since he controlled the trade route between Egypt and Cilicia, he became middle man in the trade; this business was an important source of his wealth.

1 Kings 10:28

King Solomon imported horses from Cilicia. His merchants would buy them at their market price and bring them to the king. A chariot bought and delivered from Egypt cost 600 silver shekels and a Cilician horse 150 silver shekels. These were sold through the agency of Israelite merchants to the kings of the Hittites and the Syrians.

New Buildings

a) The Palace   *1 Kings 7:1-10; 10:18-21*

The palace took thirteen years to build. There were four main buildings.
'The House of Lebanon Forest' (so called because it was built with
cedar-wood from Lebanon) was 150 feet long by 75 feet wide and 45
feet high. It was built in three rows of cedar-wood columns, fifteen in a
row, on which were laid forty-five cedar-wood beams. The beams were
covered with cedar-wood. Window faced window and door faced door
on each of the three storeys – windows and doors having square frames.
'The Hall of Pillars' – 75 feet long and 45 feet deep – had a porch in
front of it, with pillars and canopy in front of the pillars. 'The Hall of the
Throne' (used also as the Court of Justice) was finished with cedar-wood
from floor to rafters. The same wood was used in building the king's
own domestic quarters in the court at the back of the palace; and similar
quarters were built for his wife, the Egyptian princess. The buildings
themselves were built of heavy blocks of stone, sawn to fit, and set in a
large encircling court. The throne was made of ivory overlaid with gold,
and all the utensils used in the palace were of gold. The throne itself
had six steps, with a lion at each end of each step; a lion stood by each
arm-rest, and on the throne was a calf's head.

b) The Temple   *1 Kings 6:2-22; 7:15-26*

The temple was built by a Tyrian architect on the pattern of Syrian temples.
First there was the vestibule, then the main hall (the 'Holy Place', a
large rectangular room lit by small windows under the roof); then a
small windowless room shaped like a cube ('The Holiest Shrine').

Two free-standing bronze columns, 27 feet high, dominated the
porch. The capitals mounted on the columns were made of molten
bronze. The southern column was called Jachin, and the northern
Boaz. There was a large 'bronze sea', resting on the backs of oxen facing
north, south, east and west (representing the underground fresh-water
ocean on which, it was believed, the earth rested); and there was the
central altar, on which sacrifices were made (representing the 'mountain
of the gods').*

* This is a short summary of the historian's very long and elaborate account of the temple
and its furniture. It was a magnificent building – very different from the building his
father worshipped in.

The temple was both the Royal Chapel (its chief priest was appointed by the king and was a member of his government) and the national shrine of the whole people. Here future kings were crowned and the great public festivals were held. Although the temple was built for the Israelite worship of God, its Tyrian architect embodied many pagan features in its structure; here lay a real danger for Israelite religion as Moses understood it.

c) The Labour Corps   1 Kings 5:13

To carry out all these immense building operations, King Solomon organised a conscript army of labourers, especially to work in Lebanon felling and transporting trees. Conscripts served one month in every three on active service.

A Note on Religion   1 Kings 11:1, 4, 7-8

King Solomon had a large harem, and many of his wives (as we have seen) were pagan women. He was not as loyal to the worship of GOD as his father had been. He built hill-shrines for Chemosh, the Moabite god (on the top of the mountain facing Jerusalem City itself), and for Molech, the Ammonite god. He built many altars to pagan gods for his foreign wives.

King Solomon's reign was a long and prosperous one. The population grew and the standard of living rose. The cities expanded; Jerusalem City spread beyond the great wall he built.

Outwardly there was peace and prosperity. But underneath the peace and prosperity there was growing resentment and unrest – especially in the North. His death was the signal for revolt.

Northern Rebellion (922 BCE)

1 Kings 11:26-31, 40

The story of the rebellion begins while King Solomon was still alive.

He was building the Great Tower and extending the walls of Jerusalem City. He had a very able young officer, a Northerner called Jeroboam, and he liked the very thorough way in which this officer carried out his duties. He promoted him and made him the officer commanding the northern labour force – a Northerner in charge of Northern conscripts.

One day Jeroboam took the road leading north out of Jerusalem City, and as he was walking along he met the prophet Ahijah, a Northerner like himself. Ahijah stopped him, and the two of them left the road and talked together alone in a field.

Ahijah was wearing a new cloak. He tore it into twelve pieces – representing the twelve tribes of the old tribal league – and gave ten pieces to Jeroboam.

'Take ten pieces,' he said. 'This is GOD's word: "King Solomon has abandoned me and has not lived in my Way. I am going to tear the kingdom from him and give you the ten northern tribes. I appoint you king over the North. If you live in my Way, I will be with you."'

Jeroboam began to plan the rebellion of the North. King Solomon got to know about it and sentenced him to death. But he escaped to Egypt into the protection of Pharaoh Sheshak, and stayed there until King Solomon's death.

1 Kings 12:1, 3-14, 16-18, 2, 20, 25, 28-29

No sooner had King Solomon died than rebellion broke out in the North. It happened in this way.

King Rehoboam had already been crowned king of the South. He had now to meet the assembly of the Northern Israelites at Shechem, the meeting place of the old tribal league, to be crowned king of the North.

The assembly spoke plainly.

'Your father was a tyrant,' they told him. 'Put an end to the hard labour and the heavy burdens he laid on us, and we will be your loyal citizens.'

King Rehoboam wanted to talk the matter over with his advisers first.

'Give me three days,' he said. 'I will then give you my answer.'

'What do you suggest I do?' he asked the elder statesmen.

'A real king is the servant of his people, not a tyrant,' they said. 'If this is the sort of king you want to be, meet the people's requests; they will be your loyal subjects ever after.'

He didn't like this kind of advice, and turned to his young companions, the friends he had grown up with at court.

'Put the people in their place,' they said. 'Tell them you little finger is thicker than your father's loins! Tell them you'll add to your father's "heavy burdens", that you'll use lashes instead of your father's whips if there's any trouble. That's how to deal with them!'

The king met the assembly on the third day.

The Northern Israelites saw that it was a waste of time arguing with him. Their mood is shown in this Northern song:

'We don't belong to David!
The Bethlehem farmer's no good to us!
Home you go, men of the North!
Let David look after himself!'

They went angrily back to their tents.

King Rehoboam ordered the Labour Force Commander, Adoram, to pacify them. The crowd stoned him and killed him.

That frightened King Rehoboam. He climbed into his chariot and made off for Jerusalem. Never again were North and South one country.

Jeroboam had already come home from Egypt. When news of King Solomon's death had reached him, he had set off for his native town of Zeredah in Ephraim territory, where he bided his time. The Northern leaders now summoned him from his village to meet the Northern Assembly and crowned him king of the North.

He rebuilt Shechem as his royal city and made it his headquarters. As a precaution, he also fortified Penuel in the highlands east of Jordan River.*

He also established the worship of GOD at Bethel and made it the great religious centre of the North. GOD's throne in the temple there was supported on two golden bulls instead of winged sphinxes as in the temple at Jerusalem.

'You have worshipped in Jerusalem long enough,' he told the people. 'This is the old temple where GOD who brought us out of Egypt is to be worshipped.'

---

* Some time later, he made Tirzah his capital city. Tirzah remained the Northern capital until King Omri built Samaria.

Stories of the North (922-721 BCE)

Attack on the South (c. 900 BCE)   *1 Kings 15:16-22*

War broke out between North and South, and it lasted for more than twenty-five years.

King Baasha of the North began it. He declared war on King Asa of the South and built and fortified Ramah Town, five miles north of Jerusalem City, to stop anybody crossing the borders between the two countries.

King Asa replied by making a treaty with King Benhadad of Syria, the country to the north of King Baasha's territory. He took silver and gold from the temple and the palace treasuries and sent them, in charge of his officers, as a gift to the Syrian king in his capital, Damascus City.

'We are allies,' he said in his message to the king, 'as our fathers were before us. I send this gift to you. King Baasha is attacking me. Cancel your treaty with him and make him withdraw his forces.'

The Syrian king willingly agreed and ordered his army south to attack the Northern cities in the Jordan Valley near Galilee Lake. King Baasha had to stop fortifying Ramah and withdraw to his fortified capital city of Tirzah seven miles north-east of Shechem. King Asa immediately issued an order to pull the fortifications of Ramah down. The Southerners carried its stones and timbers away and used them to fortify two other cities to the north of the site of Rama – Geba and Mizpah – to guard their northern frontier.

Civil War   *1 Kings 16:8-11, 15-18, 21-22, 24*

King Elah – King Baasha's son who had now succeeded him – had been on the throne barely two years when he lost his life in an army revolt. Captain Zimri, one of his senior chariot officers, plotted his death. The king was drinking himself drunk in the house of the mayor of the palace in Tirzah City. Captain Zimri with his soldiers broke into the house and murdered him, and proclaimed himself king. He murdered all the members of the old royal family.

But he himself was king for just one week.

Northern troops were at the time besieging the Philistine city of Gibbethon, some twenty miles north-west of Jerusalem City in the low hills between the mountains and the sea. When news of the king's murder reached him, the troops in the field immediately elected Captain Omri as king and marched from Gibbethon back to Tirzah City. They broke into it. When Zimri saw that it was lost, he went into the palace citadel, set the whole place on fire and died in the flames.

The country was now torn by civil war. Another claimant to the throne, a man called Tibni, raised the standard of revolt. Half the country supported him, and half supported Captain Omri. For four or five years fighting went on, until Captain Omri proved the stronger man. Tibni died fighting. Captain Omri was then crowned king of all the North.

He proved a strong king. During his reign of eight years he built a new capital city. Tirzah City – the old capital city – faced the Jordan Valley; King Omri wanted a city which could control the whole country and command the roads to the north and to the east. So he bought a hill from a landowner named Shemer, built a strong city there and called it 'Samaria' after its original owner.

King Ahab (869-850)

Syrian Invasion   *1 Kings 20:1-12*

King Benhadad of Syria invaded the North. He mustered his army – cavalry and chariots – and troops from allied countries and cities. He marched through the country and besieged the capital city, Samaria. King Ahab, King Omri's son, had stayed in the city with his people.

King Benhadad sent messengers to King Ahab. What he had to say was short and to the point.

'All your wealth is mine,' he told him.

'If you say so,' was all that King Ahab answered.

The Syrian messengers came back again.

'You don't seem to understand,' said King Benhadad's second message. 'My first message was a command to surrender to me all your wealth – and your harem. My soldiers will show you what I mean. Tomorrow, about this time, they will ransack the city – your palace and your ministers' quarters. They'll take what loot they want.'

King Ahab called a meeting of his government.

'You see what the situation is, who the aggressor is,' he told them. 'He has now asked me to surrender my family. I didn't give him a direct No when he demanded my silver and gold.'

'Stand up to him,' they answered. 'No surrender.'

King Ahab then sent this reply to King Benhadad.

'I was ready to meet your first demand,' he told him. 'But I'm not surrendering my family.'

King Benhadad's reply was an angry one.

'By God!' he said. 'I've so many troops that they will each have less than a handful of dust to take away from the rubble of your city when I've finished with it.'

King Ahab's reply was just as brief:

'Tell him to remember the proverb: Boasting's for the end of the day, not its beginning!'

King Benhadad was drinking in the Royal Tent with the kings who had come with him when King Ahab's reply was handed to him.

He turned to his officers.

'To arms!' he ordered.

1 Kings 20:13-21, 23-25a

While this was happening, one of the Northern prophets sought an audience with King Ahab.

'These are GOD's words,' he said. '"Cast your eyes over this vast rabble round the city. I am about to put it at your mercy. You will know that I am really GOD!"'

'By whom will he do it?' asked King Ahab.

'By the young commandos,' the prophet answered.

'Who is to take the offensive?' asked the king.

'Your Majesty,' answered the prophet.

The king called out his troops. The commandos made a surprise attack on the Syrian camp at noon.

King Benhadad and his royal friends were drinking themselves drunk in the royal tent at the time.

Patrols reported the attack of the Northern soldiers.

'Let them come!' said King Benhadad carelessly. 'If it's peace they want – or if they want a bit of a fight – just take them all prisoners.'

The commando attack – with the main troops coming up behind them – routed the Syrian army. Every soldier got his man. King Benhadad escaped on a horse with some of his cavalry, leaving King Ahab to capture the main body of cavalry and chariots. The Syrian casualties were very heavy; those who escaped were chased back over the border.

A Syrian Council of War was held. The generals had their own explanation why they had lost.

'The enemy's gods are mountain gods,' they argued. 'That's why they beat us. Our gods are gods of the plain – we can beat these men if we fight them on the plain. And more: the kings who are our allies are no generals. Replace them with veteran captains and muster another army, horse for horse and chariot for chariot like the one we lost. Then fight the enemy in the plains; we'll defeat them.'

1 Kings 20:25b-27, 29-34

The king accepted his generals' advice. The next spring he mustered his army, marched to Aphik Town, north of Galilee Lake, and attacked the Northerners there. The Northern army was drawn up facing them. The Syrians seemed to be everywhere; beside them, the Northern troops looked like two small flocks of goats.

For a whole week the two armies just watched each other. Then the fighting started. The Northerners routed the Syrians – their casualties in the first day's fighting were very heavy. The survivors fled back into Aphik Town. But the city wall collapsed in the siege and the town was taken. King Benhadad himself had to hide in the small inner room of the citadel.

'Your Majesty,' said his officers, 'the Northern kings are known to be merciful men. Let us, we pray you, dress in sackcloth with ropes on our heads and surrender to him. It may be he will spare your life.'

They did just that, and asked for an audience with King Ahab.

'King Benhadad, Your Majesty's servant, surrenders,' they reported. 'He asks for his life to be spared.'

'Is my royal cousin still alive?' asked King Ahab.

The officers were watching the king closely to see which way the wind was blowing; they weren't slow to catch his meaning.

'Yes,' they said, 'King Benhadad – Your Majesty's royal cousin.'

'Bring him to me,' he said.

King Benhadad came, and King Ahab called him up into his chariot.

'I will give you back the cities my father captured from your father,' King Benhadad told him. 'My father established bazaars in Samaria City; you may establish bazaars in my capital city of Damascus.'

'I will accept a treaty on these terms,' said King Ahab. 'You are free to go home.'

The Last Battle (850)

1 Kings 22:1-6, 29-37

For three years there was peace. But King Benhadad did not keep his promises; he did not hand back the cities as by treaty he had agreed to do.

One day King Jehoshaphat, king of the South, paid a state visit to King Ahab. He was present at a meeting of the Council when King Ahab reminded his officers that one of the towns had not been handed back – Ramoth-Gilead, thirty miles east of Jordan River.

'The town is ours and it is still not in our hands, you know,' said the king, 'and here we sit doing nothing. It's about time we took it by force.'

He turned to King Jehoshaphat.

'Will you be my ally?' he asked.

'Of course I will,' said King Jehoshaphat. 'Count my soldiers as your soldiers, my cavalry as your cavalry.' *

The two kings marched on Ramoth-Gilead.

'I'll disguise myself,' said King Ahab, 'and fight like a private soldier. You can wear your royal armour.'

So he fought in disguise.

Now King Benhadad had given strict orders to his chariot captains.

'There's one man you've got to go for – and one man only,' he told them. 'That man's King Ahab. Don't waste your time over anybody else.'

The chariot captains spotted King Jehoshaphat and surrounded his chariot.

'We've got King Ahab all right,' they shouted.

King Jehoshaphat shouted back at them. They realised that they had got the wrong man, and wheeled their chariots round.

An unknown soldier took a chance shot with an arrow into the mass of Northern troops – and it struck King Ahab between his scale armour and his breastplate.

He called to his charioteer.

'Wheel round,' he commanded. 'Drive me out of the fighting. I am badly wounded.'

Bitter fighting went on all day. The king kept himself standing upright in his chariot facing the Syrians, as an example to his men. He managed to keep himself standing like that till darkness began to fall. Then he collapsed and died.

As the sun set, news of his death spread through the army.

'The king's dead!' the cry went round. 'Every man to his home!'

* A story about the prophet Micaiah has been inserted at this point. It did not belong to the original story and takes an unfriendly view of Ahab. We have used it later (p. 219).

His soldiers drove the chariot with the dead king back to his capital city, Samaria, and buried him there.

King Jehu (842-815)

Army Revolt *2 Kings 8:29; 9:1-6, 9-13, 16-27, 30-35*

King Joram of the North had been badly wounded in a battle for Ramoth-Gilead; he had retired to his royal city of Jezreel to recover from his wounds. King Ahaziah of the South went to visit him.

Elisha,* the Man of GOD, sent for one of the younger members of his prophetic guild.

'Get ready to go to the army at Ramoth-Gilead,' he told him. 'Hitch up your cloak and take this flask of oil with you. When you get there, find Captain Jehu. Ask for a private interview with him in an inner room, away from his fellow-officers. Take the flask of oil and pour it on his head. Say: "These are GOD's words: I anoint you king of the North!" Then open the door and get out – as quickly as you can.'

The young man crossed Jordan River to Ramoth-Gilead. When he got there, the officers were holding a staff meeting.

'Captain Jehu,' he said, 'I've a message for you.'

'For me?' asked the captain, 'or for one of the other officers?'

'For you yourself, Captain,' he said.

Captain Jehu got up and went into an inner room. The young man poured oil on his head.

'These are GOD's words,' he said, "I anoint you king over my people, over the North!"'

He opened the door and vanished.

Captain Jehu went back to the staff meeting.

'Is everything all right?' they asked. 'What did that madman want with you?'

'What do you think?' he retorted. 'You know how these fellows talk!'

'Go on,' they said. 'You can't get away with that! Tell us what he said.'

'Well,' said Captain Jehu, 'he just said this: "These are GOD's words: I anoint you king over the North."'

His brother officers turned the stone steps up to the house into a throne, spreading their military cloaks on them. They sounded a fanfare of trumpets and shouted, 'Long live King Jehu!'

---

* Many legends were told about Elisha as miracle-worker and adviser of kings.

Captain Jehu ordered his chariot out and rode to the royal city of Jezreel where the two kings were – King Joram, still a sick man, and King Ahaziah, still on his visit.

The sentry on the top of Jezreel Tower noticed something moving along the eastern road.

'I can see riders coming!' he shouted.

'Send a cavalryman to see if there's anything wrong,' commanded King Joram.

A cavalryman rode out to meet the chariot.

He challenged the charioteer.

'In the name of the king, is it peace?' he asked.

'Peace be damned!' shouted King Jehu. 'Fall in behind me!'

'The cavalryman's staying with the chariot!' shouted the sentry on the tower.

King Joram ordered a second cavalryman out.

The same thing happened.

'He's staying too!' the sentry shouted down. 'The charioteer's driving like a madman – only Captain Jehu drives like this!'

'To arms!' commanded the king.

The royal chariots were driven out, and the two kings met Captain Jehu at Naboth's farm.

'Is it peace, Captain?' asked King Joram.

'Peace indeed!' said the captain. 'How can there be peace with all this paganism the Queen Mother's spreading throughout the land?'

The king wheeled his chariot round.

'We're betrayed, Ahaziah!' he shouted.

Captain Jehu shot him through the heart with an arrow, and he collapsed in his chariot.

'Throw his body on farmer Naboth's field!' he ordered.

King Ahaziah saw what his fate would soon be, and drove his chariot along the southern road. Captain Jehu followed him and caught up with him seven miles along the road in the valley near Ibleam.

'Get him!' he shouted. 'Pin him to his chariot!'

The soldiers hit him, but he drove his chariot on to Megiddo Fortress. And there he died.

Captain Jehu turned back to Jezreel and rode into the city. When the news was brought to Jezebel, the Queen Mother, she dressed as if for a royal party – painted her eyes and adorned her hair – and sat looking out of a palace window. As Jehu rode through the palace gates, she called down to him.

'Is it peace?' she sneered. 'You Zimri! Murderer of your King!'

Captain Jehu stopped and looked up at the window.

'Who's for me?' he shouted up at the palace officials. 'Who's on my side?'

Two or three officials were looking down.

'Throw her out of the window!' he shouted.

They threw her out. Her blood splattered the wall and her body was trampled by the horses' hoofs. Captain Jehu went on into the palace to celebrate.

'She was a king's daughter, wicked woman though she was. Give her a royal burial,' he ordered.

By the time the officers found her body, the street dogs had been scavenging around – only her skull, her feet and the palms of her hands were left.

Brutal Reform   *2 Kings 10:1-11, 15-27*

King Jehu – as he now was – made sure that all the descendants of King Ahab were got out of the way. He arranged the murder of all who remained in the capital city of Samaria or in the royal city of Jezreel, and so got rid of any possible claimants to the crown. He left none alive – members of the royal family, relatives and friends, even priests who had favoured the old regime.

He was on his way from Jezreel to Samaria. Rechab's son, Jonadab, a fighter for the old religion of the North and an enemy of Ahab – an extremist like himself – was coming along the Jezreel road to meet him.

'Are you an out and out friend of mine,' Jehu asked, 'as I am yours?'

'I am!' said Jonadab.

'Fine!' said King Jehu. 'Give me your hand!'

Jonadab gave him his hand and the king helped him to climb up into his chariot.

'Come with me,' he said. 'I will show you how much I care for the true worship of GOD!'

When he reached Samaria City, he first of all made sure that all the relatives of King Ahab were dead.

Then he called a public meeting of all the citizens.

'King Ahab worshipped Baal,' he told them. 'But his worship of Baal will seem as nothing beside my worship of Baal. I am holding a great religious service in Baal's temple here, and I command all his prophets and worshippers and priests to attend it – and I mean all of them. Those who are absent will face the death penalty.'

All this was a deliberate trick on King Jehu's part – his real aim was to murder everybody who had anything at all to do with Baal worship.

'Arrange a temple sacrifice,' was his royal command.

A proclamation was made to the whole country. Worshippers of Baal came from near and far and packed the temple from wall to wall.

The king ordered the wardrobe-master to bring out all the sacred vestments for the worshippers to wear. Then he and Jonadab entered the temple.

'We want no worshippers of GOD here,' he told the congregation. 'Just make sure that none of them have slipped in unnoticed.'

He then began the service, offering sacrifices and burnt offerings.

Meanwhile he stationed eighty soldiers outside.

'You are under orders,' he said. 'Make sure nobody escapes – or you'll pay for it with your lives.'

When the burnt-offering had been made, the king turned to his guards.

'Go in and butcher them,' he ordered. 'See that nobody gets away.'

The guards went in and butchered the whole crowd and threw their bodies out into the courtyard. They broke into the inner room and tore down the sacred pillar and took it outside and burned it. They demolished the whole building and turned it into a lavatory.

That's how King Jehu stamped out pagan religion in the North.

Six Kings and Four Rebellions (746-721)

2 Kings 15:8, 10, 14, 16, 19-20, 25, 29-30; 17:3-6, 24

Zechariah, Jeroboam II's son, was king for only six brief months. Shallum, a usurper, murdered him on the road between the royal cities, near Ibleam.

Tirzah – the capital city of the North for the forty years before King Omri built Samaria City – had become the headquarters of rebels led by a man called Menahem. He marched on Samaria City, murdered Shallum and seized the throne. (Shallum had been king for barely a month.)

Menahem was a cruel man; he destroyed the whole town of Tappuah (fourteen miles south-west of Tirzah) because they had once refused to open their gates to him. In his anger he murdered all the pregnant women with horrible brutality.

King Menahem reigned for about ten years, but only because he became a vassal of the Assyrian Emperor, Tiglath-pileser III. This emperor invaded the North and King Menahem only saved himself by paying an enormous sum of money as tribute. He had to make all the wealthy farmers pay a heavy tax – each of them had to give as much money as would buy a slave. Only on these conditions did the invading armies go home.

King Menahem's son was king for only two years. Pekah, his aide-de-camp, rose in rebellion with fifty men from east of Jordan River and murdered him in the palace fort. King Pekah reigned for four or five years. The Assyrians again marched west when King Pekah made an alliance with King Rezin of Damascus and rose in rebellion against them. They captured many cities and most of the territory in the North. Many of the leading men were deported to Assyria, and all that was left of the North was a small area of land round Samaria City itself.

A usurper called Hoshea murdered King Pekah with the help, probably, of Assyrian soldiers. He reigned for nine years, but he too had to suffer an Assyrian invasion of his country. He became an Assyrian vassal and had to pay an annual tribute.

The end came suddenly. King Hoshea thought he could safely defy the Assyrian armies. He sent messengers to the vizier of Egypt to come to his help and he stopped sending tribute to Assyria. The Assyrian emperor moved quickly. He marched west, captured and imprisoned him – and besieged Samaria City. It held out for three years. When the Assyrians captured it, they deported thousands of its inhabitants to the east.

The story of the North was over.

The Assyrian emperor now settled people from the other parts of his empire – from Babylon and its neighbourhood, and from the country through which the Orontes River flows – to colonise Samaria and the villages which had been left empty when the Northern prisoners were deported.

Stories of the South (922-586 BCE)

Egyptian Invasion (917)

1 Kings 14:25-28

King Rehoboam had been king for only five years when Egyptian armies attacked and captured his capital city, Jerusalem. The city escaped destruction by the payment of an enormous tribute. All the treasures of the temple and the palace were ransacked – among them King Solomon's gold ceremonial shields. All King Rehoboam could do was to make bronze shields to take their place. These were kept in the guard-room of the Palace Guards, whose officers were personally responsible for their safety. They were taken out, as the old gold ones used to be, on the king's official visits to the temple. After each ceremony, they were taken back to the guard-room.

King Asa (913-873)

1 Kings 15:9-15

King Asa was a good king and tried to rule the country in the spirit of his ancestor David. He banished all the male temple prostitutes and destroyed the images of pagan gods his father and grandfather had set up there. His mother, now the Queen Mother, had ordered a private image of the goddess Asherah to be made; he took away her rank as Queen Mother and burned the image in Kidron Valley. She had removed the gifts he and his father had dedicated to the temple; he had them brought back and set up again.

It was in his day that civil war broke out between North and South.*

Edomite Rebellion (c. 845)

2 Kings 8:20-22

King Joram had to face trouble beyond Jordan River in the eastern highlands. The Edomites had long been subjects of the Southern kings, but when King Joram ascended the throne, they rose in revolt and were

* See p. 148.

strong enough to make their country independent. King Joram mustered his chariot force and crossed the river. He was surrounded at the town of Zair and only escaped by breaking out of the besieged town in the darkness of the night. The Edomites never again lost their independence.

Ruthless Queen (842-837) *2 Kings 11:1-9, 11-16, 18-20*

News of the murder of King Ahaziah,* her son, reached Athaliah, the Queen Mother, in Jerusalem City. She at once made herself the sole ruler of the country. She got rid of all her possible rivals by murdering the royal family – all of them except a little baby boy, Joash, son of the dead King Ahaziah. When the princes were being hunted out, King Ahaziah's sister, the wife of Jehoiada the priest, kidnapped the little baby, pushed him and his nurse into a bedroom, hid him there and saved him from the fate of all the other princes. For the six years the Queen Mother ruled the country, he was kept hidden in a room in the temple.

A revolt against the Queen Mother and all she stood for was now brewing. It was led by Jehoiada, the priest of the true worship of GOD, the man who had helped to keep King Ahaziah's little son hidden. When the boy was seven years old, at the New Year Festival, Jehoiada sent for the officers of the royal guards and took them into the temple. He showed them the boy – the murdered king's son and rightful king – and made them swear an oath of loyalty to him. Then he gave them their orders:

'You will strike when the guard is mustered at full strength – that is, on the Sabbath at the changing of the guard when two companies are being marched in force into the temple. At this moment the two companies will form up, with drawn swords, as the young king's bodyguard. Anyone approaching the bodyguard will be killed on the spot. Remember – the king's life is in your hands.'

The officers carried out the orders. The whole guard – those off duty and those on duty – reported to Jehoiada the priest and took up their positions, with swords drawn, right across the court from the south wall to the north wall, in front of the altar and the king's rooms. Jehoiada brought the boy out, put the crown on his head and the bracelet on his arm, and anointed him.

The guards and the crowd clapped their hands and shouted, 'Long live King Joash!'

* See p. 154.

The Queen Mother heard the noise of the shouting and went across from the palace to the temple. She stared at the crowd – the new king standing by the column (as was the custom at a coronation), the captains and the trumpeters standing by his side, the common people shouting and blowing trumpets.

'Treason! Treason!' she shouted, tearing her clothes.

'March her out under guard,' commanded Jehoiada, 'and kill her.' (He had already given orders that her execution should not take place in the temple courts.)

The guards arrested her and killed her as she went through the Cavalry Gate.

The crowed rushed off to the temple of Baal. They smashed the altar and the idols, killed the temple priest in front of the altar and razed the building to the ground.

Jehoiada stationed sentries in the temple. He and the guards' officers escorted the king down from the temple, through the Guards' Gate into the palace, and seated him on the royal throne. The common people welcomed the young king's coronation and there was no violence in the city streets.

Brilliant King (783-742)   *2 Chronicles 26:3, 6-15; 2 Kings 15:5*

King Uzziah was sixteen years of age when he became king. He reigned for fifty-two years in Jerusalem City and made the South into a powerful state.

He put an end to Philistine rebellion. He destroyed three of their great cities – Gath, Jabneh and Ashdod – and built fortified cities in their territory to keep it in order.

He then dealt with the Arabs who lived to the south-east and forced the Ammonites east of Jordan Valley to pay him tribute. He became master of all the country down to the Egyptian border.

He then turned his attention to the questions of defence, water supply and agriculture. He built fortified towers in the capital city itself – at the Corner Gate, the Valley Gate and the Angle – and on his desert borders. He had large herds both in the western plains and in the eastern highlands; he built many cisterns to keep them supplied with water. He was a lover of the soil and had farms and vineyards in the hills and wherever the land could support them, and many farmers to look after them.

He built up a large standing army with the help of one of his commanders, General Hananiah, and of his Civil Service. He overhauled the army's equipment, the soldiers' armour and weapons (shields, spears, helmets, coats of mail, bows and stones for slinging) and engines of war for shooting arrows and throwing heavy stones (these he stationed on his fortified towers and at the corners of the city walls in Jerusalem).

His fame spread far and wide. He was a good king and ruled in the spirit of King David.

But one thing overshadowed his reign. He became a leper and suffered from it until his death. This forced him to live alone in a separate part of the palace; his son, the Crown Prince Jotham, took charge of the palace and the affairs of state.

Northern Attack (734)

Invasion   *2 Kings 16:5-18*

King Ahaz had been king for only a year when the two kingdoms, the North and Syria, rose in revolt against the Assyrian empire. They formed an alliance and tried to make him join them. They marched south and attacked Jerusalem City, but he kept them at bay.

Meanwhile he had sent to the Assyrian emperor for help.

'I am your vassal state,' he sent word. 'Come and rescue me from the alliance of Syria and the North. They are besieging me in my capital city.'

He sent a costly present to the emperor – silver and gold from the temple and palace treasuries. The Assyrian emperor was quick to move. He marched west and captured the Syrian capital city, Damascus. The Syrian king had had to march north to defend his own country. He lost his life in the fighting and his people were deported to Mesopotamia.

King Ahaz paid a state visit to the Assyrian emperor in Damascus City. He noted the altar in the pagan temple there and sent a sketch and plan of it to his priest in Jerusalem, Uriah, with orders to make an exact model and have it installed before his return home. When King Ahaz got back from his state visit to the emperor, he inspected the altar and worshipped at it. He had the old bronze altar (which had been left standing between his altar and the shrine) moved out of the way over to the north side. He gave orders that his new altar was to be used for morning and evening worship and for all public sacrifices. He kept the old altar for his own personal use when he wanted to pray to GOD himself. He made other large alterations to the temple.

A Remembered Story

2 Chronicles 28:8-15

This happened in the early days of the Northern invasion of the South.

The Northerners took many of their Southern kinsfolk prisoner – women and children; they looted the Southern villages and took the loot to Samaria City.

But the prophet Oded met the returning army on the road to the city.

'GOD was angry with our Southern kinsfolk,' he protested. 'That's why you've won; but butchering them was just your ungovernable anger – and that GOD hates. Now you are treating them as if they are your slaves. Have you done nothing wrong yourselves? Send them back home! GOD's as angry with you as with them!'

Four of the Northern leaders stood up to the returning soldiers too.

'We're not having any Southern prisoners here,' they said. 'We don't want any further guilt laid at our doors.'

The soldiers handed over the prisoners and loot to the leaders and representatives of the people.

The four Northern leaders who had led the protest against the brutality of the soldiers took charge of the prisoners. From the loot they clothed those who were naked, put sandals on their feet, fed them and anointed those who were wounded. They put lame people on donkeys and took all the prisoners back to their kinsfolk at Jericho, the City of Palms. Then they themselves went back to their Northern capital, Samaria City.

Besieged City (701)

Earliest Account

2 Kings 18:13-16

King Hezekiah had been king in the South for fourteen years when his country was invaded by the emperor Sennacherib of Assyria. The emperor's army overran all the fortified cities in the country, and he himself established his headquarters in Lachish, a Southern fortified town, thirty miles south-west of Jerusalem City.

King Hezekiah sent a message to the emperor.

'I have done wrong,' he said. 'Withdraw your forces; I will pay whatever tribute you impose upon me.'

The emperor required King Hezekiah to pay a very heavy tribute to him in gold and silver. It was so crippling a fine that King Hezekiah had to hand over all the silver in the temple and palace treasuries – and even break up the temple doors and columns which he himself had decorated with gold.

Assyrian Account

Hezekiah, the Jew, did not submit to me. I besieged forty-six of his strong cities, walled forts and the many small villages around them. I captured them; I built earth-ramps and used battering rams against their walls which the sappers mined and broke through, and then sent my infantry in. I drove out 200, 150 people, young and old, male and female, together with horses, mules, donkeys, camels and cattle beyond counting. All this was my booty.

King Hezekiah himself I shut up in Jerusalem, his royal residence, like a bird in a cage. I surrounded him with earthworks in order to stop anybody leaving the city. His towns (which I had plundered) I took away from his country and gave them (over) to the kings of Ashdod, Ekron and Gaza. I reduced his territory but increased his annual tribute. Later Hezekiah himself . . . sent to me in Nineveh, my royal city, gold and silver, precious stones, antimony, large cuts of red stone, couches and armchairs (inlaid with ivory), elephant hides, ebony wood, box wood (and) all kinds of valuable treasures, his (own) daughters, concubines and male and female musicians. In order to deliver the tribute and do obeisance as a slave he sent his personal messenger.

Based on *Ancient and Near Eastern Texts, p. 288.*

Later Account   *2 Kings 18:17-37; 19:1-6, 8-9, 36*

The Assyrian emperor sent his Chief Administrator with a large army from Lachish to King Hezekiah in Jerusalem City. He stood by the conduit of the Upper Pool on the road to the Fuller's Field.

Three officers of state – the Prime Minister, the Secretary of State and the Royal Herald – came out to meet him.

The Chief Administrator spoke to them: 'Tell King Hezekiah: These are the words of the emperor – "Why this boldness? Is mere gossip enough to go on when you're waging war? Whose help gave you courage to rebel against me? Egypt's – that broken stick! Or was it your GOD's help? Why, King Hezekiah has been destroying your GOD's hill shrines and altars all over the country and making people worship only at the altar in this city! Come, I'll make a bet with you – I'll give you two thousand horses if you can find riders for them! But if you're relying on Egyptian horsemen, how do you think you could stop even one of my master's lieutenants?"'

And so he went on.

The Southern officers of state begged him to speak in the official language, Aramaic, not in the local Hebrew dialect.

'We don't want the people on the wall to hear what you say,' they said.

'I wasn't sent to talk just to you and your king,' retorted the Chief Administrator. 'I was sent to talk to the men sitting on the wall – they are the ones who're doomed to starvation.'

The Chief Administrator shouted in the local Hebrew dialect:

'Listen to what the emperor says!' he called. 'These are his words: "Don't let King Hezekiah trick you." He can't rescue you from the emperor's armies. And don't believe him when he talks about trusting GOD to save the city. Take no notice of what he says. "Make peace with me," the emperor tells you, "and surrender. You can go on living as you do now until I come to take you to a richer land where there's grain and wine, bread and vineyards." King Hezekiah is talking nonsense when he says GOD will rescue you. Has any other land's god rescued it from Assyrian armies? Where are the gods of Hamath and Arpad now? And where are the gods of Samaria? Did they rescue Samaria? What happened to all these gods gives you no hope that GOD can rescue you!'

There was dead silence on the walls; nobody said anything. King Hezekiah had given orders that nobody should answer.

The three officers of state went back to Hezekiah, with their clothes torn, to report what the Chief Administrator had said.

The king tore his clothes in grief and went into the temple. He sent the Prime Minister, the Secretary of State and some older priests to the prophet Isaiah.

'This is a day of distress, rebuke and disgrace,' was the king's message to the prophet. 'The people are starving to death. Perhaps GOD, whose prophet you are, has heard what the Chief Administrator has been saying (the emperor sent him to mock him) and perhaps he will deal with him. Offer a prayer for those of us who are left.'

'Take this message back to the king,' said Isaiah. 'These are GOD's words: "Don't be frightened at the blasphemy of the emperor's officers."'

The Chief Administrator went back to the emperor and found him besieging the fortress town of Libnah – news had already reached him that he had left Lachish Town and marched north.

Then, suddenly, the emperor raised the siege and marched back to Nineveh.

Last Days

Brave King (640-609)   *2 Kings 21:3-4, 23-24*

For more than forty years King Manasseh ruled the country. He had no love for prophets; because he was a puppet of the Assyrian emperor he celebrated pagan religions even in the temple itself. As a later historian summarised it:

'He built again the hill shrines which his father, King Hezekiah, had suppressed and altars to Baal. He made an image of the Canaanite Mother-Goddess, and worshipped the sun, moon and stars. All this went on in the very temple itself.'

His son, King Amon, had a brief reign of two years. His officers assassinated him. But the common people rose against the court conspirators, put them to death and crowned Josiah – the king's son, grandson of King Manasseh and great-grandson of King Hezekiah – as king to take his father's place.

About this time the Assyrian empire began to break up. First Egypt revolted and claimed her independence. Then, away to the north and east of the empire, Medes and Babylonians revolted too, and sacked the capital city of Nineveh in 612. King Josiah could thus make a bid for the independence of his country.

2 Kings 22:1, 6, 8-20; 23:1-14, 29-30

King Josiah was only eight years old when he became king. Eighteen years later – when he was twenty-six – he made up his mind to call his people back to the true worship of GOD. The first thing he did was to repair the temple in Jerusalem. He gave orders to his Secretary of State, Shaphan.

'Go to Hilkiah the priest,' he told him. 'He can use the money in the temple treasury to pay the workmen who are repairing the temple.'

'I have found a law book in the temple,' Hilkiah told Shaphan.

He gave the book to him to read. Shaphan went back to make his report.

'We have taken the money out of the treasury,' he told the king, 'and have paid the workmen with it.'

'Hilkiah gave me a book,' he added, and he began to read from it.

The king listened, and, as Shaphan went on reading, he was deeply disturbed.

'Go back to the temple,' he ordered Hilkiah and four of his officers. 'Pray to GOD for me and the people of this country. Ask him about this book. He must be angry, for our ancestors have taken no notice of what it commands.'

So the five men went to Huldah the prophetess who was living in the Second Quarter of the city and talked to her.

'The king is right,' she said. 'What GOD has to say is this: first to the whole nation – "The neglect of this book and its laws will bring a great disaster upon the whole people"; then to the king himself – "Because you were penitent and humble enough to listen carefully to all the book says, I have heard you. The disaster shall not fall in your time."'

They reported her words.

The king called a great assembly of all the priests and prophets and of the people from the country villages and the city. The Book of the Covenant – the book found in the temple – was read aloud in their presence. Then the king stood by the great bronze pillar and renewed the Covenant with GOD, promising to live in GOD's Way. All the assembly confirmed the Covenant.

Then he commanded that all signs of pagan religion should be removed from the temple. The wooden image of the Mother-Goddess was carried out to Kidron Valley and burned and the ashes scattered over the common graveyard. The rooms occupied by the temple prostitutes were torn down – rooms where the women used to weave vestments for the image of the Mother-Goddess and her worshippers. He closed all the local village hill-shrines throughout the whole country and brought their priests to the city. He destroyed the hill-shrines of the goat-demons which stood outside the entrance of the City-Governor's house, on the left as you came in by the city gate. The country priests, however, when they came up to the city, were not allowed to share in the temple sacrifices; they became 'second-class priests', eating unleavened cakes with their kinsmen.

He also destroyed 'The Place of Fire' where child-sacrifices had been made to the Ammonite god, 'The King' – there were to be no more child-sacrifices. He stopped the worship of the Sun God, destroying the statues of horses at the Temple Gate (they stood near the rooms of the chamberlain, among the summer houses) and burning the 'Chariots of the Sun'. He pulled down the roof-shrines on King Ahaz's upper rooms and the altars King Manasseh had built in the two temple courts. He

166

broke them down and scattered their dust in Kidron Valley. He got rid of the pagan shrines which stood east of the city and south of the Olive Hill and which King Solomon had built for the worship of the Mother-Goddess, the Moabite god Chemosh and the Ammonite god 'The King'. He broke down their sacred pillars and sacred poles and filled their places with human bones.

He then issued a royal edict.

'Let us keep the Passover Festival,' he ordered, 'as the Book of the Covenant sets it out. GOD saved us from the Egyptians; he has saved us again today!'

A Passover like this had not been held for a very long time – a great service of the whole country in the temple in Jerusalem City. It was the climax of King Josiah's reformation of the religion of his people.

In 609 the Egyptian Pharaoh marched north to help the Assyrian emperor against the rebels. King Josiah threw his army across his path, blocking the Megiddo Pass. In the battle that followed, King Josiah was killed. His officers carried his body in a chariot from Megiddo to Jerusalem City and buried him in his own grave. The citizens crowned his son, Jehoahaz, king in his place.

Fall of the City (609-586)

2 Kings 23:31-37; 24:1-12, 15-18; 25:1-15, 18-21

The new king, Jehoahaz, was only twenty-three, and he had been king only a few months when the Pharaoh had him deported to the north, to prevent his being a real king in his own country and causing trouble there. He demanded a heavy tribute from the South and crowned Eliakim – another son of King Josiah, an older brother of the deposed king – in his place, changing his name to Jehoiakim. Then he moved Jehoahaz to Egypt where he died a prisoner.

King Jehoiakim paid very heavy tribute to the Egyptians – so heavy that he had to use a graded tax to raise the money from farmers and merchants; the money in the palace and temple treasuries was not enough. He was Pharaoh's vassal until the new Babylonian empire (which had succeeded the Assyrian empire) defeated Egypt at the battle of Carchemish three years later (605).

Then the Babylonian armies marched south to secure their hold on the plain between Jerusalem City and the Great Sea. For three years King Jehoiakim was forced to be the vassal of the Babylonian emperor. Then he revolted. But he was attacked by raiding guerrilla bands from the surrounding countries, sent by the Babylonians to harass him until they could strike with their regular armies.

Then King Jehoiakim died and was succeeded by his son, King Jehoiachin, a young man of eighteen. He had only been three months on the throne when the Babylonian armies marched south again and besieged Jerusalem City. The Babylonian emperor himself joined his armies while the siege was on. So Jehoiachin surrendered (597).

The emperor deported him, the Queen Mother and the harem, the court officials and leading citizens, seven thousand soldiers and a thousand craftsmen to Babylon. To act as regent in the deposed king's place, he chose the king's uncle, Mattaniah – a young man of twenty-one – changing his name to Zedekiah.

King Zedekiah had been regent nine years when, pressed by extreme nationalists, he too rebelled against his Babylonian overlords.

In January 587 the Babylonian armies marched south to attack Jerusalem City. They camped outside the city and built a siege wall all round it, to prevent anybody leaving or entering it. The siege lasted till July 586. At the end of the siege, no food was left; starvation stared everybody in the face.

On 9 July the city walls were breached. In the darkness of the night, the king and his troops slipped through the King's Garden, out by the gate 'Between the Two Walls' (near Siloam Pool) and made for the Arabah Valley south of the Salt Sea. The Babylonian troops were busy occupying the city. But when they discovered the king's escape, they went after him and caught him in the flat country near Jericho City in the Jordan Valley. They took him before the Babylonian emperor in Riblah in the far north where he was court-martialled. The king's two sons were executed in his presence; he himself was blinded, handcuffed and deported to Babylon where he remained a prisoner for the rest of his life.

On 7 August the Babylonian commander-in-chief entered Jerusalem City and burned down the temple and the palace and every important house. He then ordered the soldiers to break down the city walls. He deported all the people who mattered – survivors of the siege and deserters to the invading forces alike. He left only the peasants to look after vineyard and field.

He then looted the temple; the bronze columns (known as 'Jachin' and 'Boaz'), the stands, and the great bronze bowl (called 'The Sea') were all broken up and the metal carried away. He melted down pots, shovels, snuffers, incense dishes, all the bronze vessels used in worship, and took away the gold and silver (of which the firepans and bowls were made) as ingots. Everything was looted.

He then rounded up representative citizens – from the priesthood, the army and the common people – to be executed as a warning to the whole nation: the two most important priests, Seraiah and Zephaniah, and three doorkeepers, the chamberlain in charge of the troops, five members of the King's Council who were discovered still hiding in the city, and the Army Secretary in charge of mobilisation; and sixty common citizens found at random in the city. He deported all these to Riblah, where the emperor had them flogged and executed.

Some thousands of Southerners were exiled to Babylon, far from their own country.

Murder of the Governor*   *2 Kings 25:22-26*

The Babylonians appointed Gedaliah as governor – many people, of course, were still left in the South. He set up his headquarters in the small town of Mizpah, 'Watch Tower', some eight miles north of the ruined city. Army officers and their men who had escaped to the hills as guerrillas came to swear allegiance to their new governor.

'Don't be frightened of the Babylonian officials here,' he told them. 'We have to live as vassals of the empire. If we go quietly about our work, everything will be all right.'

But peace was soon shattered – by a man called Ishmael, a fanatical member of the exiled royal family. He broke into the governor's residence and assassinated Gedaliah – and fellow-citizens and Babylonian officers who happened to be with him. Then, in panic, army officers and citizens fled to Egypt – they knew the sort of revenge the Babylonian authorities would take.

King in Exile   *2 Kings 25:27-30*

In March 561 – after thirty-seven years of imprisonment – King Jehoiachin's fortune changed. In that month a new emperor ascended the Babylonian throne. He summoned King Jehoiachin into his presence and spoke kindly to him. He allowed him to live in the palace. So King Jehoiachin changed his prison dress for royal robes. From this time on, he dined at the royal table; he was given regular daily allowances from the Babylonian treasury.

* See the fuller account on p. 247.

The New Lawbook

We have already read of the finding of the lawbook in the temple (p. 165). We know something of what it contained, for it was used in the writing of Deuteronomy, which was an expansion of it.

The last hundred years before the fall of Jerusalem had been a frustrating time for all who cared for the traditions of Moses – and a dangerous time too. The North was an Assyrian province; the South, in all but name, was an Assyrian province too. King Manasseh had given up any attempt to carry on the old traditions. Loyal followers of the old worship of GOD were suppressed.

A group of loyal worshippers of GOD went into hiding, and began to plan for the time when there would again be a loyal king on the throne. They drew up a 'Plan of Reform' which they hoped would one day become the law of the land. The 'Plan' itself had perhaps a long history behind it; a rough sketch of it may have been drawn up in the North in the dark days before the fall of Samaria, its capital city, when true worshippers of GOD there were facing as grave a situation as the South were now facing under King Manasseh. When Samaria fell, a copy was taken to the South, and there it became the 'Plan of Reform', the law book, which was later found in the temple when King Josiah began to restore it to something of its old glory. The selections from it which follow show what kind of 'Plan' it was – a recall of the people of the Covenant of Moses.

To make this very clear, the planners wrote their 'Plan of Reform' as speeches put into the mouth of Moses, imagining him making them to the Hebrew people before they crossed Jordan River on their way to the highlands. This was their way of saying 'We are not telling you anything new; we are calling you to be real followers of Moses.'

You Must Love GOD   *Deuteronomy 6:4*

Listen, you who are GOD's People: GOD, our GOD, is one GOD: you must love him with all you are – with your heart, your soul, your strength.

Don't Despise GOD's Kindness   *Deuteronomy 8:7-20*

GOD is leading you to your homeland – and a fine big country it is. Rivers and streams and springs gush out in the valleys and on the mountainsides; everywhere there is wheat and barley, grapes and figs, and pomegranates and olives and honey. There will be no desert rations there – you won't lack anything. There's iron in the rocks and copper in the hills. You will eat as much as you want and thank GOD for giving you such a wonderful country.

And that's the danger point. Take care that you don't then forget GOD or begin to disobey him. When you live in your fine houses, remember all he has done for you – rescuing you from Egypt; leading your march across the vast and frightening desert, with its poisonous snakes and scorpions and its dry and waterless tracks; getting you water from the flinty cliffs and feeding you with desert 'manna' (your ancestors never knew such food). All through these years he was caring for you, keeping you humble and testing you. Don't start being proud and talking about your capturing this wonderful country 'in our own strength'. Remember that GOD gave you whatever strength you needed. He gave his promise to your ancestors; today he is keeping his promise. I warn you: if you forget GOD and start worshipping other 'gods', you will meet with disaster – the same disaster that has overtaken the tribes who were living here before you. And disaster will have only one cause – your disobedience.

Only One Centre of Worship   *Deuteronomy 12:2-14, 32, 30-31; 16:21-22*

The people who lived here before you worshipped their 'gods' on high mountains and beneath trees – you must not copy them. You must wipe all this out – break the altars down, smash the stone pillars, burn their sacred poles and cut down the images of their 'gods'. Not even a memory all of this must remain.

When you worship GOD, you must only worship him in the one place he will choose, from all the tribal centres, as his home, where his name is to be known. You must bring all your sacrifices there; and there, together with your families, you must eat the sacred meal in GOD's presence, happy in the celebration of any success he may have given you.

You must not worship GOD as we are now worshipping him here in the desert, where everyone does what they think is right. For here we are not yet living in our homeland. But when you have crossed Jordan River and settled down in your homeland, and the war, with all its dangers, is over, it will be very different. You must bring your sacrifices (note what I am telling you) to the one place GOD chooses as his home, and there you shall enjoy yourselves in his presence – you and your families and your farm-workers and the priests (these, unlike you, have no land of their own). You are not to offer sacrifices to GOD at just any place that catches your eye. You must, as I am now telling you, offer your sacrifices only at the one place in your homeland GOD chooses.

You must carry out these orders to the letter. You must not copy the customs of the country which will be your home. You have not taken their place just to start doing what they do, asking how they worshipped their 'gods' and copying them. That's not the way to worship GOD – he detests all that goes on in the old temples. Why, they even burn their own children – and think that that is real religion!

There must be no sacred pole standing by GOD's altar, nor any stone pillar. That's the very sort of thing he loathes.

Look After the Poor   *Deuteronomy 15:1-18*

At the end of every seven years, there must be a cancelling of debts – GOD's 'Cancellation of Debts'. This is what you must do: if a man has lent money to a fellow-citizen, he must cross the debt out – he mustn't try to get him to pay up. He can make a foreigner pay up; he mustn't make a fellow-citizen do so. Indeed, there shouldn't be any poor people at all in the country – GOD has given you enough for everybody (that is, if you listen to what he wants and do what he tells you). GOD will give you prosperity, just as he said he would. You can lend money to foreigners, if you want to, but there's to be no borrowing from them. You can govern others; you are not to be governed by them.

But if there happens to be a poor man among you – one of your own countrymen, for example, in one of your own towns – you mustn't be selfish or mean; you must be open-handed, lending him whatever he needs. And there's to be no jiggery-pokery, either – turning mean just when the seven years are nearly over and refusing to give a needy fellow-citizen any help at all. He will appeal to GOD, and you will be known for what you are – a rebel against GOD. Help him, and help him generously and don't begrudge him anything. It's treating people like this that will make your country really prosperous. There will always be some poor people about, of course; that's why I'm telling you to be generous to your fellow-citizens – to any who are needy or poor.

And you must deal with slavery in the same way, too – where an Israelite man or woman, one of your fellow-citizens, is sold to you as a slave. What must happen is this: they work for you for six years; in the seventh year you must set them free. What is more: when you set them free, see that they don't go away empty-handed. Treat them generously – give them a present from your flock or threshing-floor or winepress. GOD has been good to you; be good to them. Don't begrudge them their freedom. They have worked hard for you for six whole years – and only cost you half of what you would have had to pay a hired servant; and you've got GOD's blessing as well. You know what it feels like to be a slave – you were slaves once in Egypt and GOD set you free. That's why I am talking to you like this.

If your slave doesn't want to leave you – perhaps they have grown fond of you and your family or they enjoy working for you – that's another matter. They must be marked on the ear, and then they stay your slave until they die. You must treat men and women alike in this matter.

God's Way Is for King and Citizens Alike   *Deuteronomy 17:14-20*

When you are settled in your homeland, you may want to follow the practice of surrounding peoples and have a monarchy instead of a tribal league. This is a perfectly proper kind of government. But no foreigner must ever be king; GOD will choose one of your fellow-countrymen and you must make him king. But when he's elected king, he must not try to ape foreign kings – no large cavalry divisions (why, he would have to send fellow-countrymen to Egypt to buy war-horses – Egypt indeed! – hasn't GOD forbidden his people ever to go back along that desert road?) – no harem (that will make him forget GOD all right), no vast personal wealth.

When he becomes king, he must make a copy in a scroll of all I am now telling you (he can write it out from the priest's copy), keep it by him and make a habit of studying it. He will learn there what worshipping GOD really means – obeying him and living in his Way. That will keep him from ever lording it over his fellow-countrymen, and help him to make his rule like GOD's rule. That will make his reign long and his dynasty secure.

Treat People as Persons   *Deuteronomy 22:1-4, 6-8*

You must always help your fellow-countrymen.

For example, if you come across his ox or sheep or goat straying, you musn't just pass by and do nothing about it. Take it back to him. If he lives a long way off – or you don't know whose it is – take the animal home with you and keep it until it is claimed; then let him have it back. It doesn't matter what it is that he has lost – his donkey, his overcoat, anything. You mustn't just pass by. If you ever find his donkey or ox lying in the road, don't go on as if it didn't concern you; give him a hand to get it on its feet again.

If you come across a bird's nest – either in a tree or on the ground – when you're out walking, and you notice eggs or young in the nest and the mother-bird sitting on them, you must leave the mother-bird alone. You can take the young birds, if you like; you must let the mother-bird go free. This, too, is something you must do, if you want to live long in your homeland.

Again, when you build a house, build a parapet round the flat roof. Somebody may one day go up on to the roof; if he falls over into the street to his death, that will then be his carelessness and not your fault. Your family cannot then be held responsible.

Generosity and Justice for Everybody   *Deuteronomy 24:6, 10-22*

You must not take a man's mill or even his mill-stone as security for debt. That is to take his very livelihood away from him.

When you lend anything to one of your neighbours, you must not force your way into his house to take something as security. Stand outside, and let the man himself bring his security out to you. If he is poor, you must not keep the cloak he gives you as security all night; give it back to him before sunset so that he may sleep in it – and feel grateful to you. That's what GOD thinks is the 'right' thing to do.

You are not to treat a poor hired servant brutally, and it doesn't matter whether he is a fellow-countryman or a resident-alien in your town. Pay him his wages promptly at the end of the day – and before sunset. Remember that he has little money and the day's wages mean everything to him. If you treat him wrongly, he will appeal to GOD and that will mark you down for what you are – a wicked man.

Capital punishment can be inflicted on a man only for a crime he himself has committed. You must execute the man himself – not his father or his son in his stead.

Don't exploit a resident-alien or a fatherless child and rob him of his legal rights; and you must never take the cloak of a widow as security for debt. You know what it feels like to be a slave – somebody who has no one to stand up for him. Don't forget Egypt and the way GOD rescued you. This lies behind all I am telling you to do.

And let your generosity be real down-to-earth generosity. For example: sometimes at harvest you overlook a sheaf of corn and leave it in the field. When you find out what you've done, don't go back for it. Some resident-alien or orphan or widow will find it a god-send. This is what GOD wants and he will bless you for it. Or again: when you shake the fruit off your olive-trees, don't shake the branches a second time. Let the resident-aliens, the orphans, the widows have the fruit that remains. And do the same when you clip the grapes off your vines; don't pick the branches twice – let the resident-aliens, the orphans, the widows have the grapes that remain. Remember what it was like to be an Egyptian slave.

Limits of Citizenship   *Deuteronomy 23:2-8*

Nobody whose mother is a foreigner can be admitted to GOD's assembly – nor any of his descendants for ten generations.

No Ammonites or Moabites can be admitted to GOD's assembly – nor any of their descendants for ten generations. The reason is this: on the march across the desert to Jordan River, you were in need of food and water; but these people, instead of helping you, hired a foreign prophet to bring a curse upon you. GOD, indeed, didn't listen to him but turned his curse into a blessing, because he cared for you. So you are never at any time to help them or do them good.

But you are not to despise the Edomites (they are your kinsmen) or the Egyptians (you once lived as resident-aliens in their country). The great-grandchildren of Edomites and Egyptians and their descendants can be admitted to GOD's assembly.

Thanking God   *Deuteronomy 16:16-17, 1-3, 7-15*

Three times each year you must meet – not anywhere but in the one place GOD has chosen – to thank him for his kindness to you: at the Pilgrim Festival of Cakes-made-without-yeast, at the Pilgrim Festival of Weeks, and at the Pilgrim Festival of Tents. You must not come to these festivals empty-handed; every man must give what he can, remembering how GOD has helped him. Treat April as a special month by celebrating Passover at the Pilgrim Festival of Cakes-made-without-yeast. For it was in April that GOD rescued you from Egypt. Offer as your 'Passover' sacrifice a lamb or a kid or a calf, and eat cakes made without yeast – iron rations that will remind you of the panic of that night of escape and will keep it in your mind as long as you live.

Count seven weeks from the time you began reaping the standing corn; that will give you the date for the Pilgrim Festival of Weeks to begin. Make your gift match GOD's kindness to you, and enjoy your worship of him. You must not come alone, but bring your children, slaves, the priests, foreigners, fatherless children and the widows of your town.

At harvest time, when you are cleaning your threshing-floors and wine-presses, meet again for a whole week to celebrate the Pilgrim Festival of Tents and thank GOD for blessing your farming and your business. Again, do not come alone, but bring your children, your slaves, the priests, foreigners, fatherless children and widows. You are to have a thoroughly happy time.

The Harvest Festival *Deuteronomy 26:1-2, 5-11*

When you've settled down in your homeland, take some of the produce of the first harvest of the year and carry it in a basket to the place GOD has chosen for his worship.

At the harvest festival you shall always make this statement of your faith: 'My ancestors were a small company of homeless nomads who entered Egypt and lived there as resident-aliens. We became a strong and large tribe. The Egyptians gave us a hard time and treated us brutally and forced us to work as slave labourers. We appealed to GOD, our ancestral God. He took note of us and saw what a brutal life we were forced to live as slaves. He rescued us with terrifying deeds of violent strength – with many signs and wonders – and led us here to this rich and fertile homeland of ours. Look! I bring the harvest of the soil which you, O GOD, have given me.'

Put down your basket in GOD's presence, and bow in reverence before him.

And then – because GOD has given you all these good things – enjoy yourselves, not alone by yourselves but with all your family and the priests and the resident-aliens who live in your neighbourhood.

A Final Word *Deuteronomy 30:11-14*

All these things I have told you to do are not beyond your powers or out of your reach. They are not, as it were, 'high up in the sky'; you can't say, 'Who can get up so high and tell us what they are all about and make them plain to us so that we can do something about them?' Nor are they, as it were, foreign laws from some country far beyond the sea; you can't say, 'Who can sail across the seas for us and translate them into our language and make them plain to us so that we can do something about them?' GOD's Way is right here within your reach – you can talk about it, understand it and walk in it.

Not the End
but the Beginning

9 July 586 was the Black Day of Israelite history. The historians describe what happened on that day and tell us a little about the twenty years that followed. Then silence. We do not come again on any contemporary historical records for more than 140 years. What was there to write down?

Many thought that the end had come – there was nothing left to live for. But there were others whose trust in God was deeper and for whom the words of men like Amos and Jeremiah (now written down in scrolls) began to take on a new meaning. For them the terrifying disaster of political extinction was not the end; it was rather a strange and unexpected beginning. They recovered their sense of God's presence, and began to look forward to new life in the old homeland.

Historians reckon that about 250,000 people were living in Palestine at the time of the fall of the city. Many escaped to Egypt and elsewhere; this was the beginning of the dispersion of the Jewish people throughout the world. Several thousands were deported to Babylon – probably much less than 10,000, a figure given in one of their later accounts. But it was among these few thousand that life was reborn.

The deportees in Babylon were allowed considerable freedom to live their own lives in their own community, to meet for worship and to carry on trade; and they kept in touch with their fellow-countrymen in Palestine.

Life for those who still lived in Jerusalem and its surrounding villages was pitiful. The city itself was in ruins; temple, buildings, city wall were a mass of rubble. A contemporary poem (from *Lamentations*) paints a vivid picture –

> City gates gone,
>   only rubble and broken bars;
>   king and government in exile,
>   everyone for himself;
>   no prophets any more,
>   no visions of GOD!

There were no priests and no temple. All the hopes of the Israelite people in GOD's purpose – that Palestine should be the land of his people – were destroyed.

People had no heart – and no resources – to start building again; the ruins were to lie there, little changed, for more than sixty years. They were merely a neglected part of the Babylonian empire, at the mercy of a hostile governor in Samaria.

In 538 a great upheaval took place in international affairs. The Babylonian empire collapsed; the Persian empire, under its remarkable leader, Cyrus, took its place. The rise of Cyrus to power brought new hope: was not GOD at work in this imperial upheaval? Was not this the signal for their return home?

This lively hope was the theme of the poems of 'The Prophet of the Exile' (see p. 272). So it happened, and a few thousand began the long trek home.

Those who returned home in 538, full of high hopes, soon faced disillusion. The immensity of the task that faced them – the sheer work of rebuilding houses and temple – overwhelmed them. Some twenty years went by before, fired by two prophets, they had vigour enough to rebuild the temple, but even this was a 'poverty-stricken affair'. They had, of course, already rebuilt many houses; but much of the city and its surrounding wall lay still in ruins.

It was some fifty years later – in 444 – that their first outstanding leader arose – Nehemiah, a high official at the Persian court. He spent two terms as governor (444 and 432). Some forty years later – in 398 – another Persian official, Ezra, was made 'Commissioner for Jewish Religious Affairs', and came, with royal authority, to complete Nehemiah's work. Nehemiah rebuilt the city; Ezra re-established the religious life of the people. Both kept diaries. Here is what they had to say.

Nehemiah (444-432 BCE)

News from Jerusalem
Nehemiah 1:1-4

I was a royal cupbearer and in December of the year 445 I was in the fortress in the city of Susa, the winter residence of the Persian emperor, when Hanani my brother and some of my fellow-countrymen arrived with news from Palestine. I asked them how people were faring there and what Jerusalem City was like.

'There's been a great disaster,' they told me, 'and the survivors are in trouble. The walls of the city have been levelled to the ground and the city gates burnt.'

I broke down and cried. I spent several days mourning and praying.

Emperor's Commissioner

It was now April. One day I took wine to the emperor (the empress was with him) and was offering it to him. I was feeling very unhappy. It was forbidden to show grief in the royal presence; but the emperor noticed something in my looks.

'You aren't ill, are you?' he asked. 'Why are you looking so depressed? You seem very upset these days.'

I felt afraid to tell him. But I spoke up.

'Long live Your Majesty!' I said. 'I can't help feeling upset. My family graves are in disrepair and my city's gates have been burned down.'

'Well, what do you want me to do for you?' he asked.

'If it pleases Your Majesty and Your Majesty thinks well of me,' I said, 'send me back to my own city where my ancestors are buried. Give me authority to rebuild it.'

'How long will you be away?' he asked. 'When will you get back?'

I told him and he was gracious enough to send me as governor of Jerusalem City.

'If Your Majesty pleases,' I said to him, 'give me your written authority to present to the governor of Beyond-Euphrates for any help I may need. And I shall need written authority to present to the Warden of the Royal Forest to bring timber for the rebuilding of the gates of the Temple Fortress and for my own Residence.'

The emperor gave me an escort of army officers and cavalry. My coming displeased Sanballat the governor of Samaria (he was in temporary charge of Jerusalem City) and a Persian official, an Ammonite called Tobiah. They didn't want anybody to come and take over the cause of the Israelites.

Inspection of the City
Nehemiah 2:11-20

So I came to the city.

For three days I stared at the devastation. On the third night, I got up. I told nobody about my plans. I ordered two or three men from my escort to come with me and I rode out on the only animal there was – my own. In the darkness I went out by the Valley Gate in the west to the Dragon Spring and the Dung Gate in the south which led me out to the refuse dump where once human sacrifices had been made. I inspected the ruins of the city walls and the burned gates from the outside, but at the Dung Gate I had to follow the eastern walls inside the city – the cliffs fell steeply into the Kidron Valley. I went on to the Fountain Gate and the King's Pool. Beyond this my animal could not get through. In the darkness I went down into the valley and looked up at the ruined walls. I went back by the way I'd come and entered the city again by the Valley Gate. And so home. The city officials had no idea what I'd been up to. I had said nothing to them or to the workmen who were to help me in rebuilding the city.

I now called them together.

'You see the devastation of the city,' I told them. 'Let us start the rebuilding of the walls.'

I made it quite clear to them that God had given me this work to do. They all agreed and began with a good heart.

Three men opposed us – the two I've mentioned and Geshem the Arab, the governor of Idumea, the old land of Edom to the east. They spread vicious rumours about us.

'What do you think you're up to?' they said. 'Starting a rebellion?'

'You've got nothing to do with this,' I told them. 'This is God's work; we are his servants. We're going on with the rebuilding.'

From an Old Labour Register   *Nehemiah 3:1-32*

A record was kept of the men who worked on the rebuilding and the work each did. Everybody took part from the High Priest himself to farmers from neighbouring villages – and the girls, the daughters of one of the city magistrates. Men from Jericho and Tekoa (though the gentry here at first resented taking orders as common workmen) and Mizpah and Gibeon came along. Magistrates worked alongside caretakers. Goldsmiths, perfumers and merchants gave a hand.

Most of the men were organised in gangs to rebuild the city gates or particular stretches of the city wall. But some men preferred to rebuild that part of the wall opposite their own houses.

Here is a list of the city gates that were rebuilt, beginning from the north and going round the city anti-clockwise: Sheep Gate, Fish Gate, Old Gate, Valley Gate, Dung Gate, Fountain Gate, The Angle, Water Gate, Horse Gate, East Gate, Muster Gate.

Trouble from Outside   *Nehemiah 4:6-23*

So we went on rebuilding the wall. We built the whole length of it but only to half its proper height. The people worked with a will.

The governor of Samaria, Sanballat, and Tobiah the Ammonite and representatives from Ammon and the Philistine city of Ashdod were in conference when news reached them that the city walls were actually being rebuilt and the great gaps in the wall closed. This made them bitterly angry. They put their heads together to plot a military attack on the city and throw us into confusion. But we prayed to God and posted a twenty-four-hour guard on the walls.

We had trouble with some of the workers. They went on strike. They were actually singing a strike song –

We can never, never
   build the wall –
   mountains, mountains of rubble,
   no strength left to shift it.

Our enemies were talking too.

'We'll steal secretly into the city,' they were saying, 'and catch them unawares. We'll have them dead and the work stopped in no time.'

Our countrymen living in enemy territory came to us again and again.

'They're calling up their men from all over the country,' they warned us.

So we doubled our guard. We stationed spearmen in the exposed open places behind the wall and called out the citizens with their swords, spears and bows.

'No panicking,' I said. 'Remember God's terrible power and fight for your fellow-citizens, your families and your homes!'

Our enemies soon discovered that their secret plot was public news and that their plans were now useless. Each of us could take up our work on the wall again.

But we didn't relax our guard. We worked in shifts, half of us working on the wall, half of us armed and standing guard. The leaders stood behind the countrymen who had come in to work on the wall. We saw to it as well that all the men carrying loads were armed – they worked with one hand and carried a sword in the other – and that the builders wore their swords like soldiers. The bugler stood beside me.

These were the orders of the day: 'We are scattered over the whole city, and we are far from one another on the wall. Rally at the sound of the bugle – it will be blown where fighting has broken out. Our God will fight for us.'

So we went on with the rebuilding. Half of us were armed from dawn till the stars came out.

The men from the villages used to come into the city each day and go home at night. This was becoming dangerous. So I issued further orders: men from the villages – and their servants – must spend the night in the city; they can carry on their work as usual in the daytime, but through the night they must help in guarding the walls.

None of us ever took our clothes off; we kept our weapons at the ready all the time.

Trouble in the City   *Nehemiah 5:1-13*

Then we had trouble between rich and poor – between wealthy citizens who had made their money in Babylon and brought it back with them and the peasants who had been left to carry on when the city fell. The poor peasants were full of angry protests.

'We are reduced to giving our children in pledge as slaves,' some said, 'just to buy corn to keep alive.'

'And we,' said others, 'we've got to mortgage our fields and vineyards and houses to get corn. There isn't enough food – that's the trouble.'

'And we've had to borrow money to pay the royal taxes,' said others.

The burden of their complaint was that there was no real sharing.

'We're as hungry as they are,' they said. 'Our children are no different from theirs! Yet we have to sell our children as slaves – some of our girls are slaves already. And we can't do anything about it – these tycoons have taken our land.'

This made me very angry.

I thought the matter over, and then charged them, at a public meeting, with taking interest from their fellow citizens.

'We've done what we could to bring you back from foreign slavery,' I told them, 'and now we're going into the slave trade ourselves!'

There was dead silence. They hadn't anything to say.

'It's a dreadful thing you're going,' I went on. 'Doesn't our religion mean anything to you? Are you going to make us the laughing-stock of the world? I myself have been lending money and corn to these needy people. Drop this business of taking persons as pledges for debt. Give them back their land you've taken and pay them back the interest you've been charging.'

'We'll give them back whatever we've taken from them,' they said at last. 'We'll do what you say – we'll charge no interest.'

I called the priests and made the men swear an oath to do what they had promised. I shook my cloak as though I had been carrying something in it and was emptying it on the ground.

'May God throw you away – just like that,' I said, 'if you go back on any of your promises!'

They did as I ordered.

My Own Practice

Nehemiah 5:14-19

I have just mentioned my own practice. Let me say something about it.

There had been governors before me. All of them had taxed the people heavily in money and kind. Minor officials had been petty tyrants. My religion meant something to me and I never did that sort of thing. I bought no land while I was governor – I had enough to do with the building of the wall. I actually used my own servants only for work on the wall.

Besides this, a hundred and fifty people shared my table – common people and officials as well as refugees from abroad. Every day we had to find oxen, sheep, fowls, skins of wine – and I could afford to do this. But I refused to take the official allowance – my people were suffering too much.

Remember, O my God, what I've tried to do for these people!

Trouble Again

Nehemiah 6:1-19

The wall was now finished. All the places where it had been breached had been dealt with. Only the doors of the gateways had not been set up.

News of all this reached our enemies.

Sanballat and Geshem tried to draw me into a trap.

'Meet us for peace talks,' was their first message. 'We suggest Kephirah village in the Ono plain on the road to Joppa.'

I saw through their cunning.

'I have important work to do,' I replied. 'I can't go down to the plain. Why should the work stop just to meet you?'

Four times they pressed me to meet them there; four times I said No.

They tried another trick.

Sanballat sent one of his officers with an open letter: 'There are rumours in the surrounding countries (Geshem confirms this) that you and the citizens of Jerusalem are plotting rebellion. That's why you are rebuilding the city walls. Rumour has it that you intend to proclaim yourself king, and that prophets are proclaiming it openly on your streets. You know rumours like this get round to the emperor. Be sensible and let us talk it all over.'

'There are no such rumours,' I replied. 'You've invented them.'

They were only trying to scare me. I just worked all the harder. But Sanballat tried to trap me again.

'We had a man called Shemaiah, a false prophet with contacts abroad, detained in house-arrest. I went to his house one day.

'Let us meet in the temple,' he said, 'and have the doors shut. Men have been sent to assassinate you, and they'll do it under cover of darkness.'

'Should such a man as I run away?' I said. 'Would any man in my place go into the temple just to save his life? I stay where I am.'

It was clear he had been bribed by Tobiah and Sanballat; God had not sent him to me. They had hired him to try and frighten me and bring me into bad odour with the people and hold me up to ridicule.

Remember Tobiah and Sanballat, O my God, and all their deeds – and Noadiah the prophetess and the other prophets who wanted to frighten me from doing my duty.

So in October 444 – in fifty-two days – the city wall was finished. It was reported to our enemies in Samaria. News about what we had done spread, too, throughout the surrounding countries. There, people didn't think much of the citizens of Samaria – they had lost much of the reputation they once had – but they respected our religious convictions.

Quite a number of the Jewish nobles in the city were bound in loyalty to Tobiah the Ammonite who had married into the family of one of the 'Founding Fathers', those who had come back to Palestine a hundred years before. (His son also had married the daughter of one of the builders of the wall.) Letters passed between these nobles and Tobiah. All I did was reported to him and the nobles spoke well of him to me. He wrote to me, but all he was concerned with was scaring me off the work I was doing.

Dedication of the Walls　　　　　*Nehemiah 7:1-5; 11:1-2; 12:27-43*

The walls had now been built, the city gates finished and regular gate-keepers appointed.

I now handed over the control of the city to my brother Hanani and to Captain Hananiah, the governor of the Fortress – a man whose loyalty to God could be trusted more than that of many others.

The city covered a large area and the citizens were too few to defend it properly; houses for the people had yet to be built. So I gave special instructions about the city's safety: the city gates were not to be left open during the heat of the day when the guards were taking their

185

siesta; they must be kept shut and barred. Each citizen was to be held responsible for sentry-duty or for guarding that part of the wall opposite his own house.

I called a full conference of officials and people. They decided that for the present only one in ten of the citizens should come to live in the city; the rest must still stay in the villages round about. All the leaders, of course, had to live in the city. The others to live in the city were chosen by lots or were volunteers. The volunteers were cheered by the people.

Then we held a great procession to dedicate the city walls. We divided ourselves into two great companies – one went southwards round the walls and the other northward. We started and finished in the temple. We sang and offered sacrifices – a very happy company, men and women and boys and girls. The joy of the city was public news in the surrounding countries.

Religious Reform (432)   *Nehemiah 13:4-31*

Twelve years went by. Eliashib, the High Priest, was now a very old man. He was related by marriage to Tobiah the Ammonite and let him live in the disused tithe-room in the temple.

I was not in the city at the time. In the year 434 I went back to report to the emperor. I stayed there some time and then asked the emperor's permission to visit Jerusalem again.

I discovered Tobiah living in the tithe-room. I was very angry and pitched all his furniture out in the street. I re-established the tithe-system and rededicated the tithe-room to its proper use.

The whole organisation of the temple had collapsed. The temple caretakers (whose wages were paid from the tithes) had had to earn their own living by farm work. I put all this right.

Remember me, O my God, and this work I did – don't let my work for you be forgotten.

I next tackled the question of the Sabbath. I found that the Sabbath was not being kept. Farmers were treading wine-presses; loading grain on donkeys and driving them into the city; and the markets were open – all on the Sabbath. Tyrian merchants were bringing fish and all kinds of wares into the city and selling them – all on the Sabbath. I warned the people and argued with the leaders.

I put this right. The city gates were to be closed at sunset on Friday night, the beginning of the Sabbath; they were to remain shut until the Sabbath was over. I stationed my own officers at the gates to see that there was no traffic through them while the Sabbath lasted. The merchants started lodging just under the walls outside the city. I threatened to arrest them if they stayed there. That settled that.

Remember this work of mine, O my God, and have mercy on me according to the greatness of your steadfast love.

There was a third matter to put right.

I noticed how many mixed marriages there were. When the exiles first came back, there were very few Jewish girls; so even Jewish priests had married girls from Ashdod, the Philistine city, and from Ammon and Moab. The children spoke the Ashdod or Ammonite or Moabite language – they hadn't even learned to speak Hebrew. I condemned all this – and even lost my temper with them, man-handling some of them.

'No more mixed marriages,' I ordered. 'It doesn't matter what you have to say – marrying foreign women is disloyalty to God.'

I was having no more quislings in the city. I deported the grandson of Eliashib the High Priest – he had married Sanballat's daughter.

Remember them, O my God, to their shame.

So I got rid of every foreign influence in the city.

Remember this, O my God, to my credit.

Ezra (398 BCE)

Royal Commissioner   *Ezra 7:1-9*

Artaxerxes II, the Persian emperor, appointed Ezra the priest Commissioner for Religious Affairs for all the Jewish people.

In the year 397, Ezra with other leading Jews, paid a visit to Jerusalem City – the journey took him five months. On the way, he stayed in Ctesiphon, on the Tigris River, and met the Jewish community there.

Renewing the Covenant   *Ezra 8:32-36; Nehemiah 7:73; 8:1-18*

We reached Jerusalem, and three days after I arrived I inspected the temple. I was given an account of the enormous wealth the returned exiles had brought back and handed over.

The people gathered in a packed crowd in the Water Gate Square. They asked me to get the scroll of the Law from the temple to read it to them.

I stood on a wooden pulpit (made specially for this occasion) well above the crowd, and when I began to read the whole crowd stood. I read from the scroll, facing the Water Gate Square, from early morning till noon. The crowd listened quietly.

Officials, who stood by me on my right and on my left, helped the people to follow what I was reading, summarising and explaining it, passage by passage.

The people wept when they understood what the Law said.

'No weeping or mourning,' I said. 'This is a day holy to GOD. Go home and have a good meal – don't forget to share it with those who are starving. Remember, GOD's joy is in your strength.'

The people went home in great happiness.

Next day, the heads of families and temple officials met with me to study the scroll in detail. We found the regulations about the Festival of Tents which ought to be celebrated just at this time of the year. We decided to hold the Festival together. The people went out into the countryside and cut down leafy branches to make tents. These they set up on their flat roofs, in their courtyards, in the temple courts and in the Water Gate Square and the Ephraim Gate Square.

Each day of the Festival – it lasted a week – I read to them the scroll of the Law. On the eighth day we held a great religious service, just as the scroll set it out.

Mixed Marriages   *Ezra 9:1-5; 10:1-4, 7-17*

It was then reported to me that mixed marriages were still taking place. I was appalled at this news and spent the day in confession and prayer.

A great crowd gathered outside the temple.

Then Shecaniah – who himself had married a foreign girl – spoke to me.

'We have broken faith with God,' he said. 'But we can put it right. Let us make a covenant with God to divorce our foreign wives. This is your task, and we will stand by you in this.'

So they all took an oath.

A proclamation was issued calling a great assembly in the city; anyone not coming within three days would have his property forfeited and himself excommunicated.

The crowd gathered in the open square before the temple. They were rather nervous, both because of the reason for the meeting and because it was raining heavily.

I addressed the crowd and told them what we had decided about mixed marriages.

'We agree with you!' the crowd shouted. 'We must do as you say. But we can't go on standing here in the open. We are a large crowd and it's raining heavily. Nor can we settle this matter in a day or two. Let it be dealt with, on our behalf, by our officials.'

It took three months to clear it all up.

The Story in Worship

The story has now been told. What did it mean to the Israelite people?

The very stories we have been reading tell us something; they were selected by their historians, as we have said, to bring home to those who heard them read in the synagogue the truths they had learned. But a people's deepest convictions are seen most clearly in their songs and poetry and hymns; here we can 'read their hearts'. The hymns of the Israelite people are gathered together in *The Psalms*.

The Book of Psalms, as we find it now in the Old Testament, is 'The Hymnbook of the Second Temple', the temple that was rebuilt when the exiles returned to their homeland. But like all church hymnbooks, it had a long history behind it and it contained hymns both old and new.

The building of the great temple in Jerusalem in King Solomon's time made a great difference to the people's worship. Village worship went on in the old hill-top shrines. But in the temple, king and religious leaders made their influence felt, and poet and musician developed a deeper and richer form of worship. Here the great national religious festivals were held; here the king was crowned at the New Year Festival; here were sung their joys and sorrows, their fears and hopes, their praise and penitence as 'GOD's People'. The heart of their worship was what GOD had done for them, and through them, for the world.

The hymns sung in the first temple were gathered together in what might be called 'The Prayer Book of Solomon's Temple'. As time went on, before and after the Exile, other collections of hymns were made. At last, all these were gathered together in 'The Hymnbook of the Second Temple', *The Psalms*.

There were different kinds of hymns.* Most of them were hymns for Congregation and Choir – praise to God as Lord of History and Lord of Nature, New Year hymns and hymns for the king's coronation, national laments (for dark days of national danger) and national thanksgiving (for times of deliverance). Some of the hymns were for individuals – hymns of lament for those who were sick and in trouble, hymns expressing individual joy and thanksgiving. At their most important festival, the New Year Festival ('the Festival of Tents'), held in late September or early October, they celebrated their national story – how GOD rescued them from Egypt and made them his People.

---

* In indicating the different types of psalms and the way some of them have been sung in worship I have followed Elmer A. Leslie, *The Psalms*.

190

Some of the hymns that follow here were sung in Solomon's temple; others were written and sung after the Exile in the rebuilt temple. They all celebrate the story we have been reading – a story not just to be recited but a story to be sung. Here are real hymns. Here are real convictions, with their greatness and their littleness, their high vision (which has inspired all later generations) and their inhibiting bitterness (when their suffering robbed them of their generosity and dimmed their sense of humanity). They hide little.

GOD – Lord of History

Psalm 105

Thank GOD and call upon him,
    tell the whole world what he has done;
sing to GOD, sing his praise,
    remember his wonderful deeds!

When our ancestors were few in number,
    mere strangers in the land,
trekking from country to country,
    from people to people,
he guarded them from tyrants,
    rebuking kings.

When famine broke out in the land
    and their livelihood was lost,
he sent a man ahead of them,
    Joseph, sold as a slave.

His feet were hurt by fetters,
    his neck clamped with an iron collar –
until GOD's word came true,
    GOD's promise was made good!

Pharaoh ordered his release,
    the people's ruler set him free,
made him master of the palace,
    governor of his dominions,
giving courtiers their orders,
    teaching royal advisers wisdom!

GOD made his people grow
    in numbers and in strength;
the Egyptians hated them
    and deceived them.

He sent Moses and Aaron,
    his chosen servants;
showing his signs and wonders
    in the land of Egypt.

He turned day into deep darkness
    but they ignored his commands;
he turned their rivers to blood
    and killed their fish.

Frogs swarmed over the country,
    even into the royal palace;
at his word, flies and gnats
    covered the countryside.

He turned their rain to hail,
    lightning flashed
blighting vine and fig-tree,
    splintering the trees.

He sent locusts,
    innumerable locusts,
eating the greenness,
    the fruits of the fields.

He struck their eldest sons,
    the flower of their youth.

He led his people out
    laden with silver and gold,
    marching, not stumbling;
the panic-stricken Egyptians
    were glad to see them go.
He screened them with a cloud by day
    and lit the night with fire.

When they were hungry
    he gave them quails and manna;
water gushed out of the struck rock,
    a river in the desert.

He remembered his promise
    to his servant Abraham –
he led his people out
    singing victory songs.

He gave them a homeland
    aliens had worked for –
that they might obey him
    and live in his Way.

Psalm 114

O praise GOD!

When God's People escaped from Egypt
    and its barbarous speech,
the South became GOD's home,
    the North his country.

The sea stared and fled,
    Jordan River flowed back,
the mountains skipped like rams,
    the hills like lambs.

What made you flee, O Sea?
    What turned you back, O Jordan?
Why skip like rams, you mountains?
    and like lambs, you hills?

Dance, O Earth, in GOD's presence,
    in the presence of our God –
he turned rocks into clear water,
    granite into living spring!

Songs of the New Year

Psalm 2 *(A Coronation Hymn)*

Choir   Why is the world in a welter,
              foreigners in futile ferment?
            Kings stand on guard,
              rulers are rebels
                against GOD and his King –
            'Shake off their shackles!' they shout.
            'Throw away their chains!'

            GOD laughs from the sky,
              holds them in scorn,
            speaks in anger,
              terrifying them with his fury.

King   'I have crowned my King
              on my Holy Mountain!'
                GOD said to me.
            'You are my son,
              I have made you my son today!
            Ask, and I will give you the world
              as your inheritance,
            the whole world
              as your empire –
            you shall smash them with iron clubs,
              shatter them like a clay pot!'

Choir   Take care, you kings!
              Learn your lesson, you governors!
            Submit to GOD as loyal subjects,
              reverence the king's authority –
            or you will lose your way
              in GOD's sudden anger!

            Happy are they
              who find GOD their fortress!

Psalm 72 *(A Coronation Hymn)*

Help the king, O GOD, to rule as you do
    and to live in your Way,
dealing with your people as you deal with them,
    seeing the poor get justice.
So shall the mountains be dressed with peace
    and the hills with justice
    as with the greenness of spring.

May he stand by the helpless,
    rescue the poor,
        crush their oppressors!

May he live for ever
    like the sun and the moon!
May he be like rain falling on fields,
    like showers watering the earth!
May enduring justice and lasting peace
    flourish under him
        till the moon is no more!

May he rule from sea to sea
    from the Euphrates to the world's end.
May his enemies pay him homage,
    his foes meet defeat.
From the western lands of the Great Sea
    to Arabia and Egypt,
kings shall pay him tribute-money
    and bring him gifts.
All kings shall do him homage,
    all nations be his servants!

For he shall rescue the poor from the rich,
    sufferers who have none to help,
looking on them with pity
    and saving their lives,
        guarding them from violence.
The lives of common people
    are precious to him.

So the poor man shall share his country's wealth,
   praying for the king,
      blessing him every day.

There will be abundant harvests
   waving on even the hill-tops,
corn like Lebanon Forest,
   sheaves as common as grass!

May his fame last for ever –
   as long as the sun in the sky!
May the whole world
   speak his name as a blessing!

Psalm 124

If GOD had not been on our side –
   let GOD's People say –
If GOD had not been on our side
   when armies attacked us,
they would have swallowed us alive
   in the flood of their fury:
waters would have swept us away,
   torrents overwhelmed us,
   raging rivers drowned us!

Praise GOD
   who never gave us up
   to their wild hunger.
We have escaped
   like a bird from a farmer's trap.
The trap is broken!
   We have escaped!

Our help is in GOD
   who made earth and sky!

Psalm 132 *(A Coronation Hymn)*

Congregation Remember King David, O GOD,
      and the hard times he went through,
his vow to you,
      the God of his people:
'I will not go home
      or go to bed,
I will not sleep
      or take my rest,
until I find a home for GOD,
      a home for my people's God.'

Choir We heard of the Ark in Bethlehem,
      we found it in Kiriath-jearim.
Let us bring it to its true home,
      let us worship GOD!

Congregation O GOD, come home,
      you and your Ark!
Let the priests live in your Way,
      let your people shout for joy!
For your servant David's sake
      do not reject your anointed king!

The official GOD made a vow to David
Prophets   and he will faithfully keep it:
addressing 'From your descendants I will raise
the King   kings on your throne.
If they keep my Covenant
      and walk in my Way,
their descendants, too, for ever
      shall sit on your throne.'

GOD has chosen this mountain
      for his home:
'This is my home for ever,
      my desire is to live here.

'I will bless her destitute people,
      I will satisfy her hungry with bread,

I will clothe her priests with true religion –
   her citizens shout for joy.

'I will give David's dynasty new strength,
   giving my anointed king a burning lamp,
humiliating his enemies,
   making his crown sparkle on his head!'

National Lament

Psalm 74

Why have you abandoned us, O God?
   Is it for ever?
Why does your anger smoke
   over the flock in your fields?
Remember your people –
   the people you established long ago!
Remember your Holy Mountain,
   your home!
Come – rebuild the untouched ruins,
   the temple wrecked by the enemy!
It's your enemies who have stampeded
   and run riot in your temple,
hacking wood and swinging axes
   like timbermen in the forests,
ripping the panels out,
   smashing them
   with hatchets and hammers,
firing the buildings,
   desecrating your home –
'We'll smash it all!
   We'll burn all God's temples down!'

No sign! No prophet!
   Nobody to tell us how long!
How long, O God, will the enemy scoff?
   Will he curse your name for ever?
Why do you hold back,
   why hide your hand?

Yet you are our king from of old,
    conqueror of the earth.
Your power split the sea-monster
    and broke the heads of the sea-serpent;
you crushed the sea-dragon,
    fed him as food for sharks!

You struck open springs and torrents,
    dried up the unfailing waters
        to make dry land appear!

Yours is the day, yours the night,
    you made the moon and the sun,
you fixed the regions of the earth,
    you planned winter and summer!

Remember this, O GOD! –
    it's you the enemy slanders,
    your name pagan soldiers insult!
Do not surrender us who acknowledge you,
    do not forever forget your suffering people!
Look at the men you have made –
    they have corrupted the earth,
    turned it into fields of violence!

Don't let the oppressed be humiliated!
    Let the poor and needy praise you!
Arise, O God, and take your stand,
    remember the insults of brutal men!
Don't forget your enemies' threats –
    their rage rising to a roar!

Psalm 77

I shout to God for help,
    I shout to God to listen to me.
I seek him in the day of my distress,
    stretching out my hands to him.
Through the night I cannot stop weeping,
    I can find no peace of mind.

I groan at the very thought of God,
   my mind dark with questions.
I shut my eyes
   lying dazed and speechless.

I remember the story of my people,
   the years of long ago,
thinking – thinking – in the darkness,
   questioning and searching:
Will GOD ignore us for ever,
   forever be against us?
Has his love utterly gone?
   Do his promises no longer stand?
Has he forgotten what kindness means?
   Has his sternness silenced his compassion?
'Has his hand lost its grip,' I say to myself,
   'hanging limp at his side?'

I will recall what GOD has done,
   his great deeds of long ago;
I will think quietly and deeply
   about what he has really done.
Your Way, O God, is the good Way –
   what other god is like you?
You act – you do not just talk –
   everybody can see your strength;
you rescue your people
   with your power.

The waters saw you, O God,
   the waters saw you and writhed,
      the deeps were in storm.

Clouds poured the rain down,
   thunder rolled across the sky,
      the lightning flashed everywhere.

The crash of your thunder was like chariot wheels,
   your lightning lit the world,
      the earth quaked.

The sea was your highway,
  the oceans your pathway,
    your footprints unseen.

You led your people like a shepherd
  by the hand of Moses and Aaron.

Psalm 83

This is no time for peace, O God,
  for 'silence' and 'stillness'.
Look – your enemies are crowding in,
  those who hate you are on the march,
with crafty plots like conspirators,
  against your people, your treasure –
'Come, let us wipe them out as a nation
  from the memory of man!'
They come as one man,
  sworn enemies of yours –
Arab tribes from the east,
  Tyrians and Philistines from the west.

Treat them as you treated Sisera
  at the Kishon River;
destroy them as you destroyed the Midianites
  at Harod Well.
Scatter them like a dust-storm,
  like chaff in the wind,
like a forest fire
  in the blazing mountains!
Hunt them with your whirlwind,
  terrify them with your hurricane!
Fill their faces with shame,
  till they confess your greatness, O GOD.
May they forever be shamed and dismayed,
  destroyed and disgraced!

Let them know that you alone
  rule as GOD
    over the whole world!

Psalm 129

'All my life I have been bitterly persecuted,' –
  let GOD's people say –
'All my life I have been bitterly persecuted,
  but never beaten.
They have driven me like a beast of burden,
  ploughing their own long furrows;
but GOD cut the pagan harness off
  and set us free!'

May all who hate GOD's people
  be shamed and defeated!
May they be like grass growing on the roofs
  scorched by the hot east wind,
grass no harvester bothers with,
  no binder can use,
like people nobody greets
  as they pass in the streets!

Psalm 137

By Babylonian rivers
  we sat down in tears
remembering Jerusalem,
  hanging our harps on the poplars.

Our captors called for a song,
  our plunderers for a tune! –
  'Sing us one of your Jerusalem songs!'
How can we sing GOD's song
  on alien soil?

If I forget you, O Jerusalem,
  let my right hand hang helpless!
Let my tongue stick in my mouth
  if I stop remembering you,
if I don't think more of you
  than anything else in the world!

Don't forget the Edomites, O GOD,
   their 'Day of Jerusalem',
the attack and the shouting – 'Down with it,
   Down with it to the ground!'

And you, O Babylon, Babylon the Destroyer! –
   he'll be a happy man who treats you
   as you have treated us!
Happy if he seizes your children
   and dashes their heads on the rock!

Individual Thanksgiving

Psalm 66

Choir   O wide, wide world!
   Raise a shout of joy to God,
   sing the honour of his name,
   speak the glory of his praise!
Make this your theme –
   'How awe-inspiring your deeds, O God!
   Your enemies cringe
   before your greatness and your strength!
Let the whole earth worship you,
   sing to you,
   praise your name!'

Come and see what God has done,
   his awe-inspiring deeds among us!
He turned the sea into dry land,
   his people crossed the sea on foot!

Listen! Let us rejoice in him
   who rules in strength for ever,
keeping watch over the world –
   no rebel can rise against him.

O peoples, bless our God,
  make his praise heard near and far –
he has given us life,
  kept us from slipping.

You tested us, O God,
  you refined us as silver is refined;
you led us into the siege –
  our backs broken with their burdens,
  men riding rough-shod over us.
We went through fire and water,
  but you led us into freedom.

Individual   I offer my sacrifice in your temple
worshipper   to honour my vows,
vows my lips uttered,
  my mouth spoke, when I was hard-pressed.

Come, listen, all you who worship God,
  I will tell you what he has done for me!
I cried out to him for help,
  sang his high praise.

I had said to myself,
  'God won't bother with me!'
But that's just what he did,
  he listened to my voice!

Blessed be God –
  who didn't ignore my prayer,
  who didn't stop loving me!

Psalm 107

Priest   Thank GOD for his goodness!
Congregation   His steadfast love endures for ever!

Priest   Let those GOD rescued make it plain –
  those he rescued from oppression

and brought back from foreign lands,
   from the east and from the west,
   from the north and from the south!

Pilgrims come forward
  Choir   Some got lost in the desert wastes,
    looking in vain for a city home.
Hungry and thirsty
    they lost all hope.
They shouted to GOD for help
    and he rescued them,
leading them along the right road
    to their city home.
      Let them thank GOD for his steadfast love
        and the wonderful help he gives to them,
      quenching their thirst,
        satisfying their hunger with good food!

Former prisoners come forward
  Choir   Some were living fettered
    in the pitch-darkness of a prison cell.
They had not listened to what God had to say
    and they refused to walk his Way.
They were utterly miserable,
    there was no lifting hand when they stumbled.
Then they shouted to GOD for help,
    and he rescued them,
leading them out of their prison darkness
    and breaking their fetters.
      Let them thank GOD for his steadfast love
        and the wonderful help he gives to them.
      He shattered prison gates, though made of bronze
        and prison bars, though made of iron!

Sailors come forward
  Choir   Some went down to the sea in ships,
    trafficking on the great oceans.
They watched what GOD can do,
    the wonder of his way in great waters.

At his word, the storm broke,
  whipping up the waves.
Lifted to the sky,
  plunged to the deeps,
they staggered like drunken men,
  sailors though they were.
They shouted to GOD for help
  and he rescued them.
The storm died down
  and the sea was still;
they were glad to be on calm water again,
  sailing safely into port.
    Let them thank GOD for his steadfast love
      and the wonderful help he gives to them.
    Let them speak GOD's praise
      in the public assemblies of the people
      where the elders sit.

Making Sense of the Story

Introduction

The story of this small highland people has now been told: we have listened to what they have had to say, in their own records, about their rise and fall; and we have seen something of the vision that helped them to survive the loss of their political independence.

We come now to the inescapable question – as inescapable for us as for them: 'How can anybody make sense of such a brutal story?' 'What kind of world is it in which this sort of thing can happen?' 'Was the vision of Moses and David merely an idle dream?' We have now to see what kind of answers they gave to questions like these.

The Israelite people took what we call 'politics' and 'economics' and 'social questions' quite seriously. But the answers to the questions they were asking were not to be found there; they went deeper. Rightly or wrongly, they found them in their 'religious' experience.

But what is 'religion' about? And what do you mean by 'religious experience'? It was Nels Ferré who wrote: 'Religion is facing reality. Religious thinking is deciding what reality is all about and how to deal with it.'*

If religion is 'facing reality', it cannot be just one specialised activity among a lot of other specialised activities; it can only be the way we live the whole of our lives.

This is the truth that the Israelite people – or the best minds among them – had been slowly learning from the day when they escaped from Egypt to the time when, their cities in ruins and their political independence destroyed, they faced their darkest hour and lived through it. That is why, in the long run, the popular religions they encountered in Palestine held no enduring meaning for them. They had outgrown them.

Those who saw this clearly were the 'great prophets', of whom Amos was the first to appear. So we come now to listen to three of them: Amos himself who spoke as the storm clouds were gathering on the northern horizon; Jeremiah who was caught up in the siege and fall of Jerusalem itself; and the unknown prophet who was one of the exiles in Babylon.

These prophets stood above the panic of their contemporaries. They looked the real world in the face and refused to be intimidated by what must have seemed to others overwhelming human disaster. But they did

---

* Nels N. F. Ferré, *Making Religion Real*, p. 12.

not come suddenly 'out of the blue'. There was a long story behind them.

For a thousand years at least there had been people in the Middle East who were known as 'prophets'. The word 'prophet' itself probably means 'spokesman'. 'Prophets' spoke on behalf of the god – or gods – their people worshipped; they announced the god's will. We have, for example, an account of a prophet who spoke to his king in the name of his god as far back as 1700 BCE in the city of Mari on the River Euphrates. From the time of the Philistine attack on the highlands, we meet them in the story of the Israelites themselves.

Earlier prophets were very different from people like Amos. Most of them lived in groups and were associated with local shrines and temples as officials. They spoke in excited speech, and they stimulated this frenzy and excitement with music. There were groups of 'royal prophets' who advised the kings and announced God's will to them (see the stories on pp. 30, 219).

There were, however, others who belonged to no such group but lived independent lives. These 'independent prophets' were the real predecessors of people like Amos. We shall begin this part of our book with the stories of two of them, Elijah and Micaiah, to show what kind of people these earlier 'prophets' were.

The great prophets themselves were not eager to be called 'prophets'; and they would have nothing to do with the 'official prophets'. They had a new and original approach; they looked beyond their own nation to the world of nations, and they spoke out of their own intimate experience of God with a freshness and directness which we have not met before – and which moves us still.

As we read their poems we must note and remember three things.

First, they begin with their own personal experience of God: 'GOD spoke to me.' They believed they were 'called' by God to speak to his people in his name; some of them have left accounts of their 'call'. This experience had a compelling quality – they dared not say No. They chose to face death itself rather than keep quiet. This compelling experience came out of their everyday life as farmers or villagers or city dwellers. The convictions to which it led did not come easily; they had to think hard and live dangerously to get them clear. They claimed no authority for their experience except the reality of the experience itself; they believed what they had to say ought to be clear in everybody's conscience.

Secondly, when they spoke about events in their own country or in neighbouring countries, they knew what they were talking about. They took the trouble to find out what was happening, probably through the merchants and travellers they met in market or temple. As far as they could, they 'got their facts right'. They were dealing with the real world.

Thirdly, they found their clue to the meaning of their total experience (their experience of God and their experience of the world as they knew it) in the religious traditions of their people – the story of the escape from Egypt and the Covenant on the Holy Mountain – about which they had thought long and deeply. They worked out the convictions of Moses afresh in the light of the new world in which they and their compatriots found themselves.

They had no use for mere 'nationalism' or the 'national religions' either of their own people or of other countries. Their eyes were on the whole world. They judged their own people and foreign peoples by the same standards. The God in whose presence they stood was the God of the whole universe. They had no interest in religion as 'social custom'; they wanted to know the truth about the human situation in which they all stood. They spoke to people face to face – on the street, in the Temple court. They took their lives in their hands.

There is one other thing to remember. The great prophets were poets; what they had to say must be read as poetry. They were seeing the whole world in the light of their experience of God and in the light of the religious traditions of their people. They were making their 'vision' clear – what they had heard and what they had seen; they were calling their people to 'listen' and 'look'. Poetry was their natural language; they wanted to change people's hearts as well as their minds, get them to feel and think and live in a new way, God's Way. Their charge against their people – and the world – was that they would not 'look' and they would not 'listen'.

As we read, we must put ourselves in their place to listen with their ears and look with their eyes, and try to see the world we live in as they saw the world they lived in.

Two Ninth-century Prophets

Elijah (850 BCE)

Elijah comes suddenly into the story, like a thunderbolt, out of the eastern desert – a bold and unforgettable figure. He was an independent prophet, though he had some connections with the prophetic groups of his time. His name came, in later centuries, to represent the whole prophetic movement.

We see him, in gaunt outline, through the mists of the popular stories told about him, with their love of miracle and marvel. But his greatness shines through the stories – his passionate loyalty to GOD alone and his fearlessness in denouncing a king's crime to his face.

He was concerned with a very vital issue: there could be no toleration of any worship other than the worship of GOD among his own people. A treaty had been made between Tyre and the North, and in this alliance the North was very much the weaker partner. Under its provisions King Ahab had married a Phoenician princess; she was a dominating woman as well as a princess of a great and famous country, and she was determined to introduce the worship of her own god, Baal, into the country of her adoption.

King Ahab himself seems to have been a sincere worshipper of GOD; he gave his son the name 'Ahaziah', 'GOD holds me'. His marriage treaty with Jezebel would include, however, her right to have a temple of her own in the capital city; she wanted more than this.

Elijah was concerned to see that no Baal worship was established in the North where GOD alone should be worshipped. The stories of the great drought and of the incident on Carmel Mountain make this issue clear. He was also concerned with the laws of his people, which were laws for king and commoner alike. Kings, thought Jezebel, could do what they liked, as they did in her own country. 'Not so,' said Elijah, 'GOD's law rules here – for everybody.' This is the issue in the story of Naboth's vineyard. That Elijah was concerned to see that the traditions of Moses were maintained is shown in the story of his visit to 'GOD's Mountain'.

The Drought   *1 Kings 17:1-10; 18:1-2a*

Elijah, whose home was in the wild country of Gilead, east of Jordan River, sought an audience with King Ahab.

'As GOD lives, whose servant I am,' he told him, 'there will be drought here for two whole years – no rainy season in the winter, no dew in the summer – unless I say so.'

And he went out of the presence of the king.

GOD spoke to him again.

'Go east,' he said. 'Hide in the Cherith Valley, east of Jordan River. You'll find water in the stream to drink; ravens will bring you food.'

He went to the Cherith Valley. Ravens brought him bread in the morning and meat in the evening; and he drank from the stream. After some time, the stream in the valley dried up; the great drought had come.

GOD spoke to Elijah again.

'Get up and go north to Sidonian territory. A widow there will look after you.'

He got up and went north.

Nearly two years passed by. One day, GOD spoke to Elijah.

'Go and seek an audience with King Ahab,' he told him. 'I am going to end this drought with a storm.'

Elijah set off to meet the king.

'You Trouble-maker!' 1 Kings 18:2b-20

Now the drought was very severe in Samaria, the capital city.

Ahab's Chief Minister was a good man called Obadiah, loyal to the true worship of GOD. In the persecution of GOD's prophets which Queen Jezebel had ruthlessly carried out, he had hidden two hundred of them, in groups of five, in the hilly limestone country where there were many caves, and sent them bread and water.

The king summoned Obadiah.

'Let us survey the land,' he said, 'and examine all the streams and valleys to see if there is any green grass still growing. We don't want to lose our war-horses and mules if there is any chance of saving them; and we don't want to lose the cattle either.'

They divided the country between them, the king going in one direction, Obadiah in the other.

Obadiah was out in the open country when, suddenly, he found himself face to face with Elijah. He knew at once who he was and fell on the ground in reverence before him.

'Is it you, my lord Elijah?' he said.

'Yes, it is,' said Elijah. 'Go to your master the king. Tell him I am here.'

'What wrong have I done?' asked Obadiah. 'Why do you want me to risk my life like this? The king's been looking for you everywhere. When anyone tells him, "Elijah's not here" he makes him swear an oath on pain of death that he is telling the truth. And now you command me to tell the king you're here – just like that! I know what will happen. When I'm gone, GOD's spirit will whisk you away. I shall tell the king you're here; he'll come – and you'll have gone! He'll have me executed on the spot. I've worshipped GOD all my life – you know that. Haven't you heard what I did for the prophets when Queen Jezebel was murdering any she could find? And you say, "Tell him I'm here" – and send me to my death!'

'I speak in GOD's name,' said Elijah. 'I swear to you I will meet the king here, where we are now standing, today.'

'It's you, is it, you trouble-maker!' said the king to Elijah as soon as he saw him.

'I'm no trouble-maker,' said Elijah. 'You and your family are the trouble-makers. You've abandoned the true worship of GOD for all these pagan cults. Call an assembly of the people on Carmel Mountain. And make sure the dervishes of the pagan god Baal and the pagan goddess Asherah – the dervishes the queen's so fond of – are all there.'

The king called an assembly of people and dervishes on Carmel Mountain.

Carmel Mountain   *1 Kings 18:21-46*

Elijah faced the crowd.

'How long are you going to stand shilly-shallying at the crossroads?' he asked them. 'If our GOD is God, follow him. If Baal is God, follow him.'

There was dead silence.

'I am the only prophet of GOD left,' he went on. 'There are more than four hundred prophets of Baal here; I stand alone. Let us be put to the test. Bring two bulls. Let them choose one, prepare it for a burnt-offering, and put it on the wood – but no fire, if you please. I'll dress the other bull and put it on the wood – and I'll have no fire either.'

He paused and turned to the pagan prophets.

'You pray to your god and I will pray to mine,' he told them. 'The God who answers by fire will be God!'

'It's a fair test!' shouted the crowd.

'You begin,' said Elijah to the prophets. 'There are more of you.'

They prepared the bull and the wood.

'O Baal, answer us!' they prayed. They went on praying like this from morning to noon, dancing a ritual dance around the altar. But there wasn't a sound or a word in answer.

Elijah could keep quiet no longer.

'You'll have to shout louder!' he taunted them. 'He's a god, isn't he? Perhaps he's just thinking – or somebody's called him away – or he's on a journey – or he's dozed off – you'll have to see if you can wake him up!'

They shouted out at the top of their voices, and cut themselves with knives and lances till blood flowed (this is a custom of pagan worship). This went on till early evening – but no voice, no answer, nothing.

Elijah spoke to the watching crowd.

'Come nearer to me,' he said.

There was an old ruined altar to GOD on that part of the mountain. Elijah chose twelve stones from it (representing the twelve tribes of the old tribal league), and made a new altar. He dug a trench round it, deep enough to take about twelve gallons of water. He stacked wood on it and put the bull on the wood.

He told the crowd to pour water over it.

'Do it a second and a third time,' he said.

The water drenched the altar and filled the trench as well.

He went up to the altar.

'O GOD,' he prayed, 'God of our ancestors, let nobody here today doubt that you are God in this country and that I am your servant, carrying out your orders. Answer me, O GOD, answer me! Let everybody here know that you are God and that you are bringing them back to your true worship!'

Lightning suddenly fell out of the cloudless sky and burned up bull and wood and stones and dust – and all the water in the trench.

The crowd fell down on their faces in reverence.

'GOD is really God!' they shouted. 'GOD is really God!'

'Arrest the pagan prophets!' Elijah told the crowd. 'Don't let any escape!'

The arrested them and marched them down the mountainside to the Kishon River in the valley below and butchered them there.

Everybody had been fasting all day.

'You can eat and drink now,' Elijah told the king. 'There's the sound of beating rain!'

The king went up to the altar to eat and drink; Elijah climbed almost to the top of the mountain and squatted on the ground with his face between his knees. He called to the lad, his servant.

'Go up to the very top, and look out to sea,' he told him.

'I can't see anything,' the lad called back.

This happened six times. But the seventh time there was something to see.

'I can see a cloud coming in from the sea!' he shouted down. 'It isn't a very big one – it's about the size of a man's fist.'

'Up!' said Elijah. 'Run back to the king. Tell him to harness his horses if he doesn't want to be held up by the rain!'

The sky grew black with clouds and wind and there was a great storm of rain.

King Ahab mounted his chariot and made for the royal city of Jezreel. Elijah tied his cloak round his waist and ran in front of the royal chariot all the seventeen miles to the city – GOD gave him superhuman strength to do it.

Panic and Rebuke   *1 Kings 19:1-18*

The king told the queen what had happened, and especially about the butchery of the pagan prophets. She immediately sent a message to Elijah:

'You're not Elijah and I'm not Jezebel – if you're not as dead as my prophets before tomorrow's out!'

Elijah was in a panic, and fled for his life to the south. He reached Beersheba and left his lad there. He himself went on for twenty miles into the desert. He found a broom-bush and rested in its shade.

'Let me die,' he prayed to GOD. 'I can't stand any more, O GOD! Kill me – I'm not the leader that I thought I was.'

He lay down and went to sleep.

Suddenly an angel was waking him.

'Get up and eat something,' he said.

Elijah looked round and saw a round flat cake of bread and a flask of water. He got up, ate the cake and drank the water; and then lay down again.

The angel came back a second time and wakened him.

'Get up and eat something,' he said. 'You've a long journey in front of you and you'll need all your strength.'

Again Elijah got up and ate and drank. He felt a new man now and went on and on until he reached the Holy Mountain where Moses had met GOD. He found a cave and spent the night there.

Then GOD passed by.

A storm of wind swept over the mountain, pulling up great rocks and smashing them to pieces. But the storm wind wasn't GOD's presence.

An earthquake shook the mountain. But the earthquake wasn't GOD's presence either.

Then a forest fire swept the mountainside. But that wasn't GOD's presence.

After all this, there was a silence so deep that it was almost like a sound itself.

Elijah left the cave, hiding his face in his cloak, and stood at the cave's mouth.

He heard a voice:

'What are you doing here, Elijah?'

'Because I've been utterly loyal to you,' said Elijah. 'The people of the North have abandoned you. The Covenant means nothing to them, your altars are deserted ruins, your prophets butchered. I'm the only one left – and I'm a wanted man!'

'Go back!' said GOD. 'Sow the seed of revolution. Anoint Hazael king of Damascus, Jehu king of the North – and Elisha to carry on your work. Refugees from King Hazael will be killed by King Jehu, and anybody escaping from King Jehu will be killed by Elisha. You are not the only one loyal to me – there are many who have never worshipped a pagan god, and never kissed Baal's image.'

Elijah went back.

On the way he came upon twelve men ploughing, each driving a pair of oxen in harness. Elisha was the last of the ploughmen. Elijah walked over the ploughed land and threw his cloak over him. Elisha dropped the reins of the oxen and ran after him.

'Let me say goodbye to my parents,' he asked. 'I'll come with you then.'

'Go home,' said Elijah. 'But don't forget what I've just done.'

Elisha went home. He sacrificed his two oxen, using the wooden plough as firewood, and he and his companions had a religious meal together. In this way he dedicated himself to the service of GOD with Elijah, and swore in his companions to help in his new work. He then left home and became Elijah's follower and friend.

A Farmer's Murder
1 Kings 21

Naboth was a farmer. His vineyard had belonged to his family for many generations and lay next to the palace grounds in Jezreel City.

King Ahab asked Naboth one day about it.

'I'm wanting a vegetable garden,' he told him. 'Your vineyard is just what I want – it's next-door to my palace. Will you let me have it? I'll give you a better vineyard for it; or I'll pay you a fair price, just as you like.'

217

'No,' said Naboth. 'The vineyard was my father's and my grandfather's. I should be an irreligious man if I sold my ancestral lands.'

The king went back to his palace a vexed and sullen man; he'd set his heart on that vineyard. He went to bed and sulked and wouldn't have anything to eat.

'Why are you sulking?' asked the queen. He told her what had happened.

'You're a fine king,' she said (she was a foreign princess, and was thinking of what her father, the king of Tyre, would have done). 'Get up and eat your food and stop worrying. I'll see you get the vineyard.'

She sent a royal letter, sealed with the royal seal, to the aldermen and freemen of the city, all Naboth's fellow-councillors:

'Proclaim a religious fast, and put Naboth where everybody can see him. Get two witnesses – you know what kind of men to get – to sit facing him and to charge him with cursing GOD and the king. You know what the sentence is – death by stoning.'

The city council carried out the royal orders to the letter. They held the fast, suborned the witnesses and had Naboth executed outside the city.

They sent a brief report: 'Naboth has been executed.'

The queen received the report and went straight to the king.

'Get up and go down to the vineyard,' she told him. 'It's yours now. Naboth wouldn't sell it to you, would he? Well – he's dead!'

The king got up and went down to the vineyard to take possession of it. (By law the property of rebels and criminals became the king's.)

GOD spoke to Elijah.

'Get up,' he said, 'and go and meet King Ahab face to face. He's in Naboth's vineyard; he's gone to take possession of it. Give him this message from me: "You've committed murder to get hold of a vineyard. Where the street-dogs are licking up Naboth's blood, they'll one day lick up yours!"'

'Have you caught up with me, my enemy?' the king said to Elijah.

'I've caught up with you, all right!' said Elijah. 'You've sold your soul in this foul deed; you've signed your own death-warrant – and that of your family. "I'll get rid of you all!" says GOD.'

When King Ahab heard these words, he tore his robes and wore sackcloth. He accepted Elijah's rebuke.

Micaiah (850 BCE)

1 Kings 22:7-28

King Ahab of the North and King Jehoshaphat of the South were together in Samaria, the Northern capital. They were discussing with their ministers the attack on Ramoth-Gilead, east of Jordan River. King Jehoshaphat asked that GOD's will should be sought, and the professional court prophets told the two kings that GOD's will was that they should attack the city. At this point in the story later editors inserted the following prophetic story (see p. 152).

'Isn't there another prophet here?' asked King Jehoshaphat, 'to tell us what GOD's will is?'

'There is,' said King Ahab, 'there's Micaiah. But I've no use for him – he's always against me!'

'You mustn't say that,' said King Jehoshaphat.

King Ahab sent for Micaiah.

The Council of War was, of course, a state occasion. The whole court was there; the kings were sitting on their thrones, in full regalia, in the open square by the City Gate. All the professional prophets were shouting, 'GOD's word': 'Go up and conquer – GOD will put the town at Your Majesty's mercy!' They were in a wild frenzy. One of them, Zedekiah, had made some iron horns and was wearing them and shouting: '"You will gore the Syrians like a bull," says GOD, "and destroy them!"'

Meanwhile, the officer sent to fetch Micaiah had found him and was talking to him.

'Now remember,' he was saying, 'all the prophets are for the king and his plans. Take the same line yourself.'

'As GOD lives,' said Micaiah, 'I will say only what GOD tells me to say.'

He came into the presence of King Ahab.

'Micaiah,' said the king, 'shall we attack Ramoth-Gilead or shall we not?'

'Go up and conquer!' said Micaiah (mimicking the professional prophets). 'GOD will put the town at Your Majesty's mercy.'

'How often have I to command you to tell me what GOD really says,' said the king, 'the truth and nothing but the truth?'

'I saw the Northern soldiers scattered on the mountains like sheep without their shepherd,' said Micaiah. '"They have no king," GOD told me. "Let them disband and go peacefully home."'

'Didn't I tell you he would talk like this?' said King Ahab to King Jehoshaphat. 'Didn't I tell you he would be against me and not for me?'

'You asked me to tell you what GOD had to say,' Micaiah went on. 'I saw GOD sitting on his throne, surrounded by his heavenly court. "Who knows how to mislead King Ahab?" GOD asked them, "so that he may die in battle at Ramoth-Gilead?" There was a debate among his counsellors. Then one of them stepped out before him. "I know how to mislead him," he said. "How?" asked GOD. "I will go down and fill the minds of the professional prophets with lies," he said. "Do just that," said GOD. "You've got your orders: go!" GOD is surely against you; the court prophets are all lying.'

Zedekiah stepped up to Micaiah and struck him on the face.

'How did GOD's spirit go from me to you?' he shouted.

'You'll know the answer to that question,' said Micaiah, 'when you find yourself hiding as a refugee in the back room of a house.'

'Arrest the fellow!' ordered King Ahab, 'and hand him over to Governor Amon and Prince Joash. Tell them to lock him up, and feed him on bread and water till I come for my victory parade!'

'If you come home as victor,' said Micaiah, 'then GOD hasn't spoken through me!'

Voice of a Farmer: Amos (760 BCE)

We know little about Amos. All we know comes from the brief account of the 'Incident in the North' which follows and the impressions his poetry gives us. He was a shepherd.

The times he lived in were times of great prosperity for the North and the South; both kingdoms were ruled over by able kings – Jeroboam II in the North and Ahaziah (Uzziah) in the South. There is little about these kings in Israelite historical records. Jeroboam is dismissed as a bad king; though we are told he was 'the Saviour of the North' and ruled an empire 'like Solomon's'; what is told of Ahaziah is found on p. 160. Prosperity for both kingdoms was possible because Assyria and Egypt were preoccupied with their own internal affairs. Within a few years, however, Assyria was to resume her march to the west.

So, for a moment, the North was revelling in her wealth and in the expansion of her trade. But the wealth brought with it corruption in the courts of justice, contempt for the rights of ordinary citizens, the growth of large estates (with their summer houses) at the expense of small landowners, the neglect of the poor. The worship at GOD's Temple was a 'contemptible side-show, its religious tradition merely a cloak for pride and complacency'. Everybody seemed so engrossed in 'getting on' and 'keeping up with the Joneses' that nobody bothered about what was happening in the world outside or noticed the storm clouds blowing up beyond their northern borders.

Amos was a Southerner; but he spoke in the North, where perhaps his business took him to the market at Bethel.

Incident in the North   *Amos 1:1; 7:10-17*

Amos was a farmer, dealing in sheep and cattle and sycamore figs in the Southern village of Tekoa. He spoke openly in GOD's name in the famous royal city of Bethel in the North.

Amaziah, the temple priest there, sent a report to the king:

'Here, in the heart of the country, Amos is plotting revolution; he is a danger to the state. The theme of his harangues is – "King Jeroboam shall die in the war that's coming and the people will be deported!"'

Amaziah faced Amos himself.

'Get back to the South, you visionary!' he told him. 'Earn your living by preaching there! And don't you ever come back here to Bethel with your wild talk. This is a royal city with a royal temple and a royal palace!'

Amos was not slow to defend himself:

'I was no professional prophet – I'd no official standing!
I was a cattleman, growing the fruit the poor eat!
GOD seized me when I was out with the sheep,
and told me to give his message to the North.

Now listen to what GOD has got to say to you!

You tell me to keep my mouth shut,
    stop dribbling prophecies over you Northerners!
You yourself will know what war means –
    your wife driven to live on the streets,
    your children dead in the fighting,
    your estate shared out as booty,
    yourself dying in a foreign land.
The Northerners shall be deported!'

Amos's Call

These four 'visions' probably represent Amos's account of his call by GOD to be his 'spokesman'. They are set in the form of brief conversations. Amos had been thinking deeply about the story of his people in the light of what he knew of his time and what life was like in his own country and in the North. Incidents from his own village experience (as with Jesus) gave him the imagery with which to express his sense of GOD's presence: a plague of locusts, a forest fire, building the wall of a village house, carrying the fruit for the autumn festival at the end of the agricultural year. He was aware of the terrible threat of Assyrian invasion, to which both North and South seemed blind. The experiences he describes seem to have taken some time: in the first two he thinks that the people may change their ways; in the last two there is no hope at all. These, then, were his marching orders.

Brief though the 'visions' are, they are crowded with meaning. The words echo not only his farming experience but the language of temple worship and the religious traditions of his people. For example, the forest fire blotting out the hillside calls to mind the Great Deep that, in the ancient story, covered the world. These are the words of a poet and carry more meaning than a first reading reveals. They are the clue to all that he later had to say.

The Vision of Locusts *Amos 7:1-3*

GOD opened my eyes and I saw him at work:
the spring crops were beginning to grow when a plague of locusts blotted out the countryside. When they had eaten up everything that was green, I prayed to GOD:

> 'O GOD, forgive us,
> how can the North face this?
> It's a very small country!'

GOD changed his plans.
'Very well, it won't happen,' he said.

The Vision of the Forest Fire *Amos 7:4-6*

GOD opened my eyes and I saw him at work:
a great fire was raging, devouring the Great Deep* and threatening the whole countryside. I prayed to GOD:

> 'Stop the fire, O GOD, stop the fire!
> How can the North face this?
> It's a very small country!'

GOD changed his plans.
'Very well, this won't happen, either,' he said.

---

* A reference to the watery chaos mentioned in the story of creation (see p. 293); it is to be found under the earth and from it flow springs and rivers.

The Vision of the Plumb-line
Amos 7:7-9

GOD opened my eyes and I saw him at work:
a man had taken up his stand by the wall of a house and was holding a
plumb-line to test it.

'What are you looking at, Amos?' GOD asked me.

'A plumb-line,' I said.

'I am testing my people of the North,' he said, 'as the man is testing
this wall – I cannot keep overlooking things!

> Northern hill-shrines shall be deserted;
> Northern temples tumble into ruin;
> the Northern royal house perish in war!'

The Vision of Autumn Fruit
Amos 8:1-3

GOD opened my eyes and I saw him at work:
there was a basket of autumn fruit in the street, ready for the autumn
festival at the end of the year.

'What are you looking at, Amos?' he asked me.

'A basket of autumn fruit,' I said.

'It's autumn for the North, too,' he said. 'Autumn – and the end. I
cannot go on overlooking things!

> Temple songs will turn to temple laments –
> war and many deaths,
> streets choked with dead soldiers
> and silence!'

GOD's Way: the Common Law of the World

Damascus in the North-east
Amos 1:3-5

These are GOD's words:

> Crime upon crime upon crime –
> that is the rebellious story of Damascus.
> I will not come
> to save them from their fate!

They beat up Gilead villagers
like a threshing sledge
threshing grain.

Therefore
the royal family shall know what war means:
palaces and fortresses
in flames;
peasants driven from their fields,
the king from his throne;
people deported
back to their ancestral home!

This is GOD's Word!

Philistine Gaza in the South-west *Amos 1:7-8*

These are GOD's words:

Crime upon crime upon crime –
that is the rebellious story of Gaza City.
I will not come
to save them from their fate!

They deported a whole people
to the slave-markets of Edom.

Therefore
they shall know what war means:
city walls and fortresses
shall go up in flames,
sister cities
perish with them:
citizens killed,
kings dethroned,
the last Philistine dead!

This is GOD's Word!

Ammon in the East *Amos 1:13-15*

Crime upon crime upon crime –
that is the rebellious story of Ammon.

225

I will not come
to save them from their fate!

They murdered helpless women
in their border warfare.

Therefore
kings and nobles shall know what war means:
the royal city
in flames,
fortresses crashing in ruins
with battle cries
like thunder on a stormy day,
kings and nobles together
deported as prisoners!

This is GOD's Word!

Moab in the South-east
Amos 2:1-3

Crime upon crime upon crime –
that is the rebellious story of Moab.
I will not come
to save them from their fate!

They burned to lime
the bones of Edom's king –
a shameful outrage!*

Therefore
Moab shall fall in flames,
its fortresses in fire.
They shall die
with stormy shouting
and bugles blowing,
sheik and his captains
perishing in battle!

This is GOD's Word!

---

* Such treatment was reserved for the worst of criminals.

Crime upon crime upon crime –
   that is the rebellious story of the North.
I will not come
   to save them from their fate!

They sell innocent men for money,
   destitute men for land,
   trampling on poor men's heads,
   robbing them of their rights.
A man and his father
   sleep with the same slave-girl,
   holding my true worship in contempt.
They use pledged clothes to sleep on
   by every altar,
   drink wine taken in fines
   in every village temple.

Yet it was I who gave them their homeland,
   destroying the Amorites who lived there –
     men tall as cedars,
     strong as oaks –
   destroying them root and branch.
It was I who rescued them from Egypt,
   and led them across the desert
   to occupy Amorite territory.

I gave you prophets
   and dedicated men;
   you corrupted the dedicated men
   and told the prophets to shut their mouths.
Is not this the plain truth,
   you Northerners?
I will shake you
   to the depth of your being,
   like a loaded harvest wagon
   creaking over rough ground!

Swift runner
   shall fall with fatigue,

strong man
become a weakling,
soldier die in battle,
bowman be beaten back.
In that day
army-runner and horseman
will be captured,
bravest hero
will run naked away!

This is GOD's Word!

Is This the Way GOD's People Should Live?

Your Wealth Won't Save You!   *Amos 3:9-10, 12, 14-15*

A Proclamation to be made in Philistine and Egyptian Palaces:

Gather in the central highlands,
    survey the confusion in Samaria City,
    the oppression in her streets:
        honesty means nothing to her people,
        violence and robbery are their way to wealth!

This is what GOD has to say:

Like the knuckle bone or tip of an ear
    which is all the shepherd grabs from the lion's mouth,
    there will barely be a survivor
    from the North and its capital city –
    only here a man cowering on the corner of a couch,
    there a man sitting on the cushion of a bed.
Temple altars shall be toppled
    and tumbled to the ground;
    winter house and summer house
    be smashed down;
    great houses with their ivory and ebony
    be shattered wreckage.

This is GOD's Word!

You Did Not Turn Back to Me!   *Amos 4:6-12*

Starvation in your cities,
    famine in your villages –
    yet you did not turn back to me,
      says GOD.

No rain in spring,
    no harvest coming in summer –
    yet you did not turn back to me,
      says GOD.

Blight and mildew,
    ravaged gardens and vineyards –
    yet you did not turn back to me,
      says GOD.

Commandos dead on the battlefield,
    stink of corpses –
    yet you did not turn back to me,
      says GOD.

Everywhere devastation,
    only a charred stick snatched from the fire –
    yet you did not turn back to me,
      says GOD.

That is why I deal with you as I do,
    O North!

'GOD's Day' Indeed!   *Amos 5:7, 10-12, 16-19, 21-24; 6:1a, 3-8, 12-14*

Woe
    to you who make justice bitter –
      trampling on the common rights of men;
      hating the honest witness,
      bold speaker of the truth;
      robbing the peasant of his land,
      raping his harvest with your 'fines'!

Therefore
 build your stone houses –
  they will never be your home!
 plant your vineyards –
  you will never drink their wine!

I know all about your untold crimes,
 your bold rebellion –
  bullying innocent men,
  taking any blood-money you can,
  brow-beating poor people in the courts!

When I pass through your homeland,
 there'll be moaning in the market-place,
 anguish in the streets,
 farmers off their farms, away at funerals,
 professional mourners howling in the villages!

Woe
 to you who want 'GOD's Day' –
  what good will that Day do you?
 Day of Darkness,
  not Day of Light! –
 like a man running from a lion
  and meeting a bear!
 like a man leaning on a house-wall
  and being bitten by a snake!

I hate and loathe your harvest festivals –
 your religious services mean nothing to me!
Make your offerings –
 I won't accept them!
Give your richest gifts –
 I won't bother to look at them!
Stop singing your noisy hymns –
 your harps are no music to me!
Let justice roll down
 like the winter rains,
and righteousness
 like an unfailing river!

Woe
    to those who fancy themselves safe
        on Samaria Mountain!
    who can't be bothered about 'the evil day',
        forcing frightening disaster nearer –
    lounging on ivory beds,
    sprawling on couches,
    fetching from their farms
    fresh lamb and fatted veal,
    bawling their 'new songs'
    to the music of the harp,
    swilling bowlfuls of wine,
    painted with costly cosmetics!
For the break-up of their country
    they don't care a damn!

Therefore
    they'll be the first to be marched away –
    no sprawling revellers then,
        just silence!

I despise this Northern insolence
    and hate their proud palaces.
I will surrender the city
    and everybody in it!

Do horses gallop up a cliff?
    Can you drive an ox-plough on the sea?
Can you get justice in your corrupt courts?
    An honest man might as well poison himself!
Yet you boast about the Gilead war –
    'Oh, the capture of Karnaim was a walk-over!'

I am calling out an empire against you,
    O men of the North!
They will be your masters
    from your farthest north
    to your farthest south!

You'll Pay for Your Sharp Practice! *Amos 8:4-7*

Listen –
    you who trample down the common people
        and tyrannise the needy –
    moaning and groaning
        all Sabbath day:
    'Will the Sabbath never be over?
        Then we can get back to
        selling our corn,
        giving short measure,
        tampering with the weights,
        tilting the scales,
        slipping in the sweepings!'
    I swear by all your accursed insolence:
        'I won't forget!'

Is This the Way GOD's People Should Worship Him?

Hold to Me! *Amos 5:4-6*

'Hold to me
    if you want to be really alive!
No pilgrimages to Bethel or Gilgal!
    No travelling to Beersheba!'

Hold to GOD
    if you want to be really alive –
lest he leap like a forest fire
    over the North:
there'll be no putting
    that fire out!

Listen! *Amos 3:2-8*

With you alone I have been intimate
    among all the peoples of the world, have I?
It is you, then, I will punish
    for all your crimes.

Do two men walk together along a country road
    without having planned it?
Does a lion roar in the forest
    without having caught its prey?

Does a bird drop to the earth
    without being lured down?
Does a ground-trap snap
    without being triggered off?
If the bugle blows in the city
    aren't the people terrified?
Does a town meet disaster
    without GOD having something to do with it?

The lion has roared –
    who can help shuddering?
GOD has spoken –
    who can help announcing what he has said?

You Do Have a Good Time! *Amos 4:4-5*

Worship at Bethel –
    and be a rebel!
Worship at Gilgal –
    and be a traitor!
Bring your sacrifices
    every morning!
Take three days
    to offer your tithes!
Burn your thank-offering –
    make sure there's no leaven in it!
Shout out your subscriptions –
    let everybody hear!
You do have a good time,
    you Northerners!

This is GOD's Word!

> Don't you know that the Africans
>   matter to me,
>   matter as much as you Northerners?
> Wasn't it you I led
>   out of Egypt?
> I know it was!
> I also led the Philistines
>   from Crete,
> and the Syrians
>   from beyond Damascus!

> > > This is GOD's Word!

A Hymn   *Amos 4:13; 5:9, 8; 9:5, 6*

When Amos's friends gathered his poems together (he may have written some down himself), they put with them verses from a hymn which seemed to them to make clear how Amos thought about GOD. GOD, for him, was the God of creation, Lord of the universe. This is the theme of these verses. They probably come from a temple hymn. Their style is very different from Amos's style, but they match the thought of God which shines through his 'visions' and his poetry.

> Look! –
>   he who shapes the thunder clouds,
>   makes the storm,
>   shares with us his thoughts,
>   makes early morning dark with cloud,
>   walks on earth's high hills –
>   GOD is his name!
>
> He who makes 'The Bull'
>   rise after 'The Goat'
>   and set after 'The Grape-gatherer',
>   made the Pleiades and Orion,
>   turned pitch darkness into the morning,

darkened day into night,
summoned the ocean
and poured it over the earth –
   GOD is his name!

He at whose touch the earth heaves –
   rising like the Nile,
   sinking like the Nile –
   who builds his terraces in the sky,
   his dome over the earth –
      GOD is his name!

Voice of a Villager:
Jeremiah (626-585 BCE)

Jeremiah's story is a tragic story set in tragic times. Over a hundred years had passed since Amos spoke in Bethel; the whole situation of the Israelite people had dramatically changed. What Amos foresaw had happened: Assyrian armies had marched westward, trampling into subjection the little countries between them and the Mediterranean coast. The North had fallen in 721 and had become an Assyrian province. The South was an Assyrian province in all but name, and now the sky was darkening for it too. For a moment in the last years there had seemed a chance of escape: Assyria collapsed. But Babylon took its place and carried on its policy of westward expansion. Jeremiah lived through it all – the fall of Assyria, the march of Egyptian armies north to save it (when King Josiah died in the fight at Megiddo Pass), the decisive battle of Carchemish (605) when Egyptian power was smashed, the march west of the Babylonian armies, the first capture of Jerusalem in 597 (when the king and some of his high officers were deported), and the final fall of the city in 586 and the end of Israelite political independence.

Jeremiah was a poet to his fingertips; sensitive, shy and retiring, he was driven into the very heart of the storm that overwhelmed his people –

'desperate tides of a whole world's anguish
forced through the channels of a single heart.'*

Some of his private poems have survived, poems he made for himself and never intended for anybody else; we owe their preservation probably to his friend and secretary, Baruch. We call them his 'Confessions'; we have to wait for a thousand years before any writing like them appears again. They tell the story of his heart.

We know so much about Jeremiah because Baruch wrote down an account of the last thirty years. He was rather a prosy writer (unlike his master), but in the stories he gives us we can see what Jeremiah had to face. The background of the story we have already read on pp. 158-169; read it again before you begin this account of Jeremiah.

* Dr A. S. Peake prefaced these lines from F. W. H. Myers' *S. Paul* to his great commentary on *Jeremiah*.

We give first Baruch's stories; then the poems of Jeremiah in this order: 1. his call; 2. his 'Confessions'; 3. poems about contemporary events; 4. as with Amos's poems, what he had to say about everyday life and about religion.

Baruch's Stories of Jeremiah

In the Stocks   *Jeremiah 19:1-2, 10, 12-15; 20:1-6*

Jeremiah was speaking to the people in the valley outside Jerusalem City. He had a potter's earthen jar in his hand. He smashed it on the ground.

'These are GOD's words,' he said. '"When you smash a jar like this, nobody can mend it again. That's what I mean to do with this city and its inhabitants – smash it and make it like this burial ground. House and palace alike shall be as cursed as this valley; on their flat roofs you have made sacrifices to the sun and the moon and the stars, and worshipped the foreign gods of the country."'

He left the burial ground and went to the temple court.

'These are GOD's words,' he told the crowd there. '"You have been obstinate. You would not listen to what I have to say. I am about to bring on this city and the surrounding villages the disaster I have announced."'

The Chief Temple Officer, a priest called Pashhur, was standing by listening. He immediately arrested Jeremiah, and had him flogged and put in the stocks near the Benjamin Gate on the north side of the temple.

Next day, he came back and set him free.

'GOD's changed your name,' Jeremiah said to him. 'You're no longer Pashhur ("Safety"); you're Magor-missabib ("Total Terror"). These are GOD's words: "You and all your friends will know the Terror when it comes. You'll see your friends die in the fighting. The Babylonian emperor will capture the city, loot the houses and the palace, and march the people away to Babylon. You and your family will be among them. You will all die and be buried in a foreign land – you and all your friends who have listened to your lies."'

In the Temple Court   *Jeremiah 26:1-24*

King Jehoiakim, son of the good King Josiah, had just succeeded his father (the Egyptians had put him on the throne in place of his younger brother).

237

God spoke to Jeremiah.

'Go and stand in the temple court,' he told him, 'and speak to all the crowds there. Tell them everything I command you to tell them; keep nothing back. They may listen and change their ways; if they do, I will not send the disaster their present behaviour deserves. Tell them this from me: "If you won't listen to me, live in my Way, take note of what my servants the prophets tell you (which is just what you haven't done), then I will make this temple like burnt-out Shiloh.* I will make this city the sort of city the whole world will despise."'

Priests, temple prophets and people listened while Jeremiah was speaking. As soon as he finished, they arrested him.

'You shall die for this!' they shouted. 'Speaking in GOD's name indeed! Talking about the temple being burned to the ground and the city becoming an empty desert! Death's what you deserve!'

The crowd hemmed him in.

The incident was reported to the king's ministers and they immediately left the palace and held court at the New Gate of the temple.

'Lynch him!' the priests and prophets were shouting. 'You've heard how he's attacked this city!'

'GOD sent me to speak against this temple and this city,' said Jeremiah. 'What I've said is what GOD told me to say. What you've got to do is clear – change your ways and listen to GOD's warning; then the disaster GOD speaks of may not happen. You can do what you like with me – I am at your mercy. But don't forget this: if you kill me, an innocent man, you will have to face the consequences of such a brutal act. What I said is what GOD sent me to say; I am sure of this.'

'The man's innocent,' was the judgement of the ministers. 'It's obvious he speaks with GOD's authority.'

Some elder statesmen were present, and they spoke up.

'We'd better remember what happened once before in King Hezekiah's days,' they said. 'Micah told the people just what Jeremiah's told us – he was telling them what GOD had to say:

> Ploughland, tumbled-down walls, sprouting trees –
> that's what this stronghold, this city,
> this temple will be like.

---

* It is now known that the destruction of Shiloh Jeremiah refers to was a recent event and not the Philistine destruction of the town five hundred years before.

'Did the king – did the people – kill him for talking like that? Didn't they take GOD seriously and ask his forgiveness? And didn't GOD listen to them? The disaster never happened. We're just making it dead certain.'

'Ah, but what happened only a short time ago to Uriah?' the crowd protested. 'King Jehoiakim didn't treat his bitter words about this city like that – he held them to be treason. Uriah escaped to Egypt, but he was brought back to this country and executed and his body thrown into a common graveyard!'

It was at this moment that a man called Ahikam stood by Jeremiah and saved him from being lynched by the crowd.

The Burning of the Scroll   *Jeremiah 36*

A little later – King Jehoiakim had been on the throne for three years – GOD spoke again to Jeremiah.

'Write down in a scroll all I have told you to say since I first spoke to you,' he told him, 'all I have told you to say about the North and the South and the surrounding countries. If they'll listen, perhaps the Southerners will take some note of what I have to say about the disaster which threatens them; they may yet change their ways and be forgiven.'

Jeremiah sent for Baruch. He dictated all he had said and Baruch wrote it down. Then he gave Baruch some careful instructions.

'I can't go into the temple,' he told him. 'You can. There are special services being held at the great December Fast; the courts will be crowded with people from the city and the country villages. Go and read this scroll to the crowds there. These are GOD's words. Perhaps the people will change their ways and worship GOD as they should; the disaster which is threatening them is a very real and terrible disaster.'

Baruch did as he was told. He read Jeremiah's words in the room in the upper temple court by the New Gate used by one of the king's ministers, Gemariah.

Micaiah, Gemariah's son, was in the crowd listening. When the reading was over, he went post-haste to the Adjutant-General's room in the palace where a cabinet meeting of the king's ministers was being held. He told them what he had just heard.

The ministers sent an officer to fetch Baruch and his scroll.

'Read it again to us,' they ordered.

Baruch read it to them.

As the reading finished, they turned in panic to one another.

'We must tell the king about this,' they said.

'How did you come to write it down?' they asked Baruch. 'Did Jeremiah dictate it?'

'He did,' he said. 'He went on dictating, and I wrote it all down as accurately as I could in ink in this scroll.'

'You and Jeremiah had better keep out of the way,' they warned him. 'Don't let anybody know where you're hiding.'

The ministers left the scroll in the Adjutant-General's room and went to seek an audience with the king. They reported all they knew about the incident in the temple.

The king ordered one of the secretaries to fetch the scroll.

He was sitting in his winter house with a fire burning brightly in the brazier in front of him. The secretary began to read.

When he had read three or four columns, the king leaned forward and slashed them off with a penknife and threw them into the fire. So it went on until the whole scroll had been burned.

The king and his court weren't in the least troubled by what they heard; they showed no sign of fear at all. Three of his ministers tried to stop him burning the scroll. But he took no notice. All he did was to order two of his officers to arrest Baruch and Jeremiah. GOD saw to it that they weren't found.

GOD spoke to Jeremiah again.

'Get another scroll,' he told him, 'and write it all down again. Then tell the king in my name: "You have burned the scroll, but no son of yours shall succeed you on the throne. You will die in the fighting and your body will lie in the city streets – burned in the midday heat and frozen by the night frost."'

Jeremiah dictated the words again, and Baruch wrote them down on another scroll. Other words that GOD had spoken were also added, words dealing with the coming disaster.

Two Prophets Meet   *Jeremiah 28*

Jeremiah was wearing a wooden halter on his shoulders as a sign to the people that what had happened to King Jehoiachin would happen to them all. (In 597, King Jehoiachin and leading citizens had been deported to Babylon – they had no more choice than a farm animal which has to go where its driver makes it go.)

One day, that winter, Jeremiah went into the crowded temple courts. Hananiah, the prophet from Gibeon, accosted him. Everybody could hear what he said.

'This is what GOD says,' Hananiah called out to him, '"I have broken the harness which the Babylonian emperor has put on you – in two years everything he looted from the temple will be recovered, and King Jehoiachin and all Jewish prisoners will be back home again!"'

Jeremiah faced Hananiah with the crowds standing round.

'Very well!' he said. 'May GOD do just that – as you say. May loot and exiles all come home again. But there's something else to be said. Listen, you and all this crowd: in days gone by, the prophets, our predecessors, spoke only of disaster; a prophet who talks about peace can only be proved a true prophet when peace has come.'

Hananiah got hold of the halter Jeremiah was wearing round his neck, took it off and broke it up.

'These are GOD's words,' he told the crowd. '"In the same way, within two years, I will break the harness the emperor has put on your necks!"'

Jeremiah went home.

Some days later, GOD spoke again to him.

'Go and tell Hananiah this,' he said. '"You have smashed the wooden halter; I will make an iron halter to take its place. Listen to me. It is I who have made all these nations the slaves of the Babylonian emperor – they shall stay his slaves."'

Jeremiah went to Hananiah.

'Listen to me, Hananiah,' he said. 'GOD never sent you. You have made these people trust a lie. These are GOD's words to you: "I have finished with you!"'

Hananiah died in April.

Letters to Babylon (after 597) *Jeremiah 29:1-7, 10-13, 21-32*

This is the letter Jeremiah sent from Jerusalem to Babylon to the leaders of the exiles there (he got King Zedekiah's envoys to Babylon to deliver it for him):

These are GOD's words: 'This is what I have to say to all those I sent as exiles to Babylon:

> Make Babylon your home –
>   build houses,
>   grow food in your gardens,

marry and rear families;
  you will not die out,
  you will become a great community.
Work for the good of the country
  I have made the place of your exile.
When you pray to me,
    remember Babylon in your prayers –
    you and she stand or fall together.

This is what I have to say to you:

Remember my plans for you,
    plans of peace, not plans of disaster,
    a future to hope for.
Pray to me and I will listen;
    seek me and find me;
    when you seek me with all your hearts,
    you shall find me.'

Jeremiah received an answer to this letter. This is his reply to it:
  'You answer me by saying, "GOD has given us prophets here in Babylon. We don't need any words from you." Then hear what GOD has to say about your prophets, Ahab and Zedekiah: "I will deliver them into the emperor's power; he will execute them in your sight. Their names will become by-words among you – all this because of their infamous conduct and their false prophecies. I never gave them the right to speak, but I noticed what they did. These are my words."'

Shemaiah sent a letter from Babylon to Zephaniah the supervisor in Jerusalem:
  'GOD appointed you to take the place of the priest Jehoiada to keep order in the temple – to arrest any madman who plays the prophet and put him in irons. Why, then, haven't you arrested the self-styled prophet Jeremiah? He sent a letter to us here in Babylon telling us that we are here to stay for a very long time and that we must settle down and make Babylon our home.'
  Zephaniah read the letter to Jeremiah.
  GOD spoke to him:
  'Send a message in my name to the exiles in Babylon. "What Shemaiah has told you is a lie. This is what I have to say: I will punish Shemaiah and his descendants; they will not live to see the good I mean to do to you."'

The Scroll and the River   *Jeremiah 51:59-64*

Seraiah, the Quartermaster, brother of Baruch, had business in Babylon.

Jeremiah had written in a scroll what GOD had told him about the Babylonian empire: that it would not last for ever, doom would one day overtake it.

Jeremiah went to Seraiah.

'When you get to Babylon,' he said, 'make sure that you read all the words of the scroll to the exiles there. Then pray this prayer: "O GOD, you have spoken against this great empire. You will bring it to an end; the city will become desolate ruins, abandoned by people and animals." This done, tie the scroll to a stone and throw it into the Euphrates River. Then repeat God's words: "So shall Babylon sink, to rise no more; I am bringing her doom upon her!"'

Slaves – Pawns in the Political Game (between 597 and 586)

Jeremiah 34:8-22

King Zedekiah made a solemn agreement with the citizens of Jerusalem to free all Israelite slaves – men and women; no citizen was to hold a fellow-citizen as a slave. So all slaves were set free.

After a time, the citizens went back on their word; they forced the freed slaves into slavery again.

GOD spoke to Jeremiah.

'This is what I have to say to them: You did a fine thing when you set the slaves free and made a solemn agreement to do so in my presence. But you have gone back on your word. You have put me to shame by forcing men and women back into slavery.

'This is what I now have to say to you: You have flouted me in this matter of a Declaration of Freedom. I will therefore set you free – to become yourselves the slaves of a new master: war and hunger and the disease they breed. The whole world shall hold you in horror. As for the men who broke my Covenant by disowning their solemn Declaration of Freedom, I will hand them over to their enemies, and they will know what war means. The Babylonian army has raised the siege – for the moment. But king and ministers shall become its victims – I order it back to the city. Jerusalem shall be attacked, captured and burnt to the ground. Its villages shall be left desolate and deserted.'

King Zedekiah – son of the good King Josiah – was now on the throne, put there by the Babylonian authorities. Neither he nor his ministers nor the common people took Jeremiah seriously. They did not believe that GOD was speaking to them through him.

But one day King Zedekiah sent two men to Jeremiah with a message. 'Pray to God for us,' he asked.

Jeremiah was still a free man; he had not yet been put into prison. The Babylonian armies had been besieging Jerusalem; but news that the Egyptians were marching north had forced them to withdraw their troops to the coast.

GOD spoke to Jeremiah.

'This is what I have to say,' he told him. 'The king sent to you to pray for him. Tell him: "The Egyptian armies have retreated: the Babylonian armies will come back to carry out their attack on the city. They will capture it and burn it down. Don't fool yourself and think that they will abandon their attack; they won't. Even if you had troops enough to defeat their entire army and the soldiers in their camp were all wounded men, they would still march and burn the city down!"'

There was a lull in the siege while the Babylonian armies were back on the plain facing the advancing Egyptian troops. Jeremiah set off through the Benjamin Gate of the city to go to his native village of Anathoth to deal with some property there. A sentry challenged him.

'Running away, are you?' he said.

'That's a lie!' said Jeremiah. 'I'm no deserter.'

The sentry wouldn't listen. He arrested him and marched him to the city authorities. The officials were so angry with Jeremiah that they had him flogged and kept him in the secretary's house which was being used as a prison. And there he stayed, shut up in an underground pit, for a long time.

The king, at last, heard about his arrest, and had him brought secretly to the palace.

'Has GOD said anything to you?' he asked.

'He has,' said Jeremiah. '"You will become a prisoner of the Babylonian emperor."'

'What wrong have I done to your Majesty or your ministers or my fellow-countrymen?' he went on. 'What have I done to deserve prison? And what's happened to all the prophets who said the Babylonian armies would never come back to attack you or the city? Your Majesty, I beg you to listen to me. Grant me this petition: don't send me back to that pit or I shall die there.'

The king gave orders for Jeremiah to be detained in the Guards' Barracks; and he was to have a loaf from the Bakers' Bazaar until bread rations gave out.

So that's where Jeremiah stayed.

Four of the king's ministers were noting down the kind of message Jeremiah was still giving to the people about the Babylonian attack on the city. Here are two they seized on:

'The man who stays in the city will face death; war or starvation or disease will see to that. The man who surrenders to the Babylonians will at least save his life, if only by the skin of his teeth. At any rate he will stay alive.'

'The city will certainly fall to the attack of the Babylonian armies.'

The four men asked for an audience with the king.

'Order this man's execution,' they advised him. 'This kind of talk is undermining the resistance of both troops and civilians. This fellow isn't trying to help his country; he is merely making sure of its defeat.'

'Well,' said the king, 'he's at your mercy' – by this time he was a mere figurehead.

The men arrested Jeremiah and threw him into a pit in the Guards' Barracks. The pit was empty but muddy, and Jeremiah sank in the mud.

One of the palace chamberlains, an African named Ebed-melech, was on duty at the palace and heard about what had happened to Jeremiah. He left the palace and found the king at the Benjamin Gate.

'Your Majesty,' he said, 'your ministers have done a dreadful thing in throwing Jeremiah into the pit. If he's left there, he'll die.'

'Take three men,' said the king, 'and get him out. I don't want him to die.'

Ebed-melech and the men got some rags and old clothes from a wardrobe. They lowered them by ropes, so that Jeremiah could put them under his armpits to stop the ropes chafing his skin. Then they pulled him up and got him out of the pit. But he stayed on in the Guards' Barracks.

One day, King Zedekiah again summoned Jeremiah to a secret interview. They met at the gate where the king's bodyguard entered the temple.

'I've a question to ask you,' said the king. 'Tell me the truth.'

'If I tell you the truth,' said Jeremiah, 'you'll only order my execution. You never listen to what I have to say.'

The king swore an oath:

'As GOD lives who made us,' he said, 'I won't execute you and I won't hand you over to the men who want to get rid of you.'

'Well,' said Jeremiah, 'this is what GOD has to say: "If you surrender to the Babylonians, you will escape with your life and the city will escape being burned down – and your family will escape with you. If you don't surrender, the city will be captured and burned to the ground; you yourself certainly won't escape."'

'I am afraid of the Jews who have already deserted to the Babylonians,' said the king. 'I don't want to be handed over to them and beaten up.'

'You won't,' said Jeremiah. 'Do what GOD tells you through me; you will be safe, your life spared. If you don't surrender, this is what GOD has shown me: I have seen in a vision the women abandoned in the royal harem being led out by the Babylonian officers and chanting this lament about their country as they walked along –

> Even your friends have let you down,
>> they've had their way with you,
>> they've pushed you into the deep mud
>> and left you there!'

'If you want to escape death,' said the king, 'don't breathe a word about this conversation. If the officials hear about it and question you, tell them you were presenting a petition to me not to be sent back to certain death in Jonathan's house.'

News about this secret interview with the king did leak out; the officials came and questioned Jeremiah about it. He answered them as the king had told him to. They let him be; the conversation with the king had not been overheard.

Jeremiah stayed in the Guards' Barracks until the fall of the city.

Freedom Again

Jeremiah 39:1-3, 13-18; 40:1-6

The city was captured in the summer of 586. The Babylonians entered it and set up their headquarters at the Middle Gate. They sent for Jeremiah who was still in the Guards' Barracks and put him into the custody of Gedaliah to be taken out to his Residence. (Gedaliah, son of his old friend Ahikam, was soon to be made governor of the Jersualem area by the Babylonian authorities.)

Before Jeremiah left the Guards' Barracks, GOD spoke to him.

'Send this message to the African Ebed-melech,' said GOD. '"I am about to carry out all I have threatened against this city – words of disaster, not words of victory – and you will see it happen. But I will rescue you and see that you do not fall into the hands of the men you fear. I guarantee your escape – you will not be killed in the fighting. Your life will be saved because you trusted me. These are my words."'

Some months later, Jeremiah was rounded up with the crowd of prisoners being taken on the long journey to Babylon. The assembly-point was Ramah, some five miles north of the city. Here he was found in chains by Captain Nebuzaradan, the commander of the Babylonian Guards. He ordered him to be unchained.

'You are a free man,' he told Jeremiah. 'If you want to come with me to Babylon, I will see that you are in no danger. But do what you like. Stay here if you want to.'

Jeremiah chose to join Captain Gedaliah in Mizpah, a town some few miles to the west, where he had set up his headquarters, and those who had rallied round him.

Murder of the Governor

Jeremiah 40:7-16; 41:1-18

Jewish soldiers who had escaped from the city were fighting as guerrillas in the hills. News reached them of Gedaliah's appointment as governor of the remaining population (mostly poor peasants). The guerrilla captains – Ishmael, Johanan and Jonathan, Seraiah, Ephai's sons, Jezaniah – marched their men to Mizpah to serve under him.

'Don't worry about the Babylonian officers here,' the governor told them. 'Settle down in the country, accept our new masters loyally and everything will be all right. My work's clear: I will deal directly with the Babylonian authorities from my headquarters here. You can get on with your farming wherever you want to.' He swore an oath of loyalty to all his countrymen.

Many Jews had fled as refugees across the eastern frontiers. When they heard of the new government in Mizpah, they came back and took up their farming again. There were splendid harvests that summer.

Captain Johanan and the guerrilla leaders came in to Gedaliah to report a plot against his life; it was being hatched, they said, in a neighbouring state.

'Haven't you heard what King Baalis of Ammon is up to?' they asked him. 'He's sent Prince Ishmael to assassinate you.'

Gedaliah thought it was only a rumour – there was nothing in it. But Captain Johanan saw him privately about it.

'Let me deal with Prince Ishmael,' he said. 'Let me get rid of him; I can do it without any public fuss. Why should we take any risk? Your death would be a disaster for the whole country. We should have to take to the hills again.'

'I forbid you to do any such thing,' said Gedaliah. 'There's nothing in this rumour, I tell you.'

In the spring, Prince Ishmael and ten conspirators arrived in Mizpah and were entertained by the governor. In the middle of the meal, the eleven men carried out their plot, murdering the governor and the Jewish advisers and Babylonian officials who were with him. They sealed off the Governor's Residence; nobody in the town suspected anything.

Next day, eighty pilgrims from three northern towns arrived; they were going to Jerusalem to share in a service in the ruined temple there. Prince Ishmael went out to meet them as they walked along singing hymns of lament, and lured them into the town.

'Come and meet the governor,' he said.

When they reached the town centre, he and his men butchered them and threw their bodies into a well. Ten of them begged for mercy.

'Don't kill us, don't kill us!' they pleaded. 'We've lots of wheat and barley and oil and honey hidden out in the open countryside.'

He spared their lives.

But he rounded up the Mizpah townspeople and some royal princesses Captain Nebuzaradan had put in the care of the governor, and at dawn next day marched them off as prisoners toward the eastern frontier and Ammonite territory.

News of the governor's murder quickly reached Captain Johanan and his friends. They called out their men and caught Prince Ishmael at the Pool of Gibeon. The crowd of prisoners were filled with joy when they recognised the soldiers and soon showed whose side they were on. Prince Ishmael and eight of his men made good their escape across the frontier.

Captain Johanan gathered together the people he and his men had rescued. But instead of going back north, they marched south and stopped at Kimham's Sheepfolds near Bethlehem with the idea of going on to Egypt. They were terrified at the thought of the reprisals the Babylonians would take.

Panic   *Jeremiah 42:1-22; 43:1-7*

Captain Johanan and Captain Azariah and the crowd of survivors consulted Jeremiah (he had been marched away with the others).

'Do what we ask you,' they said. 'You have often told us what GOD has to say to us. Ask him to guide us now and tell us what to do. There are not many of us left.'

'Very well,' said Jeremiah. 'I will do what you ask and tell you what GOD has to say. I won't hide anything from you.'

'GOD knows that we mean what we say,' they said. 'We will do whatever he tell us to do. We will obey him – whether we like it or not. That's why we're asking you to pray for us. We want to do the right thing, and we know we can only do the right thing if we obey what GOD says.'

Jeremiah waited ten days before GOD spoke to him. He called the captains and the people together.

'This is what GOD has to say to you,' he told them. '"Stay here in this country and I will build you up as a strong people – you need not fear ruin or death. I will not deal with you as I have done in the past. I know you are terrified of the Babylonian emperor and what he may do. Don't be frightened. I am with you and I will deal with him. I will show my kindness to you by making him treat you kindly and let you settle in your own country. But if you refuse to listen to me, if you say, 'No, it's Egypt for us – we've finished with fighting and hunger – we're going to live where there's peace and plenty. We're going to Egypt' – if you talk like this, then listen, I have something to say to you. You're only a handful of refugees; you'll find in Egypt only what you're trying to escape from here – fighting and famine and death. And there'll be no escaping from Egypt; you'll never see your native land again. I have warned you. You go to Egypt at your own risk. You asked for my guidance and you promised to do whatever I told you. I have now told you. But in your hearts, I fear, you are not keeping your promises."'

Jeremiah finished.

'You're lying,' the captains had the insolence to say to him. 'GOD never said that. Baruch's been putting you up to talking like this. All he wants is for the Babylonians to capture us – and we know what that means: death or deportation.'

They refused to stay in Palestine. The captains led the whole crowd of refugees south across the Egyptian border and made Jeremiah and Baruch go with them. They settled in the Egyptian town of Daphne.

In Egypt   *Jeremiah 43:8-44:30*

GOD spoke to Jeremiah in Daphne.

'Take some large stones,' he told him, 'and bury them in the pavement in front of the Government House in Daphne – let the Jewish refugees see you do it. Then tell them: This is what GOD has to say to you – "I will bring my servant, the Babylonian emperor, to this place. He will set up his throne on these very stones and raise his pavilion over them. He will conquer Egypt with all the horrors of war – the very things you are trying to escape – and rob and burn the Egyptian temples, even the obelisks of the great temple of Heliopolis. He will deal with Egypt as a shepherd deals with his coat – picking lice out of it. Nobody will stop him."'

Jewish refugees in Egypt were now living in Migdol, Daphne, Memphis (the old Egyptian capital) and even in the south in Upper Egypt. GOD told Jeremiah to speak to them when they met together for an act of worship.

'This is what GOD has to say to you,' Jeremiah told them. '"You have yourselves seen the disaster which has overtaken your native land and its capital city. It all lies desolate. You know the reason: you were not loyal to me; you worshipped the pagan gods of the country. I told you plainly that this was wrong; I sent my servants the prophets to tell you. But nobody took any notice. That's why disaster overwhelmed you. Why are you following the same suicidal path here in Egypt? Why are you worshipping in Egyptian temples? You are only courting disaster again – the same disaster which has overtaken your country and your capital city. You will meet the same fate: there will be no survivors!"'

The women and their husbands screamed at Jeremiah.

'We won't listen to you!' they shouted. 'We've made up our minds. We'll worship Ishtar, the Queen of Heaven. That's what our fathers did and we were happy and well fed and safe then. We've had nothing but trouble since we listened to men like you and stopped worshipping her.

'We made cakes stamped with her image,' the screaming women

went on, 'and we poured libations out to her – and our husbands knew all about it!'

'All right, you've made up your minds,' said Jeremiah. 'Go on with your Egyptian worship. But remember what GOD is saying to you: "I have sworn by my name that you will never use my name in worship again, and you will suffer the disaster you deserve – the very things you came here to escape. The refugees from that disaster will be few indeed. You will discover then whose word is the truth – mine or yours. And this will be the sign of disaster: the Egyptian Pharaoh will be defeated by his enemies as surely as King Zedekiah was captured by the Babylonian emperor!"'

A Word to Baruch   *Jeremiah 45*

'That is what GOD has to say to you, Baruch,' said Jeremiah one day when Baruch had finished writing down his poems in the scroll:

'"I know what you have been saying, that all I've meant to you is trouble and sorrow, that you're tired of complaining and that you can't settle down. Listen to me.

> I am about to pull down what I built up
>   root up what I planted.
> You're a very ambitious man –
>   this is no time for ambition.
> I am about to bring disaster
>   on the whole world.
> You'll have to live dangerously;
>   all you'll get will be strength to see it through!"'

Jeremiah's Call

Jeremiah was quite a young man when he became aware of GOD's call to be his 'spokesman'. When this happened is not quite clear but it was a time of international turmoil and uncertainty. The date given in the records is 626. Whatever the truth about this, most of Jeremiah's poems and Baruch's stories come from the years after the death of King Josiah (609).

He described his Call (as Amos had done) in symbolic language. The sight of almond blossoms in spring, the first flowers to appear, stirred his mind; the word for 'almond blossom' (shaqed) and the word for 'wakeful' (shoqed) sound very much alike; one word recalled the other. The open oven he passed by was facing north and being fanned by a northern wind; this reminded him of the danger from the north – where all real danger – Scythian horde or Assyrian army – came from. It was his people's danger that brought Jeremiah from the seclusion of his little village of Anathoth (where his father was village priest) into the public life of the nation.

GOD's Spokesman

Jeremiah 1:4-10

God spoke to me:

> 'Before you were born
>> I chose you,
>> and set you apart,
>> appointed you
>> to speak in my name to the whole world.'

'But GOD,' I said, 'I am too young. I don't know how to speak to people at all!'
GOD's answer came clear:

> 'Don't talk like that!
>> You shall go
>>> to whomever I send you!
>> You shall speak
>>> whatever I tell you!
>> Don't be afraid of anybody –
>>> I am with you,
>>> I am looking after you!'

GOD touched my mouth with his hand and told me:

> 'Look, I have given you the power
>> to speak my words,
>> power over the whole world
>> to pluck up and plant,
>> to break down and build up.'

252

Almond Blossom   *Jeremiah 1:11-12*

God spoke to me:

'What are you looking at, Jeremiah?' he asked.
'Almond blossom,' I said.
'Just so,' he said.

'I stand wakeful over my Word
to make it my deed!'

A Boiling Pot   *Jeremiah 1:13-14, 16-17*

God spoke to me again.

'What are you looking at, Jeremiah?' he asked.
'A boiling pot,' I said, 'and a fierce north wind is fanning the fire!'
God's words came clear:

'A north wind wildly blowing
on the people of this land!
I will pass sentence on them
for deserting me so falsely,
sacrificing to village gods
carved with their own hands.

'These are your marching orders:
up and tell them what I tell you.
Don't let them frighten you –
or I will really make you frightened
when you meet them.

This is GOD's Word.

Jeremiah's 'Confessions'

These poems are prayers in which Jeremiah lays bare his heart to God.
Here we can see what questions and conflicts went on in his mind, and
how he had to fight his way through to his faith in God.

Alone Against the World

Alas, my mother,
I wish you had never given me birth –
   a man at odds with the whole world!
I stand in no man's debt –
   yet all men curse me!

You know all about me, O GOD –
   remember me and come to me!
Set me right with those who are against me –
   and set me right quickly.
It's men who care nothing for you
   who have heaped insults on me.

My joy and my happiness
   is to listen to your words.
I am wholly yours,
   O GOD of the whole world!
I never joined the village merry-making –
   that gave me no pleasure at all.
I sat alone –
   you were urging me on,
   your anger was my anger.

Why does my pain go on and on,
   my wounds incurable?
You are to me like a waterless gorge,
   and a dried-up spring!

God answered me:

   I will heal you, if you stay loyal,
      and you will indeed be my servant;
      call right right and wrong wrong,
      and you will be my ambassador.

   It's for others to take your side,
      and not for you to take theirs.
   Against the assault of this people
      I will make you like bronze battlements!

They will attack you
    but they will not conquer you.
I am with you,
    I will rescue you
    from the power of vicious men,
    from the grip of ruthless men.

The Human Heart   *Jeremiah 17:9-10*

GOD once said to me:

How deep is the human heart –
    deep as an unfathomable sea!
Its sickness defies cure –
    who knows its secret?

I, GOD,
    plumb the secret mind
    and test the secret heart.

'Let's dig a pit to catch him!'   *Jeremiah 18:18-20, 22b*

'Come!' they said, 'let's put him in his place,
    frame charges against him
    and take no notice of what he says!'

Watch them, O GOD,
    listen to my accusers!
Is evil all I get for doing good?

Remember: I stood before you
    to plead for them,
    to stave off your anger!

And all they could do
    was to dig a pit to catch me,
    set a trap for me to walk into!

Out of the Depths   Jeremiah 20:7-11

You have deceived me, O GOD,
   and I let myself be deceived!
You were too strong for me,
   you did with me what you wanted.
I'm everybody's laughing-stock,
   a daily joke.

I've only to speak to be laughed at
   with my 'Violence!' and 'Wrong!' –
'God's Word' I talk about
   is no joke!

'I'll give it all up,
   I'll be no ambassador of his!' –
my protest dies
for his word within me
sets my heart ablaze,
scorches my very soul.
I can stand no more of this,
   I can't go on.

I know what they're all whispering,
   my old friends whispering:
'He and his "Terror is coming!" –
   let us denounce him!
He'll slip up somewhere
   and we'll get our own back!'

But GOD is with me,
   giving me a hero's courage.
It's they who'll slip up,
   they'll not get the better of me!
It's they who will fall
   and fail.
Their shameful behaviour
   shall not be forgotten!

Why Was I Born? *Jeremiah 20:14-18*

> I hate the day
>> when I was born,
> I don't want
>> any birthday greetings!
>
> I hate the man
>> who told my father the happy news –
> 'You've a son now!'
>> 'Happy' indeed!
>
> May his fate be like the fate of the towns
>> that died in the Sodom earthquake –
> its morning disaster,
> its noon black with battle!
>
> Why didn't he kill me
>> there and then –
> making my mother my grave
> big with my dead body?
>
> Why was I born
>> for trouble and hard labour,
> a lifetime of shame?

The Tragedy of GOD's People

Why Go to Egypt? *Jeremiah 2:14, 16-18*

> Was the North a slave bought in the slave market
>> or born on bondage?
> Why, then, is he at the mercy of invaders,
>> his towns smoking ruins?
>
> Egyptian legionaries
>> are shaving you bald –
> and your abandonment of GOD
> is the cause of it all!

Why go off to Egypt
  to quench your thirst in the Nile?
Why go off to Assyria
  to quench your thirst in the Euphrates?

Disaster will teach you
  the error of your ways –
  how bitter a thing it is
  to abandon your GOD,
  to scorn my help!

Danger from the North

It used to be thought that this danger was the raiding of the Scythians from the north. But it is now doubted whether there were any such raids. However, whether Jeremiah is referring to Scythians or Assyrians, his argument is clear – the danger to the Israelite people was what was happening over their northern borders, and to this they were strangely blind.

Watchman's Shout   *Jeremiah 4:5-8*

Blow the bugle,
  shout across the hills –
'Fly from the villages!
Gather in the walled towns!'

Hoist the signal in Jerusalem city!
Escape while you can!
Danger and disaster
  march down from the north!

The lion has leapt from his lair!
Destroyer of Nations is marching,
  marching south,
  harrying your homeland,
  murdering your people
  in town and village!

Put on mourning,
    lament and wail!
GOD's fierce anger
    pursues us still!

Gathering Storm   *Jeremiah 4:13, 15-17a*

Look!
    Soldiers like thunderclouds!
    Chariots like storm-winds!
    Cavalry like vultures!
    All is lost!

Look!

Runner from the frontier,
    herald from the highlands:
'Enemy troops are marching,
    marching on Jerusalem!'

Invaders pour over the border,
    threatening our Southern towns,
    sleepless pickets
    ring them round!

The Pity of It All!   *Jeremiah 4:19-21*

My heart! My heart! The pain of it!
The wild beating of my heart!
The tumult of my mind!

Bugles blowing,
    soldiers shouting,
    crash upon cruel crash
    in the deserted towns!

Tents and curtains
    of my beloved city
    torn in tatters!

How long must I watch
   the signal on the hills?
How long listen
   to the blare of bugles?

Vision of Chaos   *Jeremiah 4:23-26*

I looked at the earth beneath me –
Chaos again!
   stared at the sky above me –
   starless dark!

I looked at the mountains –
   they were quaking!
   at the highlands –
   they were shaking!

I looked and looked again –
   empty roads,
   empty skies!
I looked and looked again –
   everywhere
   deserted and smoking cities
   before GOD's anger.

Invasion   *Jeremiah 4:29*

Thud of galloping cavalry!
Swish of archers' arrows!
Roads crowded with fugitives,
   crawling into caves,
   hiding in thickets,
   climbing crags!
Towns
   empty and deserted!

Dreadful City   *Jeremiah 4:30-31*

Dressing in scarlet still?
Flaunting your trinkets?
Painting your face?
You are wasting your time!

Your lovers don't want your beauty,
    they want your blood!

Scream like a woman's scream
    in her first child-birth! –
Scream of the city
    clenching her fists:
'Woe! Woe! Woe!
    I faint at my murderers' feet!'

Death of King Josiah (609)   *Jeremiah 22:10*

No dirge for the late king,
    no lament!
Keep your tears
    for the king in exile –
    no home-coming for him,
    no sight of his native land!

Megiddo (609)   *Jeremiah 8:18-9:1*

My grief knows no relief,
    my heart sinks!
Far and wide
    my people shout for help:

'Is GOD no longer
    on the Temple Hill?
Has her king
    deserted her?
Harvest's over, summer's gone
    and we're not rescued!'

My people's wounds
    have broken my heart;
    sorrow and dismay
    overpower me.

Is there no healing oil in Gilead,
    no doctor there?
Why, then, is my people's wound
    raw and bleeding?

Would to GOD my head were a sea,
    my eyes a river –
I would weep for ever
    over the dead of my people!

Jehoiakim's Palace   *Jeremiah 22:13-16*

Woe to him who builds his palace
    on injustice,
    its upper rooms
    on fraud!
    conscripts labourers
    and robs them of their pay!
    with only one thought in his head –
    'A spacious palace!
    airy rooms!
    wide windows!
    cedar panels!
    scarlet paint!'

What kind of a king do you think you are?
    Is cedar all you can think about?
Your father was a different king –
    eating and drinking indeed,
    but caring for justice and right,
    defending the humble and poor.
He was a king indeed,
    his was honest religion!
                         This is GOD's Word!

Lament for King and Queen Mother (after 597)   *Jeremiah 13:18-19*

Tell the king and queen mother:
'No throne now – only a peasant's chair!
Your splendid crown
    fallen on the palace floor!

'Towns of the steppes blockaded!
Guards at the gates gone!
The South swept away,
    swept away into exile!'

King Jehoiachin's Surrender (597)   *Jeremiah 22:28-30*

King Jehoiachin! – a broken pot
   nobody wants any more!
Why – why was he flung headlong
   into an unknown land?

O Earth – Earth – Earth!
   Listen to what God has to say:

'Write this man down as an outlaw,
   a stumbler all his life.
No descendant shall succeed him
   sitting on David's throne,
   king of the South!'

Is This the Way GOD's People Should Live?

No Covenant for Them!   *Jeremiah 5:1-5*

'Explore the city's streets,
   search the market-places;
   find, if you can, anybody who acts justly
   or values honesty,
   that I may forgive the city,'
      says GOD.

Its people use your name
   but it doesn't mean anything.
Yet it's honesty
   that matters to you, O GOD.
You have punished them
   but they didn't even wince!
They won't learn –
   they've set their faces like flint,
   no repentance for them!

They're only peasants (said I),
   they know no better,
   they haven't really understood,
   their 'worship' is all mixed-up.

I'll try the 'important people',
    I'll talk with them,
    they understand what you want,
    their worship is real worship.

But even they just please themselves
    like a runaway horse –
    no Covenant for them!

Violence Everywhere   *Jeremiah 6:6b-7*

False city,
    full of oppression!
Like cool water in a well
    your heart is cool with evil!

Everywhere victims shouting
    'Violence!' 'Robbery!'
I can see nothing
    but a sick and wounded city!

Hard Hearts   *Jeremiah 8:4-7*

These are GOD's words:

If a man falls down
    he gets up again;
    if he loses his way
    he finds the track again.
My people have wandered from the road –
    why don't they find their way back?

They cling to deceit,
    they won't repent.
I've been listening hard –
I can't hear a whisper.
Nobody stops and says,
'What have I done?'
They are as headstrong

as a horse
    galloping into battle!
Stork flying in the sky
    knows how to find her way;
    dove and swallow
    keep their appointed time.
My people have no sense
    of my time or way!

Nobody Trusts Anybody   *Jeremiah 9:2-6*

    O for a traveller's hut
        in the desert,
        to be quit of my folk
        and far away!

    Adulterers all!
    Gang of traitors!
    They use words as men use a bow,
        loyalty means nothing to them!
    They heap crime on crime,
        they've no use for religion!

                              This is GOD's Word!

    Guard against your friend!
    Don't trust even your brother!
    Brother cheats brother like Jacob,
        neighbour slanders neighbour!

    Cheating is a common game,
        truth doesn't matter,
        lies are a habit,
        nobody says 'I'm sorry'!
    Violence is their easy answer,
        cheating their trade!
    Nobody wants to know about me,
        says GOD.

A Word to the Government   *Jeremiah 12:11-12*

> Listen to what GOD has to say,
>   O dynasty of David!
>
> Make justice your concern,
>   rescue the robbed from the robber –
>   lest my anger blaze like a fire –
>   and no fitful fire! –
>   lit by your foul play.

Is This the Way GOD's People Should Worship Him?

'I remember!'   *Jeremiah 2:1-2*

> GOD said this to my people through me:
>
> I remember
>   your youthful affection,
>   the love of our honeymoon –
>   the love with which you followed me
>   on the desert march!

Strange Ingratitude   *Jeremiah 2:4-12*

> Listen to what GOD has to say to you:
>
> What fault did your fathers find in me
>   to leave me,
>   becoming as false
>   as the false gods they followed?
>
> They never asked,
> 'Where is GOD
>   who rescued us from Egypt,
>   marched us across the desert
>   with its wild and shifting sands,
>   its drought and desolation,
>   where nobody travels
>   and nobody lives.'

It was I who
    brought you to the arable lands
    with their happy harvests!
And all you could do when you got there
    was to become pagan as the pagans,
    no priest asking, 'Where is GOD?'
    no judge aware of my Way.

This is what I have to say:
I will stand up to you,
I will stand up
    to all your descendants!

Search – and search again –
    in the west, in the east:
    can you find anywhere
    a people changing its religion?

Yet my people have changed me, their glory,
    for a helpless idol –
    the very heavens stare aghast,
    scared and shocked!

This is GOD's Word!

Springs and Wells *Jeremiah 2:13*

My people have done
    two evil things:
They have abandoned me,
    a mountain spring of running water;
    they have hewed out for themselves
    cracked and leaking wells!

'Can't you hear the bugles blowing?' *Jeremiah 6:16-20*

Stand by the cross-roads and look,
    ask where the old paths are –
    then use them
    and learn what quietness of heart means.
'Not likely!'
    is all they said.

I gave you watchmen –
   can't you hear the bugles blowing?
'No, we can't!'
   is all they said.

I call the nations to witness,
   the earth to listen:
   the disaster I bring upon them
   is of their own evil making!
They would not listen,
   they flouted my Way.

What good's Arabian incense,
   sweet spices from overseas?
I can't stand your 'Sabbath services'!
I hate your temple 'worship'!

Snow on Hermon Mountain *Jeremiah 18:13-17*

   These are GOD's words:

Ask anybody:
   have you heard anything like this? –
   my unravaged people
   are guilty of shameful wrong.

Does the white snow
   melt from Hermon Mountain?
Do the waters
   fail from the Great Sea?

Yet my people have forgotten me,
   given their heart to idols,
   stumbling on the road,
   walking along rough by-paths.

They've made their homeland a desert,
   a thing of scorn for all time;
   passers-by are shocked
   and shake their heads.

I will scatter them before their enemies
   like the east wind blowing.
I will turn my back on them and not my face
   in the day of their disaster!

GOD and Our Conscience   *Jeremiah 23:16-24*

   These are GOD's words:

   Don't listen to the professional prophets
      who talk – talk – talk,
      filling you with false hopes,
      dreaming their own dreams:
      not a word is mine!

   They talk – talk – talk
      to those who care nothing for me:
      'You're all right!'
      to those who are stubbornly selfish:
      'You've nothing to worry about!'

   He who has really stood in GOD's presence
      must listen with awe;
      is there any other way
      to hear and understand?

   Look – a great storm
      is sweeping down,
      a great wind whirling round
      shattering injustice!

   There'll be no calm weather
      till GOD's will is done;
      in the years ahead
      you will face this plain truth.

   I never sent these professional prophets –
      but what a time they've had!
   I never spoke a word to them –
      but they talked as if I had!

If they had really stood in my presence
    they would have told my people the truth –
    and persuaded them to repent
    of their dishonesty and injustice!

Am I not GOD –
    God of the near and the far?
Can anybody escape
    my all-seeing eye?
Do I not fill
    heaven and earth?
                  This is GOD's very Word!

Recognising a Prophet
Jeremiah 23:28-29

    Let the prophet who's just dreaming
        go on dreaming!
    Let him I have really spoken to
        say honestly what I have said!

    Can't you tell chaff from wheat?
        (asks GOD)
    Isn't my word like fire?
        (asks GOD)
        like a hammer smashing rock?

But There's Still Hope

Learn from Experience
Jeremiah 31:21-22

    Set up signals on the hills,
        signposts along the road,
        the long, long road
        you've walked along!

    Come home, my people,
        come home!
    Are you in two minds still?
    Has your disloyalty taught you nothing?

In the days that are to come,
   GOD says,
I will make a new covenant
   with both North and South.

It won't be like the old covenant
   I made on the desert march
   when I led your ancestors
   out of Egypt.
That covenant was broken long ago –
   that's why I said No to them.

This is the new covenant
   I will make with the whole people:
My Way shall be clear to everybody's conscience,
   something everyone can recognise;
I will really be their God,
   they shall really be my people.

There'll be no need for teachers,
   for anybody to say,
'Live in GOD's Way'
   to neighbour or brother.
Each shall know for himself
   what my Way is –
   humble peasant
   and king on his throne alike,
   says GOD.

I'll forgive them
   the wrong they've done –
   their disloyalty
   shall be a thing of the past.

Voice from Babylon:
The Prophet of the Exile

We know very little about what happened during the fifty years of the exile in Babylon. The exiles there were not imprisoned; they were allowed to lead normal lives in their own community, trading and worshipping as they wished.

About 540, there was a great international upheaval. The Babylonian empire fell, two years later, to the Persian leader, Cyrus; and the Middle East became the Persian empire.

It was in the years when Cyrus was rising to power that the unknown Prophet of the Exile gave his message to the Jews in Babylon.

His message was one of liberation and deliverance: God, the creator of the world, is also he who will now rescue his people from the nations who have oppressed them. This is the Good News: God will lead them out of Babylon as long ago he led his people out of Egypt.

The most remarkable poems of the prophet deal with GOD's 'Suffering Servant'. In his portrait of the Servant we can recognise features drawn from the story of Jeremiah; but the Servant represents the Israelite people, GOD's People who have suffered at the hands of the nations but through whom GOD's love and power are to be made clear to the whole world. 'Supreme power is in love rather than in coercion.'

The Road Home

Our Slavery Is Over!   *Isaiah 40:1-2*

> 'Comfort, comfort my people,'
>   says your God.
> 'Speak to the heart of Jerusalem,
>   tell her
>   her slavery is over,
>   her penalty paid,
>   she has suffered, under GOD,
>   full measure for her sins.'

The Voice   *Isaiah 40:3-8*

Listen! Someone is calling! –

'Build GOD's road
    across the wastelands –
    clear a highway for our God
    across the desert!

Valleys shall be raised,
    mountain and hill levelled out,
    rough ground and rugged heights
    smoothed to a plain.
GOD's glory will dawn
    and the whole world stand in its light.
        GOD himself has spoken!'

Listen!

'Shout!' someone is calling.
    'What shall I shout?'
'Men are like grass,
    their devotion like a fading flower.
Grass dies,
    flower fades
    when great winds blow!
Grass dies,
    flower fades:
        GOD's Word stands for ever!'

Good News   *Isaiah 40:9-11*

Climb the Olive Hill,
    herald of good news to Zion!
Shout with all your strength,
    herald of good news to Jerusalem!
Shout aloud –
    there's nothing to fear –
    shout to all the Southern cities:
'Look! – your God!'

273

He comes
>with vigour
>and victory!
His reward and his wages are with him:
>his people marching ahead of him!
He feeds his flock like a shepherd,
>carrying the lambs in his arms,
>holding them to his breast,
>and gently leading
>the ewes heavy with young.

A Word to the World   *Isaiah 40:12-18, 21-26*

Who has measured the oceans
>in the palm of his hand?
>marked off the skies
>with the span of his fingers?
>picked up the earth's dust
>in a pan?
>weighed the mountains with scales
>or the hills with a balance?

Who grasped GOD's intention
>or stood by him as his Counsellor?*
Whom did he consult
>for guidance?
Who taught him
>how to order the world
>or how to use his skill?

Open your eyes!

The very nations
>are like a drop of water
>dripping from a bucket!
>like damp
>on the pan of the scales!

* The reference here seems to be to God's Heavenly Court (see also pp. 342, 359 where this Court is mentioned) which acted as his Advisory Council; God needed, they thought, his advisers and ministers as kings do. The poet here suggests that God created the world without any such help.

He picks up the coasts and islands
   like specks of dust!

To whom, then, can you liken God?
What image can show you what he is really like?
Don't you know?
Haven't you heard?
Isn't it old news?
Haven't you ever learned anything?

He sits on the dome of the earth,
   people like grasshoppers below him!
He stretches out the skies
   like fine gauze,
   spreading them out like a tent
   as his home!

He puts emperors and governors
   in their place,
   treating them
   as though they didn't even exist!
They are only just planted,
   only just sown,
   their roots only just gripping the earth –
   when he blows on them
   and they shrivel up,
   the storm sweeps them away like straw!

'To whom, then, can you liken me
   that he should be my equal?'
      asks the Holy One.
Look up at the sky – look up! –
   who made the stars?
GOD marshals them like a mighty army
   and numbers their ranks!
He is the Great Commander –
   none dares desert!

A Word to GOD's People   *Isaiah 40:27-31*

> Why do you talk and grumble,
>   you who are my people? –
> 'GOD can't see what's happening to us,
>   he isn't bothered about us and our rights!'
>
> Don't you know?
> Haven't you heard?
> GOD is always God,
>   creator of the whole universe!
>
> He does not faint or fail,
>   he knows what we can never know.
> He gives new life
>   to those who are worn out;
>   he revives
>   those who are ready to drop!
> Commandos get tired and faint,
>   seasoned veterans fall out with fatigue;
>   but those who trust GOD
>   grow stronger and stronger –
>   soaring like eagles,
>   running without tiring,
>   marching without flagging!

GOD's New Deed

GOD's Servant – First Song   *Isaiah 42:1-4*

> Look – my servant whom I steady,
>   my chosen one, in whom I delight!
> I have given him my spirit,
>   showing the whole world
>   what religion really means.
>
> His is no clarion voice,
>   no demagogue he
>   haranguing at street corners!
> He is too gentle to break a bruised stalk,
>   to snuff a flickering wick!

But his is no flickering wick,
 his no timid heart;
 honest and plain-spoken
 he makes the heart of religion clear.
And he'll go on
 till he has made religion real
 throughout the world –
 the world that longs for what he has to say.

The Servant's Commission   *Isaiah 42:5-9; (45:1)*

These are GOD's words –
 the God who made and stretched out the skies,
 created the richness of the earth,
 the source of all human life,
 the source of all living things:

I, GOD, have called you – really called you –
 I have grasped you by the hand
 to help people everywhere to see,
 to rescue prisoners from their prison,
 from the darkness of the dungeon cell.

I am GOD – that is my name –
 I come myself,
 sharing my presence with no one,
 least of all with man-made idols.

Emperor Cyrus has gone from victory to victory –
 this is nothing to the new triumphs I now proclaim;
 and before they happen
 I announce them to you!

New Song   *Isaiah 42:10-13*

Sing a new song to GOD,
 sing in far-off lands!
Let the sea and its vast waters thunder,
 and the island people of the west!
Let desert villages and Bedouin tribes
 shout aloud!

Let the Rock Dwellers sing,
  shouting from the mountain tops.
Let them give GOD glory
  till all the islands ring!

GOD shall march out like a soldier
  in the excitement of battle
  with war-cry and shouting,
  a hero facing his foes!

GOD Is Coming!   *Isaiah 42:14-16*

Far too long have I held my peace,
  saying nothing, holding myself back!
I will groan like a woman in child-birth,
  gasping and panting!

I will demolish the mountains,
  scorching the mountain grass!
I will turn rivers into deserts,
  drying up their pools –
  that I may lead blind people along unknown roads,
  guiding them along strange paths,
  turning the darkness ahead of them into light,
  making rough country level plain!

These are the things I will do –
  I will not leave them undone!

GOD's Servant – Second Song   *Isaiah 49:1-6*

Listen to me, you islands!
Listen, you far-off peoples!

GOD called me from my birth,
  the day I was born he gave me my name.
He made my tongue a sharp sword,
  holding me in the grip of his hand;
  he made me a polished arrow,
  ready in his quiver.

'You are my servant,' he told me,
   'my people through whom I shall be known
   as I really am.'

'All I've done has come to nothing,' I answered,
   'I have wasted my strength on an empty dream.
Yet my cause is safe in GOD's keeping,
   he will make all I do worthwhile.'

GOD took me to task –
   GOD who made me his servant at my birth
   to bring his people back home:

'Is being my servant
   and bringing my people home
   too little a thing for you?

'I will make you
   the light of the whole world,
   through you deliver
   the remotest people on earth!'

'I will lead them home!'   *Isaiah 49:8-11, 13*

   These are GOD's words:

      I have answered and helped you
         in this day of good fortune and deliverance,
         rescued your homeland,
         replanning its desolated countryside,
         calling to prisoners, 'You're free!'
         to those in darkness, 'Stand in the light!'

      They shall go home like a flock
         finding pasture on sand-dune and desert;
         they shall not be hungry or thirsty,
         at the mercy of the scorching sun.

      I who love them will lead them,
         showing them where the springs are;
      I will make mountains into good roads,
         build my highways for them.

Shout for joy, O Skies!
Triumph, O Earth!
Break into singing, O Mountains!
GOD has comforted his people,
    showing mercy to his suffering folk!

New City   *Isaiah 49:14-18, 12, 19-21*

'GOD has abandoned me,' says GOD's People,
    'GOD has forgotten me!'

Can a mother forget her baby,
    neglect her own son?
Yes, she can –
    but I will not forget you!
Look! I have branded your name on my hands,
    your city walls are never out of my sight!
Your builders outnumber your destroyers,
    your overlords are marching away!

Look up and look around –
    my scattered people are coming home!
As I live (says GOD),
    you will wear them like pearls
    like a bride putting her finery on!

Look! They are coming from far away,
    from the north and from the west,
    from the cataracts of the Nile!
Your empty and deserted villages,
    your devastated land,
    will be too narrow for all your people
    when your conquerors have marched away!

Those who were deported in your dark days
    will tell you plainly –
'The land isn't big enough for us;
    find us room to live!'
'Where have all these children come from?'
    you will say to yourself.

'I was bereaved and childless –
 who looked after them all?
I was left all alone –
 where have they all come from?'

The World – GOD's People   *Isaiah 45:18-19, 22-23*

These are GOD's words –
 the God who made the sky
 and the firm and solid earth,
 an earth which is no wasteland
 but a home for people to live in:

I am God –
 there is no other.
My word is clear
 making plain what is true and right –
 no secret muttering
 in murky darkness.
I have never told my people
 to seek me in any wasteland.

O wide, wide world
 turn to me for rescue.
I am God –
 there is no other.
I have sworn by myself,
 I have given my unbreakable word
 that everybody everywhere
 shall find themselves
 in my worship and service –
 only in GOD (shall they say)
 can we find victory and strength.

GOD's Servant – Third Song   *Isaiah 50:4-9*

GOD has given me
 the tongue of a teacher,
 to cheer with a word
 those who are tired out.

Morning by morning
   he wakens me,
   wakens me
   to listen as his disciple.

GOD helped me really to listen;
   I wanted to learn,
   I've always walked with him.

I let my accusers whip my back,
   pluck my beard;
I stood facing
   the insult and the spitting.

GOD stands by me to help me –
   that's why I stand my ground;
I've set my face like flint –
   nobody can put me to shame.
My Defender stands by my side –
   who can take me to court?

Let us stand together
   at GOD's judgement bar!
Who is my accuser?
Let him approach me!

See! GOD helps me –
   who can win their case against me?
They'll all be worn out
   like a moth-eaten coat!

GOD's Servant – Fourth Song   *Isaiah 52:13, 15; 53:1-2; 52:14; 53:3-12*

GOD   See! My servant shall win through;
           he shall be exalted and lifted up,
           lifted up high!
        The world was shocked,
           kings were sneering –
           looking at an unknown man,
           listening to an unheard-of story.

The World Who could have believed what we've heard?
Who has ever seen GOD at work?
This man grew up like a young plant
 with its roots in arid soil.
He was nothing to look at,
 with neither beauty nor charm.
He seemed inhuman,
 not like an ordinary man.
We despised and ignored him
 in his sickness and sorrow –
 a figure you don't like to look at.
We held him in contempt,
 took no notice of him.

Yet it was our sickness he was suffering,
 our pains that hurt him.
We thought that it was he who was doomed,
 his suffering a punishment by GOD.
But he was the victim of our violence,
 crushed by our wrong-doing;
 his punishment was for our good,
 his whipping brought health to us.
We had all wandered where we pleased
 like silly sheep;
GOD laid on him
 the guilt of us all.

He was brutally treated,
 humble and quiet though he was.
Like a sheep on the way to the butcher,
 like a ewe in the hands of the shearer,
 he was dumb.
He was marched off to execution –
 who gave a thought to his fate?
He was cut off from the living world,
 beaten to death for our rebellions.
He was buried in a criminal's grave –
 buried with vicious men –
 he who was never guilty of any violence,
 never pretended to be other than himself!

Yet GOD remembered and healed
   his suffering servant
   who had given himself
   that the world might be forgiven.
Others will follow him
   to make life worth living –
GOD's work shall go on
   because of him.

GOD   After his terrible torture,
            after his disgrace
            my servant shall step into the light.
He shall be the world's saviour,
   bearing its evil-doing himself.
I will give him the world for his inheritance,
   his 'spoil' will be too vast to be counted.
He faced death in the depth of his being,
   standing alongside the rebels themselves.
He took the whole world's sin
   on his own shoulders!
He stood between them
   and their deserved fate!

Come!

Isaiah 55:1-5

GOD   Hi! You who are thirsty
            come and drink!
You who are starving
   come – buy and eat!
Come and buy!
You don't need money –
   everything is free!

Why waste money
   buying what isn't bread?
Why work so hard
   for what gives you no joy?
If you listened to me
   you could enjoy a real feast!

Come here to me
and hear what I have to say
and learn the secret
of being really alive:
I will make an unbreakable covenant with you,
give you my steadfast love
as I gave it to King David!
I made him a witness to the world,
a leader and commander;
so shall you hail nations you never heard of,
they shall come running to you –
for GOD, the Holy One of his people,
has shone his glory upon you!

Delay Will Be Fatal! *Isaiah 55:6-13*

Seek GOD while he is here,
pray to him while he is close at hand!
Let the wicked have done with their evil deeds,
and change the way they think!
Let them come home to GOD,
home to our God –
his mercy and his pardon
are for everybody.

These are GOD's words:

'I don't think as you think,
I don't live as you live.
The sky towers over the earth –
my Way towers over your way,
my thoughts over your thoughts!
Rain and snow fall from the sky,
watering the earth,
refreshing everything,
giving the sower his seed,
the eater his bread;
so is the word I speak –
it does not come back to me empty:

285

it does what I mean it to do,
carrying out my purpose.

You shall go out in joy,
    be led out in peace.
Mountains and hills
    shall break into singing before you,
    wild trees
    clap their hands,
    pine trees grow
    where there were only thorns,
    myrtles
    where there were only briars!

All this is a sure sign
    of GOD's presence.

Enduring Convictions

Introduction

We can now look back on the long, stormy story of this highland people – what happened to them (Parts I-III) and what their greatest men had to say about it (Part IV). What did they learn from it all? What convictions about God and humanity and the world did they find they were driven to hold to be able to live through it?

We can summarise them as three: 'God is with us'; 'We must live as God's People'; and 'God has the last word'.*

These three convictions underlie their deepest thought and their daily life. They prompt their poets and psalmists and inspire their historians. They explain their power to survive.

God is with us. The temptation to interpret this as meaning simply 'We are God's favourites' or 'God is on our side' was – and is – always very strong; for many Israelites it meant no more than this. But its real meaning is very different. We may put it in this way: God loves and cares for all people everywhere, and comes to us in our day-to-day experience in village and town. We have to learn how to be aware of his presence; we can never take him for granted. He gives us no easy answers – and sometimes seems to give us no answers at all (see *The Book of Job*, pp. 341-352). What he does, however, is to be 'with us' all the time, stand by us and call us to be his 'co-workers'. It is not an accident that it was in their dark days that the profoundest Old Testament thinkers came to be more sure of God's presence with them – just when conventional religion broke down in despair. This conviction finds its supreme statement in the Twenty-third Psalm (p. 386).

We must live as God's People. From the very beginning, religion was never for Israelite or Jewish thinkers a solitary adventure of individuals; it was an adventure for individuals living together in community. God's world is always in the making; religion is taking our part with God, as his 'co-workers', in the making of his family. The Old Testament knows nothing of 'solitary religion'; we must live as 'God's People' and help the whole world to live as his people. What this means finds one of its greatest expressions in the 'Servant's Songs' of the unknown prophet of the exile (pp. 276-285).

God has the last word. The story which the Old Testament records might well be read as a story of a people's defeat – their political

* So Martin-Achard, *An Introduction to the Old Testament*, pp. 52ff.

independence is lost, their homeland becomes a foreign province, most of their people are scattered as exiles in distant lands. Powerful empires, with their military might and economic wealth, dominate the story and do what they will – or so it seems to the outside observer. But Egypt, Assyria, Babylon, Persia, Greece pass away. The world is not in their hands – it is in God's. Ultimately, they are his 'servants', for the world itself is not theirs but God's, and we can live in it with joy and confidence only in so far as we live in 'God's Way'. God is always Lord – Lord of history and Lord of nature.

These three convictions are found it the Old Testament in many different forms and with a great variety of interpretation. They undergird it all – prophetic poetry, temple hymn, historical narrative and law. They are the theme of the great preface to the Old Testament – Genesis – with which we begin this final part.

But there is a remarkable fact to keep in mind. These convictions were held (in Old Testament times) without any awareness of a real life beyond this. The Israelite people present us with 'the only example of a specifically religious civilisation and yet they do so without any belief in life after death'. They thought their convictions out in terms of this world only; they held that, after death, humans entered a subterranean land of gloom where they lived a shadowy existence that could hardly be called 'living' at all. Only in the centuries just before the Common Era – after the story we have told in this book was over – did they develop any belief in a real life after death.

The centuries that followed the exile – when they had little but their faith to sustain them – were a great 'testing-out ground' for their central convictions. The Jews were but a handful of people in a vast empire, strangers in a hostile world. Their convictions must sometimes have seemed to them as grandiose and unreal as they did to outsiders.

Many just accepted the new situation and ceased to care. Others held on to their faith and believed that GOD who had revealed himself to their ancestors was indeed the Lord of history and could bring triumph out of overwhelming disaster. For some this triumph would be a military triumph over his enemies, for others (in whom the spirit of the prophets still lived) the conversion of the world to his Way.

A violent change in their life occurred in the second century when the powerful king, Antiochus Epiphanes, tried to exterminate their religion. This provoked a violent reaction and the Jewish Resistance Movement was born – with a hardening of all hearts. The temptation to keep themselves to themselves in so hostile a world had been there since the exile; now, for many, it hardened into hatred of the foreigner and the practice of apartheid.

So we give, after the great preface of Genesis, a selection of passages to show the very varied responses found among the Jewish people. The three convictions, however, survived and became the heritage of the world.

What Kind of World Do We Live In?

Genesis is, as it were, the great preface to the story which follows it. It is world-wide in its sweep, dealing with the character of human society and the world which is its home (chapters 1-11), and with the question of how people ought to live, God being what he is (chapters 12-49). Much in it was written down in King Solomon's reign (about 950), but it was added to, commented on and expanded throughout the next six hundred years. In reading it, we are listening to people of many generations asking fundamental questions about the world they lived in, and working out their answers.

How do we deal with fundamental questions like 'What kind of world is it?' or 'What is the meaning of human existence?' These are not scientific or historical questions like 'How was the earth made?' or 'How did civilisation arise?' Such questions can only be answered by scientific and historical methods. We are asking religious questions, and religious questions about the fundamental meaning of things can only take the form of stories or pictures – of poetry in fact. The scientist and historian tackle the question 'How?'; the poet asks the question 'Why?'. That is why the Old Testament contains so much poetry.*

The early peoples of the Middle East accounted for the world they lived in by stories (historians call them 'myths') which often seem to us crude and sometimes even repulsive. But these old stories can embody profound insights, and we must distinguish between the form and the insight the form embodies.

The Israelites drew their stories about the world they lived in from the common stories of their time and culture.† But they told them in their own way and in the light of their new experience of God. They made great changes in them, for they were using them to express their new convictions. As they went on using these stories over the thousand years of their history, they constantly revised their 'science' (compare

* Even modern scientists, when they are concerned with fundamental questions, use myths as a tool of explanation or exploration – what Plato called 'a likely story'. Note, too, the use of myth and folk tale in modern literature, especially in countries where freedom of speech is limited (e.g. Ferenc Juhász, *The Boy Turned into a Stag*, Penguin Modern European Poets, pp. 97ff).

† See, e.g., *The Epic of Gilgamesh*, version by N. K. Sanders, Penguin Classics.

the two accounts of creation) but enlarged their faith.

When they came to consider what kind of people God wants us to be, the Israelites used old tribal stories of their famous ancestors, and added comments and notes as the years passed. They were, of course, deeply interested in their own remote past (as all peoples are); these old stories were their only source of information. But they were more concerned with the future – what sort of people God wanted them to be and how they could live in God's Way; they used these stories to make this clear.

The opening words of Genesis are a prose statement based, so some scholars believe, on an old poem. Hence the verse form in which we give them.

God's Intention

The Later Account (450 BCE)   *Genesis 1:1-2:4a*

> This is the story of the making
> of earth and sky:
> in the very beginning,
> God made them both.
>
> Earth was formless chaos
> lost in darkness
> with stormy winds
> sweeping over the vast waters.
> 'Let there be light!' said God –
> and everywhere there was light,
> splendid in his eyes.
> He marked off light from darkness,
> calling light 'day'
> and darkness 'night':
> so came the evening and the morning
> of the first day.
>
> 'Let there be a vault,' said God,
> 'separating the waters above the vault
> from the waters on the earth below!'
> The great vault was made;
> he called it 'sky':
> so came the evening and the morning
> of the second day.

293

'Let all the earth's waters
    be gathered together,' said God.
'Let dry land appear!'
He called the dry land 'earth'
    and the gathered waters 'sea' –
    splendid in his eyes.
'Let the earth grow plants and trees!' said God,
    'seed-bearing plants and fruit trees!'
Plants and trees appeared –
    splendid in his eyes:
    so came the evening and the morning
    of the third day.

'Let there be lights in the sky,' said God,
    'marking off day from night,
    signs for festivals,
    for seasons and years!
Let the lights of the sky
    shine down on the earth!'
He made the sun,
    dominating the day,
    the moon and the starts
    dominating the night –
    he set them in the sky
    to shine on the earth,
    day and night,
    light and darkness –
    splendid in his eyes:
    so came the evening and the morning
    of the fourth day.

'Let there be fish in the waters!' said God,
    'and birds flying in the sky!'
And there they were –
    great sea-monsters,
    shoals of fish,
    flocks of birds –
    splendid in his eyes.
God blessed them all –
'Be fertile,' he said,

'swarms of fish in the sea,
flocks and flocks of birds in the sky':
so came the evening and the morning
of the fifth day.

'Now for the animals!' said God.
'Let there be living creatures on the earth,
    domestic animals,
    reptiles and wild animals!'
He made all the animals –
    splendid in his eyes!

'Let us now make mankind in our image,
    said God,
        'like ourselves,
        to be masters
        of fish and wild birds,
        of domestic animals,
        of reptiles and wild animals!'
He created mankind in his own image –
    in his image both sexes were created.
He blessed them too –
    'Be fertile,' he said, 'and increase!
Fill the earth and conquer it,
    be masters of all living creatures.
Plants and trees
    shall be your food;
    green plants
    food for all living creatures –
    animals, birds, reptiles,
    everything alive.'

It was all splendid in God's eyes:
    so came the evening and the morning
    of the sixth day.
Earth and sky were made,
    crowded with life.
On the sixth day
    God finished his work;
on the seventh day
    he stopped working.

He blessed the seventh day –
　　the day he stopped work.
He had brought into being
　　everything he had set himself to make.

The Earlier Account (950 BCE)　　　　　　　*Genesis 2:4b-9, 15-25*

In the very beginning no prairie bush was yet to be found anywhere; no wild grain had started to sprout. No rain had fallen on the ground; there was nobody to till the ground if it had – there was only the water rising up from beneath the ground and covering the land.

Then GOD moulded Man* from the ground† itself and breathed into him the breath that made him a living creature.

He then planted a park away in the east, in Eden, and gave it to Man as his home, planting all sorts of lovely and useful trees. In the heart of the park he planted two special tress – the Tree of Life (the fruit of this tree made those who ate it immortal) and the Tree of Knowledge.

GOD put Man in the park to work in it and guard it.

'You can eat the fruit of any tree you like,' GOD told him. 'But the fruit of one tree you must never eat – if you do, it will mean certain death. That tree is the Tree of Knowledge.

'It is bad for Man to live here all alone,' GOD went on. 'I must make a mate for him.'

So GOD moulded all the wild animals and the wild birds – again, out of the ground itself. He led Man to them to see what names he would give them – these would be the names they would always be called by. Man gave names to all the domestic animals, the wild birds and the wild animals. But none of the animals could be a mate for him.

So GOD put him into a deep sleep. While he slept, he took one of his ribs, healing his body afterwards. He then built the rib into Woman, and led her to Man. As soon as he saw her, Man exclaimed –

　　This one at last
　　　　is from my very bone,
　　　　from my very flesh.
　　She shall be called 'Woman',‡
　　　　from Man§ was she taken.

---

* Hebrew 'adam'.　　† Hebrew 'adamah'.　　‡ Hebrew 'Ishshah'.　　§ Hebrew 'Ish'.

Man and Woman were naked. This was quite natural – there was nothing to be ashamed of.

(This story explains why a man leaves his parents to marry his wife – he is united with her and the two of them become one flesh again.)

Man's Tragedy

'Can't I do what I like?' *Genesis 3:1-24*

The cleverest of the wild animals was the snake.

'So, you can't eat the fruit of any of the trees in the park?' the snake said to Woman.

'Oh yes, we can,' she answered. 'We can eat the fruit of all the trees – except one, the tree in the heart of the park. GOD told us we would die if we ate it.'

'He did, did he?' said the snake. 'You wouldn't die! GOD knows, of course, what would happen if you were to eat its fruit: you'd become clever and know what things are really like, as gods themselves do.'

When Woman saw that the fruit of the tree was good to eat and lovely to look at – and moreover, found it more tempting the more she thought about it – she plucked some and tasted it. She took some to her husband, and he tasted it, too.

Suddenly, their innocence was over – they became aware that they were naked. They made loin-clothes for themselves out of fig-leaves.

It was now evening – the breezy time of the day. They both heard the rustle of GOD walking in the park. They hid themselves among the trees.

'Where are you?' GOD called out.

'I heard you coming,' said Man. 'I was frightened – you see, I am naked. That's why I did myself.'

'How did you know you were naked?' asked GOD. 'Have you been eating from the forbidden tree?'

'It was Woman's fault – Woman you gave me for a mate,' he said. 'She gave it to me to eat.'

'What's this you've done?' GOD asked Woman.

'The snake tricked me,' she said. 'That's why I ate it.'

GOD said to the snake:

'Because of what you have done
   you shall be banished
   from all the animals of the earth.
You shall crawl on your stomach,
   eating dirt,
   as long as you live.

You and Woman,
   your brood and hers,
   shall be deadly enemies.
They shall strike at your head,
   you shall strike at their heels.'

GOD said to Woman:

   'I will make child-birth
      very painful for you –
      in pain you shall bear children.
   You will love your husband
      but he shall be your master.'

GOD said to Man:

   'You listened to your wife
      and ate from the forbidden tree.
   The ground is cursed now
      because of you:
      you will labour all your life
      to make a living.
   The soil will only grow
      thorns and thistles,
      and wild plants for you to eat.
   You will have to sweat
      to get your food –
      until you are buried
      in the ground you come from.
   You are dust –
      and to dust you shall go back!'

Man gave the name 'Eve' to his wife ('Eve' means 'Life'). God made clothes from skins for the two of them.

'Look!' said GOD. 'Man has become like one of us – he's become clever. What would happen if he plucked the fruit of the other tree – the Tree of Life – and started to eat it? He'd live for ever!'

So GOD banished him from Eden to work for his living farming the soil he came from. He drove him out. He posted angelic sentries, with fiery, ever-turning swords, to guard the way to the Tree of Life.

'Am I my brother's shepherd?' *Genesis 4:1-16*

Two sons were born to Man and his wife Eve – Abel the shepherd and Cain the farmer. Cain brought some of his farm produce as a gift to GOD, Abel some of the finest firstlings of his flock. GOD honoured Abel and his gift; he took no notice of Cain and his gift. Cain was angry and sullen.

'Why so angry and sullen?' GOD asked him.

> 'If you've been doing what is right,
>   you can hold your head up.
> If you haven't,
>   sin crouches like a wild beast
>   at your farm-door,
>   savage to get at you,
>   too strong for you to kill.'

'Let's go out into the fields,' said Cain to his brother one day. Out in the fields, Cain attacked Abel and murdered him.

'Where's your brother Abel?' GOD asked him.

'How do I know?' said Cain. 'Am I supposed to shepherd my brother the shepherd?'

'What have you done?' asked GOD. 'Listen – your brother's blood is calling for justice from the ground where he's buried. You murdered him. You shall be banished, with a curse on your head, from the ground which drank your brother's blood. Your farming days are over – the soil will serve you no more. Fugitive and vagabond you shall be wherever you go.'

'I can't face it!' cried Cain in horror. 'You've banished me today from the soil. I must keep away from you and wander aimlessly through the world; I shall be an outlaw at the mercy of everybody I meet!'

'No,' said GOD. 'If anybody murders you, he will be punished seven times more severely than you have been punished.'

GOD put a protective mark on Cain's body. So Cain left GOD's presence and made his home east of Eden, a fugitive all his life.

God's Response
Genesis 6:5-8, 13a, 14a, 22; 7:1-5, 10, 16b-17, 22-23; 8:2-3, 6-13, 20-22

GOD saw the sort of thing that men and women were doing on the earth – just downright evil, giving all his plans an evil twist. He was deeply hurt; he was sorry he had ever made the human race.

'I will end the whole dreadful business – humans, animals, reptiles, wild birds – everything,' he said. 'I am sorry I ever began it.'

One man, however, was different from the others – Noah. GOD thought well of him; he was trying to live in GOD's Way.

'Build a ship on dry land,' GOD commanded him.

Noah did what GOD told him to do.

'Now go on board,' GOD said. 'Take your family with you. You're the only good man I can find. And take some animals and birds with you – seven pairs (each with its mate) of the "clean" kind; only a pair each of the "unclean" kind. In a week's time, I'm going to send torrential rain. It will rain for a long, long time – long enough to drown all living things everywhere.'

Noah again obeyed.

At the end of the week, down came the floods of rain. GOD shut him in the ship.

The water rose and lifted the ship off the ground.

All life on land – humans, animals, reptiles, birds – died. Only Noah and those who were with him were left alive.

At last the rain stopped, and the level of the waters began to fall.

After a very long time, Noah opened the hatch and let a raven fly away to see if there was any dry land. But it kept flying to and fro until the water was gone and the land was dry.

A week went by. Then Noah let a dove fly off, to see if there was any land free of water. The dove could find no resting place; she just came back to the ship. Noah put out his hand and caught her and took her into the ship again.

A week later, he let her fly off again. She came back as darkness fell – and there, in her beak, was a fresh olive leaf! Noah knew now that the water was really going down and the land appearing. He waited another week, and let the dove fly away again. She never came back.

So Noah took the covering off the ship. All around him the land was dry. He disembarked and built an altar to GOD and sacrificed some of the 'clean' animals on it. GOD smelled the pleasant odour.

'I will never again drown the world because of what humans have done,' he said to himself. 'Their very nature has an evil twist in it; but I will never again do what I have just done.

> As long as the earth lasts,
>   seedtime and harvest,
>   cold and heat,
>   summer and winter,
>   day and night
>   shall never cease.

'Isn't "being somebody" the most important thing?'   *Genesis 11:1-8*

Once upon a time, all the people of the world spoke the same language and used the same words.

Now there was once a great migration of people; they settled at last in the Babylonian plain where the Euphrates and Tigris rivers approach the sea.

'Let us make bricks,' they said, 'and bake them hard. And let us build a mighty city and a tall tower – tall enough to touch the sky. We must be somebody – or else we shall be nobody.'

GOD came down to look at the city and the tall tower, rising higher and higher.

'If this is the sort of thing they start to do,' said GOD, 'when they are a single people speaking a common language, there's no limit to what they may plan and carry out. Let us go down and turn their common speech into a babble of languages. They won't know what they are talking about, then.'

So GOD broke up the family of humankind into different nations, scattering them over the whole earth. That stopped the building of the city.

What Kind of People Should We Be?

Abraham: Facing the Unknown

Destination Unknown   *Genesis 11:27-28, 31-32; 12:1-4, 6-9*

Once upon a time there were three brothers living with their father in Mesopotamia. The youngest brother died while his father was still alive. The two others brothers married and settled down in the Balikh Valley. Then their father died.

'Abandon your country,' GOD said to Abraham one day. 'Leave your relatives and your ancestral home and go to a land I will show you. I will make a great nation of you and bless you. You will become famous – people will use your name when they bless one another.

> I will bless those who bless you;
> I will curse those who curse you.
> By you all the families of the earth
> will bless one another –
> 'May you be as happy as Abraham!'
> they will say.

Abraham set out at GOD's command, and travelled south.

He came to the shrine at Shechem in the highlands. Here GOD spoke to him again. 'I am going to give this country to your descendants,' he said. So Abraham built an altar to GOD there. Then he went on to the highlands east of Bethel and set up camp; he built another altar to GOD and worshipped him there. He then went on by stages to the Negeb in the south.

Egyptian Incident   *Genesis 12:10-13:1*

One year, the whole of Palestine was threatened with famine. Abraham moved over the border into Egypt.

'You're a very beautiful woman,' he said to his wife, Sarah, as they were crossing the frontier. 'I know what will happen as soon as people see you. Your beauty will be my undoing; they'll murder me to get hold of you. The only thing to do is for you to say you are my sister. I can get away with it then.'

That is what she did. The Egyptians – even members of the royal family – were struck by her beauty. Her praises were sung to Pharaoh himself. He took her into his harem; and, because he liked her, he lavished gifts upon Abraham – sheep, oxen, servants and camels.

Then everything went wrong in the palace – plague broke out – all because of Sarah, Abraham's wife. Pharaoh found out what had happened.

'Why did you treat me like this?' he asked Abraham. 'Why didn't you tell me that she was your wife? Why say she's your sister – and let me take her as one of my wives? Here she is – take her and get out!'

He sent him out of Egypt under military escort; and Abraham, with his nephew Lot, found himself again in the Negeb.

Back in the Highlands   *Genesis 13:2-18; 15:1-2, 4-12, 17-18*

Abraham was now a rich man. He trekked north with his nephew Lot as far as Bethel in the highlands – the very place where he had first set up camp and built an altar to GOD.

Then trouble began. His nephew was also a rich man with many flocks and herds and tents. Fighting broke out between their herdsmen – there were too few good wells and not enough land.

'I don't want trouble between us,' said Abraham. 'We are kinsmen; I can't have this fighting. We must go our separate ways. The country lies before you: if you go to the west, I'll go to the east; if you go to the east, I'll go to the west.'

The Jordan Valley could be seen from the high hills. Lot looked down on the valley with its rich, tropical vegetation, a wonderful garden. (This was before the great disaster in the valley happened.) It reminded him of the wealth of Egypt. He chose the valley and went eastward, as far as the town of Sodom, a notorious city.

When Lot had gone, GOD spoke to Abraham.

'Take a good look from these high hills,' he said, 'survey the land – north, south, east and west. This is the home I am going to give your descendants. They'll be a great people, vast in number. Go through the country and take stock of it. It is my gift to you.'

Abraham struck camp and went south. He settled by the famous Oak of Mamre, in Hebron territory, and built an altar to GOD there.

Time passed. Then GOD spoke to Abraham in a vision.

'Don't be afraid,' he said. 'I am your Shield. You will have a great future.'

'What sort of future can there be for me, O GOD?' said Abraham. 'I've no family; my servant Eliezer will inherit all I have.'

'He shall not be your heir,' said GOD. 'Your own son shall be your heir.' He led him outside his tent.

'Look up at the sky,' he said, 'and count the stars – if you can. Your descendants shall be as many as the stars.'

Abraham trusted GOD; it was his trust that made him a truly religious man.

'I am your GOD,' said GOD. 'I brought you here to give you this country as your home.'

'How am I to be sure?' asked Abraham.

'Bring me animals and birds for a sacrifice,' said GOD.

Abraham brought them, prepared them and laid them out. Carrion birds swooped down out of the sky on to the carcases, but he drove them off.

The sun was now setting. He fell into a deep trance – everything was blacked out in a great and fearful darkness.

The sun had now set and it was pitch dark, except for a smoking fire-pot and a blazing torch moving between the carcases.

GOD made a covenant with him.

'I give this land to your descendants,' he said, 'from the Egyptian border in the south to the Euphrates River in the north, with all the tribes living there.'

Trouble at Home

Genesis 16:1-2, 4-12

Sarah had an Egyptian slave-girl, Hagar.

'I've no children myself,' she said one day to Abraham. 'Make Hagar your secondary wife; her children can count as my children.'

This is what he did.

When Hagar knew she was going to have a baby, she began to sneer at her mistress.

'I've been wronged,' said Sarah to Abraham, 'and it's your business to put it right. My slave-girl treats me with contempt. May GOD see justice done between you and me!'

'You can do what you like,' said Abraham. 'The girl's in your hands. But, remember, she's the mother of my child.'

Sarah began to ill-treat the girl, and she ran away into the southern desert, trying to get home. GOD's angel found her at a desert oasis on the way to the Egyptian border.

'Where have you come from, Hagar,' he asked, 'and where are you going?'

'I'm running away from my mistress,' she said.

'Go back,' said the angel. 'You must go on being her slave.'

'Your descendants will be so many that they won't be able to be counted,' he went on. 'You're going to have a baby; you must call him Ishmael. He'll be a wild and roving wanderer – always spoiling for a fight, at odds with his kinsmen!'

Strange Visitors   *Genesis 18:1-16*

One day, when it was getting hot, Abraham was sitting at his tent door. He looked up – three men were standing not far away. He got up and hurried to them.

'Sirs,' he said as he greeted them, 'don't go on without staying a while with me, humble as I am. Take a rest under the tree – I will fetch water for your feet and bring you something to eat. That will refresh you. Then you can go on with the journey that brought you this way.'

'Very good,' they said.

He went into the tent.

'Quick!' he said to his wife. 'Get some food ready.'

He hurried off to the herd, chose a tender, choice calf, and gave it to the lad who had run over to help him.

Then he set curds and milk and meat before his visitors, and stood under the tree, waiting on them.

'Where's Sarah, your wife?' they asked.

'She's in the tent,' he said.

'These are GOD's words,' they said. '"I will certainly come back to you in the spring and Sarah your wife will give birth to a son."'

Sarah was eavesdropping at the tent door, which was quite near.

She laughed to herself – both she and her husband were growing old.

'At my time of life and my husband an old man!' she said to herself. 'It's absurd!'

'Why did Sarah laugh?' GOD asked Abraham. 'Why did she say it was absurd? Is there anything GOD can't do? I will come back at the appointed time and she shall give birth to a son.'

'I didn't laugh,' said Sarah.

'You did,' said GOD.

The three men got up to go on their way and looked down into the

Jordan Valley, towards the town of Sodom. Abraham walked with them along the road to see them off.

An Argument with GOD   *Genesis 18:20-33*

GOD had told Abraham what he was going to do.

'I have heard a cry for help against the two towns Sodom and Gomorrah,' said GOD. 'I must go down to see what it's all about. I must know if their conduct is what I think it is.'

Abraham's three visitors went on down towards the town; Abraham remained standing in GOD's presence. They were on the high hills and the valley lay all below them.

'Would you sweep away the good people with the bad?' Abraham asked GOD. 'Suppose there are fifty good people in the town, would you sweep it away – and not spare it for the sake of those fifty? I don't think you could do such a thing – treat good and bad alike. Must not the Judge of all the earth himself be just?'

'I will spare the whole town,' said GOD, 'if I find fifty good people living there.'

'I am a mere man, and yet I dare to speak to you who are GOD,' Abraham ventured. 'Suppose there aren't fifty; suppose there are five short? Will you sweep away the whole town just because there are five short?'

'If I find forty-five good people in the town,' said GOD, 'I won't sweep it away.'

'Suppose there are only forty?' said Abraham.

'For the sake of forty,' said GOD, 'I will not sweep the town away.'

'Don't be angry with me if I go on,' said Abraham. 'Suppose the number is thirty?'

'I will not do it,' said GOD, 'if I find thirty.'

'I am daring to speak again,' said Abraham. 'Suppose there are only twenty?'

'I will not sweep the town away,' said GOD, 'for the sake of those twenty.'

'Don't be angry with me for speaking again,' said Abraham. 'Suppose only ten good people are to be found there?'

'For the sake of those ten,' said GOD, 'I will not sweep it away.'

GOD had no more to say and went on his way; Abraham went home.

A Test of Loyalty   *Genesis 22:1-13, 19*

Isaac was Abraham's only son,* and he loved him very deeply.

One day, GOD put Abraham to the test.

'Abraham!' he called.

'Here I am,' said Abraham.

'Take Isaac with you,' he said, 'and go to the distant highlands. I will point out one of the mountains there, and on that mountain you must offer him as a sacrifice.'

At dawn, Abraham saddled his donkey and took two of his men with him – and Isaac. He split the wood for the offering and set off to the mountain GOD had told him about. After two days' march, he looked up and saw the mountain in the distance.

'Stay here with the donkey,' he told his men. 'I and the boy are climbing that mountain to worship. We'll come back to you here.'

He gave Isaac the split wood to carry; he himself picked up the fire and the knife. They both set off.

'Dad,' said Isaac.

'Yes,' said Abraham.

'We've got the fire and the wood,' he said, 'but where's the sheep for the sacrifice?'

'GOD will look after that, my boy,' said Abraham.

They went on together and came to the appointed spot.

Abraham built an altar and put the wood on it. He then bound Isaac, laid him on the altar and picked up the knife. Suddenly he heard a voice.

'Abraham! Abraham!' called the voice.

'Here I am,' answered Abraham.

'Don't touch the boy,' said the voice (it was GOD speaking). 'I know now your trust in me is real trust. You didn't say No when I asked for your son, your only son.'

Abraham looked up, and there, behind him, was a ram caught by its horns in the brushwood. He sacrificed the ram instead of his son.

He went back to the men he'd left with the donkey; and they all went back to Beersheba where he made his home.

---

* The historian apparently is not counting Ishmael, Abraham's son born to his secondary wife, Hagar, as a full son.

Jacob: Coming to Terms with Yourself

Brothers' Quarrel *Genesis 25:11, 21-34; 27:1-45*

After Abraham's death, his son Isaac made his home at Beer-lahai-roi, the oasis which Hagar, the Egyptian slave-girl, reached when she ran away from her mistress.

Isaac had no children. So he prayed to GOD, and GOD answered his prayer. In due time his wife, Rebecca, gave birth to twins. The first to be born was called Esau, and the second Jacob.

Esau grew up into a skilful hunter who loved out-door life; Jacob was a quiet fellow who liked to stay at home in the camp. Isaac made a favourite of Esau – he was very fond of the game he caught. Jacob was his mother's favourite.

One day, when Esau came in hungry from the hunt, Jacob was cooking soup.

'Give me some of that red stuff to swallow,' Esau said. 'I'm famished!'

'Sell me your rights as the first-born,' said Jacob.

'What do my rights matter?' said Esau. 'I'm dying with hunger.'

'I want your solemn word on that,' said Jacob.

Esau gave him his solemn promise and made his birthright over to him. Jacob then gave him his bread and lentil soup. Esau ate and drank his fill, and then got up and went off. That's how much Esau thought of his birthright.

Isaac was now old and blind. One day he called Esau to him.

'I'm an old man and I might die any time,' he said. 'I want to give you my blessing. Take your weapons and hunt some game for me. Make my favourite dish and bring it to me.'

Rebecca overheard this. As soon as Esau had gone hunting, she got hold of Jacob.

'Your father's been talking to Esau,' she said. 'He's sent him out hunting – he's going to give him his blessing. Now listen to me and do as I say. Fetch me two kids from the flock and I'll make him his favourite tasty dish. You shall take it to your father and get his blessing before he dies.'

'It won't work,' said Jacob. 'My brother's a hairy man. My skin's smooth – my father's only got to touch me to find out who I am. It will be obvious I'm playing a trick on him, and I'll get his curse instead of his blessing.'

'Let the curse fall on me,' said his mother. 'You just go and do what you're told.'

The tasty dish was made, and Rebecca made Jacob put on Esau's best clothes which she kept there in the tent. She covered his hands and the smooth skin of his neck with goat skin, and put the tasty dish and bread in his hands.

He went in to his father.

'Hello, Dad!' he said.

'Eh?' said the old man. 'And who are you, my son?'

'I'm Esau,' he said. 'I've got your favourite dish – sit up and eat it. Then you can give me your blessing.'

'However did you find the game so quickly?' asked Isaac.

'GOD gave me happy hunting,' said Jacob.

'Come close to me,' said Isaac. 'I want to feel you. I want to know who you really are.'

Jacob let him feel him.

'Your voice is Jacob's,' he said, 'but your hands are Esau's.'

He didn't tumble to the trick, and he got ready to give him his blessing.

'Are you really Esau?' he asked again.

'Of course I am,' said Jacob.

'Bring me my tasty dish, then,' said the old man. 'I'll eat it and give you my blessing.'

Jacob gave it to him – and wine; and he ate and drank.

'Come near and kiss me, my son,' he said.

Jacob kissed him. When Isaac smelt his clothes, he blessed him:

> 'My son's smell
>   is the smell of the open country.
> May God give you
>   the sky's dew and the earth's richness,
>   corn and wine in plenty.
> People will be your slaves,
>   nations acknowledge your lordship.
> Be master of your brothers,
>   let them be your subjects.
> A curse on him who curses you!
> A blessing on him who blesses you!

Jacob had hardly left his father when in came Esau from hunting. He, too, made a tasty dish for his father and took it in to him.

'Sit up, Dad,' he said, 'and eat some of the game I've caught. Then give me your blessing.'

'Who are you?' Isaac asked.

'I'm Esau, you elder son,' he said.

The old man trembled with shock.

'Who was it, then, went hunting,' he asked, 'and brought me a tasty dish to eat? Who was it I blessed? The blessing stands – I can't alter it now.'

Esau broke down in a wild and bitter sobbing.

'Give me a blessing, Father!' he cried. 'Give me a blessing too!'

'Your brother's tricked you,' said the old man.

'He's got the right name!' said Esau. 'He's a Jacob* all right! That's twice he's tricked me. He stole my birthright – and now he steals my blessing! Haven't you kept a blessing for me?'

'I've made him your master – and the master of his brothers!' said Isaac. 'I've given him the wealth of fields and vineyards. What can I do for you, my son?'

'Haven't you even one blessing left, Father?' cried Esau. 'Give me a blessing, give me a blessing too!'

Esau broke down sobbing.

So Isaac told him:

> 'Far from earth's richness and sky's dew
>   shall be your home.
> You shall live by fighting
>   and be your brother's slave.
> You will rebel
>   and break his tyranny!'

This last trick of Jacob's made Esau hate him.

'When my father's funeral is over,' he swore, 'I'll murder him!'

He didn't keep quiet about his threat, either, and his mother was told about it.

She immediately sent for Jacob.

'Your brother's threatening to murder you,' she told him. 'Now do what I tell you. Get away from here, and go north to our ancestral home, to your uncle Laban in the Balikh Valley. Stay with him a few months; your brother's anger will die down and he'll forget all about it. Then I'll send for you and fetch you home. I don't want to lose the two of you in one day.'

---

* The popular explanation of 'Jacob' was 'usurper'.

Night at Bethel
Genesis 28:10-12, 16a, 17-18, 20-22

Jacob set off north and reached a lonely spot in the highlands. The sun had set and he stopped there for the night. It was a stony place; he used one of the stones as a pillow and went to sleep.

He had a dream. In his dream he saw a great stairway, rising from the ground right up into the sky. God's angels were going up and coming down it. He woke up – a very shaken man.

'How frightening this place is!' he said. 'This is indeed God's house, this is heaven's gate!'

He got up at dawn, lifted the stone he'd used as a pillow and set it up as a sacred pillar. He poured oil on it and made a vow:

'If God stays with me and guards me on my journey and sees I don't starve to death and brings me safe home again, then GOD shall be my God and this pillar be God's house.'

This was his vow:

'Of all you give me I will give a tenth to you.'

In the Balikh Valley
Genesis 29:1-30; 30:25, 27, 29-34, 36, 43

Jacob set off and came to the country of 'the people of the east'. He looked round and caught sight of a well in the open countryside, and three flocks of sheep resting beside it. A huge stone lay over the mouth of the well – so huge that it took several shepherds to move it.

Jacob went on to the well.

'Well, my friends,' he said to the shepherds there, 'and where do you come from?'

'The Balikh Valley,' they said.

'Do you know the farmer Laban?' he asked.

'We do,' they said.

'And how's he keeping?' he asked.

'Oh, he's all right,' they said. 'Here's his daughter Rachel with his flock.'

'It's still the middle of the day,' said Jacob. 'It isn't time to round the animals up yet. Get on with watering the sheep, and you can take them back to pasture.'

'We can't,' they said. 'We need all the shepherds here to shift that huge stone.'

While all this talk was going on, Rachel came up with her father's flock – she was his shepherdess. Jacob went over to her. He himself

311

shifted the huge stone and watered her flock for her. Then he kissed her in greeting and tears of joy rolled down his cheeks. He told her who he was and she, in her excitement, ran off to tell her father.

Laban ran out to meet him, kissed him and took him home.

'Fine!' he said. 'You belong to my own family!'

Jacob stayed a whole month with him.

'You know,' said Laban to Jacob one day, 'you shouldn't be working for me without pay, just because you're a relative; what sort of wages would you like?'

Now Jacob had fallen in love with Rachel. Her older sister, Leah, had lack-lustre eyes; but Rachel was a lovely girl.

'If you'll let me marry Rachel,' he said, 'I'll put in seven years' work for you.'

'I'd rather give her to you than to anybody else,' said wily Laban. 'Stay with me as a resident-alien.'

Jacob's love for Rachel made the seven years pass like a flash. He went to Laban.

'I've served my time,' he said, 'and I want to marry Rachel. Give her to me.'

Laban held a wedding-feast – everybody was there. But when evening came, he brought his elder daughter, Leah, and gave her to Jacob (she was heavily veiled; Jacob couldn't see who it was) and the marriage ceremony was completed.

Next morning, Jacob found that it was Leah had had married, not Rachel! He tackled Laban.

'What a dirty trick to play!' he said. 'I worked for Rachel. Why have you cheated me like this?'

'Carry through with this wedding,' said Laban, 'and I will give you Rachel in return for a further seven years' work.'

That's what Jacob did. He did not repudiate his marriage with Leah, but he married Rachel as well, accepting a new contract for seven years' service. He was very much in love with Rachel.

One day, Jacob went to Laban.

'Let me go back home,' he said.

'Now, listen to me, please,' said Laban. 'I can see that GOD is blessing me through you.'

'No doubt,' said Jacob. 'You know how hard I've worked for you and how big your farm's grown since I've been looking after it. You had little enough before. GOD has certainly blessed you since I came here. But what about me? I've got my family to look after.'

'Well,' said Laban, 'what pay do you want?'

'I don't want any pay,' said Jacob. 'I want part of the farm for myself. I'll go on looking after your flock; but give me all the spotted animals for my own – the rest will be yours. You can inspect the two flocks whenever you like. I'll be quite straight with you.'

'That's all right by me,' said Laban. 'Do as you say.'

He moved his encampment three days' journey away and left Jacob in charge of the flock.

Jacob became a wealthy shepherd with large flocks of his own. He grew richer, with slaves and camels and donkeys as well.

Escape South
Genesis 31:2, 4-7, 13-50, 54-55

Jacob now saw that Laban's attitude to him had quite changed. So one day, when he was out with his flocks in the open country, he sent for Leah and Rachel to meet him there.

'Your father doesn't like me,' he told them. 'I've worked honestly for him, but he has cheated me again and again. God, who met me at Bethel where I set up a pillar and swore a vow to him, has told me to leave this valley and go home.'

'We've nothing here to stay for, either,' they both said. 'Our father treats us like foreigners. He's had our dowry and he's made it pay good interest. What we've got isn't his – it's ours. Do what God has told you to do.'

Jacob mounted his family on camels and drove his cattle away. He crossed the Euphrates River and made for the Gilead highlands.

Meanwhile (Jacob knew nothing of this) Rachel had stolen her father's household gods while he was away shearing.

When, three days later, Laban heard that Jacob had set off home, he went after him and caught up with him after a week's hard riding.

'What do you mean by keeping me in the dark like this,' he asked, 'running off with my daughters like prisoners of war? You didn't even let me kiss my grandchildren goodbye! You've gone mad – I could soon overpower you. I won't, but only because last night your father's God told me to leave you alone . . . So you're homesick and off back home. But why steal my household gods?'

'I admit I was afraid of you,' said Jacob. 'I thought you'd rob me of your daughters. But if anybody's stolen your gods, he shall die. Call your men in; if you find anything that's yours, take it!'

Laban searched the camp, but could find nothing. Rachel had hidden the household gods in her camel saddle. She was sitting on the saddle when her father came into her tent.

'I'm sorry I can't get up,' she said. 'I don't feel well. I hope you won't be angry with me.'

He had a good look round but he didn't find the household gods.

'Now what's my crime?' asked Jacob angrily. 'You come storming after me and rummaging through my goods! Have you found anything? Put what you've found out here for my men and your men to see. They can settle the dispute between us.

'For twenty years,' he went on, 'I've lived with you – worked fourteen years for your daughters' hands, and six years just for you. You cheated me again and again. If God wasn't looking after me, you'd have sent me away with nothing!'

'The girls are my daughters,' said Laban. 'The children are my grand-children. The flocks are mine. Everything's mine! But what can I do about them? Come, let's swear a covenant together.'

So Jacob took a stone and set it up as a sacred pillar; his kinsmen built a cairn.

'May GOD keep watch over us both,' Laban said, 'when we are far away from one another. If you ill-treat my daughters or marry other women, remember God is witness between us.'

Jacob held a religious service on the hill and invited his relations to share the sacred meal beside the cairn. This over, they spent the night there.

Laban got up at dawn. He kissed his daughters and grandchildren goodbye, gave them his blessing and set off home.

Jacob went on south

Brothers Meet Again

Jacob was now going home – after twenty years in the north. His mother had long been dead; it was meeting his brother that scared him.

Genesis 32:3-13a, 22-24, 26, 29, 31a; 33:1-4, 6-17; 35:21

Esau had has camping grounds south of the old home in Beersheba. Jacob sent messengers ahead to get in touch with him.

'Talk to him like this,' he told them. 'Tell him his servant Jacob sends him greetings: "I've been living with Laban in our ancestral country.

I've been with him these twenty years. I've become quite rich – I've oxen, donkeys, flocks, slaves. May I hope for your friendship?"'

'We met Esau riding north to meet you,' the messengers brought news back. 'He has four hundred men with him.'

That put Jacob in a panic. He divided his caravan into two companies – people as well as animals. If Esaw attacked one, the other had at least a chance of escaping.

Then he prayed.

'O GOD,' he said, 'God of my grandfather Abraham and God of my father Isaac, you told me to come home. You promised too that you would take care of me. I don't deserve such steadfast love and loyalty as you have shown me. I am only your servant. I had only my staff when I crossed Jordan River twenty years ago on my way north; now I am master of these two encampments. Save me from my brother Esau. I am afraid of him – afraid he may murder us, children and mothers as well. You remember what you promised me – prosperity and many descendants.'

That night Jacob stayed where he was. In the darkness, he got up and sent his two wives and eleven children and all he had across the Jabbok Ford. He stayed behind alone on the hill – and a man wrestled with him till daybreak.*

'Let me go,' said the man. 'The day's breaking.'

'Tell me who you are,' said Jacob.

'What do you want to know my name for?' asked the man. But he gave Jacob his blessing.

As Jacob crossed the hill the sun rose.

He looked up – and there, coming to meet him, was his brother Esau and his four hundred men.

He hurriedly rearranged his caravan. He divided his children between the four women, Leah, Rachel and their two maids. He put the maids and their children at the head of the caravan, then Leah and her children, and, last of all, Rachel and her son Joseph.

He himself went on ahead of the caravan, bowing to the ground in greeting until he met his brother.

Esau ran forward, threw his arms around his neck and kissed him. They both wept for joy.

Then the women and the children arrived and greeted him.

* The Jabbok River was the border; Jacob was crossing the threshold of new country. He therefore had to meet the river demon who guards frontiers. But because God's blessing was on him, he could meet and conquer it.

'What's all this company mean?' he asked.

'To win your friendship,' said Jacob.

'I've enough, brother, more than enough,' he said. 'You keep it.'

'No, no, no,' said Jacob. 'You must have a present. It's good to see you again. And you've been so friendly. God's been very good to me. I have plenty.'

And he insisted until at last Esau accepted the present.

'Now let's get going,' said Esau. 'I'll ride along with you.'

'I travel slowly, as you know,' said Jacob. 'There are the little children, and I daren't over-drive the cattle – I should just lose them if I did. You ride on ahead, my lord, and I'll come along at my own pace. I'll join you again in the south.'

'Well, let me give you an escort, then,' said Esau.

'Oh no!' said Jacob. 'You are too kind!'

So Esau rode south.

Jacob went only a short journey east and camped where the Jabbok Gorge enters the Jordan Valley. Then he went on by stages, through the highlands, as far south as 'The Cattle Tower'.

Joseph: Learning To Be Adult

Joseph was the son of Rachel, Jacob's favourite wife. He had been born in the Balikh Valley. It was after his birth that his father made up his mind to go back to his old home in southern Palestine; Rachel died on the journey south and was buried near Bethlehem. Jacob went on to the Hebron Valley where Joseph's story begins.

Boasting Boy *Genesis 37:3-11*

Joseph was now seventeen. His father had been quite an old man when he was born, and he had always openly treated him as his favourite son. He made him a princely coat (a coat with long sleeves) to wear. His brothers resented all this; they hadn't a kind word to say for him.

Now Joseph used to dream, and he couldn't keep his dreams to himself.

'Listen to the dream I had last night,' he would chatter to his brothers. 'It was harvest-time and we were out in the fields binding sheaves. My

316

sheaf stood up; your sheaves gathered round it like a court and kept bowing down to my sheaf!'

'So, you're to be our king, are you?' sneered his brothers. 'High and mighty, eh?'

They couldn't stand either his dreams or the way he chattered about them. It made their hate boil over.

'I had another dream last night,' he told his father and his brothers some days later (he had ten older brothers). 'This time the sun, moon and stars were bowing down to me – I was the earth!'

This time even his father told him to be quiet.

'What nonsense!' he said. 'The very idea! – you the earth, and I and your mother and brothers bowing to you!'

But his father didn't forget about these dreams; his brothers were just jealous of him because he was his father's favourite son.

Brothers' Revenge
Genesis 37:12-20, 22, 24, 28-36

The time came for the brothers to lead the flocks away to the north, to Shechlem, to summer pastures. The grass was more abundant there than around Hebron.

His father spoke to Joseph one day.

'Your brothers are away in the highlands,' he said. 'I want you to go and visit them for me.'

'All right,' said Joseph.

'See how they and the sheep are getting on,' he said, 'and bring me any news.'

And off he sent him.

Joseph reached Shechem. His brothers were nowhere to be seen. A man found him wandering about the countryside.

'What are you looking for?' he asked.

'I'm looking for my brothers,' said Joseph. 'Do you know where they've gone?'

'They've left here,' said the man. 'They were talking about going on to Dothan.'

Joseph went after them, and found them near Dothan, an ancient Canaanite city.

They saw him coming. Here was their chance to get their own back. By the time he'd got up to them, they'd made up their minds.

'Here's that dreamer coming!' they said to one another. 'Let's get rid of him and throw his body into one of these rain-pits. We can make up a story about his being eaten by a wild animal. We'll make his dreams come true all right!'

'Let's have no murder,' said Reuben, his eldest brother. 'Throw him into one of these rain-pits, if you want, but keep your hands off him.'

He intended to come back and get him out of the pit and take him home.

They threw him into one of the empty rain-pits.

Quite by chance, some Midianite traders passed by. They pulled the boy out of the pit and took him off to Egypt with them.

Reuben came back to the pit – but there was no Joseph in it. He tore his clothes in grief and ran back to his brothers.

'The lad's gone!' he told them. 'And now what am I to do? How can I go home?'

The brothers had taken Joseph's fine long-sleeved coat off him before they threw him into the pit. They tore it up and took it home with them to their father.

'We found this,' they said. 'Can you recognise it?'

'It's my son's cloak!' said the old man. 'A wild animal's mauled him. He must have been torn to pieces!'

In his grief, Jacob tore his clothes and put sackcloth on. He broke down in tears.

The Midianite traders meanwhile sold Joseph on the Egyptian slave-market. Potiphar, a royal officer, commander of the guard, bought him.

Egyptian Slave   *Genesis 39:2-23; 40:2-23*

So Joseph found himself a slave, but a slave in a good home. He lived in his master's house and he was very industrious. GOD watched over him even there. His master was so impressed with him that he made him his house-overseer, general manager of all his affairs. From this moment onwards, all his master's affairs prospered, at home and in his official work. He left everything to Joseph. Only in the matter of food did he keep things in his own hands, for here religious taboos had to be observed.

Joseph was a well-built, good-looking fellow. His master's wife fell in love with him.

'Come to bed with me!' she pleaded.

He told her bluntly – No.

'It would be a sin against your husband,' he said, 'and a sin against your husband is a sin against God. My master has left everything in my hands. He doesn't even question me about his business now – I am in sole charge. I can do what I like about anything – except you: you are his wife. How do you think I could bring myself to wrong him so grievously?'

She was so passionately in love with him that not a day passed without her trying to seduce him. Joseph wouldn't listen to her and avoided her company.

But one day she caught him by himself. He'd come into the house to get on with his work, and nobody else was about. She caught hold of his cloak.

'Oh, do come to bed with me!' she pleaded.

But he left her holding his cloak and ran out into the courtyard.

That finished it. He'd run away from her, would he? She shouted to the servants, holding his cloak in her hands.

'Look!' she told them. 'My husband had to bring this Hebrew to seduce me! He's just tried to rape me! He ran away when I screamed – and left his cloak in my hands!'

She waited for her husband to come home, and then told him the same tale.

'That Hebrew you've taken up with tried to rape me,' she said. 'He ran off when I screamed out – here's the cloak he left.'

Her husband was furious and had Joseph thrown into the Round Tower (where royal prisoners were kept).

But GOD looked after Joseph even when he was in prison. He got on well with the Tower governor. Before long he was put in charge of the other prisoners and he was soon managing the Tower itself! The governor left the day-to-day work in his hands.

One day, there was trouble in the palace. Two high officials – the Lord High Chamberlain and the Royal Baker – fell from favour and were sent to the Round Tower to await trial. The commander ordered Joseph to look after them, and he waited on them.

Some months went by. One morning, Joseph found them scared and frightened.

'What's the trouble?' he asked. 'Why so glum?'

'We both had dreams last night,' they said. 'We don't know what they mean and there's no means of finding out in this prison. That's what's frightening us.'

'The interpretation of dreams is God's business,' said Joseph. 'Tell me what they were about.'

'I dreamed about a vine tree,' said the Lord High Chamberlain. 'It was growing right in front of me. It had three branches. It budded, broke into blossom and ripened into grapes. I was back in my old job, standing in Pharaoh's presence with his cup in my hand. I took the grapes, squeezed them into the royal cup and offered the cup to Pharaoh.'

'I can tell you what that means,' said Joseph. 'The three branches mean three days. In three days' time you will be called back to the palace and restored to your old position. You will be Lord High Chamberlain again.'

'By the way,' he went on, 'don't forget me when you're back in office. Do me the kindness of mentioning my name to Pharaoh. I was kidnapped in Hebrew country. I've done nothing to deserve prison.'

The Royal Baker had been listening to this happy explanation of his friend's dream.

'I was dreaming, too,' he said. 'I was walking along with three open-work baskets on my head. The top basket was full of cakes and bread for the royal table; but birds kept pecking away at them.'

'I can tell you what your dream means, too,' said Joseph. 'Again, it's a matter of three days – that's the meaning of the three baskets. In three days' time you too will be called back to the palace – but for execution. The birds will peck the flesh from your dead body.'

Three days later was Pharaoh's birthday when he entertained his officers at a feast. The two men in prison were summoned to court – the Royal High Chamberlain back in favour, the Royal Baker to execution, exactly as Joseph had said. But the Lord High Chamberlain never gave a thought to Joseph – he forgot all about him.

Viceroy   *Genesis 41:1-56*

One night, two years later, Pharaoh himself had a dream. He was standing (in his dream) on the banks of the Nile. Seven fine cows waded ashore and began to crop on the sedge of the bank. Seven scraggy cows followed them out of the river. The scraggy cows ate up the fat cows – and Pharaoh woke up.

He fell asleep and dreamed again. This time he was looking at a cornfield. Seven good, solid ears of corn were growing on a single stalk. Seven thin, shrivelled ears (so thin they seemed to have been blighted by the dry east wind) sprouted after them and swallowed the good ears – and again Pharaoh woke up.

He was so scared by these dreams that next morning he summoned the Egyptian magicians and wise men to the palace. He described his dreams, but not one of them could make head or tail of them.

Then the Lord High Chamberlain suddenly remembered what had happened in the Round Tower two years before.

He sought an audience with Pharaoh and told him about the dreams he and the Royal Baker had in the Round Tower that night.

'There was a Hebrew lad there,' he went on, 'the commander's slave. He explained our dreams to us. What he told us happened – I was given back my post, the Royal Baker was executed.'

Pharaoh immediately sent for Joseph who was hurriedly brought out of the dungeon, shaved and given a new suit of clothes. He was presented to Pharaoh.

Pharaoh again described his dreams.

'None of these magicians,' he added, 'has any idea what they mean.'

'The dreams are quite clear,' said Joseph. 'God is telling Your Majesty what he is about to do. Both dreams are saying the same thing. The number seven in both stands for seven years. There will be seven years of rich harvests; then seven years of severe famine – people will forget what the very word "harvest" means. The reason for the dreams is clear: God's mind is made up – he will soon do what he says.

'Let Your Majesty act at once,' Joseph went on. 'Let an Overseer of the Granaries be appointed for the whole of Egypt with full power to commandeer one fifth of the seven years' good harvests and store them in city granaries against the bad times coming. The famine will not then be a disaster.'

Pharaoh and his court were deeply impressed by Joseph.

'Can we find anybody better than Joseph himself?' exclaimed Pharaoh. 'God's spirit obviously inspires him!'

He turned to Joseph.

'God has clearly told you what he is about to do. You are the shrewd and responsible man we are looking for. I appoint you Viceroy, second in power only to myself, Great Steward of the Lord of the Lands.'

He put a signet-ring on Joseph's finger, had him dressed in the linen robes of a viceroy and gave him the gold chain of office. He was to ride in the 'Second Chariot' with troops riding ahead and shouting, 'To your knees!' and clearing the road.

The Viceroy had to be a full member of the Egyptian Court. So Joseph was given an Egyptian name – Zaphenath-paneah ('the God speaks and he lives') – and was married to Asenath, the daughter of the High Priest of Heliopolis ('City of the Sun').

Joseph left the palace and carried out an inspection of the whole country. The harvests of the next seven years were wonderful harvests. He commandeered all the good grain and stored it in central city granaries, each granary dealing with the farms in its neighbourhood.

Two sons were born to him – Manasseh and Ephraim.

Then the harvests failed and the whole country and neighbouring countries too faced famine. People were clamouring for food. Pharaoh issued an edict making Joseph Overseer of the Granaries of Upper and Lower Egypt, and Joseph put the grain on sale to all who needed it.

Joseph and His Brothers   *Genesis 42:1-26, 29-38; 43:1-45:14*

There was famine in Palestine as well as Egypt. Jacob heard about the great Egyptian granaries.

'Why do you stand staring at each other?' he asked his sons. 'There's corn in Egypt, they say. We don't want to starve. Go and buy some.'

So Joseph's ten older brothers set off for Egypt to buy grain. Joseph's younger brother, Benjamin, stayed at home; his father wouldn't let him out of his sight.

Joseph immediately recognised them (they had no idea who he was); he remembered his boyhood dreams.

'You are spies,' he told them. 'You've come here just to see what the situation is and how we can be attacked.'

'That's not true,' they retorted. 'We've come to buy food. We are brothers and honest men. We are not spies.'

'No!' said Joseph. 'You've come to find the weak spots in our defence.'

'Your servants are a family of twelve brothers,' they insisted. 'We live in the land of Canaan, sons of one father. Our youngest brother has stayed at home; our other brother is dead.'

'There you are!' said Joseph. 'You are spies as I said.'

He whisked them off to prison for three days to think it over.

Then he summoned them back into his presence.

'If you want to save your lives, do what I tell you,' he said. 'I am a man of my word. You are honest men, you say. Well, one of you can stay in prison as hostage; the rest of you can go home with food and then bring the youngest brother back here. That will prove the truth of your tale and save you from the death penalty.'

They all agreed.

'It's our brother's death that's brought us to this,' they said to one another. 'We are guilty men. He pleaded for mercy and we wouldn't listen. That's why we're now in trouble.'

'I told you at the time,' said Reuben. 'I told you that you were treating the boy brutally, but you took no notice. Now you've got to pay for his death.'

They didn't know that Joseph could follow all they were saying. The interpreter standing by him made them think that he spoke only Egyptian. Joseph couldn't face them any longer; he went out of the room and tears streamed down his face. Then he went back in. He had Simeon seized and bound in their presence. Then he played a trick on them. He gave secret orders for their sacks to be filled with grain and their money to be put in with it. They were given food for the homeward journey.

The men loaded their donkeys and set off.

When they got home, they told their father all that had happened – how they had been arrested as spies; how they had protested their innocence and told the Viceroy about their family; how he had imprisoned Simeon and told them to bring Benjamin back with them.

Then they opened their sacks – and there were their money-packets in the sacks with the grain! When they saw the money, they and their father were filled with dismay.

'You've robbed me of all my children,' said Jacob. 'Joseph's gone; Simeon's gone; and now you are taking Benjamin from me! And I've got to suffer it all!'

'I'll bring him back safely,' said Reuben. 'You can kill my own two sons if I don't. Let me take charge of him. I'll bring him home.'

'He's staying here,' said Jacob. 'His brother's dead; he is all I've left. If anything should happen to him, I should die with grief.'

The famine grew worse, and the grain the brothers had brought from Egypt had all been eaten.

'Go back again,' their father told them, 'and get some more grain.'

'Now, be sensible,' said Judah. 'You know what the Viceroy said – no brother, no audience with him. If you'll send Benjamin with us, all right – we'll go and buy grain; if you won't let him go, we stay here. The Viceroy warned us quite clearly.'

'You could have spared me all this trouble,' said Jacob. 'Why did you tell him you had another brother?'

'The man asked all sorts of questions,' his sons answered. 'He asked about the family – "Is your father alive?" "Have you another brother?"

All we could do was to answer him honestly. How could we know he would want us to bring Benjamin back with us?'

'Let the lad go with me,' said Judah, 'and we'll get off and escape dying here – with you and the children – from starvation. I will go bail for him; hold me responsible. If I don't bring him back to you, you may blame me for it all my life. If we hadn't been held up like this, we could have been to Egypt and back twice by now.'

Jacob gave in.

'All right,' he said. 'If it must be, it must be. But take a present for the Viceroy. Put some fine fruit in your sacks, and a little balm, a little honey, gum, myrrh, pistachio nuts and almonds. Take twice the money needed – the money-packets in the sacks were perhaps a mistake. And take your brother too. May God Almighty look after you and get the Viceroy to send both Simeon and Benjamin back to me. But if I am bereaved, I am bereaved.' So the men set off for Egypt.

They were ushered into Joseph's presence – and Joseph caught sight of Benjamin. He immediately gave orders to the Master of Ceremonies.

'Bring the men into the palace,' he said. 'They are to dine with me at noon.'

The officer led the men to the palace. When they saw where they were being taken, they were in a panic.

'It's that money,' they said to one another. 'He just wants an excuse to set his guards on us, make us slaves and take our donkeys.'

Once through the palace gates, they went up to the Master of Ceremonies and tried to explain.

'If you please, sir,' they said, 'when we came here the first time, we came to buy food. We found the money-packets only when we opened our sacks at home; we've brought them back – and more money to buy more food. We don't know how the packets got into our sacks.'

'Don't worry,' said the officer. 'There's nothing to be frightened of. Your God must have put the money there; you settled up with me all right.'

He brought Simeon out to them.

They were taken on into the palace, and given water to wash their feet and fodder to feed their donkeys. They got their present for the Viceroy ready to give him when he came in at noon – they had already been told they were to have dinner with him.

Joseph came back to the palace. The men gave him the present they had brought, bowing to the ground before him. He asked about their welfare and about the family.

'Is your father well, the old man you told me about?' he asked. 'Is he still living?'

'Your servant, our father, is alive and well,' they said.

Joseph looked up and saw Benjamin, his own brother.

'You told me about your youngest brother,' he said. 'Is this your youngest brother? May God be gracious to you, my son.'

Joseph hurried out of the room. He couldn't hold back his tears any longer, he was so deeply moved by meeting his own brother again like this. He was overcome by emotion and had to stay in his room for some time. At last, he washed his face and came out. He now kept his feelings in hand.

'Let dinner be served,' he said.

Dinner followed Egyptian custom: Joseph dined by himself, the Hebrew shepherds by themselves and the members of Joseph's court by themselves – eating with foreigners was taboo.

The brothers sat in order of age; this surprised them. Food was taken to them from Joseph's table; Benjamin's portion was five times that of any of his brothers. They all drank and had a good time together.

Joseph again gave orders to his Master of Ceremonies.

'Fill the men's sacks with as much food as they can carry,' he said, 'and put my cup – the silver cup – in the youngest brother's sack.'

This was done.

At dawn next day, the men were sent off home. They had not gone far when Joseph summoned an officer.

'Up and after the men,' he said. 'When you overtake them, ask them why they have returned evil for good and stolen the silver cup I use for drinking and divining – a wicked thing to do!'

This the officer did.

'How can you say this, sir?' the men protested. 'We would never do anything of the sort. We brought our money back, didn't we? Why should we try to steal gold or silver from the palace? If you find the cup, let the man whose sack you find it in die; the others can be your slaves.'

'Fair enough,' said the officer. 'But only the man himself will be my slave; the rest can go free.'

Soon the sacks were on the ground and being opened. The officer began with the eldest brother and worked down to the youngest. The cup was found in Benjamin's sack.

The men were in a panic. They loaded the donkeys and went back to the city.

Joseph was still in the palace when they got back. They flung themselves on the ground before him.

'What have you been up to?' he asked. 'Didn't you know that a man in my position can easily find out things by divination?'

'What can we say, sir?' said Judah. 'We don't know how to explain it or how to clear ourselves. God has found out our crime. We are your slaves – all of us.'

'No, no,' said Joseph. 'Only the man who stole the cup shall be my slave; the rest of you can go back home to your father.'

Judah went up to Joseph.

'May I have a private word with you, sir?' he asked. 'Don't be angry with me – I know you are a viceroy. My lord asked us if we had a father or a brother. We told you, "We have a father, an old man, and a young brother, born to him in his old age; his brother is dead – he alone is left of his mother's children and he is his father's favourite son."

'We told our father about this. When he asked us to come here again to buy food, we told him plainly that we couldn't come unless the lad came with us. Then your servant my father said, "My wife Rachel bore me two sons. One disappeared – surely mauled by a wild beast; I have never seen him since. If this lad leaves me and comes to harm, I shall die of grief – and it will be your fault." What will happen if, when I get home, the lad he loves so much is not with us? It will be the death of him. I guaranteed his safe return. I now ask one thing: let me stay here as your slave instead of the lad; let him go home with his brothers. How can I go home without him? I fear to think what will happen to my father.'

Joseph could hold back his feelings no longer. He ordered all officials out of the audience room. Then he broke down – everybody in the palace could hear his weeping.

'Come near to me,' he said to his brothers.

They gathered round him.

'I am your brother Joseph,' he told them. 'Now don't be angry with yourselves for what you did. There are five more years of famine ahead of us; God sent me here so that our family might survive. You must go back home with a message from me to my father: "God has made me Viceroy of Egypt. Make haste and come down to me. You can live in the land of Goshen, near me – you and the whole clan with your flocks and possessions. I will look after you and see that you don't starve."

'You and my brother Benjamin,' he went on, 'can see that I really am Joseph.'

He put his arms round his brother's neck and they both wept for joy.

Joseph and His Father

Genesis 45:21-28; 46:28-34; 47:1-6, 29-31; 50:13

Joseph gave his brothers all they needed for their journey home; and he also gave them each a splendid coat – he gave Benjamin five coats and a large sum of money. To his father he sent ten donkeys loaded with fine Egyptian food and ten donkeys loaded with bread and grain, and food for his journey to Egypt.

'Joseph is still alive!' they told their father when they got home. 'He is Viceroy of Egypt!'

The old man was stunned by the news; he wouldn't believe a word of it until he saw the cavalcade Joseph had sent. Then he began to realise what had happened!'

'It's enough!' he said. 'My son Joseph is still alive; I will go and see him before I die.'

He set off with all his possessions and reached the land of Goshen.

Meanwhile Joseph had ordered his chariot out and went to meet him. He put his arms round his father's neck and wept for joy.

'I can now die happy,' said Jacob. 'I have seen you – you are still alive!'

'I'll report your arrival to Pharaoh,' Joseph said.

Now his brothers were shepherds and had brought their flocks and herds and possessions with them.

'When Pharaoh asks about your occupation,' Joseph went on, 'tell him you are herdsmen. That will secure the border land of Goshen for you – Egyptians have a taboo about shepherds.'

Joseph sought an audience with Pharaoh.

'My father and my brothers have arrived in Goshen,' he reported. He had brought five of his brothers with him to present to Pharaoh.

'What's your occupation?' he asked.

'Your servants are herdsmen, Your Majesty, as our fathers were,' they answered. 'We have come to settle here as immigrants. There's no pasture left at home – the famine there is terrible. We ask permission to settle here.'

'Let them settle in Goshen,' said Pharaoh. 'If they have any competent men among them, they can be my cattlemen.'

Jacob was now very old, and he knew he had not long to live. He asked Joseph to come and see him.

'I want you to make me a promise,' he said. 'I want you to give me your solemn word that you won't bury me in Egypt. Bury me with my fathers in our ancestral burying ground.'

'I will carry out your wishes,' said Joseph.

'You swear that you will do it?' said Jacob.

'I do,' said Joseph.

Jacob lay back in his bed. Not long afterwards he died; Joseph buried him in the ancestral burying ground in Canaan, and then went back to Egypt.

The Last Test   *Genesis 50:15-21, 26*

Now that their father was dead, Joseph's brothers were frightened; they wondered what he would do now.

'He'll perhaps pay us back for what we did to him,' they said to one another. 'He must hate us.'

So they sent a message to him:

'Your father told us before he died to tell you this: "Tell Joseph to forgive his brothers for what they did to him." We beg you to forgive us. We are the servants of your father's God.'

Then they sought an audience with him.

Joseph was deeply moved when he met them. They flung themselves down on the ground before him.

'We are your slaves,' they said.

'Don't be afraid,' said Joseph. 'I am not God. You meant to do me harm, but God planned to bring good out of it – to save the lives of many people, as he has done. So don't get frightened. I will look after you and your children.'

He reassured them and spoke kindly to them.

Joseph went on living in Egypt. At last he died. His body was embalmed and laid in a coffin. Years later, his bones were carried to Shechem and buried there.

Two Prophetic Stories

The men who wrote these stories were trying to keep alive the old prophetic faith and to recall their countrymen to their world-mission – to be 'God's Servant' and the servant of all people. They were protesting against the 'isolationist' and 'apartheid' policies of their contemporaries. They could no longer speak openly on the streets (the small community of city and villages was too tightly knit); they probably put what they had to say down in writing.

The Story of Jonah is centred on Nineveh, the capital city of their hated enemies, the Assyrians. It is the story of how this city repented at the preaching of an Israelite prophet who symbolised the Israelite people. The Story of Ruth is a story of a Moabite girl and her loyalty to GOD's Way (see Nehemiah's and Ezra's attitude to such foreign girls, pp. 186-189). The sting of both stories is in the ending.

Jonah: Enemies Are People

Jonah 1:1-7; 2:10; 3:1-11; 4:1-11

Once upon a time GOD spoke to Jonah.

'Get up,' he said, 'and go to that great city, Nineveh. Pronounce its doom – its shameful wickedness has been reported to me.'

Jonah set off – but he made for Tartessus in the far west, right away from GOD. He went down to the port of Joppa. There was a large cargo-boat in the harbour. He paid his passage and went on board; he didn't want to have anything to do with GOD and his commands.

Out at sea they ran into a hurricane. The sea was so rough that the ship seemed about to break up. The sailors were in a panic, each shouting out to his own god for help. They threw the cargo overboard to lighten the ship.

Jonah had gone down into the hold, and was lying there fast asleep. The captain went down to see what he was doing.

'What do you mean by sleeping like this?' he shouted. 'Get up and pray to your God. He might take some notice of us and come to our help.'

Meanwhile the sailors were talking together.

'Let's toss up,' they were saying, 'and find out who's to blame for this bad luck.'

They tossed up – it was Jonah!

'Tell us your business,' they said. 'Where do you come from? What's your country? Who are your people?'

'I'm a Hebrew,' he told them. 'I'm running away from GOD – the God of heaven who made the sea and land.'

'What a thing to do!' they said. 'What shall we do with you to quieten the storm?'

The sea was growing rougher and rougher.

'Throw me overboard,' said Jonah. 'That will calm the sea. I know I am to blame for this hurricane.'

But the men didn't throw him overboard. They rowed as hard as they could to get the ship into harbour. All in vain – the sea grew stormier and stormier still.

Then they prayed to Jonah's God:

'O GOD,' they prayed, 'don't let us die if we throw this man overboard; don't hold it against us. The storm is your doing.'

Then they threw Jonah overboard – and the storm died down.

The sailors were filled with awe in GOD's presence; they worshipped him and vowed to serve him.

GOD sent a great fish. It swallowed Jonah, and there he stayed, inside the fish, for three whole days. He then ordered the fish to put Jonah on shore, and it vomited him out on to the dry land.

GOD spoke to Jonah a second time.

'Get up and go to the great city, Nineveh,' he repeated, 'and pronounce its doom, as I shall tell you.'

This time Jonah got up and went to Nineveh as GOD ordered him.

Now Nineveh was a large city. To walk across it, from city wall to city wall, was three days' walk. Jonah entered the city and walked for a whole day. He stood and announced its doom.

'In forty days' time,' he shouted, 'this city will become a heap of ruins!'

The citizens of Nineveh at once accepted GOD's word. All of them – from the greatest nobleman to the poorest worker – covered themselves with sackcloth and sat down in grief.

News of all this reached the royal palace. The king got up from his throne and stripped off his royal robes. He, too, put on sackcloth and sat down in grief.

He issued a proclamation and the heralds carried it through the city:

'By order of the king and his ministers! A fast is proclaimed for all citizens and all animals. Nothing shall be eaten and nothing drunk.

All shall put on sackcloth and pray to God with their whole heart. All citizens shall turn from their evil ways and from every act of violence.'

'Who knows?' thought the king. 'GOD may yet change his mind, and stop being angry with us; the city may be saved.'

Indeed, when GOD saw what they had done – how they had given up all their evil ways – he changed his mind. He did not destroy the city.

Jonah was burning with anger.

'Isn't this just what I said would happen when I was back home?' he said to GOD. 'That's why I ran away to the west. I know the sort of God you are – "Kind and merciful, slow to anger, quick to love people with all your heart", as the hymn* says. I knew you would change your mind. I'd rather be dead than alive!'

'Why are you getting so heated?' asked GOD.

Jonah just walked out of the East Gate of the city and sat down to see what would happen.

God made a plant grow up to cool Jonah down – the great heat of the sun was too much for him. That made Jonah happier. But at dawn, next day, a worm attacked the plant and it died. The sun rose, a scorching east wind blew and the heat beat down on Jonah. He nearly fainted.

'I'd rather be dead than alive!' he groaned.

'Is it right for you to burn with anger like this?' asked GOD.

'It is!' said Jonah. 'I could die with anger!'

'But Jonah,' said GOD, 'you are sorry for a plant which grew up and died in a night – a plant you hadn't done anything for and which grew without your help. Shouldn't I be sorry for the great city of Nineveh (even if it is a foreign city) with its hundred and twenty thousand ignorant people – and its animals?'

Ruth: Race Doesn't Count with God

Naomi and Ruth   *Ruth 1:1-22*

Once upon a time, in the days when the Hebrew tribes were settled in the highlands, there was a great drought; the villagers were facing starvation. A family in Bethlehem were forced to emigrate to find food – Elimelech and his wife Naomi and their two sons Mahlon and Chilion.

* Psalm 103:8

They settled in Moab, and the two sons married Moabite girls, Orpah and Ruth.

Then Elimelech died. The family stayed on in Moab, and for ten years everything went happily. Then both the sons died. Naomi, who had now lost both husband and sons, decided to go home to Bethlehem (news had come that there was no shortage of food there) and, with the help of her two daughters-in-law, she began to get ready for the journey.

The three women left the village and set off down the road to the Jordan Valley.

'Now you must both go home to your families,' said Naomi to the two girls. 'May GOD be as good to you as you have been to me and my husband. He will help you to marry again and find another good home.'

She kissed them goodbye, and they both burst out crying.

'No, no!' they said. 'We'll go with you to your ancestral home.'

'Now listen to me,' said Naomi, 'you must go home. There's no point in going with me. I've no more sons for you to marry, and I'm too old to marry again and have children. You wouldn't want to stay unmarried all that time, anyhow, just to marry sons of mine. No. I'm very sorry for your sakes that all this trouble has happened to me.'

The girls burst into tears again. Then Orpah kissed Naomi goodbye. Ruth held her in her arms.

'Look!' said Naomi. 'Orpah's gone back to her own people and her own religion. You go back with her.'

'Don't make me leave you!' said Ruth. 'Don't make me go home! I want to go where you go and to live where you live. Your people are my people now, your God is my God. I'll die where you die and be buried where you are buried. Only death itself will separate us from one another!'

When Naomi saw that Ruth was not to be argued with, she said no more. They went on together across the river and climbed the mountain road to Bethlehem.

When they got there, the village buzzed with gossip.

'It can't be Naomi, can it?' the women were saying.

'Don't call me Naomi (My sweet one) any more,' said Naomi. 'You'd better change my name to Mara (Bitter). I've had a dreadful time. When I went away we were all happy together; but I've come home alone. Naomi is no name for me now!'

That is how Naomi and Ruth, the Moabite girl, came home to Bethlehem. It was April, the beginning of the barley harvest.

Ruth and Boaz

Ruth 2:1-23; 3:1-18

There was a rich farmer living in Bethlehem, Boaz, a relative of Elimelech's and a member of the same clan.

'Let me go down to the harvest fields,' said Ruth to Naomi one day. 'Someone will be kind enough to let me follow them and pick any barley that's dropped.'

'Yes, you go,' said Naomi.

Off she went. She followed some reapers in a field and started picking up barley stalks. The field happened to belong to Boaz. Just then, Boaz himself came into the field from the village.

'God bless you all!' he called out to the reapers.

'Who's that girl over there?' he asked a reaper.

'Oh, it's the Moabite girl who came back with Naomi,' he said. 'She asked if she could follow us up in the field. She's been busy picking up barley ever since dawn.'

Boaz went over to her.

'Now listen to me, my girl,' he said. 'Stay in this field and don't go wandering off. And keep close to the women – go where they go. I've told the young fellows they're not to start interfering with you. The water jugs are there – use them when you're thirsty.'

Ruth flung herself on the ground before him.

'You're very kind,' she said. 'I don't know why you should be so kind to a foreigner like me.'

'Oh, I've heard all about you,' said Boaz, 'how you've looked after your mother-in-law since she's been widowed – and how you left your home and country to come and live here among strangers. God bless you!'

'You've cheered me up, sir,' said Ruth, 'and made me feel quite at home – even though I'm not one of your workers.'

It was now noon.

'Come and help yourself to some bread,' said Boaz, 'and dip it in the wine.'

Ruth sat down with the other reapers and he passed her some popped corn. She had more to eat than she needed. Then she went back into the field.

'Let her pick up what she wants,' Boaz told his men, 'and no getting fresh with her. You can drop some of the barley for her to pick up. And remember – leave her alone.'

Ruth stayed in the field until dark. She beat the barley stalks and found she had nearly a bushel of barley grain. She carried it back to the village and gave it to Naomi.

'Where did you go?' she asked. 'Where was the field? GOD bless the man who took so much notice of you.'

'Well, the man's name was Boaz,' said Ruth. 'I worked with him.'

'GOD bless him!' said Naomi. 'You know he's a relative of ours, don't you?'

'He told me to keep close to his reapers,' said Ruth, 'and I can stay there till harvest's over.'

'You keep close to the women,' said Naomi. 'You'll get into trouble if you go wandering off into another field.'

So Ruth spent all the days of both the barley and the wheat harvests out in the fields, and went back home each night to Naomi.

'I think you ought to be married,' Naomi said to Ruth one day. 'What do you think of Boaz? Now I'll tell you what to do. He's winnowing the grain tonight down at the threshing floor. Make yourself as pretty as you can and put your best dress on. Go down to the threshing floor. Wait till supper is over before you let him know who you are. Notice where he lies down to sleep. Then go and lie down at his feet and pull his blanket over you. He'll tell you what to do.'

'As you say,' said Ruth.

So she went to the threshing floor and did just what Naomi told her.

At last, supper was over. Boaz was in a merry mood and he lay down beside a heap of grain. Ruth crept quietly up, lifted the blanket at his feet and lay down. Boaz was fast asleep. In the middle of the night, he suddenly awoke, and, turning over, he found the girl lying at his feet.

'Who on earth are you?' he asked.

'I'm Ruth,' she said. 'I'm asking you to marry me – it's your duty, you know.'

'GOD has blessed you, my girl!' he said. 'You've proved to me your loyalty to your family – in the field and here tonight at the threshing floor. You haven't been flirting with the boys and trying to find out who's got money and who hasn't. You're a good girl – everybody knows that. I'll do what you ask – it's my duty. But I'm not your nearest relative, you know. There's a man who's a closer relative and it's really his duty to marry you. Stay here tonight, and tomorrow morning I'll have a word with him. If he'll fulfil his legal duty to you, well and good – he can do so. But if he won't, then, as GOD lives, I will. Now go to sleep.'

She went to sleep again. But she got up before it was light; she didn't want anybody to recognise her. Boaz thought it best that nobody should know she'd been on the threshing floor that night.

'Hold out the wrap you're wearing,' he said.

He filled it with a bushel of barley grain and helped her to put it on her back. She went back into the village.

'Well, how did it go?' asked Naomi.

Ruth told her.

'And he gave me this bushel of barley,' she added. 'He said I mustn't go home without something for you.'

'Now, take it quietly,' said Ruth. 'We'll see how it all turns out. Boaz won't rest until he has cleared the matter up.'

Happy Ending   *Ruth 4:1-17*

Boaz went up to the village gate (where the law-court was held) and sat down. After a time, he saw the man whose duty it was, as her nearest relative, to marry Ruth. He called after him as he was walking by:

'Hi, friend! Come and sit down here!'

Boaz got ten of the village elders to form a court. Then he spoke to the man.

'Now,' he said, 'you know all about Naomi. She's come back home and she's going to sell her husband's field. I thought you ought to know. You're her nearest relative. You ought to have the chance of buying it in the presence of these elders as witnesses. If you want to buy it, say so. If you don't, I'd like to know. You have first claim; I come next.'

'Right,' he said, 'I'll buy it.'

'But wait a moment,' said Boaz. 'If you buy the field, you must also marry Ruth the Moabite girl – she's the widow of the heir. The field must go eventually, as you know, to his family.'

'That puts a different light on the matter,' said the man. 'Buying it under those conditions will reduce my estate. I renounce my claim. You can have it.'

The man took off his sandal and gave it to Boaz.

'You buy the field,' he said.

Boaz turned to the assembled court.

'You are witnesses,' he said. 'I have agreed to buy all the property that belonged to the three men – Elimelech, Chilion and Mahlon. And I have agreed to marry Ruth and see that the property eventually goes to her children, so that Elimelech's name shall not die out. I call you all to witness the contract.'

'We are witnesses,' they said. 'May GOD bless you and your bride and give you prosperity.'

Ruth and Boaz were married; and in due time a son was born.

'May GOD be blessed!' all her neighbours said to Naomi. 'He isn't leaving you without somebody to look after you. May your grandson become a famous man! He'll be a joy to you in your old age – isn't he Ruth's child and hasn't she been as good as seven sons to you?'

Naomi picked the baby up and cuddled it.

'We must give the baby a name,' said the neighbours. 'Let's call him Obed.' So Obed was his name.

Obed was King David's grandfather.

Two Prophetic Poems: Living in One World

The second poem may be older than Isaiah; the first poem may be a temple hymn that Isaiah and Micah knew and used. The nationalism they protest against can be found in every century: the century of Amos, the century of Nehemiah – and the twenty-first century!

Micah 4:1-3 (Isaiah 2:2-4)

In the days that are to be
   the mountain of GOD's temple
   shall tower high above
   the highest mountain ranges.

The people of the world
   shall make pilgrimages to it:
'Come, let us climb GOD's mountain
   to the temple of his people's God;
   he will teach us the good life
   and help us to live in his Way.
From Jerusalem and its holy mountain
   GOD's true word – true religion –
   spreads over the whole earth!'

GOD shall quell the world's quarrels –
   even among distant empires:
   sword and spear shall be forged
   into ploughshare and pruning knife;
   there shall be no more war,
   no more training camps,
   no more parade grounds.

When GOD's Day comes
    there will be an open road
    from the Nile to the Euphrates!
Assyrians will go as pilgrims to Egypt,
    Egyptians as pilgrims to Assyria,
    worshipping together.

In that day
    Israel will be the Third People,
    comrade of Egypt and Assyria,
    living for the good of the world
    which GOD has blessed:
'Happy is Egypt my people,
    happy Assyria my workmanship,
    happy Israel my heritage!'

A Scholar's Poem: Real Wisdom

Scholars ('wise men'), as well as prophets and priests, played their part in the life of GOD's people. We give here a scholar's poem which is now found in *The Book of Job*. The scholars were not philosophers (as in Greece) but askers of questions – some sceptical like the author of *Ecclesiastes*, many deeply religious like the author of *Job* or the writer of Psalm 73, some historians like the author of *The Court History* (pp. 62-87). Here is a scholar's meditation on GOD's Way which for him was real wisdom.

Job 28

Where can Wisdom be tracked down?
Where are the springs of Understanding?

Silver is mined, iron dug,
   gold refined, copper smelted –
   from seams that run into darkness,
   into earth's far darkness.

Unknown workers hew out tunnels,
   lost from human sight:
   above – corn shining in the sunlight;
   below – miners raking earth like fire,
   wresting from rock the sky-blue stone
   speckled with gold,
   beyond the flight of carrion-crow,
   unseen by falcon's eye,
   unknown to the lion,
   unvisited by the snake.

Yet excavators find their way there –
   smashing the granite,
   uprooting the mountains,
   thrusting tunnels
   into the gem-starred rock,
   damming the sources of streams,
   tapping the hidden wealth of the earth.

But where can Wisdom be tracked down?
Where are the springs of Understanding?

No one knows the way to Wisdom
    or can find it in this world:
    the Ocean and the far seas confess –
    'It is not in us.'
Nobody can buy it in the market
    with gold or silver,
    or weigh it against Arabian gold
    or African topaz,
    cornelian, chrysolite,
    crystal, coral.

Where, then, can Wisdom be tracked down?
Where, then, are the springs of Understanding?

Wild beasts and wild birds
    know nothing of it,
    disaster and death hear
    only distant rumours.

God alone,
    surveying earth and sky,
    knows the way to Wisdom,
    to the place where it is found.

When, in the beginning,
    he curbed wind and water,
    set bounds to rain and thunder,
    he discovered it,
    weighed its worth,
    dug down to its depths.

To all humankind he said:
    Living in GOD's Way
    is Wisdom,
    having nothing to do with evil
    is Understanding.

Job: What Can We Know About God?

The Book of Job is one of the greatest poems in the literature of the world. It comes from the circles of the 'wise men', the scholars; *A Scholar's Poem* (p. 339), may actually have been written by the author of *The Book of Job*. The pattern of the book is this:

The Prologue
The Poem
    Job speaks
    Job and his friends state their case
    Job speaks again
    God answers Job
    Job answers God
The Epilogue

The Prologue and the Epilogue are in prose and give the beginning and ending of an old folktale about a legendary figure of the distant past: a very rich man, Job, and his family fall on evil days but finally all live happily ever after. The poet uses only the beginning and the ending; we do not know what other adventures the main body of the folktale recounted. The poem begins at the point in the folktale when overwhelming disaster has fallen on Job. The poem itself may have been many years in the making. Perhaps the poet-scholar began it by discussing the folktale with his students and using it as a starting point for a wider enquiry into some important religious questions. The undeserved suffering of an innocent man provokes not only the question 'Why suffering in a world controlled by a good God?' but also the deeper question 'What can we know about God at all?'

It has been suggested that the original work consisted of the Prologue and Epilogue and the poems where Job and God speak to one another,[*] and that, as the poem grew, poems about Job and his friends were added. Later still, other poems were added by the poet or by the poet's students or later editors, to give the book the form it now has.

We give the folktale and the main argument of the poem – the speeches of Job and God.

---

[*] See N. H. Snaith, 'The First Book of Job', *The Book of Job*, pp. 34-44.

(Note: 'Satan' here is not a proper name. The Hebrew has 'The Satan', that is 'The Adversary', the officer of the Heavenly Court charged with the supervision of the human race – God's Inspector-General.)

The Prologue

Job 1:1-2:10

Once upon a time there was a wealthy Edomite sheik called Job, the most outstanding sheik in all the East. He was, moreover, a good man, a genuinely innocent man. His religion was real religion and he would have nothing to do with evil of any kind. He had a large family – seven sons and three daughters – and immense wealth.

One day GOD summoned the Heavenly Court. It met in his presence, and among the members of the court was 'The Satan' – God's Inspector-General.

God turned to him.

'Where have you been?' he asked.

'On the earth,' he reported. 'I've been wandering north, south, east and west.'

'Did you come across my servant Job?' GOD asked. 'Now he's a good man for you – a genuinely innocent man. His religion is real religion and he won't have anything to do with evil of any kind.'

'Yes, I met him,' said the Satan. 'He's a good man, I admit. But then – he has every reason to be! He has nothing to fear – you stand guard over him and his family and his wealth. Indeed, it is you who have made him as wealthy as he is. But just touch that wealth of his – or his family – and he'll curse you to your face!'

'Very well,' said GOD. 'He's in your hands – you do just that. But leave the man himself alone.'

The Satan left the court.

One day the young people were having a banquet at the eldest son's house. Job himself was at home.

Then – disaster followed disaster.

One after another, messengers came running with news –

'Arab raiders have carried off the oxen and asses from the fields and murdered your herdsmen! I'm the only one to escape!'

'Lightning has killed all your sheep and shepherds! I'm the only one to escape!'

'Wild tribes from the desert – three bands of them – have driven your camels off and killed all your camel drivers! I'm the only one to escape!'

'A desert hurricane has blown your son's house down. The young people were buried in the rubble – and they're all dead! I'm the only one to escape!'

Job was hard hit. But he knelt down in prayer –

> 'I came naked from the earth,
>> to the earth I shall go naked back.
> GOD gave,
>> GOD takes back –
>> blessed be his name!'

All through these disasters Job never lost his trust in God – or said a word against him.

The Heavenly Court was again in session. The Satan was there to give his report.

'Well,' said GOD. 'Where have you been this time?'

'Wandering on the earth,' he said, 'north, south, east and west.'

'And what about Job now?' GOD asked him. 'He's still the kind of man I said he was – in spite of the disasters you prompted me to send to ruin him. You haven't broken him.'

'Skin for skin, as the proverb puts it,' retorted the Satan. 'You touch the man himself – and see what happens. You'll get his curses then!'

'Very well,' said GOD. 'You are free to do what you want to him – short of actually killing him.'

The Satan left the court and went back to earth. He struck Job with Egyptian boils* from head to foot, and Job sat itching in the ash-pit, scratching himself with a piece of broken crockery.

'And you still trust him!' his wife scolded. 'Curse him – and die!'

'That's a wicked thing to say,' said Job. 'You're talking just like a scurrilous street gossip! You know that we must take GOD on his own terms, whether it's good or evil he sends. That's no more than our duty.'

---

* 'The traditional and shameful disease of the wicked', N. H. Snaith, *The Book of Job*, p. 28; cf. Deuteronomy 28:27, 35.

The Poem

Job Speaks*

Job 3:1-26

May the day when I was born
   vanish from the calendar –
   vanish into dawnless darkness,
   into fog and gloom,
   lost under smothering cloud
   and sunless skies
   and the blind blackness of the night;
   with no touch of life
   or cry of joy;
   cursed by sorcerer and magician
   whose spells bind the sea monster himself!
May it never see
   the stars shining in a lightening sky,
   may it wait in vain for the dawn
   and the eyelids of the morning! –
   it did not make my mother childless
   and keep me out of sight of sorrow.
Why didn't I die
   when I was born?
Why live to lie on her knees
   and feed at her breasts?
Why wasn't I buried
   like a still-born baby?
I would now have been lying
   with kings and viceroys and princes,
   (palace and gilded house
   tumbled to rubble!)
   dead in a quiet grave,
   resting and sleeping.
Where the dead are –
   the wicked's bullying ways,
   workers' hard labour,
   are done with;
   prisoners, left alone at last,
   jogged awake by no gaoler's shout.

* See Jeremiah's poem, p. 257.

Everybody is there –
   king and commoner alike,
   and the slave,
   a free man at last!
Why are the grief-stricken
   forced into the light?
Why are the broken and bitter
   burdened with life?
All they can do is to dream of death,
   hunting it down like hidden treasure –
   death that never comes!
Their only joy
   the burial mound and the grave!
Why are they doomed
   to grope their way blindfold,
   shut in by God's unceasing No?
All that I have to sustain me
   are my sighs;
   all I have to give
   the tumbling torrents of my groans.
All I feared and dreaded
   has happened to me.
I don't know the meaning
   of peace and quiet –
   I toss and toss in restless torment.

Job 29:1-3, 7-10, 21, 15-20; 30:1, 9-10, 26-31

Oh for the old days
   when God was my guardian –
   his lamp shining down on me
   lighting my way through the darkness!
When I took my seat in the Council
   in the square by the Town Gate,
   young men stepped aside,
   old men stood up,
   the talking stopped,
   leaders were silent –
   everybody hung on my words,
   waiting for what I had to say.

I was eyes to the blind
    and feet to the lame,
    father to the poor,
    defender to the stranger,
    a terror to the criminal,
    rescuer of his victims.

I dreamed of my old age –
    'A man of vigour
    to the last –
    like a tree
    with its roots drinking the water,
    its branches bright with dew –
    gripping a new bow,
    arrows enough in my sheath!'

But now –
    young people
    laugh at me,
    young people whose fathers
    I wouldn't put with my sheepdogs!
I am sung about in street ballads,
    chattered about in gossip –
    loathed and passed by
    and spat at.

I looked forward to good –
    but evil has overtaken me.
I dreamed of light –
    but I walk in darkness!
I am ill and restless,
    miserable day following miserable day.
I have neither hope nor friends;
    if I ever speak in the Council
    I speak but as a beggar.
I am an outcast –
    the wolf my brother,
    the desert owls my friends!
The sun blackens my blistered body,
    fever burns my bones.
Harp and flute
    are fit only for mourners' dirges.

Job 31:2-5, 1, 6-10, 13-17, 19-21, 23-27, 29, 31-37

What fate or reward
  does God Almighty hand out –
  if not ruin for the wrongdoer,
  calamity for the criminal?
Doesn't he mark, then, what kind of man I am,
  count every step I take?

Neither falsehood nor fraud
  has found a friend in me;
  I made a covenant with my eyes
  not to look at a girl.
Let God test my innocence
  in the scales of justice.

If I have wandered from the right way,
  let my eyes rule my heart,
  dirt stick to my hands –
  may others eat my harvests,
  my spring crops be rooted up!

If I ever lusted after a woman
  or haunted a neighbour's door –
  may my wife grind another's corn
  and sleep in other men's beds!

If I have ever been unjust
  to slave or slave-girl,
  what answer can I give
  when God faces me as my judge?
The same God who created me
  created them!

If I have done nothing to help the poor
  or been untouched by a widow's tears;
  if I have eaten my food at home
  without sharing it with the orphan;
  if I have watched a beggar die
  for want of clothing,
  giving him no reason at all to thank me

for warming him (as I could have done)
with a fleece from my flock;
if I have charged the innocent falsely,
knowing the Court would take my side –
God's terror would crush me;
how could I stand
in the presence of his greatness?

I have never put my wealth first,
set simply on making money.
I have never worshipped the splendour of the sun
or the majesty of the moon –
either in the secrecy of my heart
or in public worship.
The ruin of my enemy
never made me happy –
the disasters that destroyed him
were no joy to me.
Has it not been a family saying:
'We can't say a word against him;
no stranger has ever had to sleep in the street'?
My home has been open
for every traveller.

I have never hidden my sins,
keeping my guilt to myself –
for I have never been afraid
of street gossip or public scorn,
holding my tongue
and hiding at home.

Oh that someone were listening!
I am hiding nothing –
let God answer me!
If he would write his charges out plainly
I would flaunt them on my shoulder
or wear them on my head like a crown!
I stake my case
on the record of my life –
I will enter his presence
like a prince!

God Answers Job out of the Storm Wind

Job 38:1-22, 24-35, 37-38; 40:8-14, 2

Who darkens debate
   with ignorant talk?
Pull yourself together like a man
   and answer my questions.

You're a knowledgeable man –
   you must know!
Were you there
   when I made the world –
   settling its shape and size
   and measuring it off?

Tell me –
Where were its pillars sunk,
   who laid the cornerstones
   when the morning stars burst into song
   and the hosts of heaven shouted aloud?
Where were you when the sea was born
   tumbling in tumult from the earth –
   blanketed in cloud
   and swathed in fog? –
   when I fixed its final shores
   like a bolted door:
'So far and no further –
   here shall your surging stop!'?

Tell me –
Have you ever ordered the dawn,
   commanded the morning
   to grip the edges of the world,
   shake the stars from the sky,
   cut the skyline clear like sculpture,
   dip it in dye like a dress?
Have you watched the Dog-star grow dim
   and the points of the Plough go out?

Tell me –
Have you seen the springs of the Sea,
    gone down into the great deep,
    discovered the gates of death
    and the guardians of the dark?
Have you ever studied
    the vastness of the earth?
Tell me about it –
    if you really know:
    how do you reach the home of light
    or the dwelling of darkness?
Can you put them at their proper stations
    and lead them home again?
How old you must be
    if you were born when they were born!

Tell me –
Have you ever visited the snow-fields
    or the home of the hail?
Where does the hot wind come from
    or the east wind go?
Who cut the channels for the rainstorm
    and a road for the thunderstorm
    over no-man's-land,
    thunder over the desert,
    clothing desolate wastes with green,
    dry land with grass?
Has the rain a father
    and the dew a sire?
Who gave birth to the ice
    and was mother to the frost? –
    the frost that freezes
    the very seas to stone?

Tell me –
Can you bind the Pleiades
    or break Orion's fetters,
    tame the Zodiac
    or guide the Bear and her cubs?
Have you taught the sky its duty
    or the earth its routine?

Can you make the clouds hear you
and command a cloudburst?
Can you send the lightning on errands
and does it salute you, 'Sir!'?
Who musters the cloudy battalions
and tips up the pitchers of the sky? –
making the soil set hard as iron
and clod cleave to clod?

Do you really think I'm unjust –
or are you just proving me wrong
to prove yourself right?
Are you as strong as I am,
can your voice thunder like mine?
Put on your might and majesty,
your glory and grandeur –
then humble the proud with your anger,
crush criminals in their tracks,
bury them all in the dust they came from,
silenced in an unknown grave!
And I – even I – will praise you
for being strong enough to save yourself!

Is my prosecutor sticking to his case?
Is my critic answering me back?

Job Speaks   *Job 40:4-5; 42:5-6*

What can I say?
I'm a man of no account,
I can only keep quiet.
I've had my say –
I'll not say it again.
I've said too much,
I'll say no more.

All I said was hearsay,
but now we stand face to face.
I take back what I said,
I repent of my empty and foolish talk.

The Epilogue

God gave Job everything back – indeed he made him twice as wealthy as he had been before.

His kinsmen and friends held a banquet in his honour. They sat down together at table and consoled him for all the misfortunes he had gone through. They each gave him a silver coin and a gold ring.

Job's wealth was now immense. And he had a second family – seven sons and three daughters as before. The girls were the most beautiful girls in the world (he called the youngest 'Bright Eyes'!) and in his will he went beyond the law and treated them like their brothers.

He lived for a very long time after this. He had great-great-grandchildren, and was a very old man when he died.

Daniel: Backs to the Wall

In 168 BCE the Jews faced one of their gravest crises. The year before, they had revolted against Antiochus IV (whose capital city was Antioch in Syria) and defied his attempt, with the help of influential Jews in Jerusalem, to force a Greek way of life upon the city and its citizens. Antiochus learned about all this on his way back from defeating the Egyptians and turned aside to deal with the situation. What began as a civil war (between liberal and orthodox Jews) became a major struggle between rebel Jews and the whole military power of the empire. The Syrian soldiers ran riot in the city and many people died at their hands. The temple was desecrated and plundered – a pig was sacrificed on the altar.

The story of what happened afterwards is told in *First Maccabees* in *The Apocrypha*. The Jewish religion was proscribed and a garrison stationed in Jerusalem to enforce obedience. The standard of revolt was raised in the village of Modein. The Jewish rebels fled to the hills. Guerilla warfare against the Syrian army followed and the rebellion spread. Eventually Jerusalem was recaptured and the temple rededicated (163) and full religious freedom secured (163). The rebellion is known as the Maccabaean Rebellion after its most famous leader, Judas Maccabaeus, 'the Hammerer'.

It was in the early days of the rebellion that *The Book of Daniel* appeared, as a tract for the times. It is a strange book containing stories and visions. The stories are of Daniel and his friends who had been taken prisoners to Babylon after the fall of Jerusalem in 586 and who refused to compromise their Jewish faith; Daniel's visions, which follow the stories, are full of strange symbolism, proclaim the fall of the great military empires of Assyria, Babylon, Persia and Greece, and predict the defeat of Antiochus IV and the rise of the Jewish people to power and world dominion.

The stories of Daniel and his friends are old popular stories. The author retells them to inspire common people to stand firm in the face of persecution. 'Look at your ancestors,' they say. 'They faced death for their faith but God took care of them. You must fight for your ancestral faith as they did. Take your courage in your hands. God will again give us the victory.' The visions, with their summaries of world history, confirm the message of the stories. Here are three of the stories and the first vision.

A Faith To Live For

Daniel 1:1-21

Long ago, the emperor of Babylon, Nebuchadnezzar, captured Jerusalem and took King Jehoiakim back to Babylon as a prisoner.* He ransacked the temple and looted its precious plate for the treasury of his own pagan temple.

He ordered his Lord High Chamberlain to choose some of the young men of the Jewish royal family and nobility for the service of the palace – fine, good-looking, well-educated, bright and clever young men – and to teach them to speak the Babylonian language. He made them a handsome allowance of food and wine. They were to be given three years' training.

Among those chosen were four young men, Daniel, Hananiah, Mishael and Azariah. The Lord High Chamberlain gave them Babylonian names – Belteshazzar, Shadrach, Meshach and Abednego.

Daniel was a sincere worshipper of God and he made up his mind that he would not deny his Jewish convictions by eating forbidden foreign food. He explained this to the Lord High Chamberlain and asked him not to make him do anything against his conscience. The Lord High Chamberlain rather liked Daniel.

'It's the emperor I'm afraid of,' he said. 'His orders must be obeyed; he settled what food you should be given. If, at the end of your training, you weren't as fit as the others, I'd be executed.'

Daniel tackled the guard in charge of the four of them.

'Give us ten days' test,' he said. 'Vegetables and water are all we want. In ten days' time compare our fitness with the fitness of the others.'

The guard agreed. When the ten days were over, they looked better and fitter than all the young men who had been given the rich food and wine the emperor had ordered. That settled the matter. They could have their vegetables.

The four young men proved brilliant students in all the subjects they had to study; Daniel himself also proved his skill in interpreting dreams and visions.

The three years' training were at last over. The emperor ordered all the young men into his presence; he wanted to talk to them himself. The four young men – Daniel, Hananiah, Mishael and Azariah – stood the test far better than any of the others; and the emperor chose them as his personal attendants. He often consulted them and he found them ten times better than all his official magicians and enchanters.

* There is some confusion of dates and names here. See p. 168 where it is Jehoiachin who is deported.

A Faith To Die For

Daniel 3:1-30

One day the emperor, Nebuchadnezzar, ordered a huge golden statue to be made – ninety feet high and nine feet wide. He had it set up on the Dura Plain, and issued an edict summoning all the important officers of the state – from viceroys to provincial officials – to attend its dedication.

The Dedication opened with a proclamation by the Royal Herald:

'Peoples and nations. Whatever language you speak, you are commanded at the sound of the musicians and choir, to fall down on your faces and worship the Golden Statue the Emperor has set up. The penalty for disobedience will be death in the raging fire of a furnace.'

The music burst on the great assembly, and the vast crowd fell on their faces and worshipped.

Certain Babylonian officials sought an audience with the emperor to lay a charge against their Jewish fellow-officials.

'Long live Your Majesty!' they said. 'Your Majesty issued an edict about the Service of Dedication: that at the sound of musicians and choir, the assembly were to fall down on their faces and worship the golden statue; the penalty for disobedience would be death in the raging fire of a furnace. We beg to report that three Jewish officials – your royal officials, Your Majesty – of the province of Babylonia disobeyed your royal edict. They refused to worship Your Majesty's god – or the golden statue Your Majesty set up.'

The emperor was furious. He ordered Shadrach, Meshach and Abednego to be arrested and brought into his presence.

'Shadrach, Meshach and Abednego,' he said, 'tell me the truth. Do you refuse to worship my god and to fall down on your faces before the golden statue? I'll give you another chance. If at the sound of musicians and choir you fall down on your faces before my statue, we will say no more. If you refuse to do so, you will be thrown into the raging fire of a furnace. Who is the god who will rescue you then from my power?'

'Your Majesty,' the three men answered, 'this is no time for words. Our God, the God we worship, can rescue us; and he will rescue us – from the furnace's raging fire and from Your Majesty's power. But even if he doesn't, we want to make it plain to Your Majesty that we will not worship either your god or your golden statue.'

This made the emperor blaze with anger. His face was distorted with rage at the sight of the three men before him.

He gave orders for the heating of the furnace – it was to be made seven times hotter than usual. His guards were to tie up the three men and throw them into the furnace fire.

The men were tied up just as they were – with their clothes and hats on – and thrown into the furnace. The heat was so great that the execution squad themselves died in the flames belching out of the furnace. The three men fell, bound as they were, into it.

The emperor watched through the side hole of the furnace.

Suddenly he stepped back in alarm.

'It was three men we threw into the fire, wasn't it?' he asked his ministers.

'Your Majesty is correct,' they replied.

'But there are four men in there,' he said. 'They are all walking unbound in the heart of the fire, quite unhurt. The fourth man looks like a god!'

The emperor went back to the side hole of the furnace.

'Shadrach, Meshach and Abednego, servants of the Most High God!' he called out. 'Come out and come here to me!'

The three men climbed out.

The emperor and his ministers stared at them: the fire hadn't touched them – their hair wasn't even singed, their clothes weren't scorched, there was no smell of burning.

'Blessed is the God of Shadrach, Meshach and Abednego!' the emperor exclaimed. 'He sent his angel to rescue his servants – men who trusted him, defied my Royal Edict and would rather die than worship any other god than their own God. Let a new edict be issued:

"Whoever speaks against the God of Shadrach, Meshach and Abednego shall be torn limb from limb and his house burned down."

'There's no other God who can rescue like this!' he added.

The three men were promoted to high office.

A Faith To Witness For   *Daniel 6:1-28*

This happened at the time of the Persian Emperor Darius.

The emperor divided his empire into one hundred and twenty provinces, each under a viceroy. He appointed three presidents over the viceroys, to receive their reports and to prevent any government corruption. Daniel was one of the presidents – the most distinguished of the three; he was a very able administrator. It was the emperor's intention to make him his president-in-chief with responsibility for the whole empire.

The other two presidents and the viceroys were jealous of him; they tried to find some incident in his administration that would give them ground for complaint. They could find none; his skill and reliability were outstanding.

'We shall have to go for his religion,' they said. 'We can't find anything else to complain of.'

So they laid their plans.

They sought an audience with the emperor.

'Long live Your Majesty!' they said. 'The presidents and viceroys in council have been concerned about the religion of the empire. We beg Your Majesty to issue an edict that, for a whole month, nobody shall make any petition to God or person except to Your Majesty. The penalty for disobedience shall be death – by being thrown to the lions. We beg Your Majesty to issue this edict in written form; it will then be unalterable, as is the customary practice of Persian law.'

The emperor signed the document publishing the edict.

Now Daniel had always been a faithful Jew. He had had windows put in the room in the roof of his residence facing west towards Jerusalem. It was his habit to go there three times a day, to kneel down and pray to God.

When he heard about the edict, he went straight up to the room on the roof and did what he had done every day – he knelt down by the window and prayed to God.

The Persian officials knew this, and they came to his residence at the time of prayer and found him on his knees praying to God.

They quickly sought an audience with the emperor.

'Your Majesty!' they said. 'You are aware that you signed the edict prohibiting any prayer to person or God except to Your Majesty, for a whole month, on pain of death?'

'I am,' said the emperor, 'and I made it an unalterable law.'

'Daniel the Jew has defied Your Majesty,' they said. 'He has ignored the edict. He still prays to his God three times a day.'

The emperor was deeply troubled when he heard this. He was determined to save Daniel somehow; he wracked his brain till sunset in vain. His officials came back to the palace – the whole crowd of them.

'Your Majesty!' they said. 'You are aware that no edict or statute, issued by Your Majesty's authority, can be altered in any way?'

There was nothing else for the emperor to do but to order Daniel's arrest and execution.

'Your God, to whom you are faithful, will rescue you!' he said to him.

Daniel was thrown into the lions' pit. A large stone was placed over its entrance, and sealed with the emperor's own seal and the state seal. There was to be no altering of the law for Daniel's sake.

The emperor went back to the palace and spent a worried, sleepless night, refusing all food and entertainment.

At daybreak, he hurried anxiously out to the pit. He had hardly reached it when, with broken voice, he called out Daniel's name.

'Servant of the living God!' he called out. 'Has your God, to whom you have been so faithful, rescued you?'

To his glad surprise, Daniel called back, 'Long live Your Majesty! God sent his angel and shut the lions' mouths. I'm quite unhurt. I was innocent before God; I never did Your Majesty any wrong.'

The emperor quickly ordered Daniel's release. He was taken up out of the pit unhurt. He had put his whole trust in God.

The emperor ordered the arrest of his accusers and sentenced them and their families to the fate they had intended for Daniel – they were thrown into the lions' pit themselves. They had scarcely fallen on the pit's floor when the lions leaped on them and crunched them up.

The emperor then sent a letter throughout the whole empire:

'May everybody enjoy peace! I am issuing a new edict that everybody throughout the whole of my dominions shall worship in sincerity the God of Daniel.'

So Daniel went from strength to strength.

A Vision of the Future   *Daniel 7:1-28*

Daniel wrote down the dreams and visions which he saw when he was lying on his bed at night. This, in his own words, is the first vision:

In my vision I was staring at the stormy sea – all the winds of heaven were blowing. Four monstrous Beasts came up out of it, each quite unlike the others: a Lion with an eagle's wings; a Bear half crouching; a Leopard with four heads and four bird's wings growing out of its back; and a powerful, terrifying Beast I could find no name for. This last Beast was stamping round and crunching with its terrible teeth, and, unlike the others, had ten Horns – an eleventh little Horn grew up while I stood staring. The little Horn had a man's eyes and spoke with a loud boasting voice. I kept on staring; then –

Thrones were set up,
> and the Everlasting God
> with hair like wool
> and snow-white robes
> took his seat on a throne
> swirling with flaming fire.

The Court was crowded –
> there were thousands upon thousands
> and myriads upon myriads there.

The trial began,
> the books were opened.

Judgement was passed on the Beasts – the last proud Beast was condemned to death (his carcase to be burned); the other Beasts to be tamed and their lives spared for a short time.

I was still staring at the scene when –

A Being in human form,
> escorted by the clouds of heaven,
> approached the Everlasting God
> and was presented to him.

This Being was crowned king,
> with all the glory and honour
> of a great king –
> with authority over the whole world,
> authority lasting for ever.

His kingdom
> shall never know defeat.

I, Daniel, was troubled and frightened at the vision. I went up to one of the angelic attendants and asked him what it all meant. He explained it to me.

'The Four Beasts,' he said, 'represent Four Empires* rising out of the earth; but it is to God's People† that enduring, imperial authority will be given.'

'But what does the last Beast represent?' I asked. 'The terrible Beast with the ten Horns and the little boastful Horn that overshadowed the others?'

* Babylonia, Media (not known), Persia, Greece.
† God's People are represented by the 'Being in human form' in the first part of the vision.

'The Fourth Beast (he said)
   shall be the Fourth Empire*
   unlike the other empires –
   a brutal tyranny
   trampling down the whole earth.
The Ten Horns
   are ten emperors.
The Eleventh Horn
   another very different emperor†
   murdering those who stand in his way,
   defying even God himself,
   persecuting God's people,
   changing their Festivals and Law,
   holding them in his grasp
   for three years and a half.
The Heavenly Court
   shall condemn him to death,
   stripping him of his sovereignty;
   all his imperial power and authority
   shall be given to God's people;
   much more shall be given to them –
   the splendour and obedience
   of the whole earth.
Their universal rule
   shall last for ever!'

The vision ended. I was greatly troubled and turned pale. But I went on thinking about what I had seen.

---

* Greece or Alexander the Great.
† Antiochus IV (popularly known as 'the Madman' throughout his empire). See p. 353.

Other Voices

'Nothing's Worthwhile!'

These three passages come from a book whose main theme is the meaninglessness of all human experience. Life is just one thing after another. There is no meaning in the disastrous story of God's people. The author was an out-and-out sceptic who says what he has to say with 'shocking honesty'. The last poem we give puts his scepticism bluntly, pouring scorn on the convictions of his fellow-countrymen: 'If you are going to be religious, you'd better be religious when you're young. You'll learn better when you grow older and find out what life is really like – just meaningless.' But there is something deeply moving in the almost savage picture he paints, and what he has to say is not to be glibly dismissed.

Ecclesiastes 1:2-11

Empty and meaningless (says the Preacher),
    everything is meaningless!
What does a man get by endless toil,
    sweating under the hot sun?
Families come, families go,
    only the earth goes on for ever.
The sun rises in the east, sets in the west,
    then back to the east again!
The wind blows south today,
    tomorrow it blows north –
    going round and round,
    turning and returning in its tracks.
Rivers run down to the sea –
    the ever-greedy sea –
    flowing, flowing
    where rivers have to flow.
The world tires a man out –
    there's no telling how tired!
The eye tires of looking,
    the ear tires of listening.

What has been will be,
  what's done must be done again,
  there's nothing new under the sun!
Can anybody say of anything –
  'Look – I've found something new?' –
  it was old
  centuries ago!
We can't remember what happened yesterday;
  in the years to come
  nobody will remember
  what happens now!

Ecclesiastes 2:12-17

I began to think about what we mean when we say 'He's wise!' or 'He's mad!' or 'He's stupid!'

I can see one thing – wisdom is like light, stupidity like darkness: the wise man can see where he's going; the fool stumbles in the dark.

I can see another thing: they both come to the same end.

'What happens to the fool,' I said to myself, 'will happen to me. Why have I been bothering about "wisdom"?'

'It's all meaningless,' I told myself.

Nobody remembers either the wise man or the fool – in a hundred years' time they'll both be dead and forgotten.

The wise man dies like the fool.

I hated being alive; all humanity just disgusted me!

Everything is meaningless – like chasing the wind.

Ecclesiastes 11:10; 12:1-6, 8

Being young –
  excited by a dawning world –
  is all meaningless.
You'd better remember your Creator
  when you're young:
  for you'll soon be telling yourself –
  'I'm bored stiff!'
Everything goes sour
  or grows old.

So remember your Creator –
before
light, sun, moon, stars grow dark
and cloudy skies come black with the rain;
and the day comes when
householders hobble along,
strong men are bent double,
women no longer grind at the grindstone;
daylight through the windows is failing,
street doors are shut;
a man can't hear the village mill
or a bird singing
(all songbirds are silent for him!)
and climbing a hill is scaring,
just walking is frightening –
and all the while
the almond tree is in flower,
the grasshopper too full to hop,
the caper bursting into bloom!

Before
the light goes out –
the silver cord snaps,
the golden lamp is smashed!

and winter wastes away –
pitcher and spindle
are broken at the well!

Everything is meaningless (says the Preacher),
everything is meaningless!

The Loveliest Song

One book in the Old Testament stands out from all the others. Tucked away among histories, hymn books and the books of the prophets we suddenly come across a book of love poems – a lyric poet celebrating human love. His poems are probably based on traditional village songs, reminding us that the grim story we have been reading is not the whole story. Life in the villages went on as usual – boys and girls fell in love, weddings were celebrated with dancing and singing. (Some of these songs were still being sung, we are told, at banquets in the time of Jesus.) The setting of the poems is the countryside; the characters are a girl and her lover. We give verses that describe their meeting.

Song of Songs 2:8-14, 16-17; 3:1-5

Girl   My sweetheart's voice!
He's coming to me –
   leaping over the hills!
He's standing
   outside our wall,
     peeping in at the windows,
     peering through the lattice!

Her Lover   Awake, my sweetheart!
My lovely one, come away!
Winter's gone,
   skies are clear,
   flowers colour the countryside,
   birds will soon be singing,
   fig-trees are touched with red,
   vine-buds full of scent!
Up, my sweetheart,
   my lovely one, let's away!
I want to see your face
   and hear your voice –
   no hiding away, like a bird
   in the cranny of the cliffs!

Girl   My love's my very own –
   and I am his!

While the air is cool,
   and the twilight lingers,
   come back to me, my sweetheart,
   let me gaze at you
   strong and supple
   like a wild goat
   on the Bether hills!
How I dreamed of him!

Night after night
    I lay awake
    watching for him,
    vainly watching.
'I will up and scour
    the squares and streets,'
    said I,
    'seeking my sweetheart.'

I looked and looked –
    he was nowhere to be found!
I called his name –
    no answering voice!
I asked the passing watchmen,
    'Haven't you seen my sweetheart?' –
    they vanished into the night.

Then –
    there he was!
I crushed him in my arms,
    I clung to him,
    I brought him home
    to my mother's room!

Her Lover   By the spirits of the countryside,
    by the goddesses of the fields,
    don't wake her,
    don't touch her –
    she's asleep.

The Voice of Worship

We come now, finally, to listen again to the hymns the Jewish people sang (see notes on p. 190). Here we can see what their convictions really were, with their depth and their limitations. All hymns bear the marks of their time, but the greatest hymns speak to all times. They need no comment.

A Song of Trust in GOD

Psalm 91

People   Happy are those who are kept safe by GOD,
who live in his shadow,
who can say to him, 'I trust you,
my refuge and my fortress!'

He will snatch you from the bird-catcher's trap,
and his treacherous pit!
He will shelter and protect you
with his wings.

By night, there is no terror to fear,
by day, no sunstroke;
in darkness or broad daylight,
no plague or pestilence.
It may strike thousands of your fellows,
it shall not strike you.

His faithfulness guards you
like a shield or a city wall.
You will see for yourself
what really happens to wicked people.

GOD is your shelter,
the Most High your refuge;
your home is safe
from deadly dangers.

His angels will escort you
wherever you go:
their hands will carry you –
you'll not stub your foot on a stone;
you will tread and trample
on asp and cobra and dragon,
snake and serpent
without hurt.

Priest   Since they love me with their whole heart
(speaking in   I will rescue them;
GOD's name) I will guard them from danger
for they know who I am.
I will answer their prayer,
I will be with them in trouble.
I will give them the joy of a long life,
they will know what my rescue means!

GOD – Lord of Nature

Psalm 29

People   Give GOD his due, you pagan gods!
and Choir   Acknowledge his glory and strength!
Acknowledge the glory due to him,
worship him in festal dress!

People   GOD's voice sounds over the great waters,
the glorious God thunders!

Choir   GOD over great waters!

People   GOD's strong voice!
GOD's majestic voice!
GOD's voice shattering the cedars!

Choir   GOD splits the forest cedars –
makes Lebanon Mountain skip like a calf,
Hermon Mountain like a wild ox!

People	GOD's voice shakes the Desert!
Choir	GOD shakes the Kadesh Desert!
People	GOD's voice sets the oak trees whirling, strips the forest bare! In his temple everything cries 'Glory!'
Choir	GOD rules the Great Deep, king enthroned for ever! giving his people strength, blessing his people with peace!

Psalm 104

Bless GOD, O my soul!

My GOD, how great you are,
   dressed in splendour and majesty,
   clothed with light;
   stretching out the sky like a tent,
   laying its foundations in the Great Deep;
   driving the dark storm as your chariot,
   riding on the clouds as your horses –
   the winds your heralds,
   the lightnings your ministers!

You built the earth on its pillars,
   set firm for ever,
   the ocean covering it like a cloak,
   drowning the mountains!

At your command the waters took flight,
   at the sound of your thunder they fled –
   over the hills,
   down the valleys,
   rushing to their appointed place!
You set their final frontiers,
   never again to drown the earth!

You make springs
  flow down the valleys
  between the mountain ranges,
  giving drink to wild beasts,
  quenching the zebra's thirst –
  while the wild birds
  are singing in the trees.

You water the mountains
  and saturate the earth
  from your storehouse in the sky,
  making green grass grow for the cattle,
  fodder for the farm,
  food from the soil
  and wine to make us happy,
  oil for our faces
  and bread for our strength.

The great trees are green with leaves,
  the mighty cedars of Lebanon
  where the birds nest –
  the stork in the topmost branches;
  the high hills are the home of wild goats,
  the rocks the refuge of wild badgers.

The moon marks the seasons,
  the sun knows where to set.
You make it dark and it is night
  when the wild beast goes out prowling;
  young lions roar after their prey,
  asking you for their food.
Day dawns and off they slink
  to lie down in their lairs.
People start their work,
  labouring on till dark.

How many things you have made, O GOD,
  made in your wisdom,
  crowding the earth!

There is the vast and endless sea
    with its innumerable living things;
    there go the ships,
    there the sea-monster you made for a plaything!

All of them look eagerly to you
    at their feeding times –
    you give and they gather,
    you open your hand, they eat their fill.
You hide your face, they are frightened,
    you take their breath away, they gasp;
    you breathe on them, they are revived,
    and you renew the whole earth!

I will sing to GOD as long as I live,
    I will sing his praise all my living days!
Bless GOD, O my soul,
    praise GOD!

Psalm 148

Praise GOD
    from the sky
    and from far above the sky,
    all his heralds,
    all his host!

Praise him –
    sun and moon,
    you shining stars,
    the high sky
    and waters above it!
Praise GOD's name!

At a word of command he made them,
    established them for ever!
GOD's law
    can never pass away!

Praise GOD –
   from the earth,
   water-spouts and oceans!
Fire, hail, snow, ice,
   storm-wind blowing at his command!
Mountains, hills,
   fruit trees, cedars!
Wild beasts, farm animals,
   snakes, birds on the wing!
Kings, princes,
   governors, judges!
Boys, girls,
   old people, children!
Let them all praise GOD's name!

His name alone is exalted!
His splendour shines down
   on earth and sky!
Praise GOD!

Songs of the New Year

Psalm 8

O GOD our king,
   how majestic you are!
Your glory is in the earth,
   your splendour in the skies!
When I gaze at the sky
   your fingers formed,
   the moon and the stars
   you have set there –
'What are we,' I cry,
   'that you should notice us,
   mortal beings,
   that you should care for us?'

Yet you made us
   a little lower than gods,
   crowning us

with glory and majesty,
giving us authority
over all you have made,
over all creation,
over sheep and cattle,
wild beasts and wild birds,
fish and the teeming life of the sea.

O GOD our king,
how majestic you are
in all the earth!

Psalm 98

It's a new song
you must sing to GOD –
his deeds have been marvellous.
His power and his goodness
have won him a great victory;
he has shown to the whole world
the just deliverance of his people –
he has remembered them
in steadfast love and loyalty.
The whole world has seen
the victories he has won!

O world! Lift up your voice
in singing and praise to GOD!
With harp and guitar and trumpet
raise your voices high
to GOD our king!

Let the sea's thunder
match the music of human voices!
Let the storm floods
clap their hands,
the mountain ranges
sing with happiness
in GOD's presence!

For he comes
  to judge all people,
  to judge the world
  with truth and justice!

Psalm 93

GOD is king!

Splendour and strength his armour,
  his belt tightened on!

'You have made the earth
  firm and fixed,
  your firm and ancient throne;
  from all eternity
  you are God!

'Yet the vast waters heave, O GOD,
  filling the sky with thunder,
  the boom of battering waves.'

Mightier
  than the waters' thunder,
  than the sea's breakers
  is GOD on high!

Psalm 96

Sing a new song to GOD,
  O wide, wide world! –
  sing to GOD and bless him,
  announce his victory day by day,
  tell his glory and great deeds
  to everybody everywhere!

The false gods people worship are mere idols –
  but our GOD made the sky!
Majesty and splendour,
  strength and beauty
  attend him in his temple!

You peoples of the world,
    ascribe to GOD –
    ascribe to GOD glory and strength,
    the glory which is his due!
Worship in his temple,
    bringing your gift for him,
    doing him homage
    in the splendour of holiness!
O wide, wide world!
    dance to the praise!

Let everybody everywhere know –
    'GOD is king!
He has made the earth
    firm and fixed!
He will judge the world
    with justice!'

Let earth and sky be glad,
    let the sea and all its creatures roar,
    let the fields and all that grows rejoice,
    let the wild trees shout for joy
    in GOD's presence –
    he has come to judge the earth;
    he will judge the world justly,
    the peoples fairly!

Songs of the Temple

Psalm 46

God is our unconquered stronghold,
    helper in our distress!
We are not afraid of earthquakes,
    of mountains tumbling into the sea!
Let the seas surge and thunder!
Let the waves be white with foam!
Let the proud mountains tremble!

GOD is with us!
Our fathers' God is our high fortress!

A river with its streams gladdens the city
which God, Most High, has made his home.
God lives in her –
she will stand firm!
God will help her
at the first light of day!
Raging storms rock the world:
God speaks – the earth quakes!

GOD is with us!
Our fathers' God is our high fortress!

See what GOD has done –
he has defeated the whole world!
War everywhere is over –
bows broken,
spears snapped,
shields burned to ashes! –
'Stop! Know that I am God,
Lord of the nations,
Lord of the earth!'

GOD is with us!
Our fathers' God is our high fortress!

Psalm 81

People

Sing aloud with joy to God our strength –
our God and our fathers' God!
Let the song ring out to the music
of the whole orchestra!
At new-moon festival, at full-moon festival
let the trumpet sound!

Celebrate the Covenant,
the Covenant made with our fathers,
the Covenant God made with our fathers
when they escaped from Egypt!

A Temple
prophet
(speaking in
GOD's name)

I heard a strange Voice –
   'Speak! I will tell you what to say:
I lifted the burden from your shoulder,
I carried your baskets of brick!
In distress you called to me –
   I rescued you,
   answering you in mountain thunders,
   testing you at Meribah Kadesh.
I fed and satisfied my people
   with fine wheat and rock honey!

'Listen, my people, and let me teach you –
   if only you would listen, my people!
No pagan god shall claim your country,
   no pagan shrine your worship!
I am GOD – your God!
I rescued you from Egypt!

'But my people did not listen –
   they would have nothing to do with me!
I left them to their own ways,
   to their stubborn, evil ways.

'If only my people would listen to me,
   if only they would walk in my Way!
I would soon deal with your enemies,
   soon conquer them –
   they would come suing for peace,
   scared and cringing!'

Psalm 100

O wide, wide world! Shout to GOD,
   worship him with joy,
   come with songs into his presence!

Know that he alone is God;
   he made us, we are his –
   his people, the flock he shepherds.

Enter his temple with gifts,
    enter his courts with praise –
    thank him and bless him!

GOD is good,
    we can trust his steadfast love
    as generation follows generation
    for ever!

Psalm 121

Worshipper   I will look up at the mountains –
    but where can I get help?

Priest   Your help comes from GOD,
    maker of heaven and earth!

Worshipper   May my helper never lose grip of me,
    never be too sleepy to take care of me.

Priest   GOD, guardian of his people,
    is never drowsy or sleepy.
GOD is your guardian,
    standing guard at your side.
No harm shall come to you
    from the sun in the daytime,
    from the moon at night.
GOD will guard your whole life
    from every danger –
    when you go out, when you come home,
    from now on and for ever!

National Lament

Psalm 90

O GOD, you have been our home
    from generation to generation!

Before the birth of the mountains,
    before the creation of the world itself,
    from everlasting to everlasting,
    you are God.

You turn us back to dust;
    back to the earth from which we came.
For you a thousand years
    are like an ended day,
    like sentry duty at night
    when the guard's relieved
    and turns in to sleep;
    like fresh morning grass
    withered and dead at nightfall!

We die in your anger –
    we have nothing to say in our defence.
You continually remember our wrong-doing,
    continually stare at our secret sins;
    our days darken in your anger,
    our years end in a sigh.

We live for seventy years –
    if we are strong, for eighty –
    brief years of toil and trouble,
    swiftly passing,
    soon forgotten.
Who knows how to bear your anger
    which our faith in you has brought home to us?
Teach us to grow old
    learning your wisdom.

How long, O GOD, before you relent
    and have pity on your people?
Match the morning with your mercy:
    help us to live with joy,
    turn our suffering into happiness,
    make good the agony of the years.

Let your people see your power,
     their descendants know your presence.
Give us your joy, O GOD,
     and make our daily work worthwhile.

Psalm 44

O God, we ourselves have heard –
     our forebears have told us –
     all you did in their days
     long ago:
     uprooting and planting peoples,
     hewing down and transplanting.
It wasn't our soldiers who conquered the country,
     or our arms that won us the victory;
     it was the strength of your hand and arm,
     the light of your face –
     your good favour.

You are my king and my God –
     you who are your people's conquering commander.
By your help we attack our enemies,
     by your help tread down our foes.
It is not my bow I trust,
     my sword will not save me.
It is you who rescue us,
     humiliate our enemies.
In God we will boast all the day,
     to your name for ever give thanks!

Yet it is us you have spurned and shamed –
     you lead our armies no more.
Our enemies have thrown us back
     plundering to their heart's desire –
     we are butchered like sheep,
     scattered over the world:
     sold cheap,
     no gain to you,
     insulted and laughed at
     by our neighbours,
     a by-word and laughing-stock
     to everybody.

I can't forget my daily disgrace,
    my face is red with shame
    listening to taunting, blaspheming voices,
    watching hostile, avenging faces.

All this is our fate;
    yet we have not forgotten you,
    nor been false to your Covenant,
    nor changed our heart's love,
    nor swerved from your Way –
    though it is us you have broken,
    not the dragon,
    us you have overwhelmed
    in blackest night!
If we had forgotten your name
    or prayed to pagan gods
    wouldn't you have found it out?
You know the secrets of our heart!

But it's for you
    we are murdered every day,
    butchered like sheep!

Rise up, O God! Why are you sleeping?
Awake! Don't abandon us for ever!
Why do you hide your face?
Why take no notice of our distress?
We fall on the dusty ground,
    clinging to the very earth!
Rise up! Come to our help!
Rescue us in your steadfast love!

National Thanksgiving

Psalm 65 (vv. 5-12)

    Answer us with deeds not words,
      with terror and victory,
      O God who rescued us! –
      hope of remotest peoples
      and far-away islands!

You build up the mountain ranges
    in your great strength;
    you calm the stormy seas
    and the wild waves;
    sea monsters cower
    at your wonders;
    you make dawn and sunset
    sing aloud for joy.

You come and water the earth,
    its richness is your gift:
    mighty rivers flow full with rain
    making the earth ready for sowing;
    in wet furrows, pressed sods,
    softened with steady showers,
    you bless the growing grain.
You crown the year with your bounty –
    wagon tracks drip with blessings.
The wild moors shout,
    the hills gird themselves
    with happiness and joy!
Sheep clothe the hills like a cloak,
    the valleys are dressed with corn,
    shouting and singing for joy!

A Morning Hymn

Psalm 19 (vv. 1-6)

The sky proclaims God's glory,
    its dome his handicraft:
    day to following day,
    night to following night
    tells his story.

No speech, no words,
    no human voice is heard.
Yet their music echoes across the world,
    their speech to remotest peoples!

The sun pitches his tent in the sea,
   happy as a bridegroom,
   exulting like a champion runner,
   eager to win the race!

From the eastern horizon
   to the farthest west
   he runs his race –
   nothing escapes his heat!

Individual Lament

Psalm 51

Be merciful to me, O God,
   blot out all the wrong I've done –
I trust your steadfast love,
   your lavish kindness.
Wash me clean
   of all my sin!

I know the wrong I've done,
   I can't forget it.
It's you I've sinned against, you only –
   I've done what you condemn.
Your sentence on me is a right sentence,
   I cannot complain of your judgement:
   I was conceived and born
   in sin.

You have searched out the truth
   in the depth of my being;
   teach me wisdom
   in my secret heart.

Make me really clean,
   whiter than snow.
Fill me with joy and gladness;
   may I, crushed as I am, rejoice.
Don't look at the wrong I've done,
   blot it all out!

Give me a clean heart, O God,
    a new and steadfast spirit.
Don't send me away,
    don't leave me.
Let me know again the joy of being rescued by you,
    hold me up and give me a willing spirit.

Teach me to sing, O God,
    and I will sing your praise!
It isn't sacrifice you want –
    if I brought a whole burnt-offering
    you wouldn't be pleased.
My only sacrifice is a broken heart –
    and this you don't despise!

Individual Thanksgiving

Psalm 139 (vv. 1-18)

You have searched the depth of my being, O GOD,
    you know all about me –
    when I'm resting,
    when I'm working.

You have probed my deepest intentions,
    tracking out the road I take
    and my camping grounds.
You know me through and through,
    understanding better than I what I'm trying to say.
You have laid siege to me
    behind me and before me;
    you have put your hand on my shoulder –
    I don't know why.
All this is beyond me,
    out of my reach –
    I can't grasp it.

Where can I go to escape you?
You are wherever I am.
If I climb the skies
   or explore the underworld,
   you are there!
If I fly with the sun
   from dawn to dark,
   your hand's still on my shoulder,
   your right hand grips me!
If I say, 'I'll lose myself in the darkness,
   vanish in the night!'
   darkness is no darkness to you,
   night is bright as day,
   darkness as light!

I thank you for being what you are –
   awe-inspiring, wonderful,
   wonderful in all you do.
You made me the man I am
   in the depth of my being;
   you've known what I am really like
   from the moment I was born.
You have watched the marvel of my body,
   the wonder of my birth;
   you've seen me grow up
   and marked all I've done –
   no day passed by uncounted,
   slipped by unnoticed.

What you think of me matters to me, O God,
   more than anything else –
   how much you know about me!
I cannot fathom your thoughts
   any more than I can count the sand on the shore!
Yet after all my searching
   I am still in your presence!

A Scholar's Hymn

Psalm 73

To the upright and pure in heart
   how good God is!

But it was the way bad people grow rich –
   and boast about it –
   that started me slipping
   and losing my foothold:
   they don't know what pain means,
   they are bursting with health;
   they have none of the troubles and suffering
   of commen men and women.
They display their pride in public
   and make violence a habit.
Their eyes shine in their fat faces
   mirroring their empty minds.
They live for sneer and slander,
   for scorn and lies;
   yet my people look up to them
   as their 'leaders' and 'heroes' (says God)
   in spite of their boasting words –
   'God's an ignoramus;
   he doesn't know or care!'
That's what bad people and rogues are like –
   yet they are the ones who make good,
   it's they who make the money!

And I began to grumble:
   what's the point of 'keeping my heart pure'
   and 'keeping my hands clean',
   when all I get is daily trouble
   and daily suffering?
But, if I'd let myself go grumbling on like this,
   I would have betrayed your family, O God.
I tried to make sense of it all,
   but it was beyond my grasp –
   until I worshipped in your temple
   and saw what really happens to evil people.

It is they whom you have set
    on slippery and dangerous ground.
They are living in a world of dreams,
    dreams which those who are awake
    know are only dreams –
    dreams suddenly and totally ended
    by death and destruction.

It was my bitter heart
    that made me envious –
I would not understand,
    dunce that I was;
I was living as a mere animal
    in your presence, O God.
Yet how different the truth is:
    I am your friend.
You hold my right hand,
    guide me with your counsel,
    receive me afterward in honour!

In the heavens above I have only you!
On earth below, having you, I have enough!
Ill and weak though I may be,
    you are mine for ever;
    all I desire now, O God,
    is to be near you.
I have made you, O God,
    my fortress!

The Heart of the Matter

Psalm 23

GOD is my shepherd!

I shall lack nothing –
    he lets me lie down on green grass,
    leads me by quiet streams,
    renews my strength.

He guides me along the right tracks,
     because he is what he is;
     when I go through the pitch-black gorge,
     nothing frightens me!

You are with me,
     club and staff at the ready –
     making me strong!

You are my host, I am your guest
     while enemies look helplessly on!
You bathe my head with oil,
     fill my cup to the brim!

Your goodness and love shall follow me
     all my days!
GOD's home is my home
     for ever!

Postscript

We have now come to the end of our account of the heart of the Old Testament. We have seen something of the story of Hebrew tribesmen, Israelite highlanders and Jewish exiles, and the convictions by which their best men and women lived – convictions forged in the face of a brutal experience that has overwhelmed more than one small nation.

The core of their faith is to be found in the memory of their escape from Egypt under Moses: told, discussed, pondered, sung, lived by for a thousand years. This faith, growing and deepening as the centuries passed, was held in many ways – with profound insight by their greatest thinkers, with more ambiguity by ordinary people. They had to fight for it against their own doubts and hesitations and fears and littleness. It was threatened, in later centuries most severely, by the sheer desperate need to survive; for theirs was a landscape across which armies and refugees moved.

It was a different thing for a Moses or a David, an Ahab or a Josiah, an Amos or a Jeremiah – kings were not always wrong nor prophets always right – for a Nehemiah or a writer like the writer of the *Book of Jonah*, or for men like the freedom fighters of the Great Rebellion of 168 BCE or young people and women of whom we hear so little. But all would say, 'God is with us', 'We must live as God's People', 'God has the last word'.

What these convictions really meant had to be worked out by every individual person – and every generation– in their own way; and, as we have seen, they can offer growing insights or become deadening clichés.

For there is no magic way to human maturity – or learning to live in God's Way as God's People. We can only walk by whatever light we have; and we have to learn to live with unanswered questions. The people without whom there would have been no Old Testament were not dreaming about some utopia – though many people, of course, especially in the later centuries, did do so; they were dealing with the world we live in as it really is and learning how to live in it with honesty and confidence and joy. Their clue was trusting, even in the darkest days, in God's 'steadfast love', and accepting it as their way too. For them, the world is God's world, and he is at work in it all the time.

We do not, therefore, turn to the Old Testament for historical or scientific information (we must get this from the present-day historian or scientist) but as a guide to human experience.

Read with insight and understanding, 'it teaches us how to look at the world in a religious light, how to experience the divine power in nature' (and, I would add, in history – in the lives of men and women), 'how to increase our ability to meet the full force of creation';* in a word, what it means to trust in God and live in his Way in the world as we know it to be today.

Further: it makes quite clear 'the menace which a supernatural religion can offer the world if it is not accompanied, at every inch of the way, with an insistence on the supremacy of charity't – steadfast love.

---

* John Wilson, *Philosophy and Religion*, p. 116.
† Herbert Butterfield, *The Methodist Recorder*, 24.7.69 – see also his *History and Human Relations*, pp. 37ff.

THE NEW TESTAMENT

'NEW WORLD'

Preface
From the author's original

The New Testament is comparatively short. Unlike the Old Testament which spans a thousand years and more, it is the creation of only three generations of a small and scattered community. Short though it is, it can be intimidating for the ordinary reader. Turning the pages over there are twenty-seven books – 'gospels', letters, 'revelation'; some passages crystal-clear, some strange and remote and obscure even when read two or three times. One incident is unforgettable – the plain and moving report of the death of a young man one Friday afternoon outside the walls of the capital city of an occupied country on the eastern borders of the Roman Empire. Four times that story is told, the climax of each of the first four books. That death in the afternoon is the obvious clue to the whole collection of writings.

I was once that ordinary reader, and *New World* has grown out of the plain guide I made for myself. I wish someone had made it for me and put it into my hands when I first picked up the New Testament to read it for myself. It was that death in the afternoon that started me reading. I wanted to know why, for these last two thousand years, it was a death people could not forget.

New World, therefore, is a translation of the essence of the New Testament as I now see it, made with a controlled vocabulary. The first three parts tell the story; the last two parts show how Christians tried to make sense of it and so came to their characteristic convictions. This, for me, is what the New Testament is about.

By 'essence of the New Testament' I mean this: first, an account of the ministry of Jesus; secondly, what Jesus himself had to say about it all; thirdly, a shortened version of the first great history of the origins and spread of the Christian community; fourthly, an account of what Christianity meant to one man – Paul; and finally, a survey of Christian convictions as seen in the letters of Paul and the gospel of John.

Here, in more detail, is the pattern of the five parts of *New World*.

The Beginning gives the account of the ministry of Jesus as it is found in the earliest gospel, *The Gospel According to Mark*. *The Gospel According to Matthew* is an enlarged edition of *Mark*; on a first reading of the New Testament it need not detain us, for Matthew's important additions are chiefly concerned with sayings of Jesus apparently unknown to Mark, and we shall be dealing with these in part two. The substance of what Luke had to say will be dealt with in part three, for Luke set his hand to something not attempted before.

The Message sets out what Jesus himself had to say. Modern scholarship enables us to go behind the collections of the sayings of Jesus which we find scattered throughout the first three gospels. It has given much attention to the *form* in which Jesus spoke, and I have therefore arranged his sayings according to their *form*. I have tried to let Jesus speak for himself – to let his words make something of the living impact he first gave them.

I give first what Dr Vincent Taylor has called 'Pronouncement Stories' – stories about Jesus which were remembered because of something he said. Note his informality. Then I give the parables and the poems. That Jesus was a poet, in the proper sense of the word, is one of the great insights of our times, the significance of which we have not yet adequately realised. To me, it makes all the difference to the way we approach him and listen to him.* Finally, I give individual sayings, each of which must be considered separately in the light of his total vision (the original occasions on which he said these has been forgotten) and the two poems in which he summed up what he lived and died for.

From Galilee to Rome gives a shortened version of Luke's two-volume work, written some fifty years after the death of Jesus, which might carry a title such as *The Origins and Convictions of the Christian Community*. Its two parts, *The Gospel According to Luke* and *The Acts of the Apostles*, were separated in the second-century arrangement of the New Testament. Luke sets the story of the first forty years against its worldwide background and shows how the friends of Jesus came step by step to grasp his fundamental conviction – that the Good News was for everybody everywhere. Nothing less than the reading of Luke's whole work will bring home the richness and range of his argument and the many issues with which he was concerned. I have tried, in this shortened version, to let his main argument speak for itself.†

The story of the ministry of Jesus and the spread of Christianity has now been told. What did this story mean to those involved in it?

---

* This insight has been accepted by scholars ever since Dr C. F. Burney published his book, *The Poetry of Our Lord*, in 1925. Those who wish to look more deeply into the matter will find a straightforward account of Hebrew poetry in Dr T. H. Robinson's *The Poetry of the Old Testament*; should consult Dr T. W. Manson's *The Teaching of Jesus*, pp. 50-56, especially the last paragraph; and can read a fascinating account of the nature of Hebrew poetry and the effect of its discovery in the eighteenth century (by Dr Louth, Professor of Poetry at Oxford) on the development of English poetry in Murray Roston's *Prophet and Poet*.
† In my selection from Luke's two-volume work, I have omitted many of the sayings of Jesus which he quoted (these will be found in *The Message*) and the passages from *Mark* with which he later expanded his own account (these have already been used in *The Beginning*); and I have kept some of his stories about Paul for part four, *Paul the Explorer*.

In *Paul the Explorer* I have tried to set out what Christianity meant to one man, Paul of Tarsus: first, in his own words; and then in the words of his friend, Luke – 'My doctor', he called him – in his account of Paul's ten years in the cities of the Aegean and of his defence before the courts in Palestine.

In *Jesus – Leader and Lord* I give the interpretation of Christianity offered by the two outstanding thinkers of its first century of expansion – Paul and the author of the Fourth Gospel.

In making this selection and arrangement, one central conviction has sustained me. It could not be better put than in the words of Dr Manson: 'Christianity had at its heart a person and a life before it had a creed and a code; and the thing that is characteristic of the great documents of the New Testament is their passionate devotion to the Person and their spontaneous reproduction of the life. "For me to live is Christ and to die is gain" . . . The New Testament has not attained to the dignity of a creed and a code; it has what is much better – a passionate love of Christ and a living fellowship of the brethren.'*

I have tried to avoid in any way distorting or misrepresenting what the New Testament has to say; I have made the selection and arrangement in the light of modern New Testament scholarship. I have long been troubled by the way in which, as ordinary readers, we keep apart our reading of the New Testament itself and the insights and discoveries of New Testament scholars. I think this is due to the fact that unless we can actually see what the text, in the light of such insights and discoveries, reads like, we find it difficult to relate what we read *about the New Testament* to what we read *in the New Testament itself* in the full editions of the Bible we normally use. I have, therefore, embodied, as far as I could, the work of scholars to whom I myself stand in great debt for what understanding of the New Testament I may have; this will be seen both in the translation itself and in the arrangement of the text. The reader who wishes to examine the reasons on which my decisions rest will find them in the books I have used.†

* *On Paul and John*, p. 117.

† These are the chief books: *The Beginning* – T. W. Manson, *The Servant-Messiah; The Message* – C. H. Dodd, *The Parables of the Kingdom*, J. Jeremias, *The Parables of Jesus*, and T. W. Manson, *The Sayings of Jesus; From Galilee to Rome* – V. Taylor, *The First Draft of St. Luke's Gospel; Paul the Explorer* – J. Knox, *Chapters in a Life of Paul; Jesus, Leader and Lord* – C. H. Dodd, *The Epistle to the Romans* (Moffatt Commentary), *The Interpretation of the Fourth Gospel* and *Historical Tradition in the Fourth Gospel*; as background for the whole volume – C. F. D. Moule, *The Birth of the New Testament*. I have, of course, used these books quite simply; but I am sure that to look at the New Testament through the eyes of such scholars is as important for the ordinary reader as for a teacher like myself.

I have also tried to help the reader to approach the records of the most important story in the world with critical awareness as well as with imagination. The clear intention of Jesus was to call everybody to fearless thought as well as to splendid living. He would have agreed with Socrates that 'the unexamined life is unlivable' ('If you can't ask questions, you might as well be dead'). He was not concerned with proselytising or indoctrination but with human maturity. He gave himself to help ordinary people to live as sons and daughters of God their Father. He didn't want mindless puppets; he wanted people to 'judge for themselves', 'to know what they believe and to love what they know'. Only so can he become for us either Leader or Lord.

A few notes about the controlled vocabulary I have used will make clear what I have tried to do.

In the later years of the nineteenth century scholars became aware that the language of the New Testament was largely the spoken language of the Mediterranean world. Whatever the faults of our twentieth-century translations, made in the language we ourselves speak, they have recaptured for us something of the directness and freshness of the colloquial idiom of gospel and letter.

I can remember a railway journey across England, lost in the pages of a Moffatt *New Testament* I had bought at a railway bookstall; and the Saturday morning when I went out and bought a copy of E. V. Rieu's *The Four Gospels* and felt as if I were reading *Mark* for the first time. Paul must have first come alive for many people in the pages of J. B. Phillips' *Letters to Young Churches* – the very title was an inspiration.

As a teacher, I have always coveted for my students such an experience. What I said to them mattered only in so far as it sent them to read the New Testament for themselves and catch something of the same excitement.

So here I set myself a limited linguistic aim. The full edition of *New World* is intended for young people in Secondary Schools; if all of them were to read it without hindrance I had to use a controlled vocabulary. I have tried to see how much of the heart of the New Testament can be put into very simple speech. I have not watered anything down (so I believe) though I have had to simplify wherever I could. I wanted them to be able to read it as I read Moffatt in the train. I have tried to face the issues straightforwardly, using, as far as I could, the work of New Testament scholars. I have had to come down on one side of the fence, of course, where there is still debate among competent scholars; but I have done so openly.

Paraphrase, especially in Paul's letters, has been unavoidable. I have done what I could to keep it within bounds. The problems which a translation with a controlled vocabulary raises troubled me most in *Jesus – Leader and Lord* with its richness of language and soaring argument. I hope that I have not entirely lost, in the search for simple language, the thrill I myself felt, and that the reader will be inspired to go on to read the full New Testament. For *New World* is not intended to take the place of the full text; it offers the reader a simplified version – first steps to the full translations.

I have found the making of this translation an exhilarating experience. Putting the New Testament into simple language has forced me to reconsider my own Christian convictions and to see the plain story of what happened in a fresh light. I hope that the reader will catch something of the excitement and enlargement I felt.

ALAN T. DALE
Dudley College of Education

May 1965

Introduction

At the heart of the New Testament lies the story of Jesus. We begin, therefore, with this story, although the books in which it was published were not the earliest Christian books or writings to be made. Mark, for example, was written probably about AD 65 when the earliest letters of Paul were already about fifteen years old.

But from the very beginning, stories about Jesus – what he did, how he talked, how he died and how his death was not the end – had been told and told again in the little Christian communities which were springing up throughout the known world. Jesus was not a dream-figure; he had really lived in Palestine. Many of his friends who had met him and known him there were still alive. So the story of Jesus was told by preachers and teachers, in discussion and debate and in worship. The Christian communities in cities like Antioch, Ephesus, and Rome gathered the stories into groups – for example, those dealing with Jesus' debates with the Jewish leaders, those of his 'mighty works', sayings dealing with how the friends of Jesus should behave. Some of the stories probably came from eye-witnesses; some were popular stories circulating both inside and outside the Christian communities. Mark had all of these to draw on when he sat down to write his account to make clear that Jesus Christ, whom Christians believed to be 'the Son of God' and their 'Lord' and 'Saviour', had lived a real human life in Palestine.

The stories about Jesus came into Mark's hands as individual stories or as groups; some of them may have come from Peter himself, for Mark had probably been his friend. But he also had the account of how Jesus died – we call it 'The Passion Story' – which the Christians in Rome had used in their worship from the very beginning; it began some days before the Jewish Passover Feast when Jesus came back to Jerusalem and told how he and his friends had spent the last days, how Jesus was arrested, tried, and executed, and (probably) what happened on the first Easter Day.

Mark also had, it seems, a picture of the course the ministry of Jesus took* from his call by Jordan River to the last days in Jerusalem. Much of this was unknown to his friends – they were not always with him – and only a few outstanding events remained clearly in their minds: the time Jesus spent in Galilee preaching in the towns and villages; his

---

* I have set out the story of Jesus as I see it in *A Source Book of the Bible for Teachers*, pp. 264-283.

meeting with the Resistance Movement at the 'Desert Meal'; the incident near Caesarea Philippi in the north; the last days in Jerusalem. Mark had to fit all his stories into this broad picture. So he gives us a portrait of Jesus as his friends remembered him and in the light of what they now believed him to be.

We begin, therefore, with the stories about Jesus which Mark used in his 'gospel'. This will help us to listen in, as it were, to the friends of Jesus talking about him; we can see the kind of stories they told, something of the way they believed events happened, and how all their stories lead up to his death and resurrection.

If we are to understand Jesus – why he did what he did, why he said what he said in the way he said it – we must remember two things: that the background of his life was an occupied country with a resistance movement ('The Zealots'); and that, like the prophets before him, he was a poet.

Occupied Country

No seas guarded the native land of Jesus. It was easy for great armies to march into it and conquer it.

Roman soldiers were soon to have barracks in the far-off island of Britain – in London, York, and Chester. They already had barracks in Palestine – in Caesarea on the coast, where they had their headquarters; in Jerusalem, the capital city, where their barracks were in the Tower of Antonia, looking down on the Temple Courts; and in Capernaum, and on a high hill near Nazareth, where they had outposts.

Julius Caesar with his soldiers first landed in Britain in 55 BC; it was eight years before, in 63 BC, that Roman soldiers first marched into Palestine. Perhaps Jesus often listened to his grandfather telling him about them, and how he was a very small boy when they came. Pompey, their general, marched along the shores of Galilee Lake and down the Jordan Valley to Jerusalem. After three months' fighting, he captured the city and the Temple, and many thousands of Jews were killed. Palestine became an occupied country; the Roman soldiers stayed to rule the country they had captured.

There was a town near Nazareth, where Jesus grew up, called Sepphoris; the villagers would go there to do their shopping. When Jesus was a boy, about twelve years of age, the people of Sepphoris rose in rebellion against the Romans. The Roman general came with his soldiers, captured the city, burned it to the ground, and sold its leading citizens into slavery.

Jesus would not forget that. Perhaps he talked with the people who had been there when it happened; his father, who was a builder, may have helped to rebuild the city.

We must remember all this when we read the story of Jesus and what he had to say to his own people. People do not like being ruled by foreign soldiers. They hate them, and dream of a time when they will drive them out of their country. The Jewish people hated the Romans; and they hated people, like the tax collectors, who helped them. Some of them were actually training what we would call today a 'resistance movement', an 'underground army'; they had to keep away from the Roman soldiers and meet in lonely places in Galilee and in the wild hills between Jerusalem and Jordan River. Jesus once told a story about a man who was attacked on one of these lonely roads. We shall meet farmers and fishermen who belonged to this resistance movement in the story of 'The Desert Meal' (page 421). One of the friends of Jesus, Simon, may once have belonged to it. We shall meet one of their leaders in the story of 'The Great Feast' – Barabbas; Pilate, the Roman Governor, set him free when he sentenced Jesus to death.

In AD 66, nearly forty years after the time of Jesus, the Jewish Rebellion broke out. After bitter fighting, the Roman soldiers defeated the Jewish people and destroyed Jerusalem city.

Stories, Poems, Sayings

The friends of Jesus gathered his sayings together into small collections. These small collections of sayings dealt with the questions people asked and helped them to see what Jesus had to say about them.

Jesus himself never wrote anything down. He talked to people and left it to his listeners to remember what he said as best they could. But he had different ways of talking to different kinds of people; this is most important to remember.

To the people in the villages, he put what he had to say in stories (or parables), like the village stories everybody loved to hear. He did not suddenly make them up when he was speaking; he had long thought about them in his own mind, ever since he was a boy. He told them in order to start people thinking about God's Way.

To his close friends, he put what he had to say in short poems, which set out, in simple language, his deepest thoughts about God's Way – what God is like and what he is doing, how he wants men and women to live, what God wants his world to be like.

This was his custom. But sometimes, of course, he told his friends a story or put what he had to say to other people in a poem.

In addition to his stories and poems, his friends remembered his many conversations with all sorts of people. Sometimes they remembered how the conversations happened; but often they only remembered the striking saying itself and forgot just how and when Jesus spoke it.

So we have arranged the sayings of Jesus to help you to feel what it was like to have heard Jesus talk.

The Poetry of Jesus

The stories of Jesus were all about the little world of Galilee – the people he had known and the things he had seen as boy and man. But they are not only about the little world of Galilee. Jesus was trying to help people to see what God wanted them to do. His stories also make us think about God's bigger world – everybody everywhere – where men and women of different races, classes, occupations, interests, and countries carry on their lives and have to learn to live together.

The poems of Jesus are about God's bigger world and everybody in it; Jews, Greeks, and Romans of the time of Jesus; British, Chinese, Russians, Indians, Africans, Americans, everybody of our own day, too. They are mostly simple and direct and clear, but sometimes he used old and famous stories of his people – of Noah and Lot, of Elijah and Elisha; of great cities of the past, Sodom and Tyre and Sidon.

All countries have their poets: famous poets whose names everybody know; and the poets whose names are forgotten, but whose poems are remembered and recited. The Jewish people had their known and unknown poets, too.

Most important of all, their great men of God like Amos and Jeremiah were poets. When they told the people what God wanted them to do, they put it in short poems which ordinary people could remember and recite to one another.

Amos was the first man of God whose poems were written down; you can find them in *The Book of Amos* in the Bible.* He believed that the worship which the people of his day offered to God was not sincere. They sang their hymns, but they did not mean what they sang, and they did not try to live in God's Way. He put what he had to say in a poem which he recited at the market in the King's town. Here it is:

* See pp. 221.

I hate, I have no use for your feasts,
   I take no delight in your solemn services.
You offer me animals and wheat,
   but I will not accept them;
Your offerings of fat beasts
   I will not look upon.

Take away from me the noise of your songs;
   to the music of your harps I will not listen.
Let justice roll down like the rivers,
   and goodness like an ever-flowing stream.

Amos 5:21-24

Jesus was a poet, as Amos and Jeremiah were. His poems had rhythm and, sometimes, rhyme, as English poems have. But Hebrew poets had a special way of writing poetry; they repeat, in a slightly different way, each line. Look at the last verse of the poem by Amos. In the first line he speaks of 'the noise of your songs'; in the second line he speaks of 'the music of your harps'. The lines are 'parallel' to one another. The last two lines of the verse are 'parallel' too. There are many ways of doing this, and you will find illustrations of it in the Old Testament, especially in the Psalms. If you look through the poems of Jesus in *The Poetry of Jesus* (page 469), you will see how he spoke in this way too.

The Beginning

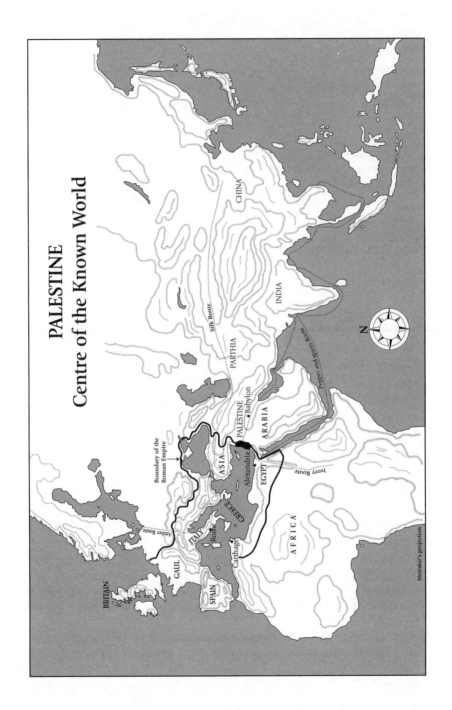

PALESTINE
Centre of the Known World

On the Banks of the River

The story of Jesus began in the hot Jordan Valley, on the banks of the river. Not very far to the south was the Salt Sea. It was a long way from Nazareth, the village in the north where he had grown up and lived as a builder.

Jesus was probably about thirty years of age. He had come south to join the hermit John and his friends.

John the Hermit had been living in the wild hills that rise to the east of Jordan River. He believed that God had called him to tell the Jewish people to change their ways and live in his Way.

People all over the country were talking about John and what he was saying and doing. Great crowds went out to listen to him. The news reached Nazareth. When Jesus heard it, he left his village and his family and friends, and went to meet John on the banks of Jordan River.

The Hermit John   *Mark 1:1-8*

There is an old poem in the Bible, written in far-away Babylon a long time before our story begins. The Jewish people were prisoners there, but they were soon to be set free to go back across the desert to their homeland. The poem is about the journey home, and it begins like this:

> The voice of a man
>   shouting in the lonely desert –
> 'Get God's road ready,
>   make his paths straight'.

John appeared, like the man in the poem, on the lonely moorland, calling people to change their ways so that God might forgive them. He told them to wash themselves in the water of Jordan River as a sign that they had really changed their ways.

All sorts of people went out to hear him – country people from Judea and town people from Jerusalem; they were washed by him in the water of Jordan River, saying that they were sorry for the wrong things they had done.

John lived as his desert ancestors had lived: he had a cloak of camel's hair and a leather belt round his waist, and he used to eat locusts and wild honey.

'A Stronger One than I am comes after me,' John told the people. 'I am not good enough to bend down and untie his shoelaces. I have used water as a sign that your hearts shall be made clean; he will really give you God's own power.'

Jesus Hears God's Call   *Mark 1:9-13*

When the crowds were going out to hear John, Jesus left his home in Nazareth and was washed by John in the water of Jordan River.

As Jesus was coming up out of the river, he saw, as it were, a flash of lightning across the skies; and, with the gentleness of a dove, God filled his heart with peace. Into his mind came God's words:

'You are my only Son; with you I am very pleased.'

Then God's Spirit sent him out on to the lonely moorland, and he stayed there many a long day. His only company was wild animals, but God looked after him.

In Galilee

We do not know how long Jesus stayed in the south after he heard God's call. But when King Herod had arrested John and put him in prison in his lonely castle of Machaerus, high on the mountains on the eastern side of the Salt Sea, Jesus went back to his homeland of Galilee. The stories here are all about what happened in Galilee.

The work of Jesus in Galilee was brought to an end when the soldiers of the 'Resistance Movement' tried to make Jesus their leader. Jesus knew that this was not God's Way. He had been telling the people what God's Way really was, but they had not listened. Even his own friends did not understand. When the 5,000 men met Jesus at a lonely spot on the shores of Galilee Lake, Jesus knew he would have to leave Galilee. The Desert Meal was the end of his work there.

The Good News   Mark 1:14-15

Jesus came into Galilee telling everybody the Good News about God. This is what he said:

> The Great Day is here.
> God's Kingdom has come;
>   change your ways
>   and trust in the Good News.

A Day in the Life of Jesus   Mark 1:21-38

Jesus and his friends were in Capernaum, a fishing town on the shores of Galilee Lake. It was Saturday, the Holy Day of the Jews, and Jesus and his friends went along to the Meeting House and took part in the Service of Worship. There was a madman among the people who had gathered there.

'What are you bothering us for, Jesus, coming here from Nazareth?' he shouted out. 'Have you come to get rid of us? I know you – you're God's Holy One!'

'Be quiet,' said Jesus severely, 'and come out of him.'

The mad spirit in the man threw him on the ground, and, shouting out loudly, came out of him. Everybody was taken by surprise, and started talking about Jesus and what he had said and done:

'What's this?'

'It's not like anything we've heard before!'

'He talks to mad spirits as though he was their master!'

'And they do what he tells them!'

Jesus and his friends left the building and went along with James and John to the home of Peter and Andrew. Peter's mother-in-law was in bed with fever. They told Jesus about her, and he went to her and took hold of her hand and lifted her up. The fever left her and she looked after the visitors.

At sunset, when the Holy Day was over, people brought all who were ill in body or mind to Jesus. The whole town crowded round the door of the house. Jesus made them all better, whatever their illness was.

Early next morning, while it was still dark, Jesus got up and went out of the house to a lonely place. Peter and his friends hunted him out and found him – praying.

'Everybody's looking for you,' they told him.

'Let's get away,' said Jesus, 'and give them the Good News in the nearby market towns. That's why I came out here.'

Jesus and His Home Folk

In Nazareth   *Mark 6:1-6a*

One day Jesus went back to his own village with his friends. On Saturday, the Jewish Holy Day, he spoke to the people in their Meeting House. Everybody listened to him with amazement.

'Where does he get it all from?' they said.

'What's this learning he's been given?'

'He does such wonderful things!'

'Isn't he the builder, Mary's son? Aren't James, Joses, Judas and Simon his brothers?'

'And aren't his sisters here with us?'

Because they knew him so well, they couldn't believe he was anybody special. They didn't want to have anything to do with him.

'You know what people say,' said Jesus. 'A man of God is always well thought of – except in his own country and among his own relatives and in his own home.'

He could do no wonderful things there. He could only put his hands on a few sick people and make them better. What surprised him was that the people of his own village didn't trust him.

In Capernaum   *Mark 3:19b-21, 31-35*

Jesus was at home in Capernaum, and people came crowding to him; he and his friends had no time even to eat their meals.

News of all this came to his family. They came over to look after him; they thought he was out of his mind.

His mother and brothers came and stood outside the house, and sent somebody in to ask him to come outside. The crowd was sitting round him.

'Look!' they said to him. 'Your mother and brothers are outside asking for you.'

'Who are my real mother and brothers?' asked Jesus.

He looked at those who were sitting in a circle round him.

'Here are my real mother and brothers,' he said. Whoever does what God wants them to do is my real brother and sister and mother.'

Jesus and His Friends

Five Friends

One day Jesus was walking along the seashore; he saw Peter and his brother Andrew casting their nets into the sea – they were fishermen.

'Come with me,' said Jesus. 'I'll show you better fishing than this – for men, not fish.'

And they left their nets and went with him.

A little farther on James and his brother John were getting their nets ready in the boat. Jesus called them, and they left their father with his men in the boat and went away with him.

Some time later Jesus was again out walking and he saw Levi at work in the tax office.

'Come with me,' said Jesus.

Levi got up and went with him.

A Would-be Friend   *Mark 10:17-30*

When Jesus was out on the road again, a man ran up and kneeled down in front of him.

'Good Sir,' he said, 'what must I do to take my place in God's New Kingdom?'

'You use the word "good",' said Jesus. 'Why do you use it about me? You can only use that word about God himself, for only God is really good . . . You know the Ten Commandments, don't you?'

'Sir,' he said, 'I've kept the Ten Commandments ever since I was a boy.'

Jesus looked at him and liked him very much indeed.

'There's only one thing you must do,' he said. 'You want to be really rich. Well then, sell what you've got and give it to people who haven't got anything, and come and join my company of friends.'

The man's face fell when he heard this, and he went away very sad; he was a very rich man.

'How hard it is,' Jesus said, 'for a rich man to live in God's way.'

His friends were amazed to hear him talk like this.

'You know,' Jesus went on, 'you haven't grown up yet. You think it's easy to live in God's way. But it's hard for anybody to live like that. It's easier for a camel to get through the eye of a needle than for a rich man to live in God's way.'

His friends were really amazed.

'Who then can live in God's way, if a rich man can't?' they said to one another.

Jesus looked at them.

'You forget,' he said. 'What people by themselves can't do, God can. Don't you remember what the Bible says about God – "I know that you can do everything"?'

Peter started talking.

'Look!' he said 'We've given up everything to come with you!'

'And I give you a solemn promise,' said Jesus. 'Nobody has left home, or brothers or sisters, or mother or father, or children or fields, for me and the Good News – for nothing. You won't have an easy time; you'll have to be ready to face prison and death. But here and now you will get a great reward: more homes, more brothers and sisters, more mothers, more children and more fields. And in the New World that's coming, you'll have a place in God's Kingdom.'

The 'Twelve'   *Mark 3:13-19; 6:7-13, 30*

Jesus went into the hills and called the men he wanted and they went out to him. He chose a small company of very close friends, and he called them the 'Twelve'.

He wanted them to be with him, and to go out telling the Good News about God and making sick people better.

These are the 'Twelve' and some of the nicknames Jesus gave them:

Simon	'Rock' (we say 'Peter')
James and John,	
the sons of Zebedee	'Thunder and Lightning'

Andrew
Philip
Bartholomew
Matthew
James, the son of Alphaeus
Thomas
Thaddaeus
Simon   'Rebel'
Judas

(Judas was called 'Iscariot' like his father; this is the friend who handed Jesus over to the Jewish Government.)

Jesus sent the 'Twelve' out, in pairs, into the villages; and he gave them power to make sick people better.

His orders were: 'Travel light with staff and sandals, no food, no bag, no money in your belt, and only one shirt.'

The 'Twelve' went off and told people the Good News about God and called them to change their ways. They made mad people better; they put ointment on other sick people and made them better too.

Then they came back and met Jesus again, and told him everything they had done and what they had said to the people in the villages.

A Stormy Night   Mark 4:35-41

Jesus had been talking to a crowd of people from a boat, and it was getting dark.

'Let's go across the Lake,' he said to his friends.

They left the crowd and took him along with them in the boat just as he was. Other boats, too, put out to sea with them. Suddenly there was a wind storm, and the waves were breaking into the boat and filling it with water. Jesus was sleeping on a cushion in the stern.

They woke him up.

'Sir,' they shouted, 'doesn't it matter to you that we're sinking?'

Jesus woke up.

'Silence!' he said to the wind and the sea. 'Be quiet!'

The wind dropped and there was a dead calm.

'Why are you cowards like this?' he said to his friends. 'Don't you trust God yet?'

They had been very frightened indeed.

'What sort of man is this?' they asked one another. 'He's master even of wind and sea!'

413

People Jesus Helped

A Man Suffering from Leprosy   Mark 1:40-45a

One day a man suffering from leprosy came to Jesus and knelt down in front of him.

'If you want to,' he kept saying, 'you can get rid of my leprosy.'

Jesus was angry and stretched out his hand and touched him.

'Of course I want to,' said Jesus, 'be clean.'

The man's leprosy left him and he was better. But Jesus sent him off.

'See you don't tell anybody,' he warned him sternly. 'Off you go to the Temple and take what the Bible orders you to take, so that everybody can see you're really better.'

But the man went off to spread the news far and wide.

A Lame Man   Mark 2:3-5, 11-12

One day some men brought a lame man to Jesus, and four of them were carrying him. The crowd was so great that they could not get anywhere near him. So they stripped the flat roof off the house where Jesus was, dug a hole and lowered the mat with the lame man on it.

Jesus saw how these men trusted him.

'I'm speaking to you,' he said to the lame man. 'Get up, pick up your mat and go home.'

The lame man got up, picked up his mat and walked out.

Everyone kept looking at him in amazement and thanked God for his goodness.

'We've never seen anything like this!' they said.

A Man Possessed by Spirits   Mark 5:1-20

One day Jesus and his friends sailed to the far shore of Galilee Lake. A man possessed by spirits lived among the graves there. Nobody had been able to tie him up even with chains. He had often been tied up with handcuffs and chains, but he had torn the handcuffs apart and smashed the chains. Night and day he lived among the graves and on the hills, shouting out and striking himself with stones. Nobody could tame him.

Jesus got out of the boat. The man saw him from a long way off, ran to him and knelt down at his feet.

'What are you bothering me for, Jesus, Son of the Most High God?' he screamed at the top of his voice. 'I beg you, in God's name, don't torment me!' For Jesus was already saying to him – 'Come out of the man, you foul spirit.'

414

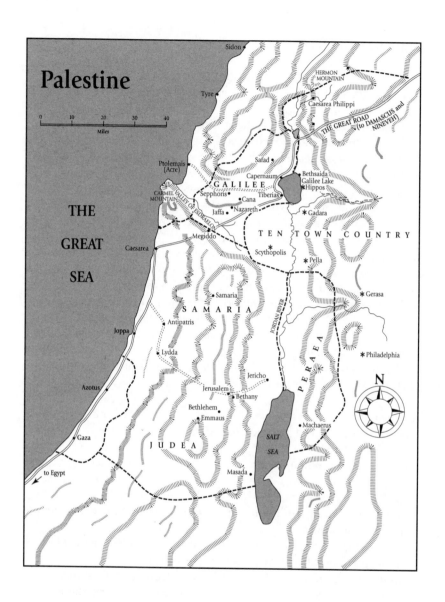

Palestine

THE GREAT SEA

Sidon

HERMON MOUNTAIN

Tyre

Caesarea Philippi

THE GREAT ROAD (to DAMASCUS and NINEVEH)

Ptolemais (Acre)

Safad

GALILEE

Capernaum

Bethsaida?

Galilee Lake

Hippos?

CARMEL MOUNTAIN

VALLEY OF ESDRAELON

Sepphoris

Tiberias

Cana

Jaffa

Nazareth

✱ Gadara

Megiddo

T E N   T O W N   C O U N T R Y

Caesarea

Scythopolis ✱

✱ Pella

Samaria

S A M A R I A

✱ Gerasa

Joppa

Antipatris

P E R A E A

Lydda

✱ Philadelphia

Jericho

Jerusalem

Bethany

Azotus

Bethlehem

Emmaus

✱ Machaerus

Gaza

J U D E A

SALT SEA

to Egypt

Masada

JORDAN RIVER

N

'What's your name?' asked Jesus.

'I'm the Roman Army,' he said. 'There are thousands of us.'

He begged Jesus over and over again not to send the foul spirits away from the graves and the hills. A great herd of pigs was feeding on the hillside.

'Send us into the pigs,' said the spirits. 'Let us get inside them.'

Jesus let them go, and the foul spirits went off into the pigs. The herd rushed down the steep bank into the sea – all 2,000 of them – and were drowned.

The herdsmen ran off and told the news in town and country; everybody came out to see what had happened. They came to Jesus and looked at the man now sitting down, wearing his clothes and quite sane, the very man who had called himself 'The Roman Army'. They were very frightened. Those who had seen what had happened told the others about the possessed man and about the pigs; and they all begged Jesus to go away. They didn't want him there.

As Jesus was getting into the boat, the man himself begged to join his company of friends; but Jesus wouldn't let him join them.

'Go home to your own people,' he said, 'and tell them what God has done for you and how he has had pity on you.'

Off he went, and everywhere in 'Ten Town Country' he told people what Jesus had done to him. It amazed everybody.

A Little Girl   Mark 5:21-24a, 35-43

One day a great crowd gathered round Jesus on the seashore. An officer of the Meeting House called Jairus, who had a little girl twelve years old, came along. When he saw Jesus, he fell down at his feet.

'My little girl's dying. Come and touch her with your hands,' he begged over and over again. 'Then she'll get better and live.'

Jesus went along with him and was talking to him when people came from his house.

'Your daughter has died,' they said. 'Why go on bothering the Master?'

Jesus took no notice of what was being said.

'Don't worry,' he said to Jairus. 'All you must do is to trust me.'

He let nobody go with him except his three friends, Peter, James, and John. When he got to the house, he saw the uproar that was going on there and the paid mourners weeping and wailing loudly.

He went in.

'What's all this uproar and weeping for?' he asked. 'This little girl isn't dead; she's asleep.'

Everybody made fun of him, but Jesus turned them all out. He took the father and mother and his friends, and went into where the little girl was lying and took hold of her hand.

'Little girl,' he said, 'get up.'

She got up and walked about. Her father and mother were too amazed to know what to do. Jesus gave them strict orders that nobody must know about it and told them to give her something to eat.

A Sick Woman   Mark 5:25-34

One day a great crowd was following Jesus and pressing round him. A woman who had suffered from bleeding for twelve years was among them. The doctors hadn't helped her very much. All her money was gone on doctor's bills, and she was no better; indeed she was much worse. She had heard people talking of Jesus and she had joined in the crowd behind him.

'If I touch just his clothes,' she kept saying to herself, 'I shall be better.'

She touched his clothes. Her bleeding stopped, and she felt better in herself at once. Her trouble was over.

Jesus noticed that power had gone out of him; he turned round in the crowd.

'Who touched my clothes?' he asked.

'You see all this crowd pressing round you,' said his friends, 'and you ask who touched you!'

Jesus looked all round him to see who had done it.

The woman, frightened and trembling all over, knew what had happened to her; and she came and fell down in front of him and told him everything.

'Daughter,' said Jesus, 'your trust in me has made you better. Go home and don't worry; your trouble won't bother you any more.'

A Deaf Man   Mark 7:32-37

One day some people brought to Jesus a deaf man with a speech impediment and begged him to touch him with his hand.

Jesus took him away from the crowd by himself. He put his finger in his ears, and spat and touched his tongue. Then he looked up and sighed.

'Be opened,' he said.

The man began to hear and use his tongue, and he talked quite clearly. Jesus told the man's friends not to tell people about it. But the more he told them not to talk about it, the more they spread the news. The were too amazed to obey him.

'How well he does everything!' they said. 'He even makes deaf people hear and dumb people talk!'

A Blind Man *Mark 8:22-26*

One day Jesus was passing through the village where Peter had grown up as a boy. People brought a blind man to him, and asked him to touch him and make him better.

Jesus led the blind man by the hand outside the village. He wet his eyes (as doctors often did in those days) and touched them with his hands.

'Can you see anything?' he asked.

The blind man looked up.

'Yes,' he said. 'I can see people – but they are like walking trees!'

Jesus put his hands on the blind man's eyes again. Now he could see quite clearly. He was blind no longer, and he could see the hills on the other side of Galilee Lake as plainly as anybody else.

Jesus sent him off home.

'Don't tell anybody else in the village,' he said. 'Don't go back there.'

Boys and Girls *Mark 10:13-15*

One day parents were bringing boys and girls to Jesus for him to touch them; his friends told them to go away. When Jesus saw them doing this he was angry.

'Let the boys and girls come to me,' he said. 'You mustn't stop them. God's Kingdom is made up of the young like these. I am sure of this: anyone who does not welcome God's Kingdom like a little boy or girl won't get inside.'

Jesus and the Crowds *Based on Mark 1:22, 28; 2:1, 2; 3:7-10; 6:2, 54-56*

People everywhere were amazed at what Jesus said; when he spoke, you had to listen. Everybody was talking about him in all the country towns and villages. He used to speak to them in their Meeting Houses and make sick people better. He couldn't go into any town without people crowding round him; he had to stay out in the countryside and people used to come to him from the villages round about.

They came to him from all over Galilee, from far in the south, from the other side of Jordan River, and even from the foreign cities of Tyre and Sidon.

When Jesus was at home in Capernaum, people crowded together so that the space about the doorway could no longer hold them.

He used to go out by Galilee Lake. Crowds came there too, and he used to talk to them.

One day, on the seashore, the crowds nearly crushed him; he had to tell his friends to keep a boat ready for him to get into. Once he had to get into a boat and the great crowd stood on the land at the water's edge.

Jesus made many sick people better. They pressed on him to touch him, and wherever he went – into villages, towns, and farms – people put the sick in the market places and begged him to let them touch the hem of his clothes. Those who touched him got better.

Our Ways and God's Ways

Jesus at Home   *Mark 2:15-17*
One day Jesus was having a meal at home with his friends. Quite a number of tax-collectors and ordinary people had been invited. Some Jewish Leaders, who had been 'shadowing' Jesus, noticed who was there.

'Why is he eating with such people?' they asked his friends.

Jesus heard them.

'Healthy people don't need a doctor,' he said, 'but sick people do.'

Religion Isn't Dull!   *Mark 2:18-19*
One day, during the Fast Days, the friends of John the Hermit were fasting. Some people came to Jesus.

'Why do John's friends fast,' they asked, 'but your friends don't?'

'Can guests at a wedding leave the wedding breakfast uneaten?' asked Jesus. 'What would the bridegroom think?'

In the Fields   *Mark 2:23-28*
One Saturday, the Holy Day of the Jews. Jesus was walking through the cornfields, and his friends were picking the ears of corn as they walked along.

'Look!' said the Jewish Leaders. 'Why are you doing what's not allowed on our Holy Day?'

'You don't know your Bibles very well,' said Jesus. 'Don't you remember what King David and his soldiers once did when they were hungry and starving? He went into God's House and ate the special bread that was kept there. That wasn't "allowed" either, you know; only the priests are "allowed" to eat that bread. He gave it to his soldiers too!'

'Our Holy Day,' Jesus went on, 'was made to be a help to men and women; men and women weren't made just to keep the Holy Day. What is more, they themselves can say what can and what can't be done on our Holy Day.'

In a Village   Mark 3:1-6

One Saturday, Jesus went to a Meeting House. A man with a withered hand was there. The Jewish Leaders watched Jesus closely to see if he would heal him, though it was a Holy Day, so that they could report him.

'Stand up for everybody to see,' said Jesus to the man.

He turned to the Jewish Leaders.

'What's the right thing to do on the Holy Day? A good thing or a bad thing?' he asked. 'Make someone better or let them die?'

They said nothing, and Jesus looked round at them in anger; he was very sad because they were so hard-hearted.

'Stretch out your hand,' he said to the man.

The man stretched out his hand and it was strong again.

The Jewish Leaders went out and met with other Leaders in the south, to see what they could do to get rid of Jesus.

Old Customs   Mark 7:1-13

The Jewish people still kept some old customs. They never ate anything without 'washing' their hands up to the wrist. If they bought anything to eat from the market, they sprinkled themselves with water. In the same way, they 'washed' cups, pots, and copper pans. This was not a proper wash, but just sprinkling; they thought that this was the sort of thing God wanted them to do. If anything had been sprinkled, they called it 'clean'; if it had not been sprinkled, they called it 'dirty'.

The Jewish Leaders noticed that the friends of Jesus ate their food with 'dirty' hands, and they came to talk to him about it.

'Why don't these friends of yours keep the old customs?' they asked. 'Why do they eat food with "dirty" hands?'

'You're just playing at being good,' said Jesus. 'The old words of the Bible might have been written about you –

> These people talk, talk, talk!
> They don't really love Me.
> What they do to 'please' Me
>   doesn't mean anything;
>   what they say 'God wants'
>   they have made up for themselves.

'You make people do what you want them to do,' said Jesus, 'not what God wants them to do. Here's an example. God said: "Respect your father and mother"; you say: "If someone says to their parents, 'I know I ought to give this to you, but I'm going to give it to the Temple', they needn't do anything for their father or mother." So your "old custom" takes the place of God's command. I could give you many other examples.'

What Matters   *Mark 7:14-23*

One day Jesus called the crowd to him.

'I want you to listen to me,' he said. 'I want you to be quite clear about what's "clean" and what's "dirty", what God wants and what God doesn't want. It's not "outside things" that matter, but "inside things"'.

When Jesus got home, away from the crowd, his friends asked him about this strange saying.

'Can't you see it, either?' asked Jesus. 'Isn't it clear that what's "outside" you can't make you "dirty"? It doesn't go into your mind, only into your body. These things make you "dirty": real badness, stealing, murder, greediness, wickedness, lying, indecency, selfishness, saying untrue things about people, having high and mighty ideas about yourself, not knowing what God wants you to do because you never tried to find out. All these wrong thoughts come out of your mind; they come from "inside" you and make you "dirty"'.

Last Days in Galilee

The Desert Meal   *Mark 6:31-46*

Everybody seemed to be coming and going; there was not time even to eat.

'Come,' said Jesus to his friends, 'you need a holiday, away from the people, by yourselves.'

So off they went in a boat right away from everybody. But a lot of people saw them going away and recognised them; the crowds who had come from near-by villages hurried along the shore and got ahead of them.

Jesus put the boat back to land and got out.

He looked at the great crowd of people – 5,000 men – and he was very sorry for them. He remembered the words from the Bible: 'Like sheep without a shepherd to look after them'. That's what this crowd was like; they had no leader. Jesus talked to them for quite a long time.

By now the afternoon was passing.

'This is a very lonely place,' said his friends to Jesus, 'and it's getting very late. Send the crowd off; they can find their way to the farms and villages over there and get some food.'

'You feed them,' said Jesus.

'What!' they said. 'Do you want us to go and buy a whole load of bread to feed them?'

'How many loaves have you got?' asked Jesus. 'Go and see.'

They found out.

'Five,' they said, 'and two fish!'

Jesus told the men to sit down in groups on the green grass, and they sat down in companies, some one hundred and some fifty strong.

Jesus took the five loaves and the two fish, and looked up and said Grace over them. He broke the loaves and gave the pieces to his friends to give to the people; and he shared the fish with them all, too. Everybody had enough to eat, and they gathered what was left of the crumbs and the fish into twelve baskets.

Then Jesus straight away made his friends get into the boat and go ahead of him over to the far shore of the lake, near Bethsaida. He stayed behind to get the crowd to go home. When he had said good-bye to them he went away up into the hills to pray.

The Night at Sea   *Mark 6:47-55*

It was now dark. The boat was out at sea and Jesus was alone on the land.

Hours passed and it was just before dawn. The men in the boat were in a bad way. A sudden storm had come down on the sea and they were struggling against the wind. Jesus saw them and came to them, walking on the sea. He was level with the boat, when they saw him. They thought he was a ghost. They yelled out in terror; all of them were staring at him.

'Cheer up!' said Jesus. 'It's me. Don't be frightened.'

He got into the boat with them and the wind dropped. They were utterly amazed; they didn't know what to make of it.

When they got across to the land, they were back again on the west shore where they started. They brought the boat into the harbour. They had just got out of the boat when the people recognised Jesus. They ran round the countryside and carried on mats those who were ill to wherever they heard he was.

In the Northern Highlands

Jesus now left Galilee and crossed the border into the countryside which was governed by the foreign cities of Tyre and Sidon. The countryside they governed stretched right across the mountains from the sea to the Jordan Valley. When he left this foreign countryside, Jesus still stayed outside Galilee. He went into 'Ten Town Country', the country governed by the great Greek cities; and then into the countryside of the new city which the Governor Philip had built in the highlands. Here he climbed snow-capped Hermon Mountain with Peter and James and John.

Jesus spent most of the time alone with his friends. He was trying to help them to understand what God's Way was really like.

Jesus in Hiding   Mark 7:24, 31

After the Desert Meal, Jesus left his own country, Galilee, and went over the border into the countryside which belongs to the foreign city of Tyre. He stayed in a house, because he did not want people to know where he was, but he couldn't hide away so easily.

He left the countryside of Tyre and went through the countryside of Sidon, through 'Ten Town Country', across the mountains to Galilee Lake.

Jesus and a Foreigner   Mark 7:25-30

While Jesus was in the countryside of Tyre, a foreign woman, whose little girl was sick in mind, heard about him. She came and fell down at his feet, and asked him to make her daughter better.

'Children get their food first,' said Jesus to her. 'You don't give the children's food to your little dogs.'

'Of course, Sir,' she said, 'but the little dogs under the table get the crumbs the children drop!'

'You're right,' said Jesus. 'You can go home, your daughter's better.'

The woman went home and found her daughter lying bed, completely cured.

On a Country Road   Mark 8:27-33

Jesus and his friends went out into the countryside near the new city which the Governor Philip had built in the highlands.

'People are talking about me,' said Jesus to his friends, as they were walking along the road. 'Who do they say I am?'

'Some say John,' they told him. 'Others say Elijah, and others say one of the great men of God.'

'But you,' said Jesus, 'who do you say I am?'

'You're God's chosen Leader!' said Peter.

Jesus warned them not to say this to anybody.

He went on to tell them that he himself – and his friends as well – would have to go through hard times. He would be treated as an enemy of the Jewish Leaders and would have to face death; but his death would not be the end. He was quite open about it.

Peter took Jesus on one side and talked seriously to him. Jesus turned round and saw his other friends. He spoke seriously to Peter.

'Out of my sight, Tempter!' he said. 'You're not thinking of what God wants. You're talking like everybody else.'

A Mountain Walk   *Mark 9:2-10*

A week later Jesus took his three friends, Peter, James, and John, and led them up into a high mountain. They were all alone together.

High up the mountain, Jesus was changed. His friends were still with him. His clothes were gleaming white; no bleach on earth could make them whiter. His friends saw two other men talking with Jesus: Moses, who had led the people out of slavery in Egypt, and Elijah, who had stood up to a king in God's name.

Peter didn't know what to say, so he started talking like this.

'Sir,' he said. 'It's great for us to be up here. Do you want us to make three shelters, one for you, one for Moses and one for Elijah?'

Peter and James and John were terrified. A cloud rolled round them. God's words came into their minds.

'This is my only son. You must do what he says.'

The three men looked round. There was nobody there but Jesus. As they went down the mountainside, Jesus told them not to talk about what they had seen to anybody, 'until I have risen from the dead'.

It was this saying they could not forget. They talked again and again among themselves about what 'rising from the dead' could mean.

At the Foot of the Mountain

Jesus, Peter, James, and John had left their friends behind at the foot of the mountain. When they got back, they saw a great crowd round them and the Jewish Leaders arguing with them.

'What's the argument about?' asked Jesus.

'Sir,' said one of the crowd, 'I brought my boy here. It's you I wanted to see. He has a bad spirit in him. He has fits and loses his speech. Every time he has a fit, it throws him on the ground. He foams at the mouth and grinds his teeth and becomes stiff. I asked your friends here to make him better, but they couldn't do anything.'

'What little trust you've got!' said Jesus. 'How long have I got to be with you? How long have I got to put up with you? Bring him to me.'

They brought him to Jesus, and the lad fell on the ground in a fit and rolled about foaming at the mouth.

'How long has he been like this?' Jesus asked his father.

'Ever since he was a child,' he said. 'It's thrown him many times into the fire and into water. He might have lost his life. If you can do anything, have pity on us and help us!'

'"If you can"!' said Jesus. 'Everything is possible to a man who trusts.'

'I trust!' cried the boy's father. 'Help me if I don't trust enough.'

Jesus noticed that the crowd was running towards him. He spoke severely.

'You deaf and dumb spirit! Come out of him, I tell you, and never go into him again.'

With a scream, the lad had a terrible fit and the spirit left him. He lay as if dead.

'He's dead!' everybody was saying.

Jesus took hold of his hand and lifted him up; and the lad stood on his feet.

The Journey South

Jesus now left the north country and went south. But he did not want people to recognise him and come crowding round him to listen to him or be healed by him. His work in the north was finished. So he passed quickly through Galilee and Samaria. He had to tell the people in the south the Good News about God, as he had told it to the people in the north.

What God wanted him to do was clear. But he knew it would be dangerous. Jerusalem, the capital city, was in the south. Here was the headquarters of the Jewish government; and here, during the Great Feast, Pilate, the Roman Governor, and his soldiers came to keep order.

Setting Off   *Mark 9:30-32*

Jesus left the northern highlands and crossed Galilee. He did not want either the Jewish Leaders or the people in the villages to know about it. He was still trying to get his friends to see the danger he was in.

Three things were clear to him. First, he would be caught by the Jewish Leaders; secondly, if he was caught, they would kill him; thirdly, if they killed him his death would not be the end – he would soon 'rise'.

His friends did not know what he was talking about and they were afraid to ask him any questions.

A Quarrel   *Mark 9:33-37*

Jesus and his friends had been out on the road.

'What were you arguing about as you came along the road?' he asked them when they were back in the house.

They said nothing; they had been arguing with one another about which one of them was the most important.

Jesus sat down, and called the 'Twelve'.

'Whoever wants to be "Number One" among my friends,' he said, 'mustn't mind being of no importance at all and spending his time looking after other people's needs.'

He took a boy and stood him among the grown men and then picked him up.

'Whoever welcomes one of these young ones, because that's the sort of thing I would do,' he said, 'welcomes me; and whoever welcomes me, welcomes not me – but God who sent me.'

Outsiders
Mark 9:38-41

'We saw a man making sick people better and using your name,' said John to Jesus one day. 'He doesn't belong to us, so we stopped him.'

'Don't stop him,' said Jesus. 'Nobody will do a good deed, as one of my friends, and then quickly insult me. If a man is not our enemy, he is our friend. If anybody gives you a cup of water as a friend of mine, because you are doing God's work, I am very sure he won't miss his place in God's Kingdom.'

On the Road
Mark 10:32-34

Jesus and the 'Twelve' were on the road going up to Jerusalem. Jesus was striding on ahead; his friends were following behind him, alarmed and frightened. Jesus took them on one side again, and told them what was going to happen to him.

'Look,' he said, 'we're going up to Jerusalem, the capital city. I shall be handed over to the Jewish Leaders, and they will want to put me to death. That means handing me over to the Romans, who won't be very gentle in the way they treat me; they will kill me. But, as I have told you, my death will not be the end. I shall soon "rise".'

True Greatness
Mark 10:35-45

James and John came up to Jesus one day.

'Sir,' they said, 'we're going to ask you for something and we want you to do it for us.'

'What do you want me to do for you?' asked Jesus.

'When you are a real King,' they said, 'make us the chief members of your Government.'

'You don't know what you are talking about,' said Jesus. 'Can you go through what I must go through?'

'Of course we can!' they said.

'You'll go through what I must go through all right,' said Jesus. 'But I can't make anybody "a chief member of my Government". God has marked out my leaders.'

The other ten friends of Jesus were angry with James and John. So Jesus called them all together.

'You know what it is like in the world outside,' he said. 'Those who think of themselves as bosses order their people about, and their great leaders are bullies. That isn't what you must do. You must turn it all the other way round. Whoever wants to be "Great" among you must be – your servant! Whoever wants to be "Number One" must be – everybody's slave! I didn't come to have servants looking after me. I came to be a servant myself and to give myself to make everybody else free.'

A Jericho Beggar   *Mark 10:46-52*

Jesus and his friends were leaving Jericho by the Jerusalem Road, and there was a large crowd with them. A blind beggar, Bartimaeus, was sitting at the roadside; he heard people saying, 'It's Jesus from Nazareth'.

'Son of David! Jesus!' he shouted. 'Have pity on me!'

The crowd told him to be quiet, but he went on shouting 'Son of David! Have pity on me!'

Jesus stood still.

'Call him over here,' he said.

Everybody then started calling the blind man: 'Cheer up!' 'Get up!' 'He's calling you!'

The beggar threw his cloak off, jumped up and came to Jesus.

'What do you want me to do for you?' asked Jesus.

'Sir,' he said, 'give me my sight back again.'

'Go home,' said Jesus. 'It's your trust in me that has made you better.'

His sight came back, and he followed Jesus along the road.

In Jerusalem

Jesus now told the Good News about God in the villages of Judea in the south and in the villages on the eastern side of Jordan River. In October, he went up to Jerusalem City for the 'Feast of Tents', when pilgrims walked up the Jericho Road and entered Jerusalem City, carrying branches, and remembered the day, 170 years before, when the Jews had recaptured Jerusalem from a foreign king.

Jesus not only told stories to help people to understand God's Way; he acted stories sometimes, as great men of God, like Isaiah and Jeremiah, had done before him. If people forgot the stories he told them, they might remember the stories he acted; for this was a strange thing to do, and people remember strange things. When he rode into the City on a donkey (not a horse, which would look like a war horse) and when he upset the market stalls in the Foreigners' Court and told them God's Temple was for everybody to worship in, he was *acting* God's Way, not just talking about it.

Reaching the City   *Mark 11:1-11*

Jerusalem was at last in sight. Near the Olive Hill, Jesus sent his friends to a village.

'Go into the village facing you,' Jesus said, 'and just as you go in you'll find a donkey. It'll be tied up, and it hasn't been broken in yet. Untie it and bring it; and if anyone asks you why you are doing this, tell them: "The Master needs it, and he'll send it straight back."'

They went off, and found the donkey tied at a door outside in the street. They untied it.

'What are you untying the donkey for?' asked some of the bystanders.

They said what Jesus had told them to say, and the men let them take it away.

They brought the donkey to Jesus and threw their clothes on its back. Jesus sat on it. People spread their clothes on the road, and others cut leafy branches from the fields and spread them out. All the crowd, those in front and those behind, shouted the words from the old Bible hymn:

Hurrah!
Happy is he who comes in God's name! -
Happy is the Kingdom of King David, our father!
A thousand times – Hurrah!

Jesus went into the city and into the Temple. He looked all round. Then, since it was getting dark, he went off with his friends out to the village of Bethany.

In the Foreigners' Court

Mark 11:15-19

Next day, Jesus walked into the city again and went into the Temple. In the great Foreigners' Court he drove out the shopkeepers who had their stalls there and the people who were buying. He upset the tables of the moneylenders and the chairs of the pigeon-sellers. He wouldn't let anybody take a short cut and carry goods through the Temple.

'Doesn't the Bible say,' he said, '"My House shall be called the House of Worship for all foreign people"? You have made it a bandits' den.'

The Jewish Leaders heard about all this and tried to find ways of getting rid of Jesus. They were frightened of him, for ordinary people listened to him with amazement.

At the end of the day Jesus and his friends went out of the city.

The Jewish Leaders Ask Questions

Mark 11:27-12:12

Jesus was in Jerusalem again. As he was walking about the Temple, Jewish Leaders came up to him.

'Who told you to do this sort of thing?' they asked. 'Who gave you the right to act like this?'

'I'll ask you a question first,' said Jesus. 'You answer my question and I'll answer yours. You remember John the Hermit; was he God's messenger, or just another of those mob-leaders? You tell me.'

They didn't know what to say.

'If we say, "He was God's messenger",' they said to one another, 'he'll say, "Why didn't you join him, then?". If we say, "Oh, just one of these mob-leaders . . .".'

They hardly dared finish the sentence. They were frightened of the crowd, for everybody thought that John was one of God's messengers.

'We don't know,' they said at last.

'Well, I'm not telling you, then, who gave me power to do what I'm doing,' said Jesus. 'But I'll tell you a story.

'Once upon a time a man cleared the ground and made a farm. He let it out to farmers and went off abroad. At harvest-time he sent a slave for his share of the harvest, but the farmers beat the slave and sent him off with empty hands. He sent another slave, but the farmers hit him on the head and insulted him.

'The landowner had an only son; he sent him to the farm.

'"They will respect my son," he said.

'When the farmers saw him, they said to one another: "This is the son himself. Come on, let's kill him and the farm will be ours!"

'They got hold of him, killed him, and threw his body outside the farm.

'What will the landowner do? He will come himself, of course, and destroy those farmers and give the farm to others.'

The Jewish Leaders now made up their minds to get hold of Jesus, for they knew that the story was aimed at them. But they were frightened of the crowd; so they left Jesus and went away.

A Trap   *Mark 12:13-17*

The Jewish Leaders sent men to catch Jesus off his guard.

'Sir,' they said, 'we know you're a man who speaks the truth. You treat everybody alike, you have no favourites and you teach God's Way as it really is. Tell us the answer to this question: Is it right to pay taxes to the Roman Emperor, or not? Should we pay or shouldn't we?'

Jesus knew that they weren't asking a straightforward question.

'What are you trying me out for?' he said. 'Get me a coin to look at.'

They got one for him.

'Whose face is this?' he asked. 'Whose name is this?'

'The Emperor's,' they said.

'Well, then, give what belongs to the Emperor back to the Emperor,' said Jesus, 'and give what belongs to God back to God.'

That made them speechless.

A Good Question   *Mark 12:28-34a*

A teacher heard Jesus talking and knew that he had given some fine answers; so he asked a question himself.

'Which of God's commands,' he asked, 'is more important than all the others?'

'The most important command,' said Jesus, 'is this:

> Listen, O people!
> There is one God only;
> And you must love God with everything you are –
> your heart, your soul, your mind, your body.

'There is another command almost as important:

> You must love the person next to you as much as
> you love yourself.

'No other command is more important than these two.'

'Splendid, Sir,' said the teacher. 'You're right when you say that there is one God, and one God only; and that to love God with everything we are, and to love the person next to us as we love ourselves, is far more important than all the Temple services.'

Jesus noted his good answer.

'You are not far from being the kind of man God wants you to be,' he said.

A Woman's Example   *Mark 12:41-44*

Jesus was one day sitting in the Temple and watching the crowd throwing their money into the great Collection Bowl. Many rich people put in great gifts. A poor widow came along, and threw in two small coins.

Jesus called his friends.

'You see that poor woman,' he said. 'I tell you that she has thrown more than anybody else into the bowl. All the others had plenty to give. She had very little money, but she gave everything she had; she really needed that money to keep alive.'

East of Jordan River

The Jewish Leaders now knew what Jesus stood for. He had come to the capital city. He had even spoken in the Temple. He had done more: he had upset the market stalls in the Foreigners' Court and said that they, the Leaders, were not using the Temple in God's Way. He was a dangerous man. The Jewish Leaders made up their minds to arrest him and put him to death.

But Jesus had made up *his* mind to speak once again to the Jewish people in the capital city and call them to change their minds. This he decided to do at the Great Feast in the spring next year, the feast the Jewish people called 'The Passover'. At this feast they remembered the day, long ago, when Moses led them out of Egypt.

Jesus knew it would be dangerous to stay in Jerusalem. So he spent the winter in the villages east of Jordan River, where the Jewish Leaders could not get hold of him.

Mark does not tell us anything about what happened during the winter; this is all he tells us:

Mark 10:1

Jesus went across Jordan River to the villages beyond. Once more the crowds came to hear him, and, as he had done in Galilee, he spent his time telling them the Good News.

The Great Feast

In the spring, a few days before the Great Feast, Jesus came back to Jerusalem City. On the Wednesday he was in Bethany, a little village not far from the City, where he had friends. On the Thursday evening, Jesus and his friends had supper together in the City itself. Armed men caught Jesus in an orchard as he was on his way back to Bethany. His friends got away. On the Friday, Jesus was brought by the Jewish Leaders before the Roman Governor, Pilate, and Pilate put him to death.

Judas   *Mark 14:1-2, 10-11*

This happened two days before the Great Feast.

The Jewish Leaders were trying to find some way of getting hold of Jesus and killing him. They did not dare to do this openly, or when the Great Feast was on, for they were afraid of a riot.

They were delighted when they heard that one of the 'Twelve', Judas Iscariot, had come and offered to put Jesus into their hands. They promised to pay him, and Judas began to look out for the chance of doing it.

In Bethany   *Mark 14:3-9*

Jesus was in Bethany having dinner with a man known as Simon the Leper, when a woman came in with a bottle of real Indian ointment that must have cost a lot of money to buy. She broke the bottle and poured the ointment over the head of Jesus. Some of the visitors spoke angrily about it to one another.

'Why should such ointment be thrown away like this!' they muttered. 'It would have made a lot of money, and the money could have been given to the poor.'

'Leave her alone,' said Jesus. 'What do you want to upset her for? It's a fine thing she has done for me. There are always poor people among you, and you can help them whenever you want to. But I'm not here for ever. What she could do, she did. She was getting my body ready for burial – before I'm dead! But you may be sure of this: the Good News will be told all over the world, and the story of what this woman has done today will be told with it. Her memory won't die.'

Finding the House

Mark 14:12-16

'Where do you want us to get the Feast ready?' the friends of Jesus asked him.

'Go into the city,' said Jesus to the two friends he was sending. 'A man carrying a water pot will meet you. Follow him and speak to the owner of the house he goes into. Tell him: "The Teacher says, 'Where is the room where I may eat the Feast with my friends?'" The owner himself will show you a large paved room upstairs. Get ready for us there.'

The men went away into the city and everything went as Jesus said. They got the Feast ready.

Supper

Mark 14:17-26

It was dark when Jesus and his friends came into the city.

'I tell you,' said Jesus, when they were having supper together, 'that one of you will hand me over to the Jewish Leaders – one who is having supper with me now.'

His friends were hurt at this.

'It can't be me?' they each said to him.

'It's one of the "Twelve",' said Jesus. 'He is sharing this very meal with me . . . What is going to happen is just what the Bible said would happen. But it will be a terrible thing for the man who hands me over to the Jewish Leaders; it would have been better for him if he had never lived.'

During the supper, Jesus took the loaf, blessed it, broke it, and gave it to his friends.

'Take it,' he said. 'This is my very self.'

He took the cup, said Grace, and gave it to them; they all drank from it.

'This means my death,' he said. 'I am dying to bring everyone to God, as the Bible says, "from the least of them to the greatest". I am sure of this: I shall drink no more wine until that day when I drink it fresh in God's Kingdom.'

When supper was over, they sang a hymn; then they walked out to the Olive Hill outside the City, on the road to the village where he was staying.

In the Street
Mark 14:27-31

'You will all let me down,' said Jesus, as they walked along. 'The Bible says:

> I will strike the shepherd
> and the sheep will run away.

But after I am "raised", I will go to Galilee before you.'

'Everybody else may let you down,' said Peter, 'but I won't.'

'I tell you, Peter,' said Jesus, 'that this very night, before dawn, you will say more than once that you're no friend of mine.'

'Say I'm no friend of yours?' said Peter hotly. 'I'd die with you first!'

Everybody else said the same.

In the Orchard
Mark 14:32-52

Jesus and his friends came to the Olive Orchard.

'Sit here,' he said to them. 'I am going to pray.'

He took his three friends, Peter, James, and John, with him. He was in very great distress.

'I am brokenhearted,' he said. 'This has nearly finished me. Stay here and keep on the alert.'

He went on a little way, fell on the ground and prayed that, if it could be, the terrible moment that lay ahead of him might pass him by.

'Father,' he prayed. 'You can do anything. Take this suffering away from me. Yet I'll do what you want, not what I want.'

He came back and found them asleep.

'Simon,' he said. 'Are you sleeping? Couldn't you keep awake for an hour? You must keep awake, and keep praying that you may not be put to the test. You are keen enough, but you aren't strong enough.'

He went away again, and prayed as he had done before.

He came back and found them asleep again. They could not keep their eyes open, and they did not know what to say to him.

He came back a third time.

'Are you still sleeping and resting?' he asked. 'The time's come! I am being handed over to the Romans! Get up! Let us go! Look – my betrayer's here!'

Suddenly, Judas came with a gang armed with swords and clubs. They had been sent by the Jewish Leaders. Judas had arranged a secret signal so that there should be no mistake.

'The man I kiss, that's Jesus,' he told them. 'Get hold of him, and take him away under guard.'

He went straight up to Jesus.

'Sir!' he said, and kissed him – as if he was just meeting him.

The men grabbed Jesus, and put him under guard. A man standing near drew his sword and struck a Jewish officer and cut off his ear.

'Do you come out armed,' said Jesus to the soldiers, 'to take me like a bandit? I was talking day by day to the people in the Temple; you were there, but you didn't take me then! This, of course, is only what the Bible said would happen!'

Everybody left him and ran away. There was a young man there with Jesus. He wasn't properly dressed; he had only a linen sheet wrapped round him. The soldiers grabbed him, but he let the sheet go and ran away naked.

Before the Jewish Leaders   Mark 14:53-64

The soldiers took Jesus to the High Court. The Jewish Leaders wanted proof against him so that they could have him put to death. They could find none. Many false reports were given against him, but they were all mixed up. People got up and told lies about him like this:

'We ourselves heard him say that he would pull down this Temple built here in Jerusalem, and without any builders build a new one in no time!'

But they could not make their stories fit together.

At last the Judge stood up and questioned Jesus.

'Have you nothing to say?' he asked. 'Why are these men saying all this against you?'

Jesus gave no answer.

'Are you God's Great Deliverer?' the Judge asked him. 'Are you God's Son?'

'I am,' said Jesus.

The Judge tore his clothes.

'We don't want witnesses any more!' he said. 'You have heard the terrible words. What do you say?'

They all voted for the death of Jesus.

Peter's Denial   *Mark 14:66-72*

Peter had followed Jesus, a long way behind, right into the courtyard. He sat down there with the servants and was warming himself at a fire.

One of the maids came along. When she saw Peter warming himself she stared at him.

'You, too, were with Jesus, the man from Nazareth,' she said.

'I don't understand you,' said Peter, 'and I don't know what you're talking about!'

He went outside into the yard and the maid saw him.

'This fellow's one of them,' she said again to the people near.

Peter denied it again, but the bystanders soon took him up.

'Of course you're one of them,' they said. 'You come from the north too!'

Peter cursed and swore.

'I don't know the man you're talking about,' he said. A cock crowed a second time, and Peter remembered what Jesus had said to him: 'Before dawn, you will say more than once that you're no friend of mine.'

Peter broke down and cried.

Before the Roman Governor   *Mark 15:1-15*

Early in the morning, the Council of the Jewish Leaders talked over what they should do with Jesus. They handcuffed him and took him off and handed him over to Pilate, the Roman Governor.

'Are you the Jewish King?' asked Pilate.

'You use the word,' said Jesus.

The Jewish Leaders brought charge after charge against him.

'Haven't you got anything to say?' asked Pilate. 'See the charges they are making against you.'

But Jesus had nothing more to say, and Pilate was very surprised.

At the Feast, Pilate used to set free any prisoner the crowd asked for.

There were some rebels in prison, who had murdered people in the Rebellion, and one of them was Barabbas.

The crowd went up and asked Pilate to do as he had done before.

'Do you want me to set "The King" free for you?' asked Pilate.

He knew that it was for their own ends that the Jewish Leaders had handed Jesus over to him. The Jewish Leaders now stirred up the crowd to get him to set Barabbas free instead.

'What, then, do you want me to do to the man you call "The King"?'

'Hang him on a cross,' they shouted.

'But what's his crime?' asked Pilate.

'Hang him on a cross!' they went on shouting.

Pilate wanted to put the mob in a good mood, so he set Barabbas free and had Jesus flogged. Then he handed him over to the soldiers to be put to death on a cross.

The Soldiers   *Mark 15:16-20*

The guard took Jesus away into the palace and called all the soldiers together. They got hold of a soldier's red cloak and threw it round Jesus and made a crown out of twigs from a thornbush and put it on his head. They saluted him.

'Hail, your Majesty!' they shouted.

They hit him on the head with a cane and spat on him and went down on their knees and bowed to him. When they'd finished making fun of him, they took the red cloak off him and dressed him in his own clothes, and led him out to die.

At Skull Hill   *Mark 15:21-41*

Simon, whose home was in North Africa, was coming into the city from the country at the time. The soldiers made him carry the wooden cross and marched Jesus to Skull Hill. They gave him drugs to deaden the pain, but he didn't take them.

It was nine o'clock in the morning. They nailed him to the cross and tossed up for his clothes and shared them out among themselves.

The charge against Jesus was fastened on the cross, THE JEWISH KING.

The soldiers put two bandits to death at the same time, one on each side of Jesus.

Passers-by shook their heads and swore at Jesus.

'Aha! You'd pull the Temple down and build it up again in no time! You'd better look after yourself and get down from the cross!'

Some of the Jewish Leaders made fun of him among themselves.

'He looked after other people,' they laughed, 'he can't look after himself! Let the Great Deliverer, the King, get down from the cross now! We'd like to see him do it – we'd believe him then all right!'

The bandits on their crosses insulted him too.

At noon, the sky went dark and the darkness lasted for three hours.

It was now three o'clock in the afternoon.

'My God, my God, why have you left me alone?' Jesus called out loudly. The words are the words of an old Bible hymn.

Some of those standing near heard him call out, but they did not catch the words.

'See,' they said, 'he's calling for Elijah!'

One of them ran and filled a sponge with sour wine and put it on the end of a cane and tried to make Jesus drink it.

'Let's see if Elijah comes to help him down!' they shouted to one another.

Jesus gave a loud cry and died.

The Roman officer in charge of the guard was standing facing Jesus and saw how he died.

'This man was a real king!' he said.

Some of the women were watching him from a distance. They had been with Jesus in Galilee and looked after him there. Among them were Mary from Magdala, Mary the mother of the younger James and of Joses, and Salome, and many other women who had come up to Jerusalem with him.

The Burial   *Mark 15:42-47*

It was now near sunset when the Holy Day of the Jews began, and all preparation for any kind of work had to be finished.

There was a good man called Joseph, a well-known member of the Jewish Council, from the village of Arimathea. He was brave enough to go to Pilate and ask for the body of Jesus.

Pilate was very surprised to hear that Jesus was already dead. He ordered the Commanding Officer to bring his report; when he heard the report from the officer, he gave the body to Joseph.

Joseph took the body of Jesus down from the cross and wrapped it in a linen sheet which he had brought. He put the body in a cave which had already been cut out of the rock and rolled a stone against the mouth.

Mary from Magdala, and the other Mary, saw where the body of Jesus was buried.

The Story Has Only Begun

You will find the earliest account of what happened after the death of Jesus in one of Paul's letters – the first letter he wrote to his friends in the city of Corinth. You can look it up in your Bibles (1 Corinthians, 15:3-8).

Here is Mark's story.

The last pages of Mark's book have been torn away and lost. The dots show you where it ends. The words in your Bible which follow this sentence were written down much later. We have used some words from Matthew's book so that the story has its proper ending.

Jesus Is Risen! *Mark 16:1-8; Matthew 28:16-20*

When the Holy Day of the Jews was over, three women friends of Jesus – Mary of Magdala, Mary who was James's mother, and Salome – brought sweet-smelling oils to anoint his body.

They got to his grave very early on Sunday, just as the sun was rising.

'Who will roll the stone away from the cave's mouth for us?' they said to one another.

It was a very big stone. They looked up and saw that it had already been rolled away.

They went into the cave and they were amazed to see a young man in white clothes sitting on the right-hand side.

'Don't be frightened,' he said. 'You are looking for Jesus of Nazareth who was put to death. He has risen. You won't find him here; you can see where they put his body. Go and tell his friends that he will be in Galilee before you and you will see him there, as he told you you would. And don't forget Peter.'

They ran out of the cave trembling with terror. They were so frightened that they didn't say a word to anyone . . .

The eleven friends of Jesus went off to the hill in Galilee which Jesus had told them about. They saw him, and worshipped him; but some had their doubts.

'I have been given world-wide power,' said Jesus. 'Go. Help everybody everywhere to follow me. Get them to join my company of friends, and show them how to live as I showed you. Remember, I shall be with you – to the very end.'

The Message

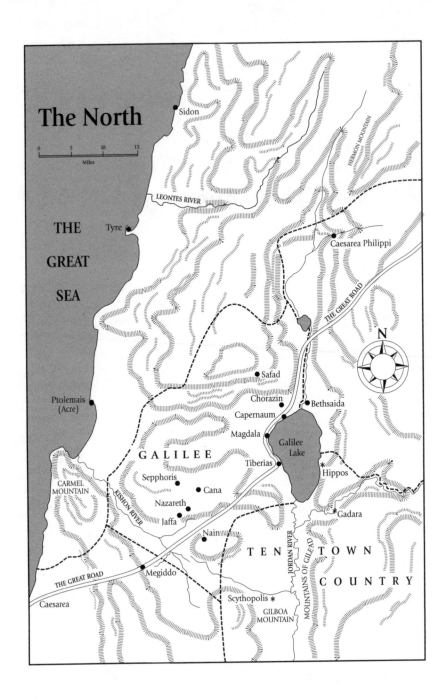

The North

THE
GREAT
SEA

0   5   10   15
Miles

Sidon

Tyre

Caesarea Philippi

HERMON MOUNTAIN

LEONTES RIVER

THE GREAT ROAD

N

Ptolemais
(Acre)

Safad

Chorazin

Bethsaida

Capernaum

Magdala

Galilee
Lake

GALILEE

Tiberias

Hippos

CARMEL
MOUNTAIN

Sepphoris

Cana

KISHON RIVER

Nazareth

Gadara

Jaffa

Nain

TEN   TOWN

JORDAN RIVER

MOUNTAINS OF GILEAD

Megiddo

THE GREAT ROAD

COUNTRY

Caesarea

Scythopolis

GILBOA
MOUNTAIN

The Conversations of Jesus

The friends of Jesus remembered some of his sayings and just what happened when he said them – where he was, the people he was talking to, and the way the conversation went. These sayings seemed to them very important sayings.

You will find many stories of the conversations of Jesus in *The Beginning*. We have not printed them again here; you can look them up for yourself. Here are other stories of the conversations of Jesus. Notice how each story ends with a saying.

1. In a Meeting House   *Luke 13:10-16*

One Saturday, the Holy Day of the Jews, Jesus was speaking to the people in one of the village Meeting Houses. There was a woman there who had been ill for eighteen years; she was bent double and couldn't stand upright at all. Jesus noticed her and called her over to him.

'My dear,' he said, 'be strong again.'

He touched her with his hands, and there and then she stood straight upright. She was so happy she started to tell everybody how good God was.

The officer in charge of the Meeting House was very angry that Jesus had done this on the Holy Day.

'You've got six weekdays for working in,' he kept saying to the crowd in the Meeting House. 'Come along with your troubles then, if you want to be made better. Don't come here with them on the Holy Day.'

'You're only playing at being good,' said Jesus to him. 'Doesn't every one of you untie his ox or his donkey from its stall and take it out to water it on the Holy Day? This woman is as good a Jew as you are. She's been kept bent double, remember, for eighteen years. It's like being chained up day after day. Wasn't it right that she should be set free on God's Holy Day?'

2. A Voice from the Crowd   *Luke 12:13-15*

One day a crowd of people were listening to Jesus.

'Sir,' said a man in the crowd, 'when my father died my brother took all he left and kept it. Tell him to share it with me.'

445

'My good man,' said Jesus, 'this is not a law-court and I'm not a judge. It's not my work to settle questions like this.'

He turned to the crowd.

'Don't get greedy,' he said. 'Being a millionaire isn't the sort of thing that makes life worth living.'

3. Another Voice   *Luke 11:27-28*

Jesus was speaking to a crowd of people.

'Your mother must have been a very happy woman!' a woman called out from the crowd.

'No,' said Jesus. 'The really happy people are those who listen to what God says – and then do it.'

4. Dreadful News   *Luke 13:1-5*

Pilate, the Roman Governor, had done a dreadful thing. His soldiers had murdered some men from Galilee while they were worshipping God in the Temple in Jerusalem.

Some people came and told Jesus about it.

'Do you think,' said Jesus, 'that their death proves that these men were more wicked than the other people who live in Galilee? I tell you, if you go on doing wicked things, when you know they are wicked, and do not change your ways, you will face something just as terrible.

'Do you remember when the tower near Siloam Pool fell down, and killed eighteen men who were standing there? I tell you, if you go on doing wicked things, when you know they are wicked, and do not change your ways, you will face something just as terrible.'

5. Meeting a Jewish Leader   *Luke 17:20-21*

'When shall we really see people living in God's Way?' a Jewish Leader once asked Jesus.

'This isn't the sort of thing that happens all of a sudden,' said Jesus. 'You can't *see* it. Nobody will say, "Ah! Here it is!" or "There it is!" It's here now.'

6. Going to Dinner   *Luke 14:1-6*

One Saturday, the Holy Day of the Jews, Jesus went to the home of a Jewish Leader to have dinner with him. The Jewish Leaders themselves were only pretending to be friendly; they were really 'shadowing' him.

There was a very sick man in front of Jesus. Somebody asked a question about him.

'Tell me,' said Jesus to the Leaders there. 'Today is the Holy Day; is making a sick man better *today* right or wrong?'

The Jewish Leaders said nothing.

Jesus took hold of the man, made him better and sent him home.

'Is there any one of you,' asked Jesus, 'who wouldn't pull his son out of the well he'd fallen into, even if it was the Holy Day? Why, he would do that even for his ox!'

That finished the conversation.

7. Out in the Fields   *After Luke 6:4 in some old copies*

One day Jesus saw a man out at work. It was Saturday, the Holy Day of the Jews. Nobody was supposed to do any work on the Holy Day; it was forbidden by Jewish Law.

'Sir,' said Jesus, 'if you know what you are doing, you are a very happy man. If you don't – if you just don't care what you do and when you do it – you are doing a very wrong thing, and you really are breaking the law about the Holy Day.'

8. Two Messengers   *Luke 7:18-23*

One day the hermit John, who was in prison, called two of his friends and sent them to Jesus to ask him a question.

'John has sent us to you,' they told Jesus when they met him.

'He wants to know if you are the Great Deliverer God promised to send us, or must we go on waiting for somebody else?'

There was a crowd of people with Jesus that day; he was making many sick people better and giving many blind people the power to see.

'Go back to John,' he said to the two men, 'and tell him what you have seen and heard. You remember what the Bible says? –

> Blind people see again;
>> lame people walk about;
>> lepers are made better;
>> deaf people are hearing;
>> dead people are alive again;
>> hopeless people are told the Good News.

'The really happy man is the man who isn't shocked at what I am doing.'

9. On a Country Road *Luke 9:57-62*

Jesus and his friends were walking along a country road. A man joined them.

'I'll go anywhere with you,' he said to Jesus.

'Foxes have dens and wild birds can roost,' said Jesus. 'I and my friends have no home.'

'Come and join my company of friends,' said Jesus to another man.

'I have to go back to my father's funeral,' said the man. 'Let me do that first.'

'There's something more important than a funeral – even your father's funeral,' said Jesus. 'You must come and tell the Good News of God's Way far and wide.'

'I'll come and join your company of friends, Sir,' said a third man. 'But let me first of all say goodbye to my family.'

'Nobody who starts ploughing and then keeps looking back at the field behind him,' said Jesus, 'is living in God's Way.'

10. Peter's Question *Matthew 18:21-22*

Peter came to Jesus one day.

'Sir,' he said, 'how often can somebody treat me badly, and I forgive them and be friends with them again? Will seven times be enough?'

'This isn't something you can add up like sums,' said Jesus. 'The answer is – every time.'

11. In the House
Matthew 17:24-26

Jesus and his friends one day came back to Capernaum. The collectors of the Temple tax stopped Peter.

'Doesn't your master pay Temple taxes?' they asked him.

'Of course,' said Peter.

When Jesus went into the house he was the first to speak.

'What do you think, Peter?' he asked. 'Do the Romans force their own citizens or foreigners to pay taxes?'

'Why, foreigners, of course,' said Peter.

'You see,' said Jesus, 'citizens are free.'

12. In the Temple
Mark 13:1-2

One day Jesus and his friends were coming out of the Temple in Jerusalem.

'Look, Sir,' said one of his friends to Jesus. 'What huge stones! What grand buildings!'

'You see these great buildings?' said Jesus. 'None of the walls will be left standing; every stone will be pulled down.'

13. On the Road to Skull Hill
Luke 23:27-31

Soldiers were marching Jesus to Skull Hill. There was a great crowd of people following him, and among them were women, very sad indeed and crying.

Jesus turned to them.

'You women of Jerusalem,' he said, 'don't cry for me. You should be crying for yourselves and your children. The time is coming when war will have broken out, and the streets will be full of fighting. People will say, "She's a very happy woman – she's got no children to worry about." Do you remember what the Bible says? – In those days

> They shall say to the mountains,
>   "Fall on us!"
> And to the hills,
>   "Hide us!"

'If this is how they behave in the springtime, what will they do when autumn comes?'

The Stories of Jesus

The Village and Its People

1. Boys on a Farm

A farmer lived on a farm with his two boys.

'Tom,' he said to the first boy, 'give me a hand on the farm today.'

'All right, Dad,' he said.

But he didn't go.

The farmer said exactly the same to his second boy, Bill.

'Not I!' said Bill.

But later on he changed his mind, and went to give his father a hand on the farm.

Did Tom, or Bill, do what his father wanted?

2. Girls at a Wedding
Matthew 25:1-11

God's Way is like this.

There was a wedding in a village. Ten village girls picked up their torches, and went out to meet the bridegroom.

Five of the girls took no spare oil; the others carried flasks of oil.

The bridegroom was a very long time coming; so long that the girls got drowsy and went to sleep. Suddenly, in the middle of the night, there was a great shouting.

'Look, the bridegroom's coming,' the watchman called out. 'Off you go to meet him.'

All the girls jumped up and trimmed their torches.

'Lend us some oil,' said the girls who had no oil, to the others. 'Our torches are going out.'

'Not likely,' said they. 'There won't be enough for us all. Go to the shops and buy your own.'

Off they went to buy oil; and, while they were away the bridegroom came.

Everybody who was ready went in with him to the feast; and the door was shut.

It was some time before the girls got back.

'Sir! Sir!' they shouted. 'Open the door for us!'

3. Playing in the Street

Luke 7:31-35

What are people today like?

They are like children playing games in the street. There they are – sitting on the ground.

'We wanted to play at weddings,' the boys call out to their playmates, 'but you didn't dance.'

'We wanted to play funerals,' the girls call out, 'but you didn't play the part of the mourners.'

John the Hermit starved himself:

'He's mad,' people say.

I go out to dinner with all sorts of people:

'Glutton and drunk,' they say, 'friend of traitors and scoundrels.'

God will be proved right; you'll see.

4. The House Door

Luke 13:24

Try as hard as you can to go in through the narrow door. Lots of people, I am sure, are trying to get in; but they can't.

5. The Lamp

Mark 4:21; Matthew 5:15

What do you light a lamp for?

To put it out?
To put it under the bed?

Or to put it on the stand
to light the whole house
and all who live in it?

6. Yeast

Luke 13:20-21

God's Way is like this.

A woman took some yeast and mixed it into a lot of flour; and *all* the flour rose.

7. Salt

Luke 14:34-35

Salt is good.
But what can you do with salt that is no longer salty?
It's fit neither for food nor for manure.
You can only throw it into the street.

8. Cloth and Wineskins   *Mark 2:21-22*

> You don't sew a patch of new cloth
> > on an old dress.
> If you do, the new patch
> > pulls at the old dress.
> Then you've got a worse tear.
> You don't put new wine
> > into old wineskins.
> If you do, the wine bursts the skins
> > and wine and skins are lost.
> New wine-skins for new wine!

9. Sawdust and Log   *Luke 6:41-42*

Why do you see a little speck of sawdust in your friend's eye but don't notice the great log of wood in your own eye?

'Tom!' you say to your friend, 'let me take that little speck of sawdust out of your eye.'

But you yourself don't see the great log of wood in your own eye.

When you act like this, you are only pretending to be good. Take the great log of wood out of your own eye first. Then you will be able to see clearly enough to take the little speck of sawdust out of your friend's eye.

10. Where the Wild Birds Roost   *Mark 4:30-32*

How shall I picture God's way of doing things? What story shall I use? It's like this.

When a mustard seed is sown in the soil, it's the smallest seed in the world. But it grows up and becomes the largest plant in the world. Its branches are so big that (you remember what the Bible says?) –

> In the shelter of its branches
> the wild birds roost.

11. The Fig Tree   *Mark 13:28*

The fig tree can teach us something.

Its branch is leafless in the winter. When it begins to bud and the leaves come out, summer is here.

12. On the Farm and in the Home *Luke 15:4-10*

Is there a farmer with a hundred sheep who wouldn't leave them on the moors – if he had lost just one of them? Wouldn't he go after that lost sheep until he found it?

When he finds it, how happy he is! He puts it on his shoulders and brings it home. He calls his friends and neighbours together.

'I've found the lost sheep,' says he. 'Let's celebrate!'

God is as happy as that, I am sure, if one bad person makes up their mind to be good; happier than he is with ninety-nine 'good' people who (so they say) 'don't need to change their minds'.

Is there a woman with ten silver coins who wouldn't light the lamp and sweep the room very, very carefully, and look everywhere – if she had lost just one of them? Wouldn't she go on looking until she found it?

When she finds it, how happy she is! She calls her friends and neighbours together.

'I've found the silver coin I lost,' says she. 'Let's celebrate!'

God is as happy as that, I am sure, when one bad person makes up their mind to be good.

13. Builders *Matthew 7:24-27*

Everybody who listens to me
and then does something about it
is like a sensible builder.

He builds his house –
and he builds it on rock.

Then winter comes.
The rain pours down,
the mountain torrents come tumbling down the
hillside,
the great winds blow
and batter the house.

But it stands up to it all –
underneath it is rock.

Everybody who listens to me
but doesn't do anything about it
is like a stupid builder.

He builds his house –
    but he builds it on earth.

Then winter comes.
The rain pours down,
    the mountain torrents come tumbling down the
        hillside,
    the great winds blow
    and hurl themselves against *his* house.

Down it comes
    with a tremendous crash!

14. Fishermen and Their Net   *Matthew 13:47-48*

God's Way is like this.

Fishermen throw their dragnet into the sea, and it catches all sorts of fish. When it is full of fish, they pull it up on to the beach.

Then they sit down and sort the fish out: the fish they want to keep go into their baskets; the fish that are no good go back into the sea.

15. The Moneylender   *Luke 7:41-42*

Two men owed a moneylender money.

One owed him £500; the other £50. They hadn't a penny in the world; so the moneylender crossed their debts out.

Which of the two men would most want to say 'Thank you' to him?

16. Getting out of Trouble   *Luke 12:58-59*

Wouldn't *you* say something like this to a man who owed a money-lender a lot of money? –

'While you are going along the road to the court with him, do your best to get things settled up. You know what will happen if you don't. He'll drag you to the judge; the judge will hand you over to the constable; the constable will throw you into jail. There you'll stay until you've paid the last penny of your debt.'

17. The Unexpected Visitor

Luke 11:5-8

There's a neighbour who's a friend of yours. One night, about midnight, you go along to his house.

'Fred!' you call out, 'lend me three loaves of bread. A friend of mine's on a journey; he's just turned up at our house, and I haven't a thing to give him.'

'I can't be bothered,' says he from inside the house. 'The door's locked, and we're all in bed. I can't get up to give you anything.'

You know what happens. You stay there knocking on the door, and up your friend gets and gives you whatever you want; not because he's a friend of yours, but because you just wouldn't be put off.

18. Thieves

Mark 3:27

A thief can't just go in and ransack the house of a very strong man. He goes for the strong man first, and ties him up. Then he sets to and ransacks the house.

Luke 12:39-40a

You can be sure of this. If the householder knew just when the thief was coming, he wouldn't let his house be broken into. Be ready!

The Big Farm

19. Brothers' Quarrel

Luke 15:11-32

A man and his two sons were farmers.

The younger son came one day to his father.

'Dad,' he said, 'it's time you handed over the farm to the two of us. Give me my share.'

That's what the father did. He divided up the farm between his two sons, and handed it over.

The younger son quickly packed his things and went abroad. There he threw his money away having 'a good time'.

At last, his pockets were empty. Then the harvest failed all over the land. There he was – no money and no food. He took a job with a farmer there, and the farmer sent him off to feed the pigs in the fields. He felt like swallowing the pigs' food himself. Nobody lifted a hand to help him.

Then he knew what a fool he'd been.

'How many of the labourers on my father's farm have more food than they want,' he thought, 'and here I am starving to death! I'm going home to my father. I've wronged God, and I've wronged my father. I'll tell him so. And I'll tell him, too, that I don't deserve to be called a son of his; he can take me on as a labourer.'

He got up and went home.

When he was still quite a long way from his father's farm, his father saw him coming. He felt very sorry for him; and he ran out to meet him, threw his arms around his neck and kissed him.

'Dad,' the boy began to say, 'I've wronged God and I've wronged you. I don't deserve to be called a son of yours . . .'

'Quick!' his father called to the servants, 'go and get his best clothes out. Get a ring and sandals and dress him properly. And kill that calf we've fattened. We'll have a feast and a great time tonight. My boy was dead and lost; and here he is alive and back home again!'

And they began to celebrate.

Now the older son had been out on the farm. He was coming home and had almost reached the farmhouse when he heard the sound of bagpipes and dancing. He called one of the farmhands out, and asked him what was going on.

'Your brother's back,' said the man. 'Your father's killed the calf because he's safe home again.'

The older son was furious, and he wouldn't even go inside the house. His father came out and begged him to come inside.

'Look,' he answered back, 'I've slaved for you all these years. I did everything you told me to do. But what do I get? Not even a kid to have a good time with my friends. This son of yours can throw his money away on girls, if he likes, and come home again – and you go and kill the calf for him!'

'My dear boy,' said his father. 'We're always together. All the farm is yours – you know that. We had to celebrate tonight. It's your *brother* who was dead and lost; it's your *brother* who's alive and back home again!'

20. Trouble at Harvest Time   *Matthew 20:1-15*

God's Way is like this.

It was harvest time, and a farmer went out to the market square to hire workmen for his vineyard. He settled with them for the proper wage for the day – a pound – and sent them out to work.

About nine o'clock he went out again. Men were hanging about the square with nothing to do.

'You, too, can go and work in the vineyard,' he said, 'and I'll pay you the proper wage.'

Off they went to work.

At noon and at three o'clock in the afternoon he went out to the market square again, and the same thing happened.

About five o'clock he went out again to the square. Men were still hanging about.

'Why are you hanging about all day doing nothing?' he asked.

'Nobody has taken us on,' they said.

'You can go into the vineyard with the others,' he told them.

By now it was evening. The farmer spoke to his foreman.

'Call the workmen in,' he said, 'and pay them their wages. And start with the last ones we took on.'

Those who started work at five o'clock in the afternoon came up and got a full day's wage – a pound.

Then those who had started work at six o'clock in the morning came up; they expected to get more than that. They, too, got a full day's wage – a pound.

They began to go for the farmer.

'These fellows who started last have only done an hour's work!'

'And you are treating them like us!'

'We've had to do all the hard work!'

'And we've had the scorching sun to put up with as well!'

The farmer tackled their leader.

'My dear man,' he said, 'I'm not treating you badly. Didn't you settle with me for a proper day's wage? Take your money and get out. I've chosen to give these fellows who started at five o'clock the same wage I'm giving you. Can't I use my own money as I want to? Does my generosity make you jealous?'

21. A Clever Rascal

Luke 16:1-8a

A rich man had a manager.

One day he was visiting his estates, and this manager was charged with letting them go to rack and ruin.

He called the manager in to see him.

'What's this I hear about you?' he asked. 'You'd better give me an account of how you've been managing things. You can't go on as manager.'

'What shall I do?' the manager thought. 'My master's sacking me. I'm not strong enough for farm work; it would be a disgrace to start begging . . . I know what I'll do; and then, when I'm out of a job, people will open their homes to me.'

He sent word to the wholesale traders who hadn't paid their debts, and asked them to come and see him. He talked to them like this.

'How much do you owe my master?' he asked the first trader.

'One hundred jars of oil,' he said.

'Here's your receipt,' said the manager. 'Sit down; be quick and write fifty jars down.'

'You,' said the manager to another trader, 'how much do you owe?'

'One hundred sacks of wheat,' he said.

'Take your receipt,' said the manager. 'Write fifty sacks down.'

(When Jesus told this story, wrote Dr Luke, he had a good word to say for this clever rascal: he was a shrewd fellow.)

22. Golden Corn   *Mark 4:3-8*

Look! A farmer went out sowing.

As he sowed his seed,
   some fell on the path
   and the birds came and gobbled it up.

Some fell on rocky ground
   where it had little soil;
   it grew up quickly
   because the soil was thin.

When the sun was high in the sky
   it was burned up;
   because it had no roots
   it withered away.

Some seed fell among thorn bushes
   which grew up and choked it;
   it never ripened.

Some seed fell into good soil
   and ripened and grew big.

When harvest came –
    some seeds bore up to thirty seeds,
    some up to sixty seeds,
    some up to a hundred seeds.

23. Out with the Sickle! *Mark 4:26-29*

God's Way is like this.

A farmer went out sowing. He scattered the seed on the earth, and then didn't bother about it any more. Every day he got up and went on with his farmwork, and every night he went to bed and slept.

The days went by, and the seeds sprouted and grew tall. The farmer didn't know how it happened, but he knew what the soil itself could do: first there would be the green shoot, then the ear, then the ripe corn. But when the crop was ready (you remember what the Bible says?) –

    He puts in the sickle –
    harvest time's here.

24. The New Barn *Luke 12:16-20*

The farmlands of a rich farmer were bearing wonderful crops.

'What on earth shall I do?' the farmer kept thinking. 'There's no room in the old barn for these grand harvests.

'I know,' he went on. 'I'll tear down my old barns and build bigger ones, big enough to hold all my wheat and wealth. "You've wealth enough for many years. Take it easy, mate," I'll say to myself. "Have a good time. Eat and drink as much as you want."'

That night he died.

What happened to his wheat and his wealth?

25. A Fig Tree but No Figs *Luke 13:6-9*

A farmer had planted a fig tree in his vineyard. One day he went to look for figs on it; there were none.

'Look,' he said to his gardener. 'I've been coming here, looking for figs on this tree, for three years; I haven't found a single one. Why should it waste good ground?'

'Sir', said the gardener, 'let it alone for another year. I'll dig the earth round it and put manure on it. If there are figs on the tree next year – that will be fine. If not, you can cut it down.'

26. Farmers' Quarrel *Matthew 13:24-30*

God's Way is like this.

One November, after the early rains, a farmer sowed his fields with corn; and he sowed good seed.

A neighbour of his had a grudge against him. One night, when everybody was asleep, he and his men came over, and sowed weeds all over the newly sown fields; and off they went.

Nobody noticed anything. The first green shoots of corn and weed all looked alike. But when the corn began to grow tall, everybody could see what had happened – everywhere weeds were growing among the corn.

'Sir', said the farmer's slaves, 'the seed we sowed was good seed, wasn't it? Where have all the weeds come from?'

'I think I know', said the farmer. 'Somebody has got a grudge against me; this is his work.'

'What do you want us to do, then?' they asked. 'Go out and pull the weeds up?'

'No', he said, 'we won't do that. We might pull up the corn as well. I'll let the fields lie, corn and weeds together. I'll deal with them at harvest time. "Get the corn into the barns," I'll tell the harvesters, "and tie up the weeds in bundles; we'll use them for the winter fires."'

Stories of Slaves

27. Three Slaves *Matthew 25:14-30; Luke 19:12-24*

God's Way is like this.

A rich man was about to go abroad. He called his slaves and handed over his property to their keeping. To three of his slaves he gave £50 each and went abroad.

The first slave did some business with his money and doubled it. The second slave did the same. The third slave went off and dug a hole in the ground and buried his master's money.

The rich man was abroad for a long time. At last he came back and settled accounts with his slaves.

The first slave came and brought his £100.

'Sir,' he said, 'you handed £50 to me. Look, I've made it into £100.'

'Fine!' said his master. 'You're a good slave. You can be relied on. You've proved yourself with a small sum of money. I'll put you in charge of something much more important.'

The second slave came to him.

'Sir,' he said, 'you handed £50 to me. Look, I've made it into £100.'

'Fine!' said his master. 'You're a good slave. You can be relied on. You've proved yourself with a small sum of money. I'll put you in charge of something much more important.'

The third slave came along.

'Sir,' he said, 'I know the sort of man you are. You're a hard man. All you think of is making money; you get rich while other men do the work. I lost my nerve. I buried the £50 in the ground; I didn't want it stolen. Here's your money back.'

'You're a bad lazy slave,' said his master. 'You knew I get rich while other men work, did you? You should have taken my money to the bankers; then, at least, I should have got some interest on it when I came back. Take the money from him, and throw him into prison.'

28. Master and Slave

Luke 17:7-9

What would you do?

Suppose you were a farmer and you had a slave out ploughing or looking after the sheep. How would you talk to him when he comes in from the field?

Something like this?

'Come along in and get on with your supper.'

I know what you'd say.

'Get my supper ready,' you'd say, 'and tidy yourself, and wait on me while I have it. You can get your own supper when I've had mine.'

Would you thank him for doing what you told him to do?

29. Slave Law

Luke 12:47-48a

If a slave knows exactly what his master wants him to do, but doesn't get things ready and do what he's told, he gets a good flogging.

If a slave gets into trouble because he doesn't really know what his master wants, he gets off lightly.

30. Testing a Slave
Luke 12:42-46

How can a man tell if a slave is sensible and can be trusted? He is going away on business, and here's his chance: he puts him in charge of the other slaves and their rations. If the slave gets on with his job and his master finds him doing everything he was told to do when he comes home, he's a happy man. His master, no doubt, makes him his manager.

But suppose this happens.

'My master's a long time coming home,' the slave thinks. So he starts bullying the other slaves; he spends his time gorging himself and getting drunk. Then, suddenly, back comes his master – just when he's not expecting him. His master will give him the flogging he deserves; he knows he's a slave who can't be trusted.

31. Waiting for the Master
Luke 12:36-37a, 38, 40a, 35

The master of the house is away at a wedding feast. The slaves are waiting for him to come home, ready to open the gates as soon as he knocks. They are happy slaves if their master finds them awake. They don't mind when he comes – before midnight or after midnight – so long as he finds them on the watch.

You must be like them – your belts fastened and your lamps alight.

32. The Gatekeeper
Mark 13:34

God's Way is like this.

A man left home and went abroad. He put his slaves in charge of everything; each had his own job.

'Keep a sharp look out,' he said to the gatekeeper.

Out on the Road

33. Bandits
Luke 10:30-35

A man was going down the road from Jerusalem to Jericho, and fell into the hands of bandits. They tore his clothes off him and beat him up. Then off they went, and left him lying half-dead on the road.

Quite by accident, a priest was going down the same road. He saw the man lying there, but he didn't stop. He went on past him – on the other side of the road. It was just the same with a Temple caretaker. He, too, came to the spot and saw the man lying there; he, too, didn't stop – he went on past him on the other side of the road.

Then a foreigner, who was on a journey across the country, came upon the man. He saw him lying there, and felt very sorry for him. He went across to him, put ointment on his wounds and bandaged them up. He lifted him up on to the horse he had been riding, and brought him to an inn and looked after him.

Next morning, he took some money out of his purse and gave it to the innkeeper.

'Look after him,' he said. 'If it costs more than what I've given you, I'll put it right with you on my way back.'

34. Farm Worker and Pearl Merchant   Matthew 13:44-46

God's Way is like this.

Money had been buried in a field. One day, a man working in the field found it, and covered it up again. Wasn't he happy! Off he went and sold everything he had, and bought the field.

Or God's Way is like this.

A merchant was travelling from town to town, looking for beautiful pearls. One day, he found a wonderful pearl. Off he went, and sold everything he had and bought it.

35. Blind Men   Luke 6:39

Can a blind man lead another blind man along the village street? Won't they both fall into the ditch?

Village Stories

36. King and Governor   Matthew 18:23-34

God's Way is like this.

Once upon a time there was a foreign king who wanted to settle accounts with his high officers. One officer, a governor of a province, was brought to him who owed a million pounds, and he hadn't a penny left. The king ordered him to be sold – and his wife and children and whatever property he had.

The governor fell down on the ground before the king in great fear.

'Give me time,' he begged, 'and I'll pay everything back to you.'

The king felt sorry for him. So he set him free, and crossed out the whole debt.

The governor went off. On the way home he met one of his fellow officers who owed him £5. He got hold of him and nearly throttled him.

'Pay me the money you owe me,' he said.

His fellow officer fell down on the ground in front of him.

'Give me time,' he begged, 'and I'll pay everything back to you.'

But he wouldn't listen to him; he threw him into prison, to stay there until he had paid everything back.

The other officers saw what was happening. They were very angry indeed, and they told the king everything that had happened.

The king called the governor into his presence.

'You're an utter scoundrel,' he said angrily. 'I crossed out your huge debt when you begged for time to pay. Ought you not to have treated your fellow officer as I treated you, and shown him some pity?'

He handed him over to the jailors – to stay in prison until he had paid every penny back.

37. Farmer and King   *Luke 14:28-32*

What does a farmer do when he wants to build a watchtower in his vineyard?

Doesn't he first sit down, and work out what it's going to cost? He wants to make sure he's got enough money. He knows what would happen if he laid the foundations of the tower, and then couldn't finish it – all the passers-by would make fun of him.

'This fellow started building,' they'd laugh, 'and couldn't finish it.'

What does a king do when he is going to meet another king in battle?

Doesn't he first sit down and work it all out: 'How can I, with 10,000 soldiers, meet my enemy who is coming against me with 20,000 soldiers?'

If he thinks he can't win, he sends officers, while his enemy is still a long way off, to ask for peace.

38. A Royal Wedding
Matthew 22:11-13

A king gave a wedding feast for his son. He came in to see the wedding guests, and saw a guest who wasn't correctly dressed.

'My dear sir,' he said, 'how did you get in here without the correct dress?'

The man couldn't think of anything to say.

The king called his bodyguard.

'Tie him hand and foot,' he said, 'and throw him out into the night.'

39. Rich Man, Beggarman
Luke 16:19-31

Once upon a time there was a very rich man who lived in a palace.

He wore rich, purple clothes and ate the most wonderful food every day.

Lazarus, a lame beggar, lay outside his palace gate. He was covered with sores, and the street-dogs came and licked him. He used to dream of gorging himself with the bread that was left from the rich man's meals.

One day, the beggar died and the angels carried him away to heaven to live with Abraham. The rich man died and was buried.

Everything was now changed.

The rich man was very miserable. He looked from where he was, and there, a long way off, he saw Abraham and Lazarus having supper together.

'Father Abraham,' he called out, 'have pity on me. Send Lazarus to dip his fingertips in water and cool my tongue. This heat is torture!'

'Son,' said Abraham, 'you've got a short memory. On earth you had your good time; Lazarus had a very bad time. Here it's all the other way round. Anyhow, there's a great gulf between us; nobody can cross it, either from us to you or from you to us.'

'Father,' he said, 'then I have one thing to ask you. Send him to my old home on earth to warn my five brothers. I don't want them to come here where I am, and be miserable like me.'

'They can read the Bible,' said Abraham, 'and do what it says.'

'That isn't enough, Father Abraham,' said he. 'But if someone like Lazarus went back from heaven and told them, they would change their minds.'

'They wouldn't,' said Abraham. 'If they won't read the Bible and do what it says, they won't listen to someone like Lazarus, even if he did go back from heaven.'

40. Rude Guests
Luke 14:16-21

Once upon a time a rich man was giving a great feast, and he invited many guests.

When the feast was ready, he sent his slave to all who were invited: 'Come along: it's all ready.'

And they all alike made excuses.

'I've bought some land,' said the first. 'I must go out and look at it. Please excuse me.'

'I've bought ten animals,' said another, 'and I'm going to test them. Please excuse me.'

'I've just got married,' said another. 'I can't come.'

The slave went back and told his master what they had said. The master was angry.

'Go out into the town at once,' he told his slave. 'Bring in the beggars and the cripples and the blind people and the lame people from the streets and alleyways.'

41. A Wicked Judge
Luke 18:2-5

Once upon a time, in a certain town, there lived a judge who was a really bad man. He didn't care about God and he didn't care about men and women and what happened to them. In the same town there lived a widow. She kept coming to him to get a money matter settled.

'I want justice,' she kept saying, 'I want justice. I've been wronged.'

The judge took no notice of her for a long time.

'I couldn't care less for God or men,' he thought at last. 'But this widow is a regular nuisance. I'd better see that she gets justice. One of these days she'll be giving me a black eye!'

42. Nobleman and Rebels
Luke 19:12, 14, 15a, 27

Once upon a time a nobleman set off on a journey across the sea to the Emperor in Rome. He wanted the Emperor to make him a king.

His countrymen hated him. Some of them went to Rome themselves to tell the Emperor what they thought.

'We don't want this man to be our king,' they told him.

The Emperor wouldn't listen to them; and home the nobleman came – a king.

'Where are these enemies of mine?' he asked. 'They didn't want me to be king, eh? Drag them here to my palace, and kill them in front of me!'

43. A Ghost Story
Matthew 12:43-45

Once upon a time a ghost lived in a haunted house. At last he was driven out. He wandered through the dry desert looking for somewhere to make his home. He had no luck.

'I'm going back to the old house,' said he.

So he went back, and there was the old house, swept clean and freshly decorated – and empty!

Off he went again, and brought seven other ghosts, much worse than himself, to live with him. They all settled down there together. Things in that house were far worse than they had ever been before.

This can happen to us.

44. Two Men
Luke 18:10-14a

Once upon a time two men went up from the city streets into the Men's Court of the Temple to say their prayers.

The first man was a 'good' man; every Saturday, the Holy Day of the Jews, he went to the Meeting House to worship God.

The other man was a tax collector; he worked for the foreign government, and, because he did that, 'good' people thought he was a 'bad' man.

The good man stood straight up and prayed aloud for everybody to hear:

'My God, I thank you that I was not born a foreigner but a Jew; not a slave but a freeman; not a woman but a man.'

While he was praying, he was thinking like this:

'O God, I thank you that I am not like other people, greedy, dishonest, wicked, or even like this tax collector here. I fast twice each week; I give one-tenth of everything I earn to the Temple.'

The tax collector stood a long way off. He wouldn't even look up; he was so sorry for all the wrong things he had done that he beat his chest with his hands.

'O God,' he kept saying, 'have mercy on me, vile wretch that I am!'

It was the tax collector, believe me, not the 'good' man, who went home forgiven.

45. Going to a Wedding Party
Luke 14:8-10

When you are invited to a wedding,
   at the party afterwards
   don't sit down in the place of honour.
Somebody more important than you
   may have been invited.
Your host will come and say
   'Go lower down the table!'
What a fool you'll feel
   doing that!

When you are invited to a wedding,
   at the party afterwards
   take the least important seat.
Your host will say
   'Sir, come higher up the table!'
What honour you will have
   doing that!

The Poetry of Jesus

How God Cares for Everybody

1. God Looks After Us   *Matthew 6:25-30*

This is what I want you to know:

> Don't worry about what you are going to eat
>   or what sort of clothes you are going to wear;
>   what you are is more important than what you eat,
>   what you are is more important than what you wear.
>
> Look at the wild birds:
>   they don't go out farming;
>   they have no store-house or barn;
> God feeds them.
> How much more than wild birds you mean to God!
>
> Look at the wild flowers:
>   they don't work like mothers at home.
> Yet, believe me, King Solomon wasn't robed
>   as gloriously as a wild flower.
>
> God dresses the wild grass –
>   blowing in the field today,
>   a bonfire on the farm tomorrow.
>
> How much more will God look after you!
> You don't trust him enough.

2. Sparrows   *Luke 12:6-7*

> You can buy sparrows five a penny;
>   yet God keeps his eye on every sparrow.
> He counts every hair of your head.
> There's nothing to fear:
>   you mean more to him than a flock of sparrows.

3. Asking, Looking, Knocking *Matthew 7:7-11*

Keep asking – it will be given you;
  keep looking – you will find;
  keep knocking – the door will be opened.
Everyone who keeps asking, gets;
  everyone who keeps looking, finds;
  to everyone who keeps knocking, the door opens.

What father will give a stone to his boy
  if he asks for bread?
What father will give him a snake
  if he asks for fish?
Fathers are not all they should be,
  but they know how to give the very best to their
    children.
God is far better than our fathers;
  of course he will give the very best
  to those who ask him.

How Jesus Was Doing God's Work

4. These Are Wonderful Days *Luke 10:23-24*

What happy people you are
  to see what you are seeing!
I tell you this:
  kings and great men of old longed to see what you
    are seeing,
  but did not see it;
  they longed to hear what you are hearing,
  but did not hear it.

5. A Prayer of Jesus *Luke 10:21*

I praise you, Father,
Lord of the world –
  very clever people have missed the secret of your heart,
  simple people have found it.
Yes, Father, I give glory to you;
  this is your way.

6. Jesus Makes God Known as Father   *Luke 10:22*

My Father has made everything clear to me:
  my Father alone knows who I am,
  and I alone know him as the Father he is,
  I – and those I want to learn the secret from me.

7. Come Here to Me!   *Matthew 11:28-30*

Come here to me
  all you who are tired with hard work,
  I will put new life into you.
Let me give you a hand and show you how to live.
I'll go your pace and see you through –
  and I'll give you the secret of the quiet mind.

Pulling with me is easy,
  the load with my help is light.

8. God Is Here Among You   *Luke 11:17-20*

(For people who said that Jesus made mad people better, not with God's help, but with the Devil's)

Civil war makes a country a desert –
  house crashes on house;
  if there is civil war in the Devil's country,
  how can he stay king?
I make mad people better (you say) with the Devil's help.
If I make mad people better with the Devil's help,
  with whose help do *your* friends make mad people
    better?
They shall be your judges.
But if I make mad people better with God's help,
  then God himself is here among you!

9. Friend of Jesus, Jesus, and God   *Luke 10:16*

Whoever says Yes to you says Yes to me;
  whoever says Yes to me says Yes to God.
Whoever says No to you says No to me;
  whoever says No to me says No to God.

10. Helping the Least of My Brothers and Sisters

Matthew 25:35-36, 40, 42-43, 45

I was hungry and you gave me food;
   I was thirsty and you gave me drink;
I was a foreigner and you took me home with you;
   I was in rags and you gave me clothes;
I fell ill and you looked after me;
   I was in prison and you came to see me.
Believe me –
   when you helped the least of my brothers and sisters,
   you helped me.

I was hungry and you gave me no food;
   I was thirsty and you gave me no drink;
I was a foreigner and you didn't take me home with you
   I was in rags and you gave me no clothes;
I fell ill and you didn't look after me;
   I was in prison and you never came to see me.
Believe me –
   when you didn't help the least of my brothers and
     sisters,
   you didn't help me.

11. First Things First

Luke 14:26-27

Those who put their father and mother before me,
   are no real friends of mine.
Those who put their children before me
   are no real friends of mine.
Those who aren't ready to face anything and follow me
   are no real friends of mine.

12. A World on Fire

Luke 12:49-53

I came to set the world on fire –
   how I wish the fire were burning now!
Mine is a dangerous life;
   how hard it will be for me until my work is done!
Do you think it is 'peace' I have come to give the world?
I tell you No – the very opposite of 'peace'!

This is what will happen
(do you remember what the Bible says?):
a home of five people will be divided,
three on one side and two on the other –
father against son and son against father,
mother against daughter and daughter against mother,
mother against son's wife and son's wife against his
mother.

How the Friends of Jesus Must Live

13. The Happy People   *Luke 6:20-21, 24-25*

Who are the happy people?
you poor people,
you belong to God;
you who are hungry now,
you shall have food;
you who are worried now,
you shall laugh.

Who are the unhappy people?
you rich people,
you have had your good time;
you who have plenty to eat now,
you shall be hungry;
you who are laughing now,
you shall be worried and sad.

14. Heart and Treasure   *Matthew 6:19-21*

Do not store up for yourself treasure on earth,
where moth and worm eat things up,
where thieves break into houses and steal.
Store up for yourself treasure in heaven,
where no moth or worm eats things up,
where no thieves break into houses and steal.
For heart and treasure
go together.

15. Bandits, Beggars, and Thieves   *Luke 6:29-30*

To anyone who hits you on the cheek
  give the other cheek to hit;
  let whoever grabs your coat
  take your shirt as well.

Give to every beggar.

Don't ask for your things back
  from the one who steals them.

16. Use Plain Words   *Matthew 5:33-34a, 37*

You know the law that was given in days of old:
  'If you swear "By God . . .," you must do what you say.'
I say to you:
  'Don't use language like that at all;
  it only spoils words.
Let your words be plain words, "Yes" and "No";
  when you swear, you are not really telling the truth.'

17. Be Clear-eyed   *Matthew 6:22-23*

Your eye is the lamp of your body:
  if your eyesight is good,
    you can see the whole world clearly;
  if your eyesight is bad,
    you can't see anything clearly;
  if you are really blind,
    how dark it is!

18. Do Everything Well   *Luke 16:10-12*

Whoever can be trusted with a small job
  can be trusted with a big one.
Whoever can't be trusted in 'things that don't matter'
  can't be trusted in things that really matter.

If you can't be trusted with money,
  who will trust you with real wealth?
If you can't be trusted in ordinary business,
  who will give you a place in God's great work?

19. Use Your Wits

Luke 12:54-56

When you see a cloud coming up in the western sky,
    you say at once, 'There's a thunderstorm coming',
    and the storm comes.
When you see the south wind blowing,
    you say, 'It's going to be scorching hot',
    and scorching hot it is!

You know how to tell the weather;
    why don't you know how to tell
    what is happening in the world of men and women?
You are only playing at being good.

20. Be Genuine

Luke 6:43-45

No healthy tree
    grows rotten fruit.
No rotten tree
    grows healthy fruit.
You can tell every tree by its fruit:
    from a thorn-bush you don't get figs;
    from a bramble-bush you don't get grapes.

The one who is good out of the richness of a good heart
    grows goodness.
The one who is evil out of an evil heart
    grows evil.

21. Don't Show Off

Matthew 6:2-6, 16-18

When you help people,
    don't 'blow your own trumpet'
    like people who are only pretending to be good;
    they want people to say, 'How good you are!'
Very good. They get what *they* want.

When you help people,
    don't let your right hand know
    what your left hand is doing;
    help people without others noticing it.
Your Father will notice, and give you what *you* want.

When you pray,
    don't make a show of it,
    like people who are only pretending to be good;
    they want people to say, 'How good you are!'
Very good. They get what *they* want.

When you pray,
    go into your own room and shut the door,
    and say your prayers to God your Father alone.
Your Father will notice and give you what *you* want.

When you fast,
    don't look sad and make your face gloomy,
    like people who are only pretending to be good;
    they want people to say, 'How good you are!'
Very good. They get what *they* want.

When you fast,
    brush your hair and wash your face;
    don't let anybody but God your Father
      see that you are fasting.
Your Father will notice and give you what *you* want.

22. Don't Be Underhand   *Luke 12:2-3*

There's nothing hidden
    that won't be brought into the light.
There's nothing secret
    that won't be openly known.
Whatever you've said in the darkness
    will be heard in the light.
Whatever you've whispered in the house
    will be shouted in the streets.

23. The World Will Be Full of Light   *Luke 17:22-24*

The time is coming when you will long to see God's
    new world
    and you will not see it.

'Here it is!' somebody will say, or 'There it is!'
Don't run after them.

For as the lightning lights up the whole sky
God himself will light up the whole world.

Leaders

24. John the Hermit   *Luke 7:24-26*

What did you go out on the moors to see?
Grass blown by the wind?
But what did you go out to see?
Somebody clothed in silk?
You must look in places for splendour and luxury!
But what did you go out to see?
One of God's great men?

Yes! I tell you –
Somebody greater than God's great men of old.

25. Leaders Should Set an Example   *Luke 11:42-44, 46-48, 52, 39-41*

What bad leaders you are!
You don't forget about the collection,
but you forget about God's justice and his love.
You like front seats in the Meeting House;
and everybody touching their hats to you in the
street.
You're like gravestones that look like a pavement:
people walk on them without knowing what's
underneath.
What bad leaders you are!
You make ordinary people carry heavy loads;
but you don't lift a finger to help them.
You build monuments to God's great men of old,
but you are like your fathers who murdered them.
You have taken away the key to the door of knowledge;
you don't want to go in yourselves,
and you won't let anybody else go in.

Alas for you leaders of the people:
    you clean the outside of a cup and a dish,
        but inside they are full of greed and violence.
    How blind you are!

    Make the inside of the cup clean first,
        then the outside may be clean too.

How We Can Learn from What Happened Long Ago

We have many stories about things that happened and about people who lived in our own country long ago. Some are happy stories; some are very unhappy stories. Jesus had many stories like our stories; stories about his own country and about his own people. We can read them in the *Old Testament*, which was his Bible.

Here are some of his poems that tell us of places and people famous long ago in the history of his people. When Jesus made these poems, everybody who heard them knew these old stories; if you don't know them, look them up in your Bible.

Here are a few words about the places and the people in his poems.

The Places

Jesus uses stories about five famous cities – all foreign cities, famous in their time. Sodom was an old city which, people believed, stood where now the Salt Sea (or Dead Sea) lies; it was destroyed in a great earthquake. Nineveh and Babylon were the capital cities of the great enemy nations; both were destroyed in war. Tyre and Sidon were famous cities on the coast – ports from which sailors took their cargo ships across the seas to Africa and Spain; their great days were long past, and now they were only small towns. Chorazin, Bethsaida, and Capernaum are three cities where Jesus himself had told the Good News about God and made many sick people better. Capernaum was his home after he left his native village of Nazareth; Bethsaida was Peter's home town; we do not know anything about Chorazin.

The People

You will have heard stories of the people Jesus speaks about. The Queen of Sheba came from a distant country to see the glory of Solomon the King. Jonah was sent by God to call the people of the great enemy city of Nineveh to change their minds and live good lives.* Elijah and Elisha were great men of God; the people they went to were all foreigners. Two old legends told about Noah who built the ark at the time of the Great Flood, and Lot who escaped just before the earthquake destroyed Sodom.

26. The Flood and the Earthquake   *Luke 17:26-30*

('Business as usual' – and everybody taken by surprise)

> As it was in the days before the Flood,
>   so will it be when God's Great Day comes:
>   everything was just like an ordinary day –
>   breakfast, dinner, tea, supper,
>   mother, father, boys and girls –
>   until (as the Bible says) 'Noah went into the ark'.
> Then came the Flood, and the old world was destroyed.
>
> As it was in the days of Lot:
>   everything was just like an ordinary day –
>   breakfast, dinner, tea, supper,
>   all the shops open,
>   farmers out in the fields, builders building houses –
>   until Lot went out of the city of Sodom.
> 'Then the earthquake happened' (as the Bible says),
>   and the old world was destroyed.
> So will it be when God's Great Day comes.

27. Six Cities   *Matthew 11:21-24*

> Alas for you, Chorazin! Alas for you, Bethsaida!
> If Tyre and Sidon had seen the great things you have seen,
>   they would have long ago changed their ways.

* This did not actually happen; it is an Old Testament story (or parable) like the stories of Jesus.

Believe me –
Tyre and Sidon will do better than you in God's Great
    Day.

Alas for you, Capernaum!
Do you remember what the Bible says about Babylon
    city?
        'These were your proud thoughts:
        "The skies I'll climb;
        "up above the highest stars
        "I will set my throne;
        "I will climb past the tallest clouds:
        "I will be like God himself!"
        How low you have been brought!
        How far you have fallen!'
        So far will you fall from your pride!
If Sodom had seen the great things you have seen,
    it would still have been a great city today.
Believe me –
Sodom will do better than you in God's Great Day!

28. Foreign Queen and Foreign City   *Luke 11:31-32*

The Queen of Sheba will stand up in God's Great Day
    and show how blind people today are:
    she came from a far-off country
    to hear King Solomon the Wise.
Look! Something much more important than Solomon
    is here.

The people of Nineveh will stand up in God's Great Day
    and show how blind people today are:
    when they heard Jonah, they listened
    and changed their ways.
Look! Something much more important than Jonah is
    here.

29. The 'Proof' *Luke 11:29-30*

People today do not really love and trust God;
　　they keep looking for a 'proof' that I am doing God's
　　　　work.

No 'proof' will be given to them –
　　only the 'proof' that Jonah was:
Jonah and what he said were the only 'proof'
　　the people of Nineveh had;
I myself today am the only 'proof' that I am doing God's
　　work.

30. Foreign Widow and Foreign Soldier *Luke 4:25-27*

There were many widows in our own country
　　when Elijah was living.

No rain fell for three long years and more,
　　famine walked through town and village;
　　but God sent Elijah to nobody in our own country,
　　but only (says the Bible) 'to a widow in a foreign city'.

There were lepers in our own country when Elisha was
　　living.
But God made nobody in our own country better,
　　only a foreign soldier.

The Doomed City

Jesus lived in an occupied country. These poems deal with the war the 'Resistance Movement' was planning to fight against the Romans; they are a warning to all who thought that hatred and fighting were God's Way and that foreign people were God's enemies.

31. Jerusalem
Luke 13:34-35a

Jerusalem, Jerusalem, killer of God's great men,
  murderer of God's messengers,
  how many times have I longed
  to gather your people together as a family,
  like a bird gathering her brood under her wings;
  you would not have it so.
Look! You've made the Temple your kind of Temple,
  not God's.

32. How Blind the City Is!
Luke 19:42-44

If only today you knew how to live for peace instead of
  war!
You cannot see what you are doing.
The time will come when
  your enemies will throw up a palisade round you,
  besiege and attack you on all sides,
  dash down your buildings and your people,
  leave not a wall upstanding:
  all because you did not see
  that God had already come to you in love, not war.

33. How Terrible It Will Be!
Luke 21:20-24

When you see the city besieged by armies,
  be sure the last days of the city have come.

Let those inside her walls escape
  and those in the villages stay in the villages.
These are the days of punishment,
  the words of the Bible are coming true.
There will be great distress in the land
  and a terrible time for this people.
They will fall at the point of the sword
  and be scattered as captives throughout the world.
Foreign soldiers will tramp the city's streets
  until the world is really God's world.

34. A Time of Sudden Violence
Luke 17:34-36

I warn you –
two men will be sleeping in the same bed,
one will be caught, one escape;

two women will be grinding at the same farm,
one will be caught, one escape;

two men will be working out in the fields,
one will be caught, one escape.

35. The Only Hope
Mark 13:15-16

The man resting on the roof must not stop to go indoors
to pick up anything in the house.
The man working in the fields must not go home
to get his clothes.

Forty years after Jesus made these poems, the Great Rebellion of the Jewish people broke out. Villages were burned, very many people were killed, and the city of Jerusalem was burned and captured by Roman soldiers.

Sayings Without Stories

The friends of Jesus remembered many of his sayings without always remembering just what happened – where he was, when he said them, the people he was talking to. But they didn't forget the sayings themselves. They wrote them down, collected them together and arranged them as they thought best. That is why you will sometimes find that Mark puts a saying in one place, Matthew in another place, and Luke in a different place still.

Here are some of these sayings of Jesus which his friends remembered and wrote down.

About the Work of Jesus

1. God has given me world-wide power. Go. Help everybody everywhere to follow me. Get them to join my company of friends, and show them how to live as I showed you. Remember, I shall always be with you – to the very end.   *Matthew 28:18-20*

2. Don't think I have come to pull the Bible to pieces. I haven't come to get rid of it; I have come to help people to see what God is really doing and to live in his way.   *Matthew 5:17*

3. Anyone who is not my friend is my enemy; anyone who does not help me to get people everywhere to live together as God's Family, sets people against one another.   *Luke 11:23*

4. Anyone who is not our enemy is our friend.   *Mark 9:40*

5. Nobody knows the date when everybody everywhere throughout the world will be living in God's Way. Angels don't know and I don't know. Only God himself knows that.   *Mark 13:32*

6. See, I am standing outside the door and knocking. If you hear the sound of my knocking and open the door, I'll come into your home, and we'll have dinner together.   *Revelation 3:20*

7. My words will outlive the world itself.
Mark 13:31; Matthew 24:35; Luke 21:33

How the Friends of Jesus Must Live

1. God is your Father, and you must live in his Way. He cares for everybody everywhere – bad people and good people, honest people and dishonest people. See how the sun shines and the rain falls on all their farms alike. *Matthew 5:45*

2. You, who are my friends, must be like salt; you must make the whole life of the world worth living. *Matthew 5:13*

3. You, who are my friends, are like daylight; you must help people to see everything clearly. *Matthew 5:14a*

4. Everybody can see a town on a hilltop. You must be like that.
Matthew 5:14b

5. If you've got ears, use them. *Mark 4:23*

6. When you listen, you must really listen. *Mark 4:24a*

7. If there is something you can really do, what a lot of other things you can learn to do too! If you don't try to do something, you won't be able to do anything! *Mark 4:25*

8. If you want to help me you must give all your heart to it. You must put yourself last. You must be ready to let people do their worst to you. And you must keep your eyes on me. *Mark 8:34*

9. Nobody can work for two masters. If you do, you will think less of one than you do of the other; or you will be devoted to one, and have no use for the other. Either God is your master – or money is. *Matthew 6:24*

10. Living in God's Way sometimes takes all the courage you've got. You'll be all right – if you never give in. *Matthew 10:22*

11. If you are always thinking of saving your skins, that's just what you won't do. But, if you forget all about yourself because you are keen on helping me, even if you lose your life, you will be all right. You will really be yourself. *Mark 8:35*

How the Friends of Jesus Must Worship God

1. You are my friends, and this is what I want to say to you: you must never worship men – not even men like the Roman Emperor; the worst they can do is to take your life away from you. You must worship God alone – both life and death are in *his* hands. *Luke 12:4-5*

2. When you are saying your prayers, you must really forgive anybody who has done you a wrong – so that God your Father may forgive you the wrong things you have done. *Mark 11:25*

3. When you say your prayers, don't babble away without thinking about what you are saying. That is what they are doing in temples all over the world; people think God listens to you if you just go on talking and talking. Don't do that sort of thing. You know what God is like: he is your Father, and he knows just what you need before you begin to ask him for it. *Matthew 6:7-8*

4. You mustn't keep on saying, 'What shall we eat?', 'What shall we drink?', 'What clothes shall we wear?'. You mustn't worry like that. People who don't know what God is like worry about food and drink and clothes. Your Father knows that you need all these things. You must make God's Way your aim, and God will give you all these things as well. *Matthew 6:31-33*

5. Can anybody add one hour to their life – by worrying? *Matthew 6:27*

6. Believe me: if two of you meet together as my friends and are sure about what you are asking, my Father will do what you ask; for, if two or three people meet together as my friends, I am with them too. *Matthew 18:19-20*

7. Trusting in God – even though it is as small as a small mustard seed – can move mountains or pull up a mulberry bush with its long roots. *Matthew 17:20; Luke 17:6*

How the Friends of Jesus Must Behave

1. Treat everybody you meet in the same way as you would like them to treat you. *Luke 6:31*

2. Be wise like serpents and innocent like doves. *Matthew 10:16b*

3. If somebody treats you badly, this is what you must do. Tell them plainly what they have done. If they say they are really sorry, be friends with them again. If they treat you badly again and again in one day, and every time come to you and say they are really sorry, be friends with them again. It won't be easy – so watch yourself.

Luke 17:3-4

4. If a Roman soldier forces you to carry his baggage for a mile along the road, go two miles along the road with him.   *Matthew 5:41*

5. Give to anyone who asks you; don't turn your back on anyone who wants to borrow from you.   *Matthew 5:42*

6. You should never think anything is impossible.   *Matthew 17:20b*

7. Why don't you make up your own minds about what is right and what is wrong?   *Luke 12:57*

8. You'll get as good as you give – and more.   *Mark 4:24b*

9. How much better off would you be if you won all the money in the world and lost – *yourself?* What would you give in exchange for – *yourself?*   *Mark 8:36-37*

10. It's a good thing to be healthy. But we may have to risk the loss of an eye or a hand sometimes; God's Way must always come first.

Mark 9:43-47

11. God will put boasters in their place – down at the bottom; he will put the humble, who never boast about themselves, in *their* place – at the top.   *Luke 14:11*

12. Don't forget this: some of those at the bottom of the class will find themselves at the top of the class; and some of those at the top will find themselves at the bottom.   *Luke 13:30*

13. You know what climbing a steep hill is like: if you slip on a stone, you can fall to your death; if you send a stone rolling down the hillside, it can kill the man following you.   *Luke 20:18*

14. When you have a party, don't always invite friends, cousins, relatives, and well-to-do neighbours; they will invite you back to *their* party, and all of you will be just having a good time together. When you have a party, give it freely; invite poor people, cripples, lame people, blind people; they can't invite you back. That's the way you'll find happiness. That's what heaven is like.   *Luke 14:12-14*

15. Giving makes us really happy, not getting.   *Acts 20:35b*

16. Worldly people deal with one another much more intelligently than religious people do.   *Luke 16:8b*

There Must Be New Standards

1. You have often heard, in the Meeting House, the law about murder read aloud: 'You shall not kill'. You know that a murderer will be arrested and tried before a judge. Believe me, God judges anyone who is even *angry* with a fellow human being.   *Matthew 5:21-22*

2. You have often heard, in the Meeting House, the law about revenge read aloud: 'An eye for an eye, a tooth for a tooth'. Believe me: there must be no fighting back – that's not the way to deal with enemies.
     Matthew 5:38-39

3. You have often heard, in the Meeting House, the law about fellow-citizens read aloud: 'Love your fellow-citizen'. My command is: 'Love your enemies'.   *Matthew 5:43-44*

4. There are religious leaders who like 'showing off'. They walk about in fine clothes. They like people to say 'Sir' when they pass them in the street. When they go to the Meeting House, they sit in the best seats. When they go out to dinner, they like to sit next to their host. They buy up the houses of widows and make them homeless. Yet, to look like 'good' people, they go to the Meeting House and make their prayers very long. God will judge them more severely than other people. Keep away from them.   *Mark 12:38-40*

5. Don't you see or understand? Are you still so dull? Don't you remember what the Bible says? –

> Listen, you foolish and thoughtless people:
>   you've eyes, but you won't look;
>   you've ears, but you won't listen.   *Mark 8:17b-18*

6. Why do you say 'Sir, Sir' when you speak to me, but don't carry out my teaching? *Luke 6:46*

7. If only you understood the Bible when you read it! There God says:

> It is your affection I delight in,
> not your Temple services.

If you had understood that saying, you wouldn't have got things all mixed up, and called innocent people wicked. *Matthew 12:7*

8. Believe me: unless your goodness is very different from the 'goodness' of your Jewish Leaders, you won't even begin to live in God's Way. *Matthew 5:20*

9. Alas for you Jewish Leaders! You are only pretending to be good. You travel all over the world to make one foreigner a Jew; when he becomes a Jew you make him twice as bad as yourselves. *Matthew 23:15*

The Heart of the Matter

Jesus has been talking about many things.

We have read his conversations, the stories he told in the villages, the poems he gave to his friends, the sayings people remembered. We know why he said all this: he was helping people to understand what God was like and what he was doing; who we are and how we should live; what the world in which we live is really like and what it will be like when everybody lives in God's Way.

Jesus put the meaning of all he had been saying in two short poems, and we have called them *The Heart of the Matter*. The two poems are 'God's Way Must Be Our Way' and 'The Prayer of the Friends of Jesus'.

God's Way Must Be Our Way   *Luke 6:27-28, 32-38*

By the side of this poem we have put some words to guide you as you read it. Here Jesus is showing us in simple words what God's Way is really like and how we must try to live in God's Way.

These are
 our
 orders
	Love your enemies,
	     do good to those who hate you,
	     bless those who curse you,
	     pray for those who treat you badly.

Living in
 God's Way
 makes a
 difference
	If you love those who love you,
	     what is there special about that?
	 Everybody does that sort of thing.
	 If you favour those who favour you,
	     what is there special about that?
	 Everybody does that sort of thing.
	 If you lend money to those you hope will help you,
	     what is there special about that?
	 Everybody does that sort of thing.

We must do
 more than
 others
	Love your enemies;
	     do good and lend,
	     expecting nothing back.

It is really	You *will* get something back:
worth while	you will be living in God's Way –
	he is kind to those who never say 'Thank you',
	and to those who are selfishness itself.
It can be put	Be merciful
quite simply	as God your Father is merciful.
So we must	Don't judge and you won't be judged;
set the	don't condemn and you won't be condemned;
pace	forgive and you will be forgiven;
	give and you will be given;
	good measure,
	pressed down,
	shaken together,
	running over,
	will be poured into your lap.
It amounts	The measure you give
to this	will be the measure you get.

The Prayer of the Friends of Jesus

We call this 'The Lord's Prayer', but this is shorter than the prayer we use in school and at home and in church or chapel. The shorter form (which we give here) is the way Jesus first put it; this is easy to say when we are alone or with one or two people. When the friends of Jesus began to use the prayer in their worship they used the longer form. Instead of saying 'Father', they used the longer saying from their Jewish prayers – 'Our Father who is in heaven'. And at the end they added words of praise to God. If you look it up in your Bibles, you will find that Luke gives us the shorter prayer, and Matthew gives us the longer one.

Here, then, is the heart of the matter. Here Jesus tells us what he wants us to do and how he wants us to live.

Luke 11:2-4

Father,
    may your name be used with reverence,
    may everybody live in your Way.
Give us today our bread for tomorrow.
Forgive us as we forgive others;
    do not put us to the test.

From Galilee to Rome

Part One – The Pioneer

A Letter to His Excellency Theophilus

We do not know who Theophilus was, except what we can learn from this letter. He seems to have been an important person; Roman governors were addressed as 'Your Excellency'. He may have been a Christian.

Luke 1:1-4

Many people have tried to write the story of what has happened among those of us who are the friends of Jesus; they used the reports which those who met Jesus face to face have handed down to us.

I thought that I too, Your Excellency, would try to write the story down. For some time now I have been trying to find out what actually happened, and I will put it down in its proper order. I want you to know the truth of what has been told to you.

The story of Jesus that Dr Luke tells us is the same story that Mark told. But he tells it in a different way; he wants us to see from the very beginning *why* Jesus lived as he did, something his friends were very slow to learn. Indeed, he wants us to see *how* his friends came at last to understand what he wanted them to do.

He wants us to see that Jesus is Lord as well as Leader, one to whom we can give our whole hearts and the service of our lives, and who gives us God's power – God's Spirit in our hearts – so that we can live in God's Way. Jesus is everybody's Lord.

Dr Luke was not born in Palestine and he was not a Jew, as we have seen; he came from one of the great cities of the Roman Empire. It was an amazing thing, he felt, that Jesus cared for *him* – and people like him – as well as for his own fellow-countrymen like Peter. And it was not just that Jesus cared for everybody everywhere, whatever their race or the colour of their skin; what amazed Dr Luke was the way Jesus cared especially for people nobody else bothered with.

How could he, then, tell the story of Jesus as if it was just a story of something that happened in Palestine? It was a story for the whole world about the whole world.

This is just where the friends of Jesus come in. His Galilean friends were only the first members of a great company of friends who were to spread all over the world. They did not realise this at first; but Dr Luke wants us to see that this was why Jesus called them – and why he calls us to be his friends today.

What Dr Luke also could not forget was what the love of Jesus cost Jesus himself. He faced death itself because he cared for everybody everywhere. Those last few days show us how great his love was.

The story begins by Jordan River, and Part One of his book ends in a capital city – Jerusalem. But this is not the end of the story (as the friends of Jesus thought at the time); it is only the beginning. So Part One of Dr Luke's story is only the story of what Jesus *began* to do and to teach, as he told His Excellency Theophilus.

The Beginning of the Venture

Dr Luke's story begins, as Mark's did, with the story of John the Hermit and the Call of Jesus by Jordan River. It is the year AD 27, and the Emperor Tiberius had been ruling the Roman Empire for fourteen years.

Dr Luke tells us more about John the Hermit than Mark did. He describes the sort of man he was and what he said to the people.

Most of all Dr Luke wants us to see what his Call meant to Jesus. Jesus had come to join John's company of friends to get ready for the coming of God's Chosen Leader. Jesus now knew that God had called *him* to be the Chosen Leader. He had to think through again what sort of Leader God wanted him to be. He made his great decision and left the moorlands to be a wandering teacher, talking to people in their villages and meeting them as equals.

John the Hermit *Luke 3:1-20*

In the year AD 27 – the fifteenth year of the reign of the Emperor Tiberius – Pilate was the Governor of Judea; King Herod and his brother Philip and King Lysanius were ruling princes in the countries to the north and east; and Annas and Caiaphas the High Priests were the Leaders of the Jewish people. However, it was to John the Hermit, out on the moorlands, that God spoke.

Now John had gone out to the banks of Jordan River and was calling people to change their ways so that God might forgive them.

He was like the man in the old poem in the Bible –

> The voice of a man
>> shouting in the lonely desert –
>> 'Get God's road ready,
>> make his paths straight.'
> Every valley shall be filled up,
>> every mountain and hill be levelled out,
>> winding roads made straight,
>> rough roads made easy.
> Everybody shall see God coming to our help.

Crowds went out to be baptised by John in Jordan River as a sign that they had changed their ways.

'You are like poisonous snakes,' John told them. 'Who told you to escape from the terrible times that are coming? If you've really changed your ways, you must show it in the way you live. You mustn't say "Oh – we are God's chosen people; we are all right." Believe me, God can make anybody his "chosen people" – even these rocks here. He's like a farmer with his axe. He's already put it at the root of the trees; and he will chop down every fruitless tree for the winter fires.'

'What must we do?' people asked him.

'The man with two coats,' said John, 'must share them with the man who has none. The man with food must share it with those who are hungry.'

'Sir, what must we do?' asked the tax collectors who came to be baptised in Jordan River.

'Collect the tax,' said John, 'and nothing more than the tax.'

'What must fellows like us do?' asked some soldiers.

'No beating up people for their money,' said John, 'and no telling lies about people. Live on your soldiers' pay.'

There was great excitement in all the towns and villages.

'Is John God's Chosen Leader?' people were asking.

'I have used water as a sign that your hearts shall be made clean,' said John. 'A Stronger One than I is coming; I am not good enough to bend down and untie his shoelaces. He will really give you God's power. He'll be like fire. He'll be like a farmer at harvest when, shovel in hand, he's cleaning out his threshing floor – storing the wheat in the barn and making a bonfire of the straw.'

This was what John told the people, day in, day out.

He was not even afraid of King Herod himself. He told him that he had done wrong to marry Queen Herodias – she was not his wife but his brother's wife. He charged him with doing many other wicked things. So King Herod did a still more wicked thing – he had John thrown into prison.

Jesus Hears God's Call   *Luke 3:21-22*

Crowds came to John to be baptised in the water of Jordan River. And among them came Jesus.

He had been baptised and he was standing on the bank of the river, praying.

Then it happened. From the open heavens, God's Spirit came down on him, like a dove.

'You are my only Son,' said a voice from heaven. 'With you I am very well pleased.'

Which Way?   *Luke 4:1-13*

Jesus went away from Jordan River, his heart filled with God's Spirit. And God led him out on to the lonely moorlands.

He was there many a long day. He was being tested; he had to think things out; what did God want him to do? All this time he had nothing to eat, and at the end he was very hungry indeed.

This conversation took place in his mind: Jesus imagined himself to be sometimes on the moorlands themselves, sometimes on the top of a very high mountain, sometimes standing on top of the Temple Gate in Jerusalem.

On the moorlands:

Voice   If you are God's Son, tell this stone here to become a loaf of bread.

Jesus   The Bible says: Bread is not the only thing a man needs to live on.

On the top of a very high mountain, where he could see so far that all the world seemed to lie at his feet:

Voice   I will give you all the power of these great countries and their royal splendour. It is all mine – mine to give to anybody I want to. It can all be yours – on one condition: you must take me for your King – not God.

Jesus	The Bible says: God himself must be your King; you must be his servant and his servant only.

Jerusalem, on the top of the Temple Gate, looking down on all the people gathered in the Court below:

Voice	If you are God's Son, jump down from this high place. The Bible says: God will command his angels to look after you. And again the Bible says: Their hands will hold you fast – you won't even stub your toe on a stone.
Jesus	The Bible also says: You must not put God to the test.

The testing time of Jesus was over – but it was not the last test he had to face.

Dangers Ahead

Jesus knew that his work would be dangerous work. We know, from Mark's story, how, at the end, Jesus would meet a lonely death on a cross. But the danger was there all the time.

For Jesus came to change the way we live, and we do not like changing our way of life. He came to call us to live in God's Way; and that calls for courage and unselfishness. We must be ready for anything, and, if we meet opposition and danger, we must not give in. Jesus knew what it was to live dangerously.

So Dr Luke now goes on to tell us what happened at the village where Jesus had grown up and where everybody knew him. We have also put here two other stories about the dangers Jesus faced.

His Own Village Is Unfriendly　　　　　　　　*Luke 4:14-30*

Jesus went back to Galilee, made strong by God's Spirit in his heart.

Everybody everywhere was talking about him. He told the people the Good News in their Meeting Houses, and everybody had a good word to say for him.

He came at last to Nazareth where he had grown up.

On the Saturday, the Holy Day of the Jews, he went along to the Meeting House there, and the leader of the Meeting House asked him to read the Bible to the people. The reading was from the book of Isaiah, one of God's great men of old. He stood up, opened the book and found these words –

God's Spirit is in my heart;
    he has called me to my great work.
This is what I have to do –
    give the Good News to the poor;
    tell prisoners that they are prisoners no longer,
    and blind people that they can see;
    set conquered people free,
    and tell everybody God's Great Day has come.

Jesus closed the book, gave it back to the leader of the Meeting House and sat down. Everybody was staring at him.

'You have been listening to the words of the Bible,' said Jesus. 'Today what God said would happen has happened.'

Everybody spoke well of him; they were astonished and charmed by the way he talked.

'Isn't he Joseph's son?' they were asking one another.

'I know what you will say to me – "Doctor, cure yourself",' said Jesus. '"We've heard all about what you did down at Capernaum. Do it here in your own village."'

'No Man of God is liked by his own home-folk,' Jesus went on.

'There were many widows in our own country
    when Elijah was living.
No rain fell for three long years and more,
    people starved in town and village;
    yet God sent him to none of our own countrymen,
    but only (says the Bible) "to a widow in a foreign city".

'There were lepers in our own country
    when Elisha was living.
Yet God made none of our own countrymen better,
    only a foreign soldier.'

The people in the Meeting House were very angry when they heard him talk like this. They got up and took him outside the village to the edge of the cliff to throw him over it.

But Jesus walked through the village crowd and went on his way.

The Government Is Unfriendly   *Luke 13:31-33*

One day, in Galilee, some Jewish Leaders came to Jesus.

'You'd better get out of here,' they said. 'King Herod's after you.'

'This is what I've got to say to that "fox", and you can tell him,' said Jesus. 'I shall go on doing what I have been doing, healing people who are sick in mind or body – today and tomorrow and the day after. I shall finish the work God has given me to do. A man of God is in no danger – outside Jerusalem City.'

A Foreign Village Is Unfriendly   *Luke 9:51-56*

This happened in Samaria. Jesus was on his way south to Jerusalem City.

He sent friends on ahead to find somewhere to spend the night. They came to a village, but the villagers turned them out, for one reason only – Jesus and his friends, it was obvious, were on their way to Jerusalem, the Holy City of their hated enemies.

'Sir,' said James and John, when they heard this, 'you remember what happened when Elijah was turned away from a village – fire came down from the sky and burned the villagers up. Do you want us to ask God to burn these villagers up?'

Jesus turned round and stopped such talk; and they went on to another village.

The Plan of the Venture: His Friends

Jesus himself could tell the Good News to only a few people, and they were his own countrymen. Time was short, and this was the work he believed God had given him to do.

But the Good News was for the whole world. So he gathered friends round him to learn to live in God's Way and to help him. After his death it would be *their* work to take the Good News 'to the ends of the earth'.

This is what happened. When Dr Luke was writing his book, there were friends of Jesus in many great cities of the Roman Empire. He wanted His Excellency Theophilus to see that this was what Jesus had planned from the beginning.

In the second part of his book, Dr Luke is going to tell how the friends of Jesus learned to follow him and carry on his work; here he tells us how they helped him in Galilee and Judea.

Jesus was one day standing right on the edge of Galilee Lake; the crowd of people, listening to the Good News about God, was pressing round him and pushing him into the water.

He noticed two boats lying just off-shore – the fishermen had landed and were washing their nets. He climbed into one of the boats – it was Peter's – and asked him to anchor it a little way out. He sat down and talked to the crowd from the boat.

At last he finished talking to them.

'Take the boat into deep water,' he said to Peter. 'Out with your nets and let's catch some fish.'

'Sir,' said Peter, 'we were out all night, hard at it, and we didn't catch one fish. But I'll get the nets out, of course, if you want me to.'

They got out the nets – and made a tremendous catch. The nets began to break, and they had to signal to their friends in the other boats to come and give them a hand. Over they came, and together they filled the two boats with so many fish that they were dangerously overloaded.

When Peter saw what had happened, he fell down in front of Jesus.

'Leave me alone,' he said, 'I'm not good enough to be a friend of yours.'

He was amazed at the catch of fish, and so were James and John his fishing partners and all the men in the boat with him.

'Don't be afraid,' said Jesus to Peter. 'From now on, you will be fishing for people instead of for fish.'

They beached their boats, gave up their fishing and went along with Jesus as his comrades and friends.

The 'Twelve' *Luke 6:12-16*

This happened in Galilee.

One day Jesus went out to 'The Hill' to pray. He spent all night thinking things out in prayer.

At daybreak he called his friends to him, and from them he chose the 'Twelve', and gave them the name 'Messengers' as well. Here is the list of the 'Twelve':

> Simon   'Rock' (we say 'Peter')
> Andrew, Simon's brother
> James and John

Philip
Bartholomew
Matthew
Thomas
James, the son of Alphaeus
Simon   'Rebel'
Judas, the son of James
Judas (who later handed Jesus over to the Jewish Leaders).

The Seventy-two
Luke 10:1-12

One day Jesus gave some special work to seventy-two of his friends. He was going through Galilee, telling people the Good News about God. He wanted them as his 'advance party' – to go ahead of him, two together, to any town or village he was going to visit.

This is what Jesus told them.

'There's a wonderful harvest; but there aren't enough harvesters. God is the owner of the harvest fields. Ask him to send harvesters out into the fields.

'Go; remember it's dangerous work; I am sending you like lambs to a pack of wolves.

'Here are your orders: no money-bag, no knapsack, no sandals, no greetings on the road.

'The first words you must say when you enter a house are – "Peace to this house". If a man who cares for peace lives there, your greeting will do his heart good. If he's not that sort of man, your greeting will at least do your own heart good.

'Make one house your home, and share meals with the people who live there – a workman should be paid. But don't go changing homes.

'If you come to a town and the townspeople are friendly, eat whatever they give you. Heal the sick people there and tell them – "God himself, in all his power, is here among you".

'If you come to a town, and the townspeople are unfriendly, go out into the streets. Tell them – "The dust of your town is sticking to our feet; we wipe it off to show you what sort of people you are. Yet your unfriendliness makes no difference to this: God himself, in all his power, is here among you". Believe me, the old foreign city of Sodom, wicked as it was, will do better than that town in God's Great Day.'*

* See the poem of Jesus, 'Six Cities', *The Message*, p. 479.

Martha and Mary
Luke 10:38-42

One day, on his travels, Jesus came to a village. A woman called Martha welcomed him into her home. She had a sister called Mary.

Mary used to sit beside Jesus, listening to him talking; Martha went hurrying about the house, doing this and that and the other.

Suddenly, she stopped in front of Jesus.

'Sir,' she said, 'doesn't it matter to you that my sister leaves me to do all the housework by myself? Tell her to give me a hand.'

'Martha, Martha,' said Jesus, 'what a lot of things you worry and fuss about! There's only one thing that matters. Mary's choice is better; nobody can ever take it away from her.'

Women who Helped
Luke 8:1-3

Jesus and the 'Twelve' were going about the countryside, visiting towns and villages, telling the people the Good News about God.

Some women went along with them too – women who had been ill and whom Jesus had cured. One of them was Mary from the village of Magdala – she had been very ill indeed. Another was Joanna; she was the wife of one of the great officers of the court of King Herod. Another was Susanna. There were many others too. They used their own money to look after Jesus and his friends.

The Purpose of the Venture: Breaking Down All Barriers

Jesus believed that God's will is that the world should be his Family and live in his Way.

Men and women were not living together as a Family. They were divided from one another by all sorts of barriers. There were barriers between rich and poor. People hated other people, as the Jewish people of his day hated the Roman soldiers. There were barriers, too, between individual people.

We must learn, Jesus believed, to break all these barriers down if we are to live in God's Way. There will always be differences between people; but we must not let them become barriers separating us from one another. We must use our differences to make our lives richer and wider.

Dr Luke was amazed at the way Jesus cared for people, especially for those whom nobody else cared for. He has told us many stories about the way Jesus took no notice of what people thought about him, but treated everybody he met, even if they were outcasts, as persons and equals.

A Roman Officer *Luke 7:1-10*

Jesus was in Capernaum; a detachment of Roman soldiers was stationed there.

One of the captain's slaves, a man of whom he was very fond, was dangerously ill. The captain heard that Jesus was in town, and he sent a message to him by some Jewish Leaders, who were friends of his, to ask him to come and cure his slave.

They found Jesus; they were very keen to get him to help the captain.

'He deserves help like this,' they said. 'He's a friend of all Jewish people. It was he who built our Meeting House for us.'

Jesus went along with them.

He had almost reached the house, when the captain again sent some of his friends to meet him.

'Sir,' he sent word, 'don't go to any more trouble. It wouldn't be fitting for you to come inside my house; that's why I didn't think it was right for me to come to meet you myself. Give the word of command, and my boy will be well. I am an officer in the army; there are generals over me and soldiers under me, and I know what orders are. I tell this soldier to go, and he goes; I tell that soldier to come, and he comes; I tell my slave to do this, and he does it.'

Jesus was filled with admiration for this Roman captain.

He turned to the crowd.

'Believe me,' he said, 'I haven't found a Jew who trusted me like this.'

The captain's friends went back to the house, and they found the slave fit and well.

A Widow *Luke 7:11-17*

On another day Jesus came to the village of Nain. His friends and a lot of other people were walking along the road with him.

At the town gate, there was a large crowd of people coming out. It was the funeral of the only son of a widow.

Jesus saw her and felt very sorry for her.

'Don't cry,' he said to her.

He went up to the coffin and touched it; the bearers stood still.

'Young man,' he said, 'get up.'

The dead man sat up and spoke.

Like Elijah in the old Bible story, Jesus gave him back to his mother.

Everybody felt that God himself was with them.

'Praise be to God!' they said.

'A great man has come among us!'

'God cares for his people.'

News of this spread throughout the whole of Palestine and beyond its borders.

A Woman Who Was 'a Bad Lot'   Luke 7:36-40, 44-50

One day a Jewish Leader, Simon by name, asked Jesus out to dinner. So they went along together to his home and sat down to dinner.

Now there was a woman in the town who, in the eyes of religious people, was 'a bad lot'; the people who went to the Meeting House wouldn't have anything to do with her. She heard that Jesus was having dinner in Simon's house, and this is what she did. She got hold of a bottle of real Indian ointment. She went and stood behind the couch on which Jesus was reclining. She was crying, and her tears fell on his feet. She wiped them dry with her hair, kissing them and putting ointment on them again and again.

Simon noticed all this.

'If this man was really a Man of God,' he thought, 'he'd know who was touching him like this, and what kind of woman she was. He'd know she was "a bad lot".'

Jesus was in no doubt about what Simon was thinking.

'Simon,' he said. 'I've something to say to you.'

'Go ahead,' said Simon.

Jesus turned to the woman.

'You see this woman,' he said. 'I came home with you, but you didn't give me any water to wash my feet; this woman wet my feet with her tears and dried them with her hair. You didn't greet me with a kiss; this woman has kissed my feet again and again ever since she came in. You didn't give me any perfume to put on my head; she's put ointment on my feet.

'Listen: because of her great love, all the wrong things she's done – and they are many – are forgiven. You don't show much love for me, do you? But then, you don't feel you need to be forgiven.'

Jesus turned to the woman.

'All the wrong things you've done are already forgiven,' he said.

The guests started whispering to one another.

'Who's this? He's even forgiving people's sins!'

'It's your trust in me that's saved you,' said Jesus to the woman. 'Go home and don't worry.'

Lepers   Luke 17:11-19

Jesus was on his way to Jerusalem. He was passing through the border country of Samaria and Galilee, and he went into one of the villages. On the road into the village, ten men met him – all lepers. But they kept their distance.

'Jesus! Sir!' they shouted to him. 'Take pity on us!'

Jesus saw them.

'You know the law for lepers who are cured,' he called back. 'Go and show yourself to the priest.'

Off the lepers went; and as they walked along the road they found they were lepers no longer – they were cured.

One of the men turned back to say 'Thank you'.

'Praise be to God!' he kept shouting loudly. He fell down on his face at the feet of Jesus and thanked him. He was the only one who wasn't a Jew; he was a 'foreigner' from Samaria.

'There were ten lepers cured, weren't there?' asked Jesus. 'What's happened to the other nine? Was this "foreigner" the only one who could come back and say "Thank you" to God?'

'Get up and go home,' he said to him. 'It's your trust in me that's made you well.'

A Chief Tax Collector   Luke 19:1-10

One day Jesus was going through Jericho City.

Now there lived in Jericho a very rich man called Zacchaeus, manager of the Tax Office there. He was very keen to see what sort of person Jesus was; but he was a little man and he couldn't see over the heads of the crowds. So he ran on ahead along the road Jesus was taking; and to get a good view of him he climbed into a fig tree.

Jesus came along the road and looked up at Zacchaeus in the tree.

'Zacchaeus,' he said, 'you'd better be quick and get down – I must stay with you today.'

He was down in a moment, thrilled to have Jesus as his guest. The crowd didn't like it.

'He's staying with that scoundrel of a fellow,' they muttered.

Zacchaeus stopped.

'I'm not the man they think I am, Sir,' he said to Jesus. 'Look, I give half my income to people in need; and if I've taken more than I ought from anybody, I give four times as much back.'

'God himself has come to this home today,' said Jesus. 'This man belongs to God's family too. You know what God said in the Bible – "I will seek the lost". That's what I and my friends are doing.'

The Cost of the Venture

Dr Luke has already told us about the dangers Jesus faced. Now he faces the greatest danger of all.

Jesus has told the Good News in Galilee. He must also tell the Good News in the capital city of his country. At the Great Feast, Jewish pilgrims from all over the world would be in Jerusalem City. Jesus would have the chance of speaking to as many of his countrymen as possible.

What drove Jesus forward was his love for people. He loved them because God his Father loved them. He knew the danger he would face in Jerusalem. His going to Jerusalem shows how great his love was, and what it cost him.

Reaching the City
Luke 19:37-48

Jesus had climbed the mountain road from Jericho and had almost reached Jerusalem City. He had come to the spot where the road begins to drop down from the top of the Olive Hill into the valley. Crowds of pilgrims were going along the road. All his friends were very happy and were singing hymns of praise to God for all they had seen Jesus do. The words came from an old Jewish hymn –

> Praise to the King
>   who comes in God's name!
> Peace in heaven!
> Glory in heaven!

There were some Jewish Leaders among the crowd.

'Sir,' they said, 'tell your friends to stop singing.'

'Believe me,' said Jesus, 'if my friends were to stop singing, the rocks would shout out!'

As Jesus went on down the road, he saw Jerusalem City across the valley. His eyes filled with tears.

'If only today you knew how to live for peace instead of war! [he said]

> You cannot see what you are doing.
> The time will come when
>> your enemies will throw up a palisade round you,
>> besiege and attack you on all sides,
>> dash down your buildings and your people,
>> leave not a wall upstanding:
>> all because you did not see
>> that God had already come to you in love, not war.'

Every day Jesus went into the Temple to tell the people the Good News about God. The Jewish Leaders had made up their minds to get rid of him, but they couldn't do anything about it. The crowds listened to him, spellbound.

The Supper   *Luke 22:14-18, 24-33, 35-38*

It was near the time for The Great Feast to begin, when all Jews remember together how God rescued them from Egypt and sent Moses to lead them to their homeland.

Jesus and his friends sat down at supper together.

'I have looked forward eagerly to sharing this Great Feast with you before I die,' he said. 'I shall never share it with you again until all it means has come true and God's Great Day has come.'

He took the cup in his hands and said Grace.

'Take this cup,' he said, 'and share it among yourselves. Believe me, I shall drink no more wine like this until God's Great Day comes.'

His friends started quarrelling about who was the most important person among them.

'Foreign kings,' said Jesus to them, 'are dictators to the people of their country; and powerful governors are called "Father and Friend" of their people. You – my friends – must turn it all the other way round. The "most important person" among you must live just as if he was the youngest among you. The "Leader" of my friends must live as the servant of all the others. Who is "the most important person" – the man who's having supper or the waiter who's looking after him? I know what you'll say – the man who's having supper, of course. Yet I have lived among you like the waiter who looks after the needs of other people.

'You are the ones who have stood by me, all through the hard times I have had,' Jesus went on. 'I will give you real "royalty" – the kind of "royalty" my Father has given me; you will have supper with me, as we are having supper together tonight, at *my* "Royal Court" and you'll be the real "Leaders" of God's People.'

Jesus turned to Simon Peter.

'Simon, Simon,' he said, 'Satan's after you to see the kind of man you are – like a farmer shaking and sifting wheat at harvest. But I have asked my Father that your trust in me may not break down. When you've won through, stand by my other friends – your brothers in God's Family.'

'Sir,' said Peter, 'I'd face prison and death with you – now.'

'When I sent you out to tell people the Good News about God,' said Jesus, 'you went without purse or bag or sandals. Did you find you were ever in real need?'

'No,' they said.

'Now it's very different,' said Jesus. 'You'll need everything you've got – purse and bag and sword; if you haven't a sword, you'd better sell your coat and buy one! You remember what the Bible says – "God's Servant was treated like a criminal"? – that's what I've got to face. It will all happen as the Bible has made clear.'

'Sir,' they said, 'see – here are two swords.'

'Enough of this,' said Jesus.

In the Orchard   *Luke 22:39-54a, 63-65*

Jesus set off for the Olive Hill – a spot he was very fond of – and his friends went along with him.

'The real test is coming,' said Jesus when they got there. 'You'd better pray that you won't have to face it.'

He went off a little way by himself.

He knelt down on the ground.

'Father,' he prayed. 'Take this suffering away from me. Yet I will do what you want, not what I want.'

God gave him the strength he needed. He was in very great distress, and he prayed with all his heart. Sweat fell from him on to the ground like drops of blood.

He finished praying and stood up. He went over to his friends and found them asleep, tired out by sadness.

'Why are you sleeping like this?' he said to them. 'Get up and pray that you won't have to face the real test that's coming!'

Before he had finished speaking a crowd of men rushed on them; and there, at their head, was the man called Judas, one of his close friends. He went right up to Jesus to greet him with a kiss, as if he was just meeting him.

'Judas,' said Jesus, 'is it with a kiss that you are handing me and my friends over to these men?'

His friends saw what was going to happen.

'Sir,' they said, 'shall we draw our swords?'

One of them hit out with his sword at one of the Temple police.

'Stop!' said Jesus. 'Let them have their way.'

He touched the man's ear and healed him.

'This is your hour indeed, the night and all its darkness,' said Jesus to the officers of the Temple guard.

The men arrested Jesus and marched him off to the High Court.

The soldiers guarding Jesus made fun of him and beat him up. They covered his face with a cloth.

'Be a real Man of God now,' they said, 'and tell us who struck you!'

And they swore at him again and again.

Jesus on Trial   *Luke 22:66-71; 23:1-25*

When it was daybreak, the Jewish Leaders had Jesus brought before their Council.

'Are you God's Chosen Leader?' they said. 'Tell us.'

'You won't believe me if I tell you,' said Jesus. 'You won't answer any questions I ask you. Do you remember the dream Daniel saw at night? –

> In the cloudy heavens
>> I saw the figure of a man
>> coming into God's presence
>> and being presented to him.

God gave him power and honour
and made him king.
His power shall last
for ever;
his kingly rule
shall never be overthrown.

'This will all come true – from this very moment.'

'You are God's Son, then?' they all called out.

'It's you who use the words,' said Jesus.

'What are we bothering about evidence for?' they said. 'We've heard it for ourselves from his own lips!'

The whole Council got up and took him to Pilate, the Roman Governor. These were the charges brought against him.

'This fellow calls himself a king,' they said. 'We've found him raising rebellion and telling citizens not to pay their taxes to the Emperor.'

'Are you the Jewish King?' Pilate asked Jesus.

'It's you who use the word,' he said.

'My judgement,' Pilate told the Jewish Leaders and the crowds, 'is that the man's innocent.'

They wouldn't have that.

'He's a mob leader,' they said. 'All over the south he's spreading his ideas. He started in the north, in Galilee, and now he's here in the capital city!'

'Is the fellow a Galilean?' Pilate asked, when he heard the word 'Galilee'.

When he found out that Jesus belonged to the country Herod ruled, Pilate sent Jesus off to him for trial, for he was in the city for the Feast.

Herod was very glad to see Jesus. He had heard many stories about him, and for a very long time had wanted to see him – he wanted to see him do a miracle. He asked him all sorts of questions, but Jesus made no reply.

The Jewish Leaders were standing near Jesus, loudly telling Herod all the crimes they said he was guilty of. Herod and his soldiers insulted him and made fun of him. At last, Herod dressed him like a real king and sent him back to Pilate.

Pilate and Herod had been enemies, but on this day they became good friends.

Pilate sent for the Jewish Leaders.

'You brought this man before me as a mob-leader,' he said. 'You were here when I examined him. I found nothing in what you had to say against him. Nor did Herod – he just sent him back to this court. He hasn't done anything that deserves the death sentence. I'll flog him and set him free.'

'Take him away!' the crowd shouted all together. 'Set Barabbas free for us!' (Barabbas had been thrown into prison as a murderer and a leader of a rebellion in the city.)

Pilate wanted to set Jesus free; so he called out to the crowd again. But they kept on shouting –

'Hang him on a cross! Hang him on a cross!'

Pilate spoke a third time to the crowd.

'But what's he done wrong? I find him innocent of anything that deserves the death sentence. I'll flog him and set him free.'

The crowd went on yelling, demanding the death sentence. The shouting of the crowd won the day, and Pilate gave orders that they should have their way.

He set free the man who had been imprisoned for rebellion and murder – the man they were asking for; and he handed Jesus over to them – they could do what they liked with him.

At Skull Hill   *Luke 23:32-49, 55-56a*

Jesus was not alone when he died; two other men, both bandits, were marched off with him to be put to death on Skull Hill. They hung all three on crosses; Jesus hung between the other two.

'Father,' Jesus kept on praying, 'forgive them. They don't know what they are doing.'

The soldiers went on tossing up for his clothes and then shared them out. The crowds stood by, watching.

The Jewish Leaders just laughed at him.

'He could save other people all right!' they sneered. 'Let him save himself now – if he really is God's Chosen Leader!'

The soldiers also joined in the foolery. They marched up to him and presented him with their sour wine.

'Get yourself out of this – if you are the Jewish King!' they called out.

Above the head of Jesus was the notice: THE JEWISH KING.

One of the bandits hanging alongside him cursed him too.

'You're God's Chosen Leader, are you?' he shouted. 'Get yourself and us out of this, then!'

The other bandit told him to be quiet.

'Aren't you afraid even of God?' he said. 'You've been given the same sentence as he has. We deserve it; we're guilty. This man hasn't done anything wrong.'

He turned to Jesus.

'Don't forget me,' he said, 'when you are King.'

'Believe me,' said Jesus, 'you'll be with me in heaven itself – today.'

Then Jesus raised his voice.

'Father,' he prayed (in the words of an old hymn), 'I put my whole life in your hands.'

With these words he died.

The officer in charge of the guard was watching.

'This man was innocent,' he said.

The crowds who had come out to see the three men die were staring at everything that happened. They went home, horrified at what they had seen.

The friends of Jesus watched all this from a distance.

The women who had come with Jesus from Galilee were among them. When his body was taken down from the cross they followed, and found out where the grave was and how his body was placed in it. Then they went home to get perfumes ready.

Not the End but the Beginning

When Jesus had been arrested and executed, his friends thought everything was over.

They had not really understood Jesus. They thought he would be the great deliverer of his people from their enemies. But he was not this sort of deliverer. Now he was dead, there was nothing more that they could do. Dr Luke wants us to see how certain they were that the story was finished.

But it certainly was not finished. To their great surprise, they found that the story had only just begun. This is his account of what happened.

We shall not discuss this important story here. But in *Paul the Explorer*, we shall see what this story meant to Paul, and, in *Jesus – Leader and Lord*, what he and John, who wrote the Fourth Gospel, had to say about it.

The Women at the Grave   *Luke 23:56b-24:11*

The women rested on the Saturday – work of all kinds on the Holy Day was forbidden by Jewish law.

At dawn, on Sunday morning, they went to the grave and took the perfumes that they had got ready. They found that someone had already rolled away the great stone from the mouth of the cave. They went inside but found it empty.

They didn't know what to do. Suddenly two men in shining clothes came right up to them. The women were very frightened – they didn't dare even to look up at them.

'Why are you looking for someone who is alive – in a graveyard where there are only dead people?' the men asked. 'Remember what he told you when he was still in Galilee – that he must be handed over to men who didn't live in God's way and face death itself, but that his death would not be the end.'

Then they remembered that Jesus had told them this. They left the grave and went back to report everything that had happened to the eleven close friends of Jesus and all the others. But their story seemed to the others a lot of nonsense; nobody believed a word of it.

On a Country Road   *Luke 24:13-35*

That same Sunday two friends of Jesus – one of them was Cleopas – were walking back to a village, the village of Emmaus, about seven miles away. They were discussing what had happened on the Friday.

As they talked and argued, Jesus himself joined them and walked along the road with them. They looked at him, but he didn't seem to be anybody they knew.

'What's all the talk about?' he asked.

They stopped, looking completely downcast.

'Are you the only visitor in the city who doesn't know what's been going on this last day or two?' said Cleopas.

'What?' he asked.

'Why,' they said, 'all this about Jesus from Nazareth. He was a Man of God indeed – you could tell that from the way he talked and what he did. He made God real – and everybody knew it. Our Leaders handed him over to the Roman Government to sentence to death, and they hung him on a cross. He'd made us all feel that he was the man to set our people free; but he wasn't.

'The story's three days old now,' they added. 'Some of our own women, though, gave us a shock this morning. They were at his grave at dawn; but it was empty, they said, and they came back with a story, if you please, about seeing angels – angels who talked about his being alive. Some of us went off to the grave there and then. The women's story about the body was true all right, but they didn't see anything of Jesus himself.'

'How dull you are!' said Jesus. 'How slow you are to see what the Bible's all about! Hadn't God's Chosen Leader got to face death like this? Wasn't this his only way to triumph?'

He told them the whole Bible story again. He began with Moses who led the people out of Egypt and went on to talk about the great Men of God like Isaiah and Jeremiah. He showed them what *they* had to say about God's Chosen Leader.

By this time they had reached the village and the end of their journey. Jesus was going on along the road beyond the village, and they had some trouble in persuading him to stop there.

'Come in and stay with us,' they said. 'It's getting dark and daylight will soon be gone.'

So he went home with them.

It was supper time, and he sat down at the table with them.

He picked up a loaf, said grace, broke it and gave it to them to eat. They were looking at him, and suddenly they knew who he was – and he was gone!

'Wasn't it thrilling to listen to him as we walked along the road,' they said to one another, 'and didn't he make the Bible come alive?'

They got up at once and were off back to the city. They found the eleven close friends and other friends in the room together.

'He's really alive again,' the men in the room told them. 'Peter's seen him!'

The two of them reported what had happened as they were walking along the road, and how they'd realised who he was when he broke the loaf at supper.

In the House *Luke 24:36-49*

The friends of Jesus went on talking together. Suddenly Jesus himself stood there in the room with them. They were scared and terrified; they thought they were seeing a ghost.

516

'What are you troubled about?' asked Jesus. 'Why are you so full of doubts? Look at my hands and my feet – it's me. Touch me and look at me – you can't touch a ghost as you can touch me.'

They couldn't believe what they saw, for joy and astonishment.

'Have you anything to eat?' he asked.

They gave him a piece of cooked fish, and they watched him take it and eat it.

He went on to make the story of the Bible plain to them so that they could see what it was really about.

'I told you all this when we were in Galilee together,' he said. 'What the Bible says about the work I've been doing must come true. You know what it says – God's Chosen Leader must face death, but his death isn't the end of everything; he will soon rise to life again. This must be told to everybody everywhere, all over the world, starting from this city. People must be told that if they change their ways God will forgive them for all the wrong things they have done. You know this is true – you have seen it all with your own eyes.

'Look, I shall give you what God my Father promised – his own power in your hearts. But you must stay here in this city until you are given it.'

At Bethany

Luke 24:50-53

Jesus took his friends out of the city, almost as far as Bethany Village.

He lifted his hands up in prayer and asked God to be with them. And while he was praying he left them.

They went back to the city as happy as could be; they almost lived in the Temple, thanking God for all he had done.

Part Two – Across the World

A Letter to His Excellency Theophilus   *Acts 1:1-5*

In the first part of my work, Your Excellency, I have told the story of Jesus – all he began to do and say. I bring this to an end by telling you what orders he gave to his friends on the day when he was taken up from us.

After his death, for a month or more, he showed himself alive again to his friends and talked to them about God's Way. While he was with them, he told them not to leave the city.

'You must wait here,' he said, 'until God gives you his power, as he has promised to do and as I have told you. John the Hermit baptised people with water; before long God will give you his own power in your hearts.'

The second part of my work tells you what happened then.

                                                                    Luke

The story now begins again. Jesus is alive again! That makes all the difference.

God's raising Jesus to life again is the part of the story that many people find very difficult to believe. 'We can believe', they say, 'that Jesus was a good and great man; but how can we believe that such an improbable and amazing thing as this happened?'

We shall come back to this in our last book, *Jesus Leader and Lord*, where we shall see what Paul and John had to say about it. For they found it just as improbable and amazing as we do; and yet they were sure it happened.

The first Friends* of Jesus did not agree among themselves just how it happened. After all, they never expected it to happen and they were taken by surprise; they had thought, when they saw Jesus executed, that it was all over and finished. (Look up 'On a Country Road', p. 515)

But now they knew that the death of Jesus was by no means the end of the story. They gave as honest an account as they could of what happened; they knew that Jesus was their Friend for ever, and now they were ready to die for him, if need be. Four of them – and these were not all – did die for him: Stephen, James (John's brother), Peter and Paul. Knowing

---

* We shall print 'Friends of Jesus' with a capital letter in this part. This was one of the names Christians used for themselves in the earliest days (look up Acts 27:3; John 14:14-15).

that Jesus was alive for ever made them new men and gave them their courage.

The World Adventure had now clearly begun. Four men took a leading part in it.

Stephen was the first to see that Palestine was too small for Jesus; only the world itself was big enough, for God's love is for everybody. He was the first man to die for Jesus.

Philip went to Samaria; he was also the first man to win an Egyptian as a Friend of Jesus.

Peter and Paul were the great leaders.

Dr Luke tells us, in a very vivid story, how Peter came to see that 'God has no favourites'. He welcomed a Roman officer as a Friend of Jesus, and told the Friends of Jesus in Jerusalem City that they must be much bolder than they had been.

But Paul was the man who saw clearly what Jesus wanted his Friends to do – the man who, when the story begins, was his bitter enemy. He knew that the Good News must be told to Jew and foreigner alike. We shall tell Paul's story in *Paul the Explorer*. Here we have chosen six stories from Dr Luke's notebook to show how the Good News was taken to Cyprus, Anatolia, Asia and Greece until at last it reached Rome itself. Dr Luke must have been very proud that it was the Friends of Jesus in his own city of Antioch who took the lead in this world adventure.

We do not know who first told the Good News in Rome; there were Friends of Jesus in the city and in other Italian towns, as you will see, when Paul got there. Perhaps Italian Jewish merchants heard the Good News when they were pilgrims in Jerusalem, and took it home with them. When Dr Luke tells us how Paul came as a prisoner to Rome, he wants us to see him as the representative of all the Friends of Jesus who took the Good News 'to the ends of the earth'.

The Venture Begins Again

You will notice, as the story begins again, how far the Friends of Jesus were from understanding him. They still thought he was going to be the deliverer of his people from their enemies.

So, at the beginning of the second part of the story, Dr Luke tells us what orders Jesus gave his Friends. They were to tell the Good News in Jerusalem City, but they were not to stop there. They were to go out all over the world.

They would need God's own power to do God's work. So Dr Luke goes on to tell us how, a few weeks later, God's power was given to them.

The Last Words of Jesus   *Acts 1:6-14*

Jesus and his Friends were together on the hill called 'Olive Orchard'.

'Lord,' they asked him, 'will you now make the Jewish people a free nation again?'

'That's God's business!' said Jesus. 'It's not your business to ask "How long are we going to be an occupied country?" or "When shall we be free?" You will be given God's own power when his spirit comes into your hearts; and then *your* business will be to go all over the world to tell everybody what you know about me. You must start here in this city first of all, go out into your own homeland, and then right to the very ends of the earth.'

With these words, Jesus was hidden by a cloud and they saw him no more.

His Friends went back to the city and to the room where they were staying. They were all there – Peter, John, James, Andrew, Philip, Thomas, Bartholomew, Matthew, James (whose father was Alphaeus), Simon (who had been a member of the Resistance Movement) and Judas (the one whose father was James). They spent their time together in prayer. The women Friends of Jesus were there too – and his mother, Mary, and his brothers.

The Great Day   *Acts 2:1-18, 22-24, 32-33, 36-41*

It was now the time of the Feast, 'The Fiftieth Day' (Pentecost), when Jewish people remembered how Moses gave them God's Law on Mount Sinai.

The Friends of Jesus were all together in the house where they were staying. Then it happened. Suddenly – as if a storm of wind and fire burst upon them – they were all filled with God's own power and they began to talk in many strange ways. God gave them the power to speak out boldly.

Jewish pilgrims from lands all over the world were staying in Jerusalem City; they came from Mesopotamia in the east, from the shores of the Black Sea in the north, from Egypt in the south, and even from Rome in the west.

Roman Empire

521

A great crowd gathered, talking excitedly; they were amazed and didn't know what to think.

'What's all this about?' they were asking.

Others thought it was all very strange.

'They're all drunk,' they said.

Peter stood up, and the other close Friends of Jesus stood up with him. He shouted over the noise of the crowd.

'Men of the South! Citizens of this city!' he called out. 'This is something you all ought to know about – so listen to me. You've got it all wrong. These men aren't drunk – after all, it's only nine o'clock in the morning. What's happened is something you'll find in your Bibles. Do you remember these words? –

> In the days that are to be
> > I will give my Spirit to everybody;
> > your people shall understand me –
> > your old men shall dream dreams,
> > your young men shall see visions.
> Even to slaves
> > I will give my Spirit.

'My fellow countrymen, listen to me.

'You yourselves know all about Jesus of Nazareth. He lived and worked among you. All he did was proof enough that God sent him and that God was with him. He cured sick people; that was a sign of God's power. You handed him over to the Romans and killed him. This, indeed, was all part of God's plan, for God raised him to life again; death could not be the end of his work. All of us here have met him and been with him since his death and know he is alive. God has given him high honour. Long ago God promised to give us his own power in our hearts; he has kept his promise and through Jesus he has given us his power. These are not idle words; you can see and hear for yourselves. Let all the Jewish people be in no doubt that God has made the man you killed Leader and Lord.'

They were very troubled when Peter spoke like this.

'Brother men,' they said, 'what shall we do?'

'You must change your ways,' said Peter, 'join the company of the Friends of Jesus as a sign that you are really sorry, and know that God has forgiven you. God will give you the power of his Spirit in your hearts. His promise is for all the Jewish people – you and your descendants; and it's not only for Jewish people; it is, as the Bible says, "for all those who live in far-off lands", everybody everywhere. What matters is not who we are but whom God calls.'

Peter told them the story of Jesus again and again and called them to make up their minds.

'This is a dishonest world today,' he said. 'Have nothing to do with its dishonesty.'

About three thousand people accepted what Peter said, and joined the company of the Friends of Jesus.

Jerusalem City

Many of the Friends of Jesus still did not understand what he wanted them to do. They told the Good News in Jerusalem City, as he had told them to do; but it looks as if they thought that this was *all* he wanted them to do.

They were certainly changed men and women, very different people from what they had been before. They were brave, and they lived together as members of God's Family. They faced the anger of the people and of the Jewish Leaders with courage, and they told the Good News fearlessly.

But they were soon to learn how much more Jesus wanted them to do.

How the Friends of Jesus Lived   Acts 2:42-47; 4:32-37; 5:14-16

The Friends of Jesus made a great stir in the city.

They lived day by day in God's Way as Jesus had shown them; Peter and James and John explained it to them.

They lived together like members of one family.

When they had supper together, they broke the loaf, shared it as Jesus had done at the last supper on the night before he died, and remembered what Jesus had done for everybody everywhere.

They spent much time in prayer.

They lived together and shared everything with one another. They sold their property and possessions and shared the money out so that nobody went without anything they needed. Every day they went to Temple worship, and met at home to 'break the loaf' together. They shared their meals together with real happiness. All this was their way of thanking God for all he had done for them. The people in the city thought well of them. Day by day, with God's help, their numbers grew.

They were one in heart and mind, and none of them thought that their own things were just for their own use – they were for everybody to share. So the close Friends of Jesus, like Peter, made it very clear what 'Jesus being alive again' really meant.

They were a happy company. Nobody went without what they needed. The rich people among them sold their lands and houses, and brought the money they got to their leaders. It was then shared out as each had need.

Here is an example. One of them, Joseph, was a rich man (Peter and his friends called him Barnabas). He was born in the island of Cyprus but he worked in the Temple, helping in the services there. He owned a field. He went and sold it and brought the money to the leaders.

More and more people, crowds of men and women, believed in Jesus and joined his company of Friends. Just as Jesus healed those who were ill, so did his Friends. People brought sick people on beds and mats out into the streets.

'Peter's shadow will fall on them as he walks along,' they said.

They brought the sick from villages outside the city, too.

Clash with the Jewish Leaders – How the Trouble Began

Acts 3:1-26; 4:1-4

Peter and John were walking one day up to the Temple. It was three o'clock in the afternoon, and people were gathering there for prayer.

In those days, a lame man whom everybody knew used to sit at one of the Temple gates – the 'Beautiful Gate'. He had been a cripple all his life, and his family put him there to beg from people as they were going into the Temple. This afternoon he was being carried to his pitch just as Peter and John came along. He caught sight of them and asked for money.

They stopped.

'Look at us,' said Peter, watching him closely.

He stared back at them both; he thought he was going to get something.

'I've no money,' said Peter, 'but I'll give you what I have: In the name of Jesus of Nazareth, get up and walk.'

He got hold of the man's hand and pulled him up. His feet and ankles became strong at once; he jumped about, stood still and walked round. Then he went into the Temple with Peter and John, now walking, now jumping, and thanking God all the time.

The crowd saw him walking round and thanking God. One after another they realised who he was – he was the beggar at the Temple Gate! They were amazed at what had happened to him. He kept holding on to Peter and John, and the people came crowding round them.

By now they had got as far as Solomon's Porch; and, when Peter saw what a crowd there was, he stood and faced them.

'Fellow countrymen,' he said, 'why does this surprise you? Why do you stare at us? There's nothing special about *us*; we didn't make this man walk about like this. Remember what the Bible says – "The God of our fathers, who has cared for us from the beginning of our history . . . has given great honour to his Servant"; the words "his Servant" there mean Jesus.'

He went on to tell them again the story of Jesus, how he died and how he was alive again.

'It was his trust in Jesus,' he said, 'that has made a healthy man of this beggar you all know so well. I know that you didn't really know what you were doing when you treated Jesus as you did. But he is God's Servant, and God raised him to life for your good, to get you to change your ways.'

At this moment the chief of police and some priests pushed their way in. They didn't want the Friends of Jesus to talk to the people like this and tell them that Jesus was alive. They arrested Peter and John and took them off to prison for the night, for it was now getting dark.

The fact was that many of the people had taken Peter at his word – the number was reckoned at about five thousand.

Next Day   *Acts 4:5-23*

Next morning, the Council of the Jewish Leaders were called together – the judges who had sentenced Jesus to death were among them. Peter and John were put in the dock.

'By what right did you do this?' the judges asked. 'Who are you?'

Peter spoke out – a man inspired.

'My lords,' he said, 'are we being questioned about a good deed done to a lame man? I can tell you the answer – and the whole country ought to know: in the name of Jesus of Nazareth, dead on a cross, raised by God to life again, this man stands before you in good health.

We know what you think of Jesus – but do you remember the words of the Bible –

> The stone the builders would not use
> has become the keystone?

'There's no other way to put things right – only by the Way Jesus made plain. One man, and one man only, matters for everybody everywhere – and that man is Jesus.'

The members of the Council stared at the boldness of Peter and John. They knew that they were laymen without any proper education, and they were amazed. And they knew, too, that they had been in the company of Jesus. But there was the beggar himself standing in the court, as healthy as any of them; how could they say nothing had happened?

They had the men taken out of court. They had to talk this matter over together.

'What are we going to do with these men?'

That was the question.

'Everybody in the city knows what these men have done.'

'We can't say it didn't happen.'

'We don't want the report to spread far and wide.'

'We'd better just let them off with a warning and tell them not to talk about Jesus any more.'

They decided just to warn them.

They called Peter and John back, and told them what the judgement of the court was: no more public speaking of any kind anywhere about Jesus of Nazareth; all this must stop.

'Well,' the two men said, 'you must make up your own minds whom we ought to obey – you or God – when we are doing God's work. Our duty is plain – we can't stop talking about what we ourselves have seen and heard.'

The Council repeated its warning and then set them free. They couldn't think of any way of punishing them. The crowds made that impossible; all over the city they were saying that God was behind it all.

'After all, the beggar was over forty years old,' the people said.

Peter and John went back to their friends, free men, and told them what the Council had said.

Prison Again *Acts 5:12, 17-42*

Peter and John and the other Friends of Jesus went on telling the Good News. They met together in the Temple. Many people joined their company, and many sick people were cured.

The Jewish Leaders were very angry about all this. So they arrested the Friends of Jesus again and put them in the common prison. But they escaped during the night, and by dawn they were back in the Temple, telling the Good News again to the people there.

While this was happening, the High Priest and the Jewish Leaders called the Council together, and sent for the prisoners. The police officers went to the prison, but the prisoners were no longer there. They went back without them.

'We found the prison safely locked all right,' they reported. 'The warders were on guard at the doors. When we unlocked the doors, we found nobody inside.'

When the Chief Constable and the members of the Council heard this report, they had no idea what to do or what would happen next. Then someone came in with a report.

'The prisoners are back in the Temple, talking to the crowds,' he said.

The Chief Constable himself went to the Temple with police officers and brought them back to the court. They were very careful not to use any violence; they were afraid the crowd might start stoning them. The Friends of Jesus faced the judges, and it was the High Priest who spoke.

'We gave you strict orders to stop talking about Jesus ,' he said. 'Now everybody in the city is talking about him, and you're trying to make it look as if we were the people who killed him.'

'It's God's orders we must obey,' said Peter, 'not yours. The story we are telling is the plain truth. We are only talking about what we've seen for ourselves. God's power in us is proof of it too, the power he gives to all those who obey him.'

These words made them very angry and they wanted to pass the death sentence.

But one of the members of the Council stood up – Gamaliel, a lawyer who was deeply respected by the people of the city. He ordered the prisoners out of the courtroom for a few minutes.

'My fellow-countrymen,' he said, 'be careful what you are about to do with these men. We've had people like them before. There was Theudas; he set himself up as a leader of the people. Four hundred men joined him. But he got killed, and all his followers were scattered. The whole affair came to nothing. Then there was Judas – he came from

Galilee too. He raised a rebellion, when the Romans were carrying out a census of the population here. He died, and all his followers were scattered. The point is this: keep your hands off these men and leave them alone. If this affair is just another popular uprising, it will come to nothing. If God is at the back of it, you can't stop these men – you'll be fighting against God himself!'

The Council agreed with him. They fetched the Friends of Jesus back into court and had them flogged. They ordered them to stop talking about Jesus, and then set them free again.

The Friends of Jesus left the court happy men, happy because it was for telling the story of Jesus that they had been treated so shamefully. But they didn't stop telling the people about him, either in the Temple or at home.

Palestine

About this time one of the Friends of Jesus, Stephen (whose story we shall tell later) told the Good News boldly in one of the city Meeting Houses. He could see what a different world Jesus wanted it to be, and he boldly said that all Jewish people must now change their way of life and begin to live in God's Way. Everything must be changed.

The Jewish Leaders arrested him and had him put to death. Other Friends of Jesus, who shared Stephen's point of view, were now also marked men and their lives too were in danger. So they escaped from the city, and went off to other towns and villages, some in Palestine itself, and some beyond its frontiers to other lands.

In this wider world they began to understand Jesus much more clearly.

We begin with those who went to other towns and villages in Palestine. Dr Luke tells us two stories of a Friend of Jesus called Philip, to show us something of what happened there.

In Samaria   *Acts 8:4-25*

Philip escaped north to a city in Samaria and told the crowds there the story of Jesus.

They listened to him and watched his good deeds – sick people were cured and lame people walked again. Everybody felt that Philip was telling them the truth about God, and the city was a very happy city.

There was a magician, Simon, living there. For many years his magic had amazed everybody, in the city and far beyond it. He called himself 'The Great Magician'. Members of the Government as well as the citizens were taken in by him.

'This man is indeed the Great Servant of God,' they said.

Now everything was changed. The people listened to Philip as he told them the Good News about God and the story of Jesus; many men and women became Friends of Jesus. Even Simon the magician became a Friend of Jesus and stayed with Philip. Philip's good deeds amazed even him.

News about all this came at last to the Christian Leaders in Jerusalem City.

They sent Peter and John to find out what was happening.

Nobody in Samaria had yet learned all that it meant to be a Friend of Jesus. So Peter and John held meetings for prayer, and asked God to give them his power. They put their hands on those who had become the Friends of Jesus – as a sign that God would give them his power – and God gave them his power.

Simon the magician was there and saw what happened. He brought some money and gave it to Peter and John.

'Show me how to do this,' he asked, 'so that I can put my hands on people too and get God to give them his power.'

'May your money perish with you!' said Peter. 'Do you think you can buy God's gift as you can buy magic – with money? You're no real Friend of Jesus; you haven't changed your heart at all. And what you've just done is a terrible thing. You must change the whole way you think and live, and you must ask God to forgive the thoughts that are in your heart, if possible. I can see how much of a magician you are still!'

'Pray to God for me,' said Simon, 'so that nothing terrible may happen to me.'

Peter and John told the people again the story of Jesus and explained the Good News to them. Then they went home to Jerusalem City; and on their way they told the Good News in many of the villages of Samaria.

On the Desert Road   Acts 8:26-40

The Desert Road goes down from Jerusalem City to the plain and then on to Egypt.

One day, a high officer of the Queen of Upper Egypt, her Chief

Treasurer, was riding in his carriage along the Desert Road. He had come all the way to Jerusalem City on pilgrimage, and was now going home. He was sitting in his carriage and reading the Bible aloud.

God had already spoken to Philip.

'At midday,' God had told him, 'be on the Desert Road.'

So Philip was on the road as the Chief Treasurer's carriage came along.

'Go up to this carriage,' said God, 'and join the traveller.'

Philip ran up to the carriage and heard the officer reading the Bible.

'Do you know what it all means?' he asked.

'How can I?' he said. 'I need someone to explain it to me.'

He invited Philip to climb up into the carriage and sit beside him.

The officer was reading the great poem in the Bible about God's Servant. Here is a verse of the poem:

> As sheep on the way to the butcher
>   and lambs in the hands of a shearer make no noise;
>   so God's Servant keeps quiet.
> He was badly and unfairly treated;
>   who will be able to talk about his descendants?
>   for at last they killed him.

'My question is this,' said the officer. 'Who is he talking about? Is he talking about himself? Or is he talking about somebody else?'

This gave Philip his chance. He began by explaining the poem to the officer and went on to tell him the Good News of Jesus.

As they were going along the road, they came to some water.

'Look – there's water here,' said the officer. 'What's to stop me from joining the company of the Friends of Jesus here and now?'

He told the driver to stop the carriage. Both of them, Philip and the officer, went down to the water. Philip baptised him there and then; and the officer joined the company of the Friends of Jesus.

They came up out of the water. God had other work for Philip to do. The officer lost sight of him, but went on to Egypt a very happy man.

Philip turned up at a nearby town, Azotus, and then went on from town to town telling people the Good News. At last he came to the port of Caesarea, the headquarters of the Roman Army.

World Adventure: Everybody Everywhere Matters

So far the Friends of Jesus have stayed in Palestine. They have been telling the Good News to the Jewish people, as Jesus did.

They now begin to realise that the Good News is for the whole world, not just for their own countrymen. Three men – Stephen, Peter and Paul – helped them to see how wide was the work that Jesus wanted them to do. The adventure Jesus called them to was a world adventure.

The Man Who Died for It: Stephen

We wish we knew more about Stephen, the first man to see that the Good News was for everybody everywhere and the first man to die, as a Friend of Jesus, in the world adventure. But all we know about him is what Dr Luke tells us in the story which follows.

His Arrest   *Acts 6:8-8:3*

There were many Jewish people in Jerusalem City who had not been born in Palestine. They had come from their homes in such far away places as North Africa and Asia. They spoke Greek and read the Bible in Greek Many were freed slaves or the sons of freed slaves. They had their own Meeting House in the city where they met together to worship God – the Freedmen's Meeting House. Most of them had come on pilgrimage. Some of these Jewish people had joined the company of the Friends of Jesus; and their leader was Stephen, a man who spoke, as Jesus had spoken, with such charm and power that people felt they had to listen.

Stephen told the Good News to these Jewish people from overseas in their Meeting House. Many of them got up and argued with him, but they could not answer *his* arguments. He spoke sensibly and with God's power.

So they made secret plans. They spread rumours about him.

'We've heard him say terrible things about Moses who led us out of Egypt,' they whispered, 'and even about God himself!'

This made the Jewish people and their Leaders very angry indeed; and they arrested Stephen and dragged him off to the Jewish Council.

'This fellow never stops insulting the holy Temple and our religion,' they got men to lie. 'Why, we've even heard him say that this Jesus of Nazareth will knock this Temple down and change the way in which Moses taught us to live.'

All this time Stephen stood there, and members of the Council were sitting and staring at him, for there was an angelic look on his face.

'Is all this true?' asked the High Priest.

Stephen then spoke to the Council, and he had a lot to say.

His Defence

He told them their national story, how they became 'the People of God' in the days of Abraham and Joseph and Moses. He tried to make clear to them what God had really wanted them to be.

'Our ancestors,' he said, 'always worshipped God in a *tent*. God told Moses to set up a *tent* in the camp on the march across the desert, and they took it with them wherever they went. They set it up here in Palestine, and here it stayed until David became King. It was only then we began to think about a *building* for God. It was King David who wanted to build a Temple for God. He didn't build it, you know; it was his son Solomon who built it.

'But you see what this means: God doesn't really live in buildings. The Bible puts it plainly –

> Heaven is my throne;
>   earth is my footstool.
> What kind of house will you build for me,
>   says God,
>   or where can I stay?
> Haven't I made everything in heaven and earth?

'Only the world is big enough for God, and we must live in his Way. But you Jewish people are always the same, as the Bible makes clear – you will never listen to God. You are just the same as your ancestors. Is there any Man of God your ancestors did not treat badly? They even killed the Men of God, although they were explaining God's Way and telling them how one day he would send his Chosen Leader. In our own day God *has* sent his Chosen Leader, and all you could do was to hand him over to the Romans and have him killed – you whom God himself has taught but who never did what he told you!'

They had listened quietly to him so far, but these last words made them wild with anger and they hissed at him. Stephen himself was filled with God's power and gazed over their heads. All he was thinking about and all he could see was – Jesus, full of God's glory and full of God's power.

'I see God's throne in heaven,' he said, 'and Jesus at God's right hand!'

His Death

The whole crowd broke into a great roar. They pressed their hands to their ears to shut out the sound of his voice; and in one great rush they tumbled over one another to get at him. They dragged him outside the city to stone him to death.

The men whose duty it was to see that he was really dead brought their clothes and put them down before a young officer of the court called Saul.

'Lord Jesus, receive me,' Stephen kept praying, even while they were throwing the stones at him.

He knelt down on the ground.

'O God,' he called out, 'forgive them this great wrong they are doing.'

It was all over. Saul was quite sure the right thing had been done.

That wasn't all that happened on that day, either. The crowds went off to get hold of other Friends of Jesus like Stephen, but they escaped into the country districts of Judea and Samaria. The close Friends of Jesus like Peter and John were left alone.

But Saul wanted more than the death of one man; he wanted to get rid of all the Friends of Jesus. He went from house to house, and dragged men and women off to prison.

The Man Who Began It: Peter

We have already seen how brave a man Peter was. He was not afraid of government or people, and he knew how dangerous it was to stand up in the Temple and tell the crowds the Good News about God 'in the name of Jesus'.

Yet he had not seen how wide God's love was and how big was the adventure Jesus had called him to. But one day he came to Caesarea, the headquarters of the Roman Army, and met a Roman Officer – a foreigner, not a Jew like himself. The officer, Captain Cornelius, was a good man who loved God and became a Friend of Jesus. It was then that Peter realised what Jesus had really cared for – the whole world, not just his own country of Palestine.

Lydda

Peter was going about the country visiting the Friends of Jesus. One day he went down from Jerusalem City to visit those who lived in the town of Lydda.

There he met a man called Aeneas, who was paralysed and who had been in bed for eight long years.

'Aeneas,' said Peter, 'Jesus cures you. Get up and make your bed yourself.' He stood straight up there and then.

All the people who lived in Lydda and the nearby town of Sharon saw for themselves that the man was strong and well again. That made them think seriously about the story of Jesus.

Joppa

In Joppa, a seaside town not far from Lydda, there lived a Friend of Jesus called Tabitha. She spent her time helping people in every way she could. She fell ill and died, and was laid in the room on the flat roof of the house.

The Friends of Jesus heard that Peter was at Lydda and they sent two men to tell him what had happened.

'Come across to us,' they said, 'and come quickly.'

Peter got up and went back with them; and when he got there they took him straight away up to the room on the roof. The widows whom Tabitha had helped crowded round him, with tears in their eyes, and showed him the coats and clothes which she had made when she was alive.

Peter had them all taken outside. He then knelt down and prayed. He turned towards the body.

'Tabitha, get up,' he said.

She opened her eyes. Then she saw Peter and sat up, and he gave her his hand and helped her to her feet. He called all the others into the room and showed them Tabitha – alive.

The news spread all over Joppa, and many people became Friends of Jesus. Peter stayed for quite a long time there, and made his home with Simon, a tanner.

Captain Cornelius: 1. The Dream   *Acts 10:1-48; 11:1-18*

Caesarea was the Headquarters of the Roman Army in Palestine, and among the officers there was a man called Cornelius, a captain of the Italian Regiment. He was a good man who, with all his family, loved

God. He was always ready to help anybody in need and prayed to God every day.

One day, about three o'clock in the afternoon, he had a dream. Everything was very clear and he saw an angel of God coming towards him.

'Cornelius,' the angel called.

He stared at his visitor in terror.

'What's the matter, sir?' he asked.

'God knows all about you, your prayers and your good deeds,' he said. 'Send to Joppa and fetch a man called Simon – he's also known as Peter. He is staying with Simon the tanner; his house faces the sea.'

The angel left him.

Cornelius, without wasting a minute, called two of his slaves and one of his soldiers who loved God as he did, told them all about the dream and sent them off to Joppa.

2. Next Day

About noon next day, the three men were well on their way and had almost reached Joppa.

And it was about noon that Peter went up on to the flat roof of the house to pray. He suddenly felt hungry and wanted his dinner, but while the servants were getting it ready he fell asleep and started to dream.

It was a strange dream.

He saw something dropping down out of the open sky – something like a great sheet, tied at the four corners and being lowered to the earth. All sorts of animals and reptiles and wild birds were inside, including things no Jew, by Jewish law, was allowed to eat.

He heard a Voice speaking.

'Get up, Peter,' it said, 'kill them and eat them.'

'Never, sir,' said Peter. 'I've never eaten any forbidden food.'

'What God calls good food,' said the Voice, 'you mustn't call forbidden food.'

This happened three times. Then the thing was suddenly drawn up into the sky.

While Peter was wondering what the dream could mean, the messengers of Cornelius stood outside the gate; all this time they had been asking people the way to Simon's house.

'Is Simon, called Peter, staying here?' they called out.

Peter was still up on the roof, wondering about the dream.

'There are three men looking for you,' God told him. 'Get up and go down to them and go along with them. There's nothing to worry about; I've sent them.'

Peter went down to the men.

'I am the man you are looking for,' he said. 'What have you come for?'

'We come from Captain Cornelius, a good man who loves God – all the Jews in Caesarea will tell you that. He was told by God to invite you to his house, and to listen to what you have to say.'

Peter asked them to stay with him. Next morning, he got up and went off with them; and some of the Friends of Jesus in Joppa went along with him.

3. At Caesarea

They got to Caesarea the next day.

Captain Cornelius had asked his relatives and close friends to come along, and was looking out for Peter and the three men. He met Peter as he was entering the house, and fell down on the ground in front of him; he thought Peter must be no ordinary man.

Peter pulled him to his feet.

'Stand up,' he said, 'I'm an ordinary man like yourself.'

Talking with Cornelius, he went on into the crowded house.

'You all know about Jewish Law,' he said. 'You know it forbids a Jew to have anything to do with a foreigner – even to visit him. But I now know better, for God has made it quite clear to me that I must not call anybody at all, whoever they are, "foreigner". I couldn't say No when you sent for me. Tell me why you wanted me to come.'

Captain Cornelius told him about his dream.

'So, you see,' he said, 'I sent at once to invite you and you have kindly come along. All of us in this room know God is here, and we want to listen to what God has told you to tell us.'

'It's as clear as daylight to me now,' said Peter, 'that God has no favourites. It doesn't matter what race or nation you belong to; if you love God and do what is right, God welcomes you.

'You know what the Bible says –

He sent out his word and healed them.
and
    How lovely on the hills
        are the footsteps of the man who brings the Good News
        and calls all the world to be at peace.

'All this is really about Jesus.

'He is God's Chosen Leader; all the world is his Kingdom, and he has brought the Good News of peace.

'You yourselves, too, know something about what has happened in Palestine in our own time – the events that began in Galilee after John the Hermit had been preaching in Jordan Valley, and the story of Jesus from Nazareth Village.

'Let me tell you what really happened.

'God called Jesus to his great work, and gave him his Spirit and power. He went from village to village doing good and healing sick people; for God was with him. We saw with our own eyes all he did in Palestine and in Jerusalem City.

'He died on a Roman cross; but God soon raised him from the dead – the same Jesus we had known in Galilee. The crowds didn't see him; only those whom God had chosen saw him – we who had dinner with him when he was alive again. He told us what to do: to tell the Good News to everybody, and to make it quite clear that, in all he said and did, God has shown us what is right and what is wrong. Jesus, not Caesar or Moses, is the judge of all people everywhere. All those who trust in Jesus are forgiven for all the wrong things they have done – because he was what he was. This is surely what the Bible tells us.'

Peter was still speaking when God's power was given to everybody who had been listening to him. The Jewish Friends of Jesus who had come along with Peter were amazed – fancy God giving his power even to *foreigners*! They themselves heard them, there in the room, singing God's praises!

'God has given his power to these foreigners just as he gave it to us Jews,' said Peter. 'Can anybody say they ought not to join the company of the Friends of Jesus?'

He gave orders for them to be baptised 'in the name of Jesus'.

Afterwards they all wanted Peter to stay a few days in Caesarea.

4. Back in Jerusalem

News about what had happened in Caesarea reached the Jewish Friends of Jesus in Jerusalem and the south – foreigners had become Friends of Jesus!

Some of them thought this was wrong. Only Jews, they thought, could become Friends of Jesus; if foreigners wanted to, they should become Jews first. So when Peter went up to Jerusalem City, they took the matter up with him.

'Why did you meet foreigners,' they said bitterly, 'and share their home life?'

Peter told them the whole story – his dream at Joppa and what happened in the home of Captain Cornelius.

'Then I remembered the words of Jesus,' he went on. 'He said, you remember, "John the Hermit used water as a sign; God will give you, my Friends, his own power in your hearts". God gave these foreigners in Caesarea his own power in their hearts. If God gave to them, foreigners though they were, the same gift that he gave to us when *we* became the Friends of Jesus, who was I to say No to God himself?'

When they heard Peter talk like this, they had nothing more to say.

'Foreigners also can change their ways,' they said, 'and live in God's Way!'

And they praised God.

Trouble Again   Acts 12:1-19

Herod again arrested some of the Friends of Jesus. He had James, the brother of John, beheaded. This made him popular. So he looked round for others, and, during the Great Feast, arrested Peter as well. After his arrest, he put him in prison with sixteen soldiers on guard. He planned to parade him before the people when the Feast was over. All the Friends of Jesus could do was to pray for him, and this they did day and night.

The Feast was over and the very next day Herod had planned to bring Peter out and show him to the crowds. It was late at night. Peter was asleep. Two soldiers lay on either side of him and he was handcuffed to them. Outside the prison door, sentries stood on guard.

A light shone in the cell and a messenger from God stood there. He tapped Peter on his side and woke him up.

'Get up quickly,' he said.

The handcuffs fell from his wrists.

'Fasten your belt,' he said, 'and put your sandals on.'

Peter did what he was told.

'Put your cloak on and follow me.'

Peter followed him out. It was like a dream; it didn't seem real.

They passed the first sentry, then the second sentry, and came to the great iron gate. Beyond the gate lay the city. Nobody was there, but the gate swung open. They went through, and along the narrow street. The messenger vanished.

By this time Peter was wide awake.

'Now I know God has rescued me,' he said to himself, 'rescued me from Herod and the show the crowds were looking forward to.'

He realised what had happened, and off he went to the house of Mary, John Mark's mother, where many Friends of Jesus were meeting to pray for him.

He knocked on the door of the outer gate, and Rhoda, a maid, came to see who it was. She knew at once it was Peter's voice. Back she ran to tell everybody – she didn't stop to open the door, she was so happy.

'Peter's outside the door,' she burst out.

'You're mad,' they told her.

'It *is* Peter!' said Rhoda.

'It's his ghost,' they said.

Peter went on knocking.

At last they opened the door, and, to their amazement, there was Peter himself!

With a wave of his hand, he got them to be quiet, and told them how God had rescued him from Prison.

'Tell James and the other Friends of Jesus,' he said.

Then he left them and went away.

There was great alarm among the soldiers when daylight came. They hadn't any idea what had become of Peter. Herod ordered a search for him, but he was nowhere to be found. He had the guards examined and ordered them to be executed. Then he went down from Jerusalem to his palace at Caesarea.

The Man Who Led the Adventure: Paul

When Dr Luke was telling us about Stephen and how he died, he gave the name of the 'young officer of the court' who was in charge of the execution. His name was Saul, and he hated all the Friends of Jesus. It is this man who is going to be the hero of Dr Luke's book. For, not long after, he himself became a Friend of Jesus.

This is the story of how it happened near the city of Damascus.

Saul is a Jewish name. It was the name of the first Hebrew King, and boys of the Benjamin Clan would be proud to be called Saul. Saul was born a Roman citizen, so he had a Roman name, Paul, as well as his Jewish name. Perhaps his full name was Gaius Julius Paulus. Later in the book Dr Luke uses his Roman name, and this Roman name, Paul, is the one by which he is best known.

On the Road

Saul was hot on the trail of the Friends of Jesus, thirsting for their blood. He went to the High Priest and asked him for warrants to search the Meeting Houses in Damascus, to arrest all 'the People of God's Way' – as the Friends of Jesus called themselves – and to bring them, men and women alike, as prisoners to Jerusalem City.

He set off along the Damascus Road.

He had almost reached his journey's end when, suddenly, a light from the sky burst on him and he fell down on the road. He heard a Voice.

'Saul! Saul!' the Voice called. 'Why do you treat me like an enemy?'

'Who are you?' asked Saul.

'I am Jesus – and you are treating me like an enemy! But get up and go on into Damascus City. You'll get your orders there.'

His fellow-travellers stood speechless with fright; they heard the Voice, but they saw nobody.

Saul got up. When he tried to see where he was, he found he was blind; they had to lead him by the hand into the city. For three days he was blind and had nothing to eat or drink.

In Damascus

A Friend of Jesus, Ananias, was living in Damascus City. He had a dream, and in the dream he saw Jesus.

'Ananias!' said Jesus.

'I'm here, Lord,' he answered.

'Get up,' said Jesus, 'and go to Straight Street. Find the house where Judas lives, and ask for Saul, a citizen of Tarsus City. You'll find him praying. He's had a dream, and in his dream he has seen a man called Ananias enter the house and put his hands on his eyes and give him his sight back again.'

'Lord,' said Ananias, 'I've heard all sorts of stories about this man; he's here with a warrant to arrest all your Friends in the city.'

'Off you go,' said Jesus. 'I've marked him out as my messenger. His orders are to tell the whole world the Good News – foreigners and their governments as well as Jewish people. And I'll not hide from him the dangers he'll have to face as a Friend of mine.'

Ananias went off and found the house and put his hands on Saul.

'Brother Saul,' he said, 'it was the Lord Jesus you saw on the road outside the city. He has sent me to you. May you have your sight back again, and may you be filled with God's power!'

His sight came back – as suddenly as he had lost it – and he could see quite clearly.

He got up, and Ananias baptised him and received him into the company of the Friends of Jesus. He had a good meal and felt quite well again.

He stayed with the Friends of Jesus for a few days. The first thing he did was to go along to the Meeting House – and tell them the story of Jesus!

'He *is* God's Son,' he said.

Everybody, listening to him talk, was amazed.

'Isn't this the man who tried to wipe out the Friends of Jesus in Jerusalem City?' they asked. 'Why, he came here with a warrant for the arrest of those who live here, to take them back as prisoners to our Leaders.'

This didn't stop Saul. He spoke all the more powerfully in the Meeting Houses. He shocked the Jewish people in the city – they didn't know how to answer his arguments. He had only one thing to say – Jesus is God's Chosen Leader.

This went on for quite some time. At last the Jewish people plotted to murder him, and they picketed the city gates the whole twenty-four hours of the day. Somebody told Saul about the plot; and one night his friends took him to the city wall, and lowered him over the wall in a basket.

To Jerusalem and Tarsus
Saul went back to Jerusalem. He tried to get in touch with the Friends of Jesus there; but they were afraid of him. They thought he was just pretending to be a Friend of Jesus.

But Barnabas introduced him to the Christian Leaders. He told them how Saul had seen Jesus on the Damascus Road and been given his orders, and how he had told the Good News boldly in the Meeting Houses of Damascus City.

That settled it, and he was welcomed into all their homes. He showed the same boldness in talking about Jesus in Jerusalem City as he had in Damascus City. His chief aim was to meet the Jews from overseas and argue with them; but they, like the Damascus Jews, made up their minds to murder him.

Somebody told the Friends of Jesus about the plot, and they took him down to the port of Caesarea and sent him off home to Tarsus City.

The Great Plan

Dr Luke now leaves Palestine and takes us to Antioch City in the north. This was a large and famous city, and roads from north, south, east and west met there. It was not an old city; it had been built, two hundred or more years before, in honour of King Antiochus.

After the death of Stephen, some of his friends escaped to Antioch, and, later, Friends of Jesus from other lands came to live there. All of them believed that Jesus cared for everybody, not just for Jewish people. Antioch was crowded with people from many lands, and these Friends of Jesus began to tell the Good News to anybody who would listen, without bothering whether they were Jews or not.

Then one day, in a prayer meeting, they were sure that God wanted them to begin to take the Good News all over the world. They made up their minds to plan this great work. This is the story of what happened, and how Paul comes into it.

The *first* great day in the story of the Friends of Jesus was the day when, in Jerusalem City, they received God's power to live in his Way (p. 520); this is the *second* great day in their story – and, it is important to note, it takes place on foreign soil.

How the Good News Came to Antioch City   Acts 11:19-26

After the death of Stephen, many of the Friends of Jesus were scattered, as we have seen. Some of them went to Phoenicia, where ships set sail for Africa and Italy and Spain. Some went to the Island of Cyprus, the homeland of Barnabas. Some went to Antioch City in the north, the third greatest city of the Empire, where the great roads from Europe and Egypt and Babylon met. It was in this city that the Friends of Jesus made the great plan to take the Good News all over the world, to foreigners and Jewish people alike. This is how it happened.

At first, the Friends of Jesus in Antioch City told the Good News to Jewish people only. But Friends of Jesus from the island of Cyprus and from North Africa came to live there; and *they* began to tell the story of Jesus to Greek people, foreigners, not Jews. This was clearly what God wanted them to do, for many of the Greek foreigners believed the Good News and became Friends of Jesus.

News of all this reached Jerusalem City, and the Leaders of the Friends of Jesus there sent Barnabas off to Antioch to find out what was happening. When he got there, he saw what a difference God's love had made to them all; and he was very glad.

'You've made up your minds to be Friends of Jesus,' he told them. 'Stick to it, and don't let Jesus down.'

He was a good man, full of God's power, and he trusted God with his whole heart.

The company of the Friends of Jesus grew. So Barnabas set off for Tarsus City to find Saul, and brought him back with him to Antioch. For a whole year they met the Friends of Jesus there in their meetings together, and explained the story of Jesus to a large company of people. It was in this city that the Friends of Jesus were first nicknamed 'Christians' – 'Christ's People'.

The Great Decision   Acts 13:1-3

Now in the company of the Friends of Jesus, there were leaders who explained the meaning of the Bible and leaders who explained the meaning of all that Jesus said and did. These are their names: Barnabas, Simon the 'Black', Luke from North Africa, Manaen who had been the close friend of King Herod, and Saul. One day they were meeting for prayer and fasting.

'I have called Barnabas and Saul to a great work,' God said to them. 'Give them this work to do.'

They went on with their prayers and fasting, asking God to guide them. Then they sent Barnabas and Saul to tell the Good News to the people of the Empire.

From East to West

The Friends of Jesus in Antioch City did not know what a great adventure they were beginning, an adventure which was to spread all over the world and go on all down the centuries. It is going on still today.

Two men started out from Antioch, Barnabas and Saul. Saul was the great leader.

Dr Luke now begins the story of Saul and his journeys across the world. (From now on we will use his Roman name – Paul.) We shall tell this story in the next part, *Paul the Explorer*. Here we tell six of Dr Luke's stories to show how the Good News was taken all over the world, until at last, one spring day, Paul walked into the capital city of the Roman Empire, Rome itself.

As the Friends of Jesus walked along the roads of the Empire, climbed the mountains and sailed the seas, they began at last to understand Jesus. As they told the Good News to everybody they met, and men and women everywhere listened to it and became Friends of Jesus, they knew why Jesus had lived and died and been raised to life again. They remembered his words, and they followed his example.

So we shall find ourselves in Greek and 'barbarian' islands, in famous cities and country towns high in the mountains, and at last we shall enter the gates of Rome itself. Everybody everywhere matters.

How the Good News Came to a Greek Island   Acts 13:4-12

Barnabas and Paul set off. They were now sure that this was the work God had given them to do.

They went down to the port of Seleucia, took ship for Cyprus and landed at Salamis Town, in the eastern part of the island. John Mark went along with them to help them.

They told the story of Jesus in the Jewish Meeting Houses, and in this way they went through the whole island.

They came at last to Paphos on the west coast, where the Roman Governor, Sergius Paul, had his headquarters. Here they met a Jewish magician, called Bar Jesus, who was friendly with the Governor.

The Governor was a thoughtful man, and when he heard about Barnabas and Paul, he asked them to come to see him. He wanted to hear the story of Jesus. Bar Jesus the magician was there, and tried to prove to the Governor that they were wrong; he didn't want to lose his job.

Paul (his Roman name was the same as the Governor's) was filled with God's power and looked straight at the magician.

'There isn't a trick or a lie in your trade you don't know,' he said. 'You're a bad man. You'd twist anything for gain – even religion! But you're dealing with God not men; you shall be blind for a time – you won't even see the brightness of the sun!'

Suddenly, the magician's world went misty and dark, and he had to feel his way about and get people to lead him by the hand.

The Governor watched all this, and became a Friend of Jesus. But what amazed him was the story of Jesus.

How the Good News Came to the Highlands of Anatolia   Acts 14:8-20

Barnabas and Paul came one day to the old town of Lystra, high up in the highlands of Anatolia, where people, though they could speak Greek, usually spoke their own strange language which Paul and Barnabas couldn't understand.

There was a man here who had been lame all his life and had never been able to walk. Paul was talking to the crowd near the town gates and the lame man sat there on the roadside listening to him. Paul looked straight at him and saw the man believed he could cure him.

'Get up on your feet!' said Paul, loudly enough for everybody to hear. 'Stand up straight!'

The lame man jumped up and walked about.

The crowd saw what Paul had done, and they started shouting in their own strange language.

'The gods have come down like men and here they are in our city!' they said.

They thought Barnabas was the great god Zeus, and Paul the messenger of the gods, Hermes – because he did all the talking!

The priest of Zeus, who looked after the nearby temple called 'The Temple of Zeus-outside-the-Town', brought bulls wreathed with flowers to the town gates, to sacrifice to Barnabas and Paul as gods.

Barnabas and Paul couldn't help but hear all this noise. When they saw what it all meant, they tore their clothes and ran among the crowd.

'Sirs!' they shouted. 'What's all this for? We are just ordinary men like you, and all we're doing is bringing you Good News. Stop all this nonsense and learn what God is really like. He's the Living God; he made the sky and land and seas. He made the whole world. Until now God let people everywhere do what they thought best. Yet even then he showed you what he was like. He looked after you all. He gave you rain from the sky and harvest time. He saw that you had food to eat. All your happiness comes from him.'

Even words like this hardly stopped the crowd from going on with their sacrifice.

Then Jews from the towns where Paul and Barnabas had already been came along and told the crowd what *they* thought about them. That turned the crowd against Paul and Barnabas, and they started throwing stones at Paul. They thought they had killed him, and dragged him outside the town.

Paul's friends stood round him; they, too, thought he was dead. But he got up and went back into the town.

How the Good News Came to a Jewish Meeting House   Acts 17:10-15

Paul and his friend Silas came one day to the town of Beroea in northern Greece. They had been travelling through the night, and when they reached the town they went into the Jewish Meeting House.

The Jewish people here were better mannered than those in other towns they had visited. They listened to the story of Jesus gladly, and every day they read the Bible carefully to see if what Paul said was true. Many became Friends of Jesus, and among them were well-known Greek women and quite a number of men. But the Jewish people in the city from which Paul had come heard that he was now telling the Good News in Beroea, and they came across to cause trouble and set the mob against him.

The Friends of Jesus there at once got Paul off on his way to the sea. Silas and Timothy stayed behind, and Paul's guides took him by boat as far as the city of Athens.

How the Good News Came to the Most Famous Greek City of All

Acts 17:16-34

Paul came to Athens by boat, and he was waiting there for Silas and Timothy.

He wandered through the streets; everywhere there were temples and images of the Greek gods. This made Paul very unhappy. He had to talk to somebody about it. He went to the Jewish Meeting House and argued there; he went to the Market Place and argued with anybody who happened to be there. There were many lecturers in the city, for its university was very famous; some of them met Paul, and he argued with them.

'What's this chatterer talking about?' sneered some.

'It's some foreign fellow talking about his gods, it seems,' said others. *

The City Council was called 'Mars Hill', after the name of the hill where it used to meet in earlier times. This Council was specially interested in all new speakers who came to teach in Athens. The citizens of Athens and their foreign visitors always had time to talk about or listen to anything strange and new; they seemed to do nothing else.

The lecturers got hold of Paul and took him before the Council.

'Tell us, if you please, something more about this "News" of yours,' they said. 'What you've been talking about sounds very strange to us. We'd like to know what it's all about.'

Paul stood before the Council.

'Citizens of Athens,' he said, 'by just wandering around your streets, I can see that religion matters very much to you. I had a good look at your temples and the images of your gods. And I noticed one altar that

---

* Paul had been talking, of course, about Jesus and how he was risen from the dead. The word he used here was 'Anastasis' which simply means 'rising from the dead'; the lecturers thought it was the name of another foreign god!

had these words on it: "To an Unknown God". You do not know him; I will tell you about him.

'The God who made the world and all that's in it by that very fact is the Master of the whole world. His home can't be a temple in a street that you can build with your own hands.* He can't need temple servants, as though he had to have somebody looking after him. He gave us the very lives we live and everything we have. We may belong to different nations now, but at the beginning God made us all one people and gave us the whole world for our home. All things are in his hands – the rise and fall of nations and the boundaries of their territories. He did all this for one purpose only – that men and women might look for him and find him.

'Yet he is very near every one of us. Your own poets have said this very thing –

> In God we live and move and exist,

and

> We, too, belong to his family.

'If, therefore, we belong to God, we can't possibly think that gold and silver and stone are good enough to show us what he is like. No artist can paint God's picture, however clever or thoughtful he may be.

'What, then, has God done? He takes no notice of the past, when we didn't know what he is like. But today, in our own time, he calls all people to change their ways. We can no longer say we do not know; Jesus has made him plain. The day is fixed when everybody everywhere will be judged by this man he has chosen – and truly judged. The proof of this he has given to everyone – he has raised him from the dead.'

Some of them laughed out loud at Paul when they heard him talk like this – about God 'raising Jesus from the dead'. But there were others.

'We'll hear you again about all this,' they said.

So Paul left them.

But there were some who went along with Paul and became Friends of Jesus. Among them were Dionysius, a member of the City Council itself, and a woman whose name was Damaris.

* See the speech of Stephen (p. 532).

This story begins in Palestine, and in the port of Caesarea, the head-quarters of the Roman army.

Acts 27:1-12

The Roman Governor decided to send us by ship to Italy. He put Paul and some other prisoners in the care of Captain Julius of the Imperial Regiment whose officers served as messengers between the Emperor and his armies. There was a boat in harbour which came from a port near Troas; it was about to sail home, calling at places along the coast on the way. We went on board and set sail.

Next day we called at Sidon. Captain Julius was very good to Paul and let him visit the Friends of Jesus there and be cared for.

We put to sea again and sailed under the shelter of the island of Cyprus, for the north-west winds were blowing against us. We left the shelter of the island and sailed across the open sea to the mainland, and came to the port of Myra. There Captain Julius found an Egyptian grain-ship bound for Italy and put us on board. There were two hundred and seventy-six passengers.

For many days we sailed slowly westward, and it took us all our time to get as far as Cnidus. The wind was too strong to let us go on across the open sea; so we sailed southward round the island of Crete, where we were sheltered from the wind. It was hard enough sailing along the coast of the island, but we came at last to a small bay called Fair Havens, not far from a city. There we dropped anchor.

We had wasted a lot of time, and the dangerous season for ships had begun, when great storms blow up. Even the Jewish Feast, which took place on 5 October, was over.

Paul spoke to Captain Julius and the pilot and the ship-owner.

'Gentlemen,' he said, 'if we put to sea again now, I can see we shall run into great danger; we shall lose not only the cargo and the ship but our own lives as well.' But Captain Julius listened more to the pilot and the ship-owner than to Paul.

The harbour at Fair Havens, it was true, was not a good place to spend the winter in. Most of the officers on board were for putting to sea and trying to get to the port of Phoenix to spend the winter there. (This was the only safe harbour, in all winds, on the south coast of Crete; it faces away from the winds, north-east and south-east.)

---

* The use of 'we' in these stories suggests that Dr Luke was with Paul at the time and recorded these events in his diary.

2. The Great Storm

Acts 27:13-26

One day the wind blew gently from the south-west. Now was their chance. They weighed anchor and sailed close along the coast of Crete. Suddenly a gale, called 'The Northeaster', blew down from the land. The ship was caught and could not face the wind.

So we ran before it and were driven out to sea. We ran under the shelter of the small island of Cauda, and even then had a hard job to get the ship's boat safely tied up on deck. The sailors fastened ropes over and under the ship to stop her from breaking up. They were frightened that they might be driven southward on to the African quicksands; they put out a sea anchor, but were still swept along.

We were tossed so violently about by the storm that next day the sailors began to throw the cargo overboard. On the third day, they threw away with their own hands everything they could. For many days we saw neither sun nor stars; we were at the mercy of the storm. At last we gave up hope of ever being saved.

All this time crew and passengers hadn't bothered to eat. So Paul stood up and spoke to them all.

'Gentlemen,' he said, 'you should have listened to me. You shouldn't have sailed from Crete; you wouldn't, then, have had such damage and lost so much. But now I'm going to tell you something to cheer you up.

'You'll lose the ship, but none of you will lose your lives. I had a dream last night. A messenger of the God to whom I belong and whom I serve stood by me. "Don't be frightened, Paul," he said. "You must stand before the Emperor. God has saved the lives of all those who are sailing with you." So cheer up, my friends. I trust God that it will all happen just as I've been told. But we shall be ship-wrecked on some island.'

3. Shipwreck

Acts 27:27-44

A fortnight passed, and all the time we were drifting across the open sea.

One night – it was about midnight – the sailors guessed that we were getting near land. They dropped the lead overboard and found we were in twenty fathoms of water. When we had sailed a little farther, they dropped the lead again – this time it was fifteen fathoms. They were now frightened that we might run on to the rocks; so they threw out four anchors from the stern, and prayed for daylight.

The sailors wanted to abandon ship, and lowered the small boat into the sea.

'We only want to let the anchors down from the bow,' they lied.

Paul spoke to Captain Julius and the soldiers.

'If these men don't stay on board,' he said, 'none of you will get ashore.'

The soldiers cut the boat's ropes and let it fall into the sea.

Just before dawn, Paul told them all to get a good meal.

'For a fortnight you've been so scared you haven't bothered to eat anything. You're starving. If you'll listen to me, you'll get something inside you – you'll need it if you're going to get ashore safely. I've told you – you'll not lose a hair of your head.'

With these words, he picked up a loaf, said Grace over it while they all watched, broke it and began to eat it. They all cheered up and had a good breakfast. When everybody had eaten enough, they threw the cargo of wheat into the sea to make the ship ride lighter.

Daylight came, but they couldn't tell where they were; they could see a small bay with sandy beach – just the place, if they could get to it, to run the ship ashore. They let the anchors go and left them in the sea; and loosed the ropes that held the rudders fast. A breeze was blowing. They set the foresail, and made for the shore.

They ran into rough water where two strong currents met and drove the ship aground. The bow stuck fast and nothing could move it; while the stern, beaten by the great seas, began to break up. The soldiers were for killing the prisoners – they thought they might swim off and escape. Captain Julius stopped that; Paul was an important prisoner and he didn't want him killed. He told those who could swim to jump into the sea first and get ashore, and the others, on cargo boards or bits of wreckage, to get there as best as they could. So it was that everybody got safely to the beach.

4. On the Island of Malta   Acts 28:1-10

When we had all reached the beach, we found out where we were – the island of Malta. The natives didn't treat us as we expected, but showed us every kindness. It was beginning to rain and everybody was very cold; so they lit a bonfire and made us all feel at home.

Paul picked up a bundle of brushwood to put on the fire. There was a viper in it and the heat woke it up; it got hold of his hand and was hanging from it. The natives were watching.

'The fellow's a murderer,' they said to one another. 'He may have escaped drowning, but the Goddess of Justice has seen to it that he won't get away with it!'

Paul shook the viper off into the fire. The natives waited – surely he would swell up or suddenly fall down dead. Nothing happened. They went on waiting and watching; and still nothing happened. That changed their minds.

'He's a god himself,' they said.

The Chief of the island, a man called Publius, owned all the lands round about the bay. He welcomed us and looked after us for three days in a most friendly way. His father was very ill with fever at the time. Paul went to see him, prayed for him, put his hands on him and cured him. Then everybody else who was ill came along, and Paul cured them too. Nothing was too much for the people to do for us. And when we went on board ship to leave the island, they gave us everything we needed.

How the Good News Came to the Capital of the Empire   Acts 28:11-31

It was three months before we left. In February we went on board another Egyptian ship which had spent the winter at the island; she had 'The Heavenly Twins' as her figurehead. We put in at the port of Syracuse. The wind dropped and we had to spend three days there. We weighed anchor at last, and made for the port of Rhegium. The south wind started blowing next day, and it took us only two days to get to Puteoli, one of the ports for Rome.

We looked up the Friends of Jesus in the town, and they asked us to spend a week with them. Then we set off for Rome.

The Friends of Jesus in the city had heard we were coming and came out to meet us – more than forty miles, as far as the Market Town of Appius and The Three Inns.

When Paul saw them he thanked God and felt ready for anything.

We came at last into Rome itself.

Paul was allowed to hire a house outside the barracks and live there by himself with a soldier on guard.

He had been there only three days when he asked the Jewish Leaders in the city to meet him, and they came along.

'I want to tell you about myself, brothers,' he said. 'I have done nothing against the Jewish people or the customs of our ancestors. Yet I was handed over as a prisoner to the Romans. This happened in Jerusalem. The Romans, after a long trial, wanted to set me free – I had done nothing, they found, to deserve the death sentence. The Jews wouldn't have it. So there was only one thing to do – appeal to the Emperor. But I have no complaint to make against my own people.

'That is why I asked you to come to see me and let me talk to you. It is because of the hope my people have held for hundreds of years that I am wearing these handcuffs.'

'We haven't had any letters from Palestine about you,' they said, 'and nobody who has come here has said anything against you. We would like to hear what you've got to say. All we know about the Friends of Jesus is that everybody says they're a bad lot.'

They fixed on a day for meeting Paul, and a great crowd came to his house. He talked about God's Way. He told them the story of Jesus and tried to show them that this is what the Bible was about. He went on talking all day.

Some of them thought he was right, and some of them thought he was wrong. They couldn't agree with one another and that ended the meeting. Paul had the last word.

'You are doing just what our people have done all down the centuries. We will not listen to what God has got to say. Well, be quite sure of this: it is to foreigners everywhere the Good News about God has been sent – they will listen.'

Paul stayed for two whole years in the house he had rented. He let anybody come to see him who wanted to. He spent his time telling the Good News and explaining the story of Jesus. He did this quite openly; nobody stopped him.

Paul the Explorer

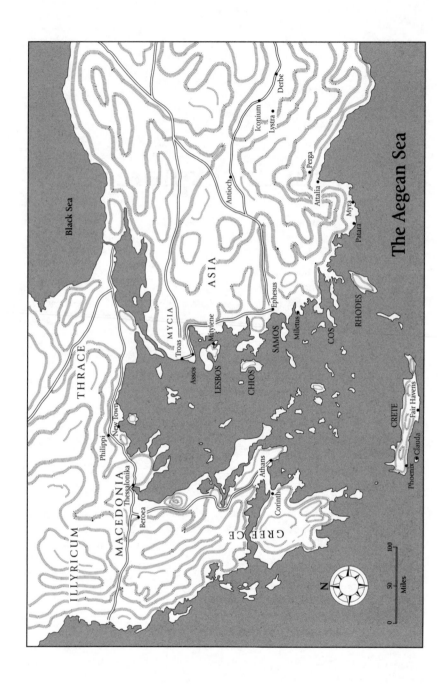

The Aegean Sea

Paul's Own Story

Paul never wrote his own life story; but he has told us a lot about himself in his letters. He often writes about himself – what he is doing, what he is planning.

Private letters are not easy for other people to follow. In letters to friends, we do not always set things out in order as we do in an essay. We write about this, and then about that, and then something else comes into our minds and we write about *that*; just as we do when we are chatting with them. Paul's letters are a little like that, for they are real letters.

So I have gathered together the passages where Paul talks about himself and his friends, and put them together, so that you can see what he had to say about himself.

I do not think Paul *talked* about himself very much to his friends; he does not seem to have said very much about himself to his good friend Dr Luke. But Paul had to *write* a lot about himself in his letters. He was bitterly attacked because of his attitude, as a Jew, to foreigners. Jewish Christians felt he was a traitor to his own country and that he had got the Good News all wrong. In defending himself he was really defending the Good News and the freedom of the friends of Jesus everywhere.

In arranging 'Paul's Own Story', one passage,* in his letter to the friends of Jesus in Anatolia, has been very helpful. People had been attacking Paul and saying that he was the kind of man who would do anything. They quoted – and quoted wrongly – incidents from his past life. He could not be trusted, they said, and he was no true friend of Jesus. To answer them, Paul tells his friends what had happened during the last twenty years of his life: he had not been the kind of man his enemies said he was – 'Here,' he says, 'is my record.' He lists the main events carefully one after another. This has given me a framework for all the other passages about himself. I have arranged them in chapters. The chapters and chapter headings are mine; the words are Paul's. I have translated them as if he were writing to us.

* Galatians 1:11-2:21

How I Became a Friend of Jesus

I am a Jew. I belong to the Benjamin clan, King Saul's clan. I grew up in a good Jewish home, and I was very patriotic. *(Philippians 3:5-6)*

When I grew up, I joined a very strict religious party, the Pharisees, and I did everything I could to become a good man; I kept every rule there was to keep. I was much more serious than many of those who grew up with me; I had a passion for all the age-old customs of my people. *(Galatians 1:14)*

But I didn't find what I was looking for. It seemed as if trying to be good made me take notice of all the bad things people do. For example, I shouldn't have known what 'envying' people was if the Bible hadn't said, 'You mustn't envy anybody'. It looked as if reading the Bible made me worse than I was! *(Romans 7:7)*

Let me be quite clear. The Bible is a good book, and what it tells us to do is good and right – it's what God wants us to do. But why should a good book not help me to be good? *(Romans 7:12-13)*

I was a real puzzle to myself: I didn't do what in my heart I really wanted to do, and I hated myself for doing what I did. All this made me most unhappy. I didn't know who could help me. And then, thank God, I found the secret of being really myself; it was Jesus who showed me God's Way and helped me to live in it. *(Romans 7:15, 24-25)*

This is indeed Good News, and I have told everybody I could about it. It's Good News about *how God helps us*; it's Good News *for everybody*, foreigner and Jew alike; and all anybody need do is to take God *at his word*. I didn't make all this up, and I certainly didn't get it from any teacher. I got it straight from Jesus himself. Haven't I myself seen him? *(Romans 1:16; Galatians 1:11-12)*

It happened like this.

You know what I was like in my old Jewish days. I was the bitter enemy of the friends of Jesus, and I tried as hard as I could to wipe them out. But God, who made this bright world, filled my heart with light, the light which shines when we know what he really is like. And I saw this light shining from the face of Jesus – Jesus who died, was buried and rose again to life. He was seen by Peter (you remember), by the 'Twelve', and by more than five hundred friends together. (Most of these are still alive, but some, of course, have since died.) He was seen by his brother James; then by all his close friends; and last of all, long after anybody could have hoped, he was seen by me, as I have said. *(Galatians 1:13; 2 Corinthians 4:6; 1 Corinthians 15:3-8)*

God had marked me out for my great work before I was born, and now, in his love, he had called me to it. He had shown me his Son; and my business now was to tell the story of Jesus to everybody all over the world. I come at the bottom of the list of his friends, far below men like Peter; I don't deserve to be called a friend of his, because I was once his enemy. I owe everything I am to God's love. *(Galatians 1:15-16; 1 Corinthians 15:9-10)*

I did not talk about this to anybody. I didn't even go up to Jerusalem City to see those who had been friends of Jesus long before I was.

I went off into Arabia, and then came back to Damascus City. King Aretas told the Governor of the city to guard the gates and arrest me. But I was lowered in a rope basket through an opening in the city wall and got away. *(Galatians 1:16b-17; 2 Corinthians 11:32-33)*

Three years went by before I went up to Jerusalem to see Peter and stayed a fortnight with him. I didn't meet any of the other close friends of Jesus, except his brother James.

None of Jesus' other friends there had ever met me face to face. They had only heard what others said – 'Our bitter enemy is telling everybody the Good News himself! And to think he once tried to stop it being told!' They thanked God for me. *(Galatians 1:18-24)*

The Crowded Years

I'm proud of what I've been able to do to make God's Way known throughout the world. But it's only through Jesus that I've been able to do what I have done.

There is one thing – and one thing only – I care to talk about: how Jesus has used me to help people of many lands to live in God's Way.

From Jerusalem in Palestine all round the world as far as Illyricum in Europe, I have made the Good News of Jesus sound like the Good News it is – Good News for everybody. For I have had one ambition: to tell the story of Jesus where his name had never been heard. I didn't want to go where others had already told the Good News. You remember what the Bible says –

> They shall see
>> who had never been told about him;
>> those who have never heard
>> shall know all about him. *(Romans 15:17-21)*

And wherever I've been they don't just talk about it either – they live it.

Let me tell you what I've had to face. I know it's silly for me to talk like this, but here's the list, for I know what it is to work hard and live dangerously.

I've been beaten up more times than I can remember, been in more than one prison, and faced death itself more than once. Five times I've been thrashed by a Jewish court to within an inch of my life; three times I've been beaten with rods by city magistrates; and once I was nearly stoned to death.

I've been shipwrecked three times; and once, I was adrift, out of sight of land, for twenty-four hours.

I don't know how many roads I've tramped. I've faced bandits; I've been attacked by fellow-countrymen and by foreigners. I've met danger in city streets and on lonely country roads and out in the open sea.

I know what it is to have false friends.

I've been so tired out that I haven't been able to sleep at night. Many a time I've been hungry and thirsty through sheer lack of food. I know what it is to be nearly frozen to death and to have only rags on my back.

I could tell you many a story.

And, as if this wasn't enough, I've had another heavy load to carry day by day – looking after and caring for the Christian churches.

I've been in some tight corners – but never cornered; I've lost my way – but never my courage; I've been on the run – but never left to my fate; I've been knocked down – but never knocked out. *(1 Thessalonians 1:5; 2 Corinthians 11:21, 23-28; 4:8-9)*

I know what people have thought of me – a feeble fool not worth bothering about. What else, indeed, could they think of a man who goes about starving and in rags, gets beaten up, lives like a vagabond, works like a common labourer? They've cursed me, made my life a misery, told lies about me. I've tried to speak kindly to them, let them do what they want and told them the Good News. But they treated me like dirt. *(1 Corinthians 4:10-13)*

Yet look at the friends Jesus has given me!

Whenever I think about them, I thank God for them – at Philippi and Thessalonica, in Anatolia, Greece and Asia. Praying for them fills me with happiness. I remember how, from the earliest days, we worked together in spreading the Good News. It's only right I should think like this about them – I am always in *their* thoughts. Whenever I was in prison or facing the judge in the defence of the Good News, I felt as if they were with me, and that we were all sharing God's love together. *(Philippians 1:3-5, 7)*

I pray that they may always be happy people, held together by their love of man and God, and sure of the Good News in all its richness because they know what they believe. I want them to know the secret of it all – God's secret – Jesus himself. *(Colossians 2:2)*

With such a story to tell, I've learned how to stand on my own feet, wherever I am. I know how to do without things, and I know how to live when I've got more than I need. It doesn't matter now what happens – I can face plenty and poverty, I can enjoy wealth and want. I've learned God's secret. There isn't anything I can't face; but I know where my strength comes from – it comes from Jesus. *(Philippians 4:11-13)*

Getting the Good News Clear

At Jerusalem   *Galatians 2:1-10*

Fourteen years after the fortnight I spent with Peter in Jerusalem, I went there again with Barnabas, and I took Titus, a foreign friend, with me. I felt it was God's will for me to go there, to put the plain story of how I told the Good News to everybody, foreigner and Jew alike, before the Christian leaders in Palestine.

I met them face to face in a private meeting. I didn't want all my work – what I had done and what I was still doing – to come to nothing.

It wasn't the leaders themselves who insisted that Titus, because he was a foreigner, should become a Jew. *That* was the idea of some so-called friends of Jesus who had slipped into the meeting. They had no right whatever to be there; they came just to put an end to the freedom I have claimed for people of all nations and races to become friends of Jesus, just as they are. These people wanted all friends of Jesus to become Jewish nationals first. I wasn't having that sort of slavery for a single minute.

The very heart of the Good News is that it is Good News for everybody everywhere, no matter what their nationality – and it was going to stay like that.

I needn't have taken the trouble, of course, to put the matter to the Christian leaders in Jerusalem. The Bible says that God doesn't take any notice of a person's rank – and it doesn't count much with me. Still, those whom everybody accepts as the chief Christian leaders – men like

Peter – had nothing to add to my 'plain story'. They went even farther. They agreed that God had given *me* the work of telling the Good News to all foreigners, just as he had given *Peter* the work of telling the Good News to the Jewish people. Both of us were doing God's work with God's help.

James and Peter and John – if anybody's word counts, theirs does – saw that it was God's work that I was doing. Barnabas and I were leaders of the friends of Jesus, they said, just as they were; and they shook us by the hand. Our work was clear: *we* were to look after the people of other lands; *they* were to look after the people of the Jewish nation.

They went on to ask us one thing: could we do something for the poor in the city who were suffering from famine? This was the beginning of the Christian Aid Fund.

The Christian Aid Fund   *1 Corinthians 16:2-4; 2 Corinthians 8:12-14*

Let me say something here about this fund. We were very keen to help, for such help might bring foreigners and Jews together. I went back to Ephesus to raise this fund to help the poor in Jerusalem.

My rule for the fund was this. Each Sunday, everybody was to put something by, in proportion to what they had earned. I should not then need to make a collection when I came myself. The money raised could be taken to Jerusalem, with a letter, by some of their leaders. I had not made up my mind then to take the gifts myself. If, when the time came, I thought I ought to go, these men could go along with me.

I told them all, when I was explaining the fund to them, that if we are really keen to give, God expects us to give only what we can afford, not to try to give more than we can afford. He doesn't want us to give so much to others that we go without what we really need ourselves. What God wants is that we share what we have together. If we've got more than we really need now and others are in need, we must help them; but some time it will be the other way round. God's will is, as I have said, that we shall share what he has given us – and share alike.

At Antioch   *Galatians 2:11-21*

But our difficulties in getting the Good News clear were by no means over. This is the sort of thing that happened. Barnabas and I, some time later, were back in Antioch, and Peter joined us there. But I had to stand up to him and tell him that he was plainly in the wrong – on this same question.

When he first came there, he ate his meals with all of us; foreigner and Jew sat down together at the same table. Then some men came from Jerusalem (they said that James had sent them), and everything changed. He started to stay away from our common meals. He was frightened of these Jewish friends of Jesus who said that you couldn't become a friend of Jesus if you hadn't first become a proper Jew. Other friends of Jesus in Antioch started to do the same – even Barnabas was deceived.

This was cheating – and cheating about the very thing that makes the Good News really Good News. It was as plain as plain could be to me.

One day, when everybody was together, I tackled Peter.

'When you first came here,' I said, 'born and bred a Jew though you are, you "lived like a foreigner, not like a Jew", as these men put it. Why have you turned round, and now try to make foreigners "live like Jews"?'

I went on to put the Good News plainly. I myself am a Jew by race and not a foreigner. But I know that a man doesn't become a friend of Jesus by carrying out all the details of the Jewish religion. He becomes a friend of Jesus by just trusting Jesus himself. That is the heart of the matter.

I know what is the secret of my own life. I go on living my ordinary life, it is true, and yet, in a sense, I don't feel I'm living it – Jesus has taken charge of me. I live by trusting Jesus, God's Son, who loved me and gave his life for me.

I'm not going to say No to God's love. If living in God's Way is just a matter of rules and regulations, Jesus threw his life away.

In Prison

My work in Asia, Macedonia and Greece was now finished; there was nothing more for me to do there. I could go now to Spain.

For many years I had dreamed of visiting Rome and the friends of Jesus there. I could call to see them on my way to Spain. I could spend a short holiday with them, and they could give me a good send-off.

But I had now made up my mind to go first to Jerusalem with the Christian Aid Fund. When I had been to visit the poor in Palestine and placed the money that had been collected safely in their hands, I would go on to Spain by way of Rome.

I wrote a letter to the friends of Jesus in Rome to tell them about these plans of mine. I wanted them to stand by me in my fight for the Good News, and to remember me in their prayers. I knew how dangerous my visit to Jerusalem would be; my life itself might be in danger. And I was afraid that the Jewish friends of Jesus there, who, as you know, didn't like me, might refuse to take the gifts I brought. But if all went well, I could go with a happy heart to Rome and enjoy my holiday there. *(Romans 15:23-25, 28, 30-32)*

What happened was very different from what I planned, and I am now in prison in Rome. Yet all this misfortune has made the Good News more widely known; it hasn't stopped my telling people about it. Everybody here in Rome knows that I am in prison because I am a friend of Jesus; even the soldiers of the Palace Guard know it. And most of the friends of Jesus here have been really cheered by my being a prisoner. They bravely go out to tell the Good News to everybody, and show no fear at all.

Of course, the friends of Jesus here don't all agree with one another – or with me. Some tell the Good News because they love Jesus; some because they are jealous of me. But they all talk about Jesus. What can I say? Only one thing. If people talk about Jesus, either honestly or dishonestly, I'm quite happy. And I shall go on being happy – even if my imprisonment is to end in my death. *(Philippians 1:12-19; 2:17)*

My Methods

Nobody can tell me what to do; I am free to live as I think I ought to live. But I've always chosen to be a slave to others – to persuade as many as I could to become friends of Jesus.

I've lived like a Jew among Jewish people. I've kept the Jewish law (though I had no need to do so) when I have been living among strict Jews. I've lived like a foreigner among foreigners (the Jews call them 'outlaws' but there's something more important than being 'Jews' or 'outlaws' – and that's being an 'in-law' of Jesus). I've tried to share the life even of people who had confused ideas about Jesus. I've done all this to get Jews (strict or not), foreigners, people who didn't share my Christian views, everybody, to become true friends of Jesus.

I have tried, you see, to live just like that people I've found myself with, and to share their way of living, as far as I could.

I've treated everybody like this, so that I might win some, in one way or another, for Jesus. *(1 Corinthians 9:19-22)*

I've tried hard not to cause anybody to stumble. I didn't want them, if possible, to start criticising what I was doing. I wanted them to see that I was God's servant, not just pleasing myself. What a lot of trouble that has caused me! I've had to put up with all sorts of things – dangers and hard times and all sorts of difficulties; I've been flogged, put in prison, and beaten up; I've had to work like a slave, go without any sleep and food.

And all through this, I've tried to live as Jesus lived. He was sincere in all he did; he knew what he stood for; he could put up with anything; he was very kind; he didn't just talk about loving people – he actually succeeded in loving them; he always told people the plain truth, for he knew God was with him and trusted in God's power. I've tried to live like that.

The only weapon I've had has been a straightforward life, but I've had to use it in a hundred different ways, and it hasn't been easy. People have sometimes honoured me, and sometimes insulted me; sometimes praised me, and sometimes blamed me. They thought I was lying – yet I always tried to tell the truth; they called me a nobody – yet everybody knew me; my life wasn't worth living – yet I have enjoyed every moment of it; I've had a rough time – yet they haven't finished me off; many things have made me sad – yet I've been a very happy man; I haven't had much money – yet I've made many people rich; I have lived like a beggar – yet the whole world's mine. *(2 Corinthians 6:3-10)*

I've lived to make the Good News known. I've tried to warn everybody I met and to teach everybody I met. I wanted them to recognise nonsense when they met it, to be really grown-up – this is what it means to be a friend of Jesus. This is what I've worked for, with every ounce of strength God has given me. *(Colossians 1:28-29)*

My Daily Rule   *Colossians 4:2, 5-6*

My daily rule? I've never been too busy to pray – I've made a habit of it. And I didn't just say my prayers; I kept wide awake and always found something to say 'Thank you' for.

I've tried to be grown-up and sensible when I've been dealing with other people, especially those who are not 'our sort' of people. I've never wasted time. I've always tried to talk to people as friends, to make what I have to say interesting and worthwhile. Everybody has different questions to ask; I've always tried to learn how to deal with all their different questions.

My Friends *From various letters, but chiefly from Romans 16:3-23*

How many friends I have had! Their kindness to me has been like the scent of flowers! Let me write some of their names down:

Timothy – he's been like a son to me; you know what a grand fellow he is;

Titus – who's worked by my side; he brought good news for me back from Corinth, you remember;

Priscilla and Aquila – who risked their lives for me, and the friends of Jesus who meet together in their home;

Stephanus and his family – the first people to become friends of Jesus in Greece, as Epaenetus was the first in Asia;

Relatives of mine – Andronicus and Junias who've been in prison with me; everybody knows them, for they have told the Good News to many people, and they were friends of Jesus before I was; and there's Herodion too;

Apelles – he's been a brave man;

Rufus – he's done fine work for Jesus (his father, you remember, carried the cross for Jesus); his mother who looked after me as if she were my mother too!

Gaius – I used to stay with him; he took care of me – and of all the friends of Jesus in his city too;

Erastus – the city-treasurer;

Stachys and Persis – both of whom I love very much indeed; what a hard worker Persis is!

Apollos – brother of mine in the service of Jesus; I began the work at Corinth, he carried it on, but God made his work and mine grow;

Epaphroditus – brother of mine, too, in the service of Jesus; we worked together and fought our battles together. He was once taken very ill when he was away from his home in Philippi, and he was upset when he knew that his friends in Philippi had heard about his illness. As a matter of fact, he nearly died. He risked his life for me; he wouldn't leave me because the friends of Jesus in Philippi had sent him to look after me.

Philemon – leader of the friends of Jesus in Colossi; and Onesimus, once his slave and now a friend of Jesus and his friend too;

Aristarchus – who is a prisoner here in Rome with me;

Mark – cousin of Barnabas, and Jesus Justus; these are the only Jewish friends of Jesus who have helped me in telling the Good News; but what a help they've been;

Tertius – who wrote down some of my letters for me; Luke – my doctor.

A Last Word

I haven't yet got anywhere near being the kind of man I want to be; and I haven't become as mature as Jesus was – by a long way. But nothing's going to stop me now; I intend to be the kind of man Jesus wanted me to be when he called me on the road to Damascus City. I know I haven't got there yet; but I've set my heart on one thing – to forget the past and live for the future. I'm like a long-distance runner; I see the tape ahead and I'm going to get there – and win the prize. *(Philippians 3:12-14)*

Who can take God's love away from us now – the love that Jesus has made real? You know the sort of thing that can happen to any of us in this world of ours – suffering, hardship, cruelty, hunger, homelessness, danger, war. It's in just such a world that we who are the friends of Jesus can now live more splendidly than the greatest world conquerors – with the help of Jesus who loved us.

I'm quite sure that nothing – neither dying nor living, neither what we're facing now nor what we may have to face tomorrow, nothing in our own world or in outer space or in our own hearts – can take God's love away from us.

Jesus is Lord in God's world. *(Romans 8:36-39)*

Don't forget I'm in prison. The scars on my body are the marks of the master I belong to – Jesus.

The graciousness of Jesus, our master, be with you all *(Colossians 4:18; Galatians 6:17-18)*. Paul, Rome.

(Note: We have put a passage from one of Paul's letters later in the book (p. 580). It gives us information, which Dr Luke does not give us, about what was happening in Corinth while Paul was in Ephesus.)

Dr Luke's Story of Paul

In his letters Paul did not need to describe the many exciting events that happened in the cities he had visited. The friends he was writing to knew all about them. So 'Paul's Own Story', which I made from his letters, had little to tell us about them. What stories he could have told we can see from his summary of his experiences in 'The Crowded Years' (p. 557).

Dr Luke fills out the picture. How much we should have missed if he had not kept a notebook. So here I have set out Dr Luke's stories, but followed Paul's own arrangement.

In this part of the book we are trying to find out two things: first, how Paul went about his work and what he tried to do ('In Anatolia' and 'On the Shores of the Aegean Sea'); second, what he had to say for himself when he was arrested and brought before Jewish and Roman judges ('On Trial in Palestine'). But we must remember that in these stories we are reading *Dr Luke's account*; we must always check up what Dr Luke tells us by reading Paul's own first-hand account of his convictions and his reasons in 'Paul's Own Story' and in *Jesus – Leader and Lord*.

Before you begin to read this part, read again Dr Luke's earlier stories about Paul which you will find in *From Galilee to Rome*. First of all read 'The Man Who Died for it: Stephen' (p. 531) and 'The Man Who Led the Adventure: Paul' (p. 539). Then read 'The Great Plan' (p. 542) and 'How the Good News Came to a Greek Island' (p. 544); these will tell you what happened just before our story begins. When you have finished reading *this* part, read 'How the Good News Came to a "Barbarian" Island' (p. 548) and 'How the Good News Came to the Capital of the Empire' (p. 551); these will tell you what happened to Paul after our story in this book is ended.

In Anatolia

Paul and Barnabas landed at the port of Anatolia (see the map on p. 521). It was probably here, in the low-lying, hot plain where Attalia and Perga stood, that Paul was taken ill.

The journey Paul and Barnabas were making was, in a real sense, a 'trial' journey. They were doing something which no friend of Jesus had tried to do before – telling the Good News to *foreigners*. They knew what to say to Jews; but how do you approach foreigners and what do you say to them? They had to find out, and it was here in Anatolia, that Paul made up his mind how this great work was to be done.

Paul and his friends left the island of Cyprus behind them and crossed the open sea. They landed at the port of Attalia on the mainland, and went on to Perga City, eight miles inland. John Mark left them and went back home, and Barnabas and Paul climbed the high mountain road to Antioch Town.

On the Saturday, the Holy Day of the Jews, they went along to the Jewish Meeting House and sat down. They listened to the reading of the Bible; and when this had finished, the leaders of the Meeting House spoke to them.

'Brothers,' they said, 'if you have anything to say to the people that would help them, come and say it.' Paul stood up and raised his hand.

'My countrymen, and those among you who are not my countrymen but are here because you care for the true worship of God, listen to the Good News I have to tell you,' he said. 'Long ago our ancestors were slaves in Egypt. But God called them, led them out of slavery, and gave them a homeland – Palestine. They lived there as tribes under the leaders God gave them. Then, in the time of Samuel, he gave them a king – Saul, a member of my own tribe – and, after King Saul, King David. The story I have to tell you is about a descendant of King David, Jesus, the Great Deliverer God promised to send us. John the Hermit, just before he died, told us God's Chosen Leader would come after him. And so it happened. To us, in our own time, the Good News has been sent.'

Then he told them the story of Jesus, and how he died and how God raised him from the dead.

'And here we are,' he went on, 'to bring you the Good News – the Good News God promised to our ancestors. He has carried out his promise to us, their descendants, by raising Jesus to life again.

'Brothers, I want all of you here to know that through this man, Jesus, God offers you now his forgiveness. See that you don't say No to him now.'

As Paul and Barnabas started to leave the Meeting House, the people asked them to tell them the Good News again the next Saturday. Many of them, Jews and foreign worshippers, went along with them to the house where they were staying. And they talked to them there and told them to hold fast to what they now knew of God's love.

Next Saturday, it seemed as if the whole town had crowded into the Meeting House to hear the story of Jesus. The Jewish leaders were jealous when they saw how big the crowds were. They got up and said outright that Paul was quite wrong and that he was a liar.

That made Paul and Barnabas speak out more boldly.

'It was right to tell the story of Jesus first of all here in this Meeting House,' they said. 'But since you won't listen, there's only one thing for us to do – to go to the foreigners who live here. The Bible itself says, you remember –

> You shall be like the sun shining on everybody,
> setting the whole world free.'

The foreigners were glad to hear Paul talk like this.
'How good God's Way is!' they said.
Many became friends of Jesus, as God wanted them to be. And the story of Jesus was told far outside the town as well.

The Jewish leaders didn't like this, and they made trouble for Paul and Barnabas. They won over to their side some of the well-known women, who came to the Meeting House, and the town councillors, and got them to drive Paul and Barnabas out of the town. But those who had become the friends of Jesus were happy people and their hearts were filled with God's love.

Paul and Barnabas travelled on to Iconium Town, and went together into the Jewish Meeting House there. Again they told the people the Good News, and a great crowd of them – both Jews and foreigners – became friends of Jesus.

But some of the Jewish leaders didn't believe the Good News; and, as in Antioch Town, they made trouble for Paul and Barnabas. They tried to win the townspeople over to their side by their talk. But the town itself was divided into two parties; one thought the leaders of the Meeting House were right, and the other was for Paul and Barnabas. So the two of them went on boldly telling the Good News day after day. God was with them, showing his love in the good deeds they did.

Then a group of Jews and foreigners got hold of the town councillors, and planned to beat up Paul and Barnabas and kill them. But they were told about the plan, and escaped from the town.

They went to the towns of Lystra* and Derbe and into the villages in the countryside, telling the Good News to everybody who would listen. Paul and Barnabas now turned for home.

---

* The story of what happened at Lystra is told in *From Galilee to Rome* in the chapter 'How the Good News Came to the Highlands of Anatolia' (p. 544).

They went back the way they had come – through the towns of Lystra and Iconium and Antioch. Here they met the friends of Jesus and told them what they would have to face.

'Living in God's Way isn't easy,' they said. 'We must be ready to face all sorts of dangers. Keep your hearts brave, and never forget the Good News.'

They chose leaders for each of the 'churches', as the friends of Jesus called their groups – older members who could look after them. This they did in simple services of prayer and fasting.

'Goodbye,' they said, 'we leave you in God's care.'

Paul and Barnabas then went down the steep mountain road to the sea. They passed through Perga Town, near the coast, and told the Good News there. Then they went down to the port of Attalia, boarded a ship and sailed for Antioch City where their journey had begun.

Home at last, they called the friends of Jesus together and told them what had happened in the island of Cyprus and among the mountain towns of Anatolia – how God had helped them and how (as they said) 'God opened a door, and foreigners have become friends of Jesus and learned to trust in him.'

They stayed on there for quite a long time.

On the Shores of the Aegean Sea

Paul's great work has now begun and he is quite clear what Jesus wants him to do. This is the first stage of that work; when this first part of his work is finished, he plans to go on to Spain, and visit Rome on his way.

Paul is now travelling through the most famous part of the ancient Mediterranean world – the home of Greek civilisation. Everywhere he goes, the names of cities will remind him of the great days of old. He will come to Troy, now a large and important city but once the scene of a famous war sung about by Greek poets (this is where the incident of the 'Trojan Horse' happened). He will come to Macedonia, the birthplace of Alexander the Great who conquered a world which stretched as far east as India. He will find himself in Athens, the most famous Greek city of all, and he will wander in the streets where Socrates, Plato and Aristotle once walked. He will come to Corinth where the Isthmian Games (like our Olympic Games) used to be held. He will live in Ephesus where the world's first scientists and philosophers had lived. We can imagine what his thoughts must be. Now he is coming on a greater work, so he believes, than the work any of those soldiers and poets and scientists had been engaged in. He too, like Alexander, is taking part in the conquest of the world – but a different kind of conquest and in the name of a greater captain than Alexander.

Looking for Headquarters   *Acts 15:36-16:12a*

One day Paul spoke to Barnabas.

'Let's go back to the towns of Anatolia, where we told the story of Jesus, and see how the friends of Jesus there are getting on.'

Barnabas wanted to take John Mark, his nephew, along with them. But Paul wouldn't agree.

'You see,' he said, 'John Mark didn't go with us on that journey – he left us at Perga and went home.'

They couldn't agree about him. So they decided to go their own ways. Barnabas took John Mark with him and went across to the island of Cyprus. The friends of Jesus at Antioch City said goodbye to Paul and prayed that God in his love would take care of him.

Paul chose Silas as his companion and set off through Syria and Cilicia, his own homeland, and encouraged the friends of Jesus there.

He went on over the mountains, visiting old friends, and came to the towns of Derbe and Lystra.

There was a friend of Jesus called Timothy in Lystra Town. He was the son of a mixed marriage – his father, who was now dead, had been a Greek; his mother, who was also a friend of Jesus, was a Jewess.

The friends of Jesus in the nearby towns of Lystra and Iconium thought he was a very fine young man, and Paul wanted him to go along with him. But there was a difficulty.

Timothy came, through his mother, as we have seen, from a Jewish family, but he had never become a proper Jew. There were many Jews living in the town, and they knew all about him. Paul didn't want them to think he didn't care at all about the Jewish Law – he was a Jew himself. So he got Timothy, half Jew as he was, made a proper Jew.

Then Paul and Silas and Timothy went on together and visited all the towns in Anatolia. Paul's visit made the churches there bold and strong, and their numbers grew day by day.

They went on over the mountains. Paul planned to go down the high road to Ephesus. But, when they were praying together about it, they felt that God did not want them to go there.

So they took the road to the north-west and came to the borders of Mysia. Here they thought of turning north and going to the towns on the shores of the Black Sea; but, again; when they prayed about it, they were quite sure that this was not where God wanted them to go.

On they went through Mysia and came down to the Roman colony of Troas.

Dr Luke's Diary
That night Paul had a dream. In his dream he saw a man from across the water, a Macedonian, standing on the opposite shore and calling to him –

'Come over into Macedonia and help us!' he was shouting.

Next day we made enquiries about getting across the water. We were sure now what God wanted us to do; we must go and tell the Good News in Macedonia.

We went aboard a ship in Troas harbour, and sailed straight across the open sea to the island of Samothrace. The following day we landed at New Town, where the road from Rome came down to the sea. We went inland to Philippi, a Roman colony and an important city in that part of the country.

A Roman Garrison Town   *Acts 16:12b-40*

Dr Luke's Diary
We stayed some days in Philippi City.

On the Saturday, the Holy Day of the Jews, we walked down to the banks of the river, outside the city gate, where Jewish people used to meet for prayer. Some women were already there, and we sat down and talked to them.

A woman named Lydia, a cloth merchant from the city of Thyatira*, was listening. She was not a Jewess, but she came to worship God in the Jewish Meeting House. As she listened to Paul, she felt God was very near. She and her family were baptised and became friends of Jesus.

'If you think I have become a true friend of Jesus,' she said to Paul, 'make my house your home.'

She was very eager for us to stay with her; so we made her home our headquarters.

That morning, as we were walking to the city gate, we passed a slave girl. She was a medium who could sound as if she were somebody else.

---

* Thyatira was a city in Asia famous for its purple cloth.

She told people's fortunes and made a lot of money for her owners. She followed us; and for days after, whenever she met us, she shouted out in her strange voice.

'These men belong to the High God. They've got Good News to give you,' she said.

This upset Paul.

He turned to the girl and spoke to the 'Voice'.

'In the name of Jesus,' he said, 'come out of her, I tell you!'

And there and then, the girl stopped talking in this strange way.

When her owners saw that they wouldn't now be able to make any money out of her, they took hold of Paul and Silas and dragged them to the market place where the law court was held.

'These Jews are upsetting the city,' they told the magistrates. 'They are telling us to do all sorts of things that are not Roman customs; they are trying to make us break the law.'

The mob started shouting, and the magistrates angrily ordered Paul and Silas to be beaten with rods. The police gave them a good flogging, locked them up in prison, and ordered the head warder to see that they didn't escape. Acting on this order, he locked them in the inner prison and fastened their feet in the stocks.

It was now about midnight.

Paul and Silas were praying and singing hymns together, and the other prisoners were listening to them, in their cells.

Suddenly there was a great earthquake. The whole prison shuddered to its foundations. All the doors sprang open and everybody's chains were broken off.

The head warder woke up, and saw the open prison doors. His first thought was 'The prisoners have gone!' and he drew his sword to commit suicide.

'Don't hurt yourself,' shouted Paul. 'We're all here.'

The warder called for torches and dashed into the cell. He was very frightened and fell down before Paul and Silas. Then he led them outside.

'Sirs,' he said, 'what must I do to know God as you do?'

'There's only one thing to do,' they told him. 'Put your trust in the Lord Jesus, and you and all your family will be all right.'

They told him and his family the story of Jesus. And there and then, in the middle of the night, he took them and washed their wounds, and, there in the prison, the warder and his family were baptised as friends of Jesus.

He led them into his own house and gave them a good meal. He and all his family were very happy, because they had come to know what God was really like and to trust him.

Daylight came, and the magistrates sent the police to the prison.

'Set the two men free,' were their orders. The head warder went to tell Paul.

'The magistrates have given orders for your release,' he said. 'You can leave the prison and go on your way. You won't have any more trouble.'

'We're Roman citizens,' said Paul. 'We've had no proper trial; we've been beaten with rods and thrown into prison. Now they want to throw us out by the back-door. Oh no! Let the magistrates themselves come and set us free properly.'

The police reported all this to the magistrates. When they heard that they were Roman citizens, they were very frightened indeed. They came along, asked their pardon, led them out of the prison and begged them to leave the city.

So Paul and Silas left the prison, and went to Lydia's home. There they met the friends of Jesus again and told them to be of good heart. Then off they went along the road to Thessalonica.

A Trading City   *Acts 17:1-10, 14-20, 34; 18:1*

Paul and Silas walked along the great Roman road. They passed through two towns and came at last to Thessalonica, the capital city of Macedonia. There was a Jewish Meeting House there, and Paul, as usual, went along on Saturday morning to the service of worship. 'It is Jesus I want to talk to you about,' he said. 'He is God's Chosen Leader.'

For three Saturday mornings he explained the Bible to them. He told them what had happened to Jesus – how he died and how he was raised by God to life again – and showed them how the Bible made all this clear.

Two or three Jews were sure Paul was right and joined him and Silas; so did many of the Greeks and the wives of important city officials.

This made the leaders of the Meeting House jealous. So they got a mob of hooligans from the market together, and started rioting in the streets. They broke into the house of a man called Jason, looking for Paul and Silas to drag them out for the mob to beat up. They couldn't find them; so they got hold of Jason himself and some of the friends of Jesus who were there, and dragged them before the city magistrates.

'These are the fellows who have been making riots all over the world,' they shouted. 'Now they've turned up in this city – Jason's been hiding them in his house. The whole lot are rebels. "Down with the Emperor and the Empire," is their slogan; "we've another Emperor – Emperor Jesus"."

The crowd was excited by these charges, and the magistrates were frightened. But they put Jason and his friends on bail, and let them go home.

The friends of Jesus had to act quickly, and that night they got Paul and Silas out of the city in the darkness and off along the road to the town of Beroea.* Even here there was some rioting, and the friends of Jesus there hurried Paul off to the coast. Silas and Timothy stayed on in Beroea, but his guides sailed with him as far as the famous city of Athens. They then left him and went back home with a message.

'Come to Athens as soon as you can,' Paul wrote to Silas and Timothy.

Paul wandered about the famous city while he was waiting for them. Many learned men lived and taught there; Paul met them and talked to them. They asked him to speak to them before the City Council. A few people – among them one of the city councillors – became friends of Jesus.

Silas and Timothy still had not come, so Paul went on without them southward to the port of Corinth.

A Great Seaport   Acts 18:1-23a

Corinth was a great seaport and ships from all over the world called there. Behind the city rose the mountain called 'High Corinth', with its famous temple on its slopes.

A Jewish merchant, called Aquila, was living here. His boyhood home was on the shores of the Black Sea. He had been living in Italy, but, not long before, the Emperor had ordered all Jewish people to leave Rome; Aquila with his wife, Priscilla, had come to live in Corinth.

Paul went to see them. He found they were weavers, making cloth from goat's hair – the trade he himself had learned as a boy. So he stayed with them and worked in their workshop. On Saturdays, the Holy Day of the Jews, he went along to the Jewish Meeting House and talked about the Bible and the story of Jesus.

At last Silas and Timothy came down from Macedonia and found Paul hard at work explaining to the Jews that God's Chosen Leader, whom they read about in the Bible, was Jesus. But the members of the

---

* You will find the story of what happened at Beroea and at Athens in *From Galilee to Rome* in the chapters 'How the Good News Came to a Jewish Meeting House' (p. 545) and 'How the Good News Came to the Most Famous Greek City of All' (p. 546).

574

Meeting House argued against him; indeed they went further and even insulted him.

'All right,' said Paul, 'you've made your minds up, and that's your business. I've done my best. In future, I'll deal with the people who are not Jews.'

He didn't go to the Meeting House any more, but made his headquarters in the house next door, which belonged to Titus Justus, a foreigner who worshipped God. Many people became friends of Jesus; among them were Crispus, the leader of the Meeting House, and his family and many citizens of the city.

One night Paul had a dream, and in the dream he heard Jesus speaking to him. 'Don't be afraid,' Jesus said to him. 'Go on telling the Good News and don't give up. I am with you. Nobody shall do you any harm, for I have many friends in this city.'

Paul stayed in Corinth for eighteen months, telling everybody the Good News.

The Jews now went further. They got hold of Paul and took him before the Governor, Gallio.

'We have our Jewish Law,' they said, 'but this fellow is telling everybody it's all wrong.'

Paul was starting to put his case, when the Governor stopped him and turned to the Jewish leaders.

'This isn't the sort of question I'm here to deal with,' he said. 'If it had been a matter of some wrong done or some crime committed, I'd have listened to your complaint. But since it's a question of mere words and names and the meaning of your Jewish religion, use your own courts. I don't intend to start judging questions of this sort. The case is dismissed.'

He had them put out of the court. The crowd got hold of Sosthenes, the leader of the Meeting House, and beat him up. The Governor took no notice.

Paul stayed on in the city for quite a long time after this.

At last Paul said goodbye to the friends of Jesus in Corinth, and, with his friends Priscilla and Aquila, the weavers, set sail for Palestine. The boat put in at Ephesus on the other side of the Aegean Sea. Paul, as he often did, went into the Jewish Meeting House and talked about the Good News with the Jews who worshipped there. They asked him to stay on in Ephesus; but he said No.

The time came to say goodbye. 'I'll come back to you,' he said, 'if that is what God wants me to do.' And he set sail for Palestine. Priscilla and Aquila stayed behind in Ephesus.

Paul landed at the port of Caesarea, which was the headquarters of the Roman army in Palestine, and went up and greeted the friends of Jesus there. Then he went on to Antioch, and stayed there for quite a time.

Paul – Right or Wrong?   *Acts 15:1-33*

This story begins in Antioch City.

Trouble began when some Jewish friends of Jesus came down from Jerusalem. They saw what was happening there; Jews and foreigners were living together as friends of Jesus – praying together and having their meals together.

'This is all wrong,' they said. 'You must become proper Jews before you can become friends of Jesus.'

Paul and Barnabas denied this, and had a long argument with them. At last it was decided to send Paul and Barnabas and some of the other Christian leaders to talk it over with the leaders of the friends of Jesus in Jerusalem. The whole church gave them a good send-off.

They went southward along the coast road through Phoenicia; and then on through Samaria. Wherever they went they told how foreigners were becoming friends of Jesus; everybody was glad to hear about it.

The Christians in Jerusalem City welcomed them when they got there, and they told them the same story.

But some of the Jewish Christians there didn't like it.

'No,' they said. 'Foreigners must become Jews first, and they must keep the Jewish Law and all that Moses told us to do.'

A meeting of the leaders was called to get this matter clear.

Peter stood up.

'Brothers,' he said, 'you know that when, in the early days, we began to tell the Good News, God chose me to be the first to tell it to foreigners – Captain Cornelius and his family – and to call them too to become friends of Jesus. God can read people's hearts, and he gave Captain Cornelius his power just as he gave it to us. He didn't ask whether he and his family were Jews or foreigners; they trusted him, and he filled their hearts with love. Why do you want to tell God what to do and make our foreign friends keep laws that neither we nor our ancestors were ever able to keep? It is by trusting in the love of Jesus that we ourselves will become what God wants us to be – just as they will. There is only one way for all of us.'

Nobody in the room spoke. Then Paul and Barnabas told them about the great things God had done, through them, among foreigners.

When their story was ended, James spoke up: 'Brothers,' he said, 'listen to me. Peter has told us how God first received foreigners as friends of Jesus, as members of his Family. After all, this shouldn't surprise us – the Bible is quite clear about it. What I have to say is this: we ought not to make it difficult for foreigners to become friends of Jesus. We should send them a letter asking them to keep four of our Jewish laws about food. That would make it easier for friends of Jesus who feel they must still keep the whole of our Jewish Law to share meals with them; for there are Jewish Meeting Houses in all the cities of the world.'

The whole meeting agreed to choose some of their number to go along to Antioch with Paul and Barnabas. They chose Judas and Silas from among their leaders, and they gave them a letter to take with them to the foreign friends of Jesus in Antioch City and in Syria and Cilicia. Here is the letter:

'We send good wishes to all our foreign friends.

'We have heard that some friends of Jesus from this city have been upsetting you with their talk. We did not send them. We are now sending Judas and Silas with our beloved Barnabas and Paul – men who have risked their lives in the service of Jesus. They will tell you themselves all about our meeting here, and explain some rules we would like you to keep. Goodbye.'

Paul and Barnabas and their friends went back to Antioch City. The letter was read aloud in a meeting of the whole church; and everybody was very happy about it.

Judas and Silas stayed with them quite a long time; for they were men who could teach the Bible and they spent the time in helping the people to understand it. The friends of Jesus then let them go back home.

Seaport and Temple City

1. The Lecture Hall   *Acts 18:23; 19:1, 8-10*
Paul left Antioch and set off across the mountains of Anatolia for Ephesus City. On the way he looked up his Christian friends in the cities he passed through and gave them what help they needed.

In Ephesus, as in other cities, Paul went along to the Jewish Meeting House. For three months, he told them the Good News and talked with them about it and begged them to live in God's Way.

Then the trouble began. Some of the members of the Meeting House wouldn't listen to him; they didn't believe a word he said. They began to insult the friends of Jesus in front of the whole meeting. When this happened, Paul left them and took the friends of Jesus along with him.

He found a hall belonging to a man called Tyrannus. Here, each day, he used to meet and talk with people about the Good News. The only time he could use the hall was during the middle of the day when, because of the heat, most people rested – from eleven in the morning to three o'clock in the afternoon.

For two whole years this is how Paul carried on his work. The story of Jesus became known far beyond the boundaries of the city itself; and not only in the Jewish Meeting Houses but among the foreign population of the province of Asia as well.

2. The Talk of the Town   *Acts 19:11-20*

Paul didn't just talk about the Good News; he healed people 'in the name of Jesus', too. There were all sorts of stories told about him and the amazing things people believed he could do.

Many people believed that evil spirits made them ill; and travelling doctors, using magic words, claimed to be able to drive the evil spirits away and make people well.

Here's a story everybody in Ephesus was talking about.

There were seven Jewish travelling doctors, sons of a Jewish leader called Sceva. They heard about Paul, and began to use the words he used – 'In the name of Jesus' – as their magic words.

'I am speaking to you,' they would say to a sick person, 'in the name of the Jesus whom Paul talks about.'

They went to a house, one day, so the story ran, to heal a sick man who believed an evil spirit was inside him. They used, as they had often done before, the words 'in the name of Jesus whom Paul talks about'.

But this time the spirit inside the man suddenly shouted out.

'I know who Jesus is,' it shouted, 'and I know who Paul is. But who are you?'

The sick man jumped on them, knocked them about and was so violent that they ran out of the house naked and badly beaten up.

This sort of story rather scared people, but at any rate they thought better of the name of Jesus.

Ephesus City was famous for magic, and it was now clear to people that God's Way had nothing to do with magic. Many of the friends of Jesus came and told Paul that they had been using magic spells. Some of the magicians even got their books of magic together and burned them for everybody to see. These books cost a lot of money; they reckoned that the value of the books burned was somewhere about £50,000.

So the Good News spread and the trade in magic dropped.

3. The Riot   Acts 19:21-20:3

At last Paul decided to go to Jerusalem, and to travel through Macedonia and Greece on his way. He believed that this was what God wanted him to do next.

'After I've been there,' he said, 'I must visit Rome too.'

So he sent his two helpers, Timothy and Erastus, on to Macedonia. But he himself stayed a little longer in Ephesus.

Just then trouble broke out about the Christians in the city.

There was a famous Temple in Ephesus City, the Temple of the Goddess Artemis. It was one of the seven wonders of the world and pilgrims came from all over the world to visit it. Many used to buy small images of the goddess and her temple to take home with them; and this kept the silversmiths and the shops busy.

Demetrius, one of the silversmiths, who was also a temple warden, called the craftsmen together.

'Men,' he said, 'you know where we get our money from. Now this fellow Paul has come along with his 'Good News'. Lots of people, not only here but throughout the province, aren't buying the images we make any more. You can see what's happening for yourselves. We're all in danger – and we shall get a bad name as well. But there's more at stake: all Asia and the world beyond worship the goddess Artemis here; soon, if this goes on, nobody will bother about her great Temple and she won't be a great goddess much longer.'

The speech turned them into a wild mob.

'Great is Artemis of the Ephesians,' they screamed and shouted.

Then the mob made one mad rush for the theatre, where public meetings were held, dragging two of Paul's friends with them.

Paul wanted to go in and face the mob. But his friends stopped him; and some of the county councillors, who were also friends of his, sent him a message, begging him not to risk it.

The meeting in the theatre was one great hullaballoo; most of the crowd hadn't a clue what it was all about – some were shouting one thing and some were shouting another.

A group of Jews pushed a man called Alexander, one of their leaders, to the front; some of the crowd thought he had something to do with the meeting and called to him. He beckoned to the mob with his hand and tried to explain that the Jews had nothing to do with the trouble. When the crowd realised he was a Jew, they burst out with one great shout – 'Great is Artemis of the Ephesians!'

For two hours there was nothing but shouting. The town clerk at last got the crowd to be quiet.

'People of Ephesus,' he said, 'is there anybody anywhere in the world who doesn't know about our city, the Guardian of the Temple of the great Goddess Artemis, and of the holy stone which fell from the sky? Nobody's going to say this is nonsense. You must calm down; you mustn't start doing anything silly. You've brought these men here – but they've neither robbed the temple nor insulted our goddess. If the silver-smiths, Demetrius and his friends, have got some trade dispute to complain about, there are law-courts and magistrates in this city; let them bring their charges against one another there. If you've got other matters to discuss, they can all be settled in the proper town meeting. We are in great danger of being charged by the Emperor with rioting here today, and we've got no excuse for going wild like this.'

With these words he closed the meeting.

When all the noise was over, Paul sent for the friends of Jesus. He told them not to be afraid but to go on telling everybody the Good News. Then he said goodbye and left the city, and went north to Macedonia. He gladdened the hearts of the Christians there as he talked to them about Jesus and the Good News. Then he went southwards to Greece, and stayed there for three months, for it was winter time.

A Note by Paul

Dr Luke has not told us all that happened while Paul was in Ephesus. While he was there, trouble broke out among the Christians in Corinth. News was brought to him that quarrelling had broken out among them; they were divided into 'parties' and were arguing which was right. Paul went over to see them to try to put things straight, but they wouldn't listen to him. He then wrote to them a severe letter. At last everything was put right. He described what happened and how troubled he had been about it in a letter he wrote to them afterwards. Here is what he wrote; we have put it as if he were telling us about it.

When I first went to Corinth to tell them the Good News there, I didn't use big words or talk as if I knew everything. I had just come from Athens, and I'd made up my mind that there was only one thing to talk about – the plain story of Jesus and how he died. *(1 Corinthians 2:1-2)*

I was hard up, but I wouldn't take a penny from them; the friends of Jesus in Macedonia looked after me. To tell the truth, I was far from well; I was nervous and jumpy. *(2 Corinthians 11:9; 1 Corinthians 2:3)*

I know what some people in Corinth said about me – 'His letters are full of big words; but when he himself turns up, you wouldn't look twice at him, and he hasn't got anything to say!' They were right. When I talked to them and told them the Good News, I didn't try to talk like a clever man; all I did was to let them see that I knew something of God's power and presence in my heart. It isn't cleverness that helps us to trust in God; it's realising what God is doing for us that makes us trust him. *(2 Corinthians 10:10; 1 Corinthians 2:4-5)*

Some time later, when I was in Ephesus, news was brought to me from Corinth that they were all quarrelling with one another there. Things got so bad that I had to go over and see them. It was a very unpleasant visit, and I made up my mind that I wouldn't let that painful sort of thing happen again. It would only make matters worse. *(1 Corinthians 1:11; 2 Corinthians 2:1)*

So I wrote a letter to them. I actually wept over it, I was so unhappy about having to write it. I didn't want to upset them; indeed I wanted them to know how much I cared for them – and I cared for them very much indeed. All this, as I have said, made me very unhappy. Yet I had to be straight with them. *(2 Corinthians 2:4)*

I told them that if I did visit them again, I was afraid of what I would find. I shouldn't find *them*, I knew, the kind of people I wanted them to be; and they wouldn't find *me* the kind of man they wanted me to be. I was afraid that they would be still quarrelling with one another, and all I'd find would be jealous, angry, selfish people, telling all sorts of stories about one another, talking nastily to one another, proud of their own little groups, and all at sixes and sevens. *(2 Corinthians 12:20)*

I warned all those who were causing trouble and everybody else as well – it's only what I had told them when I went over to see them – that if I came a third time I would just tell them, as plainly as I could, what I thought about them. *(2 Corinthians 13:2)*

Titus took this letter to Corinth. I myself stayed on in Ephesus, and then went on to Troas. I had a very happy time there; doors opened everywhere. But Titus hadn't come back with an answer to my letter, and I was all on edge to know what my friends in Corinth would do. So, although there was plenty to do in Troas, I said goodbye and went on to Macedonia. But there I had to face all sorts of difficulties – trouble in the city and fears in my heart. But God cheered me up, as he always does when we get down-hearted – Titus came back from Corinth. It was good to see him, and I felt happy again. He told me how my friends in Corinth wanted to put things right; they were sorry for what had happened, and they were keen to help in every way they could. That made me happier still.

My letter *had* hurt them. I wasn't sorry that I had written it (as I was when I had just sent it off). It had only hurt them, I could see, for a short time – they soon saw what I was really troubled about. So I was happy again, not, of course, because they had been hurt, but because that straight letter had made them change their minds and see what God's Way was. *(2 Corinthians 2:12-13; 7:5-9)*

Before all this trouble had broken out, I had planned to leave Ephesus at Whitsuntide, and go through Macedonia to see the friends of Jesus there. After that I had planned to go south and stay with the friends of Jesus at Corinth, and perhaps spend the winter with them. They could then give me a good send-off on my next journey, wherever that might be. *(1 Corinthians 16:8, 5-6)*

I could now carry out these plans.

The friends of Jesus at Corinth, twelve months before, were the first to take up the Christian Aid Fund; they were very keen about it, and began collecting money at once. I'm afraid that they hadn't done much about it while they were quarrelling with one another. But now that they had got things straight again, they should finish what they had begun. They could see how much they could still collect.

'You've started them off again,' I said to Titus. 'What about going to help them to finish it off as well?'

Titus thought this was a fine idea, and off he went. *(2 Corinthians 8:6, 10-11, 17)*

On Trial in Palestine

Paul's visit to Palestine turned out quite differently from what he had hoped. He came a free man; he left a prisoner. All his dreams of telling the Good News in Spain would now never come true.

After telling us about the riot in Jerusalem and Paul's arrest by the Commanding Officer of the Roman garrison, Dr Luke wants us to read carefully what Paul had to say in his own defence. He did not get much chance of speaking properly to either the Jewish Council or to Governor Felix. The Jewish Council was too stormy and Governor Felix was not really interested. But two speeches in his own defence are important ones – the one he made to his own countrymen from the steps of the barracks (p. 588) and the one he made before King Agrippa (p. 594). When you have read them, read again what Paul himself has told us in *Paul's Own Story* – the chapters 'How I Became a Friend of Jesus', 'Getting the Good News Clear' and 'A Last Word'. And remember that people can write much more freely and easily in a letter to friends than they can speak in a law-court.

As you read, ask yourself what are the most important points Paul is making; what does he think is the heart of Christianity?

Sailing to Palestine (Dr Luke's Diary)

1. Troas   *Acts 20:3-12*

Paul at last set off from Corinth for Palestine. As he was about to board a pilgrim ship, he learned that some Jews had made a plot to murder him on the boat. He changed his plans and went the longer way round by road through Macedonia.

The representatives from the Christians of Beroea, Thessalonica, Derbe and Ephesus were travelling with him. They were taking to Jerusalem the money they had raised for the Christian Aid Fund. At Philippi, they went ahead to wait for us at Troas.*

We left Philippi by boat after Easter to meet them there. We were five days at sea, and we spent a week in Troas.

On the Sunday we met the Christians there to 'break bread' – to have supper together, as Jesus did with his friends on the night before he died.

Paul had decided to leave Troas the next day. He had a lot to talk to them about and he went on talking till midnight.

We were meeting upstairs on the third storey of the house, and there were many lamps burning in the room. A lad called Eutychus was sitting in an open window. Paul went on talking and talking; and the lad dozed off. He went so sound asleep that he fell out of the window into

---

* Dr Luke joined Paul at Philippi and went with him to Palestine; so here he begins to use his diary again.

the street below and was picked up for dead. Paul went straight down-stairs and bent over him and put his arms around him.

Don't be frightened,' he said, 'there's life in him.'

He went back upstairs, 'broke bread' with the others and had something to eat, and went on talking until it was dawn. Then he went on his way.

They led the lad away – he was alive all right – and everybody was very glad it hadn't been worse.

2. Miletus   Acts 20:13-38

Paul decided to go by road, and we were to pick him up. So we went on ahead to the boat and set sail for the port of Assos. He met us there, and we took him on board and went on to the town of Mityline, on the east coast of the island of Lesbos.

There we stayed the night, and sailing at dawn, came that day opposite the island of Chios. We anchored for the night off the coast of the mainland, and sailed next day across the open sea to the island of Samos.

Paul had decided to sail past Ephesus; he didn't want to lose any time staying there. He wanted to be in Jerusalem by Whitsuntide, if he could, and he was in rather a hurry. So next day we sailed on to the port of Miletus, some forty miles to the south.

From Miletus Paul sent a messenger to the Christian leaders in Ephesus – twelve miles across open water and then twenty miles by road. He asked them to meet him in Miletus; and they came over.

He talked to them about the work they had done together and how he had boldly told the Good News in market square and home to Jew and foreigner alike.

'And now,' he said, 'I am going to Jerusalem and I am sure that this is what God wants me to do. I don't know what will happen. All I know is that I may find myself in prison; in every prayer meeting we have held in the towns I have passed through, this has been made clear to me. I'm not bothered about myself – I don't matter; all I want is to do what Jesus told me to do, to tell everybody the Good News of God's love, and to go on telling that Good News to the end.

'I spent a long time with you, as you know; but this is my last goodbye – I am certain you will not see me again.'

He went on to remind them how he had lived among them – working with his own hands for his own keep and that of his helpers, and telling the Good News to all who would listen.

'After I am gone,' he said, 'you will have a hard time. But I leave you in God's hands. I have shown you, by the way I myself worked, that you must always help those who can't help themselves. Remember what the Lord Jesus himself said – "It's giving, not getting, that makes us happy".

He knelt down and prayed with them all. Everybody was crying as they bade him goodbye; Paul's words about their not seeing him again had upset them very much.

They went down with him to his ship in the harbour. We said a last goodbye and went on board.

3. Tyre   Acts 21:1-6

We sailed across the open sea to the island of Cos, and came, the next day, to the island of Rhodes. From there we went across to the port of Patara on the mainland. Here we changed ships. We found a ship bound for Palestine and went aboard and set sail. We sighted the island of Cyprus to the north, made across the open sea and landed at the port of Tyre for the ship to unload its cargo.

We looked up the friends of Jesus in the town and stayed a week with them. In the prayer meeting, they told Paul that they believed God's will was that he should not go on to Jerusalem. But, when the ship was ready to sail, we left the house and went down to the harbour.

The friends of Jesus and all their families went with us through the streets and out through the city gate. We knelt down on the beach and prayed together, and then said goodbye. We boarded the ship and they went back home.

4. Caesarea   Acts 21:7-14

The day's sail from Tyre ended at the port of Ptolemais (its name was Acco in the old days). We made ourselves known to the friends of Jesus there and stayed the day with them. Next day we set sail again, and came at last to the port of Caesarea, where the Roman Governor had his headquarters.

We went up to the home of Philip, and stayed a few days with him. His four unmarried daughters were leaders in the church and taught the Bible to the others in the Sunday services.

While we were there, a Christian leader called Agabus came down from Jerusalem. In one of our meetings, he took Paul's belt and tied himself up with it, hands and feet.

'God has told me this,' he said. 'Just as I have tied myself up like this, so the Jewish leaders in Jerusalem City will bind the man who owns it, and they will hand him over to the Roman Government.'

This upset us and we begged Paul not to go up to the city; everybody in the meeting begged him not to go.

'You'll break my heart,' said Paul, 'if you go on crying like this. I'm ready for anything they can do to me in Jerusalem – I'll face prison and death itself, if that's what being loyal to Jesus means.'

Nothing could make him change his mind; it wasn't any use talking to him.

'God's will be done,' we said.

Riot and Arrest (Dr Luke's Diary)

1. Meeting James   *Acts 21:15-26*

When our stay in Caesarea was over, we got ready to go up to Jerusalem City. Some of the friends of Jesus from Caesarea went with us, and took us along to stay with Mnason. (Mnason came from the island of Cyprus and had been a friend of Jesus from the earliest days.) On our arrival, the friends of Jesus in Jerusalem gave us a warm welcome.

We went next day to see James, the chief leader of the friends of Jesus in Palestine, and the other leaders. Paul told them how glad he was to see them, and went on to tell them how he had taken the Good News to the foreign cities of the Aegean and what God had done there. He described all that had happened, city by city.

'How good God is!' they said. 'But we must be careful. You see, brother, there are many thousands of Jews among the friends of Jesus. They are all very keen still about keeping Jewish customs. They've heard a lot of untrue stories about you – how you tell the Jewish people who live abroad that they needn't bother about the Jewish religion and its laws.

'We know that these wild stories aren't true, but don't you think we ought to do something about it? They'll be certain to hear that you've turned up in the city.

'Do what we tell you – to set their minds at rest. There are four men here – Jewish friends of Jesus who feel that they themselves must still keep the Jewish law. They are going to the Temple to carry out their Jewish duty. Go along with them and pay their expenses. Everybody will then see that you yourself still care about Jewish customs, and that all the stories they have heard about you are nonsense. Foreign friends of Jesus, of course, needn't bother about our Jewish customs; we made that plain in the letter we sent to them, you remember.'

Paul agreed. He took charge of the four men, and next day went with them into the Temple. They were to spend a whole week there, carrying out their Jewish duties.

2. The Riot
Acts 21:27-36

Then it happened – just as the week was ending. A few days before, some Jews from Ephesus had happened to see Paul walking through the streets. They had recognised him – and the man who was with him, a foreigner from their own city. They now caught sight of him again. This time he was inside the Temple itself where no foreigner was allowed to go, and they jumped to the conclusion that he'd got his foreign friend with him.

They grabbed him and started shouting.

'Jews, help!' they shouted. 'Here's the traitor! Here's the man who's been attacking our customs all over the world! He's actually brought foreigners into the Temple itself – he's treating this holy place as if our law didn't matter at all!'

Everybody began shouting and there was soon a great crowd. They got hold of Paul and dragged him outside the Temple, and the great Temple gates were closed. The crowd tried to beat him to death.

News was rushed to the Roman commander, Colonel Lysias, that there was rioting in the streets.* He called out the guard at the double, and ran down and charged into the crowd. At the sight of the colonel and the soldiers, the crowd stopped beating Paul up.

Colonel Lysias went straight up to Paul and arrested him.

'Chain him up,' he told the soldiers, 'and double the chains.'

He turned to the crowd.

'Who is he? What's he been up to?' he asked.

People said all sorts of things, one man one thing, another man something else. He couldn't make out what the riot was about; so he ordered Paul to be marched into the barracks. Paul had to be carried, for the mob was heaving and pushing all around and shouting 'Finish him off!' The soldiers got him at last to the bottom of the steps and were about to take him up the steps into the barracks.

---

* The Roman barracks were in the Tower of Antonia nearby, and steps led down from them right into the Temple court.

587

3. On the Steps of the Barracks   *Acts 21:37-22:24a*

Paul stopped Colonel Lysias.

'May I say something to you?' he asked him in Greek.

'You speak Greek?' asked the colonel. 'Then you aren't the Egyptian rebel who led four thousand "Dagger Men" into the desert?'

'I am a Jew,' said Paul. 'I was born in Tarsus; I am a citizen of a very important city. Let me speak to the crowd, please.'

The colonel had no objection.

Paul stood on the barrack steps and beckoned to the crowd with his hand. There was silence. He spoke to them, not in Greek, but in their native language, Aramaic; when they heard him speak in Aramaic, you could have heard a pin drop.

He told them how he became a friend of Jesus – how he had been taught by the great Jewish teacher, Gamaliel, in Jerusalem City; and then how, on the Damascus Road, Jesus had called him to tell the Good News to everybody everywhere.

'I then came back to this city,' he said, 'and I came into the Temple here to pray. And while I was praying I saw Jesus.

'"Be quick," he said to me, "and leave the city at once; they won't listen to what you've got to say here."

'"Lord," I said, "they know all about me. They know I went from Meeting House to Meeting House and threw your friends into prison and beat them up. Why, when Stephen was murdered, I was the man in charge."

'"Go!" he said, "your business is to tell the Good News to foreigners all over the world."'

The crowd had listened quietly so far, but as soon as they heard the word 'foreigners' they started shouting again.

'Finish him off!' they roared. 'He isn't fit to be alive!'

They went on shouting, waving their clothes and throwing dust into the air.

'Into the barracks with him,' said Colonel Lysias.

4. 'I am a Roman citizen'   *Acts 22:24b-29*

'Lash him with the whips,' said the colonel when they'd got Paul into the barracks. 'Find out what they are shouting about.'

The soldiers started to tie Paul up for the whipping.

'Is is right to whip a Roman citizen,' he asked the captain in charge, 'especially when he hasn't even been found guilty?'

The captain went straight off to the colonel.

'Do you know what you're doing? he asked him. 'This man's a Roman citizen.'

The colonel came back to question Paul.

'Tell me,' he said. 'Are *you* a Roman citizen?'

'I am,' said Paul.

'It cost me a lot of money to become a Roman citizen,' said the colonel.

'I was born a citizen,' said Paul.

The soldiers didn't stop to see what happened next. The colonel, too, was very frightened – he had actually ordered his soldiers to handcuff a Roman citizen!

5. Before the Jewish Council   Acts 22:30-23:11

The colonel wanted to know what the riot was really about and what the crowds thought Paul had done. He set Paul free and gave orders for the Jewish Council to be called together. He took Paul down to meet them face to face.

Paul stared at the Council.

'Brothers,' he said, 'I have tried to do what God wanted me to do all my life.'

The High Priest told those who stood near Paul to hit him across the face.

'God will hit you!' burst out Paul. 'You're the white-washed wall the man of God spoke of long ago! Do you sit there as a Jewish judge and tell them to hit me – and break the Law yourself?'

'Do you know what you're saying?' said the men nearby. 'You're cursing the High Priest who speaks in God's name.'

'I'm sorry,' said Paul. 'I didn't know that the High Priest would talk like that. I know, of course, what the Law says.'

Now Paul knew that the Jewish Council was divided into two parties who didn't agree with one another: there were the Pharisees who believed that those who die rise to life again and that there are such beings as angels and spirits; and there were the Sadducees who thought all this was nonsense.

'Brothers,' he called out, 'I am a Pharisee myself; I belong to their party. The real charge against me is that I hope, as they do, that people rise to life again when they die.'

That put the cat among the pidgeons – the Council started arguing, and there was a lot of shouting.

Some of the Pharisees stood up and spoke up quite openly for Paul.

'We don't think this man is guilty of doing anything wrong,' they shouted. 'A spirit or an angel may have spoken to him.'

There was almost a riot in the Council Room. The colonel was afraid for Paul's safety; it looked as if he might be torn to pieces between the two parties. He told a squad of soldiers to force their way into the crowd and rescue Paul and take him back to the barracks.

That night Paul had a vision. Jesus stood over him.

'Don't be afraid,' he said. 'You have stood up for me in this city; you must stand up for me like this in Rome itself.'

6. Back to Caesarea   Acts 23:12-35

When daybreak came, more than forty Jews got together in a plot and vowed to go without food until they had killed Paul.

They went to the High Priest and members of the Jewish Council, and told them what they had planned.

'This is what we want you to do,' they said. 'Call the Council together and send word to Colonel Lysias to bring Paul down from the barracks. Tell him we want to give him a correct and careful trial. We will get him on his way here.'

Now Paul's nephew heard about this plot to ambush him. He went along to the barracks and told Paul about it. Paul sent for one of the officers.

'Take this young man to the colonel,' he said. 'He's got some news for him.'

The officer took him to the colonel.

'The prisoner, Paul, sent for me,' he said, 'and asked me to bring this young man along to you. He's got some news for you.'

The colonel took him on one side.

'What do you want to tell me?' he asked.

He told him about the plot.

'And now they are just waiting for you to say Yes,' he added.

'Not a word to anybody,' said the colonel. 'I don't want anybody to know you've seen me.'

And he sent him home.

Colonel Lysias sent for one of his captains.

'Call out two hundred soldiers and seventy cavalrymen,' he said. 'You'll need two hundred horses. Parade three hours after sunset tonight. You are to escort Paul and deliver him safe to Governor Felix. You must cover the sixty miles to Caesarea by tomorrow evening. And don't forget horses for the prisoner.'

He then wrote a letter to the Governor. It went like this:

'Claudius Lysias sends his good wishes to His Excellency Governor Felix.

'A Jewish crowd got hold of this man, and if I had not reached him and rescued him with a squad of soldiers, he would have been murdered. I found out that he is a Roman citizen. I tried to discover what his crime was, and took him down to the Jewish Council. There was a lot of talk about their religion, but nothing on which I could sentence him to death or send him to prison. I have just discovered a plot to murder him. I am sending him to you at once, and I have told the Jewish leaders to put their case before you.'

The soldiers carried out their orders. By daybreak they had taken Paul halfway to Caesarea, as far as the town of Antipatris. The infantry went back to their barracks in Jerusalem, and the cavalry escorted him the rest of the way. They delivered the colonel's letter to the Governor and handed Paul over to him.

The Governor read the letter.

'What province do you come from?' he asked.

'Cilicia,' said Paul.

'I'll try your case when your accusers get here,' he said.

He gave orders for Paul to be kept under guard in Herod's Palace.

7. *Before Governor Felix*   Acts 24:1-27

Five days passed by.

Then the High Priest, Ananias, with some members of the Council, came down from Jerusalem City. They brought with them a lawyer, Tertullus, to put their case against Paul before the Governor.

The Governor called on Tertullus to speak.

'We enjoy great peace,' Tertullus began, 'and we owe it to you, Your Excellency. In every way and everywhere the life of our people has been made better; this, too, we owe to your care. We are glad about this and we are very thankful.

'I ask you to listen, with your usual kindness, to what we have to say. I will not speak long; I don't want to waste your time.

'This fellow here is a real trouble-maker – we've found that out all right. We've three charges to make against him. First, he's caused riots among Jewish people all over the world. Second, he's the ringleader of the Nazarenes – the followers of a man called Jesus. Third, he went into the Temple with a foreigner and broke our Temple laws. That's why we arrested him.

'If you examine the prisoner himself, you can find out that all our charges are true.'

All the Jews there joined the attack on Paul and said that this was what had happened.

The Governor nodded to Paul to speak.

'I know that for many years you have been a judge over our people,' Paul began. 'This makes me glad to make my defence before you. I haven't been in the country twelve days yet – you can check that fact yourself. I went up to Jerusalem to worship. There's nobody here who can prove I started an argument or a riot, in the Temple or a Meeting House or in the streets of the city – they never found me doing anything of the sort. They can't prove any of their charges.'

He then explained that the friends of Jesus followed the teaching of the Jewish Bible and held the hope that when people die they rise again – a hope many Jews themselves hold.

'I've tried to live honestly before God and man,' he said.

'It's a long time since I was last here,' he went on. I came back this time to bring a gift of money to help the needy of my own people. This is what they found me doing. I was in the Temple carrying out my religious duty. No crowd was with me, and I was going quietly about my business. It was some Jews from Ephesus who started all the trouble. They ought to be here in this court now; they're the ones who should be making charges against me, if they think I did something wrong. Further, let these men here tell you what happened when I stood before the Jewish Council in Jerusalem. Did that court find me guilty of anything – except, perhaps, that I called out: "The one charge against me today is that I believe that people rise again to life when they die"?'

At this point the Governor said he would go on with the hearing of the case later. He knew all about 'The Way' (as the friends of Jesus were called).

'When Colonel Lysias himself comes down from Jerusalem City, he said, 'I will give my verdict.'

He gave the captain of the guard his orders.

'Keep him under guard,' he said. 'But see he has some freedom. Don't stop his friends looking after him.'

Some days later the Governor was back in Caesarea, and his young Jewish wife was with him. He had Paul brought before him and listened to what he had to say about Jesus. Paul went on to tackle the Governor about Justice and self-control and God's judgement, and this frightened him.

'You'd better go now,' he said. 'I'll find another time to talk to you, and I'll send for you then.'

He really wanted to get money out of Paul. That was why he often sent for him and talked with him.

Two years went by. Then the Emperor called Governor Felix back to Rome to give an account of himself and his government of the country.

The Governor wanted to keep the Jewish people friendly; so, when he went away, he left Paul in prison. Another Governor, Festus, was sent out to take his place.

8. Before Governor Festus   *Acts 25:1-12*

Festus took up his duties as Governor.

Three days later, he went up from Caesarea to Jerusalem City. The High Priest and the Jewish leaders at once brought their charges against Paul to his notice. They asked him, as a favour to them, to bring Paul back to the city; they intended to carry out their plot to murder him on the road.

'Paul stays in Caesarea,' the Governor answered. 'I am leaving the city quite soon, and you can go down with me. If the man has done anything wrong, you can make your charges against him there.'

He spent a week or more in the city, and then went back to Caesarea.

Next day he took his seat in the Court and ordered Paul to be brought before him. When Paul arrived, the Jewish leaders crowded round him. They made many serious charges against him, but they couldn't prove any of them.

'I have done nothing wrong,' said Paul, 'either against the Jewish religion or the Temple or the Emperor.'

The Governor wanted to please the Jewish leaders; so he turned to Paul.

'Do you want to go up to Jerusalem,' he asked, 'and be tried before me there?'

'I stand here in the court with the Emperor,' Paul answered, 'and that's where I ought to be. I've done nothing wrong against the Jewish people; you know that very well. I'm not trying to escape death – if I've done anything to deserve the death sentence. But if there's nothing in what these men say against me, nobody can hand me over to them. I claim my right to be tried by the Emperor himself in Rome.'

The Governor talked the matter over with his advisors.

'All right,' he said. 'You have appealed to the Emperor; to the Emperor you shall go.'

Some days later, King Agrippa and his sister, Queen Bernice, came down to Caesarea to welcome Governor Festus and spend a holiday in the city. This gave the Governor the chance to ask him what he thought about Paul's case.

'Governor Felix left a man in prison here,' he said, and told him what had happened.

'They didn't charge him, you see, with crimes of any sort, as I expected,' he said. 'It was all about their superstitions and about a dead man called Jesus who, Paul said, was alive. I didn't know where I was. What kind of questions do you ask in a case like this? I asked him if he wanted to go to Jerusalem and be tried there. He claimed his right to be tried before His Majesty the Emperor himself. So I ordered him to be kept under guard till I could send him to Rome.'

'I should like to hear the man myself,' said the King.

'Tomorrow,' said the Governor. 'You shall hear him tomorrow.'

Next day was a great day for the city. The King and the Queen wore their splendid robes; the army officers and important people crowded the Hall. Governor Festus gave the order for Paul to be brought in.

The Governor made a short speech.

'King Agrippa, Gentlemen,' he said. 'You see this man before you. In Jerusalem and in this city, the Jewish people have made many complaints about him. They actually demanded his death. But it was clear to me that he hadn't done anything to deserve the death sentence. When he claimed the right to be tried in Rome, I decided to send him there. But I don't know what to put in my report to the Emperor. That's why I've brought him here before this assembly, and especially before you, your Majesty. When this examination is over, I shall know, I hope, what to put in my report. It seems silly to me to send a prisoner for trial without making clear what crime he's charged with.'

King Agrippa turned to Paul.

'You may tell us what you've got to say for yourself,' he said.

Paul raised his hand, and began to put his case to the court.

'The Jewish leaders have said a lot of things against me, King Agrippa,' he said, 'and I think I'm lucky to be putting my case today to you. You're no stranger, I know, to Jewish customs and to the questions we Jewish people disagree about among ourselves. I hope you will listen to me, even if I take some time about it.

'The Jewish leaders know all about me, though they won't tell you; they've known me for a long time. They know what I was like when I was young and living in Jerusalem; what an eager Pharisee I was – some of the best Jews are Pharisees. They know what lies behind this trial. The charge against me is about one thing, Your Majesty – the hope our people have held for centuries. Why should anybody think God can't raise the dead?

'Let me begin at the beginning.

'Deeply religious as I was, I did everything I could to stamp out the name of Jesus of Nazareth. In Jerusalem City I had many of the friends of Jesus thrown into prison; I did this under a warrant from the Jewish Council itself. At their trials, I voted with the rest for the death sentence. That is not all. Again and again I hunted them out in the Meeting Houses and tried to make them say "Cursed be Jesus". I hated them. I even hunted them out in cities far beyond the borders of Palestine.

'Then something changed my life.

'I was going one day along the Damascus Road with a warrant from the Jewish Council for the arrest of all Christians I found there.

'At midday, on that very road, Your Majesty, I saw a light from the sky shining round about me and those who were with me – a light brighter than sunlight. We all fell flat on our faces. I heard a voice speaking to me – speaking in Aramaic, my native language.

"Saul, Saul," the Voice said. "Why do you treat me as an enemy? You're like a horse kicking against the sharp stick of its driver."

"Who are you?" I asked.

"I am Jesus," he said, "and it's me you are treating as an enemy. Get up and stand on your feet; I've come to you to give you your orders. I make you my servant. You are to go and tell the whole world what you know about me now and what you will learn about me later. I will take care of you, whether your own people or foreigners attack you. It is to the whole world I send you, to all those who are not Jews. You must open their eyes, so that they may turn from their evil ways, receive God's forgiveness, and become members of God's family."

'That is why, King Agrippa, I can never go back on what I saw that day; it was God's command.

'I told the Good News in Damascus first of all, then in Jerusalem, then throughout the whole country, to Jews and foreigners alike. I told them all that they should change their ways and live in God's Way. That's why the Jews got hold of me in the Temple and tried to murder me.

'From the first day to this, I have had God's help. I tell the Good News to everybody, to ordinary people and to rulers and governors. I say nothing you won't find in the Bible. God's Chosen Leader had to face death, and, by being the first to rise from the dead, brought in a new day for all people everywhere – for the Jewish people and for the people of every country in the world.

'I say that again here in this court today.'

Even while Paul was talking, the Governor Festus shouted at him.

'You've gone mad, Paul, quite mad. You've been reading too many books. You're mad!'

'I am not mad, Your Excellency,' said Paul. 'I am talking plain common sense and telling the honest truth. His Majesty knows what I'm talking about, and I'm talking from my heart. I am sure that he hasn't been blind to what has been happening – it was no hole-and-corner affair.'

He turned to the King.

'Your Majesty,' he said, 'do you believe what the Bible says? I know you do.'

'In short,' said the King, 'you are trying to make me a Christian.'

'Short or long,' said Paul, 'I wish to God that everybody listening to me now – not only you, Your Majesty – would become like me, except, of course, for these handcuffs.'

King Agrippa, the Governor and Queen Bernice stood up and the whole assembly rose.

The three of them went out, and talked together about Paul's case. They all agreed that he was doing nothing that deserved either death or prison.

'If he hadn't appealed to the Emperor,' said King Agrippa to the Governor, 'he could have left the court a free man.'

Jesus – Leader and Lord

Paul of Tarsus

Paul was a tireless traveller, and letters were the only way he could keep in touch with his many friends. Corinth and Ephesus were his headquarters for his work in the lands that bordered the Aegean Sea. They were his headquarters, not his home; for the ships and the roads often beckoned him. Perhaps it was from Corinth he once went westward through the Gulf of Corinth and up the coast of the Adriatic Sea – to Nicopolis ('Victory City', built in celebration of a sea battle) and beyond to Illyricum, modern Albania, Bosnia, Croatia and Yugoslavia. A number of the towns on this coast had been Corinthian colonies, and he would hear about them in the streets and bazaars of the city. The valley behind Ephesus must have called him and he would hear stories of the coast and the islands from sailors in the harbour. He had friends everywhere; he could hardly help being a writer of letters.

Some forty years after his death, some of his letters were gathered together and published in two volumes. That would have surprised him. Perhaps this is how it happened.

At the beginning of the second century, the leader of the Christians in Ephesus was Onesimus. It seems very likely that this was the Onesimus who owed everything – his freedom and his love of Jesus – to Paul; you can read the letter Paul wrote about him to his owner, Philemon, on p. 623. Dr Luke had recently published his book on the beginnings of Christianity, addressed to His Excellency Theophilus (*From Galilee to Rome*); and in this book, you will remember, he had told many stories about Paul. A copy of it came into the hands of Onesimus. As he read it, he remembered the letters of Paul that were still kept in the church chests at Ephesus and Colossae. These letters ought not to be hidden away, thought Onesimus; everybody ought to read them. Dr Luke's book contained the names of other churches – Thessalonica, Philippi, Corinth, Rome – to which Paul had probably written letters. Onesimus was able to get copies of the letters they had received from Paul. When he had gathered the letters all together, he published them in two volumes; and, at the end, he put the little letter Paul had written to Philemon about Onesimus himself. People everywhere could now see for them-selves how great a Christian leader Paul had been.

Paul's letters are not easy to read. I have taken passages from them, and arranged them under different headings. You can find out from his own words why he became a Christian and what he thought Christianity was about.

We begin with what he had to say about Jesus.

Paul's Story of Jesus

Paul did not need to write very much in his letters about what Jesus said and did in Palestine; everybody knew the story, and it was read and discussed every Sunday in the meeting for worship. None of the gospels had yet been written, but there were still many people alive in Paul's day who had known Jesus or been living in Palestine at the time.

Paul had, nevertheless, to remind his friends, from time to time, about what had happened to Jesus, and call their attention to its meaning. I have gathered together these passages about Jesus, so that you can read what Paul had to say about him.

Paul had a very clear picture of the kind of person Jesus was and of what he said and did. He himself had never met Jesus, but he had become a Christian only a few years after his death, and he had met his close friends (like Peter) and talked with them about him.

What Paul has to say about the story of Jesus should be compared with the fuller story in *The Beginning* and in *From Galilee to Rome* (Part One).

My Own Experience *2 Corinthians 4:6; Galatians 2:20*

Let me begin by saying what Jesus means to me. God, who made this bright world, has filled my heart with light, the light which shines now I know what he is really like. This was the light which was shining from the face of Jesus.

I can only describe my experience as a friend of Jesus in this way: I go on living my ordinary human life; and yet, in a sense, I don't feel that *I'm* living it, but that Jesus has taken charge of me. I live by trusting in Jesus, God's Son, who loved me and gave his life for me.

Here are some important points about the story of Jesus.

What Jesus Came To Do *Galatians 4:4-5; Romans 15:8-9; Galatians 5:1*

When the time was ready, God sent his Son to live among us.

He lived a life like ours, and grew up as a Jew in Palestine. But he came to help the whole world: to help his own people, the Jews, to be really 'God's People'; and to help all the peoples of the world to live as 'God's People' too.

We can put it in this way. He became the 'servant' of his own people for two reasons: he wanted them to see that all God had done for them throughout their long history from the earliest days of their Founding

Fathers (Abraham, Jacob and Joseph) was no empty dream – God was a God they could trust; but he also wanted the whole world to know what God was truly like, a God of mercy, and to worship him with all their hearts.

In a word, he came to set us *all* free that we might live as free people.

What Sort of Man Jesus Was

Romans 1:3; 1 Corinthians 9:5b; Galatians 1:19; Romans 1:4; 15:3; 1 Thessalonians 1:6; Galatians 5:22, 23a; Philippians 4:23

He was a descendant of King David. He had a number of brothers. One of them was James whom I got to know when I stayed a fortnight with Peter in Jerusalem City.

But the most important thing about him was that he made God real. That's what we mean when we call him God's Son. Yet he never did anything for his own pleasure. He is our example, and we must follow him.

These were the marks of his character.*

He cared for people – for everybody. He was a very happy man. People who couldn't get on with one another found it possible to be friends in his presence. He never gave up. He was very kind, a really good man, and he could always be relied on. He was gentle, yet master of himself. What people remembered about him was his 'graciousness'.

Jesus Made His Purpose Quite Clear Just Before He Died

1 Corinthians 2:2; 1 Thessalonians 2:15; 1 Corinthians 11:23-25; 15:3-4

Yet he met a violent death at the hands of his own people, though he was executed by the Roman Government.

On the night when he was handed over to the Jewish leaders, he had supper with his friends. During supper he picked up the loaf of bread, said grace over it and broke it in pieces.

'This is my very self,' he said. 'I am giving myself up for you. Do this to remember me by.'

When supper was over, he raised the cup in the same way.

'This cup,' he said, 'means my death. I am dying to bring all people to God, as the Bible says, "from the least of them to the greatest".

---

* In this list of the marks of Christian character, Paul seems to be describing the character of Jesus himself (see also p. 618); hence the way I have translated it.

Whenever you drink it, remember me.'
And so he died and was buried.

The Death of Jesus Was not the End but the Beginning
1 Corinthians 15:4-8, 12-19, 35-44, 54, 20, 57; Philippians 2:6-11

On the third day he was raised to life. He was seen by Peter; then by 'The Twelve'. After that, he was seen by more than five hundred at once; most of them are still living, but some have since died. He was then seen by James, his brother; then by all his close friends. Last of all, long after anybody could have hoped, he was seen also by me.

The heart of the Good News is that Jesus is not dead but alive. How, then, can some people say, 'There's no such thing as being raised from death'? If that is so, Jesus never conquered death; and if Jesus never conquered death, there is no Good News to tell, and we've been living in a fool's paradise. We've even been telling lies about God, when we said he raised Jesus from death; for he didn't – if 'there's no such thing as being raised from death'. And if 'there's no such thing as being raised from death', Jesus is just – dead. If Jesus is dead and has not been raised to life again, all we've lived for as friends of Jesus is just an empty dream, and we're just where we were, helpless to do anything about the evil in our hearts and in the world. And those who have died as friends of Jesus have now found out the bitter truth. If all we've got is a *story* about Jesus inspiring us just to live this life better, we of all people are to be pitied.

Of course, the whole idea of 'being raised from death' raises many questions for many people. For example – 'How are the dead raised to life?' 'What sort of body do they have then?' But questions like these sound silly when we remember what kind of world God's world is and what God himself is like. Take the seed the farmer sows – it must die before it can grow. The seed he sows is only bare grain; it is nothing like the plant he'll see at harvest-time. This is the way God has created the world of nature; every kind of seed grows up into its own kind of plant – its new body. This is true of the world of animals, birds, fish – all different from one another.

This shows us how to think about this matter of 'being raised from death'. There's the life we live on earth – that has its own splendour; and there's the life we live when we are 'raised from death' and live (as we say) 'in heaven' – and this world beyond our earthly world has its own different splendour.

The splendour of the sun and the splendour of the moon and the splendour of the stars differ from one another – even the stars differ in splendour.

So it is when we are 'raised from death'. Here the body is a 'physical' body; there it is raised a 'spiritual' body. Here everything grows old and decays; there it is raised in a form which neither grows old nor decays. Here the human body can suffer shame and shock; there it is raised in splendour. Here it is weak; there it is full of vigour.

This is the meaning of the words of the Bible –

'Death has been totally defeated.'

For the fact is Jesus *was* raised to life. God be thanked – we can now live victoriously because of what he has done.

It is all summed up in a hymn we sing.

> He bore the form of God;
>> yet he did not think likeness to God
>> just good fortune for himself alone.

> He gave up everything
>> taking the form of a slave,
>> living life like other men.

> As a man
>> he faced the worst;
>> obedience took him to his death.

> So God raised him to the heights,
>> and gave him the name
>> above every name –

> that at the name of Jesus
>> the living and the dead
>> should hail him as Lord,

> and everybody everywhere claim
>> 'Jesus, God's Chosen Leader, is Lord!'
>> to the glory of God the Father.

The Story of Jesus Is Part of a Much Bigger Story (To the Christians in Rome)

The letter Paul wrote to the Christians in Rome (from which this chapter is taken) is different from his other letters. He was writing to Christians he had only heard about but not yet met. He wanted them to welcome him on his way to Spain and to help him in his work in the West. He knew that they must have heard all sorts of stories about him, many of them far from the truth. So he set down in this letter, carefully and honestly, what he believed and where he stood.

Jewish Christians had attacked him on three important questions – what Christianity is in fact about, what the importance of the Jewish religion in the history of mankind is, and how Christians should behave towards one another and towards other people. In this chapter we shall hear what he has to say about the first two questions – what Christianity is in fact about, and the importance of the Jewish religion.

To Paul, Jesus was the 'clue' to understanding what God is like and what he is doing, and to understanding the world in which we live and the story of humanity. Jesus helped him to begin to answer the serious questions men and women all over the world and in all centuries ask about this strange world in which we live – Why was it created? What is it all about? What has gone wrong? How can it be put right? What kind of world ought it to be? How can it become the kind of world it ought to be? Do individuals matter?

These are the questions he discusses in the first part of his letter to the Christians in Rome.

I have set out what Paul has to say under these headings:

> What the Good News means
> God shows himself to us in the glory of his world
> God has no favourites
> What the story of the Jews means
> Jesus
> All this makes a difference to the way we use God's earth
> God's love

In 'God's Love' we have repeated some words from 'Paul's Own Story' in *From Galilee to Rome* for you to see that it is the conclusion of a serious argument.

In 'What the Story of the Jews Means', I have put only a brief passage from Paul's letter. But I have added a very vivid description of Jewish history from another letter in the New Testament. This letter carries no name, but it may have been written by Paul's friend Apollos. Where Paul only refers to a few famous names, Apollos tells us something of the story which lies behind the names and helps us to see what kind of story it was.

What the Good News Means   *Romans 1:16-17*

Let me begin by saying what I mean by the Good News. I am not ashamed of it, and this is why.

The Good News means, first of all, that God has given us the power to live in his Way.

The Good News makes it clear that all we need to do is to take God at his word; this is something that everybody, whoever they are, can do.

Last of all, the Good News is Good News for everybody everywhere; my own people were the first to hear it, but it is for the people of every other country too.

In a word, the Good News tells us how God puts right what is wrong, and how he helps people everywhere to put wrong things right.

God trusts us, and we must trust God, from start to finish. That's what the Bible means when it says: 'The good live by trusting God.'

God Shows Himself to Us in the Glory of His World

Romans 1:18-23, 28-31

God has so made the world that human beings cannot defeat the truth – about God himself or about the world itself. If they try to defeat it, they only bring disaster on themselves and their selfish schemes.

He has made himself known to everyone everywhere through the world which he has made; this is plain for all to see.

What he is really like – his tireless energy and all that makes him 'God' – cannot, of course, be seen with our eyes as we can see the earth about us and the stars above us. But that doesn't mean that we can therefore say, 'We can't possibly know anything about "God".' For, from the beginning of human history, people have been able to think about what they see in the world about them and ask questions. As we can learn what a man is like from the things he has made, so we can learn what God is like from what God has made.

People have known, therefore, something about what God is like; but they haven't acted on that knowledge and honoured him as they ought to have done. They haven't even been thankful for what he has done. So their thoughts, not only about God himself but about the world we live in, have all become twisted; their minds have become dark instead of becoming clear. They talk as if they were clever, but they are not being clever at all.

Look, for example, at what they have done – this business of idols.

> 'They have exchanged their glorious God
> for the image of an ox that eats fodder',

as the Bible says. They have stopped thinking about God himself (who never changes); they would rather have imitations instead – sometimes in the shape of a human being (who does change) and sometimes in the shape of birds and animals and snakes.

What happened then? People came to think that it wasn't worthwhile to find out what God was really like; so what they *did* think about him was nonsense. Then their treatment of one another became inhuman; they began to live more like animals than humans.

Look at what goes on. People are no longer just to one another; they go on doing what they clearly know is wrong; they grab what they want; they don't mind playing dirty tricks on one another. The list of what they do is endless: jealousy, murder, gang quarrels, plots, downright badness. They don't mind what they say about one another – they don't hesitate to tell lies. They've got no use for religion, of course. They are violent, proud of themselves, boasting of their 'triumphs', inventing all sorts of crime, showing no respect for their parents. They have no conscience, no love for anybody but themselves, and no mercy.

God Has No Favourites   *Romans 2:6-11, 14-16, 25-29*

Everybody will be judged by what they themselves have done.

Those who have tried to live splendidly and honourably – setting their hearts on what will always be worthwhile, and steadily doing what they know to be right – will find out the secret of the good life.

Those who try to grab what they can for themselves, play about with the truth and don't mind how bad they are, will have to live in the angry and furious world they have themselves made.

In all this, it doesn't matter who you are – Jew or foreigner. God has no favourites.

But the story is not all dark; there's something else to say. People all over the world, whatever race they belong to and though they know nothing about the Bible, can begin to live in God's Way. Their religion, strange though it may be, is real religion. Nobody has told them what God is like – they have only their own hearts to guide them; but they have used their minds and followed their consciences. And when God, who has shown us in Jesus his Son what his Way is like, judges them – some far from what Jesus stood for, some very near what Jesus stood for – the fact that their thoughts are all mixed-up will not be held against them.

The point is this. A good pagan is better than a bad Jew. Many people who do not seem to be religious are, in fact, doing what God asks us to do better than many whose outward lives seem to be religious. It isn't easy to tell if someone is religious; belonging to God's Family isn't just a matter of outward acts of worship. The truly religious person is the one who is such inwardly. True acts of worship spring from the heart; we don't do them because 'that's what religious people do', but because we ourselves, in our hearts, want to worship God. It's what we love with all our hearts that matters to God; it doesn't matter if we get no public praise.

What the Story of the Jews Means (The Old Testament)

Romans 3:1-2; 9:4-5

But is there anything special about the Jews? What value for us has their religion? Very much indeed, however you look at it.

The most important thing about them is that God trusted them with the Good News. Through men like Moses, Amos, Isaiah and Jeremiah he told us his purpose for all mankind.

Here is a simple statement of what God has made clear to us through the Jewish people; through, that is, the great Men of God he sent them.

He made clear:
1. that he is our Father;
2. that he lives among us in all his glory;
3. how he wants us to live as his Family;
4. how he wants us to serve him;
5. what his purposes for all mankind are; these were made clear in the stories of Abraham, Jacob and Joseph, and, in our own day, in Jesus himself.

Paul, in the passage you have just read, has briefly summarised his reasons for believing that the story of the Jewish people is important. But it was a thrilling as well as an important story. So I have put here a fuller description, from a letter of another friend of Jesus, which tells us more about what happened.

Hebrews 11:1-3, 8-10, 24-28, 32-38, 13-16, 39-40

The heart of all religion is trust in God (this friend of Jesus wrote). It is this trust which makes our hope for the future a strong hope, and makes us sure about God himself whom we cannot see, and about the world which he made to be his world.

This is what the Men of God, whose stories are in the Bible, saw very clearly; for God spoke through them. Look at what happened:

Abraham trusted God. When God called him to go out to a land which would one day be the homeland of his descendants, he did what God told him to do. When he set off, he had no idea where he was going. He had only God's command. When he reached the land which was to be the future homeland of his descendants, it was still a foreign land to him. He didn't settle down in it; he went on living in his tents, as though he might still have to move on. So did his son Isaac and his grandson Jacob. His eyes were searching the horizon for a strong city designed and made by God himself.

Moses trusted God. He refused to be a prince in the King's palace. He chose to share the hard life of his own people instead of enjoying the high life of Egypt. He knew that such high life would not last, and that God did not want him to have anything to do with it. In his eyes insults (such as God's Chosen Leader himself had to face) were greater riches than all the wealth of Egypt. He knew it would all be worthwhile. It wasn't the King's anger that made him leave Egypt; it was his trust in God. He could face anything; God was as real to him as if he could see him.

Is there any need for me to go on to tell the stories of all the others? They would take too long. But what a roll call it would be – the heroes of the early days when we fought our way through the highlands; King David, the founder of our nation, and Samuel, who played so brave a part in that exciting story; and the great Men of God like Amos, Isaiah and Jeremiah. They all trusted God.

See what they did. They defeated great empires; they made sure that justice triumphed; they proved that trust in God was not an empty dream. They took great dangers – wild animals, fire and war – in their stride.

Their very weakness helped them to find out where their strength lay.

They were tortured because they would not give in; for they knew that death itself could not defeat their hopes. Some were beaten up and lashed with whips, chained like animals and thrown into prison. Some were stoned to death and sawn in two and murdered. They knew what poverty was; the only clothes they had were the skins of sheep and goats. They were treated like dirt – people of whom the world ought to have been proud. They were outcasts, driven out on to the moors and the hills, with only caves and pits for a home.

These faithful ones were not afraid to die; their secret was their trust in God. They did not see for themselves everything that God meant his people to enjoy. They could only see it on the far horizon and greet it with a cheer. They were ready to live as foreigners and strangers in their own world.

Such people show that what they were looking for was a new homeland, a new world. If they had been content with the world they had turned their backs on, they could have gone back at any time and lived in it. They didn't go back. The plain truth is that they longed for a better world – God's world. And God was not ashamed to be called their God – though their own world was ashamed of them as citizens. God's world is in the making, and they will have their place in it.

Let us sum it all up. We remember all these people for one thing: they put their trust in God. They did not see the world they died for. God had a bigger plan than they dreamed of: he wants us all, everybody everywhere, to enjoy the world he is making. Nobody, not even such great ones as we have been remembering, can truly enjoy God's world until we can all enjoy it together.

We can now go back to Paul's own words.

Jesus *Romans 3:21-24, 27-31; 4:1-4, 14-15, 20-24; 5:1-8, 10-11; 8:14-17*
But now God has shown us clearly what he is like in a new way – how he stands for what is right, overthrows what is wrong and helps people to live in his Way.

This is not altogether a new Way, as we have seen – the Men of God of the Jewish people had begun to see how God puts wrongs right. But Jesus has made it quite plain. And if we are to live in God's Way, we must trust God; this means trusting in Jesus who has made God real to us.

This is true for everybody everywhere; for God, as we have seen, has no favourites. We have all done wrong; none of us has lived as splendidly as God intended us to live, though we were all created to live in his Way and be like him. But God treats us as if we had learned to live splendidly; his love is given to us freely. And it is Jesus who has won this freedom for us.

There is nothing in all this to make us proud of ourselves. Keeping all the rules wouldn't have stopped us being proud of ourselves. We have simply taken him at his word, and that leaves no room for boasting.

I am sure of this: everybody can really live as God wants them to live by simply trusting him, not by trying to keep all the rules. I mean everybody. Is God only the God of the Jewish people? Isn't he the God of all people everywhere? Of course he is, for there is only one God. So he puts Jewish people right – if they trust him; and he puts the people of other countries right – if they trust him.

When I talk like this, I don't make the Jewish religion worthless, as some people say I do; I am showing how important it is, for this is what it is all about.

Religion isn't a matter of rules and regulations – not even the Jewish religion, as you can see from the story of Abraham. God's Way was not a matter of rules and regulations for him. It would, of course, have been easy for him to boast if he had been the kind of man who could say: 'I'm all right; I've kept all God's rules.' But that would have counted only with his neighbours; it wouldn't have counted at all with God. The Bible is quite clear. It says: 'It was Abraham's *trust* in God that made him a truly religious man.' Keeping rules and regulations is like working for wages. Wages aren't a *gift*; they are a *right*.

Friendship is different; friends don't help one another for what they get. If religion is just a matter of carrying out rules and regulations, there's no room for friendship with God – trust doesn't mean anything, and there's no point in making promises. The world is a hard world where, if you break a law, you pay for it – and that's that.

But this wasn't the way Abraham thought about God. He never once doubted that God was his *friend* and would keep his promises. This, for him, was the glory of God, and his trust in God grew stronger the longer he lived. He was quite sure that God would not let him down. That's why the Bible says: 'It was Abraham's trust in God that made him a truly religious man.'

But the Bible doesn't mean that this was only true for Abraham; it's true for everybody. And it's true for us who put our trust in God who raised Jesus to life again.

You see what it all comes to: our simple trust in God our Father puts us right, and we've nothing to worry about. This is what Jesus made possible. He made God's love real to us; and we are happy people, because we know that we can learn to be like God himself (we were created 'in his image') and live in his Way.

We can now be happy even when we have to face hard times. We know that hard times train us never to give in; never giving in is the secret of growing up; and being grown-up (as Jesus was grown-up), we look forward with high hope to the future. We aren't dreaming; for God himself lives in us, and our hearts are full to overflowing with his love.

So Jesus died at the right time. None of us was strong enough to deal with the mess we had got ourselves into; Jesus gave his life to get us out of it.

This is the wonder of it. It isn't often that anyone will give their life even to save a decent person; sometimes, perhaps, someone will give their life for a good person. We were neither decent nor good; we were his enemies. Yet Jesus gave his life for us, and made us God's friends. This is proof of how much God loves us.

We may put it like this.

Jesus, by his death, made us God's friends – even though we were then God's enemies. Now we are God's friends, Jesus, living in our hearts, can all the more deliver us from what is evil and help us to live as God created us to live. And more: the very thought of God fills us with joy – we are his friends. This is what Jesus has done for us.

Those who, with God's help, try to live in God's Way are true members of God's Family.

You know what it was like before you became friends of Jesus. You didn't know what God was really like. You felt you were slaves, and you were always afraid. This will never happen again. God's spirit does not make us slaves but members of his Family. When we pray, we speak to God just as Jesus did; we say 'Father!' God himself makes us quite sure in our hearts that we are his children. Children, as you know, inherit their father's wealth. If, then, we are God's children, we share his wealth as his heirs along with Jesus. But note: we must remember what Jesus went through before he became what he is; we must be ready to face what he faced, as well as share in his splendour.

All This Makes a Difference to the Way We Use God's Earth

Romans 8:18-25, 28-29

We look at everything differently now – the hard time we are going through and the very earth we live on. We see it all in the light of the glorious future which God will give us.

The earth itself is being spoilt by the way people live; it is, as it were, waiting for the time when the people who live on it will live, not as they do now, but as members of God's Family, with mercy and gentleness, sharing it together.

We know that the story of the whole world has been a story of much suffering. Animals know what suffering is; men and women know what it means, too. But it is not hopeless suffering; it is like the suffering of a mother when she has her baby – something is being born. Even we, who are the friends of Jesus and who have begun the new life, also know what suffering means all too well – but we look forward in hope to the time when we shall be fully members of God's Family, our whole personalities set free.

All this, of course, is only a hope now; we don't live as we ought to do. But this hope has made us new. And we're going to hold on until the day comes when we can see it with our own eyes.

But we know now that the world is not the sort of world we once thought it was. It is a world where God works for all that is worthwhile, *alongside those who love him*. We are fellow-workers with God. This is what he was always calling us to be – with one purpose in mind, a purpose he planned and settled before history began. This purpose was that we might grow up to be the kind of person Jesus was; so that Jesus might be the elder brother of a great family of brothers and sisters.

God's Love

Romans 8:31-32, 35, 37-39

Looking back on all this, what shall we say?

If God is standing by us, what does it matter who opposes us? He did not spare his own Son; he gave him up for us all. With such a gift, will he not give us everything else as well?

Who can take God's love away from us now – the love which Jesus has made real to us?

You know the sort of thing that can happen to any of us in this world of ours – suffering, hardship, cruelty, hunger, homelessness, danger, war. In just such a world, we who are the friends of Jesus can live more splendidly than the greatest world-conquerors – with the help of Jesus who loved us.

I am quite sure that nothing – neither dying nor living, neither what we're facing now nor what we may have to face tomorrow, nothing in our own world or in outer space or in our own hearts, can take away from us God's love, made real by Jesus our Lord.

The Difference Jesus Has Made

To become a Christian makes a great difference to the way we feel and think and live. It made a great difference to those who became Christians in the early days. Here are two passages from Paul's letters where he discusses the difference becoming Christians had made in their lives.

The early Christians lived in a very different world from ours. As you read these passages, consider what difference becoming a Christian should make today.

'We've Finished With the Old Ways of Living' (To the Christians in Colossae) *Colossians 3:5, 7-11*

We once lived as many people still do. But now all that's finished with; we must have nothing to do with sexual wrongdoing, indecency, lust, evil desires, the greediness that's always wanting more and more – using the world as if it were ours, not God's. But we must go further than this. We must do away with anger in our hearts as well as with angry words, with even wanting to hurt other people, and with all bad language. And, of course, we must never do anything but tell the truth to one another.

You see, we've finished with the old ways of living with all their nasty tricks. We're living in a new world – God's world – and every day God will make us better skilled at living in it.

You've heard people talking like this, haven't you? – 'My country – right or wrong', 'Our religion's the right religion; other religions are just superstition', 'We're civilised; they're savages'. 'Some people are born slaves; they'll always be slaves'. We don't talk like that any more.

We stand – always and everywhere – for all that Jesus stood for.

Jesus has broken down all barriers. He is all that matters, and he is changing the whole life of mankind.

'We've Found Something Bigger To Live For'
(To the Christians in Corinth) *2 Corinthians 5:14-17*

The love of Jesus drives us on – when we realise that he gave his life for all mankind, so that everybody should have something bigger to live for than just themselves and what they can get for themselves. Jesus gave his life for everybody.

We don't think of people now in the way people ordinarily think of one another. (I once thought of Jesus as my enemy and the enemy of my people. I don't think of him like that any more.) We try to think of people as God thinks of them.

When anybody becomes a friend of Jesus, the world's a new world for them; the old world has gone and a new world has been born.

What Jesus Made Clear

Jesus, for his friends, was 'the light of the world'. Knowing him was like stepping out of darkness into a world full of sunlight. They no longer stumbled, as people do when they are walking in the dark (see p. 658).

'I didn't understand myself', Paul once wrote about the days before he became a Christian; and he did not understand a lot of other things too. For Paul, becoming a Christian was like hearing God say 'Let there be Light!' The world was still a place with strangeness and mystery in it,' and there were many things still to learn. But it was not a dark place any more, where he had to feel his way about; it was full of light. The day had dawned, and he could see where he was going.

I have chosen six important questions that Jesus made clear for Paul:

> What the world means;
> What freedom means;
> What God wants us to do;
> What it means to be a Christian;
> How to learn to live together;
> How to see life steadily and see it whole.

These are questions that *we* need to be clear about too. They are 'live' questions for us, as we face the making of a new world in which people of all races must have their place and part.

What the World Means (To the Christians in Corinth)

1 Corinthians 2:7-10

The world, we now know, is not a meaningless world. God has had a purpose from the beginning. He created the world so that men and women everywhere should learn to live gloriously as members of his Family.

This is God's 'secret' and his 'wisdom'.

The governments of the world didn't realise what God was doing; if they had known anything about it, they wouldn't have executed Jesus as a criminal – Jesus who showed us, in the way he lived, what God was really like.

An old poem puts it clearly:

> Human eyes have never seen,
>   human ears have never heard,
>   human minds have never thought
>   what God keeps ready
>   for those who love him.

All this God has made clear to us by giving us his Spirit – his presence in our hearts.

What Freedom Means (To the Christians in Anatolia)

Galatians 5:1, 13-15

You see what Jesus did: he set us free, to live as free men and women. Stand up, then, and live as free men and women, not as slaves.

But note this: don't let your freedom become an excuse for doing just what you feel like doing. With God's love in your hearts, be ready to do anything – and I mean *anything* – for one another. For all religion can be put in a single sentence: 'Love other people as you love yourself.'

If you live like cat and dog, you'll just destroy one another. Don't forget that.

What God Wants Us To Do (To the Christians in Corinth)

2 Corinthians 5:19-20

In Jesus, God is making everybody everywhere his friends; and he's not going to list the wrong and unkind things we have done and hold them against us.

He wants us to take this message of friendship to others; we are therefore the messengers of Jesus. It is as if God were speaking through us to everybody – 'In the name of Jesus, be friends with God!'

What It Means To Be a Christian (To the Christians in Anatolia)

Galatians 3:26-29; 4:4-7

Your trust in God your Father has made you members of his Family; Jesus has made this possible. For when you were baptised and became friends of Jesus, you began, with his help, to live in his way – as he lived in his Father's Way.

Living in God's Way means that you can't talk about one another as being 'white' or 'coloured', 'working-class' or 'upper-class', 'men' or 'women' – as though that were the only thing about them that matters. The most important thing is that as Christians you are one company of friends. And if you are friends of Jesus, you are members of God's Family as God meant you to be and promised to make you.

That is why, when the time was ripe, God sent his Son to live among us as one of us – to help us to live as his sons and daughters, grown-up members of his Family. Because this is what we now are, he has given us the spirit of his Son in our hearts. When we pray to him, we pray to him as Jesus did; we say, 'Father!'

You aren't God's slaves; God has made you, as I have said, his sons and daughters. And, as sons and daughters inherit their father's wealth, so all the wealth of God, your Father, is yours.

How To Learn To Live Together (To the Christians in Corinth)

1 Corinthians 12:1

I don't want you to have wrong ideas about the gifts which God has given us.

Different Gifts but One Spirit   *1 Corinthians 12:4-11*

First of all, God has given each of us different gifts, but he has given the one same Spirit – his presence in our hearts – to every one of us. There are different jobs to do, but we do them for the same Master. There are different kinds of work, but the same God helps all of us in whatever we have to do.

To each of us God gives his spirit in our hearts in one particular way for the good of everybody. To one he gives the gift of talking wisely; to another the power to understand difficult problems and explain them; to another a special power to trust him fully; to another the skill of a doctor or nurse.

To one person God gives wonderful powers we do not really understand; to another the insight to understand his purposes and explain them clearly; to another the power to tell whether people are inspired by good or evil; to another strange mysterious experiences; to another the power to understand what these experiences mean.

But the one same Spirit – God's presence in our hearts – is at work in all these gifts, and God gives them to each of us, one by one, as he thinks best.

An Illustration – the Human Body   *1 Corinthians 12:12-26*
Take the example of the human body. The body is one body, but it has many parts. Though there are many different parts of the body, they all together form one body. Jesus, risen to life, is like that. It doesn't matter who we are – Jews or Greeks, slaves or free.* When we became friends of Jesus, we became one 'body' inspired by one Spirit, and we all share in that one Spirit.

Look at the human body: one body, but many parts – not just one part.

Suppose all the parts of the body got jealous of one another. Suppose the foot said: 'I'm not the hand; so I'm not going to be part of the body'; it's still a foot, part of the body, isn't it? Suppose the ear said: 'I'm not an eye; so I'm not going to be part of the body'; it's still an ear, part of the body.

If the whole body were just one big eye, how could we hear? If the whole body were just one big ear, how could we smell anything? What God has done, you see, is to make the body out of many parts, arranging each part as he thought best. If all we had was one big ear or leg, there wouldn't be any 'body' at all. As it is, there are many parts, but that means that we can have something very different from the parts in themselves – a 'body' which does all sorts of things which none of the parts of the body, by themselves, could do at all.

That is why the eye can't say to the hand, 'I don't need *your* help'; the head can't say to the feet, 'I don't need *your* help'. That's nonsense. Why, we couldn't do without the parts of the body that seem to be the weakest. We know that; and we treat them, less attractive though they may seem,

* We could say now – 'White or black, worker or boss'.

with very great care. We treat our private parts with great modesty; but we don't need to do that with our hair or face or figure. God has made the less attractive parts of the body more important than the attractive parts, so that there shall be no jealousy in the body. All the parts are made to fit in with one another as equally necessary. If something goes wrong with one part, all the parts are hurt; if one part wins honour, all the parts share its joy.

Christians Are the Body of Jesus   *1 Corinthians 12:27-30*

All of you together are the 'body' of Jesus, and each one of you is part of his 'body'.

It works out like this. God has given everybody their own work to do, as a friend of Jesus.

First of all there are the messengers, those who knew Jesus in Palestine and were there when he was raised to life. Then there are the preachers, those who can explain the Bible and help us to understand what God is doing for us and the whole world. Then there are the teachers; then those to whom God has given unusual powers; then those who have the skills of healing; then those who have strange mysterious experiences. Is everybody a messenger? or a preacher? or a teacher? Has everybody unusual powers? Can everybody heal people? Is everybody a leader? Does everybody have strange mysterious experiences? Can everybody explain what these strange mysterious experiences mean? Of course not.

What Love Really Means   *1 Corinthians 12:31-13:8a*

In this matter of gifts, always put the emphasis on the most important gifts. Yet I will show you that there is something far more important than all these gifts; indeed they are worthless without it.

I may speak all the languages of earth and heaven, but, if I have no love in my heart, it's just like the old religions with the din and noise of gong and cymbal. I may be a preacher and be able to understand and explain all the wonders and secrets of God's Way; I may trust in God with all my heart, trust him as Jesus told us to trust him; but if I have no love in my heart, all this is worthless. I may give everything I've got to feed hungry people; I may be branded as a slave for what I believe; but if I have no love in my heart, I get nothing at all out of it.

This is what love is like.*

---

* Paul's description of love in the following paragraph is 'a portrait for which Christ himself has sat' (Dr C. H. Dodd).

618

Love is never in a hurry, and is always kindness itself. It doesn't envy anybody at all, it never boasts about itself. It's never snobbish or rude or selfish. It doesn't keep on talking about the wrong things other people do; remembering the good things is happiness enough. It's tough – it can face anything. And it never loses trust in God, or in men and women; it never loses hope; and it never gives in.

Love holds good – everywhere, for everybody, for ever.

Make Love Your Aim   *1 Corinthians 13:8b-14:1a*

This can't be said about even the most important gifts.

There will come a time when there will be no need for preachers to explain God's Way. And all the strange mysterious experiences we mentioned will one day come to an end. There will come a time when learning will no longer be needed.

With all our learning, we don't know very much. All the preachers have told us about God's Way is only part of the truth about him. And all these will no longer matter when we know, as one day we shall, the perfect truth.

When I was a boy, I talked, thought and made my plans as a boy does. But when I became a man, I'd grown out of all my boyish ways. Our human life is like that. *Now* we are not seeing things as they really are; we are looking at them, as it were, in a clouded mirror, and they are not very clear. *Then* we shall see them directly, face to face. *Now* I know only a little bit of the truth. *Then* I shall know the whole truth, as God knows the whole truth about me.

All these things come and go. But there are some things that do not come and go. These three – trust, hope, love – last for ever. But love crowns them all.

See that you put love first.

How We See Life Steadily and See It Whole
(To the Christians in Corinth)   *1 Corinthians 3:18-23*

Get this clear. If any of you think you are 'clever' or 'wise', think again. Other people may pat you on the back, but you're just stupid in God's eyes. You must be ready to make a fool of yourself in other people's eyes, if you want to be really 'wise'.

Let me remind you of words you will find in the Bible:

God sees to it that 'clever' people get caught in their own tricks.

God knows that the schemes of 'clever' people are stupid.

These are the facts: The whole world is yours – all your 'star' leader has been able to do (whether he's Paul or Apollos or Peter is of no importance),* all the achievements of mankind, life and death, the present moment and the unknown future. All these, of course, are yours. But remember, they are only yours because you belong to Jesus and Jesus belongs to God.

Beginning To Live in God's Way

Paul saw clearly that Jesus did not want us to dream about God's Way; he wanted us to live in it. People must often have asked Paul: 'What must we do?' 'How do we begin to live in God's Way?' It is not easy for any of us, for we have to take the world as we find it and deal with people as they are. In his letters, Paul often gave them advice and guidance. Here is his well-known advice about Christian behaviour.

Paul believed that we have to train ourselves, if we are to learn to live in God's Way, as sportsmen have to train themselves. So I have added the passage where Paul talks about the runners and boxers at the Isthmian Games at Corinth.

How To Go about It (To the Christians in Rome)

Ourselves   *Romans 12:1-3*

We are members of God's Family, and I ask you to remember two things: keep God's kindness always in your minds, and give yourselves heart and soul to him – your energy, your heart and your mind. You belong to God, and it is service like this that makes God glad.

Don't try to do 'what everybody does'; let God keep your mind alive and ready to think new thoughts, and you'll be a very different person from what you were. In this way you will be able to find out what God wants you to be and to do – what is worth-while and right and grown-up.

I've learned something of God's love, and I say this to each of you: don't go about with high and mighty ideas of your own importance. Think sensibly about yourselves, in the light of what your trust in God has already taught you about God's love.

---

* Paul is referring here to the quarrels which have been taking place in Corinth. See p. 631; and also *Paul the Explorer*, p. 580.

Ourselves as Friends of Jesus   *Romans 12:4-8*

We who are the friends of Jesus are, as I have already said, like a human body with its different parts. We are many persons, but we are one 'body'. Each of us is like a different part of the body, and we are here to help one another, as the different parts of the body help one another.

Each of us has different gifts; God has seen to that. We must use them. For example: some of us are able to understand God's Way more clearly than others; some of us deal with business better; some of us are teachers; some of us are speakers. Let us use our different gifts with God's help. And so with everything we do. If we give, let us be generous givers; if we are leaders, let us be energetic leaders; if we are helping others, let us be cheerful helpers.

Ourselves and Other People   *Romans 12:9-21*

Love must be sincere and straightforward. Have nothing to do with evil of any kind. Give your heart to everything that is good.

Be a real family, warm-hearted in your care for one another, thinking better of others than of yourselves.

When keenness is called for, let's have no laziness; on fire with the spirit of Jesus, give yourselves to his service.

Look forward to God's new world with gladness. In hard times stand your ground; never forget to pray.

Take your part in helping other friends of Jesus when they are in want; make it your aim to keep the doors of your home open to those who need it.

Remember the words of Jesus: 'Bless those who treat you badly; bless them – don't curse them.'

Share other people's happiness and other people's sadness. Learn to respect everybody.

Don't be proud. Mix with ordinary people.

Don't talk as if you knew all the answers.

Don't injure anybody just because he has injured you; do the right thing that everyone, in their heart, knows is right.

As far as you can, be friends with everybody. Never try to get your own back, my friends; leave that in God's hands. You know what the Bible says: '"I will see justice done," says God; "punishment is in my hands."'

Remember what the Bible also says:
> If your enemy is hungry,
>> give him food;
>> if he is thirsty,
>> give him drink.
> If you do this,
>> you will make him ashamed of himself.

Don't be beaten by evil; beat evil by doing good.

Ourselves and Our Duty   *Romans 13:8-10*
Don't be in debt to anybody – except in the matter of caring for one another. Those who love their neighbour, whoever that may be, have got to the heart of all religion.

The Ten Commandments – and all other commandments – can be put in a single sentence: 'Love your neighbour as you love yourself.'

This is what 'love' means, and love cannot do wrong to anybody; that is why it is the heart of religion.

The Need for Training (The Christians in Corinth)   *1 Corinthians 9:24-27*
You know what happens in a race: all the runners compete; but only one wins the prize. Run to win – that's what you must do. All the runners at the Olympic Games have to train hard. They run for a wreath that withers; we run for a prize that never withers.

I try to remember all this.

I run, and I know where I'm running. Or, if you like, I box; and when I box, I don't punch the air!

And I'm tough with my body; I let it know who's master. After spending my life training others, I'm not going to be left at the post myself.

Tackling the job

There were many problems the friends of Jesus had to tackle and do something about. Sometimes they wrote to Paul to ask him to help them. I have gathered together here what Paul had to say about seven problems.

Some are special problems they had to face.

Slavery was common in those days. What do you do if you are a slave or slave-owner when you become a friend of Jesus? If you are a slave when you become a Christian, ought you to try to get free?

The meat sold in the butchers' shops in those days had first been offered in worship to idols in the temple; ought Christians to be vegetarians and have nothing to do with it?

Other problems were ones that we know something about.

What attitude ought we to take to people in authority, many of whom are not Christian and do not try to live in God's Way?

What about sex? (We know what many people do.)

What ought we to do when, as often happens, Christians disagree with one another about important matters? (For example, the Jews kept Saturday as a Holy Day; were Christians to go on keeping Saturday a Holy Day, as many Jewish Christians did? Or were they to do what many of them were doing, keep Sunday as a Holy Day, the day when Jesus was raised to life again? Or did they not need to have a special Holy Day at all, but just live every day in God's Way?)

What ought we to do when Christians divide themselves up into groups or parties, or start quarrelling?

When you have read what Paul had to say, discuss some of *our* problems today, as Paul discussed the problems of his day.

Perhaps you don't agree with what Paul thought Christians ought to do. Why?

Slavery (A Letter to a Christian Slave-owner in Colossae) *Philemon*

My dear Philemon, friend and fellow-worker,

When I am saying my prayers and I come to your name, I always thank God for you. People often tell me how much you love and trust Jesus, and how much you love and trust all the friends of Jesus too. This love and trust is something we all share together; and sharing it together has shown us how much Jesus means to us, how good now it is to be alive. Your love has meant a lot to me and made me very happy. And what's more, you've cheered the hearts of all the friends of Jesus, too, my brother.

Now, I've got something I want you to do. I wouldn't be afraid, as a friend of Jesus, just to tell you what your duty is, and leave it at that. But I'd rather appeal to the love we both have for Jesus and one another. I'm an old man now, you know, and, what's more, I'm a prisoner as well for the sake of Jesus; and I am appealing to you for my boy.

It's Onesimus I'm talking about – I became like a father to him here in prison.* I'm sending him home to you – and sending my heart with him. I should have liked to keep him here with me; he could have been a great help, and taken your place by my side, prisoner as I am for the Good News. But I wouldn't do anything unless you said Yes. I know, of course, that you'd do the right thing; but I want it to be your choice, not mine.

He was perhaps taken away from you for a short time so that you could have him back again to stay with you always – no longer a slave but something far better than a slave, a real brother. He is a brother to me now; and he will be much more a brother to you, both as a man and as a friend of Jesus.

If you think of me as your partner, welcome him as you would welcome me.

If he's done you a wrong or is in debt to you, put it down to my account.

I, PAUL, WRITE THIS WITH MY OWN HAND – I WILL PAY YOU BACK.

I don't need to remind you that you owe your very self to me. Now I come to think of it, I'd like to make something out of this – the sort of thing that Jesus would make out of it. Cheer me up, as the real Christian you are.

I know you'll do what I ask. I wouldn't have written to you otherwise. In fact, I know you'll do more than I ask.

And while you are about it, get a room ready for me. I know you've been praying for me; I hope God will answer your prayers and give me back to you.

Remember me to Apphia our sister; and to Archippus our fellow-soldier; and to all the friends of Jesus who meet in your home.

Epaphras is a prisoner here with me; he sends you his best wishes. So do the others who are working here with me – Mark, Aristarchus, Demas and Dr Luke.

How real Jesus has made God's love and peace! May the graciousness of Jesus be with you all.

Paul (a prisoner here in the cause of Jesus) and Timothy.

* Here Paul made a pun of the name of Onesimus which I have not translated.

People in Authority (To the Christians in Rome)   *Romans 13:1-7*

Everybody must obey those who rule over us. God gives some people the right to rule, and the present government is put there by God, even though the Emperor and his officials are not friends of Jesus.

So a rebel against the government is a rebel against God, and such rebels get what they deserve. Those who are good don't need to be afraid of the magistrates; those who are bad should be. If you don't want to be frightened of the magistrates, do what is right and win their praise. For the magistrate is God's servant, working for your good. If you do wrong, you have every reason to be afraid. Government officers don't wear the sword for nothing; the government if God's servant to see that justice is done, and that those who do wrong don't escape.

You must, therefore, be good citizens – not just to escape punishment, but because that's the way you ought to live. That is why you should pay your taxes. Government officers are God's officers, and they've got to carry on the government properly.

Do your duties, then, as a citizen. Pay your rates and taxes; show respect and honour to those who have the right to them.

'My Job' (To the Christians in Corinth)   *1 Corinthians 7:17-24*

God has given us whatever gifts we have; let us go on living as we were when he called us to be friends of Jesus. That's the rule I follow in all the churches everywhere.

Were you a Jewish citizen when you became a Christian? Don't try to hide the fact. If you weren't a Jewish citizen when you became a Christian, don't try to live like a Jewish citizen.

Being a Jewish citizen or not being a Jewish citizen is a matter of no importance at all. What matters is living in God's Way.

Let each of you stay what you were when you became a Christian. Were you a slave when you became a Christian? Never mind. If you get a chance of becoming free, take it. But remember that if you were a slave when you became a friend of Jesus, you are now free with Jesus; if you were free when you became a friend of Jesus, remember that you are now his slave.

Your freedom was bought at a great price – Jesus gave his life for you. Don't become other people's slaves again.

Here, then is the rule: whatever you were when you were called to become a Christian, stay like that. God is with you.

Sex (To the Christians in Corinth)   *1 Corinthians 6:12-15, 18-20*

'I'm free to do what I want,' you say.

Yes, that's true. But not everything is good for us.

'But I *am* free to enjoy everything,' you repeat.

I agree; but there's nothing that's going to make me its slave.

'Food for the stomach; the stomach for food' – you quote that, do you? Neither of them will last for ever.

I'd rather say this: 'The body for Jesus; Jesus for the body.' For whatever our bodies were meant for, they weren't meant for any kind of sexual wrong-doing. They were meant for bigger things than that; that is why God raised Jesus to life, and why he will raise us to life – real life.

You are parts of the 'body' of Jesus, as I have said, and that means that your physical bodies belong to him, too. Can I, then, take my body, which is part of the 'body' of Jesus, and hand it over to a prostitute? Never.

So, keep clear of sexual wrongdoing. All the other wrong things people do are, in a sense, outside their bodies; those who indulge in sexual wrongdoing wrong their own body itself.

You know, don't you, that your body is the home of God's own Spirit? You don't belong to yourselves; you were bought at a great price – Jesus gave his life for you. Then use your bodies for God's praise.

Other People's Points of View

The Question of Butcher's Meat (To the Christians in Corinth)
                              1 Corinthians 8:1, 4-13; 10:25-11:1

Let us look at this matter of buying meat in the market – meat, as we know, that has already been used in the idol-worship of the temples. That's the problem. What do we do about it?

Now, let's be clear. We all know that 'an idol is just an idol and doesn't mean anything at all', and that 'there's only one God'. And even if we agree (for the sake of argument) that there are many beings called 'gods' in the sky and on earth – we know that the towns and villages are crowded with 'gods' and 'lords' – yet for us there is only one God, our Father, who made the world in which we live and whose Way is our way. And we know that there is one Lord Jesus, who has shown us what the world we live in is really like and who has helped us to come really alive.

But this is the point. There are many friends of Jesus who have not learned to think like this yet; they are only beginning to understand all that Jesus means. Some of them were once regular worshippers in the temples, and have only just become friends of Jesus; they can't eat butcher's meat, which they know has been used in the temples, without feeling that it is wrong to do so; idols still feel real to them. When they eat it, they feel guilty, for they cannot make up their minds yet what is wrong and what is right.

Now food doesn't make any difference to what God thinks of us. If we refuse to eat the meat, we are no worse off; if we eat it, we are no better off. But make sure that this right of yours to eat what you like doesn't make it difficult for these friends of Jesus, friends who honestly can't make up their minds on these questions.

For example, if somebody like this, who can't make up their mind about what's wrong and what's right, sees somebody like you, with all your understanding of God's Way, sitting down to a meal in a temple where idols are worshipped, what will happen? Might they not say, 'Oh, it's all right for them; so it must be all right for me'? So they go on into the temple and have a meal there. And all the time, in their heart they feel guilty; they feel they ought not to do it, and they're all mixed up in their mind.

With all your 'knowledge', you haven't helped them, have you? You've done them great harm, a friend for whom Jesus gave his life. You've made them do something they believed to be wrong – and that's wronging your friend and wronging Jesus.

For myself, if I thought that a question of food made it difficult for someone to be a true friend of Jesus, I wouldn't touch butcher's meat again. I don't want to do anything to make another friend of Jesus do something they feel, in their heart, is wrong.

So, as a general rule, eat the meat sold in the meat-market, and don't start asking yourself 'Is it right?', 'Is it wrong?'. For quite clearly, as the Bible says,

> The whole world belongs to God
> and everything in it.

Again, if somebody who isn't a friend of Jesus asks you out to dinner and you want to go, go and have dinner with them. Eat whatever they've got ready for you, and don't start asking yourself 'Is it right to eat this?', 'Is it wrong to eat that?'. We've settled that question.

But if somebody at the dinner table looks across at you and says, 'This meat was used in the worship in the temple, you know' that raises another question altogether – the question of what *they're* thinking and what *they* believe is right and wrong (it isn't, as we have seen, a question for you at all). For their sake, don't eat it. For the point now is this: we've got to make it quite clear what we, who are the friends of Jesus, think of idol worship; and this isn't something that doesn't matter.

'What!' you say, 'has my freedom to be spoiled because of somebody else's mixed-up ideas of what's right and what's wrong? Look, I enjoy everything I eat, and I always thank God for everything that he's given us. Why should anybody say I'm not a good friend of Jesus?'

Really, it can be put quite simply. Do everything – eating, drinking, whatever it is, everything – to the honour of God. But don't ever make things difficult either for Jewish citizens (with all *their* convictions), or for Greeks (with all *their* convictions) or for members of the Christian community (with all *their* different feelings). That's what I've tried to do – to look at things from other people's points of view, not to bother about myself but to find out what I could do to help other people. I want everybody to be a true friend of Jesus.

Follow my example, as I try to follow the example of Jesus.

The Question of Sunday (To the Christians in Rome)　　　Romans 14:5-12

One person thinks that Sunday is more important than all the other days; another thinks that every day is just as important as any other. In matters of this kind, everybody must make up their own mind carefully. If a Christian keeps one day in a special way, they keep it in honour of Jesus.

This is exactly the same question as that of buying butcher's meat in the meat-market. Some friends of Jesus eat it, and they do so in honour of Jesus and give thanks for his goodness; some won't eat it, and they also act in honour of Jesus and give God thanks for his goodness.

This, you see, is the heart of the matter: we don't live or die just for ourselves; we live and die in honour of Jesus. For both in life and death we are the friends of Jesus. Jesus died and was raised to life to be the Lord of all humanity, the living and the dead.

Why do you find fault with your brother? Or why do you look down on your sister?

God is the judge of us all.

Do you remember what the Bible says? –

> 'As I live,' God has said,
> > 'every knee shall bow before me,
> > every tongue shall praise God.'

All of us, you see, will have to give an account of ourselves to God.

Let's stop finding fault with one another. Let us make up our minds that we won't get in the way of anybody who's trying to live in God's Way.

Take this question of food.

You know what Jewish people – and many Jewish friends of Jesus – believe. They believe that God has forbidden us to eat certain kinds of food. Now, if there's one thing which Jesus has made quite clear to me and which I'm absolutely sure about, it is this: this is a mistake – no food of any kind is wrong to eat. But that isn't the end of the matter.

Here are some things to think about.

1. If anybody really believes that certain foods are wrong to eat, they are wrong to eat – for them.
2. If the feelings of another friend of Jesus are hurt because you eat anything you fancy, you are not really making love your aim.
3. Don't let mere food cause anybody to give up trying to live in God's Way. Jesus gave his life for them – as well as for you.
4. Don't let your Christian ideals get a bad name.
5. God's Way has nothing to do with food – what you eat and what you drink. But it has everything to do with (a) putting wrong things right, (b) learning to live together as friends, and (c) enjoying being alive because you know, in your hearts, that God is Father. Anybody who 'follows Jesus' by living like this is the sort of person God wants them to be – and other people respect them too.
6. Whatever we do must have two clear aims: it must help people to live together as friends, and it must help to build up God's Family.
7. Don't let questions like that of food hinder God's work.
8. Everything God has made is good; but it's a bad thing if arguing about food shakes somebody's trust in God. We ought to do nothing – eat, drink or what you will – that shakes anybody's trust in God.
9. Keep your convictions about things like food to yourself – and God. Be content with knowing that you've nothing to regret about the way you've upheld the truth.
10. If you've got any doubts about certain foods, don't eat them. If you do, you're doing wrong; you aren't, in this matter, trusting God. You're acting out of bravado, or because you don't care, or for some such reason; that's wrong. We must always let our trust in God direct our lives.

11. If we are strong, our business is to help people who are weak. We have no right just to 'please ourselves'. It's the men and women next to us we should 'please' – to help them to be themselves and to grow up. Remember – Jesus never 'pleased himself'.

Groups (To the Christians in Corinth) 1 Corinthians 1:10-13; 3:3-10; 4:6-7
You are members of God's Family, and I beg you to learn to agree with one another. We mustn't break up into quarrelling groups, arguing about who's right and who's wrong. You know what Jesus wanted. You must be real friends, sharing one another's thoughts and sharing one another's convictions.

News has been brought to me that you are quarrelling with one another; some of Chloe's business agents told me. To put it plainly, you are divided into quarrelling parties with your party-cries: 'I belong to Paul's party', 'I'm for Apollos', 'Peter's the man for me', 'I've no use for parties; I just follow Jesus'.

This is all wrong. Can the friends of Jesus be divided into parties with cries like this? It's like dividing Jesus himself. Get things straight. Have I died for you on a cross? Were you baptised 'In the Name of Paul'?

If you are going to be jealous of one another and quarrel with one another like this, you are living as though you'd never known Jesus and you're behaving like any Tom, Dick or Harry in the city. When you shout your party cries – 'I belong to Paul's party', 'I'm for Apollos' – aren't you just like anybody else in the world?

What's Apollos, anyhow? Who's this Paul? I'll tell you – just servants through whom you became friends of Jesus. That's all. We were only doing what Jesus told each of us to do. We're like gardeners: I put the plants in and Apollos watered them; but it's God who made them grow. The gardeners don't matter, whether their job is to set the plants or to water them; only God, who makes things grow, matters. The man who sets the plants and the man who waters them work together as a team, and they get paid according to the job they do. We are fellow-workers, and we work together for God, not for ourselves. You are simply God's field where we work.

Or, if you like, you are God's building. I am like a skilled master-builder. I laid the foundations. God gave me the strength to do this; I couldn't have done it by myself. Then somebody else put the building up.

I have talked like this about myself and Apollos to help you to see the real point of being a friend of Jesus – living in God's Way. You won't do it by boasting about this leader and attacking that. Who gave you the right to go about boasting of your own importance like this? Hasn't everything you've got been *given* to you? And if this is the truth about us – that everything we have is given to us by God – why all this showing off as if you were the 'big noise'?

Quarrels (To the Christians in Corinth)　　　　　　*1 Corinthians 6:1-7*
Do you mean to tell me that you go off to the ordinary law-court when something goes wrong between you and another friend of Jesus? Doesn't it occur to you that this sort of thing ought to be settled between yourselves? We who are the friends of Jesus know what God's Way is and that this is the standard by which everybody everywhere is to be judged: isn't that clear to you? What's the point of claiming to know what God's Way for the whole world is, if we can't settle little matters of this sort? Don't you know that God's Way is the Way for both heaven and earth, let alone for the everyday matters of our daily life?

And if you have to settle everyday matters like this, why choose as judges people who don't take our point of view? You ought to be ashamed of yourselves. Haven't you got anybody sensible enough to settle questions like this between one friend of Jesus and another? Must one friend of Jesus go to law against another friend of Jesus, and get people who don't accept our Christian standards to settle who's right and who's wrong?

To go to law at all with one another shows you've failed to live in God's Way.

Isn't it better to put up with wrong? Or let yourself be robbed?

Three Things To Remember

These three passages give us a summary of Paul's thoughts about the Christian life. It can be lived now – if we are prepared to 'have a go' and keep our eyes on Jesus. And it is worth it.

Remember – Everybody Is Needed (To the Christians in Ephesus)
Ephesians 2:19-22

You are no longer outsiders and foreigners in God's world; you are fellow-citizens with all the friends of Jesus everywhere and members of God's Family.

Let me make what I mean clear with an illustration.

Think of building a house. The builders lay the foundations, use the stones to build the walls and hold them together with a keystone.

God's Family is like a house. Inspired preachers among us (like Agabus)* and the first close friends of Jesus (like Peter and Andrew) are the foundations; Jesus is the keystone; you are the stones.

Jesus holds God's Family together and helps it to grow; but he needs you, as the keystone needs the stones that make the walls.

Spend Your Time on What Is Worthwhile
(To the Christians in Philippi) *Philippians 4:8*

One last word. Give your minds to what is true and noble, right and clean, lovely and graceful. Wherever you find excellence – things really worth getting excited about – concentrate on them.

Remember Who You Are (To the Christians in Colossae)
Colossians 3:12-17

Remember who you are: God has chosen you, you belong to him and he loves you. His way must be your way.

Care for people. Be kind and gentle and never think about yourself. Stand up to everything. Put up with people's wounding ways; when you have real cause to complain, don't – forgive them.†

Here is your clue: God's forgiveness of you is the measure of the forgiveness you must show to others.

It is love like the love of Jesus that makes all these things possible, holding everything in its grip and never stopping halfway. Master every situation with the quietness of heart which Jesus gives us. This is how you were meant to live; not alone by yourself, but together in company with all the friends of Jesus. Thank God that it is so.

Remember Jesus, and keep the Good News, with all its wealth of meaning, day by day in your mind. Here is real wisdom, in the light of which you can help one another, deepening one another's understanding and warning one another, if need be.

---

* See *Caesarea*, p. 585.
† Paul here gives a list of the marks of the Christian character. But, as in another letter (see p. 618), he is painting a portrait of Jesus.

How full of songs your hearts will be, songs of joy and praise and love, songs to God himself! In this spirit you can take everything in your stride, matching word and deed, as the friends of the Lord Jesus. Make him the centre of your life; and with his help let your hearts be filled with thankfulness to God – your Father.

John of Ephesus

John 20:30; 21:25; 20:31

'I have not written about the many other "signs" which Jesus did in the presence of his friends. If I had, I should have filled the world with books! I have written as I have to help you to see that Jesus is God's Chosen Leader, God's Son – to stake your life on this fact and to live splendidly as his friend.'

John's writings

The Purpose of John's Book

At the end of the first century, some forty or more years after the death of Paul, a new account of the story of Jesus was written in the city of Ephesus, Paul's headquarters during the last years he spent in the area of the Aegean Sea. We know very little about its author; his name was John.

People were asking new questions about Jesus and the meaning of his story. It was seventy years after the first Easter Day. Most Christians then living were not Jews, and Palestine and its stormy history meant little to them. They had grown up in Greek cities and they thought in Greek ways. Was the Good News, they were asking, really Good News for the Greek and Roman world? Could the story of Jesus – a story of something that happened long ago in a far-off province on the edge of the Roman Empire – really mean anything to educated people in cities like Ephesus and Corinth? Jesus had not even been a citizen of the Empire – he was a mere provincial; how could what he was and said be important in the changed world of a new century?

Many people today ask questions like those. 'Can the story of Jesus mean anything in the twenty-first century?' they ask. 'It happened so long ago and so far away. Times have changed.'

John was the first great Christian thinker to show, in the language of a new age, that the *story of Jesus matters always and everywhere to everybody.*

Mark and Matthew and Luke had told the story of Jesus much as it had been told from the beginning, using words and language that anybody who had grown up in Palestine and thought in Jewish ways could understand. Dr Luke sometimes changed a Palestinian word or phrase into its Greek form; when he described a house, for example, he pictured a Greek house, not a Palestinian house. This was not enough. Something bolder had to be done.

In the city of Ephesus, Christians met, as Christians all over the world did, on Sunday, the First Day of the week, for prayer and teaching and 'the breaking of bread' (see p. 601). At this service of worship, they heard the story of Jesus read aloud, the story that had been read aloud ever since Paul's day and that went back to the memories of the friends who had known Jesus in Palestine.

The Christians in Italy and Greece used similar stories of Jesus in their services of worship; their version of the stories of Jesus lies behind the accounts of Mark and Dr Luke in *The Beginning, The Message*, and Part One of *From Galilee to Rome*.

When these old stories had been read in the services of worship in Ephesus, John had often been asked: 'But what do these stories mean *now*?' 'What do they mean to *us*?' He had often talked about them, and shown his Greek friends how full of meaning for everybody these old stories were. He was getting old, and his friends asked him to put down in writing what he had told them in his many talks.

So he sat down to write a new kind of book about Jesus. He would not just tell the story again as Mark and Matthew and Luke had done. He would tell it in a new way so that everybody would be able to see its worldwide meaning. He would take some of the old stories and draw out their meaning in language that his Greek friends used in their conversations with one another. His theme would be, not 'What Jesus did and said', but 'What Jesus means to us now'. He would use the old stories, but he would use them in a new way.

The Plan of his Book

You will remember how Mark planned his book about Jesus. He told a straightforward story. He began with the Baptism of Jesus by Jordan River; he went on to tell of his work in Galilee, his exile in the north and his journey south; then he ended his story with the last days in Jerusalem. Matthew and Luke followed his plan, and put in other stories and sayings where they thought they best fitted in. John had a new plan.

He divided his book into three parts: the Introduction; the 'Book of Signs'; and the 'Book of the Passion'.*

* The word 'Passion' means 'suffering' and refers especially to the death of Jesus.

He begins, in the Introduction, with a poem, and then the story of the Call of the first friends of Jesus. He wants us to see what Christianity is about, and he helps us to do this by setting the story of Jesus against the background of world history, and showing us what Jesus meant to four men.

In the central part of his book, the 'Book of Signs', he uses nine stories of Jesus, familiar to his readers because they come from the stories they heard read aloud in the Sunday services. Some of them you will have already read, in Mark's and Dr Luke's versions, in *The Beginning*, *The Message* and *From Galilee to Rome*; some are new to us. But he used them in a new way, as a poet does, to make clear what Jesus means to everybody everywhere.

Then, in the last part of his book, the 'Book of the Passion', he tells the story of the last days of Jesus. But he tells us the story in his own way – first the 'Table Talk' of Jesus, then the plain story of his death, then some stories of his resurrection.

John's Method of Writing

We can see that John had a special way of writing about Jesus when we notice that he called the stories of Jesus he used, not 'stories', but 'signs'. To him they were more than stories of something that happened long ago; if we read them carefully and think about them, they tell us more than just what Jesus did in Palestine – they are 'signs' of what he means to us *now*.

How does John help us to see this?

He begins by telling the story very much as it was told in the early version of the stories of Jesus used in the worship of the Christians at Ephesus – as Mark and Dr Luke would have told it. He wants us to re-member that he is dealing with a story of something that once happened (only in one 'Sign', the 'Sixth Sign', does he put what he has to say in a story of his own making, much as Jesus put what *he* had to say in the form of stories). So, to begin with, he puts the story down very much in the words as they lay before him, though he adds a phrase here and there to bring out their meaning. If the Christians at Ephesus wished to find out just what happened, there was always Mark's *The Beginning*.

Then, when he has told the story, he adds longer 'Dialogues' (or 'Conversations'). These are his own work. He is writing as a poet does, using his imagination and his own words to bring out the meaning of the old story, though he weaves into his 'Dialogues', from time to time, actual sayings of Jesus that everybody knew. This is how he talked to his Christian friends at Ephesus when they asked him, 'What do these stories mean *now*?' He is drawing on his long Christian experience and telling them what Jesus has meant to him. 'This,' he is saying, 'is not just what Jesus did for particular people but what he always does in a different way for all of us who love him, whoever we are and wherever we are living.'

This way of writing a book about a great man had been used before. Plato, the friend of the great Greek thinker Socrates, explained what Socrates had stood for by writing Dialogues. In these Dialogues he imagines Socrates talking to all sorts of people; the words of the Dialogues are Plato's; but the picture of Socrates is a true picture, helping us to understand what Socrates stood for. In John's Dialogues, the words are mostly John's; but the picture of Jesus is a true picture.

John introduces us to friends of Jesus we have not met in Mark's and Dr Luke's stories. Nathanael came from Cana in Galilee. Others are Jerusalem friends, and one of them belonged to an important city family. He is referred to as 'the friend Jesus loved dearly' and the 'other friend'. It was the 'other friend', John tells us, who took Peter past the door-keeper into the High Court in Jerusalem. It was too dangerous to name him.

Reading John's Book

We read Mark's and Dr Luke's books (*The Beginning*, *From Galilee to Rome*) chiefly as history books. They believe that Jesus is the Son of God (as John also does) and they do not hide what they believe about him. But they are telling 'the plain story' of what happened. We must read John's book as we read a drama (like the plays of Shakespeare). John believes that it is important to be sure what actually happened, but he is telling us *what the story means*, as we have said. That is why, like a poet or a dramatist, he has arranged his story in his own way. He begins, as we have seen, with a poem. He sets out the 'Book of Signs' like a play with seven acts, and he explains the meaning of each act in his Dialogues.

As we read John's book, we must look carefully at the details of his story and ask ourselves: 'Why did he choose *that* detail?' 'What is he helping us to understand about Jesus?' He uses words, as poets do, to suggest more than they actually seem to say.

'Light', 'Day', 'Night', 'Darkness' mean for him not merely actual day and night but also the light and darkness of our minds. Jesus is 'Light' and he has come so that people do not 'stumble in the darkness'. It was

'Night' when Nicodemus came to Jesus – night in his mind as well as night in the street outside. The friends of Jesus crossed Galilee Lake *in the darkness* and alone – after the Desert Meal they, too, were puzzled about Jesus and did not understand him. John uses other words in the same way – 'running water' ('living water'), bread ('the Bread of Life'), the vine ('the true vine' means God's Family), shepherd (Jesus is the Good Shepherd), wine (the true worship of God). So, as we read, we must note first the *ordinary meaning*, and then ask, 'With what *special meaning* does John also use the word?' John deals with their special meaning in the Dialogues.

Note the characters of his stories. John seems to have chosen them to make clear that Jesus came to help everybody: men and women, old and young, religious leaders and ordinary people, friends and strangers, Jews and Greeks. Jesus meets them in many places – the house and the Temple, the village and the city, in the street and by a well and on a country road.

It may help us to realise how John uses the details of his stories, if we remember how Shakespeare uses the details of *his* plays. For example, Shakespeare begins his terrible tragedy of *Macbeth* with a scene which helps us to *feel* the darkness of his story – 'A desert heath. Thunder and lightning' – and we *feel* immediately something of the darkness and storm of the story he is going to tell us. This is what John does. He tries to help us to feel the darkness in which Nicodemus was groping for the truth by beginning his story with the words, 'Nicodemus . . . once came to Jesus *when it was dark*; he makes us feel the darkness in the heart of Judas when he tells how he left the supper in the upper room – 'He went straight out *into the night*.'

So John's stories prepare us for what he has to tell us about Jesus in the Dialogues.

There are two words John loves to use – the name Jesus used to describe God's character, 'Father', and the word 'world'. In these two words we can see what John believed was the most important thing about Jesus, made clear by what he said and the way he lived and died and rose again to life: he came to help everybody everywhere to know God as Father and to live in his Way.

A Letter

About the time John wrote his book, a circular letter, written in Ephesus, was sent to the churches in the surrounding province of Asia. It may have been written by John himself or by a close friend and pupil of his. The letter tells us simply and clearly what Christianity really means, and summarises the great theme of John's own book. These passages from the letter are worth reading before you begin to read the book itself.

1 John 1:1-5

The theme of our message is the Good News – the Word that makes real life possible.

It has always been true, but now we have direct evidence of its truth, the evidence of our own eyes and ears and hands – we have actually seen him face to face:

> The Word became human
> and lived a human life like ours. *

We have the evidence of our own eyes – we speak as witnesses – and we tell you the secret of real life, life lived in the presence of God the Father and now shown to us for us to see clearly what it is like.

What we want you to be quite sure about is that we are not guessing – we are telling you what we've seen and heard.

The message of this letter is that we all should be partners together, members of God's Family, friends of Jesus his Son.

The secret of unclouded joy – that's what our letter's about.

'The daylight's here: the night's gone for ever.' This is what Jesus had to tell us – Good News about God.

1 John 3:1-2; 4:7-12

See how great is God our Father's care of us – he calls us his sons and daughters! That, in fact, is what we really are. Here and now we are members of his Family. God has not told us what we shall one day be; but we are sure of this – when he does make it clear to us, we shall share his likeness, for we shall see him as he really is.

My dear friends, let us really care for one another; such care and love is God's gift to us. Everybody who loves and cares is his son or daughter, and knows God. Those who have no love in their hearts for anybody haven't the slightest idea what God is like, for the very heart of God is love.

* See the poem 'The Word of God', p. 641.

This is how God's love has been made clear to us: he sent his only Son to live among us to help us to live splendidly. I'm not thinking, you see, of the way we love God, but of the way he loves us. He loved us enough to send his Son to help us to get rid of all that is wrong in our hearts and lives. That's how we know what love means.

If God loves us like this, my friends, we must love one another like this too. Nobody, of course, has ever *seen* God himself; yet, if love of one another marks everything we do, God lives in our hearts, and he makes our love real love like his.

1 John 4:16b, 18-21

God is love itself. So, if we live in love – and we can see what this means by remembering how Jesus lived – we live in God's presence and he lives in our hearts. With love like this in our hearts – love for God and love for one another – there's nothing that can ever make us afraid, for such love drives all fear away. You see, God loved us first, and we learned how to love from him.

We can test our love for God. If somebody says 'I love God' and yet cares nothing about someone he meets at work or in the street or about another friend of Jesus, he is just a liar. If he can't love somebody he's seen, that shows he doesn't love God whom he hasn't seen. Indeed, Jesus told us plainly: if we love God, we must love the people we meet at work or in the street as well.

John's Gospel: The Introduction

John begins his account of the meaning of Jesus with a poem. We must read it, as we read all great poetry, many times.

It begins with an echo of the opening words of the Book of Genesis, the first book of the Bible, where the creation of the world is described. In the coming of Jesus, John suggests, God is completing the creation of the world, so that it shall be the world he intended it to be, a world where men and women live together as members of his Family.

The word 'Word' has many meanings; John wants us to keep them all in mind. It means first of all just what it says – an ordinary word (how powerful *words* can be!); it also means 'reason', 'the thought behind the word'; and finally, for John, it is the best name for Jesus, for he is God's 'Word', God explaining himself to us.

I have put the words from the Book of Genesis at the head of the poem for you to read; and then divided the poem into its three parts.

The headings of the parts are mine, to guide you in following John's argument.

Then John gives us some stories about the call of the friends of Jesus. Perhaps he put Andrew first because he was he was well-known in Ephesus, but these stories are given to us to show us that Christian experience – the experience of his friends – points to the truth of the poem. This is what Jesus means to those who love and follow him.

The poem and the stories should be read quietly. There is more in them than we shall find in one reading.

The Word of God

What Jesus Really Means *The first words of the Bible – Genesis 1:1-3*

At the very beginning of all things
God made the universe we know.
The earth lay empty and dead,
darkness blacked out the deep seas,
great winds lashed the water.
God spoke –
'Let there be Light!'
and the world was filled with Light.

The Word *John 1:1-5*

At the beginning of all things –
the Word.
God and the Word,
God himself.
At the beginning of all things,
the Word and God.

All things became what they are
through the Word;
without the Word
nothing ever became anything.

It was the Word
that made everything alive;
and it was this 'being alive'
that has been the Light
by which people have found their way.
The Light is still shining in the Darkness;
the Darkness has never put it out.

The real Light
   shining on everyone alive
   was dawning.
It was dawning on the human world,
   it was what made the world a real world,
   but nobody recognised it.

The whole world was its true home,
   yet human beings, crown of creation,
   turned their backs on it.
But to those who walked by this Light,
   to those who trusted it,
   it gave the right to become
   members of God's Family.

These became what they were –
   not because 'they were born like that',
   not because 'it's human nature to live like that',
   not because people 'chose to live like that' –
   but because God himself gave them their new life.

The Word became human
   and lived a human life like ours.
We saw his splendour,
   love's splendour, real splendour.

From the richness of his life,
   all of us have received endless kindness:
God showed us what his service meant through Moses;
   he made his love real to us through Jesus.

Nobody has ever seen God himself;
   the beloved Son,
   who knows his Father's secret thoughts,
   has made him plain.

The First Friends *John 1:35-51*

John the Hermit and two of his friends were standing one day talking together by Jordan River. Jesus walked by, and John saw him.

'Look,' he said, 'God's Chosen Leader!'*

The two friends heard what he said and went after Jesus. Jesus turned round and saw them coming.

'What are you looking for?' he asked.

'Sir,' they said, 'where are you staying?'

'Come and see,' said Jesus.

So they went along with him and saw where he was staying and spent the day with him. It was about four o'clock in the afternoon.

One of John's friends was Andrew. His first thought was to find his brother Simon.

'We've found God's Chosen Leader,' he told him, and took him back to Jesus. Jesus looked him over.

'So you are Simon?' he said. 'I'll give you a new name – Peter.'†

The next day, Jesus made up his mind to go north to Galilee.

He met Philip.‡

'Come along with me,' he said.

Philip found Nathanael.

'You know the Leader the Bible talks about,' he said, 'the Leader God is going to send us. We've found him. He's Joseph's son, Jesus, and he comes from Nazareth village.'

'You can't expect anything from a place like Nazareth!' said Nathanael.

'You'd better come and see for yourself,' said Philip.

Jesus saw Nathanael coming to meet him.

'He's a true member of God's Family,' he said. 'There's nothing false about him.'

'How do you know what sort of man I am?' asked Nathanael.

'Before Philip spoke to you,' said Jesus, 'I saw you in the shade of the fig tree.'

'Master, you are God's Son,' said Nathanael. 'You are the King of Israel.'

'You trust me just because of what I said about the fig tree,' said Jesus. 'This is nothing to what you will see. You remember Jacob's dream? He saw a ladder set up on earth and reaching up to heaven and God's

* John said 'Lamb of God', an Old Testament name meaning 'God's Chosen Leader'.

† 'Peter' means 'Rock'.

‡ Philip came from the same town as Andrew and Peter – Bethsaida on the northern shore of Galilee Lake.

angels linking heaven and earth. It was a dream for Jacob – believe me, it will be fact for the Son of Man.'

The Book of Signs

We come now to the central part of the book, the Book of Signs and its Conclusions. I have marked the Narratives and the Dialogues so that you can see which are which.

Read the Narrative first. If the same story occurs in *The Beginning* or in *From Galilee to Rome*, compare it with the version there. You can discuss, if you like, exactly what happened. But the important thing is to see how John has used the story and to find out why he has chosen just this one at this point. The title I have given the story will guide you. Then read the Dialogue which follows and think about it carefully. Here John is trying to help us to see some truth about the whole meaning of Jesus, what he does for us if we trust and love and follow him.

Each 'Sign' takes one great truth about Jesus, and all the 'Signs' together form a single argument. It runs something like this. Christianity is nothing less than a 'new creation'; *Jesus makes everything new* and, whatever we have been like, if we follow him we can start again (the First Sign). *He offers us the power to 'live splendidly'*; he is not merely a good example (the Second Sign). But we must play our part; *our new life must be sustained*, as we have to eat food if we are to be strong and healthy (the Third Sign). We are not forced to accept the offer Jesus makes us to live in a new way; *we can say Yes or No to him*, we can accept him or reject him (the Fourth Sign). And so *we judge ourselves* (Jesus does not judge us) by the choice we make (the Fifth Sign). Nevertheless, *God's purpose will succeed*, for what God cares for is that we should really be ourselves as he created us to be. Life will conquer Death; *Christianity is a victorious faith* (the Sixth Sign). Then we come to the heart of the matter. Jesus seemed weak when he died on the cross; but this was really his hour of victory. Mysterious though it may seem, *Life conquers in and through Death*; seeming weakness is strength. This is what Paul meant by 'the foolishness of God' (the Seventh Sign). So we come to the end of the Book of Signs with a simple Conclusion that leads us on to the story of the death and resurrection of Jesus.

Here is an outline of the Book of Signs. I have added beneath each title a saying of Jesus and a quotation from Paul, each dealing with the same theme. You will see that both Paul and John are helping us to realise what Jesus stood for.

First Sign – A New Beginning

Jesus	Anyone who does not welcome God's Way like a little boy or girl won't get into it. *(Matthew 18:3)*
Paul	When anybody becomes a friend of Jesus the world's a new world for him; the old world has gone and a new world has been born. *(2 Corinthians 5:17)*
Narratives	New Wine New Temple
Dialogues	A Conversation at Night A Conversation by a Well

Second Sign – New Life

Jesus: You remember what the Bible says? –

> Blind people see again,
>> lame people walk about;
>> lepers are made well,
>> deaf people are hearing;
>> dead people are alive again,
>> hopeless people are told the Good News.
>>>> *(Matthew 11:4-5)*

Paul	The Good News means first of all that God has given us the power to live in his Way. *(Romans 1:16)*
Narratives	A Boy Is Healed A Cripple Is Healed
Dialogue	New Life

Third Sign – 'Our Daily Bread'

Jesus	Give us today our bread for tomorrow. *(Matthew 6:11)*
Paul	I go on living my ordinary life; and yet, in a sense, I don't feel that I'm living it, but that Jesus has taken charge of me; I live by trusting in Jesus, God's Son, who loved me and gave his life for me. *(Galatians 2:20)*
Narrative	The Desert Meal
Three Dialogues	Living Bread
Conclusion	The Friends of Jesus Desert Him.

Fourth Sign – Yes or No?

Jesus	Why don't you make up your own mind about what is right and wrong? *(Luke 12:57)*
Paul	Everybody must make up their own mind carefully. *(Romans 14:5b)*
Narrative	Jesus Goes up to the Feast.
Seven Dialogues	Who is Jesus?

Fifth Sign – We Judge Ourselves by the Choice We Make

Jesus	The measure you give will be the measure you get. *(Matthew 7:2b)*
Paul	What you sow you reap. *(Galatians 6:7b)*
Narrative	A Blind Man Sees.
Dialogues	Many Points of View The Shepherd and His Sheep
Conclusion	'Trust what I do'

Sixth Sign – Triumphant Life

Jesus	For as the lightning lights up the whole sky God himself will light up the whole world. *(Matthew 24:27)*
Paul	We can now live more splendidly than the greatest world conquerors – with the help of Jesus who loved us. *(Romans 8:37)*
Narrative and Dialogue	The Death of Lazarus.
Conclusion	The Jewish Council Plots the Death of Jesus.

Seventh Sign – Seeming Weakness Is Strength

Jesus	If you forget all about yourself because you are keen on helping me, even if you lose your life, you'll be all right. You will really be yourself. *(Mark 8:35b)*

Paul	'My love, given freely to you, is all you need,' God once told me. 'It's when you have no strength left that you will know how strong I am.' I've proved that. It is when I'm weak I am strong. *(2 Corinthians 12:9, 10b)*
Narratives	The Anointing at Bethany Jesus Rides into the City
Two Dialogues	Foreigners Meet Jesus

The Conclusion – The Light of the World

This arrangement of the Book of Signs (as indeed the arrangement of the whole of John's Book) follows the suggestions of C. H. Dodd in the two very important books he wrote about the Gospel of John (the 'Fourth Gospel'). We owe a great debt to C. H. Dodd for the way in which he made John's argument plain.*

The First Sign – A New Beginning

Two Narratives:

New Wine   *John 2:1-10*

On the third day there was a wedding in Cana in Galilee. Jesus and his friends had been invited, and his mother was there, too.

They ran short of wine.

'There is no wine left,' his mother said to Jesus.

'You mustn't bring me into this yet, Mother,' he said. 'My time has not come.'

'You do just what he tells you,' said his mother to the servants.

Six stone water pots stood nearby (each held twenty or thirty gallons). They were kept to hold water for religious purposes.†

'Fill the water pots with water,' said Jesus to the servants, and they filled them to the top.

'Draw some of the water out,' said Jesus, 'and take it to the master of ceremonies.'

This is what the servants did.

The master of ceremonies tasted the water, now become wine. He hadn't any idea where it had come from; the servants who had got the water, of course, knew. He called the bridegroom over.

---

* The two books are *The Interpretation of the Fourth Gospel* and *Historical Tradition in the Fourth Gospel.*

† See *The Beginning,* p. 420.

'Look here,' he said, 'most people serve the best wine first. Poor wine's kept till everybody's a bit drunk. You've kept the best wine till now.'

New Temple*   John 2:13-22

Just before the Great Feast Jesus went up to Jerusalem City.

He went inside the Temple, and found the Foreigners' Court being used as a cattle market. There were oxen and sheep and doves everywhere, and money changers busy at their tables.

He made, as it were, a cattle whip of some cords and drove sheep, cattle and the whole crowd out of the Temple. He tipped the coins of the money changers on to the ground and pushed their tables over.

'Take these things out of here,' he said to the dove-sellers. 'Don't make my Father's house into a market.'

'Where's your warrant for treating us like this?' the crowd demanded.

'You can destroy this Temple,' he said, 'but in three days I'll make it into a real Temple again.'

'Indeed,' they said, 'it took nearly fifty years to build and you're going to rebuild it just like that!'

Jesus, of course, was not talking about wood and stones; he was talking about his 'body' – the company of his friends and the work he would do through them.

(His friends remembered this saying after his resurrection. They knew, then, that the Bible was right, and that Jesus had spoken nothing but the plain truth.)

Two Dialogues:
A Conversation at Night   John 3:1-12, 16-21

Nicodemus, a Jewish leader, once came to Jesus when it was dark.

'Sir,' he said, 'we Jewish leaders have no doubt that you are one of God's teachers. Nobody could do what you do without God's power.'

'Believe me,' said Jesus, 'you must begin all over again if you are to see what God is doing in this human world.'

'How can an old man begin all over again?' asked Nicodemus. 'He can't start life again as a baby, can he?'

'No,' said Jesus, 'but let me put it this way. If anyone is to live in God's Way, two things matter: they must change their ways – this is the point John the Hermit made – and be baptised as a sign that they have done so; and they must receive God's power in their own hearts.

* See *The Beginning*, p. 430; *From Galilee to Rome*, p. 508.

648

'Human power is only human power, when all is said and done; only God's power is strong enough to help someone to live in God's Way. 'Don't be so surprised when I tell you, "You must begin all over again." Strange things happen in our world. Take the wind, for example. It blows where it wants to. You can hear its noise, but you haven't any idea where it's coming from or where it's going to. Doesn't that help you to understand what God's power is like in human lives?'

'How can this sort of thing happen?' asked Nicodemus.

'You're a very learned man,' said Jesus, 'and you're a teacher yourself; can't you really understand how God works? Believe me, I am talking about what I know at first hand and reporting what I have seen; but you will not believe that these are plain reports. If what I said about the wind means nothing to you, how can what I say about God make any sense?'

This is the measure of God's love for everybody everywhere: *he gave his beloved Son.* He does not want people to destroy themselves; he wants them to live – and to live splendidly. The secret of splendid living is to stake your life on his beloved Son. God did not send his Son to judge the world; he sent him to save it.

People stand or fall by the attitude they take to Jesus; the great question is – will they risk their lives, if need be, for what he lived and died and rose again for? This is how people judge themselves; the day has dawned – and they liked the darkness better. What they were doing would not stand examination. Those who have something to hide detest the light; they keep out of it if they can – they don't want to be 'shown up' for what they are. Those who have nothing to hide welcome the light; they do not mind everybody seeing how they live – with God's help and for his sake.

A Conversation by a Well   John 4:4-42
Jesus once had to cross Samaria, and he came, about midday, to Jacob's Well, outside the Samaritan town of Sychar. His friends went off into the town to buy some food. The long walk had tired Jesus and he sat down, just as he was, near the well.

A Samaritan woman came along to draw water.

'Could you please give me a drink?' he asked.

'Indeed!' she said. 'You're a Jew – and you're asking a Samaritan woman like me to give you a drink?'*

---

* Jews, in those days, wouldn't even drink from the same cup as a Samaritan.

'If you only understood the Jewish religion,'* said Jesus. 'and who it is who is asking you for a drink, you would have asked him for a drink and he would have given you, not well water, but living water.'

'But sir,' she said, 'you've got no bucket, and it's a very deep well. Where are you going to get "living water" from? Jacob, the founder of our nation, made this well for us; he and his family and his cattle used it. Are you a greater man than he was?'

'This water will not really quench anyone's thirst,' said Jesus. 'Before long, they will be thirsty again. The water I give is not like that. If someone drinks it, they will never be thirsty any more. It will be as though they had a living spring of water in their heart, the secret of living in God's Way.'

'Sir,' she said, 'give me this water. I shan't be thirsty, then, and I won't have to come all the way to this well to get water.'

'Go and fetch your husband,' said Jesus, 'and come back here.'

'I haven't a husband,' said the woman.

'That's an honest answer,' said Jesus. 'You've been married five times, but you aren't married to the man you're living with now. You've answered quite straightforwardly.'

'You're a Man of God, I can see, sir,' she said. 'But, you know, we don't think you Jews worship God properly. Our ancestors worshipped God on this mountain here; you say God can only be properly worshipped in Jerusalem City.'

'The time is near, believe me,' said Jesus, 'when the worshipping of God as Father will not be on this mountain or in Jerusalem City alone. I said the time is near, but indeed the time has already come when God's true worshippers, who know him as Father, will worship him everywhere with their whole hearts and their whole lives. That is the kind of worship God our Father asks for. God is not Someone you can meet on a mountain. God is Spirit – you can meet him anywhere; what we must give him is the service of our lives and hearts.'

'Well, it's all rather difficult,' said the woman, 'but we know that when God's Chosen Leader comes, he will make it all plain.'

'I am God's Chosen Leader – I who am now talking with you,' said Jesus. At that moment his friends came back from the town. They were amazed to find him talking with a woman. They were too amazed even

---

* Jesus said 'Gift of God'. For Jews God's greatest gift was the Law (the first five books of the Old Testament) which sets out what religion meant to them. The Samaritans also had their own version of the Law.

to ask him if he wanted anything to eat, let alone why he was talking with her.

The woman left her pitcher by the well and went off back to town. 'Come on!' she said to people she met. 'Come and see a man who could read my life like a book!'

And out of the town they came, along the road to where Jesus was.

In the meantime, his friends asked Jesus to have something to eat.

'I've food to eat you know nothing about,' said Jesus.

'Has someone brought him some food?' his friends asked one another.

'My food is a different kind of food,' said Jesus. 'It is doing God's will and finishing the work he sent me to do. That's the food I live on.'

'You know the proverb "It takes time to grow a harvest",' Jesus went on. 'Believe me, if you'll only use your eyes and look at the fields, you'll see they are golden harvest fields already. The reaper is at work and the corn is being harvested. Sower and reaper are celebrating together.

'You remember that other proverb – "One man for sower and another for reaper". That is true too. The harvest I sent you to reap was sown by somebody else. Other people worked long and hard in the fields; you inherit their hard work.'

Crowds of the townspeople came to trust Jesus just because of what the woman told them. (You remember what she said, 'He read my life like a book!')

When they met Jesus, they asked him to stay with them, and Jesus spent two days in the town. Many more came to trust him when they heard what he himself had to say.

'You know,' they said to the woman, 'we don't trust him now just because of what *you* told us. We've listened to him ourselves and we are sure that he is indeed the Saviour of the world.'

The Second Sign – New Life

Two Narratives:

A Boy Is Healed*   John 4:46-53

There lived in Capernaum a royal official whose son was ill. He heard
that Jesus had left the south and come north into Galilee. Off he went
to meet him. He asked Jesus to come down to heal his son, who was
very near death.

'Trust based on miracles,' said Jesus, 'is not enough.'

'Sir,' he said, 'come down or my son will be dead.'

'Go home,' said Jesus. 'Your son will live.'

The man took Jesus at his word and went home.

On the way home, his servants met him.

'Your son's going to live!' they said.

He asked them the exact time he began to get better.

'It was one o'clock yesterday afternoon,' they said. 'It was then his
fever left him.'

The father realised that it was at one o'clock Jesus spoke the words
'Your son will live'. He and all the members of his household became
friends of Jesus.

A Cripple Is Healed†   John 5:2-9a

By the Sheep Pool in Jerusalem City, there was a building with five
arcades.‡ In these arcades lay a crowd of sick people – blind, crippled
and paralysed.

One of the men lying there had been ill for thirty-eight years.

Jesus caught sight of him and realised how long he had been ill.

'Do you want to get better?' asked Jesus.

'I've got no friends, sir,' he said. 'When the water bubbles up, there's
nobody to put me into the pool. Somebody always gets down before
me when I'm trying to reach it.'

'Get up,' said Jesus, 'pick your bed up and walk.'

The man was cured then and there. He picked up his bed and started
to walk.

* See *From Galilee to Rome*, p. 505.
† See *The Beginning*, p. 420.
‡ Its Aramaic name is 'New House'.

Dialogue: New Life   *John 5:9b-17, 24-26, 30*
The day happened to be Saturday, the Holy Day of the Jews.

'It's the Holy Day,' said some Jewish leaders to the man who had been cured. 'You shouldn't be carrying your bed.'

'The man who cured me told me to pick up my bed and walk,' he said.

'Who told you to do this?' they asked.

The man had no idea, for Jesus had disappeared into the crowd.

Some time later, Jesus found the man in the Temple.

'Look,' said Jesus. 'You're a healthy man now. Don't do anything that's evil. Something worse than illness may happen to you.'

The man went off and told the Jewish leaders that it was Jesus who had cured him.

It was because Jesus did things like this on the Holy Day, that the Jewish leaders became his enemies.

He made his attitude quite clear.

'My Father is always at work,' he said. 'He's at work now. So am I.'

'Believe me, whoever listens to what I have to say, and trusts God who sent me, has learned the secret of real living. They are free. They're no longer "half dead", as we say – they're full of life.

'Believe me, the time is soon coming – in fact, it is here now – when people who are living "half dead" lives will hear the voice of the Son of God, and all who listen will learn the secret of being really alive. The Father is the source of all real life; he makes the Son the source of real life too.

'I do not try to please myself; I try to do the will of God who sent me.'

The Third Sign – 'Our Daily Bread'

*Narrative: The Desert Meal**   *John 6:1-21*
One day, just before the Great Feast, Jesus went over Galilee Lake. People had watched him cure the sick, and a great crowd of them followed him.

He climbed the hillside, and he and his friends sat down.

He looked up and saw the crowd coming towards him.

'Where are you going to buy bread to feed a crowd like this?' he asked Philip.

* See *The Beginning*, p. 421.

'If you spent £50 on bread,' said Philip, 'you wouldn't have enough – they'd only get a bite each.'

'There's a boy here with five barley loaves – and two fish!' said Andrew. 'Do you think that's enough for a crowd like this?'

It was a grassy spot, and the five thousand men who had gathered there sat down on the grass.

Jesus took the boy's loaves, said Grace over them, and gave them out to the men sitting there. He did the same with the fish, too – as much as they wanted. And they all had enough.

'Pick up the bits of food left over,' said Jesus to his friends. 'We don't want to waste anything.'

They picked up enough bits of food to fill twelve wicker baskets – all left uneaten by the crowd from the five barley loaves.

The crowd had been watching, and they were soon talking among themselves.

'This is surely the Man of God we were expecting to come and save us,' they were saying to one another.

Jesus saw what was going to happen – they were planning to force him to be their king.

He slipped away, alone, to the hills.

After sunset, his friends went down to the beach, got into the boat and put across the Lake to Capernaum. It grew dark, and Jesus had not joined them. A rough sea was running before a gale. They had gone three or four miles over the water when they caught sight of Jesus walking by the sea and coming towards the boat. They were terrified.

'It's me,' said Jesus. 'Don't be frightened.'

They were about to take him on board, but at that moment the boat grounded on the beach ahead.

Three Dialogues: Living Bread   John 6:25-29

The crowd met Jesus on the western shore.

'Master,' they said, 'when did you get here?'

'Believe me,' said Jesus, 'you didn't hunt me out because you understood the meaning of what I have been doing; it's because you had a good meal. Bread like that goes stale quickly; you must not make that the chief aim of your lives. Work for the food that keeps you really alive. This is the food the Son of Man will give you. God has given him his own power.'

'What ought we to do,' they asked, 'if we are to live in God's Way?'

'Living in God's Way means just this – trust in the one he has sent.'

John 6:35, 37-39, 47-48, 50-51

'I am the living bread,' said Jesus.

'Nobody who becomes my friend ever goes hungry.

'Nobody who trusts me ever goes thirsty.

'I will never send away anyone who wants to be my friend. I have come from God, not to please myself, but to do his will – he sent me. His will is that I should keep safe everybody he has given into my charge, to share the glory of God's Great Day.* It is his will, too, that everybody who trusts in me shall know what life really means. I am the living bread – the living bread which comes from God himself. Whoever makes this bread their food will learn the secret of the life that nothing can destroy. The bread I give is my life, and I give it for the life of the world.'

John 6:60-63

'This sort of talk is more than we can stand,' said some of the friends of Jesus as they were listening to him. 'Why listen to him?'

Jesus realised that his friends were displeased with him.

'Does this upset you?' he asked. 'Suppose you saw the Son of Man going home to God! The Spirit is the source of real life; human nature by itself gets nowhere. My words – all I have said to you – are full of God's power and they are the secret of real life.'

Conclusion: The Friends of Jesus Desert Him   *John 6:66-69*

After this, many of the friends of Jesus gave him up and would have no more to do with him.

'Are you going off too?' Jesus asked the 'Twelve'.

'Sir,' said Peter, 'who else is there to go to? There's one thing we're really sure about – you are the one who has shown us what life really is. We have come to trust you, and we know you are God's Chosen Leader.'†

The Fourth Sign – Yes or No?

Narrative: Jesus Goes up to the Feast   *John 7:1-13*

Jesus could move freely in Galilee in the north; but in the south – in Judea – his life was in danger.

This incident happened shortly before the Feast of Tents in the middle of October‡ – celebrated, remember, in Jerusalem City in the south.

---

* See *The Beginning*, p. 409; *The Message*, p. 476.
† See *The Beginning*, pp. 423, 424.
‡ The Feast of Tents was the feast Jesus attended during 'The Last Days' (See *The Beginning*, p. 429).

His brothers spoke to him.

'You shouldn't stay up here in the north,' they said. 'You should move down to Judea. Your friends in the south ought to see what you are doing, how important it is. Nobody keeps to himself what he wants everybody to know. If what you are doing really means what you say it does, come out into the open.'

In fact, even his own brothers thought he was crazy.

'The right time for me has not yet come,' said Jesus, 'but you can do what you want at any time. You're in no danger; I am – because I've said publicly to government and people that their way of life is the very opposite of God's Way. You do what you like; I'm not going to be hurried by anybody.'*

With these words, he stayed on in the north, and his brothers went up to the Feast.

A few days later, Jesus himself went up, not as a pilgrim, but just quietly by himself. The crowds were expecting him to be there.

'Where's he got to?' they were asking.

There was a lot of whispering going on about him.

'He's all right,' said some.

'No, he's not,' said others, 'he's a dangerous agitator.'

People whispered this sort of thing to one another; they were scared of the Jewish leaders.

Seven Dialogues: Who Is Jesus?

John 7:14-18

The Feast was half over when Jesus went up to the Temple and spoke openly to the people. Everybody was amazed.

'Where's this man picked up his education?' they were asking. 'He's no scholar.'

'My teaching is not my own,' said Jesus. 'It is the teaching of God who sent me. Anybody who really wants to live in God's Way will realise whose teaching it is – whether it's God's truth or whether I'm just airing my own ideas. A man who is airing his own ideas is just boasting; but anybody who is really trying to understand God in all his glory is honest and straightforward.'

---

* The brothers of Jesus were making fun of him. Jesus seems a) to have refused to let his actions be determined by hostile public comment; b) to have made up his mind to go up to Jerusalem, not as a pilgrim, but incognito.

Jesus was the talk of the town.

'Isn't this the man the government want to get rid of?' some people were asking. 'And here he is talking publicly to the crowds and they don't say a thing to him! Can they have decided that he's God's Chosen Leader after all? Yet we know this man's parents; but nobody will know anything at all about the origin of God's Chosen Leader when he comes.'

'You think you know me,' said Jesus, 'and you think you know where I come from. Yet I haven't come of my own free will; I was sent by the only authority who really counts. You may think you know him, but you don't. I know him because I've come from him and he sent me.'

There was some attempt made to arrest Jesus, but it didn't get as far as actually taking him in charge – his 'right moment' had not yet come.

Many of the crowds who heard him came to put their trust in him.

'God's Chosen Leader couldn't do more than this man to make God's Way plain,' they said.

All this whispering came to the ears of the Jewish leaders and they sent the police to arrest him.

It was the last 'Great Day' of the Feast. The ceremony of the Feast included the drawing of water and the lighting of the golden candlesticks; all this was now over.

Jesus stood up and called the crowd.

'If anybody is thirsty, let him come to me,' he said. 'Whoever trusts me, let him drink.'

(In all this Jesus was speaking about our Christian experience – God's power in our hearts which those who trust in him are given. But this experience was not yet possible; it was only possible after his death and resurrection.)

These words of Jesus impressed people in different ways.

'This, indeed, is the Man of God we were told would come,' said some.

'This is God's Chosen Leader,' said others.

'God's Chosen Leader can't be a Galilean,' said others. 'The Bible says quite clearly that God's Chosen Leader will be a descendant of King David and come from Bethlehem, King David's village, in the south.'

All these different views were held. There was some attempt made to arrest him, but again, it didn't go as far as actually taking him in charge.

The police went back to the Jewish leaders.

'Why haven't you brought him here under arrest?' they demanded.

'Nobody ever talked as this man talks,' said the police officers.

'Have you been taken in by him, too?' they exclaimed. 'Have any of *us* joined him? These common people are no good; they haven't a clue about the real meaning of religion, and God's got no use for them.'

Then Nicodemus stood up. Leader though he was, he had been to talk to Jesus, you remember.

'Isn't it illegal,' he said, 'to pass sentence on a man before you've heard his own evidence and found out what he's been doing?

'Are you a Galilean patriot, too?' they retorted. 'You look up your Bible – there's nothing there about a Man of God coming from Galilee.'

John 8:12-18, 20

Jesus spoke again to the people.

'I am the light of the world,' he said. 'Those who follow me shall not wander in the darkness; they shall have light to live by.'

'We've only your own word for it,' said the Jewish leaders, 'and your own unsupported word isn't good evidence.'

'Even if you do have only my own word for it,' said Jesus, 'my own word is in itself good evidence. It springs from my deep convictions about my origin and about my destiny; and you know nothing about these. You judge people by their appearances; I don't. But if I do venture to make judgements as you do, my judgement is reliable, because it really isn't my judgement alone; it is God's judgement – God who sent me – as well as my own.*

Jesus was speaking in the Treasury at the time. Nobody arrested him; his 'right moment' had not yet come.

John 8:28-30

These are some words of Jesus.

'When you have lifted up the Son of Man,' he said, 'then you will realise that I am the man I claim to be. I do nothing just because *I* think it's right; I speak what God the Father has made clear to me. God who sent me stands by me. He has not left me to myself; for I have given my whole life to his service.'

Many people believed him, when they heard him talk like this.

---

* Jesus is here appealing to his own inner convictions, and to the true interpretation of the Old Testament which he believed the Jewish Leaders misunderstood.

Jesus spoke to those who believed him.

'If you live loyally, in the light of all I have made clear to you,' he said, 'you will be true friends of mine. You will come to understand the real truth about God's Way, and this truth will give you your freedom.'

'Our freedom?' they exclaimed. 'We're loyal Jews; we've never been anybody's slaves. What do you mean by saying that we will be *given* our freedom?'

'Believe me,' said Jesus. 'Everybody who does what is wrong is a slave. Slaves, you know, are not permanent members of a home; the son is a permanent member of the home he belongs to. If the Son gives you your freedom, you are really free.'

The Fifth Sign – We Judge Ourselves by the Choice We Make

Narrative: A Blind Man sees*   *John 9:1-7*
One Saturday, the Holy Day of the Jews, Jesus was walking with his friends through the streets of Jerusalem City. He had been in the Temple and was just coming away.

He noticed a blind man who had been born blind.

'Sir,' asked his friends, 'blindness like this is God's punishment, isn't it? Somebody must have done something wrong. Was it the man himself or his father and mother?'

'Nobody,' said Jesus, 'neither the man himself nor his father and mother, but that the power of God shall be seen in his cure.'

He spat on the ground and made some mud paste and put it on the man's eyes.

'Go and wash yourself in Siloam Pool,' he said.

The man went away and washed himself; and came back clear-eyed.

Dialogues: Many Points of View – 1. The Neighbourhood   *John 9:8-12*
Neighbours and passers-by knew the blind man as a street beggar.

'This is the street beggar, isn't it?' they began to say.

'Yes, it is.'

'No, it isn't, it only looks like him.'

'I am the beggar – I am,' the man himself kept saying.

'Then how did you get your eyes put right?' people asked.

---

* See *The Beginning,* p. 418.

'A man called Jesus made some mud paste and put it on my eyes,' he said. 'Then he told me to go and wash in Siloam Pool. I did – and now my eyes are all right.'

'Well, where *is* the man?' they asked.

'I've no idea,' he said.

2. The Jewish Leaders   *John 9:13-17*

The crowd took the beggar to the Jewish leaders.

'He used to be blind,' they said.

So he was questioned all over again.

'How did you get your eyes put right?' the leaders asked him.

'The man put mud paste on my eyes and I washed myself and now I can see,' he said.

'The man's no good,' said some of the leaders. 'Why, he takes no notice of the Holy Day.'

'How can a bad man do things like this?' asked others.

They were all at sixes and sevens.

'What have you got to say about him yourself?' they asked the beggar. 'You say he put your eyes right.'

'He's a Man of God,' he said.

3. His Father and Mother   *John 9:18-23*

The leaders just wouldn't believe that the man had been born blind and been given his sight – until they called his father and mother.

'Is this your son?' they asked. 'You say he was born blind? Well, how can he now see like this?'

'He's our son all right,' they answered. 'We know that. And we know he was born blind. But don't ask us how he can see now and who put his eyes right – we don't know a thing about it. He's old enough; ask him – he can speak for himself.'

They were frightened of what might happen to them; for the Jewish leaders had threatened to make anybody who followed Jesus an outcast. That is why they answered as they did.

4. The Man Himself   *John 9:24-34*

So, for the second time, the Jewish leaders called the man himself before them.

'Tell the truth and shame the Devil,' they said. 'This man you said put your eyes right is a bad lot.'

'I don't know whether he's bad or not,' said the beggar. 'But there's one thing I do know. I was once blind and now I'm not – I can see.'

'What did he do to you?' they asked. 'How did he put your eyes right?'

'I've told you already,' he said. 'You don't listen when people talk to you, do you? Do you want to hear it all again? It looks as if you want to become friends of his.'

'None of this impudence,' they said, 'it's you who are a friend of his. We stick to Moses; we know where we are with him – God really spoke to *him*. This man's a nobody.'

'Good gracious!' said the beggar. 'It's amazing! You don't know anything about him and you say he's a nobody; yet he put my eyes right. God doesn't listen to bad men – we know that all right. He only listens to people who take him seriously and live in his Way. I was blind when I was born and now I can see – has anybody heard of *that* happening before? If this man was a bad man, he couldn't have done a thing!'

'You were not only born blind,' they said. 'You were born bad. Are you trying to tell us our job? Get out.'

And that was that.

5. *Jesus* John 9:35-38

Jesus heard that they had stopped the beggar from going to the Meeting House. He met him again.

'Do you trust in the "Son of Man"?' he asked him.

'Who is he, sir?' he asked. 'I'd like to trust him.'

'You've seen him,' said Jesus. 'He's talking to you now.'

'I trust, sir,' he said, and knelt down on the ground at his feet.

6. *Epilogue* John 9:39-41

These are the words of Jesus.

'The kind of judgement I was born to give is this:

> Blind people see,
> the people who see become blind.'

Some of the Jewish leaders were there when he talked like this.

'Are we blind, then?' they asked.

'If you were really blind,' said Jesus, 'you wouldn't be bad men. What makes you bad is the way you say: "We can see perfectly well, thank you."'

Dialogue: The Shepherd and His Sheep   John 10:1-21

Jesus told these two stories.*

'Believe me,' said Jesus, 'the thief or bandit does not enter through the gate of the courtyard, where the sheep are kept, but climbs in over the wall. The shepherd, whose sheep they are, uses the gate, and the gatekeeper opens the gate for him.

'Again, sheep know the sound of the shepherd's voice. He calls them by their names and leads them out to the hills. He walks ahead of them and they follow; they know the sound of his voice. They won't follow a stranger; they scatter at the sound of *his* voice – they don't recognise it.'

The people who heard these two stories did not understand what he was saying.

'Believe me,' Jesus went on, 'I am the gate for the sheep. All those who have claimed to be God's Chosen Leader before me† were nothing more than thieves and bandits.‡ The sheep took no notice of them. I am the gate; anybody using this gate will be safe – he will come in and go out and find the pasturing grounds.

'The thief only thinks of stealing, killing, smashing things up. I came to help people to live – and to live splendidly. I am a true shepherd – a shepherd who will give his life for his sheep. The man who is paid to look after the sheep – no proper shepherd owning his own sheep – runs off at the very sight of a wolf and leaves the sheep to their fate, and the wolf worries them and chases them in every direction. What happens to the sheep means nothing to him.

'I am a true shepherd. I and those who are mine really know one another (as the Father knows me and I know the Father) and I give my life for the sheep. I have other sheep, too; they do not belong to this sheepfold, but I must gather them in. They will recognise my voice. There will then be one flock, one shepherd.

'The Father loves me because I give my life that I may receive it back again. Nobody takes my life from me; I give it freely. I have the right to give it and the right to receive it back again. These are my Father's orders.'

The people who listened could not agree about these words of Jesus.

'He's got a demon inside him – he's just mad,' many said. 'Listening to him's a waste of time.'

---

* See *The Message*, p. 453.
† See *From Galilee to Rome*, p. 527.
‡ The word for 'bandits' also means 'rebels', and was used to describe members of the Resistance Movement.

'This isn't the way a madman talks,' said others. 'Can a demon make blind people see?'

Conclusion: 'Trust what I do'   *John 10: 22-25, 31-39*
It was the Feast of Lights in Jerusalem City, and it was winter. Jesus was walking in Solomon's Cloister in the Temple. People gathered round him.

'How long will you keep us guessing?' they asked. 'If you are God's Chosen Leader, tell us in plain language.'

'I have told you,' said Jesus, 'and you do not believe. The evidence is simply in the life I live, for all I do is done in the service of my Father.'

The people picked up stones to stone him to death.

'I have done many good things to make plain to you that it is with God my Father's help I do everything. Which if these is the reason for your wanting to stone me?'

'We are not stoning you for doing good,' they replied, 'but for blasphemy – you, a mere man, make yourself out to be God.'

'You are forgetting what the Bible says,' said Jesus. 'Do you remember the words –

> I say, "You are gods,
>   sons of the Most High, all of you."?

'The writer, to whom God spoke, calls them "gods" – and you cannot put the Bible on one side. I said "I am the Son of God" – and God dedicated me and sent me to the world. Why do you say I am guilty of blasphemy? If I am not living in God my Father's Way, do not trust me. But if I live in his Way, trust what I do even if you do not trust me. It will be clear to you then that the Father lives in me and I live in him – and you will understand.'

They tried to arrest him, but he escaped.

The Sixth Sign – Triumphant Life

Narrative and Dialogue: The Death of Lazarus   *John 11:1-44*
Lazarus, the brother of Mary and Martha,* was ill. They lived in the southern village of Bethany, two miles from Jerusalem City.

The sisters sent word to Jesus.

---

* See *From Galilee to Rome*, p. 504.

'The friend you love is ill,' they said.

'This is not a fatal illness,' said Jesus when he received the message. 'It has happened so that God's own presence among you may be clearly seen; and that it may be clearly seen, too, that the Son of God makes God's own presence real for men and women.'

Jesus was very fond of Martha and her sister and Lazarus. So when he heard about the illness of Lazarus, he stayed on, where he was, for two days more.

'Let us go back into Judea,' said Jesus to his friends at the end of the two days.

'But Master,' they said, 'not long ago the people there were wanting to stone you to death. You're not going back?'

'There are twelve working hours in the day, aren't there?' said Jesus. 'Nobody need stumble in the daylight – they have the whole light of the sun to see by. Walking by night's a different matter – it's easy to stumble when the light's gone.'

'Our friend Lazarus has fallen asleep,' Jesus went on. 'I am going to wake him up.'

'If he's sleeping, sir,' said his friends, 'he'll get better.'

Jesus had really been talking about his death; his friends thought he had been talking about ordinary sleep.

'Lazarus is dead,' said Jesus bluntly. 'In a sense, I'm glad – for your sakes. It will help you to trust in me. Let us go to him.'

'Let us go too,' said Thomas, 'and let us die with him.'

When Jesus got there, he found that Lazarus had already been buried four days.

Many of the city people had come to console Martha and Mary in their bereavement. When Martha heard that Jesus was on his way, she went out to meet him. Mary stayed at home.

'If only you'd been here, sir,' said Martha, 'my brother wouldn't have died. But even now he's dead, God will give you whatever you ask him, I know.'

'Your brother will rise again,' said Jesus.

'I know he'll rise again when everyone rises again at the last day,' she said.

'I am the resurrection,' said Jesus 'and I am the source of life. Whoever trusts me shall come to life again, even though they die; nobody who is alive and trusts in me shall ever die. Do you believe this?'

'Yes I do, sir,' she replied. 'I firmly believe that you are God's Chosen Leader, the Son of God, the Coming One.'*

With these words, she went to call her sister Mary.

'The Master's here and wants you,' she told her in a low voice so that the others shouldn't hear.

As soon as she heard that, Mary got up quickly and went to Jesus.

He was still where Martha had left him, outside the village.

The people in the house who had come to console Mary saw her get up quickly and go out. They followed her, thinking that she was going to the tomb to mourn there.

Mary reached the spot where Jesus was standing, and, as soon as she saw him, she fell down at his feet.

'If you'd only been here, sir,' she said, 'my brother wouldn't have died.'

Jesus saw her crying – and all the people with her crying; he was deeply moved and troubled.

'Where have you buried him?' he asked.

'Come and see, sir,' they said.

Jesus wept.

'He must have been very fond of him,' the visitors said.

'He can make blind people see,' said some. 'Couldn't he have done something to stop this man from dying?'

Jesus was again deeply moved as he reached the tomb. It was a cave with a large stone closing its opening.

'Move the stone out of the way,' said Jesus.

'The smell must be very bad by now,' said Martha. 'He's been dead four days.'

'Didn't I tell you,' said Jesus, 'that you would see what God can do – if you trust in him?'

The stone was moved.

Jesus looked up.

'I thank you, Father, for listening to me. I know that you always listen to me. I say this for the sake of those who are standing round me. I want them to be sure that you have sent me.'

Then he called loudly, 'Lazarus, come out!' and the dead man came out. His hands and feet were bound with bandages, and his face was wrapped in a cloth.

'Undo him,' said Jesus, 'and let him go.'

* 'The Coming One' was a title for the Deliverer the Jewish people believed God would send to save them from their enemies.

Conclusion: The Jewish Council Plots the Death of Jesus   John 11:45-53

Many of the people who had come to visit Mary and had seen what Jesus did came to trust in him. But some of them went back to the Jewish leaders and told them all about it.

The Jewish leaders called a meeting of the Council.

'What's our line of action?' they asked. 'This man is performing many signs. If we don't do anything to stop him, everybody will be joining him. Then we shall have the Romans stepping in and that will be the end of our temple and our nation.'

Caiaphas, who was High Priest that year, addressed the Council.

'You're talking a lot of nonsense,' he said. 'Use your heads. Isn't one man's death better than the death of the whole nation?'

From that very moment they began to plan the death of Jesus.

The Seventh Sign – Seeming Weakness Is Strength

Two Narratives:

The Anointing at Bethany*   John 12:1-8

Six days before the Great Feast, Jesus came to Bethany, the village of Lazarus. They made a supper for him. Martha was in charge of the meal, and Lazarus was one of the supper party. Mary brought a pound of real Indian ointment, poured it over the feet of Jesus and wiped them with her hair. The house was filled with the smell of the ointment.

'Why wasn't this ointment sold for £30?' said Judas Iscariot. 'The money could have been given to the poor.'

It wasn't the poor he cared about. He was a thief, and stole the money in the common money box he looked after.

'Leave her alone,' said Jesus. 'Let her keep it for my burial day. There are always poor people among you; I shall not be with you for ever.'

Jesus Rides into the City†   John 12:12-14, 19

The great crowd that had come up for the Feast heard next day that Jesus was on his way to the City. They took palm branches and went out to meet him. These are the words they shouted:

> 'Hurrah!
> Happy is he who comes in the Lord's name!
> God bless the King of Israel!'

* See *The Beginning*, p. 434.
† See *The Beginning*, p. 429.

Jesus mounted a donkey he found.

'The situation's hopeless,' said the Jewish leaders. 'Everybody's on his side!'

Two Dialogues:
Foreigners Meet Jesus   *John 12:20-26*
There were some Greeks among the pilgrims at the Feast.

They approached Philip (from Bethsaida in Galilee).

'We'd like to meet Jesus,' they told him.

Philip told Andrew, and the two of them told Jesus.

'This is the great moment for the Son of Man, the crown of his work,' said Jesus. 'Believe me, a grain of wheat just remains a grain of wheat – unless it falls into the earth and dies. But if it dies, it produces many seeds. Those who just care for themselves, cease to be themselves; those who do not put themselves first become truly themselves and learn the secret of the life that is really worth living. If anybody wants to do me service, they must follow me. Where I am, my servant will be. My Father honours anybody who does me service.'

John 12:27-36

'Now I am torn in two,' said Jesus. 'What am I to say? "Father save me from the suffering that lies ahead"? But it was for this I came. "Father, bring your great work to its fulfilment."'

A voice came from heaven –

'My great work has been carried on – and will be carried on.'

The crowd nearby heard it and said that it thundered.

'An angel spoke to him,' said others.

'It was for your sake the voice spoke,' said Jesus, 'not for mine. This is the testing time of the world. The evil powers that rule the world will be defeated. I will draw everybody to myself – when I am lifted up from the earth.'

(These words of his make clear the meaning of his death.)

'We understand, from the teaching of our religion,' said the crowd, 'that God's Chosen Leader never dies. How can you say that the Son of Man must be "lifted up"? Who is the Son of Man?'

'It's only for a short time that you have the light shining on you,' said Jesus. 'Go on your way while you have the light to walk by – you do not want the darkness to overtake you. Those who walk in darkness have no idea of their direction. While the light is shining, trust it. In this way you will become people who can live in the full light of God's world.'

After saying this, Jesus went away into hiding.

Conclusion of the Book of Signs – The Light of the World

John 12:44-50

'Whoever trusts me is not just trusting me but trusting in God who sent me,' said Jesus with great urgency.

'Whoever sees what I stand for, sees what God, who sent me, stands for. I have come into the world as light, so that those who trust in me shall not stay in darkness.

'I do not judge the one who listens to what I have to say and takes no notice of it. I did not come to judge people; I came to save them. Those who have no use for me and take no notice of what I say have a judge: the very words I have spoken will be their judge on God's Great Day. What I have said is not my own idea; God my Father, who sent me, has told me what to say and what to speak. I say what God my Father has told me to say.'

The Book of the Passion

John has now finished the main part of his book where he has shown us what Christianity really means. The stories of what Jesus did and said in Palestine have a timeless meaning. He turns now to the story of the death and resurrection of Jesus.

Note, first of all, how he changes his method. In the earlier part of his book his method was to tell the story or narrative first and then to add the dialogues to explain its meaning for everybody everywhere. Here, he puts the dialogues first, and then, in simple language and without comment, he lets the story of how Jesus died speak for itself.

For John, the death of Jesus is the historical 'plain story' that most of all has timeless meaning. Although he has shown us, in the later 'Signs', how Death can be the means of Life and weakness the source of strength, he has not yet dealt with the death of Jesus and all it means to us and the whole world. So, now, he gives us more dialogue than he has given us for any of the other stories. The 'Table Talk' and 'The Prayer of Jesus' are really an explanation of what the best man in the world lived and died for.

He begins with a short story of what happened on the last night when Jesus and his friends had supper together. It is a story we have not yet heard, about how Jesus, taking the place of a slave, washed the feet of his friends. It was a slave's duty to wash the dusty feet of visitors when they came to a house. On this evening there was no slave to wash his friends' feet; Jesus had only hired or borrowed the room. He did the job himself. This is the sort of person he was.

Then comes the 'Table Talk'. Here the whole meaning of the death of Jesus is explained, in the light of this simple short story – and how his death is not the End but the Beginning.

Then, without comment, he tells us what happened in the garden and in Jerusalem and at Skull Hill.

He brings his story to its conclusion with an account of Easter morning, what happened later in the day and then, some time later, by Galilee Lake. (This last story he added after he had finished his book, as an appendix to it.)

Jesus – Servant   *John 13:1, 4-5, 12a, 15-17*

The Great Feast of the Jewish people was near. Jesus was having supper with his friends.

He got up from the table and took off his long robe. He picked up a towel and tied it round him like a belt. He poured water into a basin, and began to wash his friends' feet.

When he had washed their feet, he picked up his long robe, put it on and sat down again at the table.

'I have shown you what you must do,' he said. 'You must do what I have just done for you. Believe me –

> A slave is not greater than his master,
> a messenger than the man who sent him.

'I hope you understand all this. You will be happy if you live as I have shown you.'

Table Talk   *John 13:21-30*

Jesus was talking with his friends at the supper table. He stopped talking and became very troubled.

'One of you is going to hand me over to the government,' he said.

His friends stared at one another; they had no idea whom he was talking about.

One of his friends, one he loved very dearly, was sitting by his side on his right.

Peter nodded to him.

'Find out who he's talking about,' he whispered.

The friend leaned back close to Jesus.

'Sir,' he asked, 'who is it?'

'When I've dipped a piece of bread in the sauce,' said Jesus, 'I'll give it to the man I'm talking about.'

He dipped a piece of bread in the sauce, picked it up and gave it to Judas, the son of Simon Iscariot.

'Be quick about what you're doing,' said Jesus.

Nobody grasped what all this was about. Judas was treasurer. Some thought Jesus had told him to buy in food for the Feast; some that he was to go and help some poor people.

Judas took the piece of bread from Jesus. Then he went straight out into the night.

John 13:33-38

'I shall not be with you much longer,' said Jesus to his friends after Judas had gone out of the room. 'Love one another – this is my "new commandment". Love one another in the same way as I have loved you. This will be the mark by which everybody will recognise that you are my friends – the way in which you love one another.'

'Sir,' said Peter, 'where are you going?'

'You cannot go with me now where I am going,' said Jesus. 'You will go with me later on.'

'Sir,' said Peter, 'why can't I go with you now? I'll die in your defence.'

'You'll die in my defence?' said Jesus. 'Believe me, before the cock crows, you will say three times that you are no friend of mine.'

John 14:1-27

'Stop worrying,' said Jesus. 'Keep trusting God and keep trusting me. There are many different places in my Father's home for people to live. I would have told you long ago, if this was not true. I am going away now to make sure that there is a place for you. Then I shall be back again to welcome you into my own home, where we shall always be together.

'You know my direction and my road,' he added.

'We don't know where you're going, sir,' said Thomas. 'How can we know the road?'

'You know me – what I am and how I live,' said Jesus. 'I am the Road. The End of the Road is to know God as Father; to help people to know God as Father has been my work and mine alone. If you had known me as I really am, you would have known God as Father. From now on you know him as Father – you have seen him for yourselves.'

'Sir,' said Philip, 'help us to know God as Father; that's all we need.'

'We have been friends together for a long time,' said Jesus. Don't you know me yet, Philip? Whoever has seen what I really am has seen the Father. Why do you keep on saying "Help us to see God as Father"? Don't you believe that I live in the Father and that the Father lives in me? I don't just invent the words I speak; God the Father is living in me and at work in me. You must trust me at this point if you don't understand; my words – "I live in the Father and the Father lives in me" – are the plain truth. If you find this difficult to believe, look at my whole life and trust me for what I do. Believe me, those who trust me will be able to live as I live; indeed they will be able to do much more than I can do here – because I am going to the Father. Remember, I will do whatever you ask – if you ask *in my name*.

'If you love me, you will obey my orders, and I will ask the Father to give you another Helper to stand by you always – the Spirit who helps us to understand the whole truth about God – what he is like and what he is doing.

'I will not leave you without a teacher; I am coming back to you. In a very short time, I shall pass from human sight; but you who love me will see me. Because I live, you too will live. When I have risen to life again, you who love me will be quite sure that my words and deeds are my Father's words and deeds; and what will make you quite sure of this is the strength of our friendship – you in me and I in you.

'Those who hear my orders and obey them are the ones who really love me; and those who really love me will know in the depth of their being that God my Father loves them. I will love them, and through my love for them I will show them who I really am.'

'Sir,' said Judas (not the Judas who handed Jesus over to the Jewish leaders), 'what has happened that you are not going to show the whole world who you really are – that you are only going to show us, your friends, who you really are?'

'Those who love me,' said Jesus, 'will take what I say seriously. My Father will love them, and we will come to them and make our home in their hearts. Those who have no love for me don't bother about anything I say. What you hear me say, I do not say on my own authority; it is what God, my Father, who sent me, says.

'I have talked to you like this while I am still with you. But the Helper, the Spirit God the Father will send in my name, will explain everything to you, and call back into your minds all that *I* have said to you but which you did not understand at the time.

'When we leave one another we say "Peace be with you".* But my goodbye is no casual goodbye. Peace is my parting gift to you – my own peace which nobody else can give you. Don't panic, and don't be cowards.'

John 15:1-6, 9-17

'I am the real vine† and my Father is the farmer who looks after it. He cuts off every unfruitful branch, and he prunes every fruitful branch to make it more fruitful still. A branch dies if it gets broken off the vine – no fruit can grow on it. It is thrown on one side, and becomes a dry stick; the sticks are picked up and used for the winter firing. So it is with our friendship; if your friendship with me is not a real friendship, you will become like that dead branch. I am the vine, you are the branches. If your friendship with me is a real friendship – you in me and I in you – it will bear a great harvest; but there will be no harvest at all, if our friendship is broken – you need me.

'I have loved you as my Father has loved me. Hold fast to my love of you. The way to hold fast to my love is to obey my orders; I have obeyed my Father's orders and held fast to his love.

'In talking to you as I have done,' said Jesus, 'I have had one aim in view: I wanted you to know the happiness I know. I don't want anything to spoil your happiness. This is the secret of it – my secret, your secret: love one another as I have loved you. For someone to die for their friends – that is the greatest love we know. You are real friends of mine – if you do what I have told you.

'I don't want you to be my "slaves", just doing the things you are told to do, without knowing at all why you are doing them. I want you to be my "friends": that's why I shared with you all I have learned from my Father.

'You did not choose me, you remember; I chose you. And I chose you for one purpose: I want you to go on growing, producing a rich and lasting harvest.

'This, then, is my order: love one another.'

John 16:1-7

'I have spoken to you like this so that you will not let me down. The Jewish leaders will forbid you to worship in the Jewish Meeting House.

* See *From Galilee to Rome*, p. 503.
† In the Old Testament the vine represented 'The People of God'.

Indeed, before long, anybody who kills you will think they are being loyal to God and obeying his commands. The reason is clear – they do not know God as Father and they do not know who I really am. I have spoken to you as I have to warn you; when this sort of thing happens, you will remember I warned you. I have not talked to you like this before, because we were together. But now I am going to him who sent me. None of you asks me where I am going; my words have just made you miserable.

'Yet it is for your good that I should leave you – this is the truth. If I do not leave you, the Helper will not come to you; if I go, I will send him to you.'

John 16:12-13

'There are many things that I still have to tell you, but you could not now take what I have to say; but when the Spirit, who understands the whole truth about God, comes, he will lead you, step by step, into the whole truth about him.'

John 16:16-23a

'In a short time, you will see me no longer; again, in a short time, you will see me,' said Jesus.

His friends talked this over among themselves.

'What's he trying to tell us?' said some of them. 'We don't understand what he is talking about.'

Jesus knew that they had many questions they wanted to ask him.

'Is it what I said about your not seeing me and then your seeing me again that you are arguing about? Believe me, this will indeed happen – you will find yourselves a group of mourners and the world outside will be delighted. Your grief will be very real, but it will be changed into joy. Think of the birth of a child. The mother has to endure much pain while the child is being born. But her pain is swept away by joy – she even forgets all about it – when the child has been born: a human being has come into the world. Your experience is like hers: short sorrow, and then great joy – when I see you again. Nobody will rob you of this joy. You will be asking me no questions then.'

John 16:32-33

'See, the time is coming – it has already come – when you will go back home, scattered like sheep, and you will leave me alone by myself. Yet I am not alone; the Father stays by my side.

'I have told you all this that you may have "Peace", as I said. You will have to face hard times when you go out into the world. Don't be afraid – I have conquered the world.'

The Prayer of Jesus

John 17:1, 4, 6-9a, 11, 13-21, 25-26

'Father, the time has come.

'Glorify your Son so that your Son may glorify you.

'I have glorified you on earth. I have finished what you gave me to do.

'I have made you known – Father – to the men you gave me. They left their ordinary life to come with me (they were your choice, you gave them to me) and they have been loyal to the Good News about you. They are now quite sure that all you gave me really is *your* gift to me. I told them what you told me; they listened and are quite sure I came from you, and they have staked their lives on the fact that you sent me.

'I am praying for them.

'My earthly life is over, but they have to face the world as it is and I am coming to you. Holy Father, keep those whom you have given to me loyal to you, so that they may be one as we are one. Now I am coming to you. I speak like this now here in the world so that they may know, in all its fullness, the joy I know.

'I have given the truth about you into their keeping. The outside world treats them with hatred – they do not share its way of life as I do not share its way of life. My prayer is not for you to take them out of the world, but to guard them from its evil power. Set them apart as messengers of your truth. The Good News about you and your purpose is truth. As you sent me into the world, I also have sent them into the world; and I set myself apart for their sake, that they also may be set apart as messengers of the Good News.

'My prayer is not only for them. My prayer is also for all those who, through their message about me, stake their lives on its truth.

'I pray that they may all be one, as you, Father, and I are one – you in me and I in you. May they live in us, so that men and women everywhere may be convinced that you have sent me.

'Righteous Father, men and women in the world outside have not learned to know you. I have known you, and these, my friends, have learned that you sent me. I have made your nature as Father clear to them, and I will go on making it clear; so that the love with which you have loved me may fill their hearts, and I may be in them.'

The Last Days*

In the Garden   *John 18:1-12*

Jesus left the house with his friends and crossed the Kidron Brook to the other side of the valley. They came to a garden and went inside. They knew it well, for Jesus and his friends had often met there.

Judas knew this, and he led a detachment of Roman soldiers and a company of Jewish police straight to the spot. They were fully armed and carried lanterns and torches.

Jesus stepped out to meet them.

'Who do you want?' he asked.

'Jesus from Nazareth,' they answered.

'I'm the man you want, then,' said Jesus.

At these words, they stepped back and fell on the ground.

'Who do you want?' asked Jesus again.

'Jesus from Nazareth,' they repeated.

'I've told you – I'm the man you want,' he said. 'If it's me you're after, let these men go.'

Peter drew his sword and struck at a slave of the High Priest and cut off his right ear.

'Put your sword up,' said Jesus. 'Do you want to stop me facing what God the Father has set before me?'

The soldiers then arrested Jesus and handcuffed him.

Before Annas   *John 18:13, 15-27*

The soldiers took Jesus before Annas, the most powerful man in Jerusalem City. He was not the High Priest of the Jewish people. Caiaphas was the High Priest that year; Annas was his father-in-law.

Now Jesus had a friend whose name we do not know. He was not one of the 'Twelve', but belonged to one of the most important families in Jerusalem; the High Priest knew him well. He was the 'other friend'.

Peter and the 'other friend' followed Jesus along the road. When they got to the courtyard, the 'other friend' went straight in with Jesus; Peter was left standing outside at the door. The 'other friend' came back and had a word with the girl on duty at the door and then took him inside.

'You're one of this fellow's friends, too, aren't you?' the girl asked Peter.

'Not I,' said Peter.

---

* See *The Beginning*, p. 436; *From Galilee to Rome*, p. 510.

It was a cold night, and the slaves and court officers had lit a charcoal fire. They were standing round it, trying to keep warm. Peter joined the crowd round the fire; he wanted to get warm too.

The High Priest asked Jesus about his friends and what he stood for.

'What I have had to say,' said Jesus, 'I have said openly for everybody to hear. I have talked in the Meeting Houses, and I have talked in the Temple to Jewish people from all over the world. I have not been plotting in back rooms. Why ask me questions now? Ask the ordinary people in the villages and in this city. They heard me. They know what it was I talked about.'

One of the court officials standing near him gave him a slap on the face.

'Is that the way to talk to the High Priest?' he said.

'If I did something wrong,' said Jesus to the officer, 'prove it. If I didn't, why hit me?'

Annas had Jesus handcuffed again and sent to Caiaphas.

Peter was still standing near the fire, getting warm.

'You are one of this fellow's friends too, aren't you?' said some of the men by the fire.

'Not on your life,' said Peter.

Now it happened that one of the court officers standing there was a relative of the man Peter had slashed with his sword.

'I saw you in the garden with him, didn't I?' he asked.

'No, you didn't,' said Peter.

At that moment, somewhere in the distance a cock crowed.

Before the Roman Governor   *John 18:28-31, 33-40; 19:1-16a*
It was now Friday, the day before the Great Feast.

Just before dawn Jesus was marched into the headquarters of Pilate, the Roman Governor.

The Jewish leaders stayed outside the building (it was 'unclean'* to them because it belonged to foreigners, and, if they had gone inside, they would not have been allowed, by Jewish law, to take part in the Great Feast). So Pilate came outside.

'What's the charge against this man?' he asked.

'He's a criminal,' they said. 'Would we have brought him here if he wasn't?'

'Well, take him off and deal with him yourselves,' said Pilate. 'You've got your own laws and law courts.'

* See *The Beginning*, p. 420.

'But we can't pass the death sentence,' they replied.

Pilate went back into the building and had Jesus brought before him.

'So you're the Jewish King, are you?' he said.

'Are those your own words?' asked Jesus. 'Or are you just repeating what other people have told you?'

'Do I look like a Jew!' said Pilate. 'You've been brought here by your own leaders. What have you been up to?'

'I'm no nationalist,' said Jesus. 'My men would have been out on the streets fighting, if I were – they wouldn't have let me be arrested so easily. My "kingdom" has nothing to do with that sort of thing.'

'So you *are* a "king", then,' said Pilate.

'The word is yours,' said Jesus. 'I was born to defend the truth. Anybody who cares for the truth knows what I am talking about.'

'What is truth?' said Pilate.

And with that he went outside again.

'As far as this court is concerned,' he told the crowd, 'there is nothing this man can be charged with. I've been in the habit of setting one prisoner free for you at the Feast. What about letting "the Jewish King" go free this year?'

The crowd broke into a roar.

'Not this man, but Barabbas!'

(Barabbas was one of the terrorists in the Resistance Movement.)

So Pilate had Jesus flogged, and the soldiers – as was often their custom with prisoners – made sport of him. They made a crown out of some thorn twigs and crowned him with it, and dressed him in a soldier's purple cloak. Then they kept coming up to him, saluting him with 'Long live Your Majesty!' and slapping him on the face.

Pilate went out to the crowd again.

'Here he is,' he said. 'I'm going to bring him out to you to make it clear that there is nothing this court can charge him with.'

Jesus was brought outside, still wearing the mock crown and the purple cloak.

'There's the man!' said Pilate.

When the Jewish leaders and their officers caught sight of him, they started shouting.

'The cross! Let's have him on the gallows!'

'Take him and put him on a cross yourselves,' said Pilate. 'He's done nothing this court can deal with!'

'But we've a law of blasphemy,' they answered, 'and by that law he ought to be executed – he claims to be equal with God himself!'

That last sentence frightened Pilate. He went back again into the building.

'Where were you born?' he asked Jesus.

Jesus didn't speak.

'I'm the Governor, you know – why don't you say something?' said Pilate. 'Don't you know I can set you free or have you executed?'

'You would have no power over me at all,' said Jesus, 'if God had not given it to you. The man who handed me over to you is more guilty than you.'

From that moment Pilate made up his mind to set him free.

But the shouting of the crowd went on.

'If you let this man go, you're no friend of the Emperor! Anybody who calls himself a king is an enemy of the Emperor!'

Pilate heard what they were shouting.

He brought Jesus outside again, and took his seat as Governor and Judge at the place called 'The Pavement'. It was now just midday.

'Here's your "King"!' he said.

'Take him away! Hang him on a cross!' the crowd shouted.

'So it's your "King" I'm to hang on a cross?' he asked.

'The Emperor is the only King we've got!' they shouted back.

Pilate handed him over for execution.

At Skull Hill   *John 19:16b-35, 38-42*

The soldiers marched Jesus off, and, with his own cross on his shoulders, he went out of the building to Skull Hill, a place quite near the city. And there they hung him on the cross. Three men were hung on crosses that day – Jesus in the middle, the other two on either side of him.

Pilate had a notice written out in three languages, Jewish, Roman and Greek: JESUS OF NAZARETH, THE JEWISH KING. He had it fastened on the cross. Crowds of citizens read it.

'Don't put THE JEWISH KING,' the Jewish leaders protested to Pilate. 'Put – HE SAID HE WAS THE JEWISH KING.'

'It stays as I wrote it,' said Pilate.

When the four soldiers had carried out their orders, they picked up the clothes of Jesus and made four bundles, one for each of them. Then they picked up his tunic. This was one piece of cloth, woven from top to bottom, not made up of several pieces.

'We mustn't tear it up,' they said. 'Let's toss for it.'

That is what they did.

All this time, his mother, his aunt Mary, the wife of Clopas, and Mary from Magdala were standing near the cross itself. Jesus caught sight of his mother – and the friend he loved dearly standing by her side.

'Mother,' he said, 'take my friend as your son.'

'Take my mother as your mother,' he said to his friend.

And from that time, his friend took her into his own home.

'I am thirsty,' said Jesus.

A full jar of sour wine had been put nearby for the guard. The soldier soaked a sponge in it, stuck it on a javelin and put it up to his mouth. Jesus drank it.

'My work is done,' he said.

His head dropped, and he died.

The Jewish leaders did not want the bodies on the crosses to stay there over the Saturday, the Holy Day of the Jews, especially since this was a very important Saturday, the first day of the Great Feast. They asked Pilate to have the men's legs broken to make them die quickly, and then to have the bodies taken away.

This is what the soldiers began to do. They broke the legs of the two men hanging on either side of Jesus, one after the other. They went up to Jesus, but they found that he was already dead. They didn't break his legs, but one of the soldiers jabbed a lance into his side, and water and blood flowed out. (This is what happened; it is the evidence of an eye-witness who can be trusted.)

After all this, two men went to Pilate – Joseph from the village of Arimathea (he was a member of the Jewish Council; he had kept his friendship with Jesus a secret, for he was afraid of what the Council might do) and Nicodemus (who, as we have told, first met Jesus at night).

Joseph asked Pilate to let him take the body of Jesus down from the cross, and Pilate agreed. So his friends came and took his body away, and wrapped it in linen sheets with spices which Nicodemus had brought, more than seventy pounds weight of perfume mixture. (This is the Jewish method of burial.)

There was a large garden nearby. In it there was a new tomb – nobody had yet been buried there.

It was now getting on for six o'clock in the evening, the time when the Holy Day began. The tomb lay near at hand; so they put Jesus there.

The First Easter *John 20:1-10*

It was now early on Sunday morning and it was still dark.

Mary from Magdala came along to the tomb. She looked at it – someone had taken the stone away and it was open. She ran off to Peter and the friend whom Jesus had loved dearly.

'The Master's been taken from the tomb,' she said, 'and we don't know where he's been put.'

Peter and the other friend of Jesus ran together to the tomb. The other friend got to it first; he could run faster than Peter. He peered into the tomb – the linen cloths were lying there all right – but he stayed outside. Peter came up after him and went straight inside. He gazed at the sheets lying there and at the head-cloth, rolled up by itself, away from the sheets. The other friend now came in and saw it all. Mary's story was true. They both went home. They never dreamed Jesus had risen from the dead; the words of the Bible meant nothing to them.

John 20:11-18

Mary was standing outside the tomb crying. Still crying, she peered into the tomb. She saw two white-robed angels sitting on the slab where the body of Jesus had been lying, one at each end.

'What are you crying for?' they asked.

'My Master's been taken away,' she said, 'and I don't know where he's been put.'

She happened to turn round – and there was Jesus standing in the garden. She did not recognise him.

'What are you crying for?' he asked. 'Are you looking for somebody?'

She thought he must be the gardener.

'Sir,' she said, 'if you've carried him somewhere else, tell me where you've put him. I'll look after him.'

'Mary!' said Jesus.

She swung round.

'Master!' she said.

'Let go of me,' said Jesus, 'I have not yet gone up to my Father. Go to my brothers and tell them – "I go up to my Father and your Father; to my God and your God"'.'

Mary went off to his friends.

'I've seen the Master!' she said, and she told them what he had said to her.

The day passed, and it was now late in the evening.

The friends of Jesus were together in the house. They were frightened of the Jewish leaders, so they had locked the doors.

Then – there was Jesus standing among them.

'Peace be with you!' he said.

With these words, he let them see his hands and his side.

They saw it was Jesus, and were overjoyed.

'Peace be with you!' he said again. 'The Father sent me out: I now send you out.'

He there and then gave them God's power.

'Receive the Holy Spirit, he said.

That evening, one of the friends of Jesus was absent – Thomas 'the twin'.

'We've seen the Master!' the others told him when he came back.

'I don't believe it!' he said. 'I must see the nail-marks in his hands and touch them first – and I must put my hand in his side.'

The following Sunday, the friends of Jesus were again in the house with locked doors. This time Thomas was there too.

Then – Jesus was with them again.

'Peace be with you!' he said.

He turned to Thomas.

'Where are your fingers?' he said. 'Here are my hands. Touch my side with your hand. You must show that you trust, not that you don't.'

'My Lord and my God!' said Thomas.

'Do you trust me,' asked Jesus, 'just because you have seen me with your own eyes? They are happy people who trust me without ever having seen me with their own eyes.'

After this Jesus showed himself again to his friends. This is what happened on the beach of Galilee Lake.

Seven of his friends were together there – Peter, Thomas 'the twin', Nathanael from Cana, Zebedee's sons (James and John) and two other of his friends.

'I'm taking the boat out fishing,' said Peter.

'We'll come along with you,' said the others.

They all got into the boat there and then. They were out all night but not a fish did they catch.

And now the day was breaking.

Jesus stood on the beach. Nobody recognised him.

'Lads!' he called out, 'have you had any luck?'

'Not a fish!' they called back.

'Try the starboard side,' he called. 'There's fish there.'

Out went the net. The mass of fish they got was so great they could not haul the net in.

'It's Jesus!' said the friend whom Jesus loved dearly to Peter.

Peter had been fishing naked. When he heard the name 'Jesus' he flung his cloak round him and jumped into the water. The others brought the boat in, dragging the net. They were only about a hundred yards offshore.

They got out of the boat – and there was a charcoal fire burning on the beach, and fish cooking on it; there was bread, too.

'Get some of the fish you've just caught,' said Jesus.

Peter went on board and dragged the net to the shore. The net had not been torn in spite of the mass of fish.

'Let's have breakfast,' said Jesus.

Nobody dared ask him who he was.

Jesus picked up the bread and the fish and gave them to his friends.

After breakfast Jesus turned to Peter as they walked along, and called him by his own name, Simon.

'Simon,' he said, 'do you love me more than anything else?'

'Yes, sir,' said Peter, 'you know I love you.'

'Look after my friends,' said Jesus.

Jesus spoke to Peter for a second time.

'Simon,' he said, 'do you love me?'

'Yes, sir,' said Peter, 'you know I love you.'

'Look after my friends,' said Jesus.

Then a third time Jesus spoke to Peter.

'Simon,' he said, 'do you love me?'

For Jesus to ask him this question three times upset Peter.

'Sir,' he said, 'you know all about me. You, of all people, know I love you.'

'Look after my friends,' said Jesus.

'Believe me,' he went on, 'when you were a young man, you tied your own belt on and you went just where you wanted to. When you're an old man, you'll hold your hands out for someone else to tie your belt on and carry you where you don't want to go.'

Then he added –

'Follow me.'

Peter turned round and caught sight of the friend whom Jesus loved dearly. He was coming along behind. (This was the friend who was sitting on the right of Jesus at supper and leaned back and asked 'Who is it, sir, who's handing you over?')

'What about him, sir?' he asked.

'If I want him to wait till I come,' said Jesus, 'what's that got to do with you? I've given you your orders – Follow me.'

(The rumour spread among the friends of Jesus that this friend should not die. Jesus did not say this. What he said was 'If I want him to wait till I come.' This is the friend of Jesus who is our authority for this account of what happened and wrote it down. We know he is a reliable witness.)*

---

* The last sentence was added by the Christians in Ephesus who published this Gospel.

Notes on Some Important Words and Names

OLD TESTAMENT

Ark

This was a sacred chest or box, made of acacia wood. It was carried by the Israelites on their march across the desert and then kept in the central shrine at Shiloh. Eventually King David brought it to Jerusalem. When King Solomon built the temple there, it was kept in 'The Holiest Shrine' (see p. 144). It symbolised God's presence with his people, and was later thought of as his throne. What it meant to the Israelites changed as time went by. In earlier days it was carried into battle (see p. 26). It disappeared at the fall of Jerusalem.

Baal

This word means 'master' or 'lord'. Baal was one of the gods of the Canaanites. The chief god of the Canaanite pantheon – El – was remote; Baal was the young god of vegetation and fertility who each year died, went down into the underworld and rose again: hence autumn and spring. He was also god of storm and rain. His wife (or sister) was Asherah. The word 'asherah' was also used to describe a wooden object used in her worship.

Beersheba

The name means 'Well of Seven'. Because the Hebrew words for 'seven' and 'swear an oath' were similar, it is interpreted in some parts of the Old Testament as 'Well of the Covenant'. It was an important town in the Negeb. Isaac was associated with the shrine there. It was thought of as the southernmost limit of Israelite territory; the Israelites spoke of 'from Dan to Beersheba' as we say 'from John o'Groats to Land's End'.

Bethel

The name means 'House of God'. The site seems to have been occupied about or before 2000 BCE and was an important religious centre from earliest times. It was destroyed by the Israelites; and then, after a break, it was rebuilt. It was associated with Jacob (see p. 311). It reached the height of its fame when it became a religious centre and royal city of the North. Amos preached here (p. 221). It was destroyed again in the Assyrian invasion.

Canaan

This was the old name of the land between the Mediterranean Sea and the Desert. It was used by Semitic peoples of Mesopotamia to describe the coast from Alexandretta in the north to Gaza in the south. It means 'Purple Country' from the name of the famous purple dye ('kinahhu') which was produced by the shellfish native to this coast. The name 'Palestine' comes from the word 'Philistines' who invaded the southern part of the coast in the eleventh century, and became the name used in the West for the southern part of Canaan where the Israelites settled.

Canaanites

The name of the inhabitants of Canaan. They were Amorite in origin and therefore akin to the Israelites, but they had attained a much higher standard of culture than the latter. They were merchants and the Hebrew word for 'Canaanite' means 'merchant' as well.

Carmel

This is the name of two places: 1. a town in the south where Nabal the farmer lived (p. 46); 2. the well-wooded mountain range on the coast where Elijah met the prophets of Baal (p. 214).

Covenant

This word means 'binding' and describes a treaty or agreement between groups or individuals. It is one of the great words of the Old Testament because it was used by the Israelites to describe the great 'Agreement' which GOD made with his people at the Holy Mountain (p. 106). From it come the names which Christians use to describe the Jewish and Christian parts of the Bible: Old Testament and New Testament – 'Old Covenant' and 'New Covenant'.

Ephod

This word has two meanings: 1. a garment, especially a garment worn by the High Priest; 2. idols of some sort, sometimes used in connection with divination (p. 50). In the latter sense, the ephod may have some connection with Urim and Thummim, stones which some scholars think may have been kept in the pocket of the garment or idol and shaken to find out answers to questions. Urim and Thummim were possibly two flat stones one side of which meant Yes and the other side No. If both sides fell the same way up, that meant Yes or No as the case might be; if they showed different sides, that meant there was no answer to be given (as in the story of Saul, p. 35).

GOD
See 'Yahweh'.

Hebrews
Although we often refer to the people of the Old Testament as Hebrews, the word only occurs some thirty times, and (except for two references in *Jeremiah* and one in *Jonah*) only in *Genesis*, *Exodus*, *Deuteronomy* (once) and *1 Samuel*. Most frequently it is used by people speaking of them as foreigners and as inferiors. It is possible that the name is connected with one that appears frequently in Mesopotamian and Egyptian documents which refer to them as stateless people in many parts of the ancient world, sometimes as freebooters, as mercenary soldiers or as slaves. If this is so, the Hebrews of the Old Testament would be a particular group associated with the patriarchs, Abraham, Isaac and Jacob (Israel). The name Hebrew is replaced by 'Israelite' for the people of the covenant who were led by Joshua into Canaan.

Hebron
This was originally a Canaanite town. It became the tribal centre of the Southern tribes, and here David was crowned king of the South. Its shrine was associated with Abraham. It was the rallying point of Absalom's revolt and its people seem to have resented David's choice of Jerusalem as the capital city of all Israelites, North and South.

Israelites
This was an old tribal name ('Israel' was another name for Jacob). In the Old Testament it is used in two ways: 1. as a general name for the people of the covenant ('GOD's People') – we use it in this version in this sense; 2. as the name for the northern tribes who revolved against Jeroboam and formed a separate kingdom in the north which we call 'The North'.

Jerusalem
This was the name of the fortress which David captured and made his capital city. It was a very old fortified city, inhabited by Jebusites. The city itself was confined to the southern part of the eastern ridge which overlooked the Kidron Valley on the east and the Tyropaean Valley on the west. David called it after his own name 'Davidstown'. Solomon enlarged it by extending it to the north and building there his palace and the temple. Later on the city spread to the north and the west. The city lacked adequate water supplies – the early city was built on the

eastern ridge in order to use the only available spring, the Gihon Spring ('Bubbling Spring') in the Kidron Valley (see p. 60). Later Hezekiah cut a long tunnel to let the spring water flow into Siloam Pool on the west side of the hill. When David's attempt to weld all the people into one nation failed, Jerusalem became simply the capital city of the South. After the fall of Samaria and the Exile it became the spiritual capital of all Jewish people all over the world. See 'Zion'.

Judah
See 'The South'.

Negeb
The rocky wastes in the southernmost part of the country.

'The North'
We use this name for the Northern Kingdom ('Israel'). The deep division between North and South ('Judah') goes back to the earliest times and may be due to the fact that the Northern tribes had been in Egypt, while the Southern tribes had not. This division was strengthened in the days of the tribal league because communication between north and south was made difficult by the existence of Canaanite fortresses like Jerusalem and those of the Esdraelon Valley. The North always thought of itself as the real home of the traditions of Moses – the central shrine of the tribal league was first at Shechem and then at Shiloh, both in the north. They had their own tribal traditions which were gathered together about 750 BCE (referred to by scholars as 'E' because in their stories of the earliest days they used the name 'Elohim' for God and not 'Yahweh').

Passover
A very old spring festival, associated with the killing and eating of a lamb and daubing its blood on the lintels and doorposts of houses. In early Israelite history, the festival celebrated their deliverance from Egypt. Later it was linked with the Canaanite spring festival of Cakes-made-without-yeast (see p. 175) – perhaps because, when they settled in the highlands they found themselves celebrating their own Passover Festival at the same time as the Canaanite farmers there were celebrating their spring agricultural festival. The main importance of the festival in the Old Testament is as the celebration of the founding of GOD's people of which the escape from Egypt was the dramatic beginning, and as the supreme illustration of God's undeserved love.

Priests

Officials who looked after the worship in shrines and temples. After the Exile, Jewish priests were the civil as well as the religious authorities in Jerusalem. They undertook the rewriting of their national history (called 'P') and to them we owe the later account of the story of creation (see p. 293).

Prophets

See p. 209.

The Sea of Reeds

See p. 104.

'The South'

The name we use for the Southern Kingdom ('Judah'). Here, as in the North, the Israelite tribes had their own traditions (referred to by scholars as 'J') which were gathered together about 950 BCE.

Urim and Thummim

See 'Ephod'.

Yahweh

This is the personal name of God, usually appearing as 'the LORD' in English Bibles. The reasons for this is that the later Jew ceased to pronounce the sacred name 'Yahweh' and substituted the Hebrew word for 'Lord' when he met it in his scriptures. In order to remind themselves, Jewish scholars put the vowels for the Hebrew word for 'Lord' with the consonants of the sacred name (YHWH) and this caused Christian readers to pronounce the word as 'Jehovah'. The sacred name also appears as 'Jah' as in 'Hallelujah' ('Praise Yahweh'). The meaning of the name is uncertain, but tradition associated it with a verb which means 'He shows himself to be' or 'He is present and active' (see p. 95).

Other names for God are 'El', translated as 'God' but really a proper name of the chief Canaanite god. It is sometimes combined with 'Elyon' and translated as 'God Most High'. 'Shaddai' ('Almighty'), another name for God, seems to mean 'He of the Mountain'. In this version 'GOD' stands for 'Yahweh', 'God' for other names.

Zion

The name of the old Canaanite fortress of Jerusalem before the Israelites captured it. Later it was used, especially in psalms and prophetic poetry, as the beloved name of their Holy City.

Some Important Words

NEW TESTAMENT

Good News

This is the meaning of the word 'Gospel', a word not often used outside the New Testament. It describes all that Jesus made clear about God and men and women and the world we live in, not only in what he said, but also in what he was and did. All God had promised in the past has now been given to us ('fulfilled', said Jesus) in his coming. It is what the word 'Christianity' means – it is Good News about God and it is centred in all that Jesus was and did and said.

God's Chosen Leader and Son of Man

This translates the word 'Messiah' ('Christ' is the Greek translation of this Jewish word), the Deliverer the Jews believed God would send them. Both words mean simply 'anointed' (as kings were anointed at their coronations). Here, in T. W. Manson's words, is what they thought he would be like: he 'was an ideal figure, the embodiment of the hopes of the godly, decent, patriotic Jew of the time. He would be a man, a descendant of the royal dynasty of David and Solomon. But he would be no ordinary man. He would be unique in wisdom and knowledge, in uprightness of character, in courage and patriotism, and in loyalty and devotion to God. He would be backed by God's power and guided by God's wisdom, and so he would overthrow all the enemies of Israel and establish an Israelite kingdom in which justice, truth, and peace would be secure, where the one true God, the God of Israel, would be worshipped and obeyed, where God's people, Israel, would enjoy permanent prosperity and happiness.'* Jesus did not like this word; it had so many meanings that it did not help people to understand what he came to do. He preferred the title 'Son of Man'. 'Son of Man' really means 'Man' (it is a Jewish way of saying this). If you look up the vision of Daniel (*Daniel 7:13-18*), you will find that there it describes 'The People of God'. So, when Jesus uses it, he is thinking of more than himself; he is thinking of himself and his friends. So I have translated it 'I and my friends'. At the end of his life, when his friends did not prove loyal to him, and Jesus was alone, I have translated it 'I'. (Once, in the early

* *The Beginning of the Gospel*, p. 15.

part of the story, it meant just 'Man', and here I have translated it 'men and women' – *In the Fields*, pp. 419-420.)

Sir, Lord
Both words, 'Sir' and 'Lord', translate one Greek word, 'Kurios'. This means, first of all, simply 'owner'; it is the word used about the owner of the donkey in the story about Jesus riding into the city (Luke 19:33). It also means 'Sir', when you are addressing people you respect. It is also used as a title, 'Lord', for the Emperor and for the pagan title for God. When friends or strangers addressed Jesus in his lifetime as 'Kurios', they were using the word as we use the word 'Sir'. The experience of the first Easter made his friends believe that Jesus was 'more than a man'; he was for them 'God's Son', one who showed them, in his life and death and resurrection, what God was like, and who helped them to live in God's way. To them he was no longer just 'Sir'; he was 'Lord'. When anyone was baptised and became a Christian, they confessed their faith in the words, 'Jesus is "Lord"'. This is the meaning of the word for both Paul and John – and for all Christians.

Friends of Jesus
I have used this phrase to translate 'disciples' and apostles'. The early Christians probably called themselves just 'friends' (see Acts 27:3); and John tells us that it was the name Jesus gave them (p. 670). 'Christians' was the nickname given to them by others (see *From Galilee to Rome*, p. 543); they also called themselves 'The People of the Way'. Today we use the name 'Christians' for all who follow Jesus. So I have used 'friends of Jesus' for all who followed him, though in later books I have also used the word 'Christians', which is the word we now use. (Jesus gave the name 'apostle' to those he 'sent out'; the wider name 'disciple' probably meant, when Jesus used the word, something like our word 'apprentice'.) When the friends of Jesus thought of themselves as a group, they used the word 'church', and I have used this word in *Jesus – Leader and Lord*. But 'friends of Jesus' helps us to remember that what makes people 'Christian' is their loyalty to Jesus; and what makes them a 'church' is their carrying on the work Jesus began in Galilee.

Jewish Leaders
The Jews thought of religion and politics together, and their leaders were both their religious and political leaders. They were divided into different parties – the 'Pharisees' and the 'Sadducees' were the most

famous. I have used 'Jewish leaders' for them all; you can find out from your Bibles which they actually were.

Resistance Movement
This translates the word 'Zealots', the party that believed in armed rebellion against Rome.

Scriptural Index

697

701

2.99
13/1